RIVERS OF SAND

INDIANS OF THE SOUTHEAST

Series Editors

Michael D. Green
University of North Carolina

Theda Perdue
University of North Carolina

Advisory Editors

Leland Ferguson
University of South Carolina

Mary Young
University of Rochester

RIVERS OF SAND

INDIANS OF THE SOUTHEAST

Series Editors

Michael D. Green
University of North Carolina

Theda Perdue
University of North Carolina

Advisory Editors

Leland Ferguson
University of South Carolina

Mary Young
University of Rochester

Rivers of Sand

*Creek Indian Emigration,
Relocation, and Ethnic Cleansing
in the American South*

CHRISTOPHER D. HAVEMAN

UNIVERSITY OF NEBRASKA PRESS
Lincoln and London

© 2016 by the Board of Regents of the University of Nebraska

Chapter 2 was originally published as "With Great Difficulty and Labour: The Emigration of the McIntosh Party of Creek Indians, 1827–1828," *Chronicles of Oklahoma* 85, no. 4 (Winter 2007–8): 468–90. © Christopher D. Haveman. Portions of chapters 4 and 10 were originally published as "'Last Evening I Saw the Sun Set for the Last Time': The 1832 Treaty of Washington and the Transfer of the Creeks' Alabama Land to White Ownership," *Native South* 5 (2012): 61–94.

All rights reserved
Manufactured in the United States of America

Library of Congress Cataloging-in-Publication Data
Haveman, Christopher D., 1976–
Rivers of sand: Creek Indian emigration, relocation, and ethnic cleansing in the American South / Christopher D. Haveman.
pages cm. — (Indians of the Southeast)
Includes bibliographical references and index.
ISBN 978-0-8032-7392-4 (cloth: alk. paper)
ISBN 978-0-8032-8488-3 (epub)
ISBN 978-0-8032-8489-0 (mobi)
ISBN 978-0-8032-8490-6 (pdf)
1. Creek Indians—Relocation. 2. Creek Indians—Government relations. 3. Creek Indians—Politics and government. 4. Creek Indians—History—19th century. I. Title.
E99.C9H295 2015
323.1197'38509034—dc23
2015008315

Set in Minion by Westchester Publishing Services

*For the Haveman, Hallgren,
Kirchhoff, and DeVos families*

CONTENTS

List of Illustrations   ix

Series Preface   xi

Acknowledgments   xiii

Notes on Terminology   xv

Introduction: Water, 1848   1

1. Treason: 1825–27   11

2. Fission: 1827–28   42

3. Frenzy: 1828–29   58

4. Fraud: 1829–35   82

5. Eclipse: 1833–36   114

6. Sand: 1828–50   149

7. Chains: 1836   175

8. Coercion: 1836–37   200

9. Defiance: 1837–49   234

10. Perseverance: 1837–82   270

Conclusion: Persistence, 2014   296

List of Abbreviations   303

Notes   305

Bibliography   367

Index   395

ILLUSTRATIONS

1. Route of Echo Fixico's party, 1848   2
2. U.S. Reservation and Fort Mitchell   23
3. Lower Towns of the Creek Nation, ca. 1800–1818   33
4. Lower Creek reserves in Chambers and Tallapoosa Counties after 1832   34
5. Lower Creek reserves in Russell and Macon Counties after 1832   36
6. Lower Creek reserves in Barbour County, after 1832   38
7. Route of the first McIntosh party, 1827–28   53
8. Route of the second McIntosh party, 1828–29   67
9. Route of the third voluntary party, 1829   78
10. The town of Irwinton, Alabama   87
11. Benjamin Marshall's reservation   98
12. Benjamin Marshall's reservation   99
13. Fraud investigation notice   108
14. Wetumpka Council House   111
15. Route of the fourth voluntary party, 1834–35   124
16. Path of 1831 annular eclipse   136

17. Route of the fifth voluntary party, 1835–36   143

18. Map of Indian territory, ca. 1850–51   159

19. Route of the first detachment of prisoners, 1836   192

20. Route of the second detachment of prisoners, 1836   197

21. Route of detachment one, 1836   212

22. Route of detachment two, 1836   216

23. Route of detachment three, 1836–37   219

24. Route of detachment four, 1836   224

25. Route of detachment five, 1836   229

26. Route of Creek refugees in Cherokee country, 1837   247

27. Edward Woolf watercolor of a Creek Indian, ca. 1837   251

28. Route of detachment six, 1837 or 1838   256

29. Route of Creek refugees in Chickasaw country, 1837   263

30. Map of Creek towns in Indian territory   277

31. Map of Indian territory, ca. 1850–59   278

32. Members of the Muscogee (Creek) Nation at Horseshoe Bend, 2014   300

TABLE

1. Number of Deaths on the Journey West, 1836–37   299

SERIES PREFACE

The Creek Nation was one of the Native nations overwhelmed by the U.S. removal policy of the 1820s and 1830s. Living on lands claimed by Georgia and Alabama, the Creeks were subjected to the demands of both the states and the federal government to surrender ownership of their territory and migrate to a country west of the Mississippi River. Although the policy of removal affected dozens of Native nations and tens of thousands of Native people who lived east of the river, each story is unique.

For the Creeks, removal began not with the passage of the Indian Removal Act in 1830, but with the Treaty of Indian Springs in 1825, and it lasted into the 1840s. This extended removal crisis took a terrible toll on Creek society. Cheated and swindled before they left, harassed and intimidated on the way, the experience of the Creeks was terrible. They went west in several detachments, some composed of volunteers, some of prisoners in chains, most by heartbroken families. Everybody paid a heavy price.

But, as Chris Haveman argues in this book, religious and ceremonial life persisted and enabled the Creeks to rebuild their lives and institutions in Indian territory. Over the past several decades, many very good books have been written about Indian removal, but none have described this history with the kind of care and detail that we find here. The editors welcome *Rivers of Sand: Creek Indian Emigration, Relocation, and Ethnic Cleansing in the American South* to this series.

Theda Perdue
Michael D. Green

ACKNOWLEDGMENTS

In 2002 I left my hometown of Bellingham, Washington, to study Creek Indian history under Kathryn E. Holland Braund at Auburn University. Having grown up surrounded by the Coast Salish culture—my father worked for more than thirty years in the Lummi Nation—Alabama and Creek Indian history offered me the chance to study something new. It was the best decision I could have made. I want to thank Kathryn for her guidance, her support, and her friendship.

Behind every book are teams of people who provide intellectual, moral, logistical, and financial assistance. Christina Snyder offered valuable comments and suggestions, and this book is better because of her. I picked Andrew K. Frank's brain on a number of occasions about William McIntosh and the Seminoles. Robbie Ethridge was very helpful with portions of chapter 4. The diverse scholarly backgrounds of my colleagues at the University of West Alabama (UWA) forced me to think about my arguments in new ways. Ashley Dumas, with her vast knowledge of Southeastern Indian archaeology, proved to be a fantastic sounding board; R. Volney Riser broadened my understanding of early Alabama legal history, which proved immeasurable as I navigated the world of nineteenth-century land transfers; Richard Schellhammer, a German historian, challenged me on the term "ethnic cleansing"; and Jeff Gentsch provided answers to my many questions about the pre–Civil War military. I also want to thank my dear friend Mary Isbell at the University of New Haven for her assistance in navigating the Beinecke Rare Book and Manuscript Library, and the many others for their effort and insight, including Susan Abram, John Cottier, the indefatigable

Kiersten Fish, Marie Francois, Jim Hoogerwerf, Ron Johnson, Brian Keener, Joyce Ledbetter, Meredith McDonough, John Upchurch, Andrew K. Rindsberg, Monroe C. Snider, and Misty Will, as well as James F. Scotton and Philip Seib, two professors who helped me immensely while I was a student at Marquette University.

Archivists and librarians are the lifeline for any historian, and I want to especially thank Anna Bedsole in the Interlibrary Loan (ILL) Department at UWA and Anthony Pendleton at the circulation desk of the Ralph Brown Draughon Library at Auburn for their patience in dealing with my myriad requests. I also want to personally thank Janet Bloom at the William L. Clements Library at the University of Michigan, as well as the staff at the New York Public Library, the Department of Rare Books and Special Collections at Princeton, the Beinecke Rare Book and Manuscript Library at Yale, the W. S. Hoole Special Collections Library at the University of Alabama, and the Vermont Historical Society.

Similarly, editors are the lifeline for any writer, and I want to especially thank Matthew Bokovoy for his patience and guidance as I navigate the world of publishing. Thanks also go to Heather Stauffer and the staff at the University of Nebraska Press, as well as my colleague, wordsmith, and dear friend Lesa Shaul, who read and proofread many of my drafts.

Finally, I want to thank Michael D. Green and Theda Perdue, who generously supported this project. Mike read my dissertation and drafts of the manuscript and provided many thoughtful suggestions. My copy of *The Politics of Indian Removal* is marked up, dog-eared, and highlighted. The spine is broken and many of its pages are being held in place by the last remaining bits of binding glue. I think Mike would have appreciated that.

This book would not have been possible without the support of my family—financial, moral, or otherwise. My parents, Pat and Dale Haveman, never questioned my decision to move to Auburn for graduate school or settle and make a life in Alabama. My brother Jason, a biologist, helped me with the flora and fauna section of chapter 6, and my brother Greg provided useful information on medical history and eighteenth-century treatments. This book is for them.

NOTES ON TERMINOLOGY

Oklahoma has been called many things throughout the nineteenth century—Arkansas Territory, Indian Territory, Western Territory, Indian country. The Creeks, however, largely knew it as "Arkansaw," and no word was more despised and feared throughout the 1820s and 1830s. So as not to confuse readers with myriad names, I use the generic "Indian territory" to represent the region resettled by the Creeks and other southeastern Indians.

I also use the terms "emigrants" and "emigration" to denote the period (1827–36) when the Creeks voluntarily moved west. I acknowledge that the term "voluntary" is ambiguous—some, like those of the McIntosh party, moved eagerly; others were reluctant migrants who felt they had little choice but to rebuild their lives in the West as the Creek Nation rapidly disintegrated around them. But it is impossible to determine the motivations of every one of the approximately thirty-five hundred or more who chose to leave the land of their ancestors. For the period after 1836, I use the terms "removal" and "relocation." Removal refers to those Creeks who participated in the Second Creek War and were shackled and placed on steamboats at Montgomery alongside troops who were ordered to shoot any who tried to escape. "Relocated" Creeks were those who came west after the prisoners. They were not necessarily free to remain in Alabama but they exerted a significant amount of control over the manner in which they traveled. I consider all of it to be ethnic cleansing.

It is clear that there is no word or term that adequately conveys the emotional and physical horror of "Indian removal." My goal therefore is not to distract readers with terminology but to present a highly detailed, chronological account of the brutalities of this era, which I hope will leave little doubt in anyone's mind that the dispossession and resettlement of the Creek Indians was nothing less than a national tragedy.

RIVERS OF SAND

Introduction
Water, 1848

On 18 June 1848 Echo Fixico, an elderly Chehaw man who, by his own account, was "considerably over 100 years old," died one evening in Lewisburg, Arkansas, while on his way to the Indian territory. He was one in a party of sixty-five Creek Indian emigrants who had left their ancestral homeland for a new life in the relocated Creek Nation. The party was conducted by Ward Cochamy, a future Creek headman who had returned to Alabama initially to collect members of his family. There are no records that describe the emotions of the centenarian as he left Alabama for the final time, but it would not have been surprising if he had reflected briefly on the changes that had taken place since his childhood. Echo Fixico's life spanned the rapid decline of a once-vibrant southeastern Indian nation. He was probably born the decade after the establishment of Savannah and the founding of the colony of Georgia. During his lifetime British and American settlers methodically moved westward, annexing Creek old fields and hunting grounds. He would have been in his seventies during the Creek War, his eighties when the Creeks lost their last possessions in Georgia, and his nineties during the removal to Indian territory. With his advanced age Echo Fixico knew that when he boarded his steamboat on 30 May 1848, it would be the last time he stepped foot on his ancestral homeland. Most of the other members of the party no doubt thought the same. From Alabama the party reached New Orleans during the first week of June, then stopped in Lewisburg. It was there, while waiting for the steamboat to be cleaned, that Echo Fixico unceremoniously died. Befitting a man who had no home, the Chehaw elder was placed in a coffin and buried at the foot of

FIG. 1. Route of Echo Fixico's party, 1848. Place names correspond to stopping points or locations noted in the documentation. Route lines and locations are approximations. Cartography by Sarah Mattics.

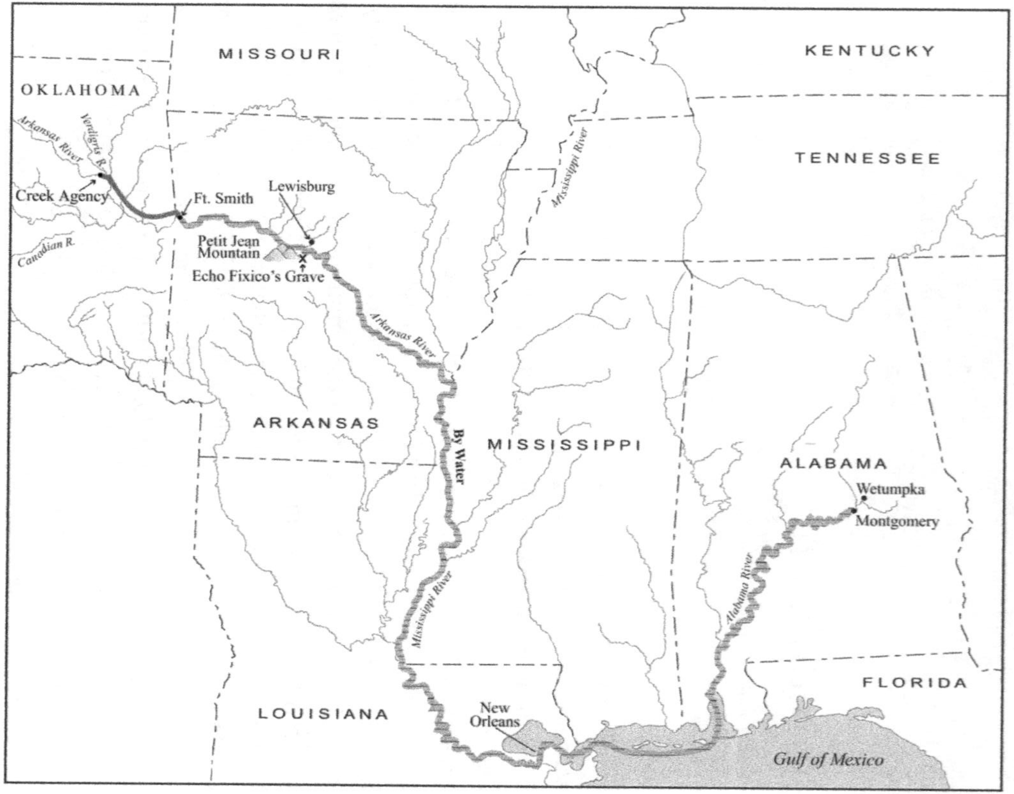

Petit Jean Mountain in the state of Arkansas. His bones never mingled with those of his ancestors in Alabama, nor would they with his peoples' remains in the West.[1]

Before he passed away Echo Fixico was following a well-worn path to Indian territory. During the previous two decades federal and state officials, aided by a proxy force of white squatters, engaged in a systematic program of ethnic cleansing in order to rid the states of Alabama and Georgia of approximately twenty-three thousand Creek inhabitants. "Ethnic cleansing" is often associated with the Serbo-Croation phrase *etničko čišćenje* (literal translation) and the breakup of Yugoslavia, although references to various forms of "cleansing" predate the 1990s. Today the term is used to describe the purging of any culture, religion, government, or race from a territory in order to secure that land for another group. Ethnic cleansing can take many forms, and its implementation can range from induced assimilation and induced emigration to coerced assimilation and deportation. At its most severe, ethnic cleansing is genocide. Under agent Benjamin Hawkins, federal officials attempted to assimilate the Creeks under the government's "civilization" program. Between 1825 and 1836, federal officials tried to cajole the Creeks into voluntarily emigrating to Indian territory. The state of Alabama attempted to destroy the economic, political, and cultural life of the Creek people by asserting legal jurisdiction over their nation while also passing laws that prohibited hunting, fishing, and trapping. In the summer of 1836, after bands of Creeks started the Second Creek War, President Andrew Jackson forcibly removed approximately 2,500 of those complicit in the uprising along with their families. Between 1836 and 1837 Jackson and his successor, Martin Van Buren, coerced the remainder of the Creek populace, without any legal right to do so, to move west.[2]

This book is about the disintegration of the eastern Creek Nation, the relocation of its people across the Mississippi River, and the reestablishment of a new nation in the Indian territory. My goal is to provide the most comprehensive account available of a native population transfer to the West. This is a case study in how federal and state officials and white illegal aliens dislodged a group of people—in this case, the Creek

Indians—from their homeland and how the Creeks desperately tried to protect their rights, their land, and their way of life. Throughout this work I argue that moving Creek Indians west was, in fact, "ethnic cleansing" and not, as Andrew Jackson asserted, about protecting the Indians from extinction or "annihilation." Indeed, a number of twentieth-century scholars took up Jackson's dangerous line of reasoning to suggest that there was a certain benevolence to Indian removal. Other scholars have argued that national security concerns and fear of foreign invasion guided Jackson's Indian policy, which seems illogical considering his administration was intent on placing disaffected southeastern Indians on the doorstep of an actual foreign country (Mexico) during a particularly volatile time (its war with the Texans, and later the United States).[3]

In reality, Creek Indian relocation was a land grab perpetrated by white politicians and squatters. Federal and state officials were determined to break the sovereignty of the Creek Nation, displace the native inhabitants, and open up millions of acres of territory to white settlement. Ethnic cleansing in the Creek country followed a systematic process that had been implemented in other places throughout the eastern United States: coerce and bribe a small faction of Indians into signing land cession treaties; force the native people onto small, often unmanageable tracts of land; allow whites (many of whom were whiskey merchants, land speculators, and squatters) to resettle on the doorstep of these Indian communities; let starvation, indebtedness, land expropriation, and alcohol abuse run its course; then assert that the salvation of these Indian peoples lay on the other side of the Mississippi River. Ethnic cleansing in the Creek country was intended to be complete and comprehensive, although, in the end, some Creeks were able to remain in the East. Emigration agents were indiscriminate when targeting people of different backgrounds, belief systems, levels of wealth, or degrees of what whites considered to be "civilization." The common denominator was that they were associated, in some way, with the Creek Nation. Indeed, many of the early migrants to Indian territory were very prosperous farmers, ranchers, plantation owners, and entrepreneurs while others were unimaginably poor and traveled west with virtually nothing. Some, like John Davis, a Weogufka man of mixed ancestry, was a Baptist missionary.

Whites married to Creek women—called Indian countrymen—were even targeted. One agent believed that the wealth, influence, and marriage connections of these people could draw large numbers of Creeks west. In perhaps the greatest insult, those who had risked their lives by aiding the United States in the first and second Creek wars, as well as during the Seminole wars, were also coerced into relocating to Indian territory.

Far from protecting the Indians, as Jackson asserted, moving Creeks westward was a demographic disaster that killed untold numbers of people. The 1825 Treaty of Indian Springs (and its replacement, the 1826 Treaty of Washington) destroyed the buffer between white and Indian society, and placed squatters and whiskey sellers on the borders of the Creek Nation at Columbus, Georgia. Whites stole Creek homes and crops. The Creek town of Eufaula was burned to the ground to make way for the white community of Irwinton. Traders infested the area with alcohol and sold merchandise on credit, and indebtedness and alcohol abuse increased exponentially. Whites blamed alcohol for hindering the Creeks' proclivity to plant, and starvation also became a widespread problem. When Andrew Jackson convinced the headmen to cede the remainder of their domain in 1832 and take individual reserves, more whites entered the Creek country to speculate on their valuable allotments. The treaties also commenced the federal emigration program in the Creek country by incentivizing voluntary resettlement west of the Mississippi River. It was a devastating one-two punch: force a large Creek population onto a greatly reduced territory while encouraging them to move west with enticements (money, food, rifles, kettles, blankets, etc.) and the promise of a better life. And yet, when they did reach the Indian territory, most Creeks discovered that their new life was anything but improved. Disease and the harsh climate killed about 18 percent of the population between 1830 and 1833. Aware of this, the Jackson administration still charged ahead moving Indians to the West. When a band of Creeks initiated a retributive uprising in 1836 in response to the starvation, land frauds, and white encroachment found in Alabama, the president finally had the excuse he needed to transfer the entire Creek population across the Mississippi River. Two detachments of Creek prisoners were chained and transferred west, while the balance—including those who were allies of the United States and had aided the government in bringing the insurgents to capture—were also ordered out of the South. After they arrived, approximately one-fifth to one-third of them were dead within a year.[4]

Although Andrew Jackson has taken much of the blame for the atrocities against the Indian people during the first half of the early nineteenth century, there are many others who are also complicit. In fact, the Treaty of Indian Springs was signed under President James Monroe, emigration commenced under John Quincy Adams, and its major operations concluded with thousands of Creeks marching west during Martin Van Buren's administration. In addition, the Creeks had been pushed westward since the founding of Savannah and had lost land through treaty cessions under every U.S. president except John Adams. The concept of moving Indians west began at least as far back as Thomas Jefferson's administration and earlier if you consider his proposal to forcibly remove the British-allied Cherokees beyond the Mississippi in 1776.[5] Moreover, no one did more to terrorize the Creek people in the 1820s and 1830s than the tens of thousands of white illegals who streamed into the Creek Nation.[6] Jackson, however, shared the spirit and the ethos of these settlers and by doing very little to stop their incursions he, by omission, sanctioned their presence.

The other purpose of this book is to show the ways in which the Creek people challenged the government's emigration program and fought to preserve their way of life on their ancestral homeland. The Creek people did not take threats to their sovereignty lying down. Far from passive victims, the Creeks and their headmen aggressively countered the federal emigration program through myriad resistance strategies. When Coweta chief William McIntosh and his cronies illegally signed the 1825 Treaty of Indian Springs—which ceded massive amounts of the Creeks' land without the permission of the Creek National Council—the Creeks executed McIntosh and others complicit in the agreement, then began a highly effective campaign to nullify the offending document. Against all odds the Creeks were successful, and on 24 January 1826 they signed the Treaty of Washington, which superseded the Indian Springs agreement—the only Indian treaty ever to be overturned after its confirmation by the U.S. Senate. The Treaty of Washington continued the federal emigration program, however, and the Creeks countered this with violence and threats of violence against would-be emigrants. They engaged in a concerted propaganda campaign that attempted to smear not only the reputation of the Indian territory's land and climate, but also the efficacy of federal officials who were charged with ensuring the emigrants' well-being. Others consistently gave agents the runaround by promising to move west without ever following through. The headmen also steadfastly refused to sign any removal treaty. As a result, Jackson administration officials were constantly frustrated by the Creeks' determination to remain on their ancestral soil. This led to disagreements among agents and officials over the best emigration strategy, and large amounts of money was wasted on gimmicky and ultimately unsuccessful ventures. In a number of cases ineffective agents were fired or reassigned. Moreover, whites failed to fully ethnically cleanse the East of all the Creek Indians and, in fact, the Poarch Band remains in Alabama to this day.[7]

The Creeks also resolutely maintained their religious and ceremonial lives during this chaotic time. They took great pains to maintain some semblance of the fundamental element that bound them together, even as they were hopelessly fracturing apart. As the Creek Nation crumbled, the people still sought unity through their annual Busk, maintained their mental and physical prowess by participating in ball plays, and continued to connect themselves to the world around them through dance. Although disrupted to a considerable extent, the Creek people were incredibly resilient and resourceful when it came to maintaining their spiritual and ceremonial lives. When the *talwa* (Creek town) of Cusseta was forced from Georgia in 1826, the townspeople rebuilt their council houses in Alabama and their Green Corn Ceremony continued on the west side of the Chattahoochee River. Many Georgia Lower Creeks forced into Alabama did not reestablish their towns or their communal fields like Cusseta, but there is some circumstantial evidence to suggest that they also held their sacred annual Busk. Rather than use their own crop harvests, these transient Lower Creeks may have stolen the green corn from local Georgians who had expropriated their land. The Creeks also may have held an abbreviated Busk while on their forced march west. In August 1836 hundreds of Creek prisoners who participated in the Second Creek War and began their journey in chains in July 1836 ate copious amounts of green corn and fruit while engaging in dances and ball plays. When a physician took measures to prevent the Creeks from obtaining it—he blamed the food on their deteriorating health—his actions were met with "much opposition and difficulty." And as the Second Creek War raged in the spring and summer of 1836, a number of Creeks hiding in the mountains of north Alabama to escape capture returned to the Creek country at great risk to their own personal freedom in order to attend a Green Corn Ceremony near Wetumpka. Dances and ball games occurred on the Alabama home front during the 1820s and 1830s and while on the march west. Opothle Yoholo and his people danced on the eve of their move to the Indian territory in August 1836. Once in the West, the Creeks continued to hold these ceremonies and dances, and the emphasis on renewal took on added importance as they consecrated new land.

Although the Creeks' long struggle to remain on their ancestral homeland was ultimately unsuccessful, they did not take the government's demand to move west lying down. After the Creek prisoners were forced west in shackles, the rest of the population (despite not having participated in the war) was also ordered to organize into camps and prepare for resettlement in the Indian territory. With no removal treaty signed, agents, including Brevet Major General Thomas S. Jesup, who oversaw the operation, conceded that the Creeks' movements were "necessarily voluntary." Hopelessly outnumbered, military personnel were therefore required to work through the headmen. These movements, which I call "coerced relocations," are so named in order to differentiate this period from that of the forced removal of the Creek prisoners who left in chains. Landless, virtually starving, surrounded by tens of thousands of whites, and with nothing to go back to in their old nation, the headmen gave begrudging consent to their resettlement west of the Mississippi River. Although the Creeks were not necessarily free to remain in Alabama—Secretary of War Lewis Cass would have certainly ordered force to be used if they had made a stand—the Creeks held an unusual amount of power, considering their circumstances, and they used it. Far from the image we have of the U.S. Army rounding up Cherokees at the end of a bayonet, most Creeks moved west through a combination of coercion and negotiation. Indeed, much of the time on the route was spent by military agents pleading with the headmen for compliance. Creeks deserted camp, raided locals' fields, purchased alcohol, and quarreled among each other. Unhappy headmen brought entire detachments to a halt when they disapproved of the manner in which they were traveling. Many Creeks traveled at their own pace and deliberately fell far behind the vanguard of the train. While traveling through the Mississippi Swamp—the region west of Memphis in Arkansas—Creek leaders dismissively notified an impatient military agent waiting near Little Rock that they would come on when they were ready. Indeed, after a particularly tedious journey, Lieutenant Mark W. Bateman, who led Tuckabatchee leader Opothle Yoholo's detachment west, complained in his journal that "the Indians [are] very discontented. Every thing appears to go wrong. I am disgusted with Indian Emigration."[8]

The Muscogee (Creek) Nation in Oklahoma is a testament to the survival of the Creek people and their culture, and this is a book about survival. And yet, even as the Creeks continue to look toward the future, they are continually reminded of their past. The Creeks' Alabama and Georgia lands are still revered today. As a child, Alfred Berryhill, the second chief of the Muscogee (Creek) Nation (2003–11), remembered driving with his father, Togo Micco Berryhill, through Oklahoma. Crossing a bridge, Togo Micco Berryhill would look down at the ravines and say "rivers of sand." It was not until Alfred visited Alabama and Georgia that he understood what his father had meant all those years before. The East was a land of water.[9]

1 Treason

1825–27

On 12 February 1825, William McIntosh and fifty of his handpicked supporters signed the Treaty of Indian Springs, ceding the Creek domain in Georgia and a large portion of their territory within Alabama to the federal government. Because the treaty evicted the Creeks from the cession and promoted voluntary emigration to Indian territory, it was both a removal and an emigration document. First, the treaty expelled all Creek residents from the ceded land and forced them into the remaining part of the Creek Nation within Alabama. Second, by trading the Creeks' eastern lands "acre for acre" for lands west of the Arkansas Territory and offering to cover the cost of their travels, the treaty commenced and incentivized voluntary emigration. The two worked hand in hand, as the problems the Creeks were sure to encounter on a vastly reduced domain would encourage them to move west. Surrounding the signatories were prominent headmen who looked on in disbelief. Ceding Creek land without the approval of the Creek National Council was illegal and punishable by death, and McIntosh had not received permission. Just moments before the signing, Opothle Yoholo, the speaker of the Upper Towns, confronted the Coweta headman and declared: "My friend, you are about to sell our country; I now warn you of your danger." McIntosh ignored the Tuckabatchee speaker and inked his mark to the document. He was followed, in order, by Etommee Tustunnuggee, Colonel Blue, Coweta Tustunnuggee, Roly McIntosh (William's brother), Chilly McIntosh (his son), and forty-five other Creeks with little or no prominence in the Creek Nation. The vast majority, however, opposed the treaty, denounced the McIntosh party, and rejected emigrating from the land of their ancestors. Declaring the Indian Springs agreement a "'national calamity,'" Creek headmen moved to overturn the treaty and punish the offenders. Although the Treaty of Indian Springs was ultimately nullified, the Creeks did not recover all their Georgia lands. In 1826, the Creeks were forced to remove from Georgia into the limits of Alabama. The Treaty of Indian Springs changed the Creek Nation forever. It was the proximal cause of the forced removal of the Creek Indians in 1836.[1]

In the darkness of 30 April 1825, more than 120 and perhaps as many as 400 Creeks, led by the Okfuskee headman Menawa, surrounded the Chattahoochee plantation of William McIntosh. The Creeks set fire to his house and then, as McIntosh tried to escape the flames, he was shot and finally stabbed to death. McIntosh's corpse was then dragged by the heels to the edge of the yard where the Creeks continued "shooting a number of balls through his head and body." McIntosh's skull was reportedly "shattered to pieces." As they desecrated his remains, the Creeks mocked McIntosh by taunting: "This is the great General—the white man's friend." Etommee Tustunnuggee, nicknamed Thomas, was also executed at McIntosh's plantation, and both bodies were riddled with nearly a hundred balls. McIntosh's execution came after two and a half months of careful deliberation by the Creek National Council. During that time, the U.S. Senate confirmed the Treaty of Indian Springs and President John Quincy Adams ratified it despite pleas from Big Warrior, a principal chief of the Creek Nation, who traveled to Washington to protest the treaty. The Creeks then turned their attention to others complicit in the signing. William McIntosh's sons-in-law, Samuel Hawkins and his brother Benjamin, were also targeted. The Creeks dragged Samuel from his home and gave him "a long talk" before he was hanged, although McIntosh associates claimed that Hawkins was "inhumanly butchered," having been "compelled to Eat fire" for two days and nights. Benjamin Hawkins escaped with only a gunshot wound. Hagy McIntosh (William's brother), Colonel William Miller, and the Derasaw brothers survived only because the high waters of the Chattahoochee River slowed their pursuers just enough to allow their escape.

Chilly McIntosh, who was at his father's plantation during the attack, slipped through a back window and fled to Milledgeville under the guise of a traveling white man. There he relayed the news to his late father's cousin, Governor George M. Troup. Most of the remaining members of the McIntosh party fled into Georgia or the interior of Alabama and sought the protection of white allies.[2]

The McIntosh party remained in exile through the spring and summer of 1825, drawing rations from four camps in Georgia. Roly McIntosh and more than two hundred Creeks hid out in Pike County while Chilly McIntosh and approximately forty supporters remained at Indian Springs. One hundred sixty-eight Creeks, all from Sand Town, were under protection at a camp in Fayette County and another in DeKalb County, Georgia. All four camps included men, women, and children. With the traitors just beyond their reach, the law menders turned their attention to the exiles' unprotected homes. Both monetarily and with regard to the sheer volume of goods, the McIntosh and Hawkins families suffered the greatest losses, although the exact amount was later disputed. William McIntosh's estate reported losses in excess of $25,000, including the destruction of two houses and the expropriation of $13,000 in cash, almost eight hundred head of cattle, clothing, agricultural tools, and housewares. Samuel Hawkins's estate claimed similar damages, including the destruction of a number of houses burned by the Creeks. Everyday items including dishes and children's clothing were taken or destroyed along with fancier possessions like earrings, silver brooches, cut glass beads, and silk frocks. The estate also claimed the loss of hundreds of head of cattle and hogs and one hundred chickens, as well as an extensive set of tools.[3]

Large numbers of black slaves were also confiscated. Slavery had long been a feature of Creek Indian society, although the practice had evolved over the centuries. While the Creeks first took native war captives (and sometimes the occasional person of European ancestry), by the late eighteenth century almost all slaves were black. Wealthy Creeks like William McIntosh lived on Southern-style plantations and had dozens of slaves to do their bidding. While laborers were bought and sold in the Creek Nation, the Creeks continued the ancient practice of enslaving people taken from an enemy. Indeed, in addition to the clothes, livestock, and jewelry confiscated or destroyed by the law menders, William McIntosh's estate lost seventy-four slaves, Chilly McIntosh seventy-two, and Samuel Hawkins fifteen, as punishment for their treason. Survivors of the attacks protested and complained that Little Prince, a principal headman of the Creek Nation, and his followers were "taking and converting to their own use all the negroes belonging to General McIntosh and Colonel Hawkins."[4]

Helpless to prevent the looting, Roly McIntosh and brothers Benjamin and Joseph Marshall, all signers of the Treaty of Indian Springs, wrote to Chilly McIntosh in June 1825 complaining that the Creeks were "still doing all the harm to us they can" and noted that "it appears that they are disposed to destroy everything." Convinced that this was the case, a number of exiles returned to their homes, at great risk to their lives, to gather any possessions they owned that had not been taken or destroyed. Large herds of cattle owned by the McIntosh party were driven eastward by their owners and quickly sold in Georgia to prevent the Creeks from destroying them.[5]

In light of the warnings given to McIntosh and his allies, and the subsequent violence and destruction they brought on themselves, the motivations of the treaty party are puzzling. The most plausible explanation is that William McIntosh wanted to usurp Creek authority by placing himself (or a close associate) as the head of government of a new western Creek Nation. McIntosh was powerful—the fifth-ranking headman on the National Council and at one time a conduit for goods and annuities entering the Creek country—but his influence had eroded since John Crowell took over the agency in 1821. Crowell redirected the flow of money away from McIntosh and toward his brother, Thomas, who ran a store in the Creek Nation. As his access to goods dried up, so did McIntosh's network of patronage. Faced with his declining power, McIntosh might have believed that he could reestablish his power base on the west side of the Mississippi River. Perhaps sensing that removal was inevitable, McIntosh knew that all Creeks who arrived thereafter would be under his charge. As a longtime friend of the United States, McIntosh had the diplomatic backing of federal officials, and the emphasis on primacy in Creek creation stories would have helped mute any dispute over authority. Historically, the first town or the first clan to arrive at a location generally held mythical importance over those who arrived after. Creek rhetoricians often manipulated the order of the arrival of clans or towns in the Southeast in order to heighten their own importance relative to others. But for the McIntosh party there would have been no dispute over who was the first in the West. Indeed, the treaty party members were asserting their origin story even before leaving the limits of the Creek Nation, when they affirmed that the "Cowetau Town is the most extensive and numerous in the nation, and claims to be the original town of the whole tribe and that all others are its branches." In fact, this is exactly how events played out going forward. The McIntosh party (minus William) created the first Creek government in the West in 1828 and held on to power for decades after relocation. When other principal headmen arrived after 1828, they were forced to accept their subservient position.[6]

Money was also a motivating factor. The McIntosh and Hawkins families were very wealthy, but so were many Creeks like Oethlamata Tustunnuggee, a signer of the Treaty of Indian Springs, who "appeared to live very well and had considerable property about him." The promise of more wealth may have motivated many to risk their lives by signing the document. Collectively, the McIntosh party stood to receive hundreds of thousands of dollars from the federal government for the "fair equivalent for the losses" of their improvements and for the "inconveniences" of removal. Indeed, William McIntosh was guaranteed $25,000 for his reservations at Indian Springs and on the Ocmulgee River in Georgia, plus an additional $15,000 for his cooperation. This explanation does not take into account all the money the Creeks stood to lose by emigrating westward, however. Although the government paid the relocation expenses of the party members, it would take time to rebuild their plantations west of the Mississippi River. Much of their large, expensive possessions like houses, cropland, rails, and livestock, to name only a few, would have remained behind in the East. And because of bureaucratic inefficiency and carelessness, compensation often took years, or even decades, to receive. Moreover, their wealth had been built, in part, by catering to white travelers passing by the inns, taverns, ferries, mills, or stores that were owned or operated by McIntosh party members. This was income that would not have been as easily replicated in the sparsely white-inhabited West.[7]

But a sparsely inhabited region may have been exactly what some McIntosh party members were looking for. Kendall Lewis was a native Marylander and Indian countryman who had settled in the Creek Nation after fleeing a murder charge in Hancock, Georgia, in 1808. Lewis had married Big Warrior's daughter and became a trusted adviser to the headman, who made use of his bilingualism. The two even shared a business interest in "Lewis' Stand," a store located at the site of old Fort Bainbridge. By the time Adam Hodgson met Lewis during the British traveler's excursion through the Creek Nation in 1820, the Indian countryman had forged an isolationist ethos and had "contracted so ardent a love of solitude, by living in the woods, that he lately removed his stand from the most profitable situation, because there was a neighbour or two within four miles."[8]

Federal officials also played a prominent role in the McIntosh debacle. The Treaty of Indian Springs was one of many post–War of 1812 land cession agreements that opened vast tracts for white settlement while reducing the living space of the Indians to uncomfortable, often unmanageable proportions. The Cherokees' 1817 Treaty of the Cherokee Agency and the Choctaws' 1820 Treaty of Doak's Stand (both negotiated in part by Andrew Jackson), like Creeks' indenture, were land-swap agreements that traded eastern soil for territory west of the Mississippi River and offered the Indians the opportunity of resettling in the West. Many other Indian treaties signed during this time, however, like the Creeks' 1814 Treaty of Fort Jackson and the Chickasaws' 1816 and 1818 agreements (all signed by Andrew Jackson), did not have a voluntary emigration component built into them. Instead, by eroding the spatial buffer with white society, these indentures made life so difficult for the native inhabitants going forward that the eastern Indians often felt that they had little choice but to move west. Indeed, after reducing the domain of the Shawnees, Wyandots, and Delawares, Michigan Territory governor Lewis Cass smugly noted that "'as our settlements gradually surround them, their minds will be better prepared'" for removal. Cass was right: the influx of white settlers drove the native inhabitants to distraction and paved the way for the removal treaties of the 1830s and 1840s.[9]

The McIntosh party also may have fallen victim to the machinations of white politicians and overzealous federal agents charged with doing their bidding. In order to wrest control of large tracts of Indian soil, federal commissioners used heavy-handed tactics to convince the Indians to sign these land cession treaties. After numerous false starts, Andrew Jackson essentially threatened the Choctaws into signing the agreement at Doak's Stand. In the Creek Nation, Duncan Greene Campbell and James Meriwether, who were "intent upon the treaty," used bribery, lies, and fraud to achieve their ends at Indian Springs in 1825. When, at the last moment, McIntosh reportedly "wavered" over concerns for his safety, Campbell and Meriwether calmed the Coweta headman's fears by halfheartedly assuring his protection. Edward G. W. Butler, as part of a federal team investigating the legitimacy of the Indian Springs agreement, believed that the treaty party was deceived by the commissioners and "sacrificed to Georgia politics." Moreover, Thomas L. McKenney, who headed the Indian Department, believed that the commissioners "flattered and caressed" McIntosh into believing "that he was consulting the ultimate advantage of the nation." The commissioners never followed through on the promise of protection and Campbell's insistence that McIntosh understood the "superior advantages" of the Indian territory is questionable considering that his brother Roly had hunted in the West on three different occasions prior to 1825 and was "not so disposed" to move there because "the muskitoes were very bad & the country was sickly, the Indians very hostile, that he had very narrowly escaped from them with life two or three times that he had been sick himself and come near dying."[10]

Finally, although it is doubtful that McIntosh's decision to sign the Treaty of Indian Springs had anything to do with a sincere desire to protect the Creeks from the corrupting influences of white society, some prominent McIntosh party members claimed, at least publicly, to have been concerned about the deterioration of Creek culture. Kendall Lewis confided to Adam Hodgson that he "regretted, in the most feeling terms, the injury which the morals of the Indians have sustained from intercourse with the whites," including alcohol abuse, greed, thievery, and deceit. Auguste Levasseur, who accompanied the Marquis de Lafayette to the United States in 1824 and 1825, recorded a similar conversation with Chilly McIntosh years later. According to the Frenchman, Chilly McIntosh's decision to emigrate was the result of his belief that the Creek Nation had become weakened as a result of its proximity to white society. Levasseur noted that Chilly McIntosh "appeared to hope that the treaty which removed them to another and a desert country, would reestablish the ancient organization of the tribes, or at least preserve them in the state in which they now were." Of course, the McIntoshes had also benefited from their ties to Georgia elites, including William's cousin, Governor Troup. It also is hard to believe that Chilly McIntosh wanted to return the Creeks to their "ancient organization," considering his father was a vocal proponent of Western-style laws, slaveholding, ranching, schooling, and concepts of landownership.[11]

Regardless of his motivations, William McIntosh did not live to see his western nation come to fruition. Roly McIntosh was quickly selected as his brother's successor by the surviving members of the treaty party. In keeping with Indian custom, he also married his late brother's widow, Susannah. Despite the apparent ease with which power was transferred, the McIntosh party never was completely unified or like-minded. The group was a mishmash of wealthy low-level headmen, intermarried families, greedy opportunists, hangers-on, and complete unknowns. Money appears to have been a strong source of friction and misgiving within the group. The infighting was made public in disputes over the claims for losses by the McIntosh and Hawkins families, where depositions show the level of distrust among some of the more prominent would-be emigrants. For example, forty-two-year-old William Lott, an Indian countryman who voluntarily emigrated with the second McIntosh party in 1828, accused Stephen Hawkins of having bad character and declared that he "would not believe him upon oath or in any other way." James Moore, another longtime resident of the Creek Nation who enrolled for emigration in 1828, also testified that he would not believe Benjamin, Stephen, or other Hawkins family members "on their oath" and accused them of circulating counterfeit money in the nation. Former Creek agent David B. Mitchell, a close McIntosh ally, countered by testifying that "the character of William Lott is notoriously bad, and I would not believe him on oath if unsupported by other credible testimony." William McIntosh's charisma was probably the glue that kept this disparate and factionalized group together. Indeed, a number of members acknowledged that McIntosh was their "head" and that they were "only the hands and feet." McIntosh's supporters had elected him as their "principal protector and chief" and appear to have followed him blindly. As a former speaker, he would have been required to articulate Creek policy with eloquence and he no doubt used these skills to craft his cult of personality. Indeed, some McIntosh party Creeks simply refused to emigrate after the death of their headman, inferring that only he had the "wisdom" to govern and protect them in the West.[12]

Still in exile, McIntosh party members reached out to their white allies in Georgia and in the federal government for assistance. Two of McIntosh's widows, Susannah and Peggy, along with Jane Hawkins, the daughter of William McIntosh and the widow of Samuel, wrote (or had written for them) scathing letters to Campbell and Meriwether. "When you see this letter stained with the blood of my husband, the last drop of which is now spilt for the friendship he has shown for your people," Peggy and Susannah chided the commissioners; then they pleaded for rations by warning that "if you and your people do not assist us, God help us, we must die either by the sword or the famine." The irascible Governor Troup also did little to hide his anger at the Creek National Council and blasted the federal government for neglecting its promise to protect the McIntosh party from retribution. Article 8 of the Treaty of Indian Springs had guaranteed the McIntosh party protection from the "incroachments [sic]" and "hostilities" of their enemies while they prepared for emigration. Troup then began mobilizing troops and threatened violence against the Creeks responsible for his cousin's execution. He had also demanded permission to survey Georgia's new territory far in advance of the 1 September 1826 deadline for the Creeks to leave the cession. The Creeks opposed to the McIntosh party refused to back down, however, and, in addition to the continued raiding of McIntosh party property, warned that they would "kill the first surveyor who stretched a chain across the land, and then kill all those who afterwards came to survey it."[13]

The failure to uphold Article 8 and the threat of more violence forced President John Quincy Adams to act. In May, Adams dispatched two special agents to the Creek Nation. Brevet Major General Edmund P. Gaines, the commanding officer of the Eastern Department of the army who had served on the Old Southwest frontier after the first Creek War, was charged with preserving the peace and convincing the Creeks to accept the Treaty of Indian Springs. Joining Gaines was Major Timothy P. Andrews from the U.S. Army's Office of the Paymaster General in Washington, who was ordered to investigate Creek agent John Crowell, whom Troup despised and had attempted to implicate in McIntosh's death. The agents quickly began to sift through the finger pointing and misinformation. During the next several weeks, countless interviews, depositions, and affidavits painted Troup as a deceitful, opportunistic schemer, and the Creeks as victims of the machinations of the governor and his McIntosh party allies. Moreover, in a council held at Thlakatchka in late June, the agents could not ignore the overwhelming opposition to the treaty. In fact, Gaines discovered that "*forty-nine-fiftieths*" of the Creeks were hostile to McIntosh and against moving west of the Mississippi River. Likewise, Andrews found that "at least nine tenths" of the entire Creek Nation opposed McIntosh during his own investigation.[14]

In many ways, the Thlakatchka council was a turning point for the Creek Nation going forward. It was at this meeting, with perhaps two thousand headmen and warriors in attendance, that Gaines became fully convinced of the fraudulence of the Treaty of Indian Springs. It was also here, on 29 June 1825, that the McIntosh Creeks were officially pardoned. This came after a number of the signers of the Treaty of Indian Springs repented and returned to the nation, including Tomoc Micco, William McIntosh's uncle. Headmen justified their act of mercy by declaring that they already had successfully "topped the tree which they had intended topping." To forestall retribution by McIntosh's kinsmen, Creek leaders issued a caveat, stating that "if the Cowetaus attempted to get revenge" for McIntosh's death, they would "cut off the branches at their leisure."

The declaration was both a warning and an invitation for the exiles to return to their homes with the promise of safe passage. Indeed, a number of former McIntosh party members, like Jacob Beavers, James Island, and Benjamin and Joseph Marshall, did so and lived peacefully among the Creeks for the next decade. Many even assumed prominent positions in eastern Creek politics. The return of these prodigal McIntosh members blurred the lines between the Creeks who vowed to remain on their ancestral homeland at all cost, and those who remained receptive to the idea of voluntarily emigrating in the future. Some, like Benjamin Marshall, helped recruit emigrants for the voluntary parties and acted, in many ways, as a cancer in the Creek Nation. Others, like Chilly and Roly McIntosh, refused to look back and continued preparations for their voluntary emigration to the Indian territory.[15]

Negotiations for a new treaty commenced in November 1825 after a delegation led by Opothle Yoholo arrived to meet with federal officials. The Tuckabatchee headman had emerged as perhaps the most influential leader in the Creek Nation after the death of Big Warrior, who passed away in Washington while protesting the Treaty of Indian Springs the previous March. Although fortunate to have been given the opportunity, the Creeks were backed into a corner before negotiations ever began. The recalcitrant Troup, who was overwhelmingly supported by his constituents, refused to budge on his demands that the Creeks not reclaim any Georgia territory under the new treaty. Jeremiah Evarts, a reformer who opposed Indian removal, observed when he traveled through the region in 1826 that "there is scarcely a native Georgian in the state, who will not get into a passion, the moment the perfect right of the state to the Creek lands is called in question." The negotiations also brought the Creeks face-to-face with the McIntosh party representatives in Washington, and witnesses to the events were struck by the favorable reception the McIntosh delegates received from the administration. The delegates and federal officials dickered for two months over a Chattahoochee River boundary favored by the Creeks and a surveyor's line north of the bend of that river favored by the Georgians. Debate over exactly how much land the Creeks would reclaim or forever lose became so contentious at times, and an agreeable resolution appeared so unlikely, that Opothle

Yoholo attempted suicide. In late January 1826, the Creek delegation reluctantly agreed to terms. The Treaty of Washington, signed on 24 January 1826, nullified the Treaty of Indian Springs—the only Indian treaty ever overturned after its ratification.[16]

The 1826 Treaty of Washington was at once a victory and a devastating defeat for the Creek people. Considering what they were up against, it is remarkable that they succeeded in reclaiming any of their ceded land. But the Treaty of Washington was only a revision of the Indian Springs treaty, and many of the worst features from the original document were carried over to the new. The Creeks reclaimed their territory within Alabama, but lost all their land within the accepted but still unsurveyed boundary of Georgia. The treaty also affected the small number of Cherokees who lived just across the border in Creek country. They too were subsequently forced off their land. The Creeks were also cajoled into giving up a two-square-mile tract of land near Fort Mitchell in Alabama, where the new Creek Agency was to be relocated. The Creeks angrily protested Crowell's decision to place the agency on top of occupied fields and homesteads, but to no avail. Soon Crowell and his minions were busy constructing the agency buildings near the garrison. Just as devastating as losing their Georgia land, the Treaty of Washington continued the federal voluntary emigration program and sought to entice three thousand Creeks westward with the promise of $100,000 to be divided among themselves. The treaties were insidiously designed to disrupt life in the Creek Nation, then lure the Creeks westward with money and the promise of amelioration. Federal officials were confident that this was all it would take to move the entire population west of the Mississippi River and, although they did not have a term for it, ethnically cleanse the South of Creek Indians. If enough Creeks left, one agent believed, it would "have the effect to break up the nation." Expounding on this theory, Duncan Greene Campbell was convinced that the Creeks would not suffer to be divided "but that the whole would come in, and that the removal would be general and entire." And even if this did not happen all at once, the influence of the McIntosh party, Campbell wrongly surmised, "would very speedily drain from our limits those who might remain."[17]

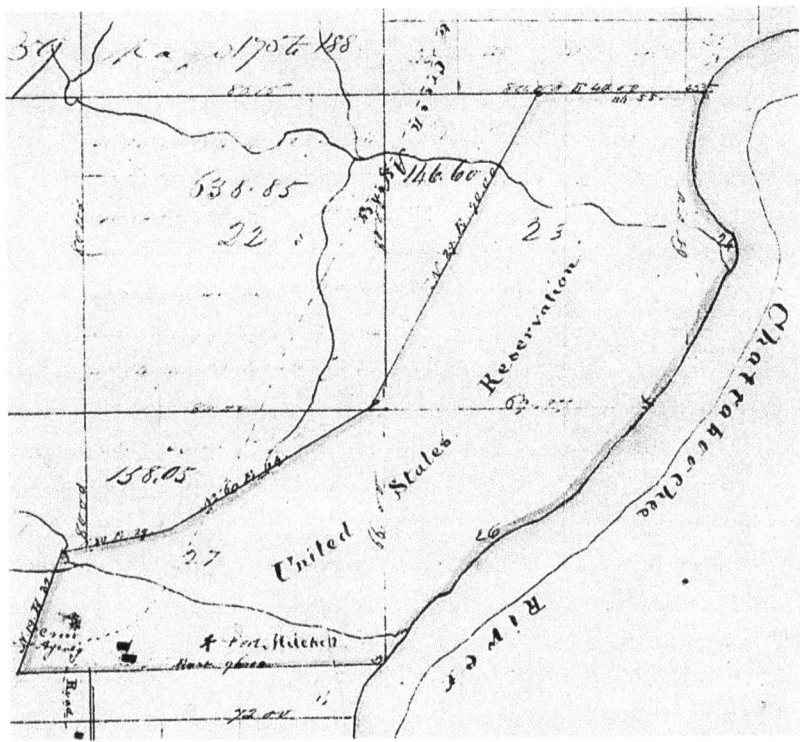

FIG. 2. U.S. Reservation and Fort Mitchell. Alabama Secretary of State, Land Plats, Tallapoosa Land District, Roll 30, 160, Alabama Department of Archives and History, Montgomery AL.

The Treaty of Washington pushed back the deadline for the Creeks to leave the boundaries of Georgia to 1 January 1827. Approximately seven thousand Lower Creeks who were dispossessed by the treaty then began the process of closing down their lives in Georgia in preparation for their forced removal onto Creek land within the borders of Alabama. It appears most Creeks made the move during the calendar year 1826, as the headmen confirmed when they declared on 16 December 1826, two weeks before the deadline to vacate Georgia, that "we had to give up a large tract of Country which Compeld our people to cross the Chatahoochy River they did so and settled on the west side among our other people."

The Creeks left behind their homesteads, which sometimes consisted of a ten- to fourteen-square-foot cabin and a field of three to eight acres "under good fence." Wealthier Lower Creeks might have owned a two-story house, complete with a plank floor and perhaps a piazza. Larger estates sometimes had a separate kitchen and a corn house, and as many as one hundred peach trees surrounding the abode. Not surprisingly, wealthier Creeks would have had more acreage, more fruit trees, and larger homes or cabins than those of lesser means. The Lower Creeks were compensated for their lost improvements. For example, Fixico of Upatoi was paid eighty-eight dollars for his property in Georgia, while Icoica, also of Upatoi, only received sixteen dollars. In order to register for the money, Creeks had to meet with agents who recorded their homestead's value. The immovable property stayed in Georgia to be expropriated by white settlers unless the Creeks took matters into their own hands. In a show of resistance over the land cession, a number of Lower Creeks burned down their houses and fences and cut down the fruit trees that grew on their land so that no white families could enjoy the benefits of their labor.[18]

As the Creek refugees were moving into Alabama, the state's general assembly attempted to dislodge the growing Indian population with a series of discriminatory laws. Two disruptive pieces of legislation were enacted in Tuscaloosa in January 1827. The first law asserted legal jurisdiction over the three million acres of land given to Alabama in the Treaty of Indian Springs but retained by the Creeks in the Treaty of Washington. Autauga County, Alabama, was subsequently expanded to include the cession. More so-called extension laws followed in 1828 and 1829. The second law prohibited the Creeks from hunting, trapping, or fishing where the state had asserted its jurisdiction. Meanwhile, in Georgia, state officials began the process of organizing counties, sheriffs, clerks, courts, and other trappings of white society on the Creeks' former territory. Advertisements for the sale of individual plots of the Indian Springs cession soon appeared in newspapers throughout the region.[19]

The Treaties of Indian Springs and Washington forever altered the composition of the eastern Creek Nation and created the two conditions that directly led to the Creeks' removal beginning in July 1836. The first problem was the erosion of the buffer between the Creek Nation and white society. Prior to the signing of the Treaty of Indian Springs, the Flint River in west-central Georgia served as the eastern Creek boundary. Although a number of small towns—Knoxville, Macon, Fayetteville, and Forsyth, to name a few—dotted the region, none of these cities were within fifty miles of the highest concentration of Lower Creeks on the Chattahoochee River. Soon after the Creeks left Georgia, however, the city of Columbus was platted. Columbus quickly became a boomtown for white settlers, traders, land speculators, and whiskey shop owners. No longer required to travel for days along stretches of dangerous road, whites could simply cross the Chattahoochee River and within minutes be commingling with thousands of Lower Creek Indians. After 1827 Columbus became the primary entrance point for white squatters into the Creek Nation, while West Point and Roanoke were also points of entry. White encroachment drove the Creeks to distraction. Many established stores and grog shops and sold whiskey and merchandise on credit. Subsequently, alcohol abuse and indebtedness rose exponentially after 1827. Many whites crossed into the Creek Nation to illegally settle on Creek soil. Some squatters cleared a plot of unoccupied Creek land and remained undetected, while others brazenly drove Creek families from their homes and stole their crops.[20]

Buffer erosion was a two-way street as the Georgians quickly discovered, however. Not all Creeks left the limits of the state in 1826. Small bands of people, mostly from the Lower towns resisted U.S. government interference in their lives, refused to acknowledge either treaty, and made no effort to comply with federal demands. As the 1 January 1827 deadline came and passed, a small number of Creeks chose to remain on their ancestral Georgia homeland. Others may have resettled into Alabama or were Lower Creeks from Alabama, but repeatedly returned to Georgia for extended periods to hunt on their traditional grounds or simply to take property from the Georgians. When the Creeks failed to find enough game—as was typically the case by the 1820s, as the deer herds were nearly depleted—they sustained themselves by killing the livestock of the Georgia settlers. Whites saw that as theft, but the Creeks felt little compunction about taking from settlers who they regarded as living illegally on their land. Hunting whites' livestock was not new to the Creek Indians and they routinely killed domesticated animals that wandered onto their territory because they considered them fair game. In other cases, Creeks who refused to ranch killed settlers' stock simply to survive. Indeed, Crowell suggested it was hunger that drove the depredations on the Georgians' property, as many of the Lower Creeks "were literally starving." But spoliation claims show that some refugee Creeks did make a good faith effort to round up their stray stock in Georgia after 1827, only to have their cattle expropriated by whites who claimed them as their own. When the Creeks went to retrieve their property, the Georgians accused them of hunting on ceded land.[21]

Many Creeks, however, continued to travel through Georgia unabated as an act of resistance. Residents living in several Georgia counties complained of temporary Creek hunting camps, disappearing livestock, and stolen crops months and years after the forced relocation deadline. The usual suspects, according to the settlers, were people from the towns of Yuchi, Oswitchee, Chehaw, Hitchiti, Cusseta, Upatoi, Thlakatchka, and Eufaula, among others, who all had town sites, individual farmsteads, or hunting grounds in Georgia prior to 1827. Some Creeks clearly took pains to avoid being detected. Many lived in temporary encampments, hid in swamps, and spent years moving about western and central Georgia in order to avoid being spotted. When discovered by the whites, these Creeks simply abandoned the encampments within a day or two and moved on. Others were clearly not as concerned about being detected. Many Creeks established traditionally elaborate hunting camps, consisting of upwards of fifty hunters and complete with shelters or lean-tos, in plain view of their white neighbors. Georgians often spotted these camps by the large amount of smoke emanating from a nearby fire. Witnesses also discovered Creek hunting trails leading to different parts of the region. The most brazen of these hunters engaged Georgians when they were spotted. Twelve Lee County residents complained of Creek camps "in every direction." When confronted, the Georgians reported that the Creeks "impudently" declared that "they will not give up this country" and would "present their guns, and by their motions tell us they will kill us if we do not hush." When threatened with the militia, the Creeks stated that they would "meet them and die on this land." Some did. In Muscogee County, a white citizen and a black slave allegedly caught a Creek man stealing from a corn house. The suspected thief, whom Crowell later described as sober and "remarkably inoffensive," was shot and killed as he allegedly reached for his gun.[22]

The close proximity to whites in Georgia and Alabama (from the 1814 Fort Jackson cession acquired by Andrew Jackson after the first Creek War) created opportunities for the Creeks, even if it meant at times adopting nontraditional means of support. George William Featherstonhaugh, a British American geologist, traveled to the Creek country in 1835 and observed a number of Creeks working as deckhands on board the steamboat *Chippewa* as it plied the rivers between Mobile and Wetumpka. Others worked poling keel and flat boats along the same watercourse. During the next several years, the town of Columbus, Georgia, and its environs became a magnet for Lower Creeks looking for work, to trade, or for rations from the local population. Each day there would "generally be hundreds, and sometimes thousands" of Creeks in Columbus, but all were required to return to their homes on the west side of the Chattahoochee River at night. Locals observed that the Creeks "were generally friendly and harmless while on this side of the river, but sometimes annoying, as they would go to private houses, to the alarm of some of the ladies. But their object was to get something to eat or steal." Lower Creeks congregated outside the doors and windows of local Columbus establishments, while the streets were filled with Creek women carrying baskets on their backs. Twenty-four Creek Indians were hired at fifty cents and a glass of whiskey to play Inca soldiers in the stock play *Pizarro* at a Columbus theater in 1831. Some Creeks were hired to pick cotton on white farmers' fields. Anne Royall, who passed through Georgia and Alabama in 1830, observed one Creek woman working as a cook and another as a chambermaid in a Columbus tavern. Other Creeks were reduced to begging door-to-door for food or money, while some Creek women turned to prostitution.[23]

The Creeks also took advantage of the increasing number of travelers passing through the Creek Nation. Some engaged in the lucrative slave trade. Swedish visitor Carl David Arfwedson, for example, noted that a number of wealthy Creeks trafficked in black slaves, with one headman owning "numberless Negro-women, who, by his own account, might any day be sold to itinerant slave-dealers for at least seven or eight thousand dollars." Other Creeks sold surplus produce to travelers. Royall reported that on the road between Fort Mitchell and Montgomery, "the whole way was strewn with Indian camps, but we saw few Indians. They live on the rivers in summer and attend to their farms, and in fall and winter live in camps on the road side, to sell their productions to travellers, such as corn and fodder for feeding horses."[24]

The second problem created by the Treaties of Indian Springs and Washington was that they caused widespread starvation among the Lower Creeks. In fact, most of the refugees entered Alabama already malnourished. There had been a long drought during the summer of 1826, and agents feared that the Creeks would be "without corn by Christmas." Others did not plant crops, probably due to the confusion surrounding their impending removal from Georgia. Linah Mims, assigned to value the improvements of the refugees, was advised in July 1826, just prior to commencing his duties, that many of the people of the Lower towns were in a "disturbed state," had not planted corn, and were subsequently "in a suffering condition." Others, who did plant, were victimized by white Georgians who drove the Creeks from their improvements and expropriated their land before they could gather their crops. A number of white businessmen formed companies; purchased dry goods, groceries, and other provisions; and established themselves near the refugee encampments in anticipation of profiting off the compensation money the Creeks received for their lost Georgia improvements. But as the money was slow in coming, and as the "extreme distress" of the Creeks grew to "alarming" levels, many were forced to sell their improvement claims for much-needed food and clothing. The hunger appears to have been so widespread that in some cases, "whole Towns headed by their Chiefs" exchanged their claims for provisions. Without money, many Lower Creeks fell into debt trying to acquire supplies to clear new fields and additional provisions to last them until they could gather their first harvest on their new land. Most of these debts were secured by their headmen and paid out of the annuity. Creeks who sold claims to white traders often protested that they were not furnished provisions equal to the value of their improvements. And even if fraud was difficult to prove, conflict of interest was not. Solomon Betton, who helped distribute the federal compensation for the Creeks' lost improvements, furnished a copy of the ledger books to his son and a business partner, who then purchased a large number of claims in exchange for goods. And, on rare occasions, the Creeks victimized each other. Some who had no improvements were caught impersonating those who had claims in order to steal the rightful owner's money or goods.[25]

The problems associated with a large population living on a reduced domain was only exacerbated by the scarcity of quality soil within Alabama. Lieutenant-Colonel John James Abert, a federal topographical engineer, believed that only a fraction of what remained of the Creek Nation after 1827 was considered quality land. With the area already "comparatively populously inhabited by Indians," the several thousand Georgia refugees were left scrambling to find the few remaining tracts of unoccupied arable soil. Many, it appears, were unable to find it or unwilling to look for it, and they began an extended period of transience. Basil Hall, a British traveler who visited Alabama in April 1828, observed firsthand the precarious condition of the Lower Creek refugees only a year after they were forced from Georgia. When Hall, his wife, daughter, and family nurse crossed the Chattahoochee and stopped by the new Creek Agency, the family observed "crowds of those miserable wretches who had been dislodged from their ancient territory to the eastward of the river, but had not yet taken root in the new lands allotted to them." Hall and his wife observed these dispossessed Lower Creeks "wandering about like bees whose hive has been destroyed." Having spent what little money they had, Hall reported that many were "bordering on starvation" and "great numbers of them actually perished from want." Hall's wife, Margaret, observed that the Creeks were "in a state of starvation" and were "flocking about" the Creek Agency, "in eager expectation of supplies of food." Another traveler who visited the agency at about the same time observed the "indiscriminate jabberings of crying hunger," as famished Creeks devoured a barrel of flour provided by Crowell. The Creeks returned the next day and petitioned for more, while on the third morning, five hundred Yuchis arrived looking for corn.[26]

A fortunate few found the remaining scraps of good land and were subsequently able to reestablish their farmsteads within Alabama. Some had to travel as far away as the Coosa and Tallapoosa Rivers to find unoccupied fertile soil. By diffusing across the Upper and Lower Creek countryside, these refugees were simply continuing a trend that had begun decades earlier when the Creek economy transitioned away from the deerskin trade to the raising of livestock. As Creeks sought out quality grazing lands in the late eighteenth and early nineteenth centuries, they moved away from town centers and left their *talwas* spread out over a wide geographic area. Many Upper Creek towns separated and moved out along the branches of the Coosa and Tallapoosa Rivers, while many Lower Creek towns (prior to 1 January 1827) spread out down the Chattahoochee or moved east to the Flint River. A number of the refugees, likely those with livestock, continued this pattern in Alabama. Gustavus H. Scott, charged with distributing the improvement money to the Georgia Creeks, discovered how spread out the refugees were throughout the Creek Nation, noting that they "are generally settled on the more fertile banks of the Coosa, Tallapoosa, Line creek, Uchee & Chattahoochee." In fact, so many Creek refugees had settled in diffused homesteads that Scott found it too difficult and time consuming to visit each Creek family. Instead, the agents proposed a central location where Creeks were ordered to come and claim their money. Similarly, Abert observed the diffused nature of Creek settlements years later and noted that although the Creeks were "always spoken of as composed of separate towns, are generally scattered up & down the water courses and not in compact settlements." One of these towns—Abert never mentions—"lies in a length of forty miles in the valey of a creek," and their homesteads are generally scattered about "in every direction."[27]

Other Creeks, it appears, clustered into sizable, multitown settlements along the Chattahoochee River. The white businessmen who purchased goods to sell to the refugees established their stand at a "location seven miles below the Creek Agency, opposit & near several large towns composed mainly of the Indians who had lately removed from the lands of Georgia." Scott believed that one of the largest encampments of Creek refugees was located two or three miles west of Miller's Bend (opposite and near West Point, Georgia) on the Chattahoochee River.[28]

Some Georgia *talwas* went about rebuilding. The largest and most prominent town reestablished within Alabama was Cusseta. In 1825 Cusseta town consisted of 1,827 inhabitants, two hundred log houses (many of which were elevated from the ground on poles), and some "very poor huts." The town was located about a mile from the Chattahoochee River in Georgia. Agent Benjamin Hawkins noted that Cusseta was "spread out," while Lukas Vischer, a Swiss traveler, observed that Cusseta homes were "sometimes close by, sometimes further away," although he later recalled that the Georgia Creeks in general were "extraordinarily dispersed." Sometime in 1826, Creeks from Cusseta moved across the Chattahoochee River and started over. Where they go exactly is unclear but after 1832, when the Creeks had ceded the last of their domain to the United States and took their land in allotments, census takers and locating agents placed Cusseta in seven different settlements that stretched for dozens of miles. Because reserves were assigned by the location of a person's improvements (if they had any), county maps perhaps offer a glimpse into where these Lower Creek refugees resettled between 1826 and 1832. Incredibly resilient, the Cussetas reestablished one, and perhaps two, town houses within Alabama. Adam Hodgson visited the rotunda (used for cold weather gatherings) and square ground (warm weather) located one mile east of the Chattahoochee River in 1820, and noted the "large building, with a conical roof, supported by a circular wall about three feet high: close to it was a quadrangular space, enclosed by four open buildings." Soon after 1826, this sacred space was taken down, the council buildings reconstructed, and a new fire lit within Alabama. According to maps, one council house was located among the Cusseta settlements "near West Point," while a second was probably constructed at Secharlitcha because the Creeks held a number of councils at that site in the early 1830s. In 1831 the Cussetas held a Busk—a purification ceremony that celebrated the new year and the bounty of their land. It was almost certainly not the first Green Corn Ceremony the Cussetas held on their Alabama soil, but it was the first that appears in the written record. There can be little doubt that the ceremony's spiritual component and emphasis on renewal took on added significance considering that they had consecrated new land.[29]

While Hitchiti and Otellewhoyanunau, a *talofa* (daughter town) of Chehaw (meaning "Hurricane Town") also reorganized in some form within Alabama, other *talwas* did not. Okteyoconnee, a town of 272 residents located some distance south of Fort Mitchell on the east side of the Chattahoochee River, never reorganized in the East, and many of its members voluntarily emigrated in 1829. Similarly, Sand Town, a settlement affiliated with the McIntosh party in Georgia, and many of whose members signed the Treaty of Indian Springs, dissolved in the East when dozens moved to the Indian territory with the first McIntosh party in 1827. Big Spring, a town of 140 residents moved west in 1827 and 1828. All three towns appear on an 1833 census of the western Creek Nation.[30]

Some Creek refugees moved into the Cherokee Nation, where at least one "small village of Full Blooded Creek Indians" consisting of fifteen families was established some fifty miles over the Cherokee line sometime before 1832. Other refugees fled south to live among the Seminoles. In 1827 a company of soldiers observed near-starving Lower Creeks fleeing to Florida. Surviving by stealing from the residents of Hog Town, the Americans noted that the refugees were "in the most miserable and wreched condition it is possible to concieve. Many of them skeletons and their bones almost worn through the skin."[31]

And yet, despite the massive upheaval caused by their forced relocation from Georgia, it is possible that even transient Creeks were able to maintain some semblance of their spiritual and ceremonial lives. Although the evidence is circumstantial to say the least, there is evidence to suggest that landless Creeks also celebrated the yearly Busk. Rather than using locally harvested green corn, the Creeks without fields might have made do by stealing from the white Georgia settlers. Theophilus Bryan of Muscogee County, Georgia, claimed in 1828 that Indians stole five bushels of corn from his property. He knew it was the work of the Lower Creeks, as he declared in an affidavit that "white people are not in the practice of stealing green corn."[32]

The Lower Creeks certainly maintained their physical and mental prowess by participating in a number of ball plays. In 1831 a Scottish visitor

FIG. 3. The Lower towns of the Creek Nation, ca. 1800–1818. Based on Ethridge, *Creek Country*, 29. Cartography by Sarah Mattics.

on his way to Charleston from New Orleans passed through the Creek Nation and observed the Yuchis and another unnamed Lower Creek town participating in a game near Fort Mitchell. He noted that the ball players' "skin was besmeared with oil, and painted fantastically with different colours. Some wore tails, others necklaces made of the teeth of animals." The traveler witnessed the Yuchis lose to their opponents. Afterward, the

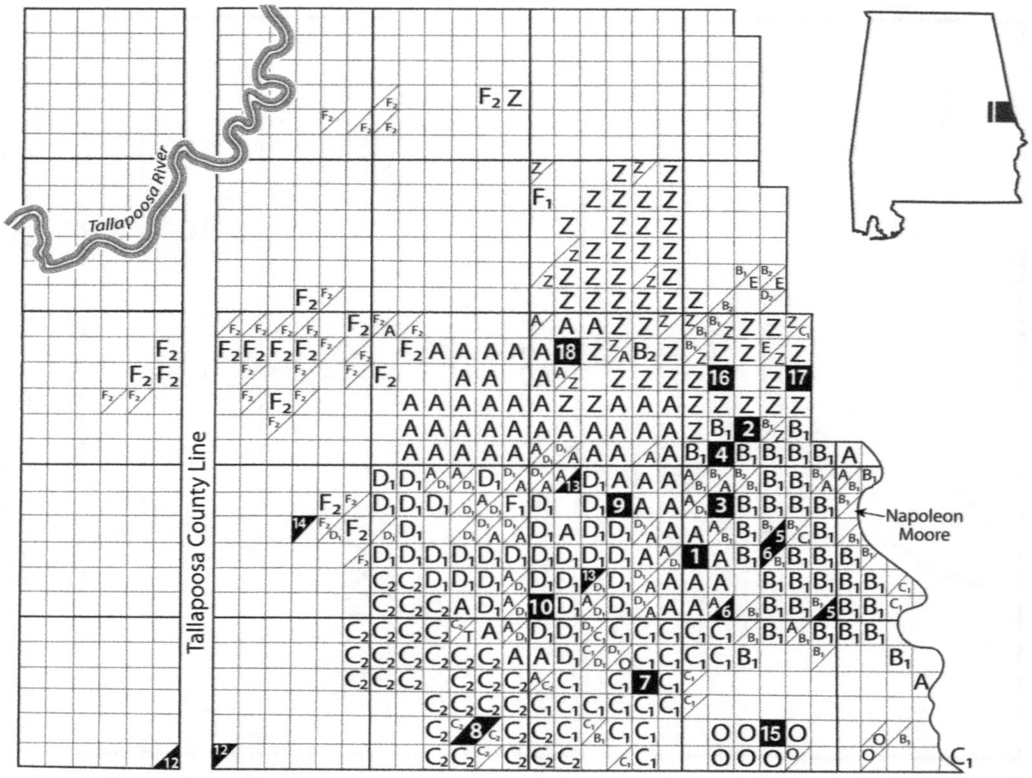

FIG. 4. Location of Lower Creek reserves in Chambers and Tallapoosa Counties, Alabama, after 1832. Map 243, RG 75, Entry 163, Central Map Files, NARA II, College Park MD. Large letters represent two half-sections owned by two different families from the same town. Numbers correspond to the reserves of the ninety principal headmen. Cartography by Sarah Mattics.

KEY

A: Cusseta (near West Point or Tuskenehaw Chooley's Town)
  1. Tuskenehaw Chooley

B1: Coweta (at Choloseparpkar or Kotchar Tustunnuggee's Town)
  2. Charlo Harjo Cochokone
  3. Kotchar Tustunnuggee
  4. Talmarse Harjo
  5. Emathla Harjo
  6. Efar Tuskenehaw

B2: Coweta (Koochkalecha Town)

C1: Coweta (on Hallewokkeyoaxar Hatchee)
  7. Absalom Island

C2: Cusseta (at Secharlitcha)
  8. Okfuskee Yoholo

D1: Cusseta (on Osenubba Hatchee or Tuckabatchee Harjo's Town)
  9. Arparlar Tustunnuggee
  10. Tuckabatchee Harjo
  11. Isfarne Emathla (reserve located in Russell County)

D2: High Log (Yuchi)

E: Yuchi (on the waters of the Chattahoochee)
  12. William Barnard

F1: Cusseta (on Little Euchee Creek)
  13. Efar Emathla

F2: Thlakatchka and Okfuskee (Echeesehogee Town on the waters of the Tallapoosa)
  14. Micco Foseke (George Grayson)

O: Thlakatchka or Broken Arrow—Wetumpka (on Euchee Hatchee)
  15. Honese Harjo

T: Cusseta (on Opillikee Hatchee/Tallassee Town)

Z: Thlakatchka (Horse Path Town)
  16. James Island
  17. Konippe Emathla
  18. Socokoba

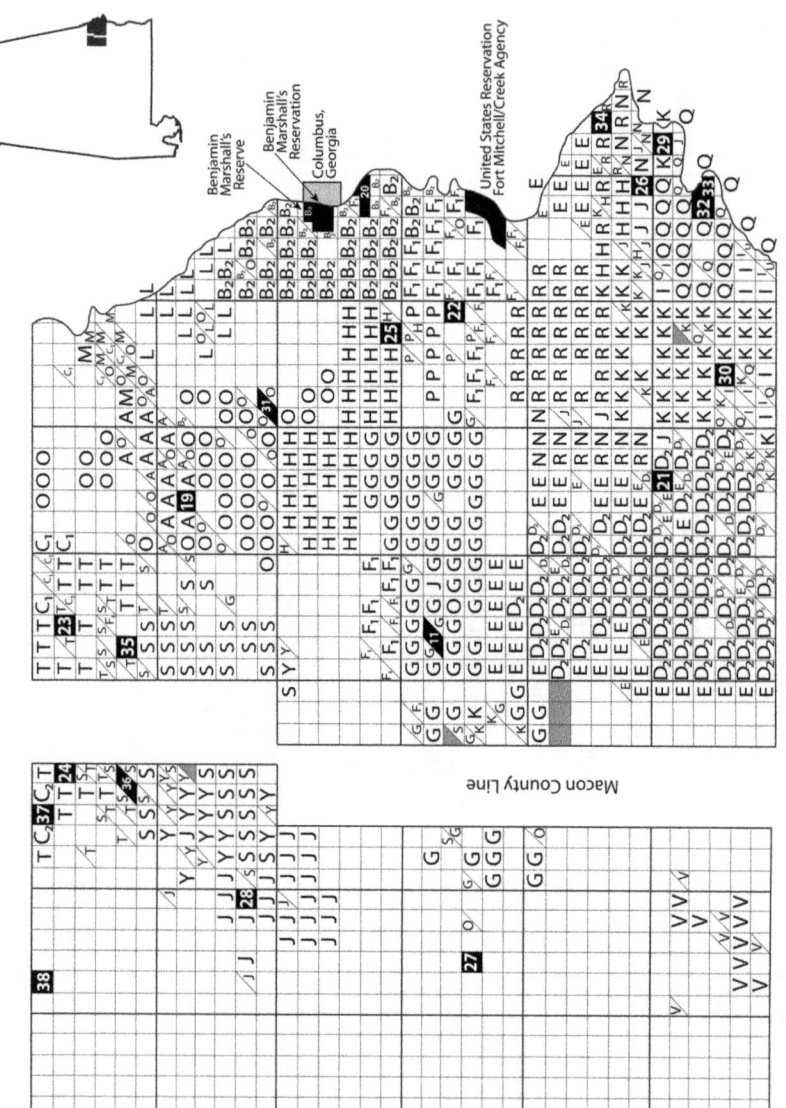

FIG. 5. Location of Lower Creek reserves in Russell and Macon Counties, Alabama, after 1832. Map 238 (Russell) and Map 256 (Macon), RG 75, Entry 163, Central Map Files, NARA II, College Park MD. Large letters represent two half-sections owned by two different families from the same town. Numbers correspond to the reserves of the ninety principal headmen. Grey areas denote portions of torn or illegible map. Cartography by Sarah Mattics.

KEY

A: Coweta (on Toosilkstookee Hatchee)
19. Joseph Marshall

B2: Coweta (Koochkalecha Town)
20. Jacob Beavers

C1: Coweta (on Hallewokkeyoaxar Hatchee)

C2: Cusseta (at Secharlitcha)

D2: High Log (Yuchi)
21. Ponaher Thlocco

E: Yuchi (on the waters of the Chattahoochee)
22. Timpoochee Barnard

F1: Cusseta (on Little Euchee Creek)
23. Neah Micco

G: Cusseta (on Tolarnulkar Hatchee)
24. Eastee Charco Chopco

H: Chehaw
25. Kotchar Harjo
26. Yoholo Harjo
27. Johnny Chopco

I: Pahlochokolo

J (Russell County): Hihagee (a Branch of the Hitchiti)

J (Macon County): Eufaula (on Chowokolo Hatchee, a branch of Lower Eufaula on the Chattahoochee and its tributary streams)
28. Woxe Micco

K: Hitchiti
29. Tunneechee
30. Neah Emathla

L: Thlakatchka (Koteofar)

M: Coweta (on Warkooche Hatchee)

N: Otellewhoyanunau

O: Thlakatchka or Broken Arrow—Wetumpka (on Euchee Hatchee)
31. Yufkar Emathla Harjo

P: Thlakatchka

Q: Tolowarthlocco (a branch of Pahlochokolo)
32. Enehar Tuskehenehaw
33. Nehar Thlocco

R: Oswitchee (on the Chattahoochee River)
34. Tuckabatchee Fixico

S: Oswitchee (on the waters of Opillikee Hatchee)
35. Oswitchee Emathla
36. Octruchee Emathla

T: Cusseta (on Opillikee Hatchee/Tallassee Town)
37. Cusseta Micco
38. Micco Chartee

U: Sawokli

V: Eufaula

Y: Cusseta (on Chowokolo Hatchee)

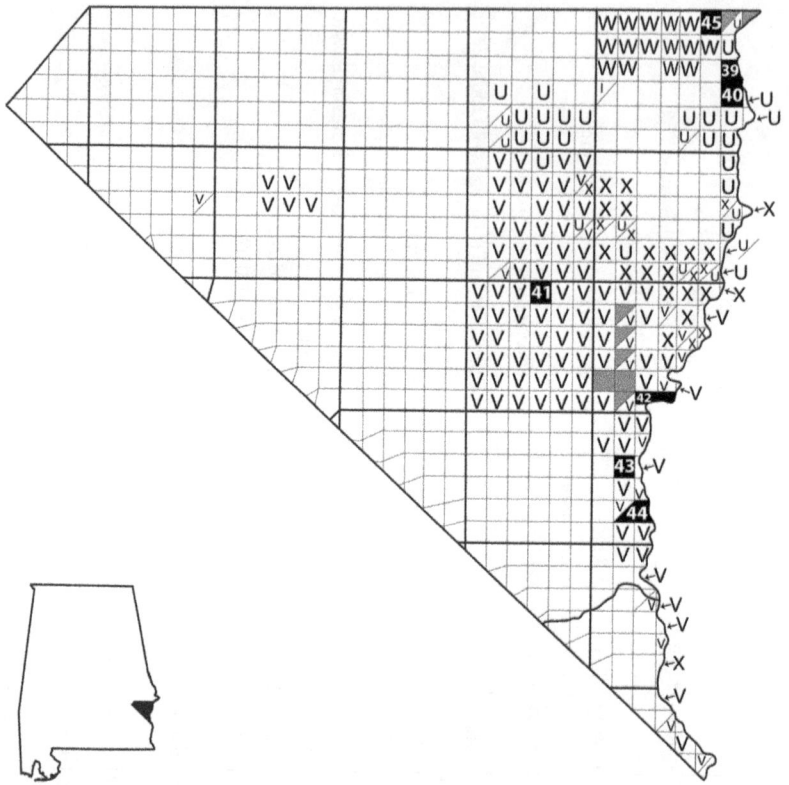

FIG. 6. Locations of Lower Creek reserves in Barbour County, Alabama, after 1832. Map 241 Record Group 75, Entry 163, Central Map Files, NARA II, College Park MD. Large letters represent two half-sections owned by two different families from the same town. Numbers correspond to the reserves of the ninety principal headmen. Grey areas denote portions of torn or illegible map. Cartography by Sarah Mattics.

KEY

I: Pahlochokolo

U: Sawokli
 39. Neah Micco
 40. Parhose Emathla

V: Eufaula
 41. Keparyar Tustunnuggee
 42. Tustunnuggee Harjo
 43. Fosehatchee Emathla
 44. Neah Tustunnuggee

W: Hatcheechubba
 45. Tallassee Micco

X: Cowyka (a branch of Sawokli)

Creeks celebrated, as "the victors danced about in all the madness of inordinate elation, and the evening terminated in a profuse jollification." Not all ball plays were for recreation, however. Called the "little brother of war," the game's speed and violence almost guaranteed injury and sometimes death, and was considered adequate preparation for actual warfare. Indeed, the Creeks held a ball play in March 1825 near the Flint River on their newly ceded territory in Georgia, perhaps in preparation for an impending assault on the McIntosh party. One white man noted that "their dissatisfaction was on account of the late treaty. Their faces were painted red; there was a ball play in that quarter," although he was not sure if those Indians were actual participants.[33]

Even as the Creek people sought to adjust to their new lives on a reduced domain, the Creek National Council faced another demand from Georgia for more soil. Soon after the ratification of the Treaty of Washington, Georgia discovered that a narrow strip of land along the Alabama border was not included in the cession. Operating under the conviction that the treaty intended to cede all Creek territory in Georgia, Troup dispatched surveyors to mark off the disputed area. Indignant at the trespass and the unyielding demands for territory, Little Prince, speaking for the council, refused to relinquish the parcel and replied to the request by declaring that the Creeks were very thickly settled and they had "no land to Spare." In January 1827 a number of Lower Creeks confronted one of the surveyors, temporarily confiscated his compass, and threatened him "very severe" if they ever found him over the line again. Still smarting from the Treaties of Indian Springs and Washington and adamant in their refusal to cede the strip, the Creeks went as far as to place towns along the boundary line to prevent the territory in question from being marked off. One surveyor observed "three settlements of Indians in my district that have in them about ten men and in two miles on the Alabama side there is a large Town that I am told have from forty to fifty warriors in it which is to be placed on the new Treaty line as spies, and prevent the land from being surveyed."[34]

Under intense internal and external pressures, the Creeks ultimately lost the disputed parcel of land. The protagonist in the Creeks' final chapter with Georgia was agent John Crowell, who pressed the Creeks relentlessly to cede the territory in question. Once again backed into a corner with few satisfying options, Little Prince relented and defied the National Council by agreeing to terms. Although his actions are puzzling, Michael D. Green suggests that Opothle Yoholo's increasing power, paranoia that Cherokees John Ridge and David Vann (who were serving as counselors to certain Creek headmen) were exerting undue influence over Creek affairs, and that even senility may have guided the aged headman. Using money and his considerable influence to ultimately gain National Council approval for the treaty, Little Prince circumnavigated Opothle Yoholo's and the Upper Creeks' opposition to the cession and in the process avoided William McIntosh's fate.[35]

The Treaty of the Creek Agency, signed on 15 November 1827, ended the Lower Creeks' long and acrimonious relationship with the Georgia government. Thomas L. McKenney, who also signed the document, later recalled of the agreement that "every foot of land remaining to the Creeks, of what was once their immense domain in Georgia, was now ceded." White immigrants soon flooded eastern Georgia. Within two years of the Treaty of Indian Springs signing, a visitor traveling through the area marveled that from the Flint River to the Chattahoochee there were "*cotton* land speculators thicker than locusts in Egypt."[36]

Despite the abrogation of the Treaty of Indian Springs, its successor, the Treaty of Washington was a devastating setback for the Creek Nation. The loss of their Georgia land forced several thousand refugees to join the rest of their population on about five million acres of land within Alabama. But much of their Alabama land was of low quality and many were unable or unwilling to reestablish their lives to any degree. This commenced an extended period of starvation and transience in the Creek country that lasted well into the 1830s. Moreover, the treaties disrupted town life and settlement patterns for a majority of the Lower Creeks. Just as insidious, the Treaties of Indian Springs and Washington were emigration documents. Hoping to entice other Creeks to follow the McIntosh party to the West, government officials began canvassing the Creek Nation, hoping to compel or cajole Creeks into enrolling for emigration. Their goal for the first party was three thousand individuals. In response to this threat, Creek headmen devised laws designed to prevent other Creeks from following the McIntosh faction west. Within this atmosphere, nearly seven hundred Creeks of the McIntosh party and their slaves made preparations to relocate to Indian territory.

2   Fission

1827–28

While most of the Lower Creeks were rebuilding their lives after the loss of their Georgia lands, members of the McIntosh party were surveying an area west of the Arkansas Territory and preparing for their emigration by packing their possessions into wagons. Although the McIntosh Creeks anticipated emigrating quickly after the Treaty of Indian Springs signing, the death of McIntosh and the reactions of those opposed to the cession derailed those plans. Some McIntosh Creeks refused to emigrate after the death of their headman. When the first McIntosh party finally left the Creek country for the West in November 1827, it included only about seven hundred Creeks and their slaves. Their departure from the Creek Nation was highly controversial, and most Creeks considered the McIntosh faction to be traitors. Any sense of relief the emigrants felt as they left the nation was short-lived, as the actual journey west proved to be dangerous and exceedingly difficult. Their destination was a location eight miles west of Cantonment Gibson—a U.S. fort built in 1824 and home to the Seventh Infantry, which was charged with keeping the peace among the western Indians. When the McIntosh party finally arrived in early 1828, they became the founders of the western Creek Nation.[1]

Would-be emigrants spent the years 1825, 1826, and much of 1827 living in fear of more retaliatory strikes from the National Council. They also spent those two and a half years without a steady supply of food and, in many cases, without adequate clothing and other provisions. Raids on the homes and property immediately after the Treaty of Indian Springs had left many members of the group with little on which to live. Exile prevented them from planting crops during the spring of 1825 or tending to any of their remaining livestock. As a result, they were forced to rely on government aid. Indeed, military personnel noted that in the immediate aftermath of McIntosh's execution, hundreds of the Coweta headman's followers came to Indian Springs in search of provisions. Most were "indifferently clothed & some with scarcely any clothing." Others were "literally naked & starving." Agents subsequently "furnished them with such articles as were generally absolutely required," but also "with some beyond what they were accustomed to." This included items such as shoes, socks, homespun, calico, blankets, soap, fishing line and hooks, saddles, pantaloons, vests, frock coats, shawls, and hosiery, as well as higher-end items such as cashmere, ostrich feathers, toothbrushes, silk, seersucker fabric, beaver hats, and tortoise combs. A small amount of food was also issued, including eggs, lard, butter, Irish potatoes, onions, molasses, sugar, and coffee.[2]

Many of the wealthy McIntosh members procured basic items for the less fortunate. For instance, Chilly McIntosh received "orders for cloak for Indians" and "sundry orders by Indians." And Joseph Marshall, a signer of the Treaty of Indian Springs, received a "verbal order for 52 Indians $5.00 each in Homespun and Blankets." Agents, including Edmund Pendleton Gaines, extended money and credit to prominent treaty party members including Chilly McIntosh, Benjamin Marshall, and Benjamin Hawkins "in the support of the hungry and naked Followers of the late Genl. McIntosh in 1825." Most of the money, it appears, was then distributed to the neediest members of the group; however, some of the funds were expropriated by whites who either cheated the Indians out of money or sold them goods at inflated prices. Indeed, Gaines conceded "that much of the money ultimately found its way into the hands of those white vultures who are usually seen hovering about the Indians at their Treaty grounds and elsewhere I can not doubt."[3]

In May 1826 Colonel David Brearley, a New Jersey native and former agent to the Quapaws and western Cherokees, was commissioned as agent to the western Creeks and ordered to conduct the McIntosh party to

Indian territory. Soon after arriving in the Creek Nation, Brearley took a tour of the area to gauge public opinion and discovered significant opposition to emigration among Creek headmen. Among the loudest was Little Prince, who complained bitterly that the government-issue gifts Brearley handed out to emigrants served as an inducement or "temptation" to move to the Indian territory. Little Prince also publicly reprimanded and threatened Hillabee resident Benjamin Hawkins for making positive representations of the western country during a meeting of the National Council held that August. Soon thereafter, Creek headmen issued an edict punishing violators with death if they emigrated or persuaded any Indian to join the McIntosh party. These threats were not extended to actual McIntosh party members, whom Little Prince described as "a few obnoxious characters who ought to have been taken away long ago." For non-McIntosh members, however, even being seen conversing with Brearley was grounds for punishment, and the agent later observed that "Men, Women & Children fled from their houses at my approach." During the voluntary emigrations, runners were often sent ahead "with the utmost speed" to all the towns in order to excite "universal alarm" that agents were about to enroll people to move west. But the hostility toward those willing to leave the Creek Nation only got worse. When Brearley returned from a visit to Washington in the fall of 1826, he discovered that "the alarming and cruel disposition" expressed toward the emigrants by the headmen "has been manifested in a greater degree during my absence, than had before come to my knowledge."[4]

The headmen's growing anger may have had something to do with what Brearley discovered when he visited would-be emigrants hiding out at "McIntosh's old place" in November 1826. They were there for a council, called by Brearley, to discuss their emigration to Indian territory. Taking a count of those in attendance, the agent discovered 176 men, 193 women, and 270 children. Including the 172 black slaves present, the total number topped out at more than 800. The 639 Creeks well exceeded the 416 people Edmund Pendleton Gaines believed belonged to the McIntosh party in 1825, and was more than double the number claimed in a government report, which declared that "all the followers of McIntosh, including *men, women, and children, do not much exceed*

300 souls altogether." Indeed, it appears that the short- and long-term crises created by the loss of their Georgia land was reason enough for the increase. As land scarcity and starvation became a looming threat, many Creeks probably decided to take their chance in the West. By May 1827 witnesses noted that many Creeks "would not only enter their names now [for emigration] but would actually follow [Brearley] like hungry dogs to be fed, anywhere he might lead."[5]

Hunger and the threats of violence against the McIntosh party convinced Brearley of the need to move the party quickly across the Mississippi River. Indeed, many preferred moving as soon as possible, while others "from necessity must do so, unless Government extend further support." Without crops and livestock, the party was forced to rely on the hunt and "wild roots," and their condition was becoming increasingly "desperate." The agent suggested the winter of 1826–27 as a good time to depart the Creek Nation, but Roly and Chilly McIntosh balked. Convinced that they needed more time to sell their property and conclude their business in the East, the two also refused to emigrate until a reconnaissance team surveyed their new lands as guaranteed in Article 6 of the Treaty of Washington.[6]

Four months later, on 15 March 1827, Benjamin Hawkins, Asseemee of Hitchiti, Lemuel B. Nichols, Arbeka Tustunnuggee, and Daniel Kennard of Thlakatchka, along with Brearley, stepped aboard the side-wheel steamboat *Fort Adams* at Montgomery for their exploratory trip to the Indian territory. These Creeks were no doubt chosen from among their peers, and for good reason. Arbeka Tustunnuggee (who signed the Treaty of Indian Springs), Hawkins, and the Kennards were all close friends or related to the McIntosh family through marriage. But, Lemuel B. Nichols, a white man married to a woman from Broken Arrow, had only lived in the Creek Nation for about seven and a half years. Nichols's presence, however, was almost certainly part of Brearley's larger strategy of attracting emigrants through what he perceived to be the powerful influence of whites who were married to Creek women. The agent was convinced that many thousands of Creeks were willing to emigrate if not for the opposition of their headmen and that the only way to neutralize the chiefs was through, what he believed to be, the wealth, influence, and marriage connections of the

Indian countrymen. Brearley also claimed that almost all of the whites living in the Creek Nation were agreeable to the arrangement, although a small number demanded "an additional sum for their services in effecting the emigration."[7]

The exploratory party reached Mobile, where they transferred to the steamboat *Columbia* for their journey to New Orleans before boarding the *Catawba* and ascending the Mississippi and Arkansas Rivers. Disembarking at Dardanelle Rock west of Little Rock, the party traveled the last leg by land to Cantonment Gibson, located on the Grand River. After arriving at the complex, the party procured additional horses, an interpreter, and guides. On 11 May the party left the complex on horseback to explore the region. The itinerary included the survey of approximately one hundred miles along the north side of the Arkansas River, although heavy rains forced the party to change direction and they crossed the Arkansas River after four days and traveling only about sixty miles. The delegates traveled southwest and crossed several minor branches before reaching the grayish and muddy waters of the Canadian River on 23 May. The party then headed in an "East and North East" direction reaching the mouth of the Grand River and arrived back at Cantonment Gibson on 27 May. What the party discovered was generally what topographical engineers would also conclude: the best land in the Creek tract was on the north side of the Arkansas River beginning near its junction with the Verdigris. After spending several days exploring their new territory, a piece of land about eight miles west of Cantonment Gibson and four miles from the territorial line was chosen. Brearley suggested that the party pick a plot on the rich north side of the Arkansas River, located at a point that offered them the protection of the garrison while allowing the government the greatest amount of ease in distributing their provisions during the first year of their resettlement. The McIntosh delegation actually liked the land between the Arkansas and Canadian Rivers better, but Brearley refused to provide them goods from that distance.[8]

Soon after the deputation returned from its four-month trip in mid-July, Creek councils were called. A meeting of the National Council was held at Wetumpka for, among other things, receiving the report on the condition of the western lands and on how the party was received by the western Cherokees and, most important, by the Osages, whose former land the McIntosh Creeks would soon occupy. The Wetumpka council ground was likely chosen because it was reasonably close to Fort Mitchell and therefore a strategically safe location to hold a fractious meeting. Among the speakers was Arbeka Tustunnuggee, the leader of the exploratory deputation, who gave a highly favorable report of their new land. He declared that with regard to the condition of the land, water, and game, the Indian territory had many advantages over their land in Alabama and Georgia. This was not necessarily true, but the party visited during the spring when the western rivers were high and the scorching summer heat had not yet arrived. They also just missed the droughts of summer and the blistering cold of wintertime. All in all, it was the best window of time to visit the Indian territory. Moreover, it was doubtful that the McIntosh party could have turned back at this point: they were fully committed, so a positive description was probably to be expected. Still, Roly McIntosh, who had hunted in the area in years past, knew the drawbacks to life in the Indian territory—the mosquitoes, the heat, and the raiding western Indians. As perhaps the person who could least afford to have a change of heart, McIntosh could only look toward the future.[9]

The council's attendance was "uncommonly numerous" and the atmosphere in the Wetumpka square no doubt was tense. Emigration was not the only controversial item on the agenda as John Crowell tried to press the headmen into ceding the last strip of their Georgia land. With the nation on the verge of fissuring, Creeks opposed to emigration, like Little Prince and Mad Tiger, implored any McIntosh party members who did not want to emigrate (but were fearful of saying otherwise) to speak up so they could remain behind under the protection of the headmen. Among the final speakers at the meeting was Chilly McIntosh who, according to newspapers, gave "a very eloquent speech." After he was done talking, McIntosh "shook hands with the head men of the Nation," then departed with his treaty party to the falls of the Chattahoochee River where a second meeting was held on 4 August. There the McIntosh faction made the necessary arraignments for their departure, received the official report of the exploratory deputation, and accepted the emblems of friendship presented by the western Cherokees and Osages.[10]

The formal commencement of voluntary emigration began with the establishment of emigration camps around the Creek Nation. These were staging areas where emigrants packed their possessions into wagons and subsisted on federal provisions until the day of their departure. One camp, containing 105 emigrants, was located near Fort Gaines, Georgia, while another, with 104, was established at Kymulga. One hundred and two emigrants probably camped at or near Coosada. For his part, Chilly McIntosh set up an enrollment camp at his house near the Chattahoochee River where he supplied provisions to an undisclosed number of emigrants. McIntosh also rented out one of his oxcarts, as well as a five-horse and a four-horse team, to Brearley in order to carry the emigrants' baggage. Other Creeks, looking to profit from the enterprise, also contributed food and fodder for the emigration and each was entitled to compensation from the federal government. Entrepreneurial Chilly McIntosh even threatened to sell his wagons if not paid the going rate for a hire, which was three dollars a day.[11]

When all the would-be emigrants had arrived and packed their belongings into the wagons, they were ordered to rendezvous at a central location for enrollment. Brearley chose Harpersville in north-central Alabama because it was outside the Creek Nation and somewhat removed from those opposed to emigration. 15 September was initially the appointed day for each camp to consolidate, with a departure date scheduled for 1 October. The party, however, ran late in part because Chilly McIntosh, who had stopped at Kymulga and merged with the camp there, arrived at Harpersville sometime after the main party. Once together, agents met with all of the adult males, each of whom gave his name and town of origin, as well as the number of women, children, and slaves accompanying the family. This information was recorded on muster rolls. Each man was promised beaver traps, guns, brass kettles, butcher knives, and blankets for enrolling, although due to bureaucratic red tape most never received these articles. When the agents had finished the muster roll on 8 November, they found that they had 707 emigrants, which included Indian countrymen and 86 slaves. There were approximately

190 men, 175 women, and 250 children. At the last minute, John Wynn, his family, and his slave left Harpersville and returned temporarily to the nation, reducing the total to 703. The number, however, was well short of the government's goal of 3,000. Noticeably absent on the roll was Roly McIntosh, who did not accompany Chilly McIntosh and the main party, but chose instead to emigrate himself while paying for the passage of members of his family along with dozens of horses.[12]

Many of the members of the first voluntary party were not actually friends or followers of William McIntosh. Approximately six hundred Creeks emigrated with the first party, while many allies of the late Coweta headman chose to remain behind and emigrate at a later date. This was reason enough for Creek leaders to issue threats against those who moved west, as a massive demographic shift across the Mississippi River threatened to tear the nation apart. Indeed, while Brearley was enrolling Creeks, a subagent was hired to run interference and allay "the angry Feelings of the hostile Chiefs" against those who chose to move west.[13]

Still, a handful of very close McIntosh family associates did move west with the first voluntary party. There were a number of signers of the Treaty of Indian Springs, including Chilly McIntosh, Arbeka Tustunnuggee, William Miller, Samuel Miller, Charles Miller, and Alexander Lashley. William McIntosh's brother Hagy and another family member, John, also enrolled, as did Stephen (the father of William's wife, Eliza) and Benjamin Hawkins (the son of Stephen), who were related through marriage. Daniel Perryman, who had been approached about using his influence to help carry out the Indian Springs treaty signing in exchange for a thousand-dollar bribe, also left the nation in 1827. Also appearing on the muster roll were four of the five members of the exploratory deputation—Benjamin Hawkins, Arbeka Tustunnuggee, Lemuel B. Nichols, and Asseemee—as well as members of somewhat prominent Creek families including Derasaw, Lovett, Marshall, Birford, and Brinton.[14]

Whatever their reasons for leaving, the actual journey to the West was difficult, especially in the dead of winter. The emigration began with an inauspicious start even before leaving the limits of Alabama, as a man was killed at the Kymulga camp. In his *Reminiscences*, Thomas S. Woodward later noted that the "half breed son" of James Seagrove "was killed by the Indians many years ago for killing another Indian at Kiemulga, when the first McIntosh party were emigrating to Arkansas territory." Moreover, while the Creeks waited for the agents to finish the muster roll, some residents of Harpersville tried to cheat the Creeks of the McIntosh party out of their money and property. An indignant Chilly McIntosh wrote a letter to the *Tuscumbia Patriot* and complained of receiving "no hospitality from the citizens of [Harpersville]" and of having been "harassed with attachments upon our property, and thrown into confusion with false accounts."[15]

The problems at Harpersville and the difficulty of land travel convinced Brearley to seek another rendezvous site for the second voluntary party he was already planning even before he had begun his journey with the first. On 8 November, a day or two before the emigrants began their march west, Brearley dispatched a letter to his subagent William Walker, ordering him to establish the new camp closer to the Tennessee River so the next group, tentatively scheduled to depart in March 1828, could take boat conveyance. Walker, an Indian countryman who married one of Big Warrior's daughters, was placed in charge of collecting emigrants while Brearley was gone.[16]

The party probably commenced their journey from Harpersville in the darkness of 9 or 10 November. As the Creeks traveled out of the town, however, whites continued to harass the party. Indignant, Chilly McIntosh complained that while they were "hoping to march our people along peaceably, we were troubled with constables every five miles, with false papers and we did not enjoy any peace until we came down the mountain; then we marched along with peace and harmony—passed through many villages, and arrived at Tuscumbia, where we encamped for a few days, intending to take boats down the waters of the Tennessee, and so on to Mighty river."[17]

Local whites only made what was already a difficult operation worse. Moving so many people of different ages and physical abilities was a massive undertaking and it appears that the party, whether by accident or by design, broke up into smaller detachments in order to better manage its movement. Each subparty had a leader who was hired to oversee its emigrants. Sometimes a Creek Indian, like Oakchonawa Yoholo of

Coosada, who received compensation for transporting twenty-one Creeks west, led these smaller detachments. The agents also came to rely on hundreds of individuals to aid in the emigration, most of whom were locals who rented out wagons, ferried the Creeks over rivers, loaded and unloaded keelboats, and provided provisions of beef, corn, cornmeal, and fodder along the route. Brearley rejected the idea of contracting ahead of time for provisions due to increased cost, and instead chose to stop along the route and purchase directly from local farmers or merchants. Runners were sent ahead to ensure a supply of food was ready once the party arrived. In cases where additional wagons were hired to haul Creek baggage or carry those too old or ill to walk long distances, the government compensated the owner for renting the wagon for that leg of the journey and paid for their return trip home. The emigrants themselves also provided provisions for the party as they commenced their journey.[18]

Poor weather and sickness plagued the Creeks as they passed by the north Alabama towns of Somerville, Decatur, Courtland, and Leighton. On 25 November 1827 the emigrants arrived in Tuscumbia. Because the town was home to a number of whiskey traders, Brearley assigned someone to suppress the sale of spirits while in camp, although the agents had purchased alcohol on a number of occasions and even compensated Creeks three gallons of whiskey for helping to overturn a wagon that fell into a river. Unlike their Harpersville counterparts, the Tuscumbians proved to be gracious hosts to the Creek emigrants. Chilly McIntosh observed that the party had "received all kind of hospitality and *good* treatment. The citizens of Tuscumbia have treated us like brothers, and our old helpless women were furnished by the good women of the town with clothing." Brearley penned a letter to the local newspaper thanking the Tuscumbians and noting that "from the inclemency of the weather during the time they were compelled to remain, many of them, particularly the aged and infants, presented extreme objects for charity, whose wretched condition was vastly ameliorated by the liberal donations [of the local women]."[19]

Although it appears that Brearley had decided that all the Creeks would walk to their new homes if able, the conditions at Tuscumbia changed his mind. The road from there to Memphis in 1827 was unfit for extended use even in dry weather, but the heavy rains made the road even more treacherous. On 28 November, Brearley broke the party into two groups. The Creeks who owned horses, along with those accompanying the baggage wagons—about three hundred total—continued by land to Memphis under the charge of subagent Thomas Anthony. The land party also consisted of a number of Creek runners who were sent ahead to organize a grand council with the principal headmen of the Chickasaw and Choctaw Nations. The purpose of the meeting, in the words of one newspaper, was to "renew their ancient friendship, and smoke the *calumet* of peace, until the smoke, to quote the language of one of their chiefs here, shall rise higher than the clouds." As the party moved westward, receipts show that the Creeks crossed the Hatchie and Wolf Rivers on 5 and 7 December, respectively.[20]

The remainder of the party, still in the vicinity of Tuscumbia, traveled by water. On 30 November, Brearley paid three hundred dollars for a keelboat that included "cooking Utensils & Tools" from which the Creek women could prepare meals. The following day he procured another keelboat in South Florence, Alabama. The water party, under the direction of David Brearley, left the Tuscumbia boat landing on 2 December, and traveled down the Tennessee River through the states of Tennessee and Kentucky. At the confluence of the rivers, the boats left the Tennessee River and entered the Ohio River and then the Mississippi River before arriving in Memphis and reuniting with those traveling on foot.[21]

Evidence suggests that the land party arrived in Memphis first, sometime around 11 December, while those traveling by boat probably arrived days later on Sunday, 16 December. To the west of their encampments was the great Mississippi Swamp—a treacherous stretch of land that was inundated with water for much of the year. Travelers through this region described it as one continuous bog, and during the rainy and flood seasons the water could reach as high as a horse's back. Due to the impracticality of traveling along dangerously muddy roads, 255 of the women, children, and elderly again boarded keelboats and began descending the Mississippi River on 25 December. The water party, now under the charge of the agent's brother, Charles Brearley, reached

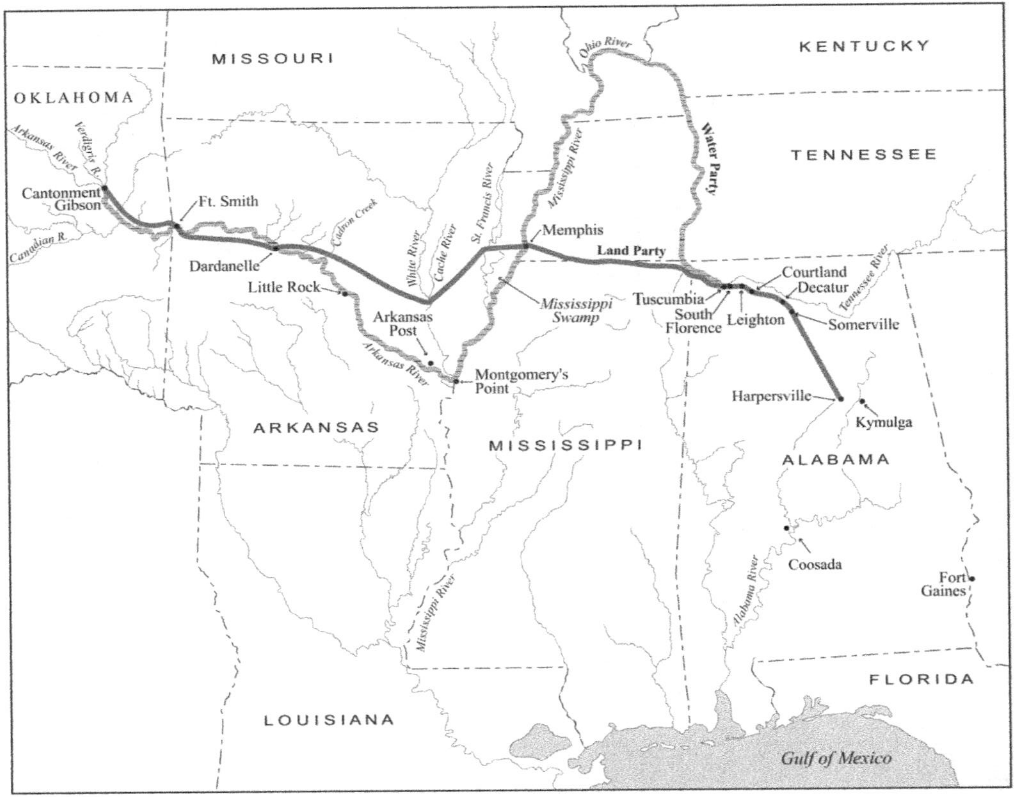

FIG. 7. Route of the first McIntosh party, November 1827–March 1828. Place names correspond to stopping points or locations noted in the documentation. Route lines and locations are approximations. Cartography by Sarah Mattics.

the mouth of the White River, and encamped at Arkansas Post before reaching Little Rock. For the women and children, travel by water, even in wet conditions, was relatively easy and uneventful, although the two keelboats were briefly detained at some point so that the travelers could bury someone who died along the route.[22]

The land party left Memphis on the same day under the command of David Brearley. For those traveling overland, the trip from Memphis to the White River through the Mississippi Swamp proved to be difficult and exhausting, and they experienced problems at almost every turn. With the "excessive rains and unusual rise of waters for the season" the roads became virtually impassable. In fact, it took almost two months to reach Cantonment Gibson from the swamp. The *Arkansas Gazette* described the journey during this stretch as primarily "'*swimming and wading*' (for it could hardly be called travelling)," and Brearley wrote to his superiors in Washington that the trek from Memphis was very "tedious and distressing to the Indians." Crossing the St. Francis proved to be particularly difficult for the Creeks and many of them were forced to leave property behind. In fact, Chilly McIntosh had to jettison two road wagons and one ox cart that he brought from his plantation.[23]

The journey from the St. Francis River to the White River took several days and the land party arrived there on 6 January 1828. The Creeks found the banks of the White River overflowed with rainfall and it took almost two weeks before they could make a safe crossing. Provisions had become scarce for the party, and with few settlers from which to purchase food, a number of Creek men swam across the White River to hunt on the less-flooded western side. In a matter of days, it was reported that Creek hunters had killed almost sixty deer. With two hundred horses and twenty baggage wagons, the party was forced to descend farther south, traveling through thick canebrakes and cypress swamps seven miles below the mouth of the Cache River in order to find a safe place to cross the White River, which was eventually done "with great difficulty and labour." Once on the western bank, the party continued toward the head of the prairie with the intention of setting out on the Cadron Road. Their route had the party bypassing Little Rock thirty miles to the north.[24]

While the land party slowly made its way toward Fort Smith, the water party was detained at Little Rock due to the high waters of the Arkansas River that rendered the current too swift for the boats to ascend. Brearley left the land party on 24 January and traveled south to meet the keelboats. At Little Rock, the agent employed the steamboat *Facility*, a brand new side-wheeler, to tow the keelboats up the Arkansas River to the mouth of the Verdigris. The Creeks later accused Brearley of stopping the boats at Fort Smith where "a great portion of [the Creeks'] property was left and destroyed—Col. Brearley said he had got the people at their place of residence and they might get their property as they could."[25]

On 30 January the water party stopped briefly at Auguste Chouteau's trading house near the falls of the Verdigris River where they were met by approximately 250 Osage Indians. The Osages had been cajoled into meeting the Creek immigrants by Colonel Matthew Arbuckle, the commander at Cantonment Gibson. Because Indian removal required the expropriation of Indian land on both sides of the Mississippi River (and the Creeks were settling on former Osage territory), repeated councils and face-to-face meetings between western and eastern Indians were necessary in order to keep the peace. Many of these councils were one-sided affairs, with federal or military officials dictating terms to each side. Indeed, with most of the prominent men in the McIntosh party still on the road somewhere between north of Little Rock and Fort Smith, and Roly McIntosh not even a part of the group, this was nothing more than a meet and greet between two Indian peoples who were soon to be neighbors. Most important, it was a chance for military agents to warn the western Indians against committing depredations. Indeed, it was here that Arbuckle issued his warning that "any offense committed by them, would be followed by the severest punishment."[26]

For their part, the Osages wanted little to do with the Creeks, and it is not surprising that they appeared "somewhat sour." Cajoled into signing massive land cession treaties in 1808, 1818, and 1825, the Osages occupied only a fraction of their once-vast domain by the time the McIntosh party arrived in early 1828. Delawares, for example, had been resettled on their land in Missouri before moving to present-day Kansas and, later, to present-day Oklahoma. The Osages resented the Delawares' occupation of their territory and the consumption of its resources, which they still claimed. Bison hunts brought the Delawares into conflict with Osage hunters, and the two peoples clashed a number of times in the 1820s. For many of the same reasons, the McIntosh Creeks would find themselves confronted by bands of Osages throughout the 1820s and 1830s. On this day, however, only niceties were exchanged. In a private meeting with Brearley, Osage headman Clermont pledged his friendship and offered his favorite son—"one of [the] finest young men in the nation"—to reside with the agent.[27]

After the council, Brearley boarded the *Facility* and traveled back toward Dardanelle to collect the land party, which was still walking toward Cantonment Gibson. The terrain between Little Rock and Fort Smith was littered with small, overflowed streams that were dangerous to cross and caused those on foot to separate into a miles-long train. A receipt for the ferriage of "one hundred and ninety six head of Horses and Oxen belonging to the Emigrating Creek Indians," issued at Dardanelle, suggests that at least portions of the party traveled on the south side of the Arkansas River, which was more common during the wet season. During the dry season, it was preferable to travel along the north side. The party was so spread out, however, that many Creeks had not even made it to Dardanelle by the time Brearley arrived to collect them. Other reports noted that the party was "scattered along the road" between Dardanelle and Fort Smith, a distance of ninety miles or more depending upon which road was used. The balance of the land party did not arrive until 12 March 1828.[28]

The Creeks arrived at their new homes noticeably exhausted. Even before collecting all of the stragglers near Dardanelle, Brearley noted in a letter to Secretary of War James Barbour that due to the poor weather and the wet roads, the land party appeared "so completely worn down" and urged patience in landing them at their destination. By spring there were still McIntosh emigrants coming in to Cantonment Gibson. These late arrivals were stragglers who had fallen sick along the route and were forced to remain while the rest of the party continued west. In fact, while near the western Cherokee settlements, a number of Talladega Creeks fell ill and had to remain behind. In March 1828 a detachment of Talladegas returned eastward along the route to recover their brethren. Also among the emigrants who arrived in Indian territory later than expected were 134 members of the party, including Alexander Lashley, who, while passing through the western Cherokee settlements near Skin Bayou, were detained for five weeks because of illness. The party was described as being "in great distress" and "destitute of provisions, or comforts of any Kind, a considerable number of them sick and altogether without the means of proceeding to their destination."[29]

During the next few years more of William McIntosh's friends and relatives trickled into the western Creek Nation. They provided transportation and provisions for themselves rather than accompany the federally sponsored emigrating party in 1827–28. These people received no immediate monetary and logistical aid, although they were later compensated for their travels by the U.S. government. Susannah McIntosh, for example, paid for the emigration of thirty-six of her family members, Peggy McIntosh thirty-five, and Jane Hawkins forty-nine. Soon after arriving in the West, Benjamin Hawkins returned to the Creek Nation to collect members of his family and thirty or forty of his slaves. Hawkins and company arrived back at Cantonment Gibson sometime in late August or early September 1828.[30]

The arrival of the approximately seven hundred emigrants and their slaves in Indian territory had broad implications for those who remained back east. Roly McIntosh and his cronies soon established a rival government in the West and federal officials were quick to point out that this new nation offered refuge from the white encroachment and starvation plaguing the Creeks in the East. This, in turn, helped pave the way for future emigrations. The deteriorating conditions in the Creek Nation in Alabama, including shortages of food brought on by the loss of their Georgia lands, had convinced numbers of Creeks that moving west was their only hope for survival. In response, Creek headmen continued their efforts to prevent the mass voluntary removal of their people, including reissuing death threats and driving Creeks from enrollment camps. Despite the intimidation, two more voluntary emigrations left the East in 1828 and 1829.

3 Frenzy
1828–29

Although approximately seven hundred Creeks and their slaves voluntarily emigrated from the Creek Nation in November 1827, this number did not represent all the people who decided to move west. Some McIntosh party members did not leave with Chilly McIntosh, but chose to wait for the second voluntary emigration almost a year later. Some decided to emigrate with the third voluntary party in 1829, while others moved west by themselves and at their own expense, with the anticipation of receiving federal compensation at a later date. The extra time allowed these Creeks to get their affairs in order and sell their property before their move to the Indian territory. There were many more Creeks who were not supporters of McIntosh yet had decided to move west as well. They were primarily Creeks most affected by the treaties of Indian Springs and Washington, and whose quality of life had declined precipitously as a result. Others likely believed that the forced removal of the entire Creek population was inevitable and wanted to choose the best land before the others. Indeed, when a three-person delegation traveled to the Indian territory to explore the region in 1828, observers noted that they were members of "the opposite party," meaning unconnected in any way with the McIntosh group. The deputation included twelve Chickasaws and six Choctaws who, like the Creeks, were also under pressure to migrate westward. While waiting to depart from St. Louis, the Creeks encountered a delegation of Potawatomis and Ottawas from the Lake Michigan region doing the same. The party also held a number of talks with the Shawnees, another relocated Indian group, before commencing their explorations west. The journey was not without incident, however, as the Creek interpreter Harper Lovett died from exposure to measles just after leaving St. Louis. After returning to the Chattahoochee, the exploratory party reported to interested friends that the West "was a fine country" and the "red children should remove there." This pronouncement was made in spite of the fact that they had not actually seen most of the land set aside for them—the Creek delegates elected to remain at the western Creek Agency visiting with Chilly McIntosh (and any other members of his party), while the Chickasaws and Choctaws explored the region on their own. The deputation arrived back too late to move with the second voluntary party that left the Creek Nation in late 1828, but perhaps due to their positive report, the 1829 voluntary emigrating party swelled to almost thirteen hundred Creeks, almost all of whom were members of "the opposite party." The size and composition of the 1829 emigration was of great concern to Creek headmen, who worked tirelessly to defeat the government's emigration program.[1]

In May 1828 perhaps as many as thirty Tuckabatchee men, allegedly under orders from Opothle Yoholo and Tuskenehaw's brother Yhargee, broke into the home of missionary Lee Compere and seized a number of blacks who were worshipping there. After the captives were led to the yard one by one, each was tied to a post and beaten "unmercifully." Among the victims was a twelve-year-old girl who was forced to watch before she too was attacked and then allegedly sexually assaulted. On its surface, the incident appeared to be another salvo in a long debate over the presence of missionaries, Christianity, and preaching in the Creek Nation. In 1822 Creek headmen, led by Big Warrior, banned public preaching, allegedly under the prodding of Creek agent John Crowell, who famously called it "all fudge" and "d——d nonsense." Methodist missionary William Capers blamed the political climate in the Creek Nation, not opposition to the Gospel, for Big Warrior's policy, however. Capers claimed the support of William McIntosh, who wanted the Methodists to build more schools and preach to the Creek people. Because Crowell opposed both Christianity and McIntosh, it was perhaps inevitable that Capers's plans would be controversial, especially if backed by the Coweta headman. McIntosh and Big Warrior were rivals long before the Treaty of Indian Springs, and the Tuckabatchee headman was a close ally of the Creek agent. Capers even rhetorically wondered if preaching would "injure some interest" in the store Crowell's brother Thomas operated at Fort Mitchell. The agent, however, claimed that he did not have a problem with the missionaries educating Creek children in areas other than Christianity. For their part, the Creeks also complained that preaching disrupted their traditional culture and that earlier missionaries had demanded too much of the Creeks' land to build their missions and had required their children to work. Moreover, as Claudio Saunt argues, the attack came at a time of increased hostility toward blacks in the Creek Nation. Traditionalists wanted to rid the nation of what they considered to be non-Creek elements, while Creek slaveholders worried that preaching would cause insubordination among their slaves.[2]

It is impossible to disregard the role emigration played in the attack, however. Compere was a proponent of the Creeks moving west, told them as much, and had been counseling individuals who were willing to emigrate. In December 1827, five months before the May attack at Withington Station, two men, purportedly under the direction of Opothle Yoholo, broke into Compere's pen and stole four pigs "by foarce." By early 1828 Compere was telling Eufaula headman Yoholo Micco that "the Indians would certainly have to remove & that they had better take the matter into serious consideration." Yoholo Micco reminded Compere of the many promises the government had made to them, including the latest: *"that if they would give up the small strip of land claimed by Georgia that the Govt would trouble them no more."* To this Compere replied that these were merely "promises of necessity." Yoholo Micco later addressed the headmen at Tuckabatchee and no doubt relayed what Compere had told him. At around the same time, John Davis, a Weogufka man of Creek and African ancestry and one of Compere's close allies and former pupils, told the Creeks that "they would all soon have to go & the *sooner they prepared for it the better."* Davis's proclamations alarmed the headmen of Tuckabatchee and may have helped set in motion the events that led to the May attack. Although some Creeks believed that preaching threatened chiefly authority in the Creek Nation, a participant in the assault noted that the attack "'originated in phrensy, bordering on despair'" because whites had come "'into their country said they were their friends, that the Government called them their children, and yet they had been promised many things which had not been done for them, and therefore the Indians did not believe that white people were any of them their friends, that it was not worth their while to think about worshipping God for . . . they would be destroyed anyhow.'"³

The targeting of Compere was in conformity with the headmen's policy of silencing anyone caught aiding or supporting voluntary emigration. In fact, "denunciations of death" were issued against people who even encouraged Creeks to move west. Even before the May 1828 attack, Davis had been threatened "with death if he did not desist from his endeavours to induce other Indians to emigrate." Creek headmen also "prohibited negroes and Indians from acting as interpreters to those persons employed in endeavouring to produce an emigration." These examples raise an interesting point about Creek governance during this period. Creek headmen were not typically vested with the power to coerce, let alone physically assault, members of their town. Their power was realized in their ability to persuade. It is possible that during this period the headmen had the support of their people to do whatever it took to keep the nation together. But William Walker, the Indian countryman and son-in-law of Big Warrior thought otherwise. Although he clearly sided with pro-emigration interests, Walker complained that would-be emigrants were afraid to even speak their mind on the subject and that the relationship between the chiefs and the people had devolved to one of "Lord, & vassall—no medium."⁴

Among the more prominent targets of these threats were Indian countrymen. As noted, when David Brearley was hired to conduct the McIntosh party west in 1826, he targeted whites married to Indian women for emigration under the assumption that they had enough influence to draw large numbers of Creeks west. Although the extent to which Brearley used this strategy is unclear, there is some evidence that it was employed. For example, James Moore, who had resided in the Creek Nation for over thirty years, enrolled with the second McIntosh party in 1828. Before he could move west, however, Opothle Yoholo threatened to confiscate his property, expel him from the Creek Nation, and prevent his Creek family from joining him if he insisted on moving. A Creek man named Red Mouth also attempted to physically impede Moore's Creek wife and children from going with him. Moore's desire to emigrate was probably reason enough for the threats, but "his endeavours to induce others to emigrate" made Moore an even more important target.[5]

Some whites were able to skirt these anti-emigration laws with impunity, however. The case of Barent Dubois, an Albany, New York, native with a Tuckabatchee wife (he married one of Big Warrior's daughters), illustrates the sometimes complex relationship between powerful Creek headmen and prominent whites living within the Creek Nation. John B. Hogan, who served as superintendent of Creek removal in 1835, was convinced that Dubois wielded great influence and control over Opothle Yoholo. Indeed, Dubois served as witness to many of Opothle Yoholo's letters, suggesting that the Indian countryman was often close by the Tuckabatchee headman's side. But, Dubois was also compensated in the 1820s for "collecting and issuing provisions" to Creek emigrants, and he accompanied twelve Creeks and two interpreters west to explore the Indian territory in 1834. Both moves were clearly at odds with the policies of anti-emigration headmen like Opothle Yoholo. Although it is unclear whether the Tuckabatchee leader knew about this, the two appear to have remained close up until relocation. Dubois, in fact, was even assigned as a subagent to Opothle Yoholo's detachment (no doubt at the behest of the headman) as the Creeks were being relocated west in 1836. But whatever it was that held their friendship together, the move to the Indian territory split it apart. While Opothle Yoholo and the rest of the Creeks left for the West in 1836 and 1837, Dubois elected to abandon his Tuckabatchee family and reintegrate himself into American society.[6]

Of course, the biggest targets were the emigrants themselves. Creek headmen were clearly concerned about pro-emigration propaganda coming from federal officials and a select number of Creeks who had visited the West. The reports were typically flattering—too flattering to be taken at face value—but in a rapidly crumbling society, many people were just desperate enough to believe it. Moreover, many Creeks were beginning to conclude that removal was inevitable. Compere, for example, believed that many Creeks were "beginning to take up the question in this light—'if we are to go we had better go soon.'" When Brearley returned to the Creek Nation in 1828 after conducting the first McIntosh party west, he met with other would-be emigrants and talked up the quality of the lands and the successes the McIntosh party was having in the West. Newspapers subsequently reported that "numbers flocked to an appointed rendezvous, and enrolled their names as emigrants, in a book prepared for the purpose." How many Creeks arrived in these camps is unclear, but it undoubtedly made the headmen nervous. Soon thereafter, unnamed Creek leaders visited an emigration camp near Fort Bainbridge on the Federal Road and used "every argument in their power to get them to return and not to go." This included providing what the emigrants called "the most foul falsehoods about the country on the arkansaw," and scaring the emigrants by telling them that the first party "has not got to the Country they started for," implying that they would suffer or die during the journey. These types of warnings were not new. In the months after the Treaty of Indian Springs signing, and still years before the first McIntosh party left for the Indian territory, Creek headmen had attempted to frighten potential traitors by warning that those who emigrated "would be certainly murdered" in the West because "there was a powerful nation there that would destroy" them all. In 1828 headmen held a meeting at Tuckabatchee and directed the heads of the most prominent clans to unite in opposition to emigration. Indeed, the leaders of the Tiger, Wind, and Potato clans were able to threaten or cajole dozens of their people into retracting their pledge to move west.[7]

Simple persuasion only went so far, however. Another effective tool, at least initially, was acts of violence. After reports circulated of people "flocking" to the camps, headmen organized a secret council; thereafter, many Creeks fearing for their safety refused to enroll, while many others deserted the camps altogether. Those who stayed were attacked, like the man at Tuckabatchee who was "badly" beaten after declaring his intention to move west. In 1829 a would-be emigrant was killed. Headmen and the men under their charge specifically targeted enrollment camps where large numbers of people were congregated in one place. Fifty Yuchis were physically driven from Fort Strother by orders of a headman, and some estimated that upwards of two hundred Creeks had abandoned the rendezvous and returned home. Only "a few mulattoes" remained, and when Brearley went to the camp to see how enrollment was coming along, he found those that were still there "wavering." At Fort Bainbridge, a child was kidnapped from his emigrating mother, the victim of an apparent clan attack. The camp at Ten Islands (at or near Fort Strother) was in a "mutaneous and disorderly situation" due to threats made against enrollees. John Berryhill of Thlakatchka town waited in camp at Line Creek when Tuskenehaw, the son of the late Big Warrior, arrived. Using "Insulting language" against the Creeks there, he told the emigrants that "for a trifle he would Cut our throats" for leaving the Creek Nation. On another occasion, Tuskenehaw, along with the former Red Stick prophet Jim Boy, drew a sword and threatened to kill William J. Wills of Thlakatchka while at the Clewalla home of John Reed's mother near Line Creek. Tuskenehaw also pointed a cocked rifle at Alexander Moniac and threatened to shoot him if he did not desist from emigrating. Moniac had already been issued his "Publick Rifle" for enrolling, but did not leave with the second party, and Walker observed that the two men were thereafter "seen together perfectly friendley."[8]

Confiscation and destruction of property was another tool in the headmen's arsenal. In a number of cases, horses were stolen in camp by Creeks opposed to emigration. Some were irrevocably lost, while others were found with the bells around their necks missing in an apparent attempt to prevent their recovery. The federal agents and government property were also targeted. Early in 1828 Long Warrior and approximately thirty Creeks, under orders from the headmen of Tuckabatchee, burned a newly built government storehouse in Sylacauga. The house was designed to store the guns, blankets, butcher knives, camp kettles, and other items that were distributed to Creek emigrants. Around the same time, Tuskenehaw physically assaulted his brother-in-law, William Walker, who was employed as an emigration subagent and had directed the construction of the storehouse. Although some claimed the assault was over personal matters, it was clear to Walker that he was targeted because of his involvement in collecting Creeks for the second voluntary emigration.[9]

The headmen's threats worked. When the enrollment camps consolidated at Fort Strother during the first week of October 1828 to prepare for their journey west, there were only about five hundred people and their slaves. Brearley's decision to target Indian countrymen for emigration did not result in a large party or in neutralizing the headmen's opposition, but probably contributed to the considerable numbers of whites (and Creeks with European ancestry) who chose to move west that year. In fact, the racial composition of the second party did not go unnoticed by the *Cherokee Phoenix*, which reported that the emigrants "are called Creeks, though we are credibly informed that there were but few full Indians, most of the party being white men, half breeds, and mulattoes." Federal agents took notice as well, and counted the number of "whites" on the muster roll, something they had not done with the first party.[10]

The most notable member of the group was Kendall Lewis, whose father-in-law, Big Warrior, opposed the Treaty of Indian Springs and no doubt would have opposed emigration had he lived. The second McIntosh party included emigrants from other prominent families like Kennard (Daniel Kennard accompanied the McIntosh exploratory deputation to the Indian territory in the spring of 1827), Berryhill, Carr, Lott (Benjamin Lott of Hitchiti was a licensed trader in the Creek Nation), and Posey. David McIntosh and fourteen of Roly McIntosh's slaves emigrated, as did John Wynn and family, who had enrolled with the first McIntosh party but elected to remain behind in 1827. Although Thlakatchka was by far the most represented town, a number of Upper Creek families from Tuckabatchee, Tallassee, Weogufka, Coosada, Tallasseehatchee, and Hillabee, among others, had decided to try their luck in the West. Others, such as the Creeks from Cusseta, Hitchiti, and Oswitchee, likely emigrated because of the deteriorating effects of the treaties of Indian Springs and Washington.[11]

The party would have been much larger had dozens of would-be emigrants not remained behind in the Creek Nation. The fifty Yuchis who had been driven off did not return to the camp and only one representative from that town appears on the roll. Many other Creeks entered their names at Fort Strother only to remain behind for various reasons when the party commenced its journey westward. William, Thomas, and Walter Grayson, all members of a prominent and wealthy Hillabee family, enrolled but later changed their minds (or were prevented from emigrating) and stayed behind in the Creek Nation. Next to their names, Brearley wrote "not gone," an indication that they had not made it to the Indian territory. Several other families also abandoned the party. Joseph Pidgeon, a student at the Withington Mission School, deserted the rendezvous site before the party left Fort Strother. In the margins of the muster roll, Brearley wrote "Joseph P. run off." Pidgeon stayed behind in Alabama and was later hanged in Mobile, as Thomas S. Woodward later recalled, for killing a "cab-man" during a robbery. Joseph's Tuckabatchee family members—Thomas and David Pidgeon—also absconded, and both heads of family have "not gone" scribbled next to their names. A receipt issued to Tom Pidgeon for steamboat transportation from Blakeley to Mobile in April 1837 suggests he moved west with over three thousand other Creeks as part of detachment six. Emigration also broke up families. William J. Wills, who months earlier had been threatened by Tuskenehaw over emigrating, enrolled with the second voluntary party in 1828. Next to his name, Brearley wrote "his wife not gone."[12]

With these losses, the second emigrating party left Fort Strother on 8 October 1828 with, according to the *Alabama Journal*, 518 people. The party traveled with thirty loaded wagons and approximately one hundred "loose horses." The emigrants traveled due north to Gunter's Landing on the Tennessee River, a decision Brearley had made a year earlier while at Harpersville. The party divided into land and water components at Creek Path, a Cherokee settlement near the Tennessee River. Approximately two hundred women, children, and elderly boarded as many as five flatboats and descended the Tennessee River, while the balance traveled by land. The emigrants' journey by water included a trip through the treacherous Muscle Shoals, where the Tennessee River dropped more than 160 feet between the eastern shoals and Florence, Alabama. Taking new boats at Florence, the water party continued down the Tennessee, Ohio, and Mississippi Rivers before arriving at Memphis. Again, the emigrants were active participants in their own movement. Pleasant Berryhill and Thomas Posey, both of Thlakatchka, received compensation for working as "boat hands" from Gunter's Landing to

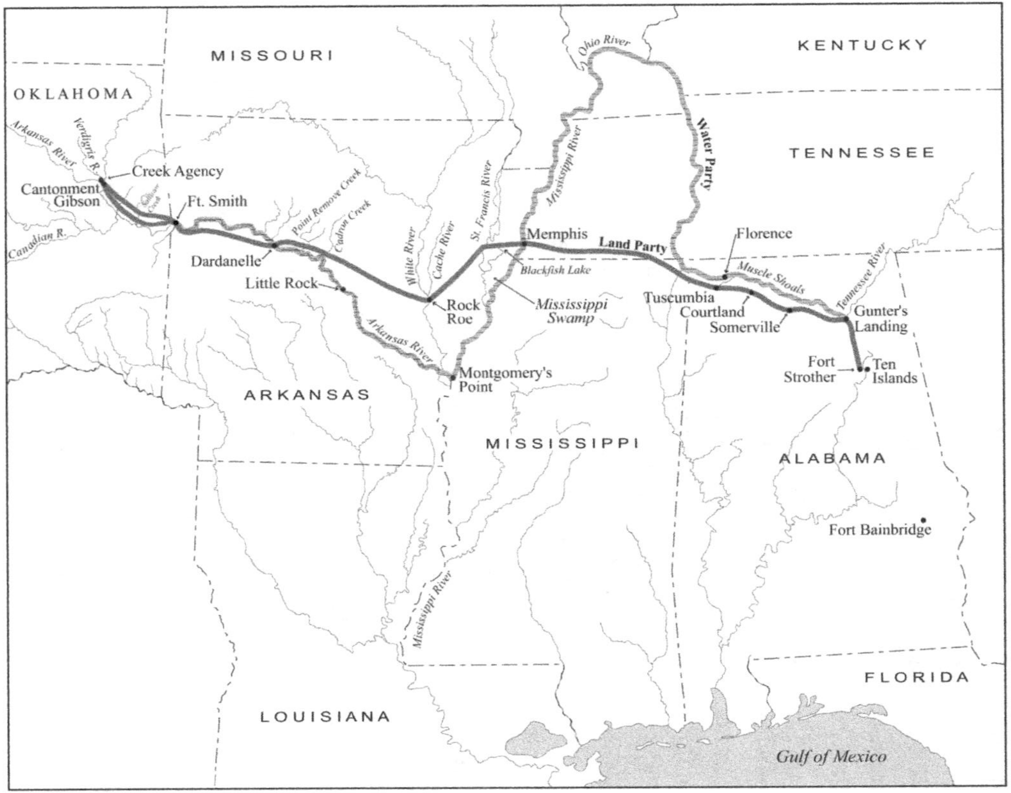

FIG. 8. Route of the second McIntosh party, October 1828–January 1829. Place names correspond to stopping points or locations noted in the documentation. Route lines and locations are approximations. The exact route across Arkansas is unclear. The *Arkansas Gazette*, 11 and 18 November 1828, implies that the party bypassed Little Rock thirty miles to the north, while a subagents' receipts for disbursements suggests that the party may have moved from Rock Roe to Little Rock; see Brearley to DeWheat, SIAC, Agent (Brearley), Account (14,487), Year (1830), NARA. Cartography by Sarah Mattics.

the bottom of the shoals, while Pleasant Austin of Tuckabatchee helped pole and steer one of the flatboats from Gunter's Landing to the Ohio River. Samuel Hopwood, of Tallassee town, was paid for steering a boat from the Tennessee River to Fort Smith and for issuing provisions to the Creeks during their journey west.[13]

Dry weather allowed the 236 members of the land party, almost all of whom were on horseback, to travel easily. After leaving the water party at Gunter's Landing, the group moved west along the south side of the Tennessee River, passing through Somerville, Alabama, and the Chickasaw Nation. The party crossed the Hatchie River on 23 October, before arriving in Memphis well ahead of the water party. Ferriages over the Blackfish (1 November), St. Francis River (4 November), and White River (8 November), as well as the Rock Roe bayou (the following day) appear to have been executed more or less without incident, although a number of people became ill and were issued provisions near the St. Francis. Continuing westward, the land party crossed the Arkansas River twice: once at Dardanelle (20 November) and again at Fort Smith (24 November). The land on the south side of the Arkansas River was gently rolling and undulating and interspersed with prairie land. The timber consisted of blackjack oak, post oak, hickory, and pine trees. The land party crossed a few streams and creeks that no doubt were easily fordable in the dry weather. In fact, the second McIntosh party encountered much less difficulty on their journey than the first McIntosh party did almost a year earlier. The only evidence of deaths along the route were receipts issued for the construction of coffins and the burial of two Creeks who died as the party was moving out of Fort Strother. Indeed, Okmulgee Micco of Thlakatchka was reported dead on the muster roll. The land party reached the western Creek Agency on 28 November 1828, after a journey of fifty-four days. Waiting to greet the new arrivals at the agency were the three members of the exploratory deputation that had left the Creek Nation months earlier.[14]

The dry weather that had allowed the land party easy travels frustrated those on the river. The keel boats were delayed at the mouth of the White River and along portions of the Arkansas because of shallow water. The steamboat *Facility*, in Little Rock discharging freight from New Orleans, towed the two keels for portions of their final leg to the Indian territory. The water party did not leave Little Rock until Monday, 22 December, and probably did not reach its destination until January 1829, several weeks behind those on foot. A receipt issued to one of Brearley's clerks for "wagoners" to meet the water party at Sallisaw Creek suggests that the Arkansas was likely too shallow for the steamer and the Creeks may have been forced to walk the last part of their journey from that stream, or Fort Smith, to the agency.[15]

Like the first McIntosh party, most of the emigrants from the second voluntary party settled near the junction of the Arkansas and Verdigris Rivers. The poorest were unable to move too far from the distribution centers of Cantonment Gibson and the western Creek Agency, which they relied on for basic necessities. Many appear to have had difficulty reestablishing their lives, and the gap between rich and poor, which was already significant in the East, no doubt grew wider. Many of the emigrants from the first two parties arrived in the Indian territory without money and "many were without clothing and the necessaries of life." Because these Creeks were in debt and had exhausted all of their credit, traders in the West initially refused to sell them provisions.[16]

After mustering the new immigrants into the western Creek Nation, Brearley turned eastward in early 1829, intent on organizing a third emigrating party. Traveling with Brearley was an Osage headman, Auguste Aristide Chouteau (a member of the legendary family who helped found St. Louis), and a number of McIntosh party leaders. Chouteau was called on to aid in the third voluntary party, while the Osage headman's role was little more than a gimmicky attempt to "promote the spirit of Emigration." The intent was to pledge friendship between the two nations, emphasize the quality of the land, and convince the Creeks of the benefits of moving west. But the reluctant headman's presence in the Creek Nation was not received warmly. Opothle Yoholo responded to the chief's presence by declaring that "if he comes as a friend, desirous of becoming acquainted with him and his people, he was welcome; but if for the purpose of inducing the Creeks to emigrate, they wanted nothing to do with him; that a great man Tecumseh once came among them, and the Creeks ever since have been suspicious of strangers." For his part, the Osage chief wanted little to do with the Creeks and was "anxious to return to his own people." Federal officials were also unhappy with the expenses related to the stunt. Although Thomas L. McKenney, head of the War Department's Indian office, declared that the decision to bring the headman west "was not a sound discretion," he conceded that "the Chief ought not . . . be cast off—or left, to find his way home."[17]

Federal officials had had enough. Brearley, who was initially only hired to conduct the McIntosh party west, had already collected a handful of emigrants for the third party when he was relieved of his duties in June 1829. The agent was in Washington when he received the news. John Crowell, who was aided by his brother Thomas, succeeded Brearley as head of the emigration effort. Brearley's ouster was the product of the new Jackson administration's decision to merge the eastern and western Creek agencies under Crowell in an attempt to streamline emigration and heal old wounds between the McIntosh Creeks and those still in the Creek Nation. The fact that prominent western Creeks led by Roly McIntosh charged Brearley with eleven grievances probably did not help his cause either. Some of the accusations dealt with fraud— the Creeks claimed that he kept for himself the money promised the emigrants in the Treaty of Washington. Prominent McIntosh members alleged that Brearley's "sole object is *speculation*." Headmen accused Brearley of buying up all the cattle and hogs in the region, then securing a contract to supply the Creeks with meat at inflated prices. Brearley also speculated in flour and sold it to the western Creeks at "a very extravagant advance." The Indians also alleged that Brearley took out all of the lard from the meat provisions, then sold it back to the Creeks and issued second-rate cuts after "selecting all the choice pieces for his own use." Brearley was also accused of bringing alcohol into the western settlements, and they listed "intoxication and disrespectful language to the Chiefs" as another complaint. However, many prominent western Creeks did not agree with the charges against Brearley. Illustrating the degree to which members of the emigrating parties were divided among themselves, John Wynn, William Lott, Samuel Berryhill (all members of Thlakatchka), "and many others" refused to sign the memorial (some refused to sign as witnesses but were ordered to by the chiefs) that was passed in council against Brearley. John Berryhill also opposed the memorial, "but was forced to Sign it by the Chiefs."[18]

The deteriorating conditions found in the Creek Nation seemed to guarantee that the Crowells would have more success than Brearley. The extension laws and white encroachment continued to place enormous pressure on the Creek people, and President Andrew Jackson, who had taken office months earlier, had already publicly declared that he had little interest in helping the Indians while they remained east of the Mississippi River. Indeed, many defenders of Jackson claim that the seventh president's removal policy was guided in part by a sincere desire to protect the eastern Indians and their culture from annihilation. In justifying Indian removal, Jackson told Creek leaders that they must be separated from the corrupting influences of white society for their long-term survival. But Jackson helped place whites on the doorstep of these very Indian communities. Jackson told the Creeks at the close of the Creek War in 1814 that they were surrounded by "bad" white men and should move west even as he expanded the American territorial domain of these bad men by millions of acres. Indeed, illegal white immigrants did not just enter the Creek Nation through Georgia—many were entering through Fort Williams, an old Creek War garrison on the Creeks' western Coosa River boundary line adjacent to the 1814 Treaty of Fort Jackson cession. By one estimate, 110 white families lived illegally within the Creek Nation just opposite Shelby County. In fact, there were so many whites living in this region that the Alabama General Assembly authorized the construction of a road from Fort Williams to West Point, Georgia. Enraged by the intrusion, Creek headmen complained that the road-building company was "Cuting and Spoiling" their land. Rather than remove the intruders, Jackson's secretary of war, John H. Eaton, told the Creeks that they were subject to the laws of Alabama and construction of the road proceeded.[19]

Many of these white intruders "were notoriously bad and infamous characters" and had become so audacious in their pursuit of property that many took forcible possession of Creek houses and fields. Others were noted livestock thieves. Some had passed counterfeit money that they used to cheat the Creeks out of their property. A number of whites were found "roving about in the mountains" looking for gold, although some believed this was only a cover for horse stealing. Other white families were squatting in the abandoned houses of Creeks who had emigrated to the West. When confronted, some lied and claimed that they had purchased the house and fields from the Creeks. Tuskenehaw, a Lower Creek headman from Cusseta, complained to Andrew Jackson that his "white sons and daughters are moving into my Country in abundance they are spoiling my lands and taking possession of the Red peoples improvements that they have made with their own labour."[20]

Hunger, which had been a chronic problem since the loss of the Creeks' Georgia land, was exacerbated when whites evicted Creeks from their planted fields. The problem was further compounded when headmen drove would-be emigrants from the camps. Most had not planted in anticipation of subsisting on government rations, and their situation became more precarious as they were left to fend for themselves. In fact, it is quite possible that the Creeks who Basil Hall observed receiving rations at Fort Mitchell in April 1828 might not have been Georgia Lower Creeks who were unable to find land within Alabama, but instead were people who had been driven from their emigration camps by angry headmen. The eviction of Creeks from their homes by illegal white immigrants and the actions of the headmen against emigration created an underclass of people living on the margins. Tuskenehaw of Cusseta lamented that many of his people were "in a dreadful Condition without any means of subsistence." Out of necessity and defiance, many continued to cross into Georgia searching for food and clothing. Georgians reported seeing five Yuchis east of the Chattahoochee carrying "their Guns and Dirks." When they tried to arrest them, the Indians cocked their weapons and "fixed themselves for battle." In another instance, residents of Randolph, Lee, Marion, and Muscogee Counties in Georgia complained that Lower Creek hunters killed their livestock and they found the carcass of a cow "with her Quarters taken off." They also reported home-invasion robberies in which guns and even the recently undressed clothing of a sleeping man were stolen. The Creeks, according to the memorial, "even make so bold as to take of young negroes."[21]

Alcohol was a pervasive problem for the Creeks as well. White squatters arrived in the Creek Nation with spirits, especially whiskey, to trade to the Creeks for portions of their annuity or on credit at "enormous rates." Crowell observed that "hundreds of families will sell the last [bit] of corn & potatoes, for liquor and leave the women and children in the most miserable state of starvation." Indeed, Swedish traveler Carl David Arfwedson observed a number of intoxicated men bartering "several fine deer" for whiskey near Fort Mitchell in 1832. Observing the white merchant take advantage of the intoxicated Creeks, Arfwedson wrote that "never, assuredly, had whisky brought a higher price, or deer been so depreciated in value." Moreover, many whites not only brought whiskey, but opened "drinking Houses" near the Creeks. Many others went to Columbus to obtain alcohol, and one man who lived in the area noted that on an average day there were as many as fifty intoxicated Creeks, "men and women, wallowing in the streets" of that town. Indeed, according to one source, alcohol was destroying the lives of the Creeks like a "pestilence." Arfwedson saw this firsthand while on the stage from Macon, when he and his fellow passengers encountered a Creek man who abruptly emerged from a Georgia swamp, looking to obtain whiskey from the travelers. With the alcohol procured, the Indian just as quickly disappeared. Arfwedson later discovered the man's lifeless body after he had apparently fallen, intoxicated, into his campfire. By 1833, it was estimated that there were almost four hundred whiskey shops in the Creek country.[22]

Georgians, primarily responsible for the creation of this underbelly of roving, starving Creeks Indians, were largely unmoved by the plight of their dispossessed neighbors. Nevertheless, they had the audacity to complain whenever Creeks were found within their own state limits, and the rhetoric reached fevered pitch whenever one of the "intruders" stole livestock or occasionally killed one of the white citizens. State officials were also concerned about the Creeks traveling through Georgia in order to meet with Cherokee leaders and plot cooperative anti-removal strategies. By 1828, Georgia's General Assembly moved to prohibit all Creeks from entering the state without a written permit from the Creek

Agency. These passports, good for only ten days, meant little to the Creeks, however, and during the next several years, large numbers still could be found throughout the western portions of the state. Once captured without a permit, the act allowed the Creek "intruder" to be jailed. In rare cases, however, a number of Creeks were killed by white vigilantes. Tuskenehaw of Cusseta wrote to the president complaining that "the Whites have Collected themselves in bodies and hunted up such as did cross into Georgia and shot them as if though they were deer" and that "there has been seventeen Red people kill'd by the whites and nothing thought of more than if they had been So many wild Hogs."[23]

As a result of these problems, the emigration camps swelled with Creeks looking to ameliorate their suffering. Approximately thirteen hundred people enrolled for emigration in 1829. The party consisted almost solely of commoners, and Roly McIntosh later recalled that "there was no particular Chief in the party," although the future principal chief of the Creek Nation (1867–75, 1879–83), Samuel Checote, a ten-year-old boy at the time, emigrated with his family that year. And, although the members of the Perryman (Benjamin), Stidham (George W.), Bruner (Thomas), and Reed (Vicey) families who were collected under David Brearley before he was fired fancied themselves members of the "third and last part of the McIntosh party," a vast majority of the emigrants had no connection to the late Coweta headman. Most moved west because life in the Creek Nation had become too difficult, while others certainly hoped that they would find more prosperity in the West. Once again, many hailed from *talwas* most affected by the Treaties of Indian Springs and Washington. Emigrants from the towns of Hitchiti and Okteyoconnee had lost their land in Georgia, while others, like those from Yuchi, probably suffered from starvation and white encroachment. Many of the Yuchis were probably those who had been driven from the enrollment camps by Creek headmen a year earlier. Some Creeks probably emigrated because they bought into federal officials' assertion that the Creeks could not live peacefully near white society. Indeed, Creek emigrants at the Fort Bainbridge encampment stated that their reason for leaving the land of their ancestors was because "it was impossible for us to [live] while we were surrounded by the whites." Many Creeks felt compelled to leave for their children's future. In a letter to Jackson, eleven Creek emigrants noted that the "old men did not come to this country for our own good but for our children who loves to hunt." The Creeks noted that the West promised them "plenty of game more than we can destroy."[24]

Others were looking to escape their past. One unintended consequence of voluntary emigration was that it allowed Creeks, who might otherwise have had no desire to leave the nation, an escape hatch if they ever ran afoul of clan law. Lawbreakers could simply enter an emigration camp, receive federal protection, and disappear into the western Indian territory before they could be brought to justice. Indeed, among the enrollees in 1829 were two Creeks accused of breaking "the sacred laws of the Creek Nation." The charge was adultery, and that spring, Hitchiti chief Neah Emathla, a veteran of the First Seminole War, led a party of twenty Creek men to Fort Bainbridge to prevent their escape. After arriving at the three-hundred-person encampment, the men "most barberously" beat both the man and the woman, then "wantonly took off their ears." The crime itself was reason enough for the attack, but this episode appears to have been as much a political statement as it was a warning to others that emigration camps were not places of refuge. Indeed, during the attack, the headman defiantly declared that "if the United States had promised them protection, he would see whether they would be protected or not."[25]

Some Creeks, however, did make their escape. Arpekoche Emathla hastily led his Fish Pond family of ten westward in the winter of 1834–35 without government money or transportation because "one of the Young men of the family was charged with being too intimate with the wife of another man, and in order to escape punishment, which was severe under the Creek law or custom, the family came to the Territory." Ironically, since clan justice left entire families vulnerable, it could actually have the effect of increasing the numbers of Creeks who moved to Indian territory. Even the politically connected used the West as a safety valve during times of emergency. Opothle Yoholo's son Dick Johnson stabbed a man to death and then fled across the Mississippi River to avoid capture. He was later murdered in Texas.[26]

Creeks hoping to make a quick escape to the Indian territory were frustrated, however, by delays caused by inadequate federal funding. Many of the emigrants entered the camps in the latter part of 1828, and had hastily sold their property far below value in anticipation of emigrating relatively quickly. But eight months later, the Creeks had not moved. William Walker, the Indian countryman from Tuckabatchee, had collected two hundred Creeks during the first quarter of 1829 while still working for Brearley, but was unable to move them without money. Crowell, who believed that four or five thousand Creeks would leave that fall if $100,000 was quickly made available, grew frustrated with Washington's inefficiency. In one of his feistier moods, Crowell exasperatedly told the secretary of war that, on the subject of funding the 1829 emigration: "I regret your having deferred acting upon it—I am required to Keep you constantly advised of the progress I am making; in reply I have to remark that no progress can be made without funds."[27]

It was not until June that the third voluntary party commenced its journey in earnest. With very little documentation available, the exact route of this party is only conjecture. Newspapers reported that nine hundred emigrants passed through Pike County to Line Creek (probably under the charge of Thomas Crowell and Luther Blake) before merging with William Walker's camp from Fort Bainbridge. Most of the emigrants of the enlarged party probably then moved north and rendezvoused in Sylacauga before traveling on foot to Gunter's Landing where the Creeks were divided into two groups. At least five flatboats laden with emigrants navigated the Muscle Shoals on the Tennessee River while the land party, with twenty wagons and 187 horses, marched through Somerville and Decatur on the south side of the Tennessee River to Tuscumbia, where they camped near town at the end of June 1829. Receipts show that members of the team (but no mention of any Creeks) passed through Mount Meigs, Coosada, and Elyton before rendezvousing with the others. These may have been provision wagons or logistical aid sent to meet the Creeks on their arrival. After navigating the shoals, newspapers reported that approximately one thousand Creeks were to board the steamboat *Pocahontas* with two flatboats in tow at Waterloo.[28]

The 405 emigrants traveling by land and conducted by Thomas Crowell and Luther Blake passed through the Chickasaw country and McNairy County, Tennessee, before arriving in Memphis days ahead of the water party. The Creeks crossed the Mississippi River and continued westward without rendezvousing with the boats. The rough road along this stretch of the journey made travel difficult and some Creeks were compensated for "Cutting Road through the [Mississippi] Swamp." As a result, the land party stretched into a long train of several miles. A post rider who came upon the party observed that while the head of the detachment was crossing the St. Francis River, the rear of the party had crossed the Blackfish and were "but a few miles behind." As the land party passed through the prairie north of Little Rock, Blake traveled south to meet the water party.[29]

Meanwhile, the boats conducted by Walker descended the Tennessee, Ohio, and Mississippi Rivers before landing in Memphis a few weeks behind those on foot. At the mouth of the White River, the Creeks were transferred to the steamboat *Virginia* for their ascent up the Arkansas River. Below Pine Bluff, the *Virginia* ran aground, and with little prospect of the water level rising, the Creeks were forced to abandon the vessel. Those who were able, walked along the north side of the Arkansas River, while those in the weakest condition waited along the riverbank for keelboats. A cryptic receipt for "dammage done" to a French man's plantation by a number of emigrants suggests that some Creeks may have loitered around Arkansas Post during their wait. The Creeks' possessions were also taken off the steamer and placed along the river to be picked up by boats that drafted less water. Receipts show that some goods were brought west, while others "rotted" along the bank. Wealthy Creeks had possessions destroyed in the *Virginia* mishap, like Rebecca Bruner, who lost eight blankets, 115 yards of homespun, two feather beds, and a set of pewter plates, forks, and knives, among other things. Other Creeks had similar misfortune, like Vicey Reed, who lost two shawls, six yards of ribbon, a pair of silver wristbands, and a feather bed; and Teehelattee, who lost two blankets, a comb, a pair of earrings, two shawls, twenty yards of heavy blue cotton fabric and fifteen yards of heavy white cotton fabric, three dressed deerskins, and four pounds of coffee.[30]

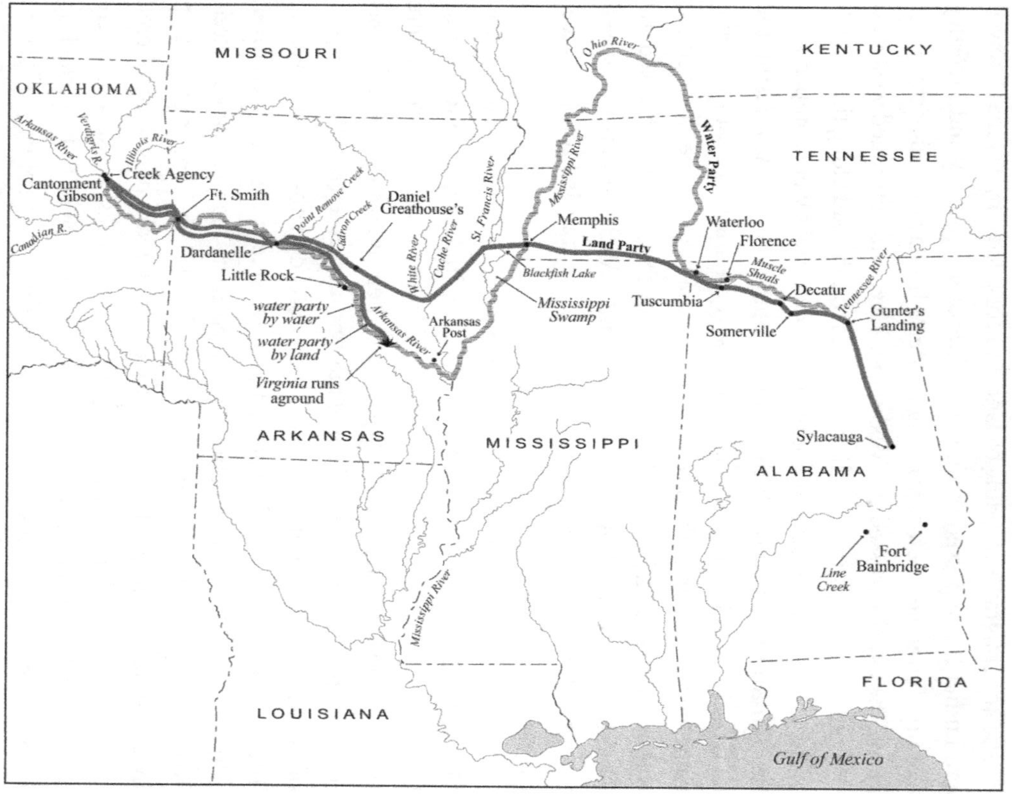

FIG. 9. Route of the third voluntary party, June–September 1829. Place names correspond to stopping points or locations noted in the documentation. Route lines and locations are approximations. Cartography by Sarah Mattics.

The *Virginia* grounding also complicated what had been an already difficult trip. Although the *Florence Gazette* reported members of the party in good health as they passed through Tuscumbia, a number of receipts were issued for the construction of coffins before the Creeks had left the limits of Alabama. By the time the water party had reached Little Rock on 13 August, however, newspapers reported considerable illness among the emigrants, with "several deaths" occurring. Indeed, a number of Creeks attached to the water party wrote Andrew Jackson and lamented that the president had "lost some of [his] red children by sickness." Those on land also suffered, and subagent Luther Blake issued receipts for "burrying and diging Graves." Some Creeks were forced to remain behind on the road and Blake subsequently "paid negroes at sundree times for bringing up the sick."[31]

The land party was well on its way to the western Creek Agency by the time the water party departed Little Rock on 15 August. The emigrants had spent their time in the river city both in and out of camp, and local residents discovered that a "considerable number of the party, of both sexes, were constantly in town" during their three-day stay. The water party recommenced its travels westward under the charge of Luther Blake, who after leaving the land party, relieved William Walker of his duties in Little Rock while the Indian countrymen returned to Alabama. The manner in which the water party arrived at the western Creek Agency remains a mystery. Receipts and newspaper accounts show that horses, wagons, and boats were all used to transport the Creeks' baggage, and it is probably not a stretch to conclude that the emigrants traveled in the same manner. A receipt for ferriage in Crawford County suggests that the land party (and perhaps the land detachment of the water party) might have passed along the south bank of the Arkansas River during the last stages of its trip. The party reached the agency sometime around the first of September 1829.[32]

The condition of the emigrants, however, was no mystery. Blake acknowledged that the party arrived sick, fatigued, and destitute of clothing, money, tools, and credit to purchase goods. Sam Houston, the former governor of Tennessee who witnessed the party as they straggled toward Cantonment Gibson, concurred and declared that the condition of the emigrants was enough to shock humanity. . . . Between fifty and a hundred Uchees were left in the swamps of Mississippi and I believe have not arrived. A considerable number of the emigrating party I heard of on the Illinois River about eighteen miles east of Cantonment Gibson; they were nearly all sick, famished, and most of them unable to turn themselves on their blankets. They subsisted principally upon what fish they could catch, and Mr. Flowers, a Cherokee Indian countryman, furnished them some provisions on his own responsibility.[33]

There is no record of how many Creeks died on the journey as the muster rolls apparently had been lost by 1848. The presence of disease was not any person's fault, as the West experienced repeated cases of small pox, influenza, and cholera. But cost-saving measures on the part of the federal government likely exacerbated the problem. The expense to transport one Creek Indian from the eastern Creek Nation to the West averaged $43.58 during David Brearley's two emigrations. The 1829 party, however, cost the government only $21.22 per person. And, considering the size and the number reported sick, the expense to conduct the third voluntary party should have been much higher than the first two emigrations. Instead, the government spent less than half.[34]

By the end of 1829, approximately twenty-five hundred Creeks, including their slaves, had voluntarily emigrated to the West. While a few emigrants were friends and followers of the late William McIntosh, most were Creeks with no connection to the late Coweta headman who had decided to start a new life in the West because of the deteriorating conditions found in the Creek Nation. Creek headmen continued their frontal assault to stop a mass population transfer across the Mississippi River and even expanded the campaign beyond their own borders. In 1833, a number of Creeks crossed into Florida and attacked John Blount, an Apalachicola chief and Jackson ally during the first Creek and Seminole Wars, who planned to move west with his band of people after signing the 1832 Treaty of Tallahassee. Blount believed his assault was, in part, retaliation for ceding his people's land and his support for voluntary emigration. In fact, Blount had been threatened before and had felt "some fear of violence" from the Creeks and Seminoles. But for those Creeks who were resolute in their determination to remain on their ancestral homeland (or were too afraid to speak of moving west), life became increasingly difficult as hunger, indebtedness, disease, and white encroachment continued unabated into the 1830s. As their desperation increased, the Creeks repeatedly went to Washington seeking redress but the Jackson administration refused to help them while they remained east of the Mississippi River. Desperate, the Creeks agreed to government demands to cede the remainder of their land to the United States in exchange for individual reserves. Far from solving the Creeks' problems, the 1832 Treaty of Washington made things much, much worse.[35]

4 Fraud
1829–35

As 1829 gave way to 1830, Creek headmen found themselves faced with assaults on two fronts. The election of President Andrew Jackson in 1828 promised a more concerted federal effort to coerce the Creeks to Indian territory. The other came in the form of whites who crossed into the Creek country illegally to squat on Creek land. In most cases, these settlers simply picked an unoccupied parcel, but there were a number of instances where Creek families were driven from their homes and their crops confiscated. Whites also exploited the Creeks by selling whiskey and establishing drinking houses near Creek towns. Starvation increased and an outbreak of smallpox killed untold numbers of people. When the headmen complained to the new president about their problems, Jackson replied that emigration was their only solution. In perhaps a last-ditch effort to preserve their way of life, the Creeks agreed to cede their entire eastern domain in exchange for individual family reserves. The 1832 Treaty of Washington was a document designed by government officials to break the Creek Nation into individual parts. The Creeks were promised title to their reserve if they remained in Alabama, but federal officials hoped the Creeks would sell their land to whites and move west. Most Creeks were resolute in their determination to remain on their ancestral homeland but were cheated out of their allotment by land speculators. Moreover, federal officials did not enforce the stipulations of the treaty to the Creeks' satisfaction. In fact, far from making their life easier, the 1832 Treaty of Washington pushed the Creeks deeper into despair.

The emigration of the third voluntary party in 1829 was a personal defeat for the leadership opposed to emigration. Approximately thirteen hundred Creeks moved west and, despite their best efforts, the headmen were unable to prevent them from leaving. Perhaps most concerning was that, once again, most of these Creeks had no connection to William McIntosh. They left because of the deteriorating conditions found in the Creek Nation. Undeterred, the chiefs continued their multipronged attack against the emigration program. Threats, especially directed at those trying to compel others to move west, continued unabated. In 1829 John Danely (Tulse Fixico), a Horse Path Town man, was driven from his town by the Okfuskee chief Menawa. Menawa told his men at a ball play that "Dannily must be killed that he talked of going to arkansas, and was trying to persuade his friends to go with him, that he should be killed, and his property taken and his children should be raised up as other Indians were, and then they would comply with the customs of the nation and that this should be the fate of all his men who spoke of going to arkansas." This followed the death of Danely's brother Jim, who was shot and killed for practicing "witchcraft." In late 1827 Jim Danely was charged by the Creeks with "rapidly accumulating wealth . . . that appeared to them so strange and unaccountable." Fearing the same fate, John fled to the Creek Agency and sought the protection of the authorities.[1]

Creek headmen also seized on any outstanding claims as a warning that the government had not fulfilled its guarantees to earlier emigrants. Circulating the reports about the unpaid compensation for improvements left in the Creek Nation as well as the still unpaid share of the money promised to the McIntosh party as guaranteed in the 1826 Treaty of Washington had the desired effect and operated, according to Creek Agent John Crowell, "injuriously to the cause." The delay in moving the fourth voluntary emigrating party, tentatively scheduled to depart in the spring or summer of 1830, also offered visual proof of the government's broken promises and left the enrollees "greatly disappointed." Opponents even tried to make enrolling for emigration more difficult by forcing people to come before the headmen and declare their intensions to move to Indian territory. Although the leadership claimed that they would not stop people from leaving, Crowell was unconvinced and believed the new rule meant that would-be emigrants needed the approval of the Creek National Council in order to go west.[2]

While the chiefs continued their campaign against emigration, proponents of removal in Washington and Tuscaloosa were bolstered by the election of Andrew Jackson, in whom they found a staunch ally. The Creeks were understandably nervous about the general taking office and dispatched a letter soon after his inauguration congratulating the president on his victory, but firmly reminding him that the Creeks viewed the preceding treaties as guaranteeing "*forever* all the Lands we now hold." While the headmen asked the president for relief from Alabama's extension laws and white encroachment, Jackson offered the Creeks no quarter and his administration quickly went about implementing the president's removal agenda. In public speeches and in communiqués to Creek headmen, the administration made clear its desire for the Indians to quickly and peacefully move to the West. After the passage of the Indian Removal Act in 1830, Jackson invited a delegation of Creeks to Tennessee to negotiate an exchange of land, but the Creeks rebuffed his overture.[3]

Despite his aggressive rhetoric and track record when dealing with land cession treaties as a general, Jackson the president was for the most part passively aggressive toward the Creeks. Although he was relentless in his determination to relocate the eastern Indians to the West, he let others do much of the heavy lifting. By the time he took office in 1829, Jackson already had a ready-made proxy force of Alabama legislators and white squatters actively engaged in dislodging the Creeks from their ancestral homeland. As conditions became increasingly unbearable, Jackson officials believed the Creeks would have little choice but to agree to a peaceful, voluntary relocation to Indian territory. Indeed, topographical engineer and emigration proponent Lieutenant Colonel John James Abert reminded the administration that while removing the Creeks by physical force was illegal, "indirect coercion, by increasing their embarrassments where they are" would be just as effective. Jackson feigned concern for the Indians' welfare, but showed little willingness to aid the Creeks while they remained in Alabama. To do so would work against the emigration program, and Abert acknowledged that the Creeks "linger" about "their homes with great fondness, and arrest any disposition to move on the Slightest evidence of adequate protection where they are." The most important tool Jackson possessed in his arsenal were the Alabama extension laws passed between 1827 and 1829, which asserted legal jurisdiction over the Creek Nation. Within weeks of taking office, Jackson wrote the Creeks and declared that "my white children in Alabama have extended their law over your country. If you remain in it, you must be subject to that law." Another Jackson-supported extension law was passed by the Alabama General Assembly in 1832, which forbade "all laws, usages and customs" of the Creek and Cherokee Indians that contradicted state law. Moreover, the Creeks could only hold councils with U.S. officials employed in paying annuities or engaged in the duties of emigration. Punishment was imprisonment. Remaining meant cultural and political annihilation. Only removal prevented such a fate, Jackson declared.[4]

Just as insidious as the assertion of Alabama law over the Creeks was the presence of whites who illegally squatted on Creek land. These intruders, in fact, took full advantage of the uncertainty surrounding the extension laws to gain a foothold in the Creek Nation, and federal and state officials in many cases sanctioned their presence. Headmen observed that brazen white settlers cleared land belonging to the Creeks, then threatened that if the Indians so much as touched their property, they would prosecute them to the fullest extent of Alabama law. When the state government authorized the construction of the town of Irwinton on land containing the *talwa* of Eufaula, whites wasted little time in driving some of the townspeople off and burning their homes to the ground. Other whites tried to establish their farmsteads secretly within the woodland section that divided the Indians' fields. As one witness described it, the Creeks would "plant a few acres of corn, and a small distance off, will plant a small patch of potatoes, and in another place, he will have his pease, or beans, leaving between each patch, a peice of wood land." Although the intruders argued that the Creeks did not occupy this portion of land, in fact, "town fences" were often used by the Creeks as grazing area for livestock.[5]

As they had done numerous times in the past, Creek headmen sought resolution through diplomacy. In carefully worded letters to officials in Washington, the chiefs again complained that whites had "abundantly moved amongst" them, and that they simply wished "to live in peace upon our own lands." Neah Micco and others also wrote to Crowell and lamented that "it is painful to us to have so frequently to complain to you of the many tresspases upon our lands by the white people." Crowell reported that most of the arable soil around the Creek Agency at Fort Mitchell had been "run up either with a compass, or choped round with an ax by white people." In fact, the Creeks were often rebuffed or ignored by officials in Washington. When the chiefs demanded that soldiers remove the white intruders, they were told that they first needed permission from President Jackson. Declaring that this "was like a clap of Thunder upon me," one chief complained that the Creeks had "never received any answer" from the president despite repeated requests. There was also the threat of resistance from the squatters over any attempt by the government to remove them from Creek land. Crowell had little reason to doubt the Creeks' complaints and noted that "far from being exaggerated, I am satisfied they fall short in many instances of the treatment of the intruders towards these helpless people."[6]

While the Creeks were trying to stem the flood of white encroachment, agent John Crowell was devising a plan to introduce more whites into the Creek Nation. Calling it "important to the cause of emigration," Crowell suggested that the abandoned homes of recently emigrated people could be rented to white people as a way of both raising money and as a method of dislodging the Creeks from their territory. Officials did not think that just any white man should be allowed to reside in the Creek Nation, however. Some Indian countrymen were considered obstacles to emigration. Although Brearley had argued that many whites were receptive to going to the Indian territory (and most did go between 1827 and 1829), Thomas McKenney, head of the Indian office in Washington, considered those who remained mostly "outlaws" who speculated in the Indian business and opposed emigration "at every inch" because they did not want to see their profits move west. McKenney recommended that Crowell expel them from the Creek Nation. Perhaps taking his

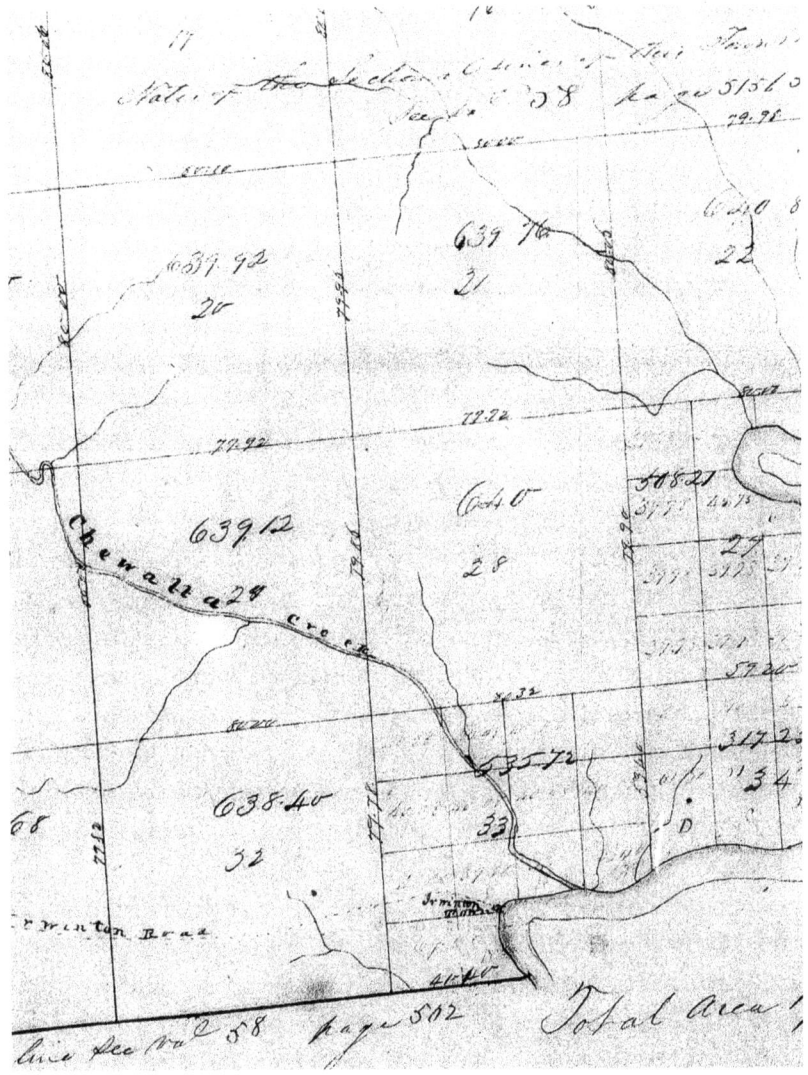

FIG. 10. The town of Irwinton, Alabama, and site of the Creek *talwa* of Eufaula. Secretary of State, Land Plats, Tallapoosa Land District, Roll 30, Page 143, Alabama Department of Archives and History, Montgomery AL.

cue from McKenney, Crowell later complained that the whites married to Creek women were "difficult to manage," and suggested to the secretary of war that "it would not be amiss to give them an alternative of emigrating or leaving the nation." Indeed, in 1828 Secretary of War Peter B. Porter had authorized Brearley to arrest and evict any Indian countryman who stood in the way of emigration. Some were. In 1830 Crowell, with the aid of a company of troops, arrested one white man—a forty-year resident of the nation—and deported him into the limits of Alabama for publicly opposing the move to Indian territory. Another man of mixed ancestry was apprehended for a similar charge and held under guard by the American soldiers.[7]

Emigration proponents continued to address the poisoned relationship between eastern Creek headmen and the McIntosh party in the West. While some argued that this east–west animosity was political—accusing Opothle Yoholo of being afraid of losing power to the McIntosh faction in Indian territory—others were quite literally afraid of the possibility of physical violence committed against them by McIntosh party members in retribution for the execution of William McIntosh years earlier. In a misguided attempt to diffuse this hostility and soothe hard feelings, officials invited Benjamin Hawkins and Roly McIntosh back to Alabama in 1830. The two became ambassadors from the West charged with securing peace between the two factions and convincing the eastern Creeks to emigrate. It was a long shot that ultimately fell flat, and Creek headmen saw right through the transparent attempt to cajole the nation into moving to across the Mississippi River. Not surprisingly, McIntosh and Hawkins had little success compelling any Creeks to go west and in fact their presence had the opposite effect and did "much injury to the cause of emigration." Secretary of War John Eaton specifically cited Hawkins's presence as a hindrance.[8]

Hawkins did take some Creeks—mostly family members and supporters—back with him, however. Along with his nephew Pinkney Hawkins, a Hillabee, Hawkins accompanied the family of Sam Sells, an Indian countryman of Thlakatchka town. Sells, a close ally of William McIntosh, emigrated with the second McIntosh party in 1828, but at the time had taken only three members of his family and seven slaves to the West. During the 1830 emigration, Sells's party consisted of twenty individuals along with two large wagons and one carriage. A former slave of Jane Hawkins who accompanied the party recalled that they "had plenty of horses," and most of the emigrants traveled west on horseback. Both the Hawkins and Sells parties traveled "near together" for the entire journey, paid for their provisions and transportation along the route, and utilized their slaves to pack provisions into the camp each night. A number of other Creeks and their slaves self-emigrated in 1830 as well. Among them was a woman from Coweta named Holo Barnett. Theophilus Perryman also self-emigrated in 1830 and was forced to abandon one of his wagons in the Chickasaw country along the way. These parties were small, consisting of one or two families or extended families of up to two dozen members. In some cases these groups did not even travel together. A slave girl who accompanied a party of self-emigrating Thlobthloccos reported that "whilst we moved in day time in separate squads we camped together at night."[9]

These small, family-sized detachments frustrated the president, who wanted to see all the Creeks on the west side of the Mississippi River as soon as possible. In June 1830 Jackson employed yet another tactic to try to compel the Creeks to emigrate. In an attempt to both save money and put pressure on the headmen to move west, Jackson stopped all government-sponsored voluntary emigrations until the entire Creek Nation left for Indian territory. The Creeks were not barred from moving, but they would have to pay their own way. Jackson also threatened to close the Creek Agency and withdraw federal protection over the Creek people. While stopping federally funded emigrations only affected those Creeks willing to move west, the closure of the agency affected all. Angry and fearful, the Creeks fired off a letter to Washington, complaining that "there is a probability of the guardian care of our country being withdrawn; this was strange news to our people, and has filled their minds with trouble. . . . Deplorable as our condition is, it would become much more aggravated should the agency in our country be abolished." There is little doubt that the administration's strategy, in accordance with its passive-aggressive style, was to let the Creeks fend for themselves under Alabama law. Jackson noted as much when he wrote that "when they find that they cannot live under the laws of Alabama, they must find, at their own expence, and by their own means, a country, and a home. . . . [I] now leave the poor deluded Creeks and Cherokees to their fate, and their anihilation."[10]

The Creeks who enrolled for emigration were the hardest hit by the government's new course. It appears that a relatively large number of people planned to voluntarily emigrate in 1830, with some reporting that there were "hundreds ready to go." Most were Lower Creeks living in the neighborhood of the agency and were those most affected by the treaties of Indian Springs and Washington. Moreover, officials believed that thousands of others were willing to emigrate if not for the obstinance of the headmen. Jackson's move was a deliberate attempt to make conditions in the Creek Nation worse by increasing the number of poor and starving thereby forcing the chiefs' hand. John Crowell later noted that "there were several thousand who expected to be removed last year at the expense of the Government, and did not plant any crop, many of whom disposed of their little property preparatory to that event." Many joined the growing underbelly of Creeks of all classes living in "a misrable and starving condition," who were "almost entirely destitute of provisions." Among those caught in this situation were approximately eighty members of the Grayson family. Three Grayson heads (Walter, William, and Thomas) enrolled to emigrate with the second McIntosh party in 1828, but remained behind for reasons known only to them. William and Walter Grayson, along with a number of other family members, however, anticipated an 1830 move to Indian territory, and most appear to have been hit hard by the government's decision not to fund a fourth voluntary emigration. They, along with other Creeks, filed claims with officials for the monetary value of the crops they had not planted in 1830. For instance, Walter Grayson claimed compensation for "the loss Sustained on 80 acres of cleared, *tendable* land, which was not cultivated in consequence of having been forbidden to do so by the Government, whereby I lost a whole crop, in the year 1830."[11]

These emigrants also faced retribution from Creek headmen who took advantage of their vulnerable condition. Many of the enrollees who had not planted crops in anticipation of receiving provisions from the government were subsisting on rations and perhaps on what livestock they had not disposed of. As punishment for their decision to move west, Creek headmen ordered the destruction of the Creeks' property. In letters to the secretary of war, John Crowell relayed that "the stock of those who had openly declared their intention to emigrate have been destroyed to a considerable extent." Left unprotected, Crowell reported that the headmen "scald at, and abuse all who avow their intention [to emigrate] and in some instances have attempted their lives."[12]

Food shortages at the beginning of the decade only made things worse. A severe drought in 1830 and 1831 created a smaller harvest than usual, while hundreds of families, Crowell noted, "seldom plant as much, as would subsist them a fourth part of the year." John James Abert blamed white squatters, who abused the Creeks and expropriated their fields, as well as traders, "who like locusts have devoured their subsistance" and inundated their homes with whiskey, for destroying the Creeks' disposition to cultivate. And, even when there was an abundant harvest, many Creeks sold their crops for alcohol. As a result, many people were reduced to eating roots, berries, and the bark off of trees. In addition, witnesses observed that "whenever an old sugar hogshead or barrel is thrown out, they hasten to it as bees to the honey comb, to lick off the few remaining particles." The problem was so widespread that even white citizens took notice. A number of Columbus, Georgia, residents wrote Andrew Jackson and declared that there were

> large bodies of Indians in a state of actual starvation with no means or Expectation of relief unless the assistance of the Government be Extended to them. In the white settlements ajacent to them they are daily begging from house to house for the means of subsistence from hour to hour they have abandoned their homes thrown themselves in crowds at the doors of the whites relying alone for Existence on the mercies and charities of the community, and if they are not speedily relieved by some general and systematic plan great numbers of them must inevitably perish.

White residents pleaded with Washington to send aid, but the Jackson administration, unwilling to promote "idleness" and "dissatisfaction," simply refused. Federal officials also denied starving Creeks relief because it would have deterred them from enrolling for emigration. Hunger was so bad that agents attempted to persuade the secretary of war to allow the neediest Creeks access to thirty or forty barrels of partially spoiled flour left by the army simply because it was "of no value to the Government."[13]

The misery was only exacerbated by disease. Smallpox struck some of the Upper Creek towns about "forty to eighty" miles from the Agency in 1831. Unaware of the full scope of the problem, the surgeon general only sent "a verry small quantity" of the treatment to Alabama—enough for only about twelve people. Untold numbers of Creeks died from the disease, most of whom were found lying on the ground outside of their homes. To sanitize the area, the houses and bodies of the dead were destroyed by fire. Hoping to contain its spread, Crowell immediately stopped issuing permits to Creeks wishing to cross into Georgia. Eventually, more than seven thousand Creeks were vaccinated during Dr. William Wharton's 137-day tour of the nation.[14]

As the Creeks sank further into despair, they made repeated trips to Washington seeking redress. Their two biggest complaints were the intrusions on their land by white squatters and the assertion of state jurisdiction over the Creek Nation. During each trip the Creeks were told that their salvation resided on the west side of the Mississippi River. Each time, the Creeks refused the offer. Officials grew tired of the impasse and of the repeated visits by different delegations of headmen. Creek leaders often received a lukewarm reception when they arrived, while other times they got nothing more than a cold shoulder. A January 1831 deputation consisting of planter John H. Brodnax and headmen Tuckabatchee Harjo and Octruchee Emathla, for instance, was ignored by the secretary of war for weeks, as the party racked up a large bill at Brown's Indian Queen Hotel in downtown Washington. Jackson believed the Creeks were in the capital city to confer with former attorney general William Wirt, who represented the Cherokees in their case against the state of Georgia. Jackson blamed Wirt for the Creeks' refusal to sell their domain and emigrate in 1830, and was convinced that the Creeks had hired him "to protect them in their rights as an independent Nation." Desperate to meet with Secretary of War Eaton or members of Congress, the two delegates clarified that they were only appointed "to attend to such business as immediately concerns our own people. We have no business in the Supreme Court."[15]

Little came of these visits. The president refused to give the Creeks what they wanted (relief from encroachments and Alabama's laws) while the Creeks rebuffed Jackson's primary demand (their wholesale emigration to the Indian territory). Aware that these meetings would yield no resolution against an intractable administration and many unsympathetic congressmen (and cognizant that federal officials were tired of footing the travel bills of the delegates), Crowell had tried to dissuade Tuckabatchee Harjo and Octruchee Emathla from going to Washington. But the Creeks were resolute. Reiterating a point that perhaps did not need to be repeated, eleven headmen dispatched a letter to Secretary of War Eaton in April 1831, once again stating that "we have been compelled to refuse a compliance with his wishes towards removing to the west; our aged fathers and mothers beseech us to remain upon the land that gave us birth, where the bones of their kindred are buried, so that when they die they may mingle their ashes together. They view a removal as the worst evil that can befall them." That December the Creeks dispatched yet another delegation to Washington and Opothle Yoholo, Tuckabatchee Harjo, Tuckabatchee Micco, and Benjamin Marshall (accompanied by George Stiggins as secretary and John Brodnax as special agent) arrived in the city sometime around the 29th. Officials then changed tactics. Convinced that the Creek National Council would never sanction a land cession or voluntary emigration, Crowell and his superiors proposed to the Creeks that they take their land in individual allotments similar to the agreement the Choctaws had signed at Dancing Rabbit Creek a year and a half earlier. The benefits for the United States were clear: allotments would open up vast tracts of Creek hunting ground for white settlement, and with the option to sell reserves individually, white purchasers could simply bypass the Creek National Council altogether. Crowell addressed the remaining headmen in council in February 1832, and after six tense days of "exertions and management," the Creeks relented. The agent quickly dispatched another delegation to Washington where they joined the headmen already in the city.[16]

There are no detailed records of the ensuing negotiations, but there was some intrigue. After behaving "in a way to give dissatisfaction to the nation," George Stiggins was sent home in February and stripped of his appointment. The primary template for the yet-to-be-written document was the Dancing Rabbit Creek agreement. Secretary of War Lewis Cass, who had replaced Eaton the previous August, asked for a list of terms the Creeks would accept, and on 12 March Brodnax responded by asking for modifications to some of the language in the Choctaw document. Like Dancing Rabbit Creek, heads of families were to take individual land reserves, but the Creeks demanded more allotments than were given to the Choctaws. Headmen also wanted safeguards that would protect them from fraud in the event that any individual wanted to sell his or her reserve. For example, Brodnax's letter proposed that there should be a number of years determined during which time all transactions would be observed by a "board of commissioners" consisting of headmen and the Creek agent. Most important, the Creeks refused to sign any removal document. With the basic parameters agreed to, the Creeks attempted to get as much as they could from the Jackson administration. On 19 March headmen sent an additional list of demands in an attempt to minimize the loss of their domain. Solemnly noting that they had historically given up large tracts of their country "for a mere song," Opothle Yoholo and others requested, among other things, that each principal chief receive five sections of land (3,200 acres); lesser chiefs, two sections (1,280 acres); and all heads of families and those without families, one section (640 acres); as well as "Four reservations Containing two sections each" set aside for town miccos (town kings), presumably for protection of the town houses and public squares.[17]

The Treaty of Washington, signed 24 March 1832, did not include many of the Creeks' demands. A census was taken and in return for the cession, 6,557 heads of families each received a half-section of land (about 320 acres), while 90 of the preeminent headmen, called "mile chiefs," each received a full section (about 640 acres). The Upper mile chiefs were chosen in council by their peers at Tuckabatchee, while the Lower Creeks assigned theirs at the Sechartlitcha settlement of Cusseta. Who made the list and who did not achieve mile chief status says a lot about the factionalism in the Creek country at the time. The ninety included a mishmash of former Red Sticks from the first Creek War (like Clewalla headman Jim Boy and Menawa of Okfuskee), men who fought on the side of the Americans against the Red Sticks (Yuchi headman Timpoochee Barnard and Natchez chief Selocta), former McIntosh party members (Jacob Beavers, James Island, and Joseph Marshall, all of Coweta), and those who approved the targeted executions of McIntosh party members (Opothle Yoholo). These selections were controversial, however, and several complained of injustice when they were not given a full section. Ottissee Micco, Efar Tustunnuggee, Tuckabatchee Fixico, and Coloma Tustunnuggee protested that certain headmen, under the manipulation of white land speculators, "concluded to make new Chiefs" at Tuckabatchee and thereby deprived them of their full allotment. Others, like John Oponee of Chehaw, John Stidham of Sawokli, and Toma Micco of Thlakatchka, were in line to receive a full reserve, but were broken at council in 1833 over their advocacy of voluntary emigration. Toma Micco had actually signed the 1832 Treaty of Washington, while Stidham publicly opposed William McIntosh at Indian Springs and signed the 1826 Treaty of Washington. At least one omission was eventually rectified: George Grayson, who is listed as Micco Foseke on the Echeesehogee (Standing Up Tobacco Town) roll, was granted mile chief status in 1846.[18]

Both parties agreed that the period to be determined for the oversight of sales by federal officials, as requested in Brodnax's 12 March letter, would be five years. All sales during this period would be overseen by a certifying agent, with final approval given by the president. After that period, the head of each family received a fee-simple patent to their land. The Creeks were allowed to remain indefinitely on their reserve, although federal agents hoped the Creeks would sell to white buyers and move west. The War Department saw the treaty as a way to ethnically cleanse Alabama of Creek Indians, and in an attempt to hurry the process along, the administration tried to enter into negotiations with the Creeks for the wholesale purchase of their allotted reserves. In outlining his goals for the prospective treaty, Lewis Cass directed locating agent John James Abert, who led negotiations, that if possible, "not one reservation should be permitted to be retained within the State of Alabama" by the Creeks.

The headmen, however, quickly rebuffed the administration's attempts to purchase the reserves en masse and stated their intention of "Setting down, and trying it awhile."[19]

In addition, the treaty reserved twenty sections for Creek orphans. These sections were later located on land considered "amongst the best in the Creek Nation" and rented to white farmers for up to two dollars an acre. Twenty-nine additional sections were allotted to the Creeks to dispose of as they saw fit. Five of the twenty-nine were later given to the western Creeks who had emigrated in the preceding years for what they called "an act of justice." But "justice" had its limitations. These five sections, eventually located in Macon County near the Barbour County line, were of low quality and valued at only 78 cents an acre. The remaining twenty-nine sections were divided among the Upper and Lower Creek towns, and one half-section was given "for various reasons" (but none entirely explained) by the headmen to Napoleon Moore. It appears that it was Moore's connection to his father, William (an Indian countryman of Cusseta and former "secretary of the nation"), that won him a special half-section of land.[20]

The way in which reserves were assigned was relatively simple. Agents visited with each town's headmen to discuss "the great outlines, which are to determine the boundaries of the reservations for each town." After visiting a particular *talwa* and locating each Creek head of family, agents called a meeting and assigned reserves in the presence of the town chiefs. Agents allowed headmen and those who had improvements to remain on their land as long as it conformed to the 320- or 640-acre reserve. If an individual's improvements extended into more than one section or half-section, then only the reserve that contained the Creek's house or residence was assigned to them. Most Creeks preferred to take their half-sections in a north-south alignment, but because locating agents were bound to assign reserves based on the location of the reserve's improvements, the reserves were arranged on both a north-south and east-west grid. In many cases, wealthier Creeks lost land while poorer Creeks actually acquired land under the treaty. Benjamin Marshall, for instance, sought a special patent for his plantation across the river from Columbus, Georgia, as a result of his extensive improvements.[21]

Creeks without improvements—typically the poor and those who were still transient in Alabama—were the last to be placed in reserves and were assigned by lot. Called "floaters," Creeks without homesteads were situated around members of their town who had improvements and as near the town's public square as possible, but not closer to the council house than those with improvements. Under Alabama law, the sixteenth section of each township was reserved for public schools and these sections remained empty (unless already occupied by a Creek homestead). Officials devised a number of ways to eliminate controversy. For instance, if two Creeks had improvements within the same section or half-section then the individual who had lived there the longest received the property. If this could not be determined, the reserve was chosen by lot. In other cases, Creeks whose land was dissected by a navigable waterway—called a "fraction"—were allowed to choose an adjacent "fraction" in order for that person to receive their full 320- or 640-acre share. If Creek heads of family resided far from other members of their town, as was often the case, they had the choice of remaining on their improvement or "floating" closer to their town. In fact, there were two instances of entire Creek towns choosing to abandon their improvements and "float" so they could reconstitute their *talwa* with all residents living together. John Ward, a Creek Indian of mixed ancestry from Hickory Ground, was accidentally floated away from his improvements on land he had occupied since 1820. Ward petitioned to be relocated back to his old reserve, stating that "the reason why he wants said land is not that it is [remarkably] fertile but because it is the land he lives on and is in the Town he belongs to and is in the midst of his relations and friends."[22]

The Treaty of Washington was a terrible deal for the Creeks, but they were convinced it was the only chance they had to remain on their native soil. While pitching the idea of taking their land in allotments, Crowell warned the headmen that it was "the only mode by which they could be protected where they now are." The Creeks were also attracted to the fact that it was not a removal document, although the treaty continued unabated the government's policy of promoting and funding voluntary emigration. With regard to solving the Creeks' concerns over Alabama's extension laws, white encroachment, and starvation,

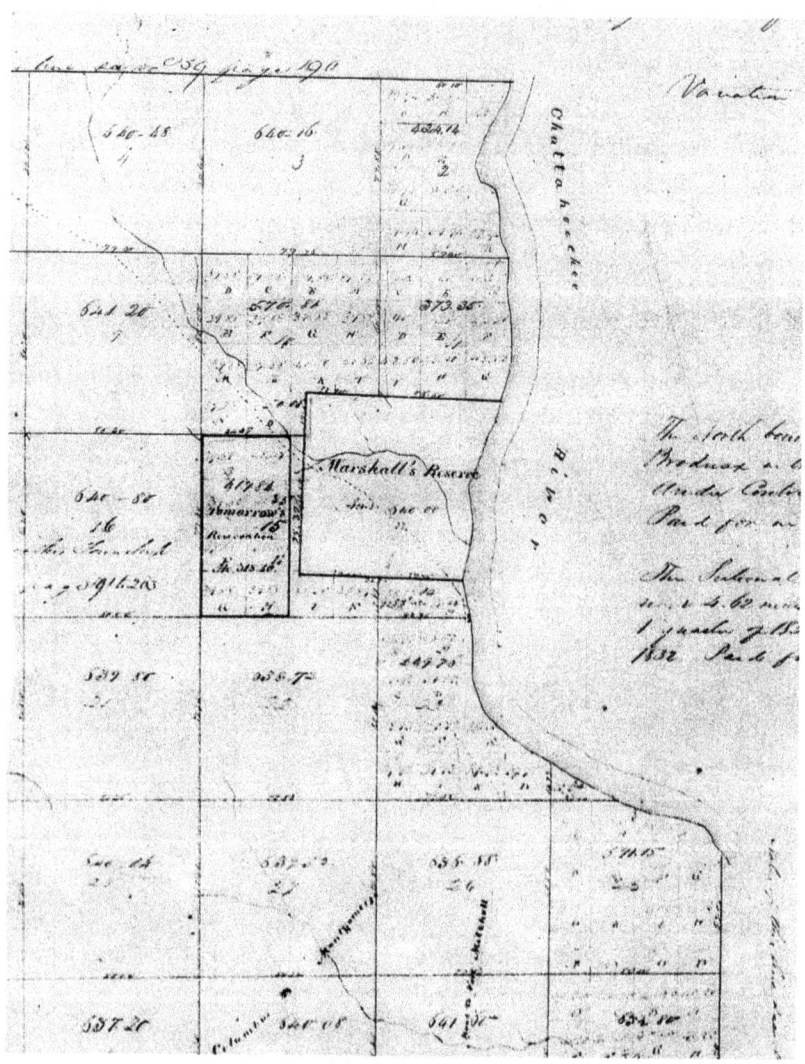

FIG. 11. Benjamin Marshall's reservation. Alabama Secretary of State, Land Plats, Tallapoosa Land District, Roll 30, Page 161a, Alabama Department of Archives and History, Montgomery AL.

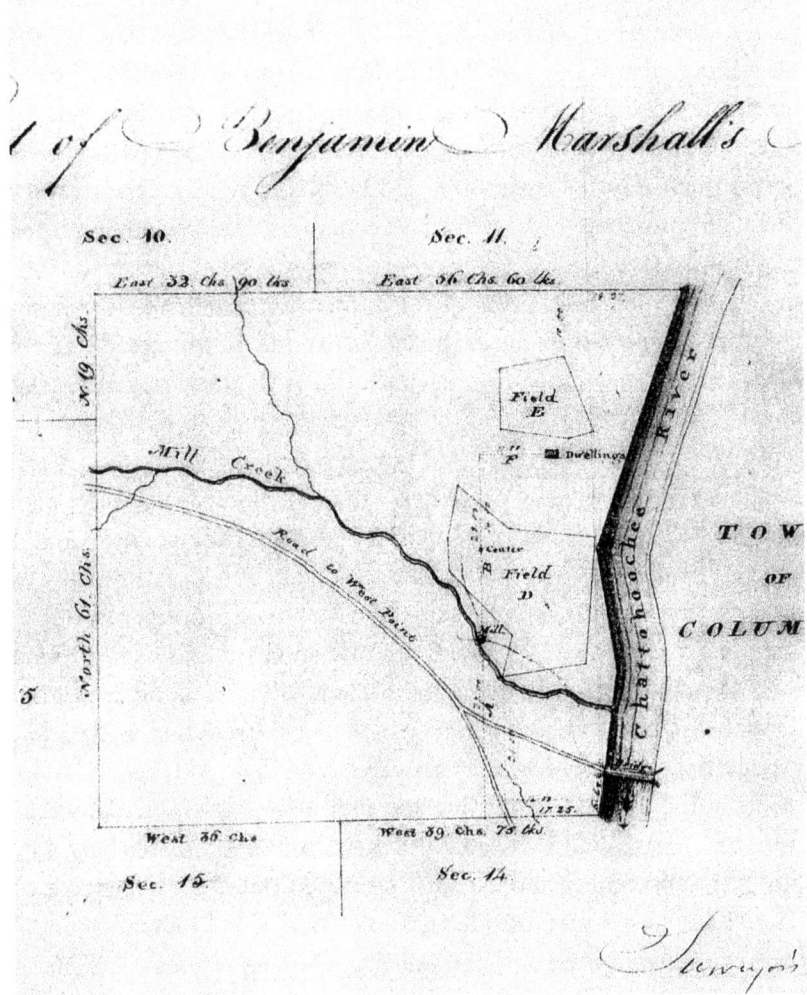

FIG. 12. Benjamin Marshall's reservation. Alabama Secretary of State, Land Plats, Tallapoosa Land District, Roll 30, Page 161, Alabama Department of Archives and History, Montgomery AL.

however, the agreement was an unmitigated disaster. The Creeks ceded their entire domain to the federal government and fell under federal and state control, which essentially ended all of the controversies over the 1827–1832 Alabama extension laws. Indeed, the former Creek Nation was quickly divided into nine new counties by an act of Alabama's general assembly and "organized so as to put the entire machinery of [the] state government into full operation." Whites made good on their earlier threats to prosecute the Creeks, and observers subsequently reported that Indians were "daily" being ordered into the state courts to answer to civil and criminal charges. Many of the accusations were frivolous. Opothle Yoholo was detained in 1836 for, as one person noted, "a debt for which he is as much responsible as he is for the national debt of Great Britain."[23]

The treaty not only increased but legalized white encroachment. Reserves not occupied by Creek heads of family were available for purchase, which meant that more than half of the Creek country would soon be settled by Americans. Moreover, squatters saw the treaty as an invitation to settle on unoccupied half-sections. Thousands, subsequently, flooded the Creek country in 1832 and 1833, joining those who were already imbedded among the Indians. Some took possession of Creek fields, evicted Creek families, and burned Creek homes. Article 5 promised the removal of white intruders, while those who had improvements at the time of the signing and had not forcibly evicted Creeks from their farms could stay only "till their crops are gathered." By 1833, however, most whites had defiantly remained. Attempts were made to remove any trespassers considered "obnoxious" to the Indians from the cession. Alabama governor John Gayle and U.S. representative Clement Comer Clay protested, however, as did many squatters, some of whom identified, if only informally, with the larger nullification movement. Whites who had extended credit to the Creeks for merchandise threatened to sue the Indians who were so fearful of being hauled into state court that they actually started defending the right of the squatters to remain illegally on their soil. Other squatters used threats of force. One speculator threated to kill Creek headmen and put others in jail if they allowed agents to force him and his cronies from their improvements.

On a larger scale, rumors swirled that regiments from Alabama and as far away as South Carolina were being organized to defend the rights of the trespassers. Dozens of white families were removed and their homes burned to prevent their return, but it failed to make much of a dent in the overall white population. The standoff reached a crescendo with the killing of Hardiman Owens—a squatter with a long rap sheet of abuses against the Creeks—who was shot and killed during his attempted arrest.[24]

The 1832 Treaty of Washington was largely incompatible with nineteenth-century Creek culture, did not take into account the condition and quantity of the Alabama soil, and its wording was vague enough that it was left open to interpretation by the agents. As a result, the document was plagued by controversy from the beginning. The 1832 treaty disrupted Creek society so significantly that it was one of the contributing factors to their forced removal beginning in 1836. Even administration officials knew that the treaty would not alleviate the Creeks' problems. In 1833, before the reserves were even assigned, Lewis Cass conceded that "it seems to be hopeless to expect that they can remain and prosper where they now are."[25]

The first problem with the treaty was that it reduced an individual's access to suitable agricultural land. Agents estimated that only "one fifth," or about a million acres, of the former Creek Nation was considered "good land." The 6,696 sections and half-sections (which included the twenty orphan reserves, the twenty-nine allotted to the headmen, and the ninety-mile chief sections) comprised a total of 2,187,200 acres, which meant that well over half of the reserves were located on poor soil. Reserves comprised of "second rate" soil were acceptable for cultivation, but in some cases, family heads were assigned land that was "wholly untillable." Sinkawhe, a "very old Blind woman," was one of many who petitioned the federal government for new land because, among other things, the reserve assigned to her "was of no account it was Hilley and Rockey and [too poor] for any use such as neither white nor Red people could make a living on." Already poor from declining fortunes, Sinkawhe and her Tallasseehatchee townsfolk pleaded for aid, claiming that they were in "grait need of Sustanance and Clothing." Tyrone Power, an Irish stage actor who traveled through Alabama in late 1834, observed firsthand the varying degrees to which the Creeks had reestablished their homes and fields on their reserves after 1832. Power noted that a few of the Lower Creeks "had erected log-houses, cleared a little land, and were also in the possession of a stove or two." A majority of the Creeks, however, remained on the edge of subsistence. Power noted that the poorer Creeks were "wretched in the extreme: most of the families were living in wigwams, built of bark or green boughs, of the frailest and least comfortable construction; not an article of furniture, except a kettle, was in the possession of this class."[26]

As farming declined precipitously, Creek men struggled to fill the void through game. Because the reserves were small by Creek standards (only a mile by a half-mile in size), hunting was severely disrupted. Federal commissioner Alfred Balch, who investigated the causes of the Second Creek War, which began in 1836, reported that hunting as a resource "failed to a great degree" after 1832 because whites, who bought the land surrounding the Creek reserves, killed much of the deer for themselves, or "frightened them off to inaccessible swamps and morasses." The Creeks continued crossing into Georgia to hunt, which often led to clashes with white residents. This coupled with the fact that the federal government forbade the Creeks from engaging in any type of hostilities, and two of the primary occupations that defined Creek manhood were essentially eliminated.[27]

The division of the former Creek Nation into townships, ranges, and sections was in conformity with eighteenth-century public land surveys. It was designed for white occupancy and did not take into account Creek settlement patterns in the 1820s. Because the Creeks' houses, and not their agricultural fields, often served as the basis of the Creeks' improvement, the most desirable land had the potential to be excluded from their reserve. Many Creeks had cleared fields on good bottomland, while their houses were established on a "distant, barren but healthy sand hill." Many Creeks were concerned that in these instances, the house with the sand hill formed the basis for the family's reserve, not the more fertile cropland. In some cases, however, entire towns were located on poor soil. The Kialigee reserves, for instance, were situated "in the most barren and secluded part of the nation." In previous generations, whenever land became exhausted or was no longer of use to the Creeks, they often abandoned the area and sought new ground. Creeks were very pragmatic in the ways in which they sought out better parcels of land when older soil no longer met their needs. Opothle Yoholo, for example, had moved his cattle onto better range land several miles away from his residence years before the treaty was signed. Even headmen who negotiated the treaty understood that one of the flaws of the document was that Creeks were confined to their reserve. Opothle Yoholo, a part of that 1832 delegation, noted as much when he and other leaders declared that "instead of the wide spread Territory comprehending almost the whole of Alabama and Georgia, the Creeks have gradually been confined to narrower & narrower limits, until at length they are reduced down to an individual tenure of a half section of land each."[28]

Many Creeks, aware of the flaws in the treaty, tried to find better land before their reserves were assigned. This was complicated, however, by conflicting language in Article 2, which states that "every other head of a Creek family [was allowed] to select one half section each," while also declaring that "all the persons belonging to the same town, entitled to selections, and who cannot make the same, so as to include their improvements, shall take them in one body in a proper form." The first part of Article 2 appears to allow Creeks to simply "select" a better piece of unoccupied land, while the latter directs agents to assign reserves based on the location of their improvements or in town clusters if the Creeks owned no property. Agents in the field also had differing interpretations of the wording, and as a result some Creeks were able to claim new land while others had their appeals rejected. Efar Emathla of Cusseta, who helped negotiate the document, claimed that he was told by Andrew Jackson that reservees would be allowed to choose any piece of unoccupied land. John Crowell backed up Efar Emathla's claim, and subsequently large numbers of Creeks quickly went about finding better soil and hastily constructing temporary improvements. Agents, for example, discovered Benjamin Marshall moving his sister onto more fertile land before her half-section was assigned. But locating agent Abert refused to allow the Creeks in his section to choose new plots and instead arranged the new landowners in town clusters for simple logistical reasons. Noting the difficulty of accommodating so many requests, Abert rhetorically asked "who was to have the first, who the second, and who the third choice[?]" Indeed, despite Jackson's alleged promises, instructions sent from the secretary of war's office were clear on this point: "No selections can be made, except by those who had improvements; at the time the Treaty was made." In fact, the instructions were so rigid that even if a Creek reservee voluntarily abandoned his or her improvements in order to live within their *talwa*, the instructions forbade other Creeks from taking the abandoned lot.[29]

The other component of the Treaty of Washington that was incompatible with the Creeks' land-use traditions was that it allowed head of families to sell their reserves. By the 1820s individual Creeks would not have been able to cede land without the approval of the Creek National Council or without great risk to their lives. William McIntosh, for example, discovered the uncompromising rigidity of this law in 1825. Administration officials considered this to be one of the biggest impediments to emigration, and in 1830 they pleaded with the headmen to "meet together in council and repeal a law which punishes any who shall offer to dispose of the land of the Creeks." The 1832 Treaty of Washington, however, allowed the Creeks not only to sell their reserve without penalty but for profit. Even more problematic, census takers and locating agents, operating from their patriarchal worldview, assigned land to the husband, including Indian countrymen, despite the fact that the matrilineages controlled Creek farmland. Headmen protested this and noted that by assigning land to husbands, the treaty placed it in "the power of the white man to dispose of the land and leave his wife." The Creeks, negotiating from a point of extreme desperation and weakness, gave up all the elements that made them powerful: their sovereignty, their polity, and their national domain. Whites no longer had to confront a unified Creek National Council when attempting to acquire Creek land; they could go directly to the 6,557 individual landowners. And this, white buyers did in spades. Many Creeks were unfamiliar with the logistics of private ownership and transferred their land unaware that the sale was permanent. When Return J. Meigs, a lawyer and Jackson confidante, was asked by the administration to come to Alabama and investigate the implementation of the treaty, many Creeks believed he was there to restore sold reserves to the original owners. Hitchiti headman Neah Emathla was one of many who did not quite understand the full scope of a land transfer when he complained on behalf of his people that white buyers were taking the Indians' fields and rails when they purchased the reserves. An agent had to explain to the unhappy headman that when a Creek sold his land, he sold the house, fences, and fields along with it.[30]

Even stipulations in the treaty that appeared to benefit the Creeks had an ulterior motive. Federal agents were directed to try and organize as many reserves as possible into town clusters. As a result, floaters and Creeks whose improvements conflicted with another person's claim were moved as compactly as possible around other members of their town. This, in effect, re-created the traditional *talwa* plat from the early eighteenth-century just before livestock raising diffused town sites. And, while scholars have used this to suggest that the Creeks had a fighting chance of maintaining their traditional lifeways, the Jackson administration designed this as a way to open up more territory for white settlement. While he acknowledged that Article 2 was created to "bring the Indians together as much as possible," Lewis Cass confided that its other goal was to "prevent their settlements from extending indefinitely through the country."[31]

Despite the headmen's decision not to sell the reserves in a bloc, instability in the former Creek Nation made holding on to their allotments almost impossible for most families. Many sold their land for quick, lifesaving cash. Indeed, one speculator claimed to have purchased five reserves from Creeks "suffering for the nesesarys of life." Others sold in anticipation of voluntarily emigrating to the Indian territory. Creeks who were floated onto poor land often sold out of indifference. Other Creeks sold in exchange for a life estate whereby they were allowed to continue living on their allotment until their death, when full ownership was transferred to the white purchaser. For example, one Creek man who sold his land in Talladega County was allowed to remain on his reserve, according to a contract drawn up, "for the term of one or two hundred years, or as long as he or his heirs may deem proper to remain where he now lives." Indeed, one agent observed that with regard to Indians who had sold their reserve but were allowed to remain, "no Indians are more opposed to emigration than many of those who have sold their land." Finally, many reserves were transferred to white ownership because of a loophole in the treaty. Because there was no provision for the transfer of land to the heirs of a Creek Indian who died prior to selling his or her allotment, many reserves were sold by administrators appointed by the orphans' courts. In a number of cases, Creek families often did not even receive due compensation for their deceased relative's land, as agents discovered that many administrators had neither the ability nor the inclination to seek out and pay the rightful heirs, especially if they had already left for Indian territory.[32]

Many Creeks, however, lost their land through the diabolical machinations of white predators. The Creek delegation to Washington anticipated that some sort of land fraud would be perpetrated on them, and demanded protections that they considered lacking in the Choctaws' 1830 treaty. The five years of federal oversight of sales did little to stop the speculation and land stealing, however. The schemes ranged from sneaky to illegal and the Creeks were utterly ill equipped to deal with the onslaught. This is no embarrassment to the Creeks, as federal officials appear to have been caught completely off guard as well. In fact, one federal commissioner recalled that "the modes of practising deceptions upon the Indians were as various as the ingenuity of men." With the natural buffer destroyed as a result of the Treaties of Indian Springs and Washington, unsuspecting Creek reservees found a bevy of land speculators and traders on their doorstep in nearby Columbus. Many Creeks who wished to remain on their reserve got caught up in a debt cycle spurred on by white traders who established stores in the Creek country and extended lines of credit with an eye toward native land as collateral. Other traders hastily tried to generate credit so they could receive a portion of the $100,000 allotted by the treaty for debt repayment. Subsequently, many Creeks suffered the same fate as Chehaw resident Kloslitco, who was arrested and tied up by a speculator to whom he owed money. Although the reservee "did not wish to sell," Kloslitco was forced to give up his land in order to cover his debt. The practice was so widespread that Meigs declared that this tactic was used as "engines" to compel the Creeks to sell to white speculators.[33]

The most brazen predators went about systematically stealing land from the Creek owners. The two most common types of fraud were "personation," where a speculator bribed another Indian to impersonate the true owner of the half-section. The impersonator was usually versed in the details of the true owner's life and provided this information to confirm his or her identity. Starving Creeks were often targeted (and bribed with food) to act as impersonators because they were just desperate enough to turn on their townspeople. Once the land was signed over to the imposter, he turned over all but a few dollars to the speculator. If the impersonator was ever reluctant to hand over the money, however, agents reported that whites, "if they cannot get it in any other way they take the indian into another house and [then] choak him untill he gives it up." Another common type of fraud was taking back most of the purchase money by force after the certifying agent walked away from the sale. Some Creeks sold land for hundreds of dollars but retained only a fraction of that after the sale, while other Creeks had the purchase money stolen and exchanged for an unequal amount in goods like homespun. In some instances, the speculators were not above simple pickpocketing. Siarh Yoholo, a mile chief of Tuckabatchee, sold his land for a thousand dollars, but soon thereafter a white man who had participated in the transaction threw his arms around him "in the attitude of hugging" and covertly took the purchase money out of the headman's pouch during the embrace.[34]

Alcohol featured prominently in many of the frauds. Speculators either used spirits to ensnarl the Creeks in debt, or established grog shops near the reserves they had bought in order to expropriate the purchase money through whiskey sales. One witness observed that "Many of the Indians have received 2, 3, 4, 5, $600 for their land and have been drunk ever since until all their money is gone."[35]

Indeed, many Creeks lost their land through the kind of fraud described by Johnson Jones Hooper, whose *Some Adventures of Captain Simon Suggs, Late of the Tallapoosa Volunteers* (published in book form

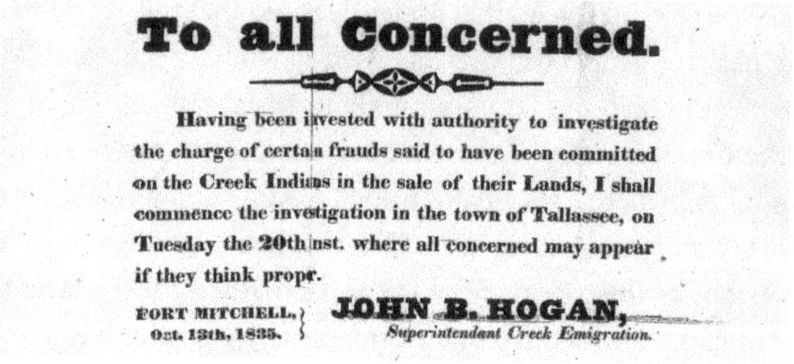

> **To all Concerned.**
>
> Having been invested with authority to investigate the charge of certain frauds said to have been committed on the Creek Indians in the sale of their Lands, I shall commence the investigation in the town of Tallassee, on Tuesday the 20th inst. where all concerned may appear if they think proper.
>
> FORT MITCHELL, **JOHN B. HOGAN,**
> Oct. 13th, 1835. *Superintendant Creek Emigration.*

FIG. 13. Fraud investigation notice, Files of the Office of the Commissary General of Subsistence, Indian Removal to the West, 1832–1840, Bethesda MD: University Publications of America, Roll 5, 462.

in 1845) lampooned the people of the Old Southwest frontier during this period. Hooper, however, also named names and places in an attempt, perhaps, to expose real people or make real people look foolish. Hooper's reference to "the great Indian Council held at Dudley's store, in Tallapoosa county, in September of the year 1835" refers to the assignment of the twenty-nine sections to the Creek headmen that took place at Peter Dudley's house at Okfuskee in Tallapoosa County. Indeed, one letter written by people recruiting the Creeks to emigrate noted that they had "succeeded, at a council of head chiefs held at 'Dudley' in September [1835] last, in obtaining their consent and fixed determination to remove west as soon as their twenty-nine sections of land were sold." "Colonel Bryan," who bought the land from Suggs was almost certainly Colonel Joseph Bryan, a judge, locating agent, and speculator, who provided legal counsel for a number of land speculators. "General Lawson" (Irvin Lawson) and "Mr. Goodwin" (Thomas or John Goodwin) were also real people. And "Sudo Micco," the "Sky chief," was no doubt Suddi Micco, number sixty-six on the 1832 census of Creeks from the town of Chatoksofke (an affiliated town of Okfuskee) and the only Creek Indian with that name on the roll. Even Bird H. Young—according to one scholar, the archetype for Simon Suggs (referred to as "the Mad Bird" by a Creek woman in the story)—was the purchaser of a large number of Creek lands in the 1830s. Moreover, in an 1858 letter published in his *Reminiscences* (which was edited by Hooper), Thomas Simpson Woodward mentions Harrison Young (a real-life speculator) as "the brother of Simon Suggs." And, a reference to a "Charly McL—e-" might have been real-life land speculator Charles McLemore who was a close confidante of Woodward. Just as in Hooper's work, these real-life speculators knew each other. In fact, a partnership consisting of "Bryan, Lawson, McLemore, & Dudley" purchased Okfuskee headman Menawa's section in May 1835. The sale was even investigated over concerns that it was not properly certified.[36]

Perhaps the most heartbreaking aspect of the frauds was that speculators were successful primarily because they took advantage of the Creeks' trusting nature. In fact, Abert lamented that the Creeks' "generally good character (for they are a well disposed people) their honesty of purpose, and general honesty of conduct, instead of establishing claims upon good feelings, seems rather to expose them to injuries. Their weaknesses receive no compassion" from the white speculators.[37]

From the Creeks' perspective, the 1832 Treaty of Washington failed on just about every conceivable level. Creek headmen were stung by the problems associated with the agreement. The pervasiveness of the frauds and the degree to which the Creek reserves were being turned over to white ownership surprised those who initially saw the treaty as a way to salvage Creek land for the Creek people. Principal headmen, who complained bitterly that the government had not abided by the stipulations of the treaty including the removal of white intruders, angrily stated that "instead of our situation, being relieved, as was anticipated, we are distressed in a ten fold manner." White squatters continued to trespass on Creek land, while many Creeks who did sell were defrauded out of their land and money. The ensuing investigations and litigation delayed the compensation due Creek sellers and white purchasers. Far from the Creeks' lives improving, the treaty only made conditions in the former Creek Nation worse. In fact, the treaty ultimately hastened their forced removal across the Mississippi. In a grim description of the conditions found in the Creek country fifteen months after the treaty signing, Abert reported that the Creeks were "brow beat, and cowed, and imposed upon, and distressed with the feeling that they have no adequate protection in the U.S. and no capacity of self protection in themselves. They dare not enforce their own laws to preserve order for fear of the laws of the whites. In consequence more murders of each other have been committed in the last six months, than for as many previous years, and the whites will not bring the offenders to justice, for like [*Othello*'s] Iago, no matter which kills, sees in it his gain."³⁸

The treaty was so unfavorable to the Creek people that it appears certain headmen who negotiated the document deliberately misled their townspeople about its full scope. Enoch Parsons, the brother of census taker Benjamin, noted that "the generality of the Indians did not understand the Treaty and were not of opinion their country was sold to the United States. The Chiefs had suppressed the information in order to secure their safety." When locating agents arrived in Tuckabatchee in late 1833, the Creeks refused to give their names because Opothle Yoholo told them that the agents were not abiding by the spirit of the treaty. According to the officials, the Tuckabatcheans were told by the headman that all Creeks, not just family heads, were to receive land.³⁹

The selling of the reserves threatened the Creeks' ceremonial life because square grounds were vulnerable to purchase by white speculators. As a result of livestock raising beginning in the latter part of the eighteenth century, most Creek towns were diffused as residents sought large amounts of grazing land. In 1826 when seven thousand Lower Creeks were forced from Georgia, this pattern continued as many refugees tried to resettle on the limited amount of good land in Alabama. In a number of cases, this left the town centers sparsely populated. As locating agents assigned reserves based in part on the locations of the Creeks' improvements, it was inevitable that at least some town square grounds would be located on public land or on half-sections owned by impoverished Creeks in need of life-saving cash. For instance, the Wetumpka council house, a popular site for important national councils, was on a half-section assigned to Yarkinhar, a man with no discernible prominence. Worse, the council house near the Cusseta settlements was located on unallotted land. And whites drove off the Creek families living on the reserves that contained the Tawarsa town house. The Creek delegation that signed the 1832 Treaty of Washington demanded that allotments be

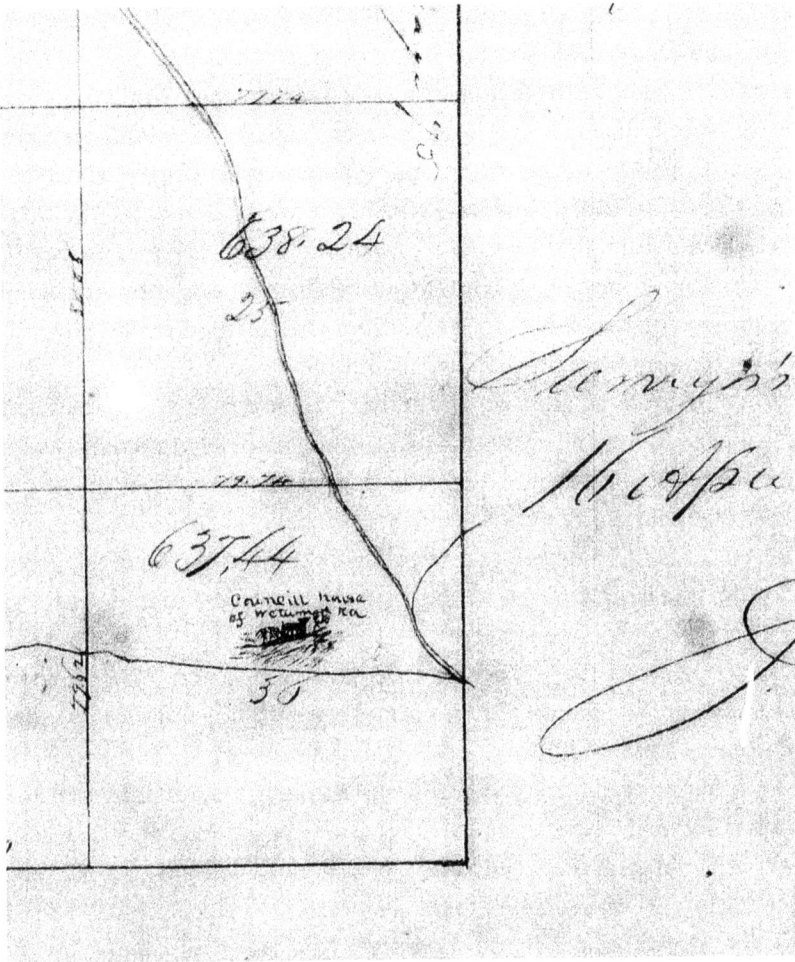

FIG. 14. The Wetumpka Council House, Russell County, Alabama. Alabama Secretary of State, Land Plats, Tallapoosa, Roll 30, 133, Alabama Department of Archives and History, Montgomery AL.

set aside for these council grounds, but this stipulation never made it into the treaty. Concerned about the prospect of their sacred ceremonial sites falling into the hands of white land speculators, in 1834 the headmen of Tuckabatchee, Ottissee, and Tallassee agreed to move chiefs and other "substantial people" onto reserves containing their *talwa*'s town house and adjacent lands. Under the plan, the chiefs agreed to give Ahalocco Yoholo, Opothle Yoholo's brother, a reserve containing the Tallassee town house despite the fact that he was a Tuckabatchee. Similarly, it was agreed that Tomathla Micco would take land containing the Ottissee town house. Creeks who claimed the half-sections containing these respective sites complained to federal officials, however, and both Ahalocco Yoholo and Tomathla Micco were floated to land in the pine woods.[40]

The 1832 Treaty of Washington completely and comprehensively destroyed the Creek Nation in the East. The Creeks remained in Alabama for a number of years hence, but there was no longer a "Creek Nation" to speak of. The treaty neutered Creek government and headmen did not consider the western Creek Nation to be legitimate. Instead, the Creek people existed in a sort of liminal state: they were no longer sovereign, but did not enjoy the same privileges as white Alabamians. Steven C. Hahn, who has written thoroughly on the evolution of the Creek Nation, argued that Creek nationhood was political and diplomatic in nature—a policy of neutrality designed to defend the Creeks' interests against the machinations of colonial Spain, France, and Britain. When treaties were signed, the Creek polity evolved to the point of meeting European nations as a "nation." Defense of territory lay at the heart of Creek nationhood, and this continued through the 1820s. By 1821 the Creek National Council had passed two laws against ceding Creek land without council approval and underscored the seriousness of the crime by attaching a death sentence to lawbreakers. The Council was considered *the* line of defense against land cessions. And when William McIntosh circumvented this body on 12 February 1825, he and a number of his allies were dealt with accordingly. But after 1832 the Creeks could no longer rely on defense of territory to bind their people together. There were 6,557 individual Creek landowners, many of whom acted as a nation of one by selling their reserve and moving west. Hahn pinpoints the early origins of the Creek Nation to 1718, the year of the "Coweta Resolution." The end of the eastern Creek Nation was 24 March 1832.[41]

The 1832 Treaty of Washington was a last desperate attempt by Creek headmen to stem the invasion of white squatters and reassert a modicum of control over their land. But certifying agents were underqualified and understaffed, and Jackson only made the situation worse when he closed the eastern Creek Agency on 31 December 1832, and dismissed agent John Crowell (a subagent was retained until the end of 1835). When the frauds exploded with a pervasiveness no one expected, Jackson sent in an understaffed group of investigators to resolve the problem. With this evidence it seems clear that, while not condoning the frauds and perhaps underestimating their seriousness, Jackson probably was not too upset with how the treaty played itself out as it hastened the removal of the Creeks across the Mississippi River. The land frauds and the slow adjudication of the claims were one of the primary causes of the Second Creek War in 1836 and the forced removal of the Creeks to the Indian territory later that summer. Still, it is difficult to fault the headmen, at the time, for agreeing to such a deal. Whites historically had little respect for the Creeks' sovereign claims to their land and trespassing had been pandemic for a century prior to 1832. The headmen likely believed they needed to adopt white conceptions of landownership, a title or deed, in order to force the Americans into taking their claims seriously.[42]

5 Eclipse
1833–36

The failure of the 1832 Treaty of Washington was a devastating setback for the Creek people. The Creeks had already surrendered more than half their domain to the United States, and hundreds more of their reserves were transferred to whites either through legitimate sales or because of fraud. Landless, poor, and backed into a corner with few acceptable options, many Creeks were pushed to the edge of despair. Their morale plummeted and there was a marked change in the demeanor of the Creek people after 1834. Some grew angry and began plotting ways to lash out against white encroachment while others grew despondent. And some of the staunchest anti-removal headmen appear to have begun contemplating moving to the West. Within this environment, Andrew Jackson reconvened federally sponsored voluntary emigration, which had been halted under his orders in 1830. Despite their best efforts, however, agents could only coax approximately six hundred Creeks and their slaves to emigrate in 1834 and about five hundred more in 1835. The remaining twenty thousand Creeks were resolute in their determination to remain behind on their reserves, which they held on to with only the faintest of legal guarantees.

In September 1832 Chilly McIntosh returned to Alabama to conduct two orders of business. First, he and Robert Tiger, a Thlakatchka man who left the Creek Nation with the second McIntosh party in 1828, were given powers of attorney by the western Creeks to sell the five sections of land conveyed to them by the eastern chiefs. The western Creek headman then planned on conducting a party of thirty or forty families connected to the McIntosh party back with him to Indian territory, but added that he would "chearfully render any assistance" in his power to remove any other Creeks west. Prominent allies, including his patrilineal relative, former Georgia governor and then–U.S. senator George M. Troup, had personally endorsed McIntosh's application to serve as an emigration agent. In February 1833 the head of the Office of Indian Affairs, Elbert Herring, notified McIntosh that if the western headman could "prevail upon a number of the Creeks to remove to the west," he would be duly compensated by the federal government. Under the impression that he had the full support of the administration, McIntosh soon established provision depots and "mortgaged his whole private fortune for means to defray his expenses."[1]

But on 4 May Herring ordered McIntosh to suspend his operations. While Herring complained that he had not been updated on the progress of the emigration and believed a party led by McIntosh would cost more than if conducted by a regular federal agent, this was clearly a decision made by the president or secretary of war. Lewis Cass, for example, claimed to have been unaware of the full scope of McIntosh's intentions—believing the western headman was only ascertaining the Creeks' disposition to move west while explaining to them "the advantages of such a movement"—not planning a full emigration. In reality, both officials were probably disappointed with the small number of people McIntosh was able to enroll. While he claimed that because of widespread hunger, alcohol abuse, and white encroachment, perhaps five thousand Creeks would emigrate that season, McIntosh had only collected three hundred people. With little prospect of more Creeks enrolling, Cass chose to pull the plug. The decision left McIntosh in the lurch. Fearful of being branded "as a liar," McIntosh complained that his life would be "hazarded" if his authority was withdrawn, rendering him "as one who had deceived his friends." Officials, however, allowed McIntosh to move the Creeks he had already enrolled, but ordered him not to collect any more. But even as he continued with his modified plans, the War Department kept its distance from the western Thlakatchka headman.

Cass gave him only lukewarm financial support and told those disbursing money to McIntosh that he would get "the smallest amount" of funding necessary to carry out the emigration.[2]

The curtailing of McIntosh's emigration scheme gives even more insight into Jackson's decision to stop government-sponsored emigrations back in 1830. In defending his decision to trim back McIntosh's operations, Lewis Cass argued that moving only small parties "would "increase, rather than diminish" the difficulty in compelling the entire Creek population to move west. The secretary of war believed that most of the people who had voluntarily emigrated were "unimportant" players in Creek affairs, while all of the principal headmen capable of convincing large numbers of people to move west were decidedly opposed to emigration. Moving only small parties of Creeks who were receptive to resettling in Indian territory meant that "the friends of the emigrating system would be gone, and its enemies would remain, with "additional influence." Cass, however, believed that "if the whole tribe remain together, they will soon perceive the necessity of removing, and a wholesome public opinion will operate in effecting it." He was not the only one who felt this way. Baptist missionary Lee Compere, for example, had groused back in 1828 that the three-person exploratory party consisted of only a few young men who had "neither rank nor influence" to convince a large body of Creeks to move west. Moreover, Compere was convinced that "if only a small portion are detatched from the rest they will always be viewed as an insignificant party whose example is in no degree worthy of imitation."[3]

Not everyone shared this viewpoint, however. Topographical engineer John James Abert believed, conversely, that emigration was "a business of reluctance and of indirect force" and would succeed "more by example" than persuasion. Stopping the emigrations in 1830, he argued, had left those preparing to move west "in a state of deplorable distress and want" and those in favor of emigrating "as destitute of influence as of means." Like a rolling "snow ball," Abert asserted, emigration would first happen in small parties. Similarly, John Crowell argued in 1830 that the administration had to keep the parties going, regardless of size, in order to "convince the chiefs that they could not stop the current of emigration." Others offered the opinion that small emigrations would "separate friends and families" and thereby compel the balance to follow their kin westward.[4]

The debate over the size of the emigrating parties notwithstanding, McIntosh's bungling of the enrollment process probably doomed his cause anyway. A reputed gambler loitered about the camp dispensing alcohol while trying to swindle the emigrants out of their money. McIntosh allegedly went on a two-day drinking and gambling binge, and witnesses noted that he "and all the Indians, men, women [and] children, were drunk." The western headman subsequently ran out of money, which delayed the commencement of the journey and left his provision-starved emigrants "in a state of suffering." Only the arrest of the gambler and the relocation of the encampment across the Alabama River prevented the Creeks from losing all of their funds. Still, there was a fear that because McIntosh was heavily in debt, any money he received from the federal government would be seized by his creditors.[5]

McIntosh hired land buyers as emigrating subagents who then tried to gain power of attorney over the emigrants' allotments. Although the reserves had not yet been assigned in May 1833, emigrant heads of families were entitled to half-sections under the 1832 Treaty of Washington and speculators were interested in their claims. Some suggested that McIntosh was the "dupe" or the "tool" of "heartless speculators" who used every argument to convince the Creeks to emigrate in order to acquire their land. Rumors swirled that these white men had convinced a number of Creeks that wagons filled with silver would be distributed to them opposite West Point, Georgia, if they signed over powers of attorney and moved west. Subsequently, many Creeks went to collect their share of the silver that never materialized. In order to sustain the lie, the disappointed Creeks were then reportedly told that "the vast wealth contained in the vaults of the Columbus Banks (Georgia) are kept in reserve for them." Indeed, being conned by a swindler would not have surprised many who knew the impressionable McIntosh. Edmund Pendleton Gaines, who offered a personality assessment of the western Creek headman in the months after the Treaty of Indian Springs signing, noted that "Chilly McIntosh is without any decided character, either good or bad; and he would be perfectly harmless, if he were left to himself; but he confides in the counsel of men, whose constant purpose, in reference to the Indians, is, to confuse and divide them, and profit by their misfortunes."[6]

As a result of these problems, many Creeks deserted the general rendezvous and returned home. Despite initially enrolling three hundred people, only sixty-two emigrants, twenty-one of whom were slaves, ultimately moved west. The emigrants left in summer and arrived in August or September 1833, although approximately twenty people (mostly slaves) belonging to McIntosh's party were conducted by Benjamin Hawkins and arrived the previous spring. Their exact route remains unclear, although a Grayson family slave who emigrated with his (or his owner's) own resources overtook the party at the White River and accompanied them for two weeks before reaching Dardanelle and going off on his own. Eight people died during the forty-two-day journey or shortly after arriving in the West, and the emigrants told officials at Fort Gibson that they were "in a starving condition."[7]

After the party arrived west, officials discovered that their apprehensions about McIntosh were well founded. The western headman inconsistently provided rations and the Creeks sometimes went a month without receiving food. In other cases their provisions did not include beef, corn, or both, and many of the emigrants were left "to beg of their neighbours." McIntosh also, at times, issued due bills—which could be exchanged only at certain western traders' stores—instead of actual rations. In some cases these stores ran out of goods, leaving hungry Creeks without subsistence, while at other times these due bills did not come close to covering the expenditures of the recipients. Sally Harrod, for example, received $132 for a family of four and eighteen slaves, which meant that each person had to make $6 last for six months. Hawkins was little better. Despite paying him to transport eighteen slaves to Indian territory, the Hillabee man never supplied more than twelve days' rations of beef or corn over a six-month period.[8]

McIntosh's failures did little to dissuade administration officials, who pushed ahead for another voluntary party in 1834. In fact, federal agents predicted a big year for Indian emigration in general. Anticipating that large parties of Choctaws and Seminoles would join the Creeks in resettling west of the Mississippi River, officials began taking steps to accommodate the movement of so many people. Agents advised the western Creeks and Cherokees to plant more corn so they could supply the new arrivals. Captain Jacob Brown, a principal disbursing agent in Little Rock, also requested that white residents along the routes clear the roads of fallen timbers, repair bridges and causeways, and asked ferry owners to perform necessary maintenance on their boats. Brown also proposed new route-selection policies for conductors in an attempt to minimize cost and maximize efficiency. The Creeks, for example, were to continue on the well-traveled road from Memphis to Rock Roe. They would stop at Mary Black's (a public house popular among travelers) before crossing Cadron Creek and reaching Dardanelle. There, Brown suggested, the parties should split in two. The Creeks most likely to settle on the Canadian River (typically those opposed to the McIntosh faction) would cross the Arkansas and use the south side of the river to reach the Choctaw Agency, the Sans Bois Mountains, and the Canadian River at or near the junction of the North Fork. The Creeks who anticipated settling above Fort Gibson (typically Lower Creeks) were advised to continue from Dardanelle along the north side of the Arkansas River until they reached the garrison. Brown then contracted for the establishment of provision depots along the routes beginning near the St. Francis River and stretching to the Indian territory.[9]

Despite their bold predictions, the agents had great difficulty convincing many Creeks to actually go west. On several occasions Creeks attacked small parties of emigrants as they had done in the past, which hindered enrollment. Captain John Page, a veteran of the Choctaw removals who was assigned to conduct the Creek emigrating party in 1834, issued warnings to Neah Micco and others opposed to emigration not to interfere with the enrollment process or prevent would-be emigrants from coming into camp. Page reported that as a result of the warning, "some of them were so mad and so excited that they actually turned pale." The Cusseta headman Tuckabatchee Harjo was particularly aggressive in preventing the Creeks from leaving, and used "every exertion to prevent & procrastinate the Emmigration." Agents also underestimated the number of Creeks who, after disposing of their half-sections and were actually willing to move west. As noted earlier, many Creeks who sold their land were granted a life estate from the white purchaser, who allowed them to remain indefinitely on their old reserve. And of the small numbers interested in emigrating, some refused to do so until their land fraud cases were adjudicated. Others wanted to wait until they received their share of the annuity, which was not paid in full until late October.[10]

Moreover, Page complained that Alexander Hill, who was appointed special agent to superintend the emigration of Creek Indians, was too "extravagant" in his spending. Hill appointed fourteen enrolling agents and positioned them in several different Creek towns, then established five camps throughout the Creek country before he had enrolled any Indians. Page, who called Hill "a very excellent man" with "little knowledge of the business," only became more frustrated with the ineffectiveness of the superintendent as the weeks went by. While on his way to Mobile to procure funds, Page visited an encampment established by Hill at Fort Hull, Alabama. On arriving, Page discovered an enrolling agent, assistant agent, interpreter, and two five-horse wagon teams, but only one Creek Indian emigrant. This camp had been operational for three weeks.[11]

The Jackson administration was also largely responsible for what would turn out to be a disastrous journey westward. Still stubborn in their refusal to fund small emigrating parties, officials demanded that the agents not commence the march until at least two thousand were collected. With only a fraction of that number enrolled, however, agents were left scurrying to find additional people. But as summer turned to fall and then winter, many Creeks who had already joined the party had second thoughts about traveling overland in the cold. Subsequently, a number of Creeks who had already committed to emigrate deserted the encampments and returned home. Most of those who remained behind were among the poorest inhabitants of the former Creek Nation and the ones desperate enough to endure the risk of traveling west in the winter. In fact, many of these emigrants probably had little to return to in Alabama. Most had likely sold or been cheated out of their reserves and probably had not planted or harvested any crops. Indeed, Page was forced to feed about 170 Creeks from "poor families" for up to three weeks. The agent noted that "the weather is getting so cold," and "what few are going are generally verry poor and destitute of clothing and it would be a prudent and humane act to give it up untill spring." By December, however, Hill believed they had come too far to turn back. The superintendent had already collected 286 emigrants and sent them to Centreville, while an additional 260 collected by Page were in camp near Fort Mitchell. Despite Page's protestations, the emigrants would travel over land in the dead of winter.[12]

Not all of the emigrants were poor, however. A small number of wealthy Creeks from prominent families migrated with the 1834 party. John Stidham of Sawokli—who signed the 1826 Treaty of Washington that nullified the Treaty of Indian Springs, but who had been broken as a principal chief and denied a full section of land a year earlier for his advocacy of voluntary emigration—enrolled with his wife and twenty-six of his slaves. Another headman who was broken and prevented from becoming a mile chief for his support of emigration, John Oponee of Chehaw, sent sixteen of his slaves west with the 1834 party. Four other Stidham heads of families appear on the emigration muster roll, as do members of the Marshall family and four McIntosh family slaves. Also listed on the muster roll is Jacob Beavers, a mile chief from Coweta and McIntosh party member, who had explored the western Creek country in 1829. Sampson Grayson, a Creek Indian from a prominent Hillabee family, and thirty-four of his slaves also emigrated along with other members of the Grayson family.[13]

John Page's muster roll shows that the party was 630 members strong, which included 115 of the Creeks' slaves. The party carried with them 213 horses and enough possessions and provisions to fill twelve large wagons and eight small ones. The party left Centreville and crossed the Cahaba River on 26 December 1834. The deteriorating weather and the crippling poverty of the migrants concerned Page as he commenced their march, and he observed that many in the party were "in a dreadful situation to move in the cold weather." The agent worried that the Creeks would "suffer so much" before they even reached Memphis. Sarah Haynsworth Gayle, the wife of Governor John Gayle, noted in her journal the arrival of the party in Tuscaloosa, declaring that "a part of the Creek tribe of Indian is in Town on its way to its new home." She also wrote that some of the Creeks sold ponies to the locals during their stay. While encamped in the state's capital, the Creeks were invited into the statehouse and seated in chairs that were "arranged around the hall below the lower tier of desks." Headman Eufaula Harjo (or possibly Yoholo Micco), who had earlier bid farewell to Alabama's senators, addressed the representatives from his seat. Speaking in the Muskogean language through an interpreter, the speech was later reprinted in the *Huntsville Democrat*. "In these lands of Alabama," the headman declared in a "low and subdued" voice, "which have been my forefather's, where their bones lie buried, I see that the Indian fires are going out—they must soon be extinguished. New fires are lighting in the west—and we will go there."[14]

The party left Tuscaloosa and struggled over bad roads and in cold, wet weather to Columbus, Mississippi. Complaining that it had "rained and hailed almost every day" of the journey, Page recorded that it was "almost impossible to get along, the roads are almost impassable. We have labored from day light till long after dark to get some days 6 miles." The rivers were also high and in some cases the bridges were "swept off," which made crossing the Cahaba, Black Warrior, and Luxapalila that much more difficult. The deteriorating conditions strained the poorest and most vulnerable of the party, and the agent observed that "the cold weather is so severe on the little children and old persons and some of them nearly naked that they would perish if they were not attended to. We have to stop the waggons to take the children out and warm them and put them back again 6 or 7 times in a day. I send ahead and have fires built for this purpose. I wrap them in tents and any thing I can get hold of to keep them from freezing; five or six in each waggon constantly crying in consequence of suffering with cold." Leaving Columbus, the party moved north along the Tombigbee River before crossing the Buttahatchee River and passing through Cotton Gin Port. The Creeks were then conducted northwest toward Memphis, crossing the Tombigbee and Tallahatchie Rivers along the way.[15]

A number of people deserted the party along the route. Many had enrolled without telling the agents that they were only going as far as the Chickasaw country. In fact, moving to live among the Chickasaws was increasingly popular among a number of Creeks. A year earlier, a delegation had visited Chickasaw headmen and sought asylum in their country. After this was granted, 236 would-be emigrants notified Jackson that they intended to move into Mississippi, claiming that the people they were going to live near were "all our family conections." How many of these Creeks migrated is unclear, but when Page's party passed through the Chickasaw country in 1834, "a Considerable number" of the Creeks absconded from the group. Page pleaded with them to continue westward and after obliging for a day or two, they "Slipd off in the Night." Other Creeks remained behind among the Chickasaws in protest after learning that they would not receive their rifles and blankets in Memphis. Eufaula Harjo complained to Page that they were promised many things by Alexander Hill and he had not delivered on those guarantees. Indeed, the muster roll lists a number of Creeks who "Deserted Near Memphis, Ten."[16]

The weather was so severe that Page decided while still in Columbus to contract for the use of a steamboat to transport the Creeks from Memphis. Seventy-two emigrants accompanied the horses and wagons through the Mississippi Swamp under the charge of subagent William J. Beattie, a Vermonter and land speculator who had moved to Alabama to make his fortune. The balance embarked on the steamboat *Harry Hill* and a keelboat to descend the Mississippi River. The swamps, inundated with water for most of the year, were completely iced over during the winter of 1834–35. Considered "almost impassable," all who traveled through it suffered. In fact, Page noted that "some places [Beattie] Cut the ice Sufficiently wide to drive [the horses] through other places . . . was So wide they had to tie their Legs and pull them over." The land party continued westward, crossing, when not frozen over, a "desolate, melancholy-looking, coffee-coloured piece of water" called Blackfish Lake that was several miles long and hundreds of yards wide. The party then forded the St. Francis and White Rivers and Rock Roe Bayou. The *Arkansas Gazette* reported that the land party also stopped at Mary Black's public house on the prairie. Black's homestead was a popular stopover among travelers passing between Little Rock and Memphis. One traveler described her as "a widow of goodly proportions: I have

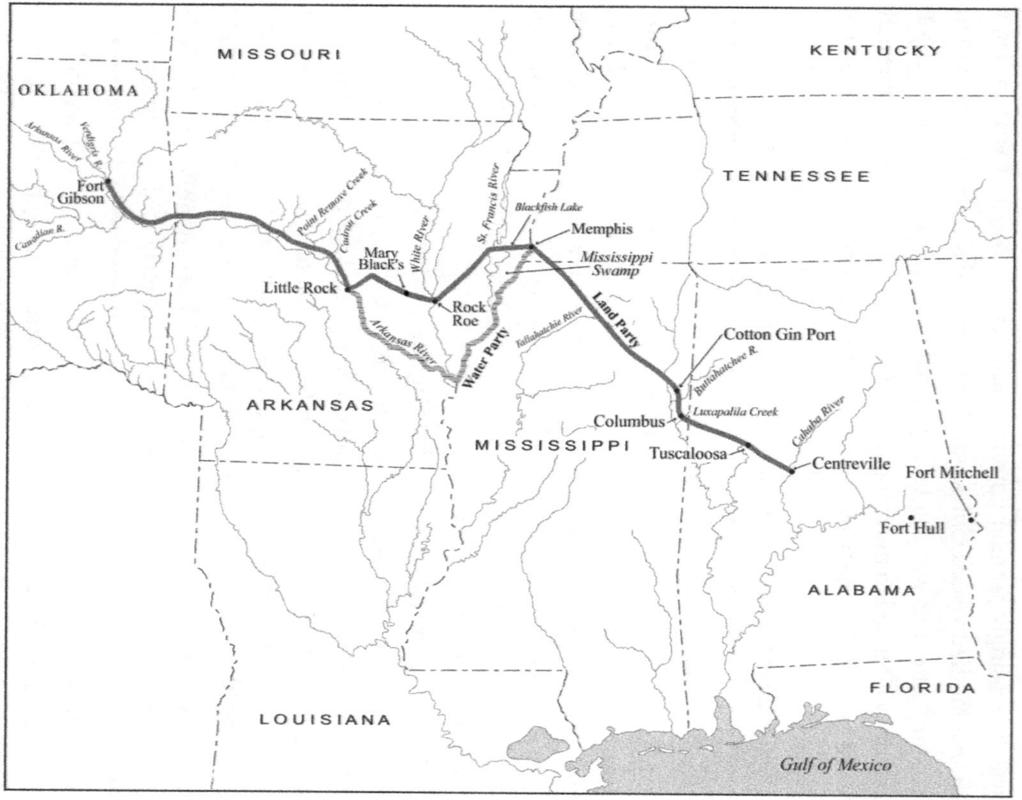

FIG. 15. Route of the fourth voluntary party, December 1834–March 1835. Place names correspond to stopping points or locations noted in the documentation. Route lines and locations are approximations. Cartography by Sarah Mattics.

seen fatter women, but not many." The public house was a log cabin in the dogtrot style—known as "two pens and a passage"—which meant that there were two rooms (from ten to twenty feet apart), all under one roof, with a passage or breezeway between. One of the rooms was a dining hall, while the other was a bedroom that contained four single beds. In the rear of the public house was the kitchen and quarters of Mary Black and her family.[17]

The party riding the *Harry Hill* was not spared from the inclement weather either. The steamboat was detained two or three days on the Mississippi River because of high winds, and once they entered the Arkansas River, ice and sandbars delayed the emigrants several days more. In fact, a five-mile stretch of the Arkansas was completely frozen over and the party spent two and a half days trying to break up the ice. Page felled a number of trees along the riverbank hoping that the weight or the impact would get the water flowing. The captain also rammed the boat into the ice in an attempt to dislodge it, while agents cut chunks of it from the river. The water party arrived at Little Rock on 24 February only after clearing a sufficient path through the river. The party remained in Little Rock for about a week, where they were rejoined by the Creeks traveling on foot. Unable to proceed by water, the entire party left the city by land on 1 March. The extreme cold strained the Creeks and their slaves, and Page reported that they

> worked hard and suffered much from day Light untill sun down to get six and sometimes Ten Miles, it rained snowed or hailed almost Every day and freezing at the same time. We were Compelled to thaw the Tents & Blankets before we Could roll them up to put them in the waggons in the morning. The Indian Children and sick Indians had to go in the waggons on top of their Baggage and to prevent them from freezing we were Compelled to have fires along the road and take them out and warm them, dry their blankets that were wrapped round them and replace them again in the waggons. Strict attention had to be paid to this or some must inevitably have perished and there was a Continual Crying from morning untill night with the children. I used to Encourage them by saying that the weather would

moderate in a few days and it would be warm but it never happened during the whole trip.[18]

The misery of the Creek emigrants was compounded by the general sickliness of the region. Several months prior to the Creeks' departure, dozens of Cherokees died of measles, dysentery, and cholera as they passed up the Arkansas River on the steamboat *Thomas Yeatman*. Joseph W. Harris, who was conducting the Cherokees, advised that future parties should travel by land, not water, in order to avoid the prevalence of disease. Despite traveling by land, the Creeks could not avoid sickness, although it was influenza that plagued the emigrants, not cholera. Page reported that the virus was so fatal to the white residents of the Arkansas Territory that when he visited one homestead along the route, he discovered "almost Every member of the family down with this disease." The muster roll shows that at least five Creeks died after leaving Little Rock—one each on 3 and 7 March, two on 9 March, and the last on 12 March—although the agent noted that only "three or four" had succumbed to the flu. Page credited the survival of his party to his decision to move them quickly through the territory. Consequently, the emigrants were hurried along over bad roads in the dead of winter. Page later noted that "many persons pronounced it murder in the highest degree for me to move Indians or Compell them to march in Such Severe weather when they were dying Every day with the influenza." On 9 March, while still 150 miles from Fort Gibson, the Creeks and their slaves had to march through "a very Severe Snow Storm."[19]

The party arrived at their destination on 28 March 1835. Most of the Creeks settled on the north side of the Arkansas River, with some even occupying the abandoned houses and farms of previous emigrants who had moved off to find choicer land. Page's muster roll lists ten entries for deaths during the journey, which was remarkable considering the severity of the weather, the sickliness of the region, and the poverty of the emigrants. Page proudly boasted that "there was not one Indian frozen to death," although there were several cases of chilblains—a painful inflammation of the skin's small blood vessels that occurs when a person's extremities are suddenly warmed from cold temperatures.

These victims, unable to walk, traveled by wagon. There are twenty entries for desertion during the journey, although how many family members per listing actually abandoned the party is not clear. Grant Foreman, for instance, notes that only 469 of the 630 emigrants from the 1834 party made it to the western Creek Nation.[20]

The 1834 voluntary emigrating party was a disaster. The cost, as Page described it, was "Enormous" and many of the expenses appear to have been incurred even before the journey had begun. With few Indians willing to move and even fewer willing to do so in wintertime, many of the five enrollment camps Hill established sat empty while assistant agents and teamsters were still getting paid. Page also complained that the expenditures increased after Hill took "the advise of people who wanted employ and had corn to sell." Delays, however, were the biggest culprit. In a letter to Commissary General of Subsistence George Gibson, sent just after the emigration had concluded, Page complained that he had to pay the wagon teams and provision the Indians for "nearly two months Longer than was nesessary." When the party finally did begin its march west, the cost of transportation and subsistence during the winter months was much more expensive than at any other time of year. Federal officials had relieved Brearley of duty in part because, at $43.58 per person, the average cost of the 1827 and 1828 emigrations was considered too high. Page, however, calculated that because of Hill's inefficiency and the severity of the season, it had cost the government $60 to transport one Creek Indian only as far as Little Rock.[21]

Federal officials were sensitive to the possibility that reports of the suffering of the Creeks during the 1834 emigration might trickle back to Alabama and hinder future enrollment. In fact, news did filter back to the Creeks. Sampson Grayson, who accompanied the 1834 party, returned to Alabama in 1835 and immediately spread rumors about neglect and abuse along the journey. Grayson asserted that agents only had enough provisions for half of the crossing and the Creeks were therefore forced to pay their own fare the rest of the way—$100 for adults and $50 for children—or "be made slaves to the sugar plantations of Mississippi." Grayson also noted that many Creeks died along the route as a result of the cruel neglect of the agents and that "their dead bodies were denied the right of sepulture." There may be some truth to Grayson's claims. Creeks who died on frozen ground may not have been buried to the satisfaction of the other emigrants, and Page's decision to hurry the Creeks across the Arkansas Territory to avoid influenza may have prevented full rations from being distributed. Still, there is no evidence to support many of Grayson's other accusations. In fact, considering the foolish decision to move the Creeks in the dead of winter, the extreme cold the Creeks encountered, and the sickness they were exposed to in the West, it is any wonder why Grayson felt the need to lie at all.[22]

Undeterred, the administration pressed ahead with plans for an 1835 emigration, albeit with some policy changes. Officials appear to have pinned much of the blame for the problems of the 1834 party on Alexander Hill. A 20 March 1835 circular sent from Washington, for example, acknowledged that the Creeks were likely prejudiced against emigration by "ineffectual operations" and advised agents that the Creeks "must be convinced that the government is in Earnest, and that the Experience derived from the Effect of the unadvised course of one of its Agents," would lead to better procedures in the future. Federal officials then went about trying to make voluntary emigration more palatable to the Creek people. First, Hill was replaced by John B. Hogan, a veteran who helped capture Fort George in Upper Canada in 1813, was in Fort Erie during the siege in 1814, and served in Florida in 1818. Hogan, who was appointed superintendent of Creek removal, had been tapped by Hill the previous September to assist with the 1834 party but had declined the appointment. In addition to Hogan, the 20 March circular was sent to John Page, who remained on as disbursing agent. The missive provided the agents with talking points when addressing would-be emigrants. For instance, agents were advised to represent to the Creeks

> the disadvantages under which they and their people labor by lingering in a Country over which they have surrendered all their rights; and the great advantages that must arise from an Emigration to the new country assigned to their tribe, which is much more fertile than that they now occupy, and from its situation entirely adapted to them. That they may there become a happy and a prosperous people. Here they must

inevitably sink lower and lower into the most abject and degraded condition. You will remind them of the advancements which those of their tribe who removed in former years, have made in agriculture; that they raise large surpluses of Corn, which they sell at good prices to the government and to traders; that their condition is Every way satisfactory to themselves and that they are rapidly improving.

The government also abandoned any hope of collecting two thousand or more Creeks at a time and instead ordered the agents to send a party west when it had reached the more modest number of five hundred enrollees.[23]

But Hogan and his subagents ran into a number of problems as they canvassed the former Creek Nation looking for emigrants. The circular advised Hogan to get to know the headmen and gain their confidence. Indeed, the agent quickly realized that "nothing can be done in emigration unless the chiefs agree to it." Hogan was also suspicious that certain prominent Creek leaders were unduly influenced by groups of powerful land speculators. Although the extent of their influence is hard to gauge, Hogan claimed that Opothle Yoholo was under the control of "Weir" (probably Dr. Robert J. Ware, a former Alabama legislator), Clement Billingslea (a physician), "Major Coules" (Thomas M. Cowles), and the aforementioned Barent Dubois. Ware, Billingslea, and Cowles opposed Jackson and were described by Hogan as the "three leading nullifiers of Montgomery county." As was the case with many speculators, these men appear to have been partners in different land companies. They belonged to the Montgomery County–based outfit Ware, Billingslea, & Co., as well as one that operated in Chambers County, Alabama, referred to as the "Blowing Up Company." Using these organizations, these men purchased a large number of Creek reserves.[24]

Moreover, Ware, Billingslea, and Cowles tried to convince Opothle Yoholo and his followers to move to a 150-square-mile tract of land on Mexico's northern frontier of Texas, northwest of Nacogdoches. In exchange, the speculators would take the extremely valuable reserves of a number of the Upper Creek mile chiefs. As Creek society continued to disintegrate and as reports of the unhealthiness of the Indian territory continued to filter back to the East, Texas had become an attractive option for many Creek leaders, including Jim Boy, who appears to have been in on the plan. Indeed, many of the Creeks who sold their reserves fairly and without any evidence of fraud, likely did so because they were hoping to move to Texas. Opothle Yoholo was receptive to Mexico, but adamantly refused to emigrate to the Indian territory, noting that "their women and children would all die there" and that "they must cut his throat before they could remove his body there." Even Sampson Grayson, in spite of his contempt for the Indian territory, became an advocate for Texas. Moreover, southeastern Indians who had moved to Texas years earlier extolled the region's bounty. Most important, it was out of the jurisdiction of the U.S. government. In 1833, the headmen of the Alabama and Coushatta towns sent the Creeks and Seminoles a communiqué in which they stated that they "doe Sympathize with their breathren in their appression by the Federal Government of the United States and doe recommend to their breathren to Leave the United States and doe reccommend them to emigrate to the Province of Texas" where they "may become powerful and happy as we were once want to be before we Left you." In the 1700s bands of Alabamas and Coushattas had migrated from present-day central Alabama to Louisiana before resettling in east Texas in the nineteenth century. The headmen also boasted that their "country abounds in all Kinds of game." Soon thereafter, a number of Creek leaders stated to the president and secretary of war their desire to move into Mexico. They emphasized the unhealthiness of the Indian territory by noting that "the inclemency of the winter Season is So Severe" that their elderly "could never endure its piercing Cold."[25]

The Texas scheme is significant only in that it appears to be the first time Opothle Yoholo seriously considered the idea of leaving the land of his ancestors. And it is quite possible that it was the first time the headman realized removal was inevitable. As his desperation grew, Opothle Yoholo even appeared willing to go into business with Benjamin Hawkins, the man the Creek National Council had targeted for execution for his association with William McIntosh in 1825. By the mid-1830s, however, Hawkins had fled the western Creek Nation and its McIntosh-led government, found his way to Texas, and as a speculator himself, became involved in the plan to colonize Creeks in Mexico. This was all a needless distraction for Hogan, however. It was illegal for Indians to resettle across the border under a treaty signed between Mexico and the United States in 1831. Moreover, Opothle Yoholo had made a large down payment of borrowed money on the tract of land. When the deal fell through, the Tuckabatchees lost the money and fell deeper into debt, which placed them further under the speculators' control. Debt also served as an anchor that kept the Creeks firmly in Alabama, as neither the Indians' sense of justice nor the speculators' obsessive greed would allow the Creeks to emigrate without first settling their obligations. In any event, Hogan soon discovered that the prospects for a large emigration to the Indian territory was unlikely for 1835.[26]

The Texas scheme was not the only speculative plan afoot in the former Creek Nation, however. Tuskenehaw of Tuckabatchee—the onetime principal headman of the Creek Nation who was deposed more than once for his unpredictability (and whom Hogan believed was under the control of his brother-in-law, William Walker, as well as speculators Thomas S. Woodward and a man named "Harris," probably Peter C. Harris)—became involved in a proposal to trade valuable Creek reserves for land near Fort Hull, Alabama. This large tract of land, just south of the Federal Road, was owned by Walker. Just as Grayson and Hawkins had done for the Texas deal, Tuskenehaw then went about deterring other would-be emigrants from moving to the Indian territory. A subagent reported to a frustrated Hogan that Tuskenehaw had sent a talk to the Eufaulas, advising them not to move west but to "come and join in his colony." It is unclear exactly what Tuskenehaw's motives were for swapping valuable reserves in the former Creek Nation for less-valuable land outside of it. He might have been trying to get out from under the ruinous unfamiliarity of private ownership. Perhaps he saw strength in numbers through consolidation. The move also may have been a power grab by a broken, disgraced former headman. Or maybe it was a last, desperate attempt to remain on his native Alabama soil. While Tuskenehaw's plan was ultimately rejected by federal agents, his consolidation strategy was adopted by at least one other Creek leader. By early 1836, the Oswitchees had abandoned their reserves near the Chattahoochee

River and settled onto a piece of land that had been purchased by their mile chief, Tuckabatchee Fixico.[27]

These land deals show the degree to which the Creeks were plagued by factionalism at a time when they needed unity. As the frauds, starvation, and talk of emigration persisted, Creek leadership became increasingly divided over the best way forward. John Page complained that the Creeks were "divided into three parties and all opposed to each other," and that it was "difficult to get any two to think alike." Some, like Opothle Yoholo, held out hope for Texas; a very small number, like Coweta mile chief Kotchar Tustunnuggee, had resigned themselves to moving to the Indian territory; while a majority wanted to remain in Alabama. Even those committed to staying on their ancestral soil differed over how best to achieve that goal, however. Most headmen no doubt believed diplomacy to be the best course of action, while a small but influential coterie of chiefs, like Neah Micco of Cusseta and Neah Emathla of Hitchiti, were being pressed by their followers to use violent resistance against white encroachment.[28]

The Creeks were also pulled in different directions by interested whites. The Indians and their annuities were a source of profit, and many traders and grog shop owners did their best to thwart emigration out of fear of seeing their incomes move west of the Mississippi River. Creek councils were also a source of money, and many traders eagerly bid on the privilege of supplying provisions to the congregants during these days-long events. At one council, "many gamblers were present and had their Banks in operations." When agents called a council in late 1832 to discuss the purchase of the Creeks' reserves and emigration, traders introduced large quantities of liquor that prevented the officials from meeting with the headmen for three days. And yet, at the same time, many other land speculators desperately tried to force the government's hand and push the Creeks west. Some chiefs complained that many of those who had stolen their allotments "wish to forstall investigation by effecting our speedy removal." Whites subsequently lied to federal officials that the Creeks were committing depredations, stealing horses, and "perpetrating murders" in the hopes that Jackson would send the army to push the Indians across the Mississippi and prevent the reservees from identifying those who had taken their land.²⁹

For many Creeks, however, there was a fourth option. As the mile chiefs' bickered among themselves over the proper course of action, many Creeks spoke with their feet and moved to other southeastern Indian nations. Although a few hundred had already fled to live among the Chickasaws and a few more might have slipped down to reside with the Seminoles, most chose asylum in the Cherokee Nation. There were several encampments of refugee Creeks living in the southern part of the Cherokee country, while an increasing number of Creeks were moving into Benton County, Alabama (the northernmost part of the former Creek Nation), ostensibly to cross onto Cherokee soil. Some agents estimated that there were upwards of twelve hundred Creeks among the Cherokees, with their numbers "still increasing daily." These Creeks, looking for a permanent home in order to avoid removal, settled in the mountains of north Alabama and Georgia, as well as Tennessee, and as far away as North Carolina. Witnesses in Georgia observed that many refugees brought along their possessions, including cattle, horses, and hogs, with the intent of forming a new town. The Creeks told Moravian missionaries in the area that they had fled to Murray County, Georgia to escape famine and "white oppression" in their former home, despite the fact that the Cherokees also suffered from a great scarcity of food.³⁰

The year 1835 was clearly a turning point for the Creek people. It was not a period marked by any significant external event, but by a perceptible change in their collective demeanor. As the land frauds continued almost unabated, as the wheels of justice moved slowly, and as increasingly more Creeks began to realize that removal was inevitable, a general fatalism enveloped the former Creek Nation. Some Creeks could not pull themselves out of the depths of despair and took their own lives. Alfred Balch, a commissioner charged with investigating the causes of the Second Creek War that began in 1836, observed that "during the years 1834 and 1835, the number of suicides committed by these people was enormously large. The warriors went into the woods, and hanged themselves with grape-vines." Other Creeks were not so despondent, but clearly their desperation showed. In June 1835 a number of headmen sent a sharply worded letter to Andrew Jackson in which they complained of the government's broken promises and noted that just as their forests had given way to the cleared fields of the farmer, "it is time then for the red man to disappear also. His council fires are now nearly extinguished." Still, they lashed out at the thought of emigrating to Indian territory and called such a move "nothing better than the final extinction of our race." Rejecting Jackson's claims that moving to the West would allow the Creeks to live unmolested by whites, the headmen pointed out that "Alabama was what Arkansaw now is"—a land inhabited almost solely by Indians. Comparing whites to "a hive of Bees," however, the chiefs predicted that "the United States must shortly swarm and this country will in a few years be filled up with our white brethren."[31]

Opothle Yoholo, who was among the signers of that letter, saw the numerous disasters the Creeks had faced as nothing less than a harbinger of the world's end. The devastating 1813–14 Creek War, the Treaty of Indian Springs in 1825, land cessions, swarming white encroachment, and even a very visible annular solar eclipse that passed almost directly over Tuckabatchee on 12 February 1831 may have been interpreted as a sign of impending doom. When Return J. Meigs, a lawyer and Andrew Jackson confidante, was sent to Alabama to investigate the land frauds, he asked the Tuckabatchee headman about emigration and the loss of Creek political sovereignty under the 1832 Treaty of Washington. The headman responded

> by alluding to the earthquakes, the eclipses of the sun and moon and stars of unusual appearance, which had been seen and felt about the time of the late war, which portended the gradual declension and final extinction of the Creeks; that since that period they had rapidly declined; that they were doomed to destruction; that Almighty God had so decreed it; that the white people also had their limit of prosperity after reaching which, and which would be beyond the Mississippi, they also would come to naught, and both they and the Creeks would disappear from the face of the earth.

Opothle Yoholo then told Meigs that "the world itself would be destroyed in time" and that it was pointless "for man to strive against his fate, but quietly await the end of things."[32]

Some Creeks turned to violent resistance as a survival technique; others, perhaps, simply as an outlet for their anger. One Creek Indian threatened an emigration subagent with death if he attempted to remove him to the Indian territory. Reports of killings and Indian attacks in the Lower Creek reserves created "such dread among the whites that they will not travel except in parties of four or five." Many Creeks continued to cross the Chattahoochee River into Georgia to hunt or steal property, and local residents reported the loss of clothing, cups and saucers, cattle, and hogs. But in addition to theft, many Creeks turned to vandalism and home-invasion robberies. Mary Lindsey, a Georgia woman who lived in Baker County, complained that a number of Creeks raided her home and stole a large quantity of her possessions, but not before grabbing her two featherbeds, ripping them apart, and dumping the contents into a nearby pond. Increased contact between whites and Indians led to more violence. One of the more prominent settlers killed was a former Georgia legislator from Appling County. The violence also became more coordinated. When seven Creeks "stole a negro man" they were pursued by eleven whites who were subsequently ambushed by approximately fifty other Indians. Moreover, the Georgians accused the Creeks not only of "robbing and plundering" local citizens but also of attempting to form an alliance with the Cherokees in order to help them "in killing up the white people, and taking their lands back again." Since the Creeks arrived in north Georgia, the whites noted that "the Cherokees have become much more impudent and hostile than they were before."[33]

And yet, in the midst of the chaos, the Creeks continued to maintain their rich spiritual and ceremonial lives. Agents in the field who were attempting to collect emigrants for the next party reported that there had been "several ball plays and green corn dances." And a number of headmen in the neighborhood of Fort Mitchell continued the maintenance of their council grounds by hewing the beams of their town houses. But with the specter of emigration in the background, the 1835

FIG. 16. "A Map of the Eclipse of Feby. 12th in its passage across the United States," *The American Almanac and Repository of Useful Knowledge, For the Year 1831* (Boston: Gray and Bowen, 1831), 13.

Green Corn Ceremonies no doubt took on a much different complexion than previous years' Busks. One emigration subagent who attended a ceremony—probably the one at Tuckabatchee—reported that at the opening and closing of the festivities, the orator acknowledged that "it was the last dance of the kind they would ever have on that ground." The speaker exhorted the people to remain sober and not to disgrace themselves so they could leave their homeland "with honor." Indeed, soon after this, Opothle Yoholo and seven other headmen of Tuckabatchee and affiliated towns announced that they would move to the Indian territory. The headmen sent word that they would consume black drink for the final time on their native soil, polish their sacred plates, and would be ready to start in a month. Opothle Yoholo also notified his people that he was "preparing his travelling clothes, and will put out all his old fire" and not rekindle it until he was west of the Mississippi. In the midst of his collapsing world, however, Opothle Yoholo fully immersed himself in his spiritual cleansing at the 1835 Busk. As agents tried to meet with the powerful headman about moving west, they were forced to wait until he had finished his black drink because "during that operation they will not talk on business or shake hands with any person for fear of spoiling the charm." Also in attendance at that Tuckabatchee Green Corn Ceremony was actor John Howard Payne, whose recorded observations of the festivities are the most comprehensive on record. Payne was well aware that the land frauds served as a backdrop to the ceremony, and even witnessed a Creek widow complain to an investigator that her land had been stolen. When the Busk began, however, these problems seemed to disappear. Indeed, the actor marveled at the fact that he had never seen "an assembly more absorbed with what they regarded as the solemnities of the occasion." One of the dances—the one signifying the four forms of warfare—took on additional meaning because one of the participants, it was pointed out to Payne, had shot William McIntosh during his execution in 1825.[34]

It is unclear exactly how many of the Creeks who promised Hogan and his minions that they would emigrate actually intended to do so—agents' estimations were almost always wrong. But whatever momentum Hogan thought he had created was dashed in September 1835, when the federal government signed a no-bid contract with John William Augustine Sanford & Company for the removal of five thousand Creeks at $20 per person. If completed by 1 July 1836, the contractors would have rights to conduct the remainder of the population west. Sanford & Company was formed sometime in the fall of 1834, apparently in response to the struggles Alexander Hill was having recruiting Creek emigrants. In fact, in laying out his reasons for the federal government's need to switch to contractors, company member Alfred Iverson, in a letter to his father-in-law, former Georgia governor and then–U.S. secretary of state John Forsyth, described Hill as "wholly unqualified to conduct this business to a successful issue."[35]

The hiring of Sanford & Company was more proof that Andrew Jackson cared little about the concerns of the Creek people. Hogan, who remained on as superintendent of removal, bluntly reported that the switch to contractors was "obnoxious to the Indians." Many worried that profit would be put over the welfare of the emigrants. In fact, a number of Creek headmen, including Opothle Yoholo, wrote the president stating they were worried that "the health comfort and interest of the Indian will never be consulted but that all their arrangements will be conducted for their own good and pecuniary benefit." The most galling part of the switch to contractors, however, was that most of Sanford & Company's partners were the very land speculators who had stolen the Creeks' reserves. Iverson and Stephen Miles Ingersoll (a physician and former Georgia legislator) were both members of M. W. Perry & Company, one of the most notorious Columbus, Georgia–based land organizations, while John D. Howell also speculated in Creek reserves. Other partners—like Samuel C. Benton, a one-time clerk to Creek agent John Crowell, and Luther Blake, who helped conduct the 1829 voluntary emigrating party—were brought on board because they allegedly controlled Neah Micco and other prominent headmen. In response to the prospect of using contractors, one Creek leader declared that "the Indians will not go with them; they are the very men, who have cheated the Indians out of their lands, and they now want to cheat them out of what little they have left, and while on the march, they will be drove like a parcel of pigs to market." Others refused to emigrate with Sanford & Company because they believed the contractors "would abuse them."[36]

These concerns were dismissed by the secretary of war. In fact, Lewis Cass candidly told the headmen that the contract had been entered into "because it would be a more economical mode of removing your people than any other." In his typical condescending tone, Cass declared that the switch to contractors "is therefore better for the government and cannot be worse for you." The contract had some built-in safeguards. Provisions were to be supplied to the emigrants and their horses at regular intervals, for example, and travel could not exceed an average of twelve miles per day. In addition, as had been the case with every previous emigration, a military agent was assigned to accompany the party west in order to ensure that the Creeks were treated "with lenity, forbearance, and humanity." In cases where a dispute might arise between the military agents and employees of Sanford & Company, the surgeon accompanying the party acted as arbiter.[37]

Regardless of the lip service paid to Creek welfare, the contract was still a business arrangement that sought to ensure the best possible outcome for the administration and the company. With promises made by the contractors that thousands of Creeks would move west that year, officials abandoned the plan to move parties of five hundred people, and opted instead to require the company to emigrate one thousand Creeks or more at a time. One six-horse wagon carrying fifteen hundred pounds of baggage was assigned to every fifty to eighty Creeks, which meant at most, each emigrant could only bring thirty pounds of personal property, at worst, just under nineteen pounds. Those who were unable to travel would be left along the route under the care of a "proper person" at the expense of the United States. The company received a prorated sum for all those who died before reaching Fort Gibson or were left along the route due to illness or infirmity.[38]

Sanford & Company fought the same general opposition to emigration that federal agents had experienced, but with the stigma of land speculation and profiteering attached. By October Hogan had declared the prospects for a large party dead and sent word to General George

Gibson, the commissary general of subsistence in Washington, that "there will be little or no emigration this fall; if the contractors get a party it will be a very small one." To facilitate enrollment, the company brought on board Benjamin Marshall, a signer of the Treaty of Indian Springs, to replace Benton, who withdrew because of illness. William J. Beattie, who worked as a subagent for the 1834 party, also became a silent partner. Marshall did not invest in the company, but was hired because he had "extensive connexions" among the Creek people. For his part, Marshall offered his services in order to "get his negroes removed" to the Indian territory. He planned on removing his family sometime later. The Coweta headman's influence was nowhere near as strong as the company suspected, however, and his presence did little to bolster enrollment. When asked whether the contractors would reach their required number of one thousand emigrants, Marshall stated that "he did not think the party would be over a few hundred."[39]

Even as expectations dropped, the contractors plodded on. Three emigration camps were established throughout the former Creek Nation—one consisting of approximately two hundred was established at the Cusseta reserves forty miles to the northwest of Columbus, Georgia, while Benjamin Marshall oversaw another encampment of 160 emigrants (half of whom were blacks) at his brother Joseph's old plantation. On 2 December 1835 these two parties merged with another camp of more than 150 members near Young's Ferry on the Tallapoosa River. Unable to muster the Creeks because of the prevalence of grog shops in the area, the camp traveled to Wetumpka before stopping at a location about four miles northwest of town in Autauga County. There agents met with each head of family and counted a total of 511 enrollees. The most prominent member of the party was Coweta mile chief Kotchar Tustunnuggee, who emigrated with his family and seven slaves. Members of the Marshall, Derasaw, and Carr families also accompanied the party, as did thirty-five of Benjamin Marshall's slaves. Opothle Yoholo, citing the need to settle unpaid debts, remained behind.[40]

The party left its encampment in Autauga County and moved toward Memphis on 7 December 1835. The Creeks were conducted by Stephen M. Ingersoll and William J. Beattie of Sanford & Company and Lieutenant

Edward Deas, who was the military agent overseeing the contractors. Although the government originally ordered the 1835 emigration to proceed along the same route as Page's 1834 party, the contractors chose the "northern route" through Montevallo, Elyton, Moulton, and Tuscumbia because the roads were better during that time of the season than the route through the state's capital. Despite the fact that the Tuscaloosa route was shorter, the contractors wanted to avoid the hazards that plagued the emigrating party that left Alabama a year earlier. Indeed, Deas noted that the roads were "very good" and the weather "uncommonly fine." As a result of the favorable conditions, the Creeks traveled more than the twelve miles per day average that was stipulated in the contract. Deas, who believed that travel would be "diminished accordingly" during winter's ensuing bad weather, adhered to the letter but perhaps not the spirit of the agreement. The Creeks' journey still began with an inauspicious start, however. A number of intoxicated Creeks engaged in "an unfortunate quarrel," and one was struck across the head and died of a fractured skull. The Creeks considered the death an accident and no clan justice was subsequently administered.[41]

The journey through Alabama took two weeks. The Creeks passed through Montevallo on 10 December, forded the Cahaba River on 11 December, passed through Elyton on 12 December, and crossed the forks of the Black Warrior River on 15 December and again the following day. A few days later, the party passed through Moulton and encamped ten miles beyond the city after a long days' march of eighteen miles in search of water. On 19 December, Lizzy Kennard decided to leave the party and join up with a number of her friends who had passed by on their way to Indian territory. The balance, including a Creek woman and a female slave who had recently joined the party, left their encampment near Moulton and, because of rain and muddy roads, detoured to Courtland before reaching the neighborhood of Tuscumbia on 21 December 1835. The contractors anticipated moving to Memphis by land, but travelers in Tuscumbia "gave such extremely unfavorable accounts of the state of the roads" that the party decided to go by water. On 22 December the party was moved to the boat landing near Tuscumbia, and the following day the baggage and some small wagons were loaded onto a steamboat with two keelboats in tow to take them as far as Waterloo, Alabama, where they would exchange that steamer for the *Wheeling*.[42]

The party split at Tuscumbia. The horses, accompanied by a handful of Creeks, left for Memphis at noon on 23 December over roads that were "almost impassable," while the water party departed the landing in the boats a few hours later. Arriving in Waterloo the following day, the water party found no signs of the *Wheeling*. Determined to move quickly, the contractors hired the steamer *Alpha*, an Ohio River boat that was engaged in running goods between Cincinnati and Rising Sun, Indiana. In December 1835 the *Alpha* was laid up in Waterloo waiting for keels to finish delivering cargo to the town of Florence when the owners encountered the Creek emigrants. They paid the operators of the *Alpha* $2,200 to transport the Creeks to Fort Gibson. Two keelboats of "nearly the largest size" were lashed to each side of the vessel.[43]

The water party left Waterloo on 25 December and descended the Tennessee River. Even as the boats plied the river, the contractors were busy on board constructing temporary cooking hearths on the decks of keelboats that enabled the Creeks to cook and keep warm. In addition, Deas reported that "other necessary fixtures have also been constructed to preserve cleanliness and pure air in the interior of the boats." John Hewitt Jones, a part owner of the *Alpha* who accompanied the boat as a clerk, took notes on some of the manners and customs of the Creeks. For example, Jones observed that the Creek emigrants traveled in their traditional turbans during the journey. He recorded the Creeks' nomenclature for circulating monies—*dollahumpkin* was a dollar; *nulcupachee* was a bit; and *calloxogee* was six and a half cents. Jones also observed that while on the boats, "a group of little Indians 6 to 8 years old sat on the forecastle flat on deck playing cards." The water party arrived in the neighborhood of Paducah, Kentucky, at nine o'clock on the morning of 28 December and encamped on the island near the mouth of the Tennessee River, opposite the town. The following day the water party continued down the Mississippi River on its way to Memphis.[44]

The boats arrived in Memphis on 31 December, where they reunited with the land party. The *Alpha* docked on the Arkansas side of the river,

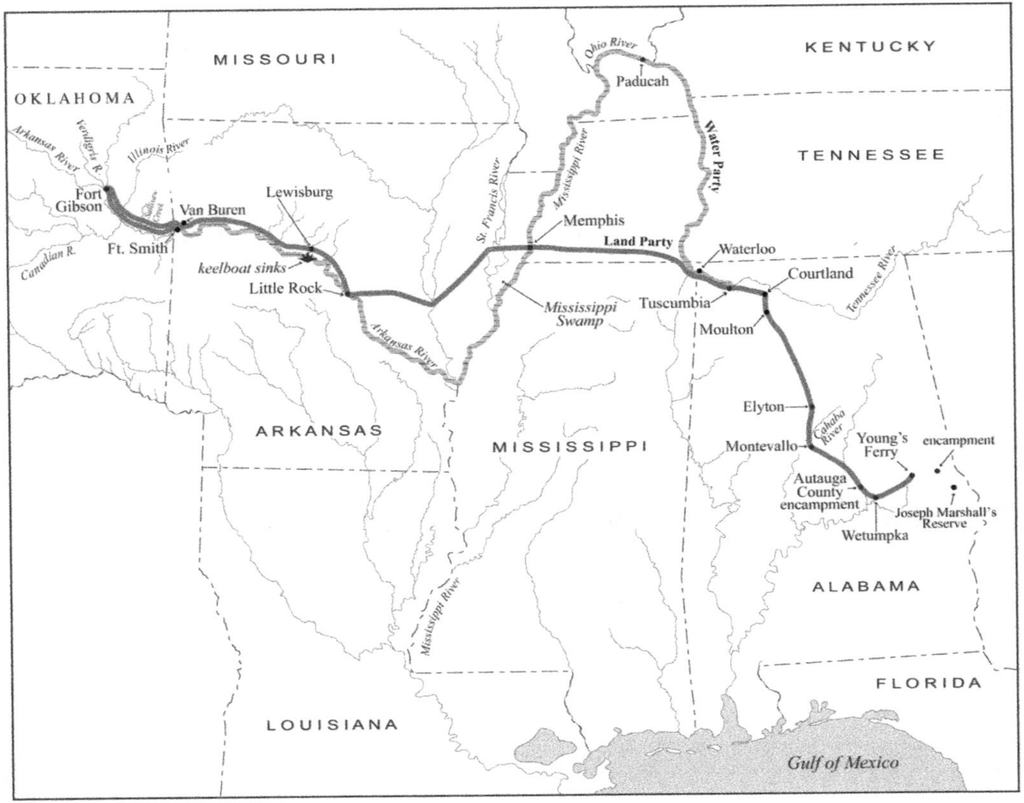

FIG. 17. Route of the fifth voluntary party, December 1835–February 1836. Place names correspond to stopping points or locations noted in the documentation. Route lines and locations are approximations. Cartography by Sarah Mattics.

while they waited for the land party to cross the Mississippi, in order to prevent the Creeks from obtaining alcohol. Those who were able to slip away purchased goods such as "saddles, gears, clothes &c." while in town. Although the party had been relatively healthy to this point (despite the fact that one of Benjamin Marshall's slave boys died in Tuscumbia) the same could not be said for the Creeks' horses. After the land party had finished crossing the river, Deas discovered that of the 154 horses that left Tuscumbia, only 132 had made it across the Mississippi River. Deas cryptically wrote that the horses "had been disposed of on the way, with the exception of two, which were lost." The contractors had marched the horses twice the distance per day as outlined in the contract without increasing the forage. But the mistreatment of their prized possessions clearly worried the emigrants and Jones noted that after reuniting the land and water parties in Memphis, "it was impossible to get away for the Indians must see their ponies and would bring them into camp and make a terrible fuss over them and were very loth to part with them. Some offered to sell a nice little pony for 5$ for fear they would not go through the trip."[45]

The Creeks had reason to continue worrying about their horses beyond Memphis. The road through the Mississippi Swamp and the numerous rivers, streams, and bayous that inundated large portions of the journey to Little Rock was in exceedingly poor condition during the latter part of 1835. In fact, relying on what travelers had reported, the contractors noted that "we have most appalling accounts of the Mississippi swamp. It is said that hundreds of people are in the mire without a prospect of getting out; and it is believed it will be very difficult to get horses through, if not impossible. Their bones may be found one thousand years hence by a different race of men than white men." The journey for the water party was less eventful. The weather was mild and the journey relatively easy. The steamer came to shore most evenings to allow the Creeks to camp and prepare meals. It also gave the contractors time to wash the facilities in order to conform somewhat to the Creeks' standards of cleanliness. Not all the emigrants slept on land, some chose to remain for the evening on board the boats, although most of the Creeks remained inside when it rained. Jones observed the Creeks as the boats came to shore during the evenings, and noted:

> It was a fine sight to see the camping of the Indians on the trip. As soon as the Boat was tied to the shore and a plank out the first to leave was the squaws, who gathered up their kit, which was usually tied up by the corners in a blanket in which was their tents, blankets, cook articles &c. They would throw it over their backs and let the tie come across their foreheads, resting on their backs and in one hand take an axe and in the other and under their arm a little papoose and run ashore and up the bank. They would chop trees and make a fire and prepare supper.

Jones often walked through the evening encampments that, he noted, "looked like a little village."[46]

Regardless of the circumstances, the Creeks took pains to maintain their normal routine as best they could. This included making *sofkee* and other traditional dishes while on the journey west. When Jones walked through the camps in 1835–36, he observed that the Creek women "parched corn in a kettle and then would pound it in a mortar or deep cut trough in a log and then boil it up and make a very fine dish." There can be little doubt that Creek women faced difficulties in preparing food for their families under such trying conditions, but perhaps the task provided comfort and a sense of continuity despite the anxiety and turmoil of their situation.[47]

The tedium of river travel also gave the Creeks time to contemplate their migration westward. An English-speaking Indian of mixed ancestry played the violin and sang a lamentation on board the *Alpha* during their journey west. Jones recorded the song, which went as follows:

"Indians"

Alas! for them—their day is o'er
Their fires are out from hill and shore:
No more for them the wild deer bounds;
The pale man's axe rings through their woods,

Their pleasant springs are dry.
Their children—look! by power oppressed,
Beyond the mountains of the west,
Their children go—to die,
By foes alone their death song must be sung.[48]

The *Alpha* passed through the mouth of the White River and the cutoff to the Arkansas River on 2 January 1836, before arriving in Little Rock on 8 January. The Creeks were not allowed to camp, and the *Alpha* remained anchored in the middle of the Arkansas River a few miles above the city while some of the agents took a small boat into the town to attend to some business. The Creeks once again stayed behind so they would not obtain alcohol. It appears that despite the contractors' best efforts, the Creeks did consume spirits during the journey. Jones wrote in his autobiography that when the Creeks did drink, "there was a tear round among the Indians. The women (squaws) would down a fellow and tie his legs and tie his arms and let him lay till he got sober." The next day the boat was delayed several hours while wood was chopped for the boilers. Consequently, the party only traveled about twenty-two or twenty-three miles that day, about half the usual distance. In order to make up time, the contractors decided to run the steamer all evening. This had been done on a number of occasions during the first leg of the water party's journey down the Tennessee River, but the vessel had come to shore each evening since they entered the Arkansas River. Running all night on the Arkansas was dangerous due to sandbars, snags, and the rapid rise and fall of the water. Another pilot was taken aboard on 10 January in order to assist in the evening runs. But despite the extra man, one of the keelboats struck a snag during their first night voyage and the Creeks were forced to abandon the craft near Lewisburg. Snags were trees that had fallen into the river and had one end imbedded in the silt on the river's bottom, with the top bobbing only a few inches under the water. They were extremely dangerous and could easily tear a hole in the bottom of a boat, causing it to sink in minutes. Hundreds and sometimes thousands of snags were pulled out of the Arkansas River by snag boats each year. In fact, from 28 August 1836 to 1 March 1837,

928 trees were pulled out of the water. Jones observed that the sinking of the keelboat "made a terrible rumpus among the Indians," and that "it was a very dark night, the stove keel boat sinking fast with about 250 Indians on board, caused great confusion and such a time to get them and their baggage on the Steam Boat. The yelling of the yellow skins, big and little, old and young was not easily forgotten." For his part, Deas only recorded that one of the keelboats "struck a snag and sprung a leak." The captain ran the keelboat onto a sandbar in order to prevent it from sinking and the party camped there for the evening.[49]

The conditions on the Arkansas River continued to plague the water party as they moved westward. The *Alpha* hit a sandbar and ran aground on 13 January and it took until the evening to free it. The vessel struck sandbars again on 15 January. The next few days were spent navigating some rapids, and the keelboats had to be unlashed from the steamer and piloted through this treacherous stretch of river. After running aground on more sandbars, the boats passed through Van Buren and Fort Smith. Because the boats could not ascend the Arkansas River any further, the Creeks were landed two miles above Fort Smith. The final leg of their journey was by land. The delays on the Arkansas allowed the land party not only to catch up with the water party, which they did on 13 January, but also to pass them. By the time the *Alpha* reached Fort Smith, the land party was about a week ahead of those on the river and had actually reached Fort Gibson.

The Creeks disembarked the keelboats and camped along the north bank of the Arkansas River while the contractors tried to procure transportation by land. The party would have used the horses of the land party, but miscommunication prevented those on foot from stopping at Fort Smith as ordered. Messengers were sent west to bring back the horses so the Creeks could use them during the last portion of their journey. Once the transportation arrived, the party again commenced its journey westward with ten wagons that were pulled by an array of horses, oxen, and mules, in addition to the small wagons owned by the Creeks. One "light four-horse wagon" was engaged to transport the family and baggage of a sick Creek woman. This wagon later overturned, although without serious injury. During the final leg of their journey, the Creeks crossed Sallisaw Creek, Illinois River, the Grand River at Fort Gibson, and the Verdigris River four miles from the garrison. It was there, on the banks of the Verdigris, that the Creeks requested to stop and muster into the western Creek Nation. They arrived on 2 February 1836, after traveling for fifty-eight days. The muster roll shows two deaths and three births along the journey.[50]

By the start of 1836, approximately 3,500 Creeks and their slaves had voluntarily emigrated to the Indian territory. Many other Creeks, whose numbers are more difficult to count, self-emigrated without the initial aid of the federal government. Perhaps as many as 150 voluntarily left Alabama and moved west with their own resources in 1834 and 1835. The federal government used a number of different strategies to entice or cajole the Creeks west, but all these efforts failed. One of their last attempts—threatening to stop the distribution of the annuity money east of the Mississippi River—caused great concern among the Indians, but did not result in a large removal party in 1835. For their part, the John W. A. Sanford & Company contractors were disappointed with their inability to get much more than five hundred emigrants and noted that "they had lost considerable money on this party." The deadline was still a few months away, however, and the contractors continued to try and collect Creeks into 1836. A vast majority of the Creeks pleaded to remain in peace on their ancestral land in Alabama, but this proved increasingly difficult as whites defrauded Creeks out of their reserves or illegally squatted on Creek land. There were likely a number of Creeks who wanted to emigrate but refused to do so until their land fraud claims were adjudicated. Many believed that if they left Alabama before their cases were settled, they would receive nothing for their land. Still other Creeks believed that rebellion was the only tool left in their arsenal. Throughout 1835 the increasingly dire situation of the Creeks compelled a small number of Lower Creeks to commit acts of violence against these white intruders. But the violence that was sporadic through much of 1835 turned into a full-scale war in 1836. The war gave Andrew Jackson the excuse he needed to both forcibly and coercively remove all the Creeks from Alabama.[51]

6 Sand

1828–50

A minority of the Creeks who immigrated to the West between 1827 and 1835 were McIntosh family members, friends, or business partners. Most of this group probably saw profits to be made from the move. There were also large numbers of Creeks with no connection to William McIntosh who emigrated for reasons known only to them. Many were Lower Creeks, formerly of Georgia, who had lost their land in the treaties of Indian Springs and Washington and likely found it difficult to reestablish their lives within the borders of Alabama. Others were squeezed out as white intruders squatted illegally on Creek soil. Still, others believed that the forced removal of the entire Creek Nation was inevitable, and wanted to settle on a good tract before the western lands filled with Indians. And a handful of Creeks emigrated to escape clan justice in the East. While most of the Creek emigrants believed resettling in the West would be difficult at times, there is no doubt that most of them did not think it would be as challenging as it turned out to be. Disease, raids by western Indians, the questionable quality of the soil, and the government's tardiness in distributing needed provisions made life for the western Creeks extremely difficult. Even the wealthy elites of the McIntosh party were not immune to the problems they faced in the West.

When the Creek emigrants arrived at Cantonment Gibson between 1828 and 1836, they discovered a ramshackle garrison and a handful of restless American soldiers. Located three or four miles above the mouth of the Grand River, the fort sat on the river's eastern bank near a natural rock ledge that extended seventeen feet to the river's edge.

This served as the complex's steamboat landing, and many people walked up this feature after stepping foot in the Indian territory for the very first time. Work had begun on Cantonment Gibson in 1824 as a replacement for Fort Smith to the southeast. The complex, described by Indian Commissioner Henry Leavitt Ellsworth as "numerous little log buildings," required continual upkeep. Letters surreptitiously sent from the garrison noted that the complex was both physically and metaphysically "rotting down"; the wood structure decayed from the harsh climate, as did the morality of the troops of the Seventh Infantry, who were often found intoxicated during their time off. But its unassuming appearance belied the importance of Cantonment Gibson to the Creek immigrants. The garrison was a place of protection as well as a site of arbitration between Indian peoples and the U.S. government. Indeed, Colonel Matthew Arbuckle, the commanding officer at Gibson, often served as witness to Indian treaties signed on location. The garrison also served as a distribution center for provisions arriving from the East and as a staging area for relocated Indians. In recognition of its importance and permanence, the secretary of war changed the garrison's designation in 1832 from cantonment to fort.[1]

The deterioration of both the fort and its inhabitants' morale was due in large part to the harsh climate of the Indian territory. Even as federal officials repeatedly tried to convince the eastern Indian nations that the environment in the West was healthy, travelers who actually visited the region had mixed opinions. The Indian territory was a land of extremes that offered little in the way of seasonal relief. Ellsworth, who accompanied author Washington Irving on his travels to the West in 1832, noted that "the flies & musquitoes abound in summer—in the spring the streams are high & the mud deep—and later in the fall the immense praries are on fire, to destroy both man & beast." Despite their rosy portrayal of the western land to the eastern Indians, federal agents understood that the harshness of the climate was a possible deterrent to emigration. General Edmund Pendleton Gaines believed that the only way to convince the Creeks to resettle in this region was to have them visit during the winter and spring months because "in Summer and Autumn, they might possibly be frightened at the unhealthiness and scarcity of water of some parts of the country through which they may pass." Indeed, during an 1850 expedition to the Creek country, topographical engineers recorded a fourteen-day stretch in August where the temperature reached at least 102 degrees during the day, with the highest recorded measurement peaking at 107 degrees. Even in the shade the temperature was sweltering, and Lieutenant Israel C. Woodruff observed that "the southerly wind, though very strong, was so heated that it seemed to have just issued from a furnace." Once the calendar turned to September, the expedition found some temperature relief but was forced to confront "the absolute want of water." It is doubtful, however, that a visit during the winter, as Gaines suggested, would have swayed the Creeks much, as the area was subjected to "a great intensity of cold" as a result of the northwest winds. In fact there was a common expression in the Indian territory that "heaps of people die here every winter," a reference to the "Cold Plague"—the seasonal pneumonia and fevers. During the spring, the rains and snowmelt in the Rocky Mountains turned previously dry riverbeds into torrents of water with "velocity so great as to carry every thing before it."[2]

The quality of the soil and water, and the diversity of the flora and fauna, varied greatly in Indian territory, depending on location. It was also a matter of opinion. Regardless of what federal agents, western traders, topographical engineers, or naturalists believed to be true, immigrating Indians saw the western lands through the prism of what they had known in the East. Many were subsequently disappointed. Indeed, Baptist minister Isaac McCoy believed that the Chickasaws and Choctaws, who explored the region with the Creeks in 1828, "did not expect to be pleased" with the country even before seeing it, and as it turned out, they were not. McCoy had this experience with a number of southern and eastern Indian peoples—once complaining that while on an expedition "when travelling over prairie lands, which, excepting timber, equalled in situation and fertility of soil the excellent lands in the vicinity of Lexington and Georgetown, Kentucky, [the Indians] complained of its poorness. It seemed not easy to correct their errors." Indeed, there was no subject, McCoy asserted, "upon which persons equally tenacious of truth so widely differ" than opinions about the quality of land.[3]

The western Creek country was a mix of rolling and gently rolling prairies, cut up by numerous rivers and streams. Timber grew in "streaks and groves" along the riverbanks and was interspersed throughout the prairie lands. Cottonwood, various species of oaks, and pecan were the most common tree types. The area is sandstone, limestone, and shale country, and the rock not only underlay much of the terrain but also was exposed in many areas near the rivers and tributaries. On the eastern shore of the Verdigris River, for instance, there were "high bluffs of slaty sandstone," while red sandstone rose along portions of both banks of the Arkansas. Topographical engineers also observed a "strange appearance" of "large oblong and cubical masses" of limestone "six feet high above the surface" on some of the timbered hills of the Arkansas River that looked "of an old fortification." Soil composition was therefore affected by the presence of sand due to the erosion of sandstone, but also from deposits of salt, clay, gypsum, iron, and coal. Various types of loam (a mix of sand, silt, and clay) were common, as well as alluvial deposits along the rivers and streams.[4]

The voluntary immigrant Creeks, who came from a forested region with well-watered streams and rivers, had mixed reactions to Indian territory. All Creeks had to confront what they perceived to be a deficiency in timber and water. McIntosh party leaders, for example, complained that their territory was "very little Timbered," and the Creeks into the 1850s were heard complaining of their "'woodless and waterless'" country. Certainly, compared to the forests of Alabama and Georgia, the western Creek territory had little woodland. The Creeks feared these lightly timbered and watered prairie lands, and they were convinced that anyone who settled there would meet "certain death." Indeed, after federal officials accidentally ceded a large portion of the western Creek country to immigrating Cherokees, Roly McIntosh and other western headmen wrote President Andrew Jackson and declared that being "driven into the open Pararia Out of Sight of Timber and there to perish it is enough to make our hearts bleed at the thought of it." McCoy feared that the absence of timber would affect the settlement patterns of the western Creeks. Noting that "the greatest defect in this country (and I am sorry that it is of so serious a character) is the scarcity of timber,"

McCoy feared that if the immigrant Indians made their fields on top of cleared forestland—as the Creeks had done in Alabama and Georgia—the woodland would become even more scarce. This made the construction of homes and plantations more difficult, but it also threatened the well-being of the immigrants. Because of the harsh winter climate, access to firewood was almost as important as access to provisions. James Logan, agent to the Creeks in the 1840s, noted that the only type of firewood the Creeks could procure within a close proximity to their settlements was cottonwood, which did not burn when green but burned too quickly when dry. Fortunately for the Creeks, the cottonwoods in the Indian territory grew large—some more than four feet in diameter.[5]

Although McCoy complained that portions of the Creek tract contained "too much prairie land," there were stretches of well-timbered country, particularly along the river bottoms. McCoy noted that the northeast side of the Arkansas River was "mostly covered with a dense growth of woods, though some prairies occur, but they are equally fertile, and are well supplied with adjacent woodlands." U.S. topographical engineering expeditions also reported that many of the rivers in or near the Creek reserve were well wooded with willow, dogwood, black walnut, birch, cedar, sassafras, and persimmon. Near the North Fork and Canadian Rivers, on the Creeks' southern boundary were—in addition to those that grew at the Arkansas River—strips of forestland consisting of hickory, hackberry, mulberry, elm, ash, sycamore, red haw, and locust.[6]

Access to fresh water was another concern for the immigrants. Water quality was determined by the composition of the sediment of the riverbeds and soil from the riverbanks. It was also affected by the seasonal climate. The best water in the region came from the Grand River, where a good supply could be obtained in both the summer and winter months. In December 1828 at a point three miles above the river's mouth adjacent to Fort Gibson, the water was "perfectly clear" and ran over a bed of gravel that was "easily and distinctly seen when the river is deepest." McCoy described the Grand as "transparent." William O. Tuggle, a Georgia lawyer appointed to settle the Creeks' outstanding claims against the U.S. government in 1879, called the Grand "clear & beautiful." The land north of the Arkansas River to the mouth of the Cimarron reportedly was "well supplied with perennial springs of water," while in other parts of the Creek country these reservoirs were "exceedingly rare." There were occasional springs along the banks of the North Fork that produced quality water on par with that of the Grand. Over much of the prairie and timber lands, however, collecting rainfall or digging wells was the best means of obtaining fresh water, although John P. Moore, the son of Indian countryman James Moore, noted that "we have sume wells of water in this country so bad [that if you] take it up and let it [stand] for one half hour you cant drink it."[7]

Indeed, whites, who thought in terms of industrial mills, considered the West "well watered." But for Creeks concerned with cleanliness and purity, many of the western rivers were dreadful. The two biggest problems the immigrants faced were both the water quality and seasonal water levels. River clarity varied from stream to stream and ranged from being simply "discolored" to, at its worst, "salt water." Some streams were characterized as "muddy" while Moore complained that, in general, the western "waters are bad and brackish" and "smell of brimstone." With no river anywhere near the western Creek Nation considered as clear as the Grand (although the Deep Fork was called "a beautiful stream"), agents were resigned to ranking the western waters by how much less disagreeable they were than the others. For example, McCoy noted that the "Arkansas and the North Fork are rather less muddy" than a river like the Missouri, while the Verdigris was "still less" muddy than the Arkansas and North Fork. Similarly, topographers Lieutenant Washington Hood and John W. Bell noted that the Verdigris was "not so clear" as the Grand, which was clearly not intended as a knock on the Verdigris (indeed, one Presbyterian missionary described the Verdigris as "deep, clear & beautiful"). In some cases, nicknames for disagreeable streams appear to have exposed their secrets: names like "Glauber Salt Creek," "Red Creek," "Salt Fork," and "Mud Creek" were shown on maps in and around the western Creek Nation.[8]

The rivers in the western Creek country were composed of a number of different hues that ran the color spectrum. The Verdigris, one of the clearer rivers, was called "melancholy" with "dark green waters," while during the autumn months of 1836, agents noticed the Arkansas River to be the color of a "half burnt brick." The North Fork appeared "greyish or muddy," perhaps due in part to the soil near its south bank, which contained sand that was reddish brown, "almost approaching to a purple." To the south, the Canadian River was described as "reddish yellow; almost as highly colored as if nature had intended its waters for a dye." In the north, the Cimarron River was so red it was nicknamed "Red Fork." Indeed, Count Albert-Alexandre de Pourtalès, a Swiss traveler who also accompanied Washington Irving on his visit to the Indian territory in 1832, observed that "the nearby rocks bordering the bloody Red Fork are very high. The river is low, and its bed is marked everywhere by little islands of red sand which can hardly be distinguished from the red water."[9]

The condition of the rivers meant that potable water could often be hard to find. Although the Arkansas River was considered "tolerably clear" for portions of the year, it was usually off limits to drink due to the salinity from the Cimarron drainage. In fact, one Creek resident of the Indian territory noted that "Diarhea & slight fever are natural to the Red Man when he first drinks the brackish waters of the Arkansaw river." Captain John Page, who helped superintend the large relocations in 1837, was more blunt, noting that during its low stages the Arkansas "will Kill any person in the world to drink." The Cimarron contained the worst water of any large stream in the western Creek country, with the Canadian probably a close second. Both rivers ran near the Salt Plain and/or gypsum region of the Indian territory. The Canadian River was considered "impotably saline," while topographical engineers noted that the Cimarron (which, in addition to its "Red Fork" moniker, was sometimes derogatorily called "Salt Fork") was dry "and its entire bed encrusted with deposits of crystallized salt" during the summer of 1850. One traveler declared that the Cimarron had a "strong brine" taste, while McCoy noted that the river was "so very salt as to be unfit for common use." In fact, much of the water in the gypsum region between the North Fork and Cimarron was impregnated with Glauber salts, a crystalline sodium sulfate that made the water "bitter and unpalatable." There was also an extensive saline near the Creeks' northeast boundary, which created one stream of "pellucid salt water," and in other places, springs of "bubbles of sulphuretted hydrogen, which deposits a slight scum of sulphur."[10]

Water levels were also a contrast in extremes. During the summer and autumn, the excessive heat dried rivers to their beds creating, as Togo Micco Berryhill observed decades later, "rivers of sand." During an expedition to run a boundary line, Isaac McCoy noted that the "Arkansas was so shallow over its wide bed of sand in November, that an effort to meander it above the mouth of Verdigris, by the help of canoes, failed." During the same month, the Cimarron was only a foot and a half deep. In September portions of the North Fork were found to be "entirely destitute of water," while the only fresh water on the Cimarron came from an underground spring that stood for a few hundred yards before disappearing and gave the appearance of "a marsh" rather than a stream. When McCoy accompanied the exploratory party of Choctaws, Chickasaws, and Creeks through the Indian territory in 1828, he estimated that half of the Arkansas River bed was a "sand beach." Counterintuitively, low water could sometimes make crossing rivers even more dangerous. The Canadian, for example, was notoriously difficult and dangerous to ford due to the prevalence of quicksand. Water scarcity would not only affect the immigrants but their livestock as well. Topographical engineers who surveyed the northern and western Creek boundary in 1850 almost abandoned portions of the project because they could not find adequate water for their cattle. At one point, as the party moved through the valley divide of the Cimarron and North Fork, their livestock, with no other options, was forced to drink bitter water that "proved very injurious to them."[11]

During the wet season, however, Indian territory flooding was particularly devastating. In 1833 the western Creek Nation experienced "one of the most destructive floods in these rivers that has ever been known in this country." Flooding was a common occurrence in the West, as the spring snowmelt caused rivers to flood their banks, but the flood of May 1833 was extreme even by Indian territory standards. The Verdigris River reportedly was fifteen feet "higher than it was ever known before," and the western Creek Agency, established shortly after the arrival of the first McIntosh party on the eastern bank of that stream three or four miles from its mouth, was flooded to the roof. The river "entirely swept off" the public storehouses and sixteen boxes of rifles were "carried [off] with the buildings." Percussion caps for the rifles were also destroyed when, during an attempt to dry them, they exploded. The flooding caused enormous destruction and western Creek agent John Campbell reported that "a great many Indian families have lost their Houses, fields, crops and every thing that they had to support on." Campbell was particularly worried for the poorer Creeks, who did not have time to replant that season. Creeks living on the Arkansas River also lost a considerable portion of their livestock when that stream flooded during the same period.[12]

Like water, soil quality also varied. When the McIntosh exploratory deputation visited Indian territory in 1827, they found that the best land was located on the north side of the Arkansas River, where arable bottomland stretched for "75 or 80 Miles" and averaged "from 3 to 5 Miles in Width." Fertile bottoms, about a mile wide, extended some distance up the south side of the Verdigris near its junction with the Arkansas as well. A dividing ridge of prairie separated these two rivers, however, and was considered "uninhabitable" due to the absence of wood. Similarly, the prairies south of the Arkansas, which stretched for almost forty miles, were described by Brearley as "barren" and "Sterril." Portions of the prairie and bottomland of the Canadian were considered inhabitable, but not equal in quality or quantity to that of the north side of the Arkansas. The bottomlands of the North Fork, however, which flowed into the Canadian River, were characterized as "abundant and of good quality," although the soil was typically very sandy on the north side.[13]

Although livestock played an increasingly larger role in Creek society toward the end of the nineteenth century, the quality of the Creek country for raising stock was initially subject to debate. Trader Auguste P. Chouteau effusively praised the western lands, claiming the "'prairies are covered with fine grass; stock do well on it winter and summer; in the winter the grass of the prairies dies and cures, and the cattle and horses prefer it and keep fat upon it.'" The bottomlands along the North Fork were considered "fine pasturage." Cane, especially good for grazing herds, did grow to twelve or more feet along portions of the Arkansas River bottoms, and was so thick in places that it was difficult to pass through. Lieutenant Jefferson Van Horne, a disbursing agent at Fort Gibson, however, argued that the western Creeks occupied land that was "not well adapted to raising stock." As a result, the Creeks not only had "very few cattle and hogs" but also had to import their meat rations from outside the western Creek Nation to feed the voluntary immigrating parties (Ellsworth, however, believed that the Creeks "had a great supply of Pork"). Indeed, surveyors reported that during the autumn months, "the grass becomes so scarce and is so destitute of nutrition, that it is extremely difficult to Keep the animals alive." In the gypsum region along the valley divide of the Cimarron and North Fork, topographical engineers described the pasturage as "very deficient" because large swaths of grass had been burned by the Comanches in their system of maneuvering bison. In other areas bison had eaten the grass down significantly the previous spring and, because of drought, it had not adequately rebounded. Attempts to raise coarse-wool sheep on a large scale failed "because of the prairie wolves which are numerous and troublesome."[14]

Federal officials would not have allocated valuable territory suitable for the tastes of American settlers to Indians. Still, a number of explorers, traders, and missionaries did find the Indian territory rich and bountiful. Surgeon-naturalist Samuel Washington Woodhouse believed that portions of the Creek territory comprised "a rich alluvial, and in many places, I think, not to be surpassed, for all ordinary purposes of cultivation, by that of the Mississippi river." Presbyterian missionary Robert McGill Loughridge, who traveled this stretch ministering to Creek settlements, observed that "the prospect in these large prairies is often sublime. With the exception of an occasional mountain rising abruptly, sometimes covered with bushes, at others with rugged rocks, one vast plain covered with beautiful green grass, is extended in every direction as far as the eye can reach, presenting the appearance of thousands of acres of rich meadow." Chouteau reported that the country was home to a variety of fine grapes, as well as plums, black haws, strawberries, blackberries, pawpaws, persimmons, may apples, and "'a species of pome-granite,

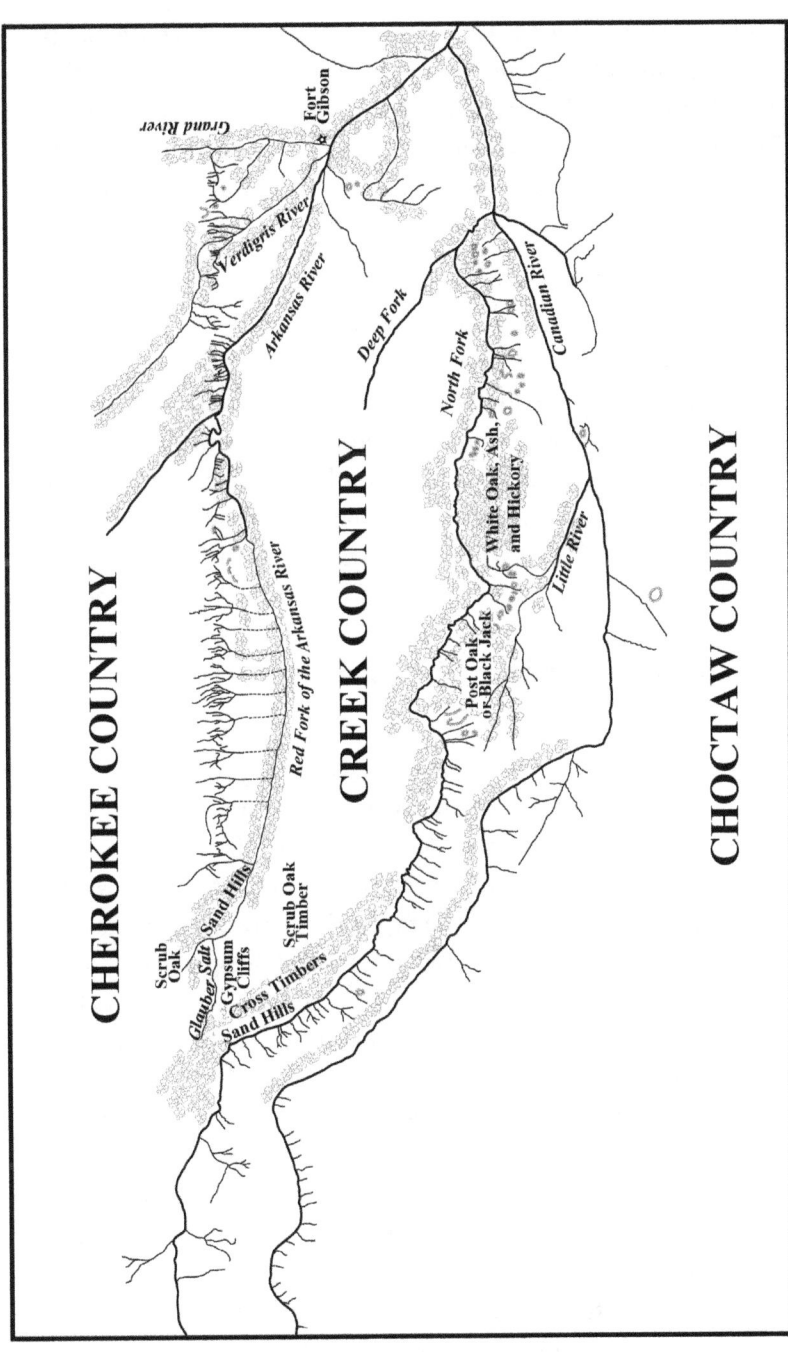

FIG. 18. Map of Indian territory, ca. 1850–51. Based on map from *Letter from the Secretary of War, Transmitting Reports of Captains Sitgreaves and Woodruff of the survey of the Creek Indian boundary line*, 35th Cong., 1st sess., 1858, H. Exec. Doc. 104, serial no. 958. Cartography by Sarah Mattics.

which is much esteemed for its flavor.'" George Catlin visited the western Creek country in the 1830s and noted that the region was "one of the richest and most desirable countries in the world for agricultural pursuits." Catlin marveled at the abundance of vines "producing the greatest profusion of delicious grapes, of five-eighths of an inch in diameter." Beyond that Catlin observed

> verdant valleys of green prairies, into which we had descended; and oftentimes find our progress completely arrested by hundreds of acres of small plum-trees, of four or six feet in height; so closely woven and interlocked together, as entirely to dispute our progress, and sending us several miles around; when every bush that was in sight was so loaded with the weight of its delicious wild fruit, that they were in many instances literally without leaves on their branches, and bent quite to the ground, Amongst these, and in patches, were intervening beds of wild roses, wild currants, and gooseberries. And underneath and about them, and occasionally interlocked with them, huge masses of the prickly pears, and beautiful and tempting wild flowers that sweetened the atmosphere above.

Near the North Fork, Woodhouse encountered small grapes growing on top of the sand drifts along with plums and American colocynth. The region was also home to a number of species of wildflowers, although due to the drought of 1850 many prairies were devoid of flowers. Many of the plant species found during the expedition were also common to Alabama, including milkweed (*Asclepias verticillata*); big potato morning glory, which has an edible root (*Ipomoea pandurata*); horse nettle (*Solanum carolinense*); and bee balm (*Monarda fistulosa*), an aromatic plant that smells of mint when its leaves are crushed.[15]

Some McIntosh party members were no strangers to the area's game, as they had hunted there on at least three occasions prior to 1825. On this subject, Chouteau was once again effusive and observed that "the country abounds in wild game, such as the buffalo, elk, deer, antelope, bears, and furred animals; wild horses are found to the north-west in numerous herds." Naturalists also found large herds of bison watering at a pond in the midst of the quality pasturage found in the bottomlands of the North Fork. On an expedition hunt between that stream and the Red Fork, the party obtained large quantities of bison meat, venison, and wild turkey. Indeed, in 1828 Chilly McIntosh and twenty-seven members of the McIntosh party went on a bison hunt that lasted almost three weeks. The men killed twenty-four, but saw almost six hundred along with a number of deer. As a result of the success of the hunt, the party planned another for the following month. The region was also home to cougar, wildcat (probably bobcat), and small game that included beaver, turkey, raccoon, marmot, squirrel, rabbit, and varieties of fox and wolf.[16]

When water levels permitted, the Creeks had an abundance of fish to choose from. In 1846, Loughridge witnessed hundreds of Creeks fishing on the North Fork of the Canadian River. Using methods that had served them well for generations in Alabama and Georgia, Loughridge estimated that as many as two hundred men, women, and children were engaged in poisoning, spearing, filleting, and barbequing their catch. The Creeks had assembled along the bank three hours before daylight where they commenced pounding twelve hundred strands of devil's shoestring (*Tephrosia virginiana* [L.] Pers.) and then "churned" the pulp through baskets placed in the water. By daylight the fish had felt the effects of the poison and were "floating upon the water, swimming around & in different directions." With their prey incapacitated, the Creeks, both in the water and in canoes, used bows and arrows, spears, and other weapons to gather the catch. Their bounty included hundreds of "fine" and large (one-hundred-pound) catfish, as well as buffalo, drum, river redhorse, suckers, perch, gar, and spadefish. Nearby, Creek women were smoking the fish for preservation.[17]

While federal officials and western agents talked up the quality of the West, many relocated Indians, including the Creeks, were unhappy with the territory allotted to them. Much of this was the result of trying to fit so many people onto the few strips of what eastern Indians considered to be good land. Indeed, while accompanying a delegation of southeastern Indians in 1828, Isaac McCoy was surprised to discover that "almost all the country of Arkansas and its waters had been previously assigned to other tribes, so that there remained none, in a manner, vacant for the examination of the Chickasaws." McCoy suggested placing the Chickasaws within the Choctaw reserve because the latter had "a great deal of excellent country." This ultimately did occur, much to the frustration of the Chickasaws. Many Creeks, unhappy with their own territory, simply moved onto the more fertile reserves of their neighbors soon after arriving, and even William McIntosh, while negotiating the Treaty of Indian Springs in January 1825, reportedly "preferred the territory selected by the Choctaws." Other Creeks moved as far away as Missouri. Indeed, a band of twenty-five Creeks were discovered living on the strips of dry land in the swamps near New Madrid. Certainly, the isolation and harshness of the western Creek Nation made a number of Creeks miss their ancestral homeland. While in Alabama in 1830, British traveler James Stuart observed one Creek emigrant who returned, if only to visit old friends, but "still seemed to regret" his decision to leave "the land of his fathers." In fact, a number of Creeks who appear in the voluntary emigration muster rolls returned to the East for various reasons.[18]

Many other transplanted Indians were just as displeased with their western territory. In 1832 seven hundred Senecas arrived from Ohio only to complain that their new lands were insufficiently timbered. Similarly, letters reached Washington declaring that the Kickapoos were also dissatisfied with the inferiority of their western soil. Like the Creeks who moved into Choctaw territory, bands of Quapaws moved into Caddo country after they had "distinctly stated that they would not reside on the land allotted to them." The Creeks also suffered from encroachments by other formerly eastern Indians. Western Creek headmen, led by Roly McIntosh, complained of "Large hords" of Delawares "killing and destroying the game" on Creek land. According to the Creeks, the Delawares had "immense droves of horses pasturing on the cane, killing up all the deer, bear and turkeys; and destroying the Buffaloe that come in or near the Creek country, killing hundreds of them for their skins and tongues, stealing horses from the neighboring tribes and bringing them to the Creek country." The Creeks feared that other Indian groups would blame them for stealing their horses, which would bring them "into collision with their neighbors."[19]

The irony of removal was that relocated Indians also became intruders on other people's land. Federal officials knew that placing immigrant nations in the Indian territory left them susceptible to raids by their western counterparts despite pronouncements that removal was designed to protect them. Edmund P. Gaines, for example, warned that great care should be taken of the Creeks to "protect them from the possibility of an attack from the war or hunting parties they may meet with, of other tribes." However, government bureaucracy or inattentiveness exacerbated the problem. On several occasions, the Creeks were attacked by small bands of Indians who lived on their southern and western borders. The attacks, which generally occurred at night and lasted for such a short time that a warning could never be sounded in time, kept them "in continual alarm for the safety of our people, more particularly our women and children." But the attacks were made worse because the Creeks had not received all the rifles promised them by the federal government. This, and the western Indians' knowledge of the topography, prevented the Creeks from protecting themselves and successfully hunting down the intruders.[20]

Most of the early confrontations the Creeks had with western Indians involved the Osages. Proximity, the harsh climate, and the fact that part of the western Creek Nation incorporated former Osage country exacerbated the hostilities. While the Creeks and Cherokees were pressing the Osages from the south, the Kickapoos were encroaching on Osage land from the northeast. Moreover, the thinning of the herds by hunters of relocated eastern nations made their situation even worse. Hunting was also complicated by the rival claims to Creek hunting land by western Indians who saw the immigrants as interlopers. When topographical engineers traipsed through the region marking the northern and western boundaries of the Creek Nation in 1849, they were confronted by bands of Osages who "declared that they would not permit the work to be carried on over the country which supplies them with game, and to which they conceived they have a common right." Isaac McCoy declared the Osages "poor and miserable," and reported that fifteen hundred of them had settled on Creek lands along the Verdigris River while twenty Osage families lived along the Grand River within the Cherokee territory. By 1831 the Osages not only had a dwindling food supply but also limited furs to trade for sustenance. To ameliorate their immediate sufferings,

Claremore's band of Osages raided the Creeks' and Cherokees' livestock and other property. Government officials blamed the depredations on the "extreme and long continued cold weather" of the 1830–31 winter in which temperatures hovered around zero for long periods of time. A council of Creeks and Osages was organized and a treaty consummated on 10 May 1831 in which both parties agreed to up to thirty-nine whippings for stealing. A similar treaty between the Cherokees and Osages was completed about a week later. The Osages blamed the severity of the winter and their poverty for the raids. But they remained poor and were encroached upon by even more eastern Indian nations throughout the 1830s, which led to more attacks. By 1835 the Creeks estimated that they had lost up to $10,000 at the hands of the Osages.[21]

The Creeks employed multipronged strategies to deal with incursions by other Indian groups. First and foremost, the Creeks sought peace through diplomacy. This meant either organized councils brokered by federal agents at Fort Gibson (as was the case with the Osage treaty of 1831) or between Indian groups themselves. In June 1843 four thousand Indians from twenty-two different nations, many of them relocated from the East, gathered to establish or reaffirm alliances and ensure mutual protection against everything from intertribal violence to further land cessions. Among the speakers at the council was Creek headman Roly McIntosh. But even as the Creeks were considered, as one historian put it, "peacemakers on the middle border," they took pragmatic steps to ensure their own safety. Indeed, by the 1840s the Creeks had invited bands of Kickapoos to live among them and serve as their mercenaries. Patrolling the Creeks' northern, southern, and western borders, the Kickapoos repulsed Pawnee horse-raiding expeditions and effectively decreased the number of raids from the Kiowas and Comanches.[22]

Early Creek settlement patterns were another strategy employed by the immigrants to ensure their protection. Fear of attack by western Indians, who viewed the Creeks as intruders, was one reason most immigrants huddled into compact settlements near Fort Gibson or the western Creek Agency. This area, on the north side of the Arkansas near its confluence with the Verdigris, was also one of the more fertile tracts of soil and was close enough to the fort for the easy distribution of provisions. By 1833 the western Creek Nation comprised approximately 2,500 inhabitants, of which 423 were Cowetas, 326 Thlakatchkas, 300 from the town of Big Spring, 251 Talladegas, 206 Okteyoconnees, 166 Hitchitis, 131 Eufaulas, 120 Cowykas, 117 Wockokoys, 100 Coosadas, 95 Chowokolos, 77 residents of Sand Town, 70 Sawoklis, 50 Newyaucaus, and 27 Hatcheechubbas. These figures included the emigrants' 498 slaves. By 1834 the north side of the Arkansas River was home to 2,135 people who lived in what appeared to be "one extended village, as thickly settled as some of the smaller parishes in New England, having some neighborhoods rather more dense than others." Creek homesteads (which, according to Count Albert-Alexandre de Pourtalès, were little more than "a long line of wooden huts") were "as near each other as their farms will admit," and extended for a length of twenty miles up the north side of the Arkansas and six miles up the south side of the Verdigris. Isaac McCoy blamed Creek bias against their Indian territory land as another reason for the creation of this dense settlement, noting in 1829 that "it appears not to be easy for the Creeks to receive just impressions respecting either the extent or resources of their country. They speak of it as being limited to a small point in the fork of Arkansas and Verdigris." By 1834, however, agents counted 175 residents on the south bank of the Arkansas, 50 on the north side of the Verdigris, and the balance—almost 700—living on the Canadian River. Most of the Creeks on the Arkansas owned a single house with a corn crib and between one half and three acres of cleared land.[23]

Most of the Creeks who lived in the dense Arkansas-Verdigris settlement were also likely too poor to move far beyond the garrison. In fact, many of these immigrants had a difficult time rebuilding their lives. When a delegation of Chickasaws visited the Indian territory in 1829, they found the Creeks "continually mourning for the land of their births." The immigrants told the delegation that "the land was poor, and that they were wretchedly situated." These Creeks had arrived in the West with little or no property, and conditions in the Indian territory made it difficult to increase their holdings. Toma Yoca, for example, appears not to have owned even a single house—instead, he claimed one "camp," a corn crib, and half an acre of cleared fields among his sole possessions. Providing the Creeks with basic provisions proved difficult due to the region's isolation. Supply lines were often cut by the low stages of the Arkansas River, which caused the prices of goods to rise and pushed the Creeks deeper into poverty. A keelboat laden with blankets, rifles, lead, powder, and other materiel bound for distribution among the western Creeks and Quapaws sank at the White Oak Shoals in the Arkansas River below Fort Smith in the mid-1830s. Many Creeks were forced to barter their crops for clothing. And some at Fort Gibson noted that while many of the poorer class of Creeks were "every day selling considerable quantities of corn which they carry on their backs and sell to the traders," several of these same people were being cheated by whites out of their produce. Agents observed that "the Creeks commonly get a beggarly price for their corn &c. The traders and contractors reap the profits." In fact, a common practice among traders and speculators was to purchase a bushel of corn from "poor hard working indians" for between twenty-five and thirty-seven and a half cents, and then resell the same corn for many times that amount. If corn was selling for seventy-five cents a bushel, the Creeks were trading it for only fifty cents in goods.[24]

The middling Creek immigrants were often compared to the lower class of white frontiersmen. One report noted that "the appearance of things among the Cherokees and Creeks of this country, is similar to that in new and poor white settlements on our frontiers generally. The Indians, perhaps, have more corn growing, more cattle, fewer wagons and less furniture in their houses than the whites alluded to, in proportion to numbers. They make houses and fences like the whites, keep sheep and hogs, and have spinning wheels &c." Creeks like Letif Harjo, who owned a house, a corn crib, 2,860 rails, and 7 acres of cleared land, and Tomma Gigee, who owned a home, a corn crib, 2,410 rails, 6 acres of cleared land, and 14 peach trees, probably fit this description. Indeed, Washington Irving rode upon a small Creek homestead or village consisting of "two or three log houses, sheltered under lofty trees on the border of a prairie." The Creek owners had cultivated "small farms adjacent" to their homes."[25]

The wealthiest Creeks, however, were able to move beyond these poorer settlements and construct multiple-building farmsteads and eventually Southern-style plantations. Kendall Lewis moved to the

Canadian River and established a homestead complete with a dwelling house, a storehouse (with a cellar, a "Passage," and a shed), a corn crib, a hen house, and a kitchen, surrounded by 4 acres of cleared land, 2,648 rails, and 54 peach trees. Benjamin Hawkins lived on the Verdigris and constructed a number of houses, including one that was described as a "Double House, Floored, Hewed, &c.," along with a kitchen, smokehouse, corn crib, and stable. Hawkins also owned 400 square and round logs for milling. James Hardage's estate included a number of dwelling houses located on the Verdigris River and one on the Grand, 5 kitchens, 4 corn cribs, 10.5 acres of cleared land, and 91 peach trees. Some of the very wealthiest Creeks owned upwards of 150 acres of cleared land. Inside these wealthier homes, Chouteau reported seeing "'chairs, tables, beds, bedsteads, and in some instances bureaus'" and described the supper tables of the wealthy Creeks as being "'neatly set; and a good comfortable dinner, supper or breakfast is served,'" and "'tea or coffee are in general use.'"[26]

Wealthy Creek farms, with slaves to do their bidding, produced more than enough to meet their needs. The very first harvest of the western Creeks in August 1828 yielded forty to seventy-five bushels of corn per acre. By 1829 the wealthiest members of the McIntosh party had produced such a large surplus that they were able to undersell white merchants and contractors in the West. In fact, it was the McIntosh party that provided provisions to the 1829 voluntary emigrating party, not white traders. In 1830, the Creeks raised in excess of fifty thousand bushels of corn, which created another huge surplus for sale. The soldiers, agents, and traders at Fort Gibson purchased provisions like poultry, butter, eggs, and wild geese directly from the McIntosh Creeks. The western Creeks also had gardens of beans, pumpkins, onions, cucumbers, cabbages, beets, peas, watermelons, lettuce, radishes, and Irish and sweet potatoes. Chouteau, a frequent visitor to the western Creek Nation, reported on the condition of the Indian immigrants. The trader noted that the richest Creeks were prospering by raising new crops such as "'all the kinds of grains and vegetables common to that latitude; patches of cotton and tobacco and of upland rice, are common to them'" on up to 150-acre plots of land. Moreover, some of the elite McIntosh Creeks raised herds of cattle, horses, sheep, goats, and hogs, as well as chickens, turkeys, ducks, and geese. These wealthy Creeks carried on a thriving trade with western Indians like the Comanches, who sponsored large Pan-Indian fairs. The Creeks and other relocated southeastern Indian nations traded their surplus crops, government-issued guns, and powder for skins, robes, horses, salt, and meat.[27]

Wealthier Creeks were still concerned about making appearances. Many western Creeks continued to wear the standard style of clothing and accoutrements they enjoyed in the East. Washington Irving noted that in contrast to the Osages who were poor, the Creeks "dress in calico hunting-shirts of various brilliant colors, decorated with bright fringes, and belted with broad girdles, embroidered with beads: they have leggings of dressed deer skins, or of green or scarlet cloth, with embroidered knee bands and tassles: their moccasons are fancifully wrought and ornamented, and they wear gaudy handkerchiefs tastefully bound round their heads." As he approached the Verdigris after leaving Fort Gibson, Irving observed a Creek man on horseback wearing "a bright blue hunting-shirt trimmed with scarlet fringe; a gayly colored handkerchief was bound round his head something like a turban, with one end hanging down beside his ear." A month later the author saw more Creeks near the Arkansas River "in their brightly colored dresses, looking like so many gay tropical birds." Observers saw Creek immigrants riding horses with women walking behind carrying "quite a heavy baggage on their backs" or riding "with three or four slave attendants, following in his trail." The noted artist George Catlin painted Benjamin and Samuel Perryman, two members of the McIntosh party who immigrated to the Indian territory in 1827, observing that they "are mostly clad in calicoes, and other cloths of civilized manufacture; tasselled and fringed off by themselves in the most fantastic way, and sometimes with much true and picturesque taste. They use a vast many beads, and other trinkets, to hang upon their necks, and ornament their moccasins and beautiful belts."[28]

Concerned about maintaining their newfound power, the western Creek government was composed primarily of these wealthy, well-connected McIntosh party family members and allies. Roly McIntosh, whom Little Prince and Opothle Yoholo described in a government report as "an underling Chief, inferior degree" in the East, became the principal chief of the Creeks in the West and held that position until 1859. In his 1835 *Annual Register*, Isaac McCoy noted that Benjamin Perryman served just below McIntosh as second chief, Fushatchee Micco was the commanding general of the militia, and Chilly McIntosh and Jacob Derasaw were judges. Derasaw replaced Cowockcochee Emarthla, who had previously served as second judge. Benjamin Perryman died sometime before 1836, and by the 1840s Benjamin Marshall was serving as second chief and was, according to some, "decidedly the most influential and reliable man in the nation." In 1834 five headmen—Roly McIntosh, Fushatchee Micco, Chilly McIntosh, Siah Hardage, and Kendall Lewis—were selected as principal headmen empowered to transact all the business of the nation including that concerning the rights and privileges of its citizens, recovering monies from the federal government, and negotiating treaties. These headmen were nominated and appointed by the town miccos and other representatives of the fifteen western Creek *talwas*.[29]

Regardless of wealth, disease was the great equalizer in the Indian territory. As was the case during the relocations of the late 1830s, the mortality rate during the first years of resettlement far outpaced the number of deaths during the actual journey west. Soon after the third voluntary party arrived in 1829, a cholera outbreak caused "extreme distress" throughout the western Creek, Cherokee, and Choctaw territories. Another "excessively fatal" cholera outbreak struck New Orleans and spread to Fort Gibson just as the Creeks were recovering from the devastating flooding of 1833. Almost immediately upon the cholera subsiding, residents of the western Creek Nation became "unusually sickly" from to the spread of bilious fevers. In addition to the cholera and fever, physicians appointed to tend to the sick discovered immigrants with dysentery, whooping cough, and measles. The rate of disease only grew worse into the early 1830s as at least 18 percent of the population died between 1830 and 1833 due to "the country being more unhealthy than usual." Several hundred Creeks perished because of the "prevailing diseases of the country" coupled with the "great want of medical assistance," and a population that was estimated to be approximately 3,000 at the start of the decade showed only 2,459 residents three years later. The child mortality rate reached almost 75 percent. When Washington Irving arrived at the frontier farmhouse of one of the members of the Berryhill family in October 1832, the Creek immigrant could offer no accommodation because of sickness in his family. Irving observed that "his log house was a mere hospital, crowded with invalids," and the author noted that Berryhill himself looked to be "in no very thriving condition." The Creeks used a mix of western medicine and traditional cures, including one of the most common—"blown water," where herbs and roots were boiled in a large kettle before a Creek doctor blew healing air into the elixir through a reed that was two or three feet long. Missionary Augustus Ward Loomis, who witnessed the blown water ceremony during an 1850s Busk, observed that "water is drawn from the spring into which the conjurer blows a blessing through his reed, and the people all drink of it, supposing they are imbibing health-insuring draughts."[30]

Despite federal officials' promise that the western lands were healthy, whites also complained about the sickliness of the region. Creek agent James Logan noted that the location of the Creek Agency—which by 1845 was situated six miles from Fort Gibson and three hundred yards from the north bank of the Arkansas River—caused him "to actually dread the approach of warm weather." Although the buildings were constructed on high ground, the area between the agency and the Arkansas was low and marshy, which produced "a miasma often creating fatal effects." Indeed, Logan further complained that he had "never escaped one summer season out of the five . . . without being prostrated, by sickness."[31]

Federal officials were concerned about the prevalence of western diseases, if for no other reason than it threatened to derail the emigration program back east. When thirteen families from the first voluntary party became "very sick" in the fall of 1828, Dr. John W. Baylor was quickly dispatched to treat the immigrants and stop the spread of the illness. In any other circumstance, the relatively small number of sick likely would not have warranted such a response, but as the physician noted, "considerable mortality, might have a tendency, to retard the views of Government in their emigration." The reports, however, did reach the Creeks in the East. In a letter to Washington, eleven Upper and Lower headmen, including former McIntosh party member James Island and Cusseta headman Neah Micco (who succeeded Little Prince as a principal chief of the Lower towns after the Thlakatchka headman's death in 1829), acknowledged that although the western Creeks had described the West as bountiful and full of game, "they cannot refrain from writing us the unhealthiness of the country, the many deaths that have taken place among them. Our people view health as the greatest happiness they enjoy. From all accounts that we have received, it is a grave yard." Still, some believed that the only cure to the sickness found in the West was to return to the healthy land they once called home. Indeed, because of the "extensive prevalence of disease," several Creek immigrants packed up their belongings and returned to Alabama soon after their immigration, believing that the West "would always be unhealthy."[32]

Bureaucratic carelessness and governmental neglect was another great equalizer. The Creeks suffered from policy makers in Washington and indifferent or corrupt agents on the ground. This was not just a Creek problem. Indian territory visitor Charles Joseph Latrobe believed that relocated Indians were "more exposed to oppression" in the West, due in part to the fact that the western agents were largely dishonest men. Indeed, John P. Moore pleaded with his father in 1836 to send him money but warned him not to put it in an agent's hands "unless you can trust him with it, for sum of the Agent that brings the Indians on to this country run away with the Indians money, &c, and the Indians did not get nothing for it." As noted earlier, David Brearley was particularly unpopular among the McIntosh Creeks for offenses ranging from speculating in provisions to appearing intoxicated in public. Luther Blake, who was appointed as a western subagent by John Crowell after Brearley's dismissal in 1829, was little better. Blake, who speculated heavily in eastern Creek reserves after the 1832 Treaty of Washington signing, was accused of withholding payments from the Creeks' sale of corn to the government. In an angry letter to President Andrew Jackson, the Creeks accused the president of not responding to their concerns. The western headmen pleaded that "the sorrows of three years now rest upon us—our load is too heavy to bear!" The Creeks threatened that if the president did not find an agent to take care of them, his "Muscogee children may seek a new home, very far to [the] setting sun" and that their warriors "will march before their women, and children, and their aged people, until they find rest & peace." Francis Audrain, a former schoolteacher for the western Choctaws, served until 1837 when ill health and a lack of "energy" forced him out of office. James Logan, who served the Creeks into the 1840s, was fired for disobeying federal orders. Logan was directed to distribute three thousand rifles to the Creeks but stopped out of fear that they would find their way into the hands of western Indians and be used in Mexico's invasion of Texas in 1842. Newspapers speculated that the lack of game prompted the Creeks to dispose of the weapons for five dollars apiece. James L. Dawson succeeded Logan in the spring of 1842, only to be fired when Dawson killed Seaborn Hill, a prominent trader who was security on Dawson's official bond. When Hill informed officials that he no longer wanted to be liable for Dawson, the agent apparently murdered him in a fit of rage. Logan, who was rehired as Creek agent shortly after the incident, believed the murder had more to do with Hill's discovery of a plan by Dawson and a partner to defraud the Creeks by replacing their annuity and other government monies with counterfeit coinage. Dawson quickly escaped to Texas with a thousand-dollar reward on his head.[33]

Nothing, however, angered the Creeks more than the accidental cession of a large portion of their land to the Cherokees. In 1828 the western Cherokees ceded their land in the Arkansas Territory for land farther west in the Indian territory. Unbeknown to federal agents at the time, portions of the seven million acres given to the immigrants ran "over a valuable portion of lands previously granted to the Creeks." Isaac McCoy blamed the "want of correct information of the geographical situation of the country" for the mistake, as well as "the absence of a superintendency, extending with equal interest to all parts, to all tribes, and informed of all." Neither the Creeks nor the Cherokees were willing to concede the land, however, and the problem was complicated by the fact that Cherokee settlers had already moved into the Creek territory and established farmsteads. But for the members of the McIntosh party who resided on the land in question, the controversy drove them to distraction. Headmen, led by Roly McIntosh, defiantly protested any loss of their domain and declared that "our people have allready settled the Country and do not intend to be removed without it is done by force" and that they would "rather meet death" on the soil guaranteed them than be forced into the prairies. The issue remained unresolved until 1833, when the two parties agreed to a treaty that adjusted the boundary line. For the Creeks—including prominent McIntosh party members Kendall Lewis, Benjamin Perryman, Benjamin Hawkins, and Susannah McIntosh—who were suddenly living in what became Cherokee country, the Treaty of Fort Gibson meant another, albeit smaller, removal. Creek land and improvements that were inside the Cherokee tract were appraised, and the Creeks were compensated accordingly. The Creeks also received, among other things, industrial materiel from the United States including tools, iron, steel, "four patent railway mills" for grinding corn, and twenty-four crosscut saws, as well as an additional blacksmith and wheelwright or wagon maker, and one thousand dollars annually for educational purposes.[34]

Although the Treaty of Fort Gibson appeared to end one controversy, it just as easily created another. This agreement, in conjunction with the Seminoles' 1832 Treaty of Payne's Landing (a removal document that set aside land for the Florida Indians in the Creek territory), merged the two parties together in the West and made the Seminoles "a constituent part" of the western Creek Nation. The dearth of quality soil and a bureaucratic misunderstanding of the geopolitics of the Creeks and Seminoles created the problem. The Creeks welcomed the Seminoles, but only if they planned to fully assimilate into their polity and dissolve their government and their claims to sovereignty. In doing so, it was assumed that the Seminoles "would be more cordially received and would live more amicably, than if they should be placed in the Creek Country as if they were a separate community." The Seminoles, however, had no desire to settle among the Creeks and give up their laws and identity, while also worrying that the western Creeks would seize their black slaves. For their part, Creek headmen were concerned that if the Seminoles refused to live within the western Creek Nation, they would be forced to cede even more of their western lands to accommodate their Florida counterparts. Federal officials were indifferent, and noted that "it is entirely optional with [the Seminoles] to agree to or reject" living among the Creeks. Still, the government did little to resolve these problems and when the Seminoles moved west in different waves in the late 1830s and early 1840s, many were placed on the Deep Fork of the Canadian River—the site agreed on by the Creeks. Others settled on the Little River. But many Seminoles refused to reside within the Creek country and live under Creek laws and instead squatted on Cherokee lands. By 1842 there were perhaps as many as fourteen hundred Seminoles living in the Cherokee territory near Fort Gibson.[35]

The first few years of settlement in the West proved to be very difficult for the Creek immigrants. Despite the reports of the Creeks producing large surpluses of crops and establishing homes and plantations, the western Creeks faced constant problems. Disease, raids by western Indians, and extreme weather were a few of the many troubles that prevented a smooth transition to western life. Compounding the problem was the inefficiency of federal bureaucrats in distributing the promised provisions necessary for survival in the Indian territory. In fact, many McIntosh party members still had not received money for emigrating as promised in the 1826 Treaty of Washington or compensation for their lost improvements in Georgia. There is little doubt that many Creeks regretted leaving the eastern Creek Nation, and a few went as far as to emigrate back to the East. But there was no looking back for the elites of the McIntosh party as their orientation increasingly pointed west. Indeed, in the late 1820s, a party of emigrants toured the far western region of the continent when "a few Creeks of the McIntosh party in Arkansas, visited California and went up the Pacific coast to the Columbia river, and returned by the way of Salt Lake." But Roly McIntosh and his allies understood that a power struggle potentially loomed if and when high-ranking eastern headmen migrated west. This became a reality in early 1836, as one of the first mile chiefs—Kotchar Tustunnuggee—arrived in Indian territory. By the end of 1837, almost the entire National Council had been relocated across the Mississippi River. Fearful of losing their authority, members of the McIntosh party moved to consolidate their power and check the influence of the immigrant eastern headmen.[36]

7 Chains
1836

Undeterred by their failures and still under contract to emigrate five thousand Creeks, the employees of John W. A. Sanford & Company charged forward enrolling emigrants. The contractors confidently guaranteed that they would get at least eight thousand Upper Creeks to voluntarily move in the spring of 1836, although they noted that the prospects for a Lower Creek emigration were not as good. The partners declared, however, that they would not be surprised if the entire Creek populace moved west that year. According to the company, the plan was to start five detachments of emigrants consisting of "not less than 1000 or more than 1500" Creeks at different intervals. They prepared to open a number of enrollment camps and anticipated a late April 1836 emigration. Just like the previous year, the contractors ran into a number of obstacles. The Creeks resented Sanford & Company in general and the contractors in particular, and the late additions to the organization of land speculators William Walker and Thomas S. Woodward only added to their dissatisfaction. Enrollment was also stymied by the general opposition to leaving Alabama and the slow adjudication of the Creeks' land fraud claims. In fact, frustrations over white encroachment, landlessness, indebtedness, and starvation caused Lower Creeks from Cusseta, Hitchiti, Yuchi, Chehaw, and other towns to lash out against whites. The violence that had been isolated and sporadic in 1835 intensified over the ensuing months. By the spring of 1836, the eastern and central portions of Alabama were in a state of open war.[1]

It was an inauspicious start to the year 1836 in the Chattahoochee Valley. In January a number of Georgians patrolling the area for wayward Creeks blundered upon a group of Chehaw men asleep around a campfire on the eastern side of the Chattahoochee River. Firing at the camp, the whites killed one man and wounded another. In a defiant act of resistance to white encroachment, upwards of "thirty or forty" Creeks avenged the attack, ultimately killing two Georgians. There were also two separate attacks against Creeks as they picked cotton on the plantations of white settlers. When General Daniel McDougald, an infamous land speculator and head of a Georgia militia, threatened to cross the Chattahoochee and preempt the escalation of Creek hostilities, John B. Hogan, knowing what a tinderbox the former Creek Nation had become, warned that "should General McDougald, however, persist in crossing into Alabama, he will be attacked, I have no doubt, and it will be the means of creating a Creek war." This was quite an about-face for Hogan, who had spent a great deal of time persuading his superiors that the threats of Creek violence were overblown. Just more than a week earlier, Hogan had sardonically noted in a letter to Washington that Columbus residents were back to "their old tricks" of inventing hostilities. Hogan blamed the rumors on the speculators who wanted to disrupt the fraud investigations, although these sporadic false alarms had occurred in the Columbus papers well before 1836. But this time was different. By the first week of February 1836, Hogan had recanted his earlier assessment and noted that "the conduct and appearance of those people are changed. *Not an Indian came* to the council fire but was armed with his rifle, *knife, pouch, horn*, &c., ready for battle."[2]

Adding insult to injury, in late 1835 or early 1836, a phrenologist traveled through the Creek reserves "digging up a number of Indian skulls and carrying them off" for examination. Traditionally, Creeks buried their dead in the sitting position underneath their homes. With an increasing number of Creek houses abandoned because of emigration or land fraud, the skulls were probably relatively easy to procure. The desecration was profoundly insulting and it was not surprising that the actions "greatly incensed" the Creeks. In fact, one Creek headman who had had his land stolen, "spoke up with great bitterness and said: 'He would stay and die here, and then the whites might have his skull for a water cup; they wanted everything, and when he was dead they might have his skull too.'" Moreover, the Creeks threatened to kill the man (probably one of the Creeks' slaves) who had shown the doctor the location of the skulls.[3]

While many in the Lower towns were militarizing, some of the most prominent Upper Creek headmen appear to have given up their fight to remain on their native soil. By the spring of 1836, Opothle Yoholo had taken definitive steps to conclude his people's affairs in Alabama. Many of the Upper Creeks did not plant crops in anticipation of an eventual emigration that year. In order to resolve the hundreds of outstanding land fraud claims, the Tuckabatchee headman entered into negotiations (but did not consummate an agreement) with a group of speculators who proposed purchasing the stolen reserves for a sum equivalent to the value of each half-section. Creek chiefs also sent some of their slaves west. On 19 May twelve of Opothle Yoholo's slaves and seven of Tuckabatchee Micco's slaves arrived in Indian territory. Another muster roll shows that Opothle Yoholo sent twenty more of his slaves west so they would be out of the reach of white speculators looking to claim a "national debt." Just as the West was a haven for Creeks looking to escape clan justice, the Indian territory was also a refuge for Creek property.[4]

Opothle Yoholo's decision to emigrate was a pragmatic one. Two thousand Creeks, mostly from the Upper towns, had already fled into Tennessee and the Cherokee country looking for food. Many other landless Creeks were "roaming listlessly about" the countryside. The headman pleaded with Captain John Page for rations, telling the agent that his people "must Eat they cannot live on air." Page replied that the only way he or his people would be rationed long-term was to come into the emigration camps and move west.[5]

Factionalism among whites also complicated matters in the Creek country and prevented a hasty emigration to Indian territory. Hogan and Sanford & Company were in the midst of a nasty feud over the scope of the land fraud investigations. The contractors accused the agent of impropriety and of inventing frauds where there were not any, while Hogan criticized the contractors for being land speculators. Indeed, Hogan investigated some frauds allegedly committed by the very people who complained about his inquiries. Sanford & Company also complained that Hogan slowed the pace of emigration because of what they considered the agent's excessively thorough investigations, and even suggested that Hogan tried to sabotage Sanford & Company's efforts so he could emigrate the Creeks himself. The company attempted to end Hogan's interference by inviting him to be a partner—even sweetening the deal by suggesting an eventual name change to John B. Hogan & Co.—but he declined.[6]

Intense competition among different land speculators also worked to undermine Sanford & Company. Because a number of the emigration contractors were also members of the land speculation organization Perry & Company (whose underhanded tactics and success in stealing Creek reserves created resentment among other whites), Hogan believed that jealous speculators poisoned the minds of the Lower Creek headmen against emigration in order to disrupt the plans of Sanford & Company as an act of revenge. Determining the speculators' loyalties and allegiances is nearly impossible, as so many of the white speculators were engaged in multiple schemes at the same time. Hogan complained in early 1836 that land speculators bribed headmen Neah Micco, Efar Emathla, Tuskenehaw, and the Cussetas on Tolarnulkarhatchee to lie to investigators and deny that their land had been stolen. The speculators told these Creeks that Hogan was there to force them to the Indian territory. If the Creeks successfully obstructed the investigation, they were told that they would have been allowed to live permanently on approximately ten sections owned by McDougald. The go-between was Paddy Carr, a Cusseta Creek Indian who was raised by former agent John Crowell. Although Carr was once a trusted interpreter—accompanying the delegation that negotiated the 1826 Treaty of Washington—Hogan called him a "rogue" because of his association with land speculators. Indeed, Carr worked as a purchaser for Perry & Company. Luther Blake, a member of Sanford & Company, was also a part of the plan, which probably explains why he was voted out of the emigrating company's contract in March 1836. For his part, McDougald's allegiance is still unclear; one document lists the Columbus militiaman as an active member of three different land companies.[7]

By March 1836 the former Creek Nation had devolved into a quagmire of confusion and despair. White residents noticed an unusually high number of ball plays and dances during the spring of 1836. Many speculated that this was an opportunity for disaffected Creeks to plot revenge, or provide an opportunity to hone the skills and strategy necessary for warfare.[8] Despite warnings that violence was imminent, Jackson did nothing, which by omission contributed to the destabilization of the region. With increased contact came increased violence, and Creek headmen complained back in 1831 that

> murders already have taken place, both by the reds and whites. We have caused the red men to be brought to justice, the whites go unpunished. We are weak, and our words and oaths go for naught; justice we don't expect, nor can we get. We may expect murders to be more frequent, should the whites be permitted to move amongst us. They bring spirits among us for the purpose of practising frauds; they daily rob us of our property; they bring white officers among us, and take our property from us for debts that never were contracted. We are made subject to the laws we have no means of comprehending; we never know when we are doing right.

The president, however, was repeatedly dismissive and advised the Creeks to move west.[9]

Even as the unrest reached a tipping point, headmen made a last-ditch effort to solve their problems through diplomacy. Jackson's recalcitrance, however, had so poisoned relations between the Creeks and the United States that the Creeks knew negotiation was doomed to fail. In February 1836, a desperate Neah Micco and fifteen other headmen (many of whom would end up participating in the Second Creek War) sent a letter to Jackson warning of hostilities between whites and Indians and pleading for a face-to-face meeting with the president. This meeting never happened, however. "We thought of sending a delegation to you," the headmen conceded, "but have been persuaded not to do so, for fear you would not like it."[10]

Sometime before 8 March 1836 a store owner (and land speculator) was killed, as was his brother, by bands of Yuchis. This was no random act and Hogan noted that "the Indians knew who they were shooting at" when they killed the men. Hogan acknowledged that the Yuchis "have a deep sense of injury, and do not easily forget it," and the agent observed that many of the contractors were deeply afraid of them. Indeed, the previous summer when Luther Blake visited the Yuchi reserves, the speculator was "glad to get away as fast as possible." Agents also feared traveling alone around the Lower Creek towns of Hitchiti, Chehaw, and Eufaula. John Page, who as disbursing agent carried large sums of money with him, was told by other Creeks not to travel alone near these Indians, and he subsequently hired another agent to accompany him through the region. The Lower towns had been pulled in different directions by special interests and different factions. Land speculators had massaged egos and filled the chiefs' heads with enough promises and lies. The Lower Creeks had reached a breaking point.[11]

The Second Creek War began in earnest the first week of May 1836 near the Russell-Barbour County line in Alabama with the killing of one of the members of the Glenn family. A premeditated event, the war was a response to the events of the past century and its causes were myriad. Alfred Balch, one of a pair of commissioners sent to investigate the causes of the uprising, argued in his report to Secretary of War Benjamin F. Butler in 1837 that the war was the result of starvation; the land frauds after 1832; indebtedness through the purchase of goods and alcohol on credit; and federal officials' repeated attempts to cajole the Creeks westward. The underlying cause of the Second Creek War, however, was white encroachment and the origins Balch traced to the first settlers of Georgia. The commissioner declared:

> It is probable that the followers of Oglethorpe, few in number, and with exceedingly limited means, crossed the Atlantic with no expectation that their coming would result either in the total extermination or entire removal of the Indians, first from the sea to the mountains, and then from the mountains to the western side of the Mississippi. And yet it would now seem that it required no prophet, even at that day, to foretell that such must be the final issue of the establishment

of strong and prosperous communities of white men at Newbern, Charleston, Savannah, and throughout the neighboring country.[12]

Some blamed a conspiracy among land speculators to instigate hostilities among the Creeks and thereby disrupt the land fraud investigations, while others suspected that the Second Seminole War, which began in 1835, had played a role in inspiring the uprising. Indeed, by the last week of December 1835, the Seminoles had won a number of battles—the Dade Massacre, the killing of Seminole agent Wiley Thompson at Fort King, and halting the army's progress at the Battle of Withlacoochee. Reports of the Seminoles' success filtered back to the Creek country, and Hogan wrote to his superiors that there were many Creeks of mixed ancestry "who read and write, and can, and no doubt do, communicate to them the Florida news." Although the government feared that many Creeks would join the Seminoles (John Page believed that "there are not one hundred Creeks among them," while agents in Florida estimated that the number of Creeks probably did not exceed six hundred), most Lower Creeks initially had little interest in helping the Seminoles, and were more concerned with making a stand on their own land. The Seminole victories merely showed the Creeks that it could be done. Some Creeks saw the uprising as a retaliatory race war, and agents in the field reported that in a number of cases only whites were targeted and the "negroes they do not kill." Moreover, when Creek rebels broke into a house, they let the three slaves live, telling them that "they intended to kill all the white people."[13]

John T. Ellisor, who has written a sweeping and definitive account of the Second Creek War, notes that Neah Micco, Neah Emathla, Tuskenehaw, and the Oswitchee chief Octruchee Emathla planned initial attacks on Fort Mitchell and Columbus, but for reasons unclear, these plans were delayed. Bands of young men from the towns of Hitchiti, Yuchi, Oswitchee, Sawokli, Chehaw, Cusseta, and Eufaula grew impatient, however, and decided to raid local plantations and farmsteads anyway. Within days of the initial attacks, the Creeks occupied all the white plantations "in three or four towns" in the southern section of the former Creek

Nation. Before the month of May was over, these Creeks had plundered stagecoaches along the roads running through the Creek country, cut off the flow of mail, attacked steamers like the *Georgian* and *Hyperion*, and sacked the town of Roanoke on the east side of the Chattahoochee. There was considerable rage behind many of the attacks. The Davis family, including their seven children, "were all killed, and their heads cut off; one child they threw into the yard and the hogs eat it nearly up." The Creeks also exacted revenge by burning the homes of former Creek agent John Crowell and Paddy Carr. And, as was tradition, the Creeks confiscated slaves whenever possible, including seventy from Carr's plantation. The violence soon spread as far north as LaFayette in Chambers County, south to Irwinton, and between the Chattahoochee River in the east to Tuskegee and Tallassee in the West. Perhaps as many as three thousand Creeks and their families were in open revolt against white settlements. Whites fled into Georgia or into larger towns like West Point, Columbus, Wetumpka, and Montgomery. Lower Creeks who did not participate in the hostilities fled to Fort Mitchell, Tallassee, Tuskegee, Ben Marshall's reserve across from Columbus, or to Upper Creek towns in Macon County. Military personnel later noted that "the country between this point & Tuskegee exhibits a mournful spectacle of devastation & waste— Every mansion is burn't the cattle driven off—Cribs of corn plundered & the whole country deserted." For those Lower Creeks, the attacks proved fruitful and many were able to procure corn cribs, houses full of meat, livestock, plenty of clothing, and money. Counterinsurgents, led by Jim Boy, who aided the United States during the war, happened upon Neah Micco's camp in June 1836 and found captured slaves, as well as expensive furniture, writing paper, china, and cut glass. They also found provisions such as "purloined beef, bacon, and pork in large quantities, both cooked and uncooked." This was a rich bounty for Lower Creeks accustomed to lean times.[14]

The commencement of large-scale violence did not come as a surprise to the Upper Creeks. Opothle Yoholo believed that the war was the result of whiskey traders and "sand-shakers" (land speculators). Several Tuckabatchee headmen who did not take up arms against white settlers wrote to Secretary of War Lewis Cass and lamented that some of the Lower Creeks had "taken the blood of their White Brothers." But the Creeks again reiterated that the extension laws and 1832 Treaty of Washington (although they did not specifically mention them by name) had usurped the National Council. The headmen noted that "we once had it in power to bring to justice such persons as acted in this way but since our laws have been taken from us we have it not in our power." The war was also not a surprise to the agents living among the Creeks; John Page wrote to his superiors in Washington that "the hostility that has broken out among the Lower Creeks did not astonish me in the least; I have been looking for it." Thomas Abbott, census taker and certifying agent, was admonished for publicly declaring that "the whites have stolen from the Indians, and the Indians are only getting it back again." George F. Salli, a Mobile resident who traveled through the Creek country the year before, was also not surprised at the outbreak of violence. He blamed white settlers and land speculators for forcing the Creeks into a starving condition, and observed during his journey that "such was the scarcity of provisions then amongst them that they had barked the oak trees on the road, just as a tanner would, to get the inner rind as a substitute for bread. There was no garbage that they would not greedily devour." The Creeks also were reduced to eating dead and decaying livestock including a hog "which had died of disease five or six days previously." Fearing that Creek violence would serve as a pretext for the annihilation of the Creek people by angry whites, Salli rhetorically asked Secretary of War Lewis Cass: "If we send an armed force among them should we not at the same time send them bread? The money laid out in a military expedition to hurry the work of death among them, if laid out in provisions, would soon restore peace and brotherly love among [them] and would make them friends instead of enemies."[15]

By the third week of May, the secretary of war had responded to the violence by suspending all investigations into the alleged frauds, dismissing Hogan, and declaring that Creek emigration had become "a military operation" to be "entrusted to the military authorities," as had been done with the Seminoles. Once the rebels were captured, Cass demanded that they be "disarmed, and sent immediately to their country west of the Mississippi." With no need to hunt while they subsisted on federal rations for a year in the West, Cass made it clear that the prisoners' weapons would not be returned to them at Fort Gibson until it was considered safe. Thomas S. Jesup, brevetted a major general, was charged with superintending Creek removal while simultaneously helping to command the forces charged with defeating the Creek rebels (along with his superior, Major General Winfield Scott). Captain John Page served directly under Jesup.[16]

Except for a handful of men from Sougahatchee and Loachapoka, among others, the Upper Creeks remained neutral or supported the United States in ending the hostilities. Prominent headmen like Opothle Yoholo, Menawa, and Tustunnuggee Chopco condemned the uprising, and this went a long way toward preventing more Creeks from joining the war on the side of the insurgents. Moreover, a number of Lower Creek headmen, like Tuckabatchee Harjo, Benjamin Marshall, and James Island, also aided the federal government. By the second week of June, Neah Micco, who had never fully committed to the rebel cause, surrendered to authorities and was stripped of his chieftaincy by Opothle Yoholo, Menawa, and seventeen other Creek leaders. Soon thereafter, Neah Emathla was captured by a detachment led by Jim Boy and placed in double irons at Fort Mitchell.[17]

While Neah Micco and Neah Emathla were arrested without incident, many other Creeks fought capture. When a number of Creeks were apprehended in August 1836, Georgia volunteers discovered that members of their party "having become so desperate in consequence of being constantly and closely pursued by the troops, that they have killed six of their own children who were unable to keep up with them in their flight." The headman Tallassee Fixico, also known as Okfuskee Yoholo, surrendered to military personnel in Tallassee by waving a white flag and professing to be friendly, but was arrested when Tustunnuggee Chopco, who was aiding the federal government, recognized him as an insurgent. He was later shot through the heart during an escape attempt. Many of the captured prisoners were held in the Montgomery County jail. Handcuffed left hand to right hand, in groups of two, approximately twenty Creeks were confined together in a twelve-foot-by-sixteen-foot cell. One-inch-diameter iron bars guarded the two cell windows. Although "each couple were further secured by a chain fastened round the neck of each by a common padlock, and down round the hand cuffs, and there again locked," the device left "one hand at liberty." Taking advantage of this, along with one of the guards' "brutish intoxication," the Creeks were able to pick their cuffs with a knife or nail, bend the window bars, and escape their cell. They subsequently dug underneath the prison fence and escaped into Montgomery. With the help of some friendly Creeks, the militia quickly tracked down some of the escapees and killed three of them in a shootout near Tallassee.[18]

Many Creeks who escaped capture continued to maintain their spiritual and ceremonial lives despite the misery of war and famine. The emphasis on purity and renewal was so strong that many Creeks took pains to attend the Green Corn Ceremony, even if it meant putting their lives and freedoms at risk. In August 1836 troops passed through Benton County, Alabama, and crossed Terrapin Creek when they picked up a fresh trail leading up the side of a mountain. When the soldiers reached the top, they found thirty-one people encamped (ten men, two boys, and nineteen women and children). The Creeks told the officer that they had just returned from a Busk near Wetumpka and "were determined not to emigrate and that they were on their way to Cherokee to avoid it."[19]

But there was no avoiding the inevitable. The war had justified ethnic cleansing in the minds of administration officials and emigration became forced removal. Those captured by the military during the hostilities were the first to be deported. On 2 July approximately sixteen hundred Creek prisoners, including women and children, began their slow, ninety-mile march from Fort Mitchell to Montgomery. This was followed by several hundred additional prisoners from Tuskegee. The Fort Mitchell detachment was broken into thirds and escorted by two companies of artillery. Neah Emathla, veteran of two Indian wars, was shackled in a group of three hundred other prisoners. Those who were unable to walk followed behind in wagons. The movement was clumsy and chaotic as the men were cuffed "two together, and a long chain passing between the double file connected them all together." The procession was quiet "except occasionally the utterance of an emphatic 'ta' whenever two of them pulling in opposite directions would jerk one another by the wrists." The stoicism of the men contrasted sharply to that of the women, who were "shedding tears and making the most bitter wailings" and "distressing cries." Locals contributed to the confusion by accosting the party along the journey in an attempt to take the slaves, guns, and horses that were in the Indians' possession.[20]

Some Creeks remained behind as Alabama and Georgia officials took a number of prisoners into custody for prosecution. Among those tried for crimes was Jim Henry of Chehaw, who once worked as an interpreter and clerk at Stewart and Fontaine's mercantile store in Columbus. Henry was accused of, among other things, murder, robbing coaches, burning bridges and plantations, and leading the attack on the town of Roanoke, Georgia, although it is doubtful he played much of a role in most of these attacks. Henry's wife accompanied the first detachment of Creek prisoners to Indian territory, and newspapers covered their "truly affecting" farewell. While Henry was ultimately acquitted in both Russell County and Columbus courtrooms, other Creeks were not as lucky. Some were tried and hanged across the river from Columbus in the town of Girard (now the site of Phenix City, Alabama). The executioner reportedly asked the seven condemned Creeks if they felt any remorse. Six of the men said no, while the seventh expressed regret for killing an infant, but nothing more. Some sang songs and gave out one final "whoop" before they were hanged.[21]

Despite capture, many Creek prisoners attempted to make one last stand. A number deserted the party at Fort Mitchell and along the route, including at Polecat Springs. Others committed suicide. One prisoner drew a knife and slit his throat as he was being wheeled down a Montgomery street in a wagon. Another "was found hanging by the neck the night before he was to leave Fort Mitchell for the far West; preferring the glorious uncertainty of another world, to the inglorious misery of being forced to a country of which he knew nothing, but dreaded every thing bad." A few attempted to make their escape. A father and son who were due to appear in Georgia court on capital offenses were killed as they were being turned over to the authorities. As his captors fumbled with the handcuffs, the son grabbed a hatchet, struck one of the men in the head, and ran about a hundred yards before he was shot dead. The father then picked up the weapon and attempted to strike the man a second time, but was bayoneted by a guard. Jacob Rhett Motte, an army surgeon embedded with a company of soldiers fighting the Creeks and Seminoles, recorded in his journal that "one of this very party of emigrating Indians on his arrival at Montgomery [Alabama] attempted his escape; but when caught and secured in a waggon, by some accident got possession of a very dull knife; with this he made several ineffectual efforts to cut his throat, but it not proving sharp enough, he with both hands forced it into his chest over the breast-bone, and by successive violent thrusts succeeded in dividing the main artery, when he bled to death." Some of the Creeks' black slaves also used the confusion surrounding removal to make their escape. Six of Neah Micco's slaves deserted him as he was being transported to Montgomery to await steamboat transportation.[22]

The first detachment of approximately 2,300 Creeks left Montgomery on the night of 14 July 1836. They were transported by John W. A. Sanford & Company, which had been ordered by John Page to remain in a state of readiness to transport Creeks throughout May and June. Although the original contract with the federal government had expired on 30 June, the contractors reached a handshake agreement with Page to take the party west. William J. Beattie and John D. Howell represented the company en route. The detachment consisted of Creeks from a number of Lower Creek towns, including nine hundred Yuchis and at least five hundred Cussetas. Many of the rebels had had their land stolen by speculators, and Hogan reported that the Sawoklis, Hatcheechubbas, and Cowykas (a *talofa*, or daughter town, of Sawokli) who had been defrauded out of their reserves had "gone in chains to Arkansas." The Creek prisoners descended the Alabama River on two steamboats with twenty-six-year-old lieutenant John Waller Barry, son of the former postmaster general and minister to Spain under Jackson, appointed as military oversight. Barry was forced to strategically separate the party into different boats because "it was found next to impossible to prevent strife between the Creek and Uchee women." Approximately fifteen hundred Creeks rode the *Meridian* while the balance traveled on the steamboat *Lewis Cass*. Both vessels towed barges "freighted with Indians." A platoon of forty men from the Alabama Artillery Number One was placed on each boat with orders "to shoot any who might evince a hostile spirit, or attempt to escape."[23]

Despite the show of force, some Creeks made at least one attempt to desert the party. John Milton, commander of the Alabama Artillery, who accompanied the prisoners on board the *Meridian*, discovered at about three o'clock in the morning "arrangements in progress among upwards of thirty of the Indians to escape." Although he did not know if the Creeks planned to use force, Milton ordered the guards to train their weapons on the Creeks in preparation for the worst-case scenario. But just as quickly and unexpectedly as the plot was discovered, it was extinguished; Milton reported that the would-be escapees had no idea their plans had been made known "until they discovered the entire guard, on the hurricane deck in readiness to fire upon them—They then became quiet." The following day, Neah Emathla, no doubt tired from his decades of struggle against white subjugation, urged his people to become "reconciled to their situation." The talk had its desired effect and the commander was relieved to find the Creeks docile for the remainder of their time on the water. The Creeks, over time, were even granted some small freedoms. Whenever the boats landed to procure wood, the prisoners were allowed to go onshore and relax. During these respites the captives swam, fished, or bathed along the shoreline. When a bell rang signaling time to embark, the Creeks "came aboard without delay."[24]

The steamboats reached Mobile, Alabama, on 16 July and landed below the city. The party passed close enough to the neighborhood of Baywood, where former emigrating superintendent and fraud investigator John B. Hogan lived, that the agent could witness the prisoners pass by him in chains. Still smarting from his battles with Sanford & Company, Hogan sardonically noted in a letter to Washington that he saw the Creeks "conducted by at least two of the very men who practiced as much cheats on them as any other." Indeed, Beattie and Howell were extensive land speculators. The party remained in Mobile for several hours while the boats were cleaned and fresh water and provisions brought on board. Comfortable that Creeks were no longer a threat to escape or commit depredations, the Alabama Artillery Number One was discharged and did not accompany the party any further. The captives recommenced their voyage that evening at six o'clock and within hours were in the Gulf of Mexico. There is no evidence describing the actual route taken to New Orleans, although steamer pilots had a number of options. Vessels from Mobile often traveled on either side of the barrier islands (Dauphin, Petit Bois, Horn, Dog, Ship, and Cat) then through Lakes Borgne and Pontchartrain; or crossed the Gulf and ascended the Mississippi River at its mouth near the village of Balize in Plaquemines Parish. Because the party encountered "a very severe gale" around midnight on 17 July, which battered the boats to the point that Barry feared some of the Creeks would be washed overboard, it is likely that the party passed on the outside of the islands and entered the Gulf, although how they reached the Crescent City beyond that is unclear. The "frightened" passengers were hastily "stowed away in the holds of the barges" and those that could not fit were "kept in the center" of the craft. Barry boasted that they did not lose one Creek to the Gulf, although he reported one infant child dead during the passage. Dr. Eugene Abadie, the physician accompanying the party, had more disconcerting news, however: an increasing number of sick passengers.[25]

The party arrived in New Orleans on the morning of 18 July and landed at the New Canal. The prisoners went onshore and walked to their encampment near the basin at the foot of Julia Street, while the increasing number of sick Creeks, as well as the infirm, children, and baggage were placed on board one of the barges and towed up the canal by Creek volunteers. The camp was poorly situated due to its "low & wet" location, but was the best the contractors could find. The large amount of standing water created by heavy rain and impermeable clay underneath the soil only added to the discomfort. A newspaper beat writer reported on the condition of the camps and observed that "with the aid of a few staves and boards, some tattered canvass and soiled blankets, they have put up a few rude tents, which afford them however but feeble protection against the driving rains." Despite the weather, Neah Emathla rejected an offer of a blanket and defiantly stated that "I am the enemy of the white man. I ask, and will accept, nothing at his hands." The contractors were eventually able to procure the use of an old ropewalk—a warehouse where rope is made—to shelter the party. The *New-Orleans Bee* reported that residents heard the Creek prisoners utter the phrase "Georgia no good" throughout their time in the city.[26]

The Creeks departed New Orleans on 21 July, after two days' detention in search of suitable steamboats. Approximately five hundred Cussetas ascended the Mississippi River on the steamboat *Majestic*, while the *Lamplighter* carried eight hundred Creeks and included the headmen Neah Emathla and Neah Micco. The balance traveled on the steamboat *Revenue*. One of the steamers, not identified, carried a barge in tow. Newspapers reported that a fourth vessel, the barque *Cumberland*, also accompanied the prisoners north. Although Barry tried to keep the party together, the boats soon separated and the *Majestic* ran about two days ahead of the others. The monotony of water travel was only broken up by the expected, and unexpected, disruptions to the daily routine. Wood procurement and a scheduled stop south of Natchez for boat cleaning, no doubt, helped break up the long days. One Creek man died on the boat the day after the party left New Orleans, although that may have gone largely unnoticed, as Barry recorded that the deceased was "very old had no complaint—no pain—his physical powers were almost entirely destroyed, so much so, that the pang of death itself passed without causing a struggle." But boredom and monotony could also set in motion events that would end in disaster. After days of watching the same tree-lined landscape pass before them, the Creeks' attention was caught by the town of Columbia, Arkansas. Congregating on the port side of the keelboat, the Creeks gathered to watch the settlement as they passed by. Without warning, the deck gave way, instantly killing a child.[27]

The boats reached Rock Roe on 30 July, after the Arkansas River proved too low to ascend. During the next eight days, the encamped prisoners suffered through "excessive" heat with "no water fit for drinking" while the contractors procured wagons and teams for their trip overland. Despite the condition of the camp, the Creeks likely welcomed the deferral, as it gave them time not only to hunt and fish but also quite possibly to celebrate an abbreviated Busk. Although the documentation is circumstantial, Barry noted that the Creeks held "their dances & ball plays for amusement" while at the same time the party surgeon,

Dr. Eugene Abadie, observed that the captives had "obtained a great deal of green fruit and corn" at the camp. Although it is quite probable that the Creeks had grown tired of the government-issue rations and longed for a traditional foodstuff, the degree to which the Creeks sought out the green food, including corn, suggests that it may have served a much more important function. The Creeks who purchased the green corn did so against Abadie's wishes, and even as the party broke camp, the physician complained that the Creeks were "eating every thing green they can find on the road." When Abadie attempted to prevent the Creeks from obtaining it, he was met with "much opposition and difficulty." Moreover, most of these Creeks would not have had much time or opportunity to hold a Green Corn Ceremony because they were confined in irons after their capture. And although the Busk celebrated the bounty of the Creeks' land, which had now been expropriated by whites, the celebration was also about spiritual renewal and, just as important, tradition. It probably would have been inconceivable to these Creeks not to hold a Busk, regardless of the circumstances.[28]

While Barry repeatedly used the term "cheerful" to describe the demeanor of the party, the Creeks did engage in small acts of resistance. A number of Yuchis rolled the barrels containing the handcuffs and chains into the river, where they were irrevocably lost. The chains had been brought up by the *Revenue* and placed onshore among the meat and other provisions. But the irons were in barrels without heads, which allowed the Yuchis to easily identify them, and they were surreptitiously disposed of under the cover of night. Neah Micco also tried to exert his control over the manner in which they traveled by threatening to remain behind once the party commenced its journey by land to Fort Gibson. Despite his bluster, when the party broke camp at Rock Roe on the evening of August 8, Neah Micco and his people accompanied the group with "apparent cheerfulness." Moreover, as the party moved westward overland, bands of Creeks raided white settlers' orchards and cornfields and they were restrained only with the aid of the headmen and the establishment of a fifty-lash punishment for stealing. Two Yuchi girls, "whipped before the whole camp," were the first and only recorded violators.[29]

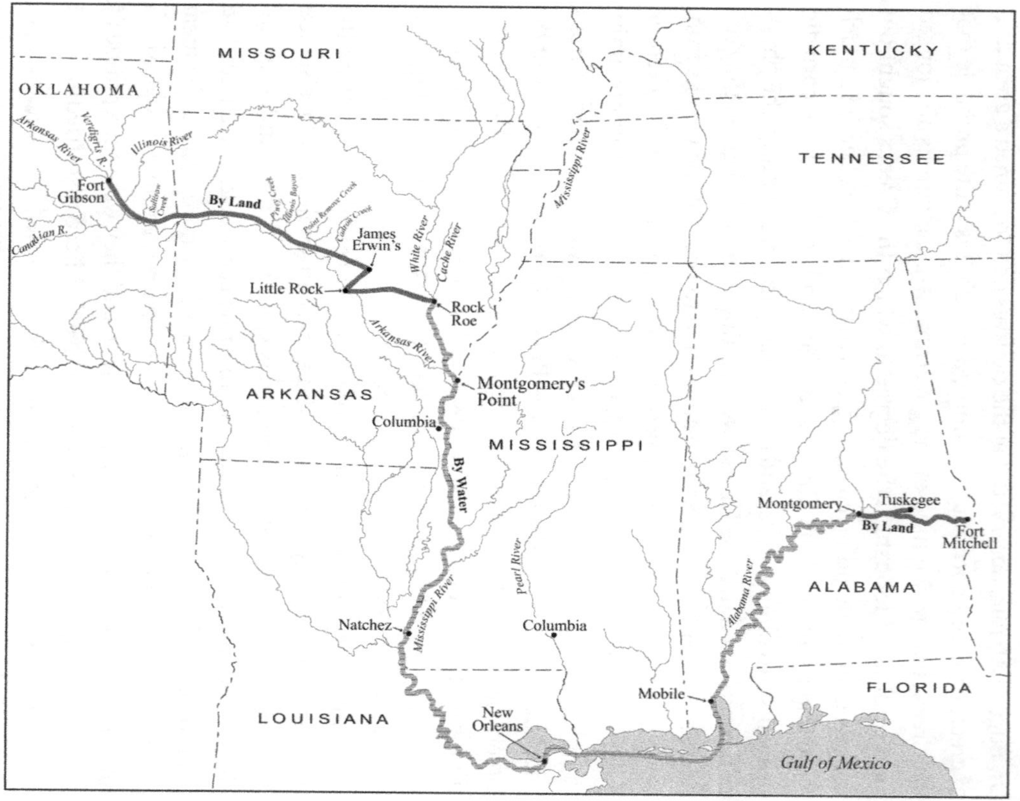

FIG. 19. Route of the first detachment of Creek prisoners, July–September 1836. Place names correspond to stopping points or locations noted in the documentation. Route lines and locations are approximations. Cartography by Sarah Mattics.

Taking advantage of the darkness in order to shield themselves from the excessive heat of the prairie, the party continued toward Little Rock. Twenty wagons—too few to handle a party of that size—were overloaded with baggage, elderly women, and sick children. Many others who were too weak to walk were unable to secure transportation. Sickness also continued to plague the Creeks. Dr. Abadie reported that that six people had died between Fort Mitchell and New Orleans, while upwards of fifty had passed away by the time the party reached James Erwin's settlement. Their passage across Arkansas was also made more difficult by the general character of the Arkansans, whom Barry described as "the most depraved, lying, cut-throat scoundrels" he had ever encountered. The settlers would approach Barry and the contractors with offers of assistance in seizing whiskey from the prisoners, while at the same time "selling it to the Indians behind our backs." But the prisoners had also gained an incredible amount of freedom. Barry allowed several of the Creeks to purchase rifles, which allowed them to hunt in the woods some distance away from the party train. Clearly unconcerned about possible escape or violent depredations, Barry noted that "the young men can easily hunt through the woods all day & be up with the party in time to camp."[30]

The Creek prisoners arrived at Fort Gibson on 3 September 1836 and camped on the western bank of the Verdigris River. Eighty-one Creeks died along the way, including those killed while trying to escape in Montgomery. Most of the deaths were caused by disease, which claimed thirty-seven children under the age of five and thirteen Creeks under the age of ten. Most of the symptoms were "bowel complaints" and fever, and Abadie diagnosed the ailments as "bilious and congestive fevers, Dysentery, Diarrhea, and cholera infantum." The physician blamed the sickness on the salt rations and overcrowding on the steamboats, as well as the excessive heat interspersed with torrential rains at New Orleans, the consumption of green fruit and corn, and drinking the dirty Mississippi River water. A few deaths were caused by accidents along the route. In addition to the small child killed by the collapse of the keelboat deck, a woman died after falling out of a tree twenty-five miles from Fort Gibson while attempting to pick grapes. The other deaths were the result of old age. The elderly High Log headman Blind King died on 25 August while on the march westward. The survivors were not in much better shape. One witness noted that he had "never seen so wretched and poor a body of Indians as this party of Creeks; they have really nothing."[31]

The arrival of Neah Micco and Neah Emathla to the Creek Nation created anxiety for members of the McIntosh-controlled government. The feeling was no doubt mutual. Concerns for personal safety and questions about leadership and power caused tension between the two groups on the eve of their reunion. The western Creeks viewed the arrivals with "jealously and distrust," and leaders like Roly McIntosh were outwardly concerned that their authority would be "superseded" or "abridged." Indeed, missionaries reported that the McIntosh faction "viewed the arrival of these new emigrants with displeasure, and declared they had no right there." McIntosh hastily sought diplomatic recognition as the principal Creek chief from both the western Cherokees and American officials. In appealing to the latter, the western headmen drew sharp distinctions between their advancement in "civilization" and the captive party who had "reduced themselves to beggary and want." Ten companies of volunteers were requested from Arkansas in order to prevent the likelihood of war and a council was arranged for the eastern and western headmen to meet. There are conflicting accounts of the ensuing negotiations. Carey A. Harris, commissioner of Indian affairs, heard secondhand that McIntosh had declared "that they were willing to meet the new emigrants as friends, provided they would submit to the laws now in force," to which Neah Emathla responded by telling McIntosh that the laws the western Creeks had created "were made for their good, and as they had prospered under them, they (the emigrants) were willing to unite under them, and try to live together peaceably." Missionaries, however, reported that on their first meeting, Neah Emathla defiantly stated to Roly McIntosh that "'it belonged to him to be chief, and he *would* be chief,'" to which McIntosh responded that he would "take the sword first" before letting the Hitchiti headman come to power.[32]

On 2 August 1836 a second detachment of 193 Creek prisoners, including men, women, and children, left Montgomery on the steamboat *Lewis*

Cass. The party included eighty Creek prisoners who had been marched in chains to Montgomery after the departure of the first detachment. While in town, the Creeks were "threatened with death" by the local whites, so Jesup hastily arranged for their removal westward. The Creeks were conducted by Captain Francis Smith Belton, a Baltimore-born veteran of the War of 1812 and Second Seminole War, who was in Montgomery discharging the Alabama volunteers when Jesup ordered him to conduct the party to Fort Gibson. The detachment arrived in Mobile at three o'clock on the morning of 6 August and by noon of that day, the Creeks had departed Alabama for New Orleans on board the steamer *Mazeppa*. Once in the Gulf, the vessel passed on the outside of the barrier islands and through Lake Borgne, which exposed the party to "very rough" waters. The passengers disembarked at the lake end of the Pontchartrain Railroad and probably took the railcars to an "old Barracks" in New Orleans, although Belton's son and biographer later wrote that the party stayed at the Old Ursuline Convent during their time in the Crescent City. The party departed on 10 August and ascended the Mississippi River on a steamboat bound for St. Louis. The decision to take a steamer only as far as Montgomery's Point was probably the result of the "enormous prices" being asked for river transportation at the time.[33]

After reaching the mouth of the White River on 15 August, the Creeks disembarked the vessel and it continued on its course to St. Louis. Belton, however, was left scrambling to find suitable transportation for the remainder of the journey, and with the health of the party "very bad," this took on added urgency. During the next week, Belton struggled to find anything remotely suitable for the conveyance of the Creek captives. Several Creeks died during their wait at Montgomery's Point—probably from "Congestive & Intermittent fevers" contracted from the local residents. On 22 August, with all of the steamboats in the area "laid up," Belton contracted for the use of a keelboat furnished "with suitable bunks or birth places, and a Cabin partition and proper flooring to keep the Indians dry and wholesome and also a fire place on deck for Cooking" to take the debilitated Creeks around a swamp, but only as far as the old Arkansas Post. The water party departed the mouth of the White River on 23 August under the charge of Dr. James Jones, a New

Orleans physician hired to accompany them. Their departure was not without drama, as many in the party showed "great reluctance" in being separated from their families and were "very suspicious of evil intended them." Belton accompanied the land party and ran into trouble almost immediately. In addition to the difficulty of traveling through the swamp, Belton griped that "the whole marching party are drunk," the result, he noted, of an Indiana flatboat stopping sometime in the evening and selling the Creeks a quantity of whiskey. Belton destroyed the alcohol, but not without "some bad feelings and threats."[34]

The land and water parties rejoined on 28 August, and after several days' delay waiting for wagons, began slowly making their way overland across Arkansas. The Creeks' journey was plagued by flies so distressing that "a horse can hardly be controlled from lying down to roll such is the torment"; excessive heat interspersed with torrential rainfall; water "of the worst description"; and sick Creeks "constantly dropping." Moreover, volunteers on their way to Fort Towson and the first detachment of Creek prisoners had taken all the suitable wagons, leaving only "miserable ox (cotton) carts, many without tired wheels or indeed, without Iron of any kind." The party passed through Angelico Island, a timber island in the middle of the Grand Prairie before reaching Mary Black's on 9 September, James Erwin's on 11 September, and Daniel Greathouse's on 14 September—all of whom were settlers who routinely contracted with federal officials to supply provisions to Indians as they were forced west. Except for a few days of "scorching sun," the party was bombarded with incessant rainfall that made crossing the myriad rivers and streams difficult, and Belton complained that "every little rill" was "a torrent." Belton's journal lists the crossing of the Cadron, Point Remove Creek at Frederick Fletcher's toll bridge, Illinois Bayou by ferry, Piney and Spadra Creeks, and Mulberry Creek. Sickness continued to plague the party and Belton complained that "the situation of the Indians is deplorable," with more than fifty people sick and where "death occasionally carries off the weakest." One teamster became "violently ill" and even Belton became so sick he was forced to turn over the party to Dr. Jones for the final six days of the journey.[35]

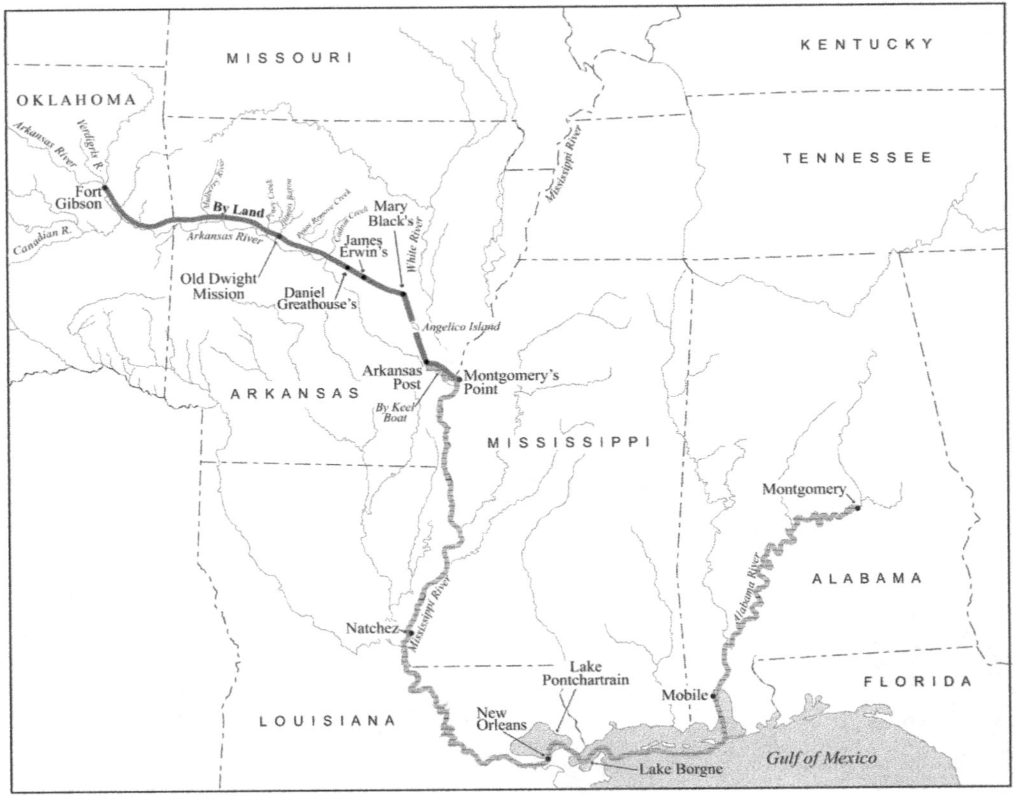

FIG. 20. Route of the second detachment of Creek prisoners, August–October 1836. Place names correspond to stopping points or locations noted in the documentation. Route lines and locations are approximations. Cartography by Sarah Mattics.

The Creeks arrived at Fort Gibson on 3 October 1836 and were mustered into the Creek Nation. Of the 210 captives enrolled at Montgomery in August, 193 made the trip west after seventeen were detained by the civil authorities in Alabama. Nineteen more Creeks died en route and nine went missing for reasons "unaccountable" (most likely, Belton believed, because of desertion in the western Cherokee territory). Only 165 Creeks from the second detachment of Creek prisoners arrived at Fort Gibson. After weeks of suffering on the road, the garrison provided little relief. The prisoners from both detachments arrived "in a state of great poverty and destitution." Captured in their summer clothing fit only for the heat and humidity of Alabama, the prisoners arrived in the West underdressed for "the inclemencies of the approaching winter." With no quick solution available, agents sent for blankets from New York. In total, 2,498 Creek prisoners departed Montgomery, Alabama, in the summer of 1836. Only 2,159 arrived at Fort Gibson between September and October 1836. Federal officials reported that 339 died, were detained in the East, or escaped during the journey west.[36]

Although a relatively small number of Creeks participated in the Second Creek War, the outbreak of violence had repercussions for the entire Creek population. Despite all their efforts, the policy of cajoling the Creeks into voluntarily emigrating westward was unsuccessful. Moreover, there was little reason to believe that many more Creeks would agree to go west, despite the best estimates of John W. A. Sanford & Company officials. But when a small band of Lower Creeks began committing depredations against local white settlers, Andrew Jackson proceeded to try and ethnically cleanse the South of Creek Indians. The administration's logic, although unsupported by evidence, was summed up by Secretary of War Lewis Cass, when he declared that although not all the Creeks were at war, "there is every reason to believe they will do so, unless prevented by a timely removal." In spite of the efforts of Opothle Yoholo, Menawa, and many other headmen to put down the Creek rebellion, Cass was wrongly convinced that "it is difficult, if not impracticable, to keep any considerable part of an Indian tribe at peace while the residue of it is engaged in war." The meaning of Cass's statement is clear: the twenty-five hundred Creeks who were chained and forced westward in the summer of 1836 was only the beginning. While the first detachment of Creek captives was encamped at New Orleans, Captain John Page was meeting with Upper Creek headmen in Alabama to notify them that they would be ordered into relocation camps by the second week of August. This was despite the fact that none of these Creeks had participated in the depredations and none had signed a removal treaty.[37]

8 Coercion

1836–37

The commencement of the Second Creek War officially ended the government's voluntary emigration program. Unsuccessful in their attempt to convince large numbers of Creeks to move west, administration officials could only concede that the policy was a failure. The war, however, gave Andrew Jackson the excuse he needed to relocate the entire population without a removal treaty. Unlike the Cherokee Trail of Tears, the Creeks who had not participated in the war were not forced west at the end of a bayonet. With "no legal right under the treaty to remove the Creeks," Brevet Major General Thomas S. Jesup conceded, "their movements was [sic] necessarily voluntary." Hopelessly outnumbered by the Indians, however, military personnel were forced to work with the headmen in order to achieve their objectives. As a result, the main body of Creeks (who left after the prisoners) were moved through a combination of coercion and negotiation rather than brute force. It was a "coerced relocation" instead of a "forced removal" in chains. Although the Creeks were not necessarily free to remain in Alabama—Lewis Cass told Jesup that those not at war "must be removed by a military force, if necessary"—Creek leaders realized that they held an unusual amount of power considering the circumstances and they demanded concessions in exchange for compliance. Indeed, the Creeks exerted myriad resistance strategies while on the road and had a large amount of control over the manner in which they traveled. On 13 August Jesup agreed to terms with the Alabama Emigrating Company to transport the Creeks west at $28.50 per person. The company, merely a reconstituted John W. A. Sanford & Company, provided the transportation, provisions, and medicine when needed. As was the case with previous movements, American military officers and a surgeon accompanied the detachments as oversight. But the movement of sixteen thousand people proved to be extremely difficult and the Creeks faced obstacles at almost every turn.[1]

Plans to ethnically cleanse Alabama of the Creek Indians began almost immediately after Andrew Jackson and Lewis Cass were briefed on the commencement of the Second Creek War. On 21 May, the secretary of war laid out the administration's case for relocating the entire Creek population westward when he noted, "as to the situation of the Creek Indians, the President has thought that the state of hostilities will justify their immediate and entire removal." As the war raged through May and June, many Creeks who had not participated in the uprising were fed at various locations in the former Creek Nation, often by the very speculators who had stolen their land years earlier. By 20 July John Page had visited the Upper Creeks and ordered them into camps on 10 August in order to prepare for their journey west. Unaware that they were to be moved so quickly, the agent noted that the Creeks were "much astonished" that they were to "be rushed off so soon." Lower Creek headmen like Cusseta chief Tuckabatchee Harjo felt the same, and they complained that the day of departure was earlier than anticipated, which gave their people little time to gather their crops and sell their livestock. After a number of appeals, an assembly of Lower Creek headmen finally relented and "gave no other than a silent acquiescence . . . but expressed among themselves strong feelings of dissatisfaction."[2]

On 17 August 1836 Jesup issued "Order No. 63," a written directive organizing two detachments of Creeks under Chief Opothle Yoholo. Out of respect for his authority, the Tuckabatchee headman was assigned to the lead party and ordered to rendezvous with his people three miles west of Tallassee. By late August this party contained approximately 2,400 Creeks and was conducted to Indian territory by Lieutenant Mark W. Bateman (also spelled Batman), a Calhoun, Tennessee, resident and former disbursing agent for the eastern Cherokees. A few Indian countrymen also chose to follow their Creek families west. Assisting Bateman was Opothle Yoholo confidante Barent Dubois, who abandoned his Tuckabatchee family after they moved west. Detachment two, consisting of 3,142 people from towns affiliated with Tuckabatchee, rendezvoused near Wetumpka under the charge of Lieutenant R. B. Screven.[3]

On 22 August Jesup issued "Order No. 67," organizing detachments three through six. These last four parties—detachment three (Jim Boy, Yelko Harjo, and their people), detachment four (Echo Harjo and his people), detachment five (Tuckabatchee Harjo and the Lower Creeks), and detachment six (the Talladega Creeks)—were eventually consolidated into three detachments when Jim Boy, Echo Harjo, and many of their followers agreed to serve in Florida against the Seminoles. Once reorganized, detachment three consisted of 2,420 people who resided along both banks of the Tallapoosa River, extending from Tallassee in the south to Horseshoe Bend in the north. The most notable among this detachment was Menawa of Okfuskee and Tuscoona Harjo, a mile chief of Fish Pond. Lieutenant Edward Deas was the principal military agent and their rendezvous was four miles east of Talladega. Detachment four, accompanied by Captain Jacob D. Shelly (and later by Lieutenant Joseph D. McCann), included 1,169 individuals from Randolph, Benton, and Talladega counties, including 400 Creek refugees captured in the Cherokee country. They encamped four miles north of Talladega. Detachment five consisted of 1,943 people, primarily from the towns of Cusseta and Coweta, led by Tuckabatchee Harjo, James Island, and Benjamin Marshall. Tuckabatchee Harjo's camp was at Cusseta in Chambers County, and James Island's party of 135 people were stationed a few miles opposite West Point, Georgia, while Marshall's people, consisting of 45 Creeks (mostly family members) and 28 slaves, was located at Girard across from Columbus, Georgia. The three converged at LaFayette, Alabama, and were accompanied to Indian territory by Lieutenant John T. Sprague.[4]

During the month of August, the Creeks closed down their ceremonial life in Alabama and prepared for relocation. The Creeks almost certainly consumed black drink for the final time on their native soil. Before departing Tallassee, Opothle Yoholo and his people, as was Creek custom before a long journey, fasted during the day and danced at night. The Tuckabatchees also polished their sacred plates in preparation for their march westward. Creek women "erected piles of light wood over the remains of their relatives and friends, and burnt them in honor of their memories." Men were chosen to carry the sacred items used in the annual Busk and other ceremonies. They traveled in advance of the detachments and no Creeks were allowed to pass them. James Island, for example, recalled how men from Coweta carried the large conch shells out of which they consumed black drink. Similarly, the Tuckabatchees selected men, "remarkable for their sobriety and moral character," to transport their sacred plates.[5]

The Creeks also extinguished their town fires. Whenever a *talwa* was relocated in the past, the public square and central fire was also moved and reestablished in its new location. Great care and ceremony surrounded the consecration of new ground, and this would have been no different during the biggest relocation the Creeks had ever experienced. There are, however, no documentary records detailing how the Creeks closed down their towns and square grounds or removed their sacred fire, although oral histories survive. In the 1930s the Works Progress Administration sent interviewers through the Muscogee (Creek) Nation in Oklahoma to collect narratives. Many deal with removal and a few stories explain the process of traveling west with the town fire. According to one, the town of Fish Pond selected two men to take a burning piece of wood from the town's fire and it was their responsibility to keep it lit until they reached their new homes in the West. These embers were used to start a campfire each night the party stopped during the march. And when camp was broken each morning and their travels resumed, two more pieces of burning wood were taken by the men. This process was repeated until they consecrated their new ceremonial ground in Indian territory. The Creeks of Okchai also chose two men, who were monitored by the *talwa*'s micco, to carry the town's fire on the journey west. These men were designated fire carriers, and no other person could handle the town's embers during the march. Moreover, these men were under strict orders to abide by the micco's commands. They could not to mingle with women or drink from a cup used by women. The fire carriers were also told to only eat certain *humpeta hutke* (white meals), such as white Indian corn bread and white *sofkee*.[6]

The Creeks also attended to practical matters. Each individual was allowed only twenty pounds of personal property to load into the wagons. One wagon and team was assigned for every seventy-five people. Still, many Creeks tried to take as much as they could carry, including seemingly valueless items like old irons and broken jugs. Prominent headmen were not bound by the twenty-pound rule and detachment one carried an excess number of wagons, in part because there were "several chiefs of distinction who required greater accommodation than others." Many women purchased jewelry, a highly portable form of personal wealth. One oral narrative recounted that Creek women bought "diamond rings, ear rings, [and] gold bracelets" because they "were celebrating before leaving their homes in Alabama." This, in fact, did occur and Lieutenant Sprague, the military agent in charge of detachment five, complained that the Cowetas and Cussetas "expended what little they had . . . for some gaudy article of jewelry." Immovable property such as fruit trees were chopped down so whites would not benefit from the labor of the former Creek landholders. This was a common practice among the Creeks when transferring their land to white ownership and had been done when they were forced out of Georgia in 1826. Certifying agents were posted in the relocation camps and many Creeks hastily sold their reserves for what little money they could. Indeed, dozens and dozens of Creeks, like Fish Pond headman Tuscoona Harjo, sold, certified, or had monies paid over to them for their reserves in mid- to late August 1836 while preparing for their journey westward. And yet, despite being given the opportunity by certifying agents stationed in the camps, some Creeks simply refused to sell their Alabama land.[7]

The Creeks also made preparations in anticipation of their arrival in Indian territory. As part of their agreeing to move west, Tuckabatchee headmen Opothle Yoholo, Mad Blue, Little Doctor, and Tuckabatchee Micco insisted that Bateman and the contractors allow the party to stop in the state of Arkansas in order to settle the difficulties between those who had participated in the Second Creek War and those who aided the government in capturing them. Citing the "bad feelings" the Creek prisoners had toward them, the mile chiefs of Tuckabatchee feared that "should we go directly into the Creek country, they would doubtless try to revenge themselves upon us." In addition, Opothle Yoholo demanded that Neah Micco and his followers "be disfranchized, receive no part of the Creek annuity, and be placed at such point within the Creek country west, as I might designate." The requested stoppage in Arkansas would also give the headmen time to negotiate with the McIntosh leadership. Opothle Yoholo, for example, noted that although he was still "recognized by the Government as the principle [sic] chief of the Creek Nation," the Tuckabatchee headman conceded that "should any of the Creeks West object to me as such, I wish time to consult, and arrange all our difficulties."[8]

During this time the contractors and military agents prepared for the logistics of relocation, such as mapping routes, arranging transportation, and setting aside the days for departure. Originally 20 August 1836 was the date selected for detachment one to commence its march west, with each successive party leaving in five-day intervals. In addition to staggering the departure days of the detachments, each party also had a prescribed route through Alabama to Memphis. This was done primarily to space the parties enough to ensure a steady supply of provisions and to avoid particularly bad roads. Contractors with the company were required to travel ahead and establish provision depots along these routes, although in many cases they negligently did not. Opothle Yoholo's party was scheduled to travel to Memphis via Wetumpka and Tuscaloosa in Alabama, and Cotton Gin Port and Pontotoc in Mississippi. The route of detachment two was established through Montevallo, Elyton, and Tuscumbia. The planned routes of detachments three and four, which rendezvoused in the northern section of the former Creek Nation near Talladega, was to travel "a few degrees west of north . . . and within a few miles of Gunter's Landing" on the Tennessee River. There, detachment four would collect an additional one thousand Creek refugees who had been captured in the Cherokee country. The fourth party then crossed the Tennessee River at Deposit Landing and passed through Huntsville, Alabama; Savannah, Tennessee; and Memphis. After reaching the neighborhood of Gunter's Landing, detachment three followed the south bank of the Tennessee River through Somerville and Decatur because the Creeks were "much opposed to crossing the River."

Detachment five left Chambers County, Alabama, and passed through Tuscumbia by way of Elyton and Courtland.[9]

By the end of August 1836 the relocation camps were in a state of chaos. Absconding from the detachments was a problem and a large military presence was used to keep the Creeks "together." Even still, the military agents overseeing the parties complained that it was difficult to get the Creeks to prepare for relocation because they listened only to their headmen and not to the agents. Traders who had sold the Creeks merchandise on credit "infested" the camps and called in their debts. The Creeks' slaves and horses were taken as collateral and even Creek women were arrested in violation of Alabama law. The Creeks also complained that those cheated out of their reserves had yet to have their claims adjudicated, and most feared that they would never see justice if they left for Indian territory. As order broke down, Jesup was forced to make concessions in order to have any hope of moving the Creeks westward. The stationary camps cost the federal government up to $10,000 per day. Meanwhile, Jesup needed the headmen's help in recruiting hundreds of Creeks to fight the Seminoles in Florida. When Opothle Yoholo declared that his people would not be ready to begin the march on 20 August, Jesup quickly pushed back the start of March to 25 August before pushing it back five more days when the headmen announced that they could not raise a force to go to Florida unless given additional time. Jesup then appeased the headmen by paying out the Creeks' 1837 annuity in advance. The general also retained the services of Colonel John Archibald Campbell—a Montgomery lawyer, Alabama legislator, future U.S. Supreme Court justice (1853–61), and son of Treaty of Indian Springs negotiator Duncan Greene Campbell—and directed him to comb through the speculators' claims and defend the Creeks against all fraudulent lawsuits. Finally, Jesup, who relied heavily on the influence of Opothle Yoholo, promised to give the headman two thousand dollars if he could convince his people to begin their march when directed.[10]

The chiefs also ordered Jesup to address the frauds. As part of his agreeing to move west, Opothle Yoholo demanded the quick adjudication of his people's land claims. The half-sections in question were more than six hundred reserves that had been set aside by John B. Hogan during his investigations. Negotiations to sell this land in a body began sometime after 21 August and concluded near midnight on 28 August 1836 when Upper Creek headmen Opothle Yoholo, Mad Blue, Tuckabatchee Micco, and Little Doctor of Tuckabatchee; Tustunnuggee Chopco of Tallassee; and Jim Boy of Clewalla entered into an agreement with a company led by James C. Watson, who at the time was a contractor for the Alabama Emigrating Company. The aforementioned John A. Campbell represented the United States as a third party. Under the terms of the contract, the Creeks sold 656 half-sections (more than 200,000 acres of land) at about 36 cents an acre.[11]

Far from settling matters, the Watson contract (also called the "big contract") created new controversies. Two of the six headmen signed the indenture without their people's consent. As Tustunnuggee Chopco of Tallassee went to sign the document, the headman publicly acknowledged that he did not have the authorization of his people to sell their land. Jim Boy also signed without consulting his people, only to later claim that he did not know he was selling his people's reserves when he penned his mark. In a sign of just how ineffective the headmen had become, Jim Boy was forced to capitulate on the contract, probably after a stinging rebuke by his townspeople. The controversy should not have been unexpected, however. The Creeks received much less for their half-sections because of this agreement than they would have if the individuals had sold the land themselves. The reserves in Jim Boy's town, for instance, were valued at one thousand dollars each and under the terms of the deal, each reservee received only about $115. Whites also complained about the Watson contract. A number of speculators who had purchased Creek reserves embraced in the deal argued that they had acquired the land legally and if the agreement was approved by the president, they would lose their investment. Federal commissioners later questioned whether the headmen even had the right to sell an individual's reserve without his or her written permission. Despite the controversy, half of the seventy-five thousand dollars was paid to the Creek claimants at the Tallassee square ground the following day. The balance was scheduled to be paid in the Indian territory four months later. Despite protestations from federal investigators, President

Andrew Jackson approved the Watson contract on the condition that federal agents receive assents from the Creek reservees embraced in the agreement. The agreement only resolved a small fraction of the Creeks' outstanding land claims, and even as the Creeks began their march westward, Opothle Yoholo repeatedly demanded to see the names of all the Creeks who had sold, or not sold, their reserves.[12]

Three days after agreeing to the Watson contract, Opothle Yoholo and his people commenced their march to Memphis. They were led by those in charge of the sacred Tuckabatchee plates. According to Albert James Pickett, six warriors transported the plates, which were "enveloped nicely in buckskin" and strapped to the back of each person. The men, who marched in single-file formation one mile ahead of the train, were led by chief "Spoke-oak Micco." They could not converse with anyone else except each other. Special medicine, prepared explicitly for the journey, was consumed to ensure that their sacred emblems arrived safely. Newspapers, however, noted that nine Creeks comprised the advance delegation, with one person carrying the plates. Witnesses who saw these men as they traveled westward noted that they were as "solumn as the grave" and refused to talk to anyone while on the road. The first party included thirty-eight wagon teams and about seven hundred horses. Detachment five left its encampments at Cusseta and West Point on 5 September, carrying forty-five wagons "of every description" and about five hundred horses. A "large herd of cattle" was "driven ahead of the train," which supplied fresh beef to the party. Detachment two, with forty-two wagons and eleven hundred horses, commenced its journey by crossing the Coosa River at Wetumpka on 6 September. This was followed by detachment four with thirty-one wagon teams, which left Talladega on 8 September, and detachment three, which began moving on 17 September 1836, with at least thirty-eight wagons.[13]

The Creeks spent their last days on their native soil in myriad ways. On the eve of his departure, Menawa—who fought Andrew Jackson at Horseshoe Bend in 1814, carried out the execution of William McIntosh in 1825, and accompanied the delegation that signed the Treaty of Washington in 1826—left his relocation camp at Talladega and spent the night before he was to move in his town of Okfuskee. With regard to his final moments on his ancestral homeland, Menawa stated that "last evening I saw the sun set for the last time, and its light shine upon the tree tops, and the land, and the water, that I am never to look upon again." Other Creeks hastily tried to finish up their business in Alabama. One elderly Creek woman remained behind, if only briefly, to certify her land sale, as the advance of her detachment marched westward from Tallassee. Similarly, Allabudder of Arbicoochee sold his land on 17 September 1836, the same day that detachment three broke camp near Talladega.[14]

The parties were slowed by large crowds of whites who milled about the camps and stole the Creeks' meager property, took their money by selling them alcohol, or had them arrested for outstanding debt. Lieutenant Deas complained that "there are many speculators hanging about the Camp, and various demands made upon the Indians." As detachment five moved through Chambers County, whites preyed on the Creeks "without mercy" and took their horses, cattle, "and even clothing." Tuskenehaw complained that many Creeks had their slaves taken from them under "forged & pretended bills of sale." While attempting to break camp near Tallassee, Lieutenant Bateman was "exceedingly annoyed by Sheriffs and Constables, who detained the Chiefs on Writs for debt." A few days later, on 3 September, as Opothle Yoholo's party passed through Wetumpka, local whites confiscated the Creeks' horses, blankets, saddles, and other property. One Creek man had six horses taken. Lieutenant Screven, overseeing detachment two, complained in his journal that "it is painful to reflect that, at the very moment of leaving their old homes peaceably in search of new ones, the Indians should have had their camps beset by a gang [of] swindlers, horse thieves and whiskey-traders, practising every species of fraud that is calculated to disgrace the human character." He even noted that the whites "anticipated" the route of the party "and an abundant supply of whiskey furnished on the road-side."[15]

Whites only exacerbated the extreme poverty of many of the Creeks. Lieutenant Sprague, the military agent overseeing detachment five, observed that the Cowetas and Cussetas of his party "were in a deplorable condition when they left their homes" and noted that "they were poor, wretchedly, and depravedly, poor, many of them without a garment to cover their nakedness. To this there was some exceptions, but this was the condition of a larger portion of them."[16]

The detachments fluctuated in size as they commenced their journey, with some Creeks belatedly joining the parties on the march. Detachment four, which left its encampment four miles north of Talladega with 1,169 Creeks, swelled to more than 2,300 people after they were joined by the refugees from the Cherokee country who were under guard at Gunter's Landing. Detachment five also grew as Creeks who had secreted themselves in the Chowokolo swamp during the Second Creek War inquired about joining the party. They were fearful of being placed in chains, and Sprague assured them that if they remained peaceful, they would be "received as friends and treated as other indians." On the ninth night of the march, perhaps as many as 350 Creeks, including women and children, joined the party. As these Creeks traveled with the detachment, they "kept themselves aloof lest they might be treated as hostiles." Tensions soon arose, however, and Sprague noted that "there has been at times great dissatisfaction in the camp originating I think with a party of hostile Indians who joined me from a swamp." Conversely, small parties of Creeks remained behind as their assigned detachments moved on without them. Benjamin Marshall, who was a defendant in a lawsuit over his late brother's estate, stayed in Alabama as the fifth detachment moved on without him. Marshall subsequently negotiated a compensation package from the Alabama Emigrating Company, and the seventy-three members of his party moved west, via Pontotoc, by themselves. Sickness was one of the reasons James Island and his people remained behind as detachment five left Chambers County in September 1836. The Coweta headman and 135 others did not rejoin the main party until reaching Memphis. Other individuals remained behind for myriad reasons. Emathla Harjo, a fifty-year-old member of Hickory Ground, did not travel in the relocation detachments because, as an associate described it, he was "a man who had crazy spells, and did not like to mix in crowds, and, therefore, would not come in the 'big Emigration.' "[17]

The typical day on the forced march west was six to eight hours of travel by foot, covering about ten to thirteen miles per day, although sometimes the parties traveled much farther in search of a suitable encampment. The agents generally broke camp at between five o'clock and nine o'clock in the morning, although there were delays in some cases. It took some time to get the entire party moving each morning. For instance, Lieutenant Deas, the military agent overseeing detachment three, noted in his journal that "in mooving a Party of the present size; a space of time of more than an hour generally elapses, between the starting of the first of the Indians & the Baggage Wagons, and the time at which the whole body has left the last nights encampment & is fairly on the road." The parties usually stopped anywhere between noon and four o'clock in the afternoon, before establishing camp for the night. Deas, who kept some of the most detailed accounts of the Creeks' journey, wrote that "in stopping also the interval between the arrival of the first of the Indians & their wagons, at the new place of Encampment, and the time at which the whole party comes up, is generally from one to two hours & sometimes more than that space of time." Life in these nighttime encampments was a flurry of activity. Deas paid "servants" to assist in the "menial offices of cooking, grooming their horses, and the like, all incidental to the camp life." These laborers also aided in erecting the large tents, preparing food, chopping firewood, and building fires. Observers traveled through the encampment of detachment four while at Huntsville and noted that the Creeks were divided into clans or families. Witnesses reported seeing the Creek women making fires and cooking food while the men were "loitering about or stretched upon a blanket" and "scores of playful children scattered around."[18]

Creek headmen exerted a great deal of influence over the manner in which they traveled and could force a change of plans or bring entire detachments to a halt. The first stand occurred just two days into the march, when the headmen of detachment two discovered that their route would not follow the same path as Opothle Yoholo's. Encamped eighteen miles west of Wetumpka, where the road forked to Tuscaloosa, the chiefs "possitively Refused to proceede" until a change was made. Although Lieutenant Screven and the contractors used "Every argument" to dissuade the Creeks from taking the Tuscaloosa road—warning that there would be provision shortages—the Creeks would not give in. Noting that they "were directed to follow in the foot-steps

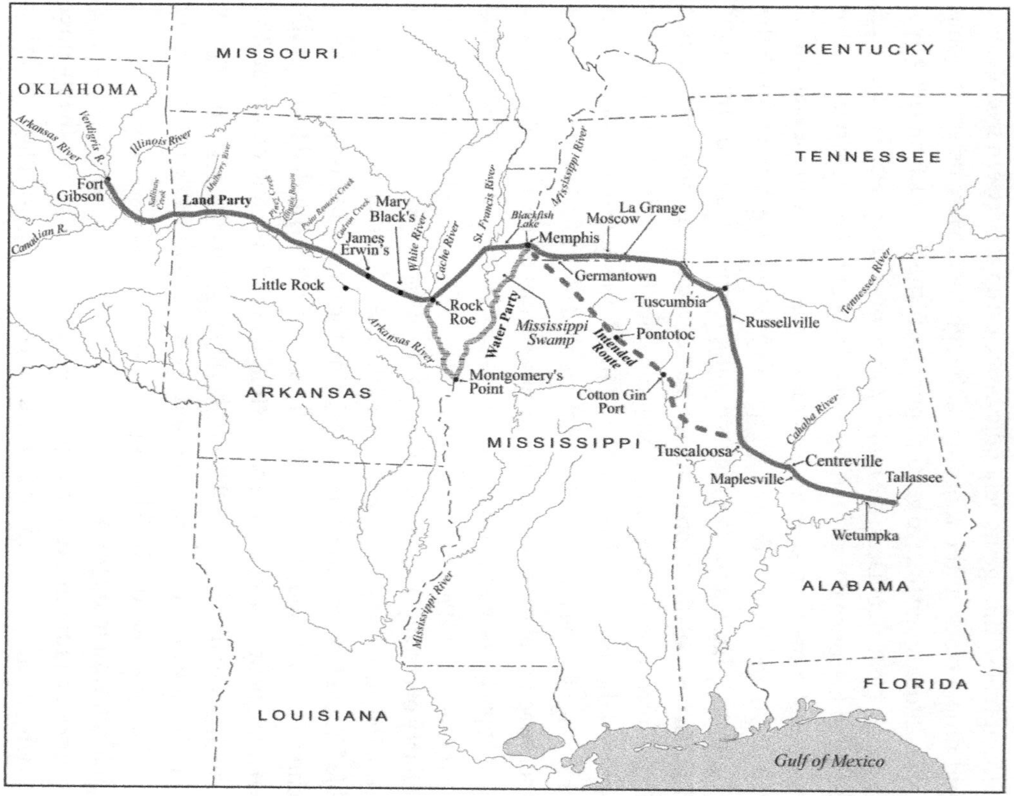

FIG. 21. Route of detachment one, August–December 1836. Place names correspond to stopping points or locations noted in the documentation. Route lines and locations are approximations. Cartography by Sarah Mattics.

of Opoth-lo-yoholo," the headmen declared that "rather than disobey this command we are willing to starve the five days." Screven finally acquiesced and the contractors were left scurrying to find food along the adjusted route. Meanwhile, Bateman had decided against passing through Cotton Gin Port because of reports of bad roads and scarce provisions and chose to go through Moulton before changing his mind again and both detachments passed through Russellville, Alabama (three days apart), without incident. The cost to the company was enormous and the contractors spent years after the relocations trying to recoup the losses. Screven, however, knew he had little choice. The agent conceded that if he had forced the Creeks to take the road to Elyton, he had the "firm conviction that it would have been disobeyed and thus have what little influence which I might possess over these people prostrated at the commencement of a long and tedious journey."[19]

In reality, the contractors and military agents had very little influence over the Creek people. While encamped in Morgan County, Alabama, the Cusseta headman Tuckabatchee Harjo and other principal chiefs met with the detachment five contactors and demanded a day of rest. The party had just completed a difficult seventeen-mile march due to the scarcity of water. To make his point, Tuckabatchee Harjo refused to accept the rations issued to him and "advised his people not to take them" either. Although Lieutenant Sprague tried to convince the Creeks to keep walking until they found a more suitable location with more provisions, the Cusseta headman "evinced much anger and left the tent saying the 'word is out.'" The next day, Tuckabatchee Harjo begrudgingly consented to go on, and the party moved fourteen miles over bad roads and through "deep swamps." The following morning, Tuckabatchee Harjo again reiterated his demands and the Cussetas "commenced throwing out their baggage from the Waggons." In spite of "all my efforts to prevent it," Sprague wrote in his journal, the headman and about two hundred of his followers remained behind as the party broke camp and continued toward Memphis without them. They rejoined the detachment two days later. With only limited power over his charges, Sprague pleaded with the Creeks that "Tuck-e-batch-e-Hadjo was not the person for them to listen to about stopping."[20]

Military agents often avoided conflict, however, by simply budgeting days of rest into the itinerary. Although the Creeks were accustomed to traveling dozens of miles per day while on the hunt or in times of war, they were in no hurry to get to Indian territory. As a result, the headmen insisted on periodic respites so they could bathe, wash clothing, relax, and perhaps most important, stall. The day after Tuckabatchee Harjo's stand, Sprague sent a communiqué ordering the contractors to halt the party on 25 September in order to allow the Creeks to rest and have "an opportunity to wash." Detachment one spent a day in camp two miles west of Tuscaloosa in order to give the Creeks a chance to relax, clean their clothes, and purify themselves in the Black Warrior River. The rest was needed, as Opothle Yoholo's party had already suffered five deaths by the time they reached the state's capital. The day off also gave the agents time to repair wagons and shoe horses. Joshua H. Foster, a student at the University of Alabama, visited the camp and observed the Creeks naked and "'paddling like ducks'" in the water. In fact, Tuscaloosans crowded the river's edge to gawk at the Creek women washing their children. These stops were expensive and the Alabama Emigrating Company was forced to provide rations to the Creeks without making any progress on the journey. On 10 October, as the party camped three miles west of Purdy, Tennessee, Deas stopped his detachment for a day "to rest, in conformity with the wishes of the people."[21]

Agents and contractors were also helpless to prevent the Creeks from consuming alcohol on the journey west. Lieutenant Screven estimated that the sale of whiskey on the roadside accounted for "more than one half" of all the problems detachment two encountered along the route. Lieutenant Deas, overseeing detachment three, argued that alcohol was "the cause of more disturbances and difficulties in the camp, than all others put together." Indeed, Deas complained that "there are almost always persons at every small town or Settlement who are base enough to persist in selling [liquor] to [the Creeks] even after the evil consequences have been fully explained." It was not just white residents and traders selling alcohol to the Creeks, however. As the first party passed through Mississippi, Lieutenant Bateman reported that the "Indians generally drunk. Got their Liquor from the Chickasaw Indians." Alcohol consumption slowed the detachments and threatened the lives of the Creeks as they marched west. Within days of setting out from Tallassee, Spony Fixico, a member of Opothle Yoholo's party, was shot by his brother during a drinking binge. He "died in a few hours." Similarly, as detachment three approached Somerville, Alabama, Nocose Yoholo of Hillabee, who was about six miles behind the rear of his party, was shot in the side with a pistol after a drunken disagreement with a white man. When Deas returned to investigate, he found the man "still very" intoxicated, but "not dangerously wounded." More than two weeks later, near Bolivar, Tennessee, a number of Creeks became inebriated and "some fighting took place." No one was killed, although "several were wounded." Lieutenant Sprague complained that intoxicated Creeks would come "singing into camp late at night, threatening the lives of all who came within their reach."[22]

The headmen's influence did not carry as much weight with indifferent contractors, however. No detachment had a worse assortment of company employees than detachment five. By the time the party had reached Memphis, Lieutenant Sprague had complained that "great inconvenience was experienced upon this entire route for the want of Depots of provisions." Moreover, there was "great dissatisfaction in camp arising from the fatigue of the party and the disregard paid to their comfort." The problem was compounded by stretches of bad roads and the lack of potable water, which often required the party to march several miles more per day in search of a clean spring or creek. This led to constant friction between the military agent and Alabama Emigrating Company employees Felix G. Gibson and Charles Abercrombie. On 5 October Sprague ordered the party to halt, but the contractors "objected and seemed determined to drive the Indians" onward. Sprague complained that on many days, "the waggons and agents are always ahead and no one remains to provide" for the Creeks who fell behind. One day, Sprague discovered that the teamsters had thrown the Creeks' possessions out of their wagon and drove off four miles ahead of the main party. Earlier, a wagon driver refused Sprague's command to pick up a "lame man" who was "seated by the side of the road." Instead, the driver "declined doing it and drove off." Sprague also accused the contractors

FIG. 22. Route of detachment two, September–December 1836. Place names correspond to stopping points or locations noted in the documentation. Route lines and locations are approximations. Cartography by Sarah Mattics.

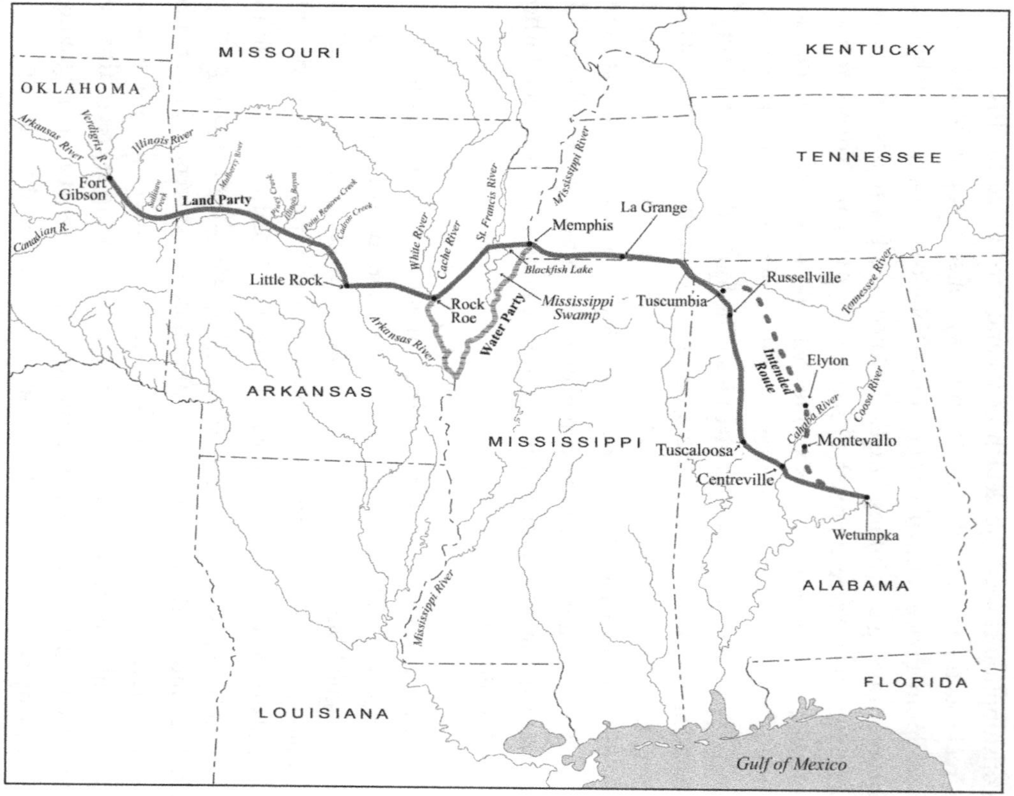

of not providing enough transportation. The agent discovered "one blind man and one in the most perfect state of decrepitude" who were forced to walk because there was no room in the wagons. Many infirm Creeks were still forced to walk and came "into camp late at night, loosing their rations, and totally unfit to proceed the following day." In fact, the morning after a particularly difficult march, Sprague counted approximately 190 Creeks "who from the distance and fatigue the day before were unable to get up, among these were many sick, feeble and the poorer class of Indians." When Sprague ordered the company to limit the amount of travel to twelve miles per day or less, one contractor glibly retorted that "he should not obey it." Sprague was forced to purchase wagons "for the purpose of bring[ing] up the lame and blind and sick which had been left through the negligence of the Agents," but the contractors refused to pay for them. The problem reached a critical mass when four Creeks attacked the party's interpreter "with the determination to kill him," claiming that he "was engaged with the white men in driving them on like dogs." By the time the party had approached Memphis, Sprague had had enough: he refused to allow the Creeks to cross the Mississippi River under the charge of Gibson and Abercrombie. Abercrombie quit under pressure while near Memphis and Gibson remained, although Sprague noted in his journal that "here, I think, Mr. Gibson for the first time read the contract" agreed to by the owners of the Alabama Emigrating Company, which established guidelines for caring for the Creeks.[23]

A combination of bad roads, harsh weather, and the lack of potable water plagued the detachments as they moved west. The roads through Alabama, Mississippi, and Tennessee alternated between "very good" and "horridly bad." Lieutenant Deas complained that a stretch of road along the south side of the Tennessee River was "dusty" and "consequently extremely unpleasant to travel" over. As detachment one passed through the Chickasaw country, Bateman reported that "the Indians and the ponies [are] lame. Their feet being worn out traveling over The Gravel roads." The following day Bateman again noted, "Roads bad. Indians' feet sore. Ponies giving out. Chiefs cross." Indeed, Tuckabatchee headmen later recalled that "the feet of our old people bled. Our young children cried, and our horses died by the way." A lack of potable water (despite periods of torrential rainfall) forced the Creeks to trek miles farther along these same bad roads in search of a clean spring. After a long ten hours of walking over "very hilly and rough" roads in the Chickasaw country, the Creeks of detachment five encamped for the evening after a seventeen-mile march. Lieutenant Sprague lamented that the distance that day "was accomplished with great difficulty and with much fatigue to the Indians; but the scarcity of water compelled the party to go much farther than was proper for the comfort and convenience of the Indians." Some Creeks did not arrive in camp until nine o'clock that night—about four hours after the main party had stopped for the evening. Some days later, a portion of the detachment did not arrive in camp until the following morning.[24]

Even before leaving the limits of Alabama, a large number of Creeks had already suffered from the effects of sickness, fatigue, and dehydration. On Wednesday, 21 September, as Opothle Yoholo's party traveled toward Russellville, Bateman wrote in his journal: "day hot. Thermometer 96°." Two weeks later, after passing through Moscow, Tennessee, Bateman observed the "number of deaths increasing. Old men & women & children dropping off." Indeed, the headmen reported that there was "much sickness among our people" on the way to Memphis, and a list of Creeks who died shows that many were children. For instance, Oche Yoholo's son, described as "a little boy," died along the road, as did a number of the other Creeks' sons and daughters. Opothle Yoholo and other headmen noted below the list that "some have died absent from their friends and we are sorry. Their friends will be sorry when they hear it, but we must all die some time, we must listen to all talks, some times they bring good news and some times bad news." Receipts show the purchase of one thousand feet of board for the construction of eleven coffins. A receipt was also issued for the construction of a coffin and "Furnishing Grave" for the Cusseta chief Okfuskee Yoholo, who died on 19 October while in Memphis. The bad roads, hot weather, long marches, sickness, and death took their toll on just about everyone. The fifth detachment was "strewn for twelve or fifteen miles" along the road near Memphis. In many cases, the journey strained the agents as much as the Creeks. One month after setting out, as his detachment passed

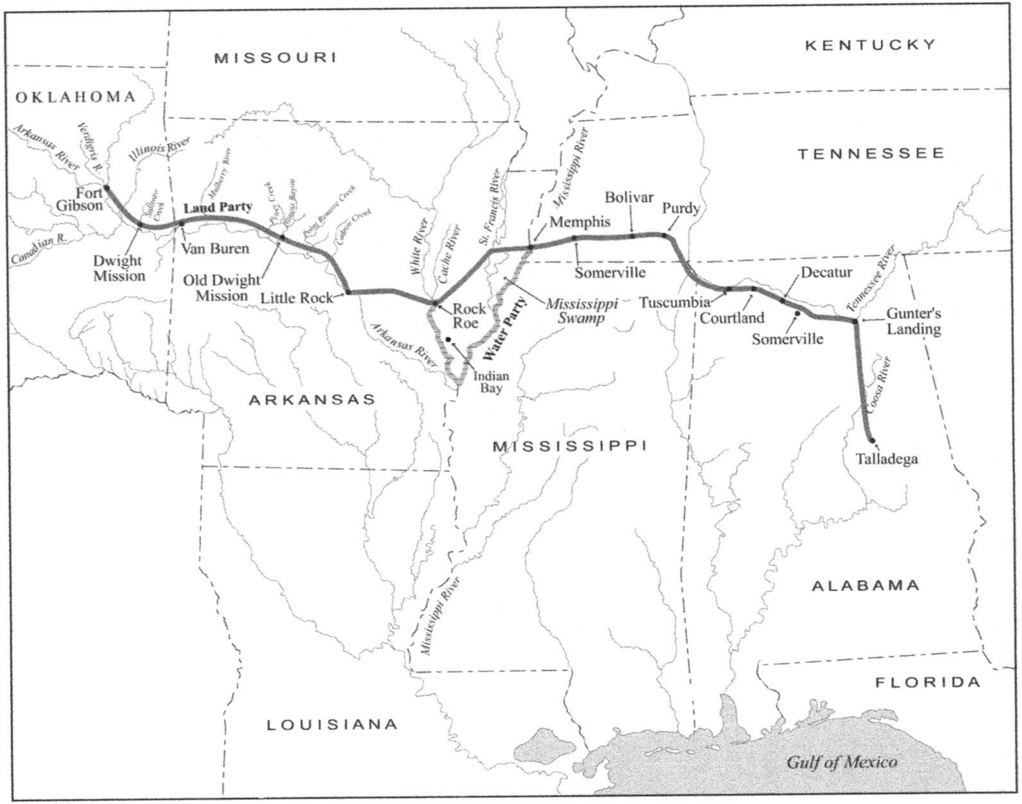

FIG. 23. Route of detachment three, September 1836–January 1837. Place names correspond to stopping points or locations noted in the documentation. Route lines and locations are approximations. Cartography by Sarah Mattics.

through Hardeman County, Tennessee, a frustrated Bateman wrote in his journal: "The Indians very discontented. Every thing appears to go wrong. I am disgusted with Indian Emigration."[25]

The scarcity of water and provisions was compounded when the once-staggered detachments began catching up to the rear of the party ahead of them. This occurred first at the end of September in the Chickasaw country, when detachment five ran up against the rear of detachment two, which was only a few days behind detachment one. Sprague observed: "We found the party of Indians /3000/ in charge of Lt. Scriven camped here which makes our situation still more unpleasant and O, poth-le-olo's party having camped here a few days previous has been the means of draining the country of its resources." Sprague and Screven met that evening and made arrangements to separate the parties. The fifth detachment subsequently took the right fork through the towns of Purdy, Bolivar, Somerville, and Raleigh in Tennessee, while detachment two—still obligated to follow in the line of Opothle Yoholo—followed the southern road through La Grange, Tennessee. The modified route forced the Creeks of detachment five to walk twenty additional miles and placed the party just in front of detachment four. While near Bolivar, the fourth party moved close enough to the rear of detachment five that Sprague felt compelled to send a communiqué eastward, ordering the party not to pass them on the road.[26]

Despite trying to separate the detachments, all the parties bottlenecked at the Mississippi River. The process was slowed due to the size of the ferry and because only smaller parties could cross the river at a time. Progress was further delayed because of the terrible condition of the roads through the Mississippi Swamp, and the contractors were forced to use steamers to take the Creeks around the inundated land to Rock Roe. The steamer *Lady Byron* was used as a ferry (with a small flatboat attached to its side) to transport the horses and wagons across the river. Once on the west bank, the Creeks took the *Lady Byron*, *Farmer*, and *John Nelson* around the Mississippi Swamp—which was nearly impassable in the fall of 1836. Subsequently, by early October all five detachments—approximately thirteen thousand Creeks—were lined up in a train that extended for more than one hundred miles. For instance, on 9 October 1836, detachment one was encamped two miles east of Memphis; detachment five was near Raleigh, Tennessee, seven miles from Memphis; detachment four was a few miles behind the fifth party near Raleigh; detachment two was encamped on the banks of the Wolf River, sixteen miles east of Memphis; and detachment three was encamped three miles west of Purdy, Tennessee, approximately one hundred miles east of Memphis.[27]

While waiting to cross the river the Creeks used their downtime to attend to important affairs. The principal headmen of Tuckabatchee, Kialigee, Talladega, and other towns held a general council to discuss "how they have been treated on the road and to consult on other matters." A Rabbit Town woman sold her half-section to Alabama Emigrating Company employee Thomas Likens while waiting to cross the Mississippi River in October 1836. Conversely, Marhoille, a Tallasseehatchee woman, used her downtime while in camp to confront another employee of the company who had purchased the woman's land in Alabama for $3,500 but had taken back $2,100 of it, claiming that he had paid too much for the reserve.[28]

Detachment one finished crossing the Mississippi River on 13 October 1836. They were followed by detachments two, five, and four. The last to cross, number three, did not leave Memphis until 5 November. After their ferriage, detachment one was divided into two groups. Approximately five hundred Creeks accompanied the horses through the Mississippi Swamp via St. Francisville, Arkansas, while the balance boarded the steamboat *Farmer* for their trip to Rock Roe. Because the wagons could not make it through the swamp, they did not accompany the horses and instead were dismantled (by separating the running gear from the body) and placed on board the steamer and flatboats. The party reached the mouth of the Cache River after dark on 17 October. Overflowed banks prevented the boat from landing, so the *Farmer* dropped down eight miles to Rock Roe, where the party pitched its tents on the bluffs. As soon as detachment one left Memphis, detachment two took up the old position of Opothle Yoholo's party. Like the first party, the second crossed the Mississippi River (completing the passage on 21 October), then with thirteen hundred Creeks, embarked on the steamboat with "two well covered substantial Flat boats in tow" and traveled to Rock Roe. The balance marched through the swamps. This process was repeated until all five parties left Memphis. Four of the detachments used steamboats to transport them around the swamp, while approximately fifteen hundred Creeks from detachment five avoided the congestion at Rock Roe by taking the *John Nelson* all the way to Little Rock. Like the other detachments, approximately five to six hundred Creeks from this party accompanied the horses through the inundated lands in eastern Arkansas.[29]

Although less arduous than traveling by foot through the swamps, steamboat travel was often unpleasant for the Creeks. The boats were cramped, dirty, and foul-smelling. The parties were also at the mercy of the weather and the unpredictable stages of the rivers. While navigating the Mississippi River, the Cowetas and Cussetas on board the *John Nelson* were delayed a few hours in a dense fog bank. A portion of the Creeks of detachment three who were traveling on board the *Lady Byron* were detained after the boat ran aground sometime after leaving Memphis. And when the weather did improve, the Creeks found that steamboat travel could be exhausting and unpredictable. For instance, concerned with the rising water on the Arkansas River the day before, Sprague discovered the waters suddenly dropping in the middle of the night. With "no time to be lost," the Creeks were awakened and forced to break camp at two-thirty in the morning, and within an hour, they were again ascending the Arkansas. The Creeks were also not guaranteed an uninterrupted passage to their destination. Rising waters on the Arkansas River created a strong current that slowed the *John Nelson* to one and a half miles per hour, which forced the agents of detachment five to jettison the two large flatboats towed by the steamer. Half the Creeks on board the flats were forced to wait along the riverbank near Arkansas Post until they could be transported to Little Rock, while the other half of the party had to squeeze on board the *John Nelson*. Consequently, their steamboat, which was "very comfortable nor much crowded" at the beginning of their journey soon became "very much crowded." Moreover, the congestion on the boats created sanitation problems. As the *John Nelson* moved closer to Little Rock, the agent overseeing the detachment noted that "the Boat for the last three days [was] very dirty and exceeding[ly] offensive." It is therefore not surprising that after camping onshore one night, the Creeks boarded the boat the next morning "with great reluctance." There was also an element of danger on the vessels. While riding the *Lady Byron*, a Creek man "was killed by falling into the Fly-wheel of the Engine, whilst in a state of intoxication."[30]

Many Creeks had "a strong prejudice against Steam Boats" and refused to go by water. The fear of sickness was one objection, but a "greater dread was being thrown overboard when dead" and denied a proper Creek burial. An incident with Opothle Yoholo in which he "actually refused to move and willfully detained the party for two days longer, without excuse or reason" just as detachment one was preparing to cross the Mississippi River may have been his protest against river travel. The Tuckabatchee headman eventually relented and boarded the boat, but others, like Menawa and Fish Pond chief Tuscoona Harjo, refused. Aware of his limited power to coerce the headmen, Lieutenant Deas noted in his journal that "it has been decided that the Indians have the Right to go the whole journey by land, and the Chiefs . . . insisted upon doing so." Hundreds of Creeks followed their headmen into the swamps.[31]

In the fall of 1836 the Mississippi Swamp was nearly impassable. The roads were good for the first twenty miles from Memphis, but once entering the swamp, mud and water made it "impossible to pass through with loaded waggons." The conditions only got worse as one continued westward and within five more miles travel was "almost impassible on horse back." The section of road between Memphis and the White River was described "as bad as possible," while near the mouth of the Cache River it was "one continued bog." In fact, conditions were worse the closer one was to the St. Francis, where "in addition to the mud, the water was nearly up to a Horse's back." Because the soil was composed of red clay, there were long stretches where the Creeks had to wade through standing water. The roads were designed to drain water and were constructed by digging "two parallel Ditches, and throwing up and forming the Earth between them." When the trenches on either side of the road were working, the route was generally good. However, in the fall of 1836 there was not "more than a mile or two" of dry road. The route through the swamp also contained occasional potholes, which were large enough

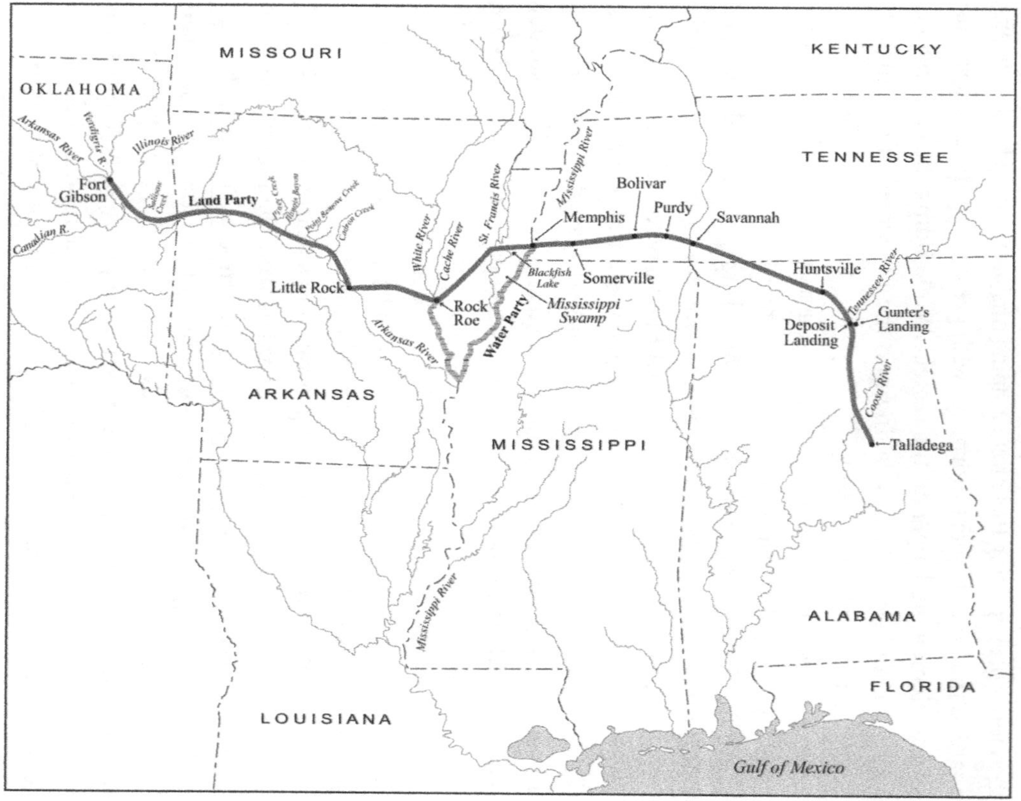

FIG. 24. Route of detachment four, September–December 1836. Place names correspond to stopping points or locations noted in the documentation. Detachment four's exact route after leaving Memphis is unclear. Route lines and locations are approximations. Cartography by Sarah Mattics.

that "it is with some difficulty that a horse can pass." Indeed, the horses suffered the most during this journey. Lieutenant Deas, who traveled from Rock Roe to the St. Francis River to investigate the condition of his land party, discovered "between 3 & 4 hundred Indians encamped at intervals of a few miles, along the whole road, many of them belonging to *other Parties* than that under my charge." In addition, Deas found "the whole road from Rock Row full of dead Horses and Indian Ponies."[32]

The Creeks' decision to walk through the swamp was about more than opposition to water travel; it was about freedom from the presence of whites. Only a handful of employees accompanied the Creeks by land through the swamp, and some of those who did abandoned the party near the St. Francis River out of neglect. Left to themselves, many of the Creeks deliberately stalled their movements. Although most of the four hundred Creeks discovered by Lieutenant Deas encamped along the road were there due to sickness or because of the negligence of the contractors in failing to secure transportation or provisions, others like Narticker Tustunnuggee (Tuckabatchee Harjo's brother) and one hundred of his people from detachment five remained in the Mississippi Swamp into the third week of November and "were determined to take their own time in coming." Even as the agents and contractors waited on the other side of the swamp, the land party refused to rendezvous "in spite of any remonstrance" and "evinced the most hostile feelings and cautioned the white-men to keep away from them." The Creeks hunted and sent word that "when they had got bear skins enough to cover them they would come on." Aware of his limited authority, Lieutenant Sprague complained that "neither the Agents or myself had any means by which we could force them into proper measures." Sprague, however, was fully aware of the symbolic nature these swamps had for the Creeks. Because of the swamp's isolation from people, "here, they felt independent" and "were almost out of the reach of the white-men."[33]

While the fifth party was ascending the Arkansas to Little Rock on the *John Nelson*, the four other detachments were encamped (on staggered days) in the neighborhood of Rock Roe. While in camp, sickness, increasingly cold weather, and "torrents" of rainfall plagued the Creeks. Bateman observed that their location at Rock Roe was "very disagreeable" and noted that although the Creeks were relatively healthy, there were two cases of sickness that "smack of Cholera." Moreover, there were very few provisions provided by the contractors in the neighborhood of Rock Roe, which forced Deas to send the *Lady Byron* down to Indian Bay to procure four thousand pounds of fresh beef and between five and six hundred bushels of corn. On 1 November, two weeks after arriving at Rock Roe, detachment one broke camp and traveled by land over the "most horrid" road, where thirty wagons were soon "bogged down" within two miles of setting out. The following day, after a brutal day of traveling along a route that Bateman called "indescribably bad," the party had to "sleep on the Prairie without any comforts." Detachment two broke camp at Rock Roe bayou almost a week later, and the Creeks "suffered exceedingly from cold" during their twelve-day march to the Arkansas River opposite Little Rock. Detachment three, which left its encampment sometime around 20 November, encountered similarly bad roads, where "the wagons cut through in many places nearly up to the hubs of the Wheels."[34]

As the detachments crossed Arkansas, the Creeks became increasingly fatigued while others grew more defiant, and the military agents were reduced to pleading with their charges for compliance. Lieutenant Bateman complained that while all the agents were on horseback by four o'clock in the morning on 2 November, it was "impossible to get the Indians to stir." The following day, after riding forty-seven miles on horseback trying to bring up the stragglers who were scattered fifteen miles along the road, Bateman bemoaned that he was in "despair of getting to Arkansas." Lieutenant Sprague continued to have problems convincing Tuckabatchee Harjo to obey orders after the *John Nelson* arrived in Little Rock on 3 November. While the steamer went back to collect those who were waiting along the riverbank after being forced to ditch the flatboat near Arkansas Post, Sprague tried to convince the Cusseta headman to begin marching westward with his people. "This he positively declined doing"; Sprague was annoyed to report that "he wanted nothing from the white-man and should rest." Tuckabatchee Harjo and about one hundred Creeks stayed behind, while the remainder of the land party commenced moving west. When the steamboat returned from Arkansas Post (with Tuckabatchee Harjo on board, having been picked up along the way) and rendezvoused with the land party on 14 October at Dardanelle, the headman disembarked the vessel and refused to reboard, citing the large numbers of his family and followers who remained behind. Most of the Creeks subsequently refused to board and the agents only succeeded in convincing three hundred to go. The following day, however, the same Creeks who had joined the *John Nelson* the day before "commenced bringing off their baggage" and refused to continue on the steamer because of a rumor, perhaps deliberately spread by the headmen, that "they were to be taken into a distant country where they were to be placed under soldiers and their men placed in irons." After much pleading, 395 Creeks, primarily the aged, feeble, and sick, reboarded the steamboat and continued toward Fort Gibson. They were the first party to arrive at the garrison on 20 November 1836. Meanwhile, Tuckabatchee Harjo persisted in taking his own time. While near Point Remove Creek the headman declared that he was west of the Mississippi and it was not in the power of any one to compel him or his people to go on. Only when threatened by an Arkansas militia did the Creeks finally break camp.[35]

Similarly, Lieutenant Deas spent the last leg of the journey pleading with defiant headmen Tuscoona Harjo and Menawa, as well as their followers, to quicken their pace. Noting the problem of leaving without the chiefs, Deas wrote that "if we were to attempt to proceed with the main Party before those in the rear arrived the consequence would be that the whole Route would be lined with stragglers. Two of the most important Chiefs are behind and many of their people are now in camp and if the Party was to proceed the latter would for the slightest cause fall to the rear and wait upon the road for the arrival of their head-men." Unable to wait any longer because of dwindling provisions, Deas sent the main party on while he traveled back toward the White River to plead with the Fish Pond and Okfuskee chiefs to join the others. Although some of the delay was due to the negligence of the contractors—several hundred Creeks were stranded on the eastern bank of the White River with no means of crossing—many of the Creeks were in no hurry to get to Indian territory and subsequently stalled their movements. After ferrying the last of the Creeks over the White River, Deas complained that "two days' delay was caused by the Indians refusing to travel in consequence of the severity of the weather." After walking six miles on 19 December, the stragglers again refused to go on. "I wished them to go 8 miles further," Deas wrote, "in order to procure provisions and to be able to overtake the main Party tomorrow. They however persisted in refusing to go any further to-day and I was therefore prevented from going on to overtake the main Party which I intended to do." On 21 and 22 December, with the weather "very fine for travelling," the headmen and four hundred of their followers, again "refused to proceed." According to Deas, Menawa was too intoxicated to travel, while Tuscoona Harjo "evinced a Stubborn obstinate disposition and every thing that could be said to persuade him to travel was in vain." Unwilling to wait any longer, Deas broke camp and most of the party continued on. The Fish Pond chief, who had "a considerable sum of money & good Poneys" demanded to walk the rest of the way "at his leasure." He was accompanied by approximately one hundred of his followers.[36]

The last leg of the journey—from the neighborhood of Little Rock to Fort Gibson—was the most difficult, as the weather turned increasingly cold. As Opothle Yoholo's party traveled through the western Cherokee country, Bateman cryptically wrote in his journal: "Roads bad. Nights cold. Indians suffer." Temperatures dropped well below freezing and as the torrents of rain turned into heavy snowfall, Bateman complained that "the ground is covered with snow and ice, The Thermometer stands at zero. The winter has set in with great severity. The Indians must suffer much." In fact, some estimated that the Creeks marched through up to eight inches of snow during the last leg of their journey. But the Creeks' condition was made worse because they traveled overland in their summer clothing. They had left Alabama in the heat and humidity of August and September, but arrived in the Indian territory in the middle of winter. Much of their heavier clothing, unnecessary at the beginning of their journey, was packed deep in the baggage wagons or, in some cases, on board steamboats. For instance, prior to leaving Alabama, the contractors were able to convince Opothle Yoholo and his people to pack all items deemed "not necessary on the march" into

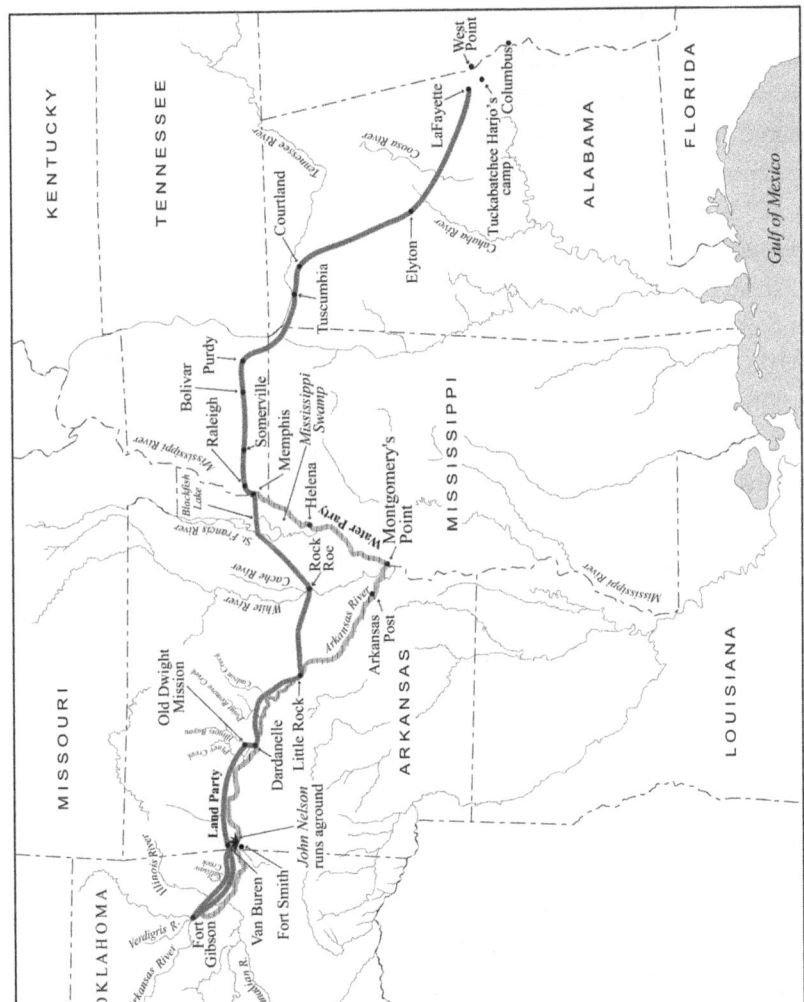

FIG. 25. Route of detachment five, September–November–December 1836. Place names correspond to stopping points or locations noted in the documentation. Route lines and locations are approximations. Cartography by Sarah Mattics.

steamboats, which would then travel ahead of the party to wait for their arrival at Fort Gibson. Most of these items were farming utensils such as plows and chains, bedding, and cookware such as pots. But agents noted that the baggage also included the Creeks' "blankets, clothing and other articles necessary for protection from the severity of the season." Subsequently, upwards of forty-three tons of Creek property was placed in a storehouse at Wetumpka prior to being shipped west. But, instead of reaching Fort Gibson in anticipation of the Creeks' arrival at the garrison, the contractors lost track of the articles at Mobile Point, Alabama, only to be rediscovered rotting on the Gulf of Mexico in 1837.[37]

The lightly clad Creeks from the other detachments suffered similarly. After the approximately four hundred Creeks departed for Fort Gibson on the *John Nelson*, the land party of detachment five recommenced their march westward. With the weather growing colder, Lieutenant Sprague observed that "the sufferings of the Indians at this period were intense. With nothing more than a cotton garment thrown over them, their feet bare, they were compelled to encounter cold sleeting storms and to travel over hard frozen ground." Observing the anguish of the travelers, Sprague sadly remembered the Creeks making "frequent appeals ... to clothe their nakedness and to protect their lacerated feet." Lieutenant Deas complained that many of the Creeks of his party were "without shoes & badly clothed," which made travel difficult "without great suffering." Indeed, oral narratives endured into the 1930s that described the Creeks leaving bloody footprints in the snow. On 25 December 1836 a witness to the arrival of the Creeks in the Indian territory penned a letter that was published in the *Arkansas State Gazette*, noting that

> thousands of [Creeks] are entirely destitute of shoes or covering of any kind for the feet; many of them are almost naked; and but few of them have any thing more on their persons than a light dress, calculated only for the summer, or for a very warm climate; and the weather being warm when they left Alabama, many of them left their heavier articles of clothing, expecting them to be brought on in steam-boats; which has as yet been only partially done. In this destitute condition, they are wading the cold mud, or are hurried on

over the frozen road, as the case may be. Many of them have in this way had their feet frost-bitten; and being unable to travel, fall in the rear of the main party, and in this way are left on the road to await the ability or convenience of the contractors to assist them.

Just as bad, many who died were denied a proper burial. The Creeks were greatly concerned about the handling of their bodies after death, and having one's corpse dissected or torn apart by animals was considered extremely disgraceful. And yet, the same letter observed that "many of them, not being able to endure this unexampled state of human suffering, die, and it is said are thrown by the side of the road, and are covered only with brush, &c., where they remain, until devoured by the wolves." Captain John Stuart of the Seventh Infantry wrote from Fort Coffee and reported that "the condition of the Creeks yet on the road to Fort Gibson, is most terrible. It is said that they are Strewed along the road for a great distance . . . many of them are almost naked, and are without shoes—The Snow for five days, has been from 4 to 8 Inches deep—and during the first and second days of the Storm, women and children were seen bending their way Onward, with most Piteous and heart rending Cries, from Cold."[38]

The approximately four hundred Creeks who arrived on 20 November aboard the *John Nelson* notwithstanding, all five detachments reached Fort Gibson between December 1836 and January 1837. Opothle Yoholo's party arrived first, followed by detachment five, detachment four, and detachment two. Detachment three arrived last, on 23 January 1837. The Creeks were turned over to the federal government and placed on provisions. The Alabama Emigrating Company tallied up the arrivals, the deaths, and the prorated cost of transporting Creeks who died along the way. In their account submitted to the government, the contractors reported that 2,318 Creeks and their slaves from detachment one arrived at Fort Gibson with 78 dying along the way; 3,095 people from detachment two with 37 deaths and 18 births during the journey; 2,818 people from detachment three with 12 deaths; 2,330 people from detachment four with 36 deaths; and 2,087 Creeks and their slaves from detachment five with 25 deaths.[39]

The physical and emotional effects of relocation were seen years after the Creeks and other southeastern Indians were forced west. In 1841 Friedrich Gerstäcker, a German adventurer, visited Arkansas and reported seeing that

> numerous square holes cut in the fallen trees showed where the squaws had pounded their maize to make bread. More melancholy traces were visible in the bones of human beings and animals which were strewed about. Many a warrior and squaw died on the road from exhaustion, and the maladies engendered by their treatment; and their relations and friends could do nothing more for them than fold them in their blankets, and cover them with boughs and bushes, to keep off the vultures, which followed their route by thousands, and soared over their heads; for their drivers would not give them time to dig a grave and bury their dead. The wolves, which also followed at no great distance, soon tore away so frail a covering, and scattered the bones in all directions.[40]

In one final insult, Opothle Yoholo was not allowed to stop for an extended period in the state of Arkansas in order to settle matters with the western Creek leaders as he had demanded back in Alabama. Arkansas governor James Conway responded to the Tuckabatchee headman's request on 10 November and declared that he could not comply unless the white residents of his state assented. Still concerned about his safety, Opothle Yoholo wrote to Matthew Arbuckle, commander at Fort Gibson, from Cadron Creek on 14 November, requesting that on his arrival the party be placed under the protection of American troops within the military reservation at the garrison. The McIntosh headmen were just as concerned, and agents reported that the western leaders "see with no pleasant feelings the prospect of being supplanted in their power and influence, by the superior numbers and authority of the main body." It was there, surrounded by an American military presence, that Opothle Yoholo met with Roly McIntosh face to face. The meeting itself appears to have been cordial and although there was "much feeling between the McIntosh party and those who have lately emigrated with their Chief Apoth le ho lo," the representatives of both parties smoked the peace pipe and drank "a glass of old rye (perhaps new corn)." This was not a lasting peace, however, only a temporary truce. There was no reconciliation between the two parties and agents believed Opothle Yoholo and his people needed to "be removed from Roly McIntosh and his people some distance." They established their new settlements near the Canadian River, many miles away from Coweta.[41]

The transfer of the Creek Nation and its people to the West would have been inconceivable prior to 1825. The Creeks worked diligently in the decade after the Treaty of Indian Springs to counter pro-emigration federal and state officials. They wrote letters, sent delegations to Washington, and expended great energy attempting to prevent their people from voluntarily moving to the West. The principal Creek headmen often clashed with each other over the best strategy to employ, but they were largely united against leaving the land of their ancestors. By the beginning of the 1830s, however, things had changed. The effects of the loss of the Creeks' Georgia buffer, the platting of Columbus, Alabama's extension laws, the election of Andrew Jackson, white encroachment, starvation, disease, and alcohol abuse created a tsunami of problems that simply overwhelmed the Creek people. The night before he left for the West, Menawa presented John B. Hogan with his portrait—painted while the Okfuskee headman was negotiating the Treaty of Washington in 1826. "I am going away," Menawa declared, "I have brought you this picture—I wish you to take it and hang it up in your house, that when your children look at it you can tell them what I have been. I have always found you true to me, but great as my regard for you is, I never wish to see you in that new country to which I am going—for when I cross the great river, my desire is that I may never again see the face of a white man!"[42]

9 Defiance

1837–49

For the over fifteen thousand Creeks who were forced and coerced from Alabama in the year 1836, their long struggle to remain on their ancestral homeland was over. Many did not go without a fight and subsequently began their journey west in chains. The rest went peacefully, but with begrudging consent. There were, however, as many as five thousand Creeks still east of the Mississippi in 1837. About eight hundred had volunteered to fight the Seminoles in Florida. As an enticement for their service, the federal government promised that the family members of the Creek warriors would be allowed to remain in east-central Alabama until their tours of duty were over. There were also hundreds of Creeks who had fled to other southeastern Indian communities and sought asylum. A thousand Creeks lived openly among the Cherokees or were in hiding in the mountains as far away as North Carolina. Five hundred Creeks lived among the Chickasaws in Mississippi, and perhaps as many or more lived with the Seminoles in Florida. Federal agents and military personnel reconnoitered in those locations looking for Creek fugitives. Although several hundred were caught, many escaped the clutches of the agents and remained in hiding until they were forced west during the Cherokee, Chickasaw, and Seminole removals. There were also a handful of Creek families living in the Tensaw region of Alabama who stayed in the East and during the next century and a half, successfully petitioned for federal recognition.

As the five large detachments of Creeks left Alabama in August and September 1836 for Fort Gibson, many Creeks remained in the South undetected. They included the Creeks who had actively participated in the Second Creek War or at least openly resisted removal and had not been captured by military personnel. Most of these Creeks were known to be hiding in the swamps or in sparsely inhabited parts of southern Georgia. Others simply refused to come into camp and enroll for relocation. Some Creeks had arrived in camp during the summer of 1836 only to abscond before their detachments commenced the journey westward. Forshatch Fixico, for example, escaped from a relocation camp and told the others that he would neither emigrate nor be taken alive. Similarly, it is doubtful that all the Lower Creeks hiding in the Chowokolo swamp joined detachment five as it moved out of Chambers County, Alabama, in September 1836. A local white resident told John T. Sprague that there were members of this party of Creeks who never intended to join but "expressed to him their enmity to the whites and their determination to remain there." Estimates placed the number of Creeks still in hiding in Alabama or Georgia at four to five hundred, and agents repeatedly discovered "*signs* of them" which were "frequently found in the corn and potatoe fields."[1]

There were, however, a few thousand Creeks who remained in Alabama with the permission of federal officials. These were the relatives of Creek men recruited to fight with the Americans in the Second Seminole War. Before leaving Alabama in the fall of 1836, military agents visited the relocation camps and asked the headmen if they were willing to offer any of their men for service in Florida. Agents visited Opothle Yoholo's party on 2 September 1836, as they camped near Wetumpka. Forty Creeks from detachment one agreed to fight, and perhaps as many as a few hundred of Opothle Yoholo's people were ultimately mustered into service. Other prominent Creeks offered their services, including the headmen Echo Harjo, Jim Boy, and Paddy Carr. Others, like Cusseta chief Tuckabatchee Harjo, were "decidedly against" offering his services and "but few of the Indians" of detachment five "were inclined to go to Florida." And, despite any difficulty they may have had in convincing the Creeks to serve, the government still met its target of recruiting between six hundred and a thousand Creek soldiers. Indeed, officials noted that 776 Creeks ultimately fought on the side of the United States against the Seminoles.[2]

Federal officials enticed the Creeks to volunteer with a number of promises. Headmen who served in Florida received ten thousand dollars "to be disposed of as they may see fit," if the people under their command performed "in good faith." The government also promised to use their 1837 annuity to pay off accumulated debts and "to get clear of the ruinous suits against them." Because many of the warriors had been defrauded by impersonation and had not legally disposed of their reserves, John Archibald Campbell was also appointed to settle their land claims. In addition, Brevet Major General Thomas S. Jesup, who later commanded the Florida campaign, agreed to allow the Creek warriors to keep all of the Seminoles' slaves they captured in battle, a common practice among the southeastern Indians during war. The Creeks who served were organized into companies and paid for their services as soldiers. Those with horses were paid as mounted volunteers. In addition to the government's offerings, the Creeks made demands of their own. The first was that their family members be allowed to remain in Alabama under the protection of the federal government until their tours of duty were completed. Military personnel subsequently placed the Creek family members in three encampments at Polecat Springs, at Echo Harjo's home thirty miles east of Polecat Springs, and at Fort Mitchell. There, the relatives of the warriors were issued provisions and protected from local white settlers. Most of the wives and children of the Tuckabatchee fighters, however, moved west with Opothle Yoholo in the fall of 1836 and did not remain in Alabama. Officials also assured the Creeks that those serving in Florida would be discharged by 1 February 1837, in order to allow the Creeks to move with their families to the Indian territory in time to plant crops.[3]

Despite the assurances given, and perhaps unbeknownst to them, the headmen actually committed their warriors to an "indefinite" length of service. This allowed the government great leeway in extending the Creeks' tours of duty, and this is exactly what they did. Despite the fact that "it was distinctly understood . . . that they were to be allowed to return to Alabama in time to remove . . . before the season for planting their corn," Jesup underestimated the time and resources it would take to put down the Seminoles, and the Creeks consequently remained in Florida long past 1 February 1837. Jesup stated as his rationale for extending their service that, "had [the Creeks] left me on the 1st of February according to the assurances given to them, I must have called into service at least two regiments of militia or volunteers to have taken their places, at a heavy expense." Jesup also believed that it would have taken too long to discharge the Creeks and replace them with a white militia. In return, Jesup told the Creeks that the government would not only issue provisions to them and their families for twelve months after arriving in the West but also until they had gathered their crops the following year. But this was small consolation. Instead of a five-month deployment, the Creek warriors remained in Florida for almost a year. The extended service strained the capabilities of the men and many were worn down by the hard service. Worse, it was yet another broken promise by the federal government.[4]

The decision to extend the Creek warriors' tours of duty had consequences far beyond just the Creeks fighting in Florida, however. Their family members also suffered, despite promises made by the government to protect them. Local whites in Alabama grew impatient with the presence of large numbers of Creeks near their settlements, especially after more depredations were committed in Alabama in late 1836 by a number of Creek Indians. Much of this renewed violence was committed by those who had not been captured during the Second Creek War. Although government officials declared the major operations of the war over by the summer of 1836, the rebels who had not been apprehended simply moved the theater of battle to southern Georgia and north Florida. Other Creeks remained in the former Creek Nation, but hid in the swamps. Once the troops left Alabama, many of these Creeks returned and recommenced their attacks. On 29 December 1836 a party of Creeks attacked a plantation in Barbour County. The Creeks burned the complex except for the slave quarters and killed one of the owner's field hands. White residents looking for vengeance, however, believed the attackers had sought protection in the relocation camps.[5]

In order to appease the excitable whites and protect the Indians from roving militias, the agents overseeing the camps ordered the Creeks to surrender their weapons and move into protective custody. Captain

John Page placed what few Creek men he had in his camp into the garrison at Fort Mitchell; while at Echo Harjo's, Lieutenant Thomas Sloan moved the party into a small complex "less than half a mile square." Page also directed Marine Lieutenant John G. Reynolds to string a chain of sentinels around the Creeks at Polecat Springs. This was done both for the protection of the Creek families and as a symbolic gesture to show the whites that the Creeks in camp were not associated with the rebels hiding in the swamps.[6]

However, as the violence continued—a planter, his overseer, and five slaves were killed on 26 January—companies of militia began indiscriminately targeting the family members of the Florida volunteers. On 5 February a group of white men arrived at Echo Harjo's and placed a number of Creeks under their guard "without provisions, & in most instances a blanket to shelter them from the inclemency of the weather." The whites then pillaged Creek property, stole some of their money and guns, then apprehended the Creek men and boys and placed them in the stockade under armed guard at Tuskegee. Weeks later, another company arrived and ordered the women and children to Tuskegee. Outgunned, Sloan could only concede to the whites' demands. On the morning of 23 February he ordered the Creek women and children to Tuskegee and "in half an hour the whole camp was on the march. In consequence of having no means of transportation, I directed them to deposit their Effects in my quarters, &c, until wagons could be procured to remove them to Tuskegee; but in the mean time the house was broken open and plundered of most articles of any value." The whites stole 145 of the Creeks' ponies, 60 head of cattle, 200 hogs, 100 bushels of corn, 100 beehives, 63 guns, cooking and farming utensils, crockery, and money. The total losses exceeded $8,300.[7]

At the Polecat Springs camp, white militia members killed ninety-year-old Lochchi Yoholo, who had been excused from mustering due to the "infirmities of age" and "deafness." The old man was found "lying in one corner shot in the breast and his head litterally stove in, with as I supposed butts of muskets." The men also attempted to rape a fifteen-year-old girl, then shot her in the leg as she made her escape. The Creeks reported that the whites raped or attempted to rape a number of the women in the camps, and in many instances stole their earrings and blankets. Out of fear for their lives, Creek women and even whole families fled into the swamps where Lieutenant Reynolds worried they might be confused with the rebels. Moreover, a company of troops had sent word earlier that they intended to apprehend all the Creek men in camp. Forced into a corner with few acceptable options, the agent reluctantly gave the Creeks the choice of "either of going to Tuskegee as prisoners" with the militia companies "and separating from their families or leave the nation with them." The agent noted that "there was no hesitation they preferred the latter and in thirty six hours afterwards with but four five horse teams, my party of upwards of nineteen hundred strong were on the march" to what was considered a safer location at Mount Meigs, Alabama, a place Reynolds had scouted days earlier. Before they left, however, whites pillaged Creek property including horses, cattle, corn, furniture, and farming utensils.[8]

Both John James Audubon and showman P. T. Barnum were traveling through Alabama in February 1837 and witnessed these Creeks during this chaotic time. On 24 February Audubon reported that

> 100 Creek Warriors were confined in Irons, preparatory to leaving for ever the Land of their births!—Some miles onward we overtook about two thousands of these once free owners of the Forest, marching towards this place under an escort of Rangers, and militia mounted Men, destined for distant lands, unknown to them, and where alas, their future and latter days must be spent in the deepest of Sorrows, afliction and perhaps even phisical want—This view . . . produced on my mind an aflicting series of reflections more powerfuly felt than easy of description—the numerous groups of Warriors, of half clad females and of naked babes, trudging through the mire under the residue of their ever scanty stock of Camp furniture, and household utensils—The evident regret expressed in the . . . masked countenances of some and the tears of others—the howlings of their numerous dogs; and the cool demeanour of the chiefs,—all formed such a Picture as I hope I never will again witness in reality—had Victor being with us, ample indeed would have been his means to paint Indians in sorrow.

At almost the same time, Barnum saw fifteen hundred Creeks encamped at Tuskegee and twenty-five hundred more at Mount Meigs before he reached Montgomery on 28 February. These camps would only be temporary, however. Whites, including Alabama governor Clement C. Clay, petitioned the secretary of war and Captain John Page to relocate the Creek families entirely from east-central Alabama. Cognizant of the promises made to the men fighting the Seminoles, Page complained that the requests put him in "a very awkward situation." By the third week of February, however, Secretary of War Joel Poinsett had authorized the movement of the families to Mobile Point to wait for the men to return from Florida.[9]

By early March 3,471 Creeks were congregated on the Alabama River in Montgomery. Their encampment was located on the property of a Montgomery resident who later complained that not only were his trees cut in order to procure firewood and construct temporary shelters to shield the Creeks from the weather but one of his houses was pulled "to pieces" in order to obtain shingles to complete the structure. The *Montgomery Advertiser*, a pro-Jackson newspaper critical of nullifiers and land speculators, reported the condition of the Creeks, noting in an article that "the spectacle exhibited by them is truly heart rending; with all their cruelties, they are human beings and no man of feeling can look upon their present destitute condition . . . while our citizens are rolling in ease and luxury, those who are natives of the country are in the most abject poverty, dependent for their subsistence on the charity of the government."[10]

The Creeks left Montgomery on three steamboats. The first party of approximately 650 traveled on the *John Nelson* and arrived at Mobile Point on 18 March. The second and third parties—which included 800 Creeks traveling aboard the *Chippewa* and 480 on the *Bonnets O Blue*—arrived at Mobile Point the following day. Another 1,600 Creeks left on 20 March. Unsure about how long the men would remain in Florida, the Alabama Emigrating Company kept three steamers—the *Farmer*, *John Nelson*, and *Navarino*—moored at Mobile Point in readiness to take the Creeks west at a moment's notice.[11]

The news of the Creek families' relocation to the Gulf of Mexico eventually reached the Creek volunteers fighting in Florida. Jesup reported that while some of the warriors were satisfied with the decision to move their families, many Creeks were angry and saw it as a "breach of faith" on the part of the United States. The news particularly angered the Lower Creeks and it complicated the government's war with the Seminoles. In fact, Jesup noted that the Lower Creeks fighting in Florida, "if not disposed to favour the Seminoles are at least not very zealous in our cause. With the exception of a very small portion of them they were zealous and true until they received information of the removal of their families from Alabama, and the outrages committed upon them there." Jesup noted that the Upper Creeks "do not participate with the Lower Creeks in the excitement produced by recent events," and he attributed this to the fact that most of their family members had moved west with Opothle Yoholo the previous fall. Jesup did observe, however, that the Upper Creeks were "broken down by hard service and disease—are unfit for duty and are extremely anxious to join their families." Indeed, at least one Creek soldier committed suicide while in Florida.[12]

While at Mobile Point, the agents overseeing the Creeks, along with Creek volunteers, reconnoitered around the area to search for Creek refugees hiding in the swamps. Some were believed to have participated in the Second Creek War or were aiding the Seminoles, while others fled to escape relocation. In fact, as early as 1829 a ten-person delegation representing four unnamed Creek towns visited Seminole headmen with the goal of seeking asylum "in case they were obliged to leave their own country." By late April 1837 agents collected a number of Creeks including a few Yuchi refugees hiding on Escribano Point on Black Water Bay. Agents used interpreters and even the captured prisoners to coax the refugees from their camps. On 27 April thirty-seven "friendly" Creeks gave themselves up, while thirty-three more "hostile" Creeks surrendered three days later. The Creeks, seventy in total, embarked on the steamboat *Watchman* for Pensacola. To ensure that no one escaped, the *Watchman* was escorted for part of its journey by the frigate *Constellation*. After arriving in Pensacola the Creeks were transferred to the steamboat *Champion* and arrived in Mobile Point at one o'clock on the afternoon of 1 May. Almost three weeks later the *Champion* transported thirty-three more fugitive Creeks to Mobile Point. In addition to those hiding in Florida, escapees were found as far away as Pascagoula, Mississippi, to the west and Fort Claiborne, Alabama, to the north.[13]

Apprehending the Creek refugees was complicated by the violence committed against them by whites. In late May 1837 a group of soldiers massacred a party of Indians hiding in the swamps near Alaqua Creek in Florida. The attack occurred on the edge of a large swamp in a space "of about fifteen or twenty feet in diameter" where "poor women with children upon their backs," according to reports, "were inhumanly butchered the cries of the children were distinctly heard, at a house distant a quarter of a mile, after their mothers were shot down the children's brains were deliberately knocked out—the women's Ears cut off, for the purpose of obtaining their Ear rings and in several instances scalped." Such atrocities made rounding up runaway Creeks more difficult, and as agents and their Indian scouts searched north Florida, they found nothing but abandoned campgrounds where the refugees had fled to escape a similar fate. The Creek refugees were victimized by "so many barbarous outrages" that many were afraid to emerge from their hiding places. This was even true if the Creeks wanted to surrender to the authorities. On a number of occasions Creeks attempted to give themselves up peacefully only to be shot at by whites. These refugees, who had "suffered severely in different skirmishes with their troops and were measurably destitute of clothing, much dispirited and nearly broken down with fatigue," were understandably skittish and only after a prolonged effort (with the aid of "friendly" Creek scouts and interpreters) were they coaxed out of their camps. Still, some fugitives refused to surrender and declared their intention to settle among the Seminoles.[14]

In addition to Florida, the search for Creek refugees stretched from the Cherokee country in North Carolina and Georgia to the Chickasaw territory in Mississippi. Official estimates placed the number of Creeks in the Cherokee country at about one thousand or more, while there were approximately five hundred living among the Chickasaws. In the spring of 1837, Lieutenant Edward Deas, who had recently returned from conducting detachment three to Indian territory, was appointed the superintendent of Creek removal in the Cherokee Nation. In March he traveled to Warrenton in Marshall County, Alabama, to inspect the 150 Creeks who were encamped under armed guard, then traveled to New Echota for a briefing on the locations of the Creeks in the Cherokee country. Military personnel used both Creek and Cherokee guides—and even employed Talladega chief Forshatch Fixico, who was a principal Creek headman in the Cherokee country and considered "the most influential of the Refugee Creeks" (and quite possibly the same man who escaped the relocation camp and refused to be taken alive)—to find and identify the escapees. The agents and militia subsequently scoured Coosawattee, eighteen miles from New Echota, and the area around Red Clay, on the Tennessee-Georgia line. Complicating matters, however, were the untold numbers of Creeks "scattered" in the North Carolina mountains or on the banks of Valley River. Many had married into Cherokee families and were nearly impossible to isolate and capture.[15]

Although a majority of the refugees inhabited "thinly settled, or barren" land in the Cherokee territory and were starving, the Creeks did their best to avoid capture. When troops arrived at Red Clay to apprehend two hundred refugees believed to be in the area, they discovered that many of the Creeks had fled to the mountains. Troops scoured the region looking for their encampments. When one detachment stumbled upon a refugee camp, a number of Creeks fled for safety while the balance "made Battle." One Creek man fired his rifle at the troops and another surrendered when a gun was pointed in his face. Another refugee shot arrows while "yelling and Calling on the Ballance to Return and fight." Troops shot the man and "he lived six Days and Dyed of the wound the next Day." In addition to the 122 Creek refugees arrested by these soldiers, the Valley River troops apprehended 90, the Georgia troops about 100, and another detachment 17. Unhappy about being captured, the soldiers observed that "the Creeks all appear very sulkey." Others died in skirmishes trying to escape, and captured Creeks lamented that "two of our men were killed, one man shot through the thigh and arm and three children lost in the flight of their mothers and have not been found." Even when the refugees were not attacked, many reported that whites destroyed their crops and carried off much of their property, which made their situation even more precarious. Still, this was only a fraction of the number of people still hiding in the mountains.[16]

Only 543 Creek refugees were captured in the Cherokee country. By May 1837 the party was encamped four miles south of Gunter's Landing in preparation for its removal westward. Approximately 100 of these Creeks had been captured in the North Carolina mountains, while the balance had been apprehended near Coosawattee and Red Clay. These Creeks, about 350 in number, were conducted from Ross Landing to Gunter's Landing by boat. There, they joined 195 Creeks already under guard of the Tennessee volunteers. Deas's muster roll shows that the refugees were primarily Upper Creeks who were extremely poor and "found in the most wretched condition and in some cases, naked, & starving." Dysentery, which primarily affected the children, made life in the camp even more miserable and delayed the commencement of the removal for almost a week. Considering their condition and their proclivity to escape, Deas elected to take the Creeks solely by water. The Alabama Emigrating Company subsequently purchased nine flatboats to descend the Muscle Shoals on the Tennessee River. Four of the flats were "of the largest class," approximately eighty feet long, while the others were between forty and fifty feet in length. On 16 May 1837 the Creeks were turned over to the agent of the Alabama Emigrating Company, H. G. Barclay, and moved to the bank of the Tennessee River. The party embarked at sunset and by ten o'clock that evening Deas noted in his journal that the party was "progressing slowly by the force of the current."[17]

As captives, the refugees were rushed westward as quickly and efficiently as possible. The small freedoms afforded the Creeks of the five detachments in 1836 were not initially extended to this party. In addition to unpopular water travel, the agents outfitted the boats so they could run as long as possible without having to stop. On many occasions the boats ran all night rather than coming to shore to allow the Creeks to camp, bathe, and rest. At Waterloo the refugees were transferred to the medium-sized steamer *Black Hawk* with a keelboat and two of the large flatboats in tow. The contractors outfitted the boat in order to "accommodate the Indians to the best advantage on board of her." This included covering all the guards—the portion of the deck that extended beyond the hull—on the *Black Hawk* to shield the Creeks from inclement weather. Temporary sheds were also constructed on the flats and keelboat to do the same for the Creeks riding in tow. The contractors constructed cooking hearths inside the flatboat and on the deck of the keel so the Creeks could prepare meals while traveling. Deas also ordered the addition of "necessary fixtures which were essential to Cleanliness" on the boats, but this work was never completed. For people used to sanitation and personal freedoms, the journey on board the river, coupled with their deteriorated condition after being captured, meant an uncomfortable but not physically demanding removal.[18]

The Creeks tried to maintain as many of their daily habits as possible, however. On 25 May a child died from exposure as a result, according to Deas, of "the folly of its mother, in putting it in cold water" as the party passed Paducah on the Ohio River. Deas, however, might have misread this episode, as the mother was likely not guided by foolishness but by the Creeks' firmly held views on purity and strength. The Creeks bathed regularly in order to maintain health and preferred cold water for strength. Infants were even submerged, and Lieutenant Henry Timberlake believed that the Cherokee practice of bathing babies daily in cold water prevented deformities. Once in the Indian territory, Creek women rolled their offspring in the snow "to make them hardy."[19]

Although water travel allowed the party to move quickly—the whole journey took only twenty days—there were unexpected problems and delays. While descending the Tennessee River, the flatboats were forced to come to shore on a number of occasions due to high winds and storms. The first detention occurred on 17 May when the boats stopped at noon near Ditto's Landing. At two o'clock the following morning, high winds again forced the boats to come to shore, and many Creeks took advantage of the weather in order to ensure their own personal freedom. On reaching the bank of the river, fifteen Creeks jumped off the flat and escaped into the night. The boats stopped again due to wind on the afternoon of 19 May near Decatur, and once more the following morning near Brown's Ferry. With the boats separated on landing, the Creeks took advantage of the confusion and the darkness and seventy-one more deserted the party. Deas offered a dollar reward for any Creek brought in, but only fifteen were recovered. Fifty-six ran toward the mountains about five miles away.[20]

The pace of travel slowed considerably once the Creeks reached the Arkansas. The river at that time of year was not in "a very good stage," as the spring freshet had begun only a few days earlier. Several boats had run aground on the bars sometime earlier and the water's rise had only recently allowed them to proceed. Still, the party came to shore each night to avoid the sandbars and any snags in the river. This allowed the Creeks to camp on land at night, and Deas jettisoned one of the flatboats, ostensibly because the party would no longer require the deck space to cook or sleep. As the threat of escape diminished, the Creeks were allowed more freedoms. With the Arkansas River continuing to rise, which slowed the boats, more stops were required to procure wood. Deas noted that "every day a considerable stop has been made in day time at wood landings, giving the Indians an opportunity of leaving the Boats, and Bathing, and also of taking Exercise, the want of which to people of their habits is the greatest objection to Transporting them by water." Some Creeks were even hired to cut wood for the *Black Hawk*'s boilers.[21]

These stops at wood landings also afforded an opportunity to bury those who had passed away. Although a primary objection to water travel was the fear of being thrown overboard when dead, this did not happen. When a young girl who had been sick for some time died on 24 May near Savannah, Tennessee, the body was carried on board the boat until she could be buried at a wood landing that afternoon. Sickness, probably the lingering effects of dysentery that had been prevalent in camp at Gunter's Landing, as well as the refugees' already deteriorated condition, resulted in a number of other deaths. Five days after the death of the Creek girl, "an Indian man & a very old woman" passed away from sickness as the party began its ascension of the Arkansas River. Another Creek child, who was under the age of ten (31 May) and an elderly Creek woman who had suffered from tuberculosis for more than a year (1 June) both died on board the boat near Little Rock. The last recorded death was of a Creek man who passed away only twenty miles from Fort Gibson.[22]

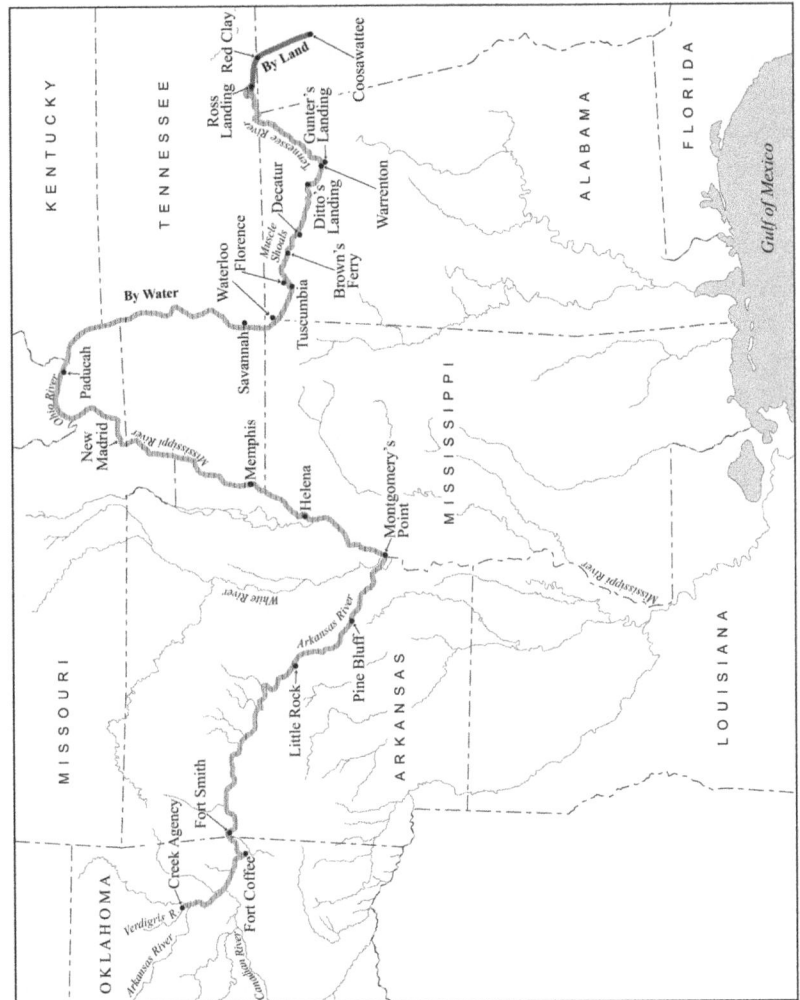

FIG. 26. Route of Creek refugees in Cherokee country, May–June 1837. Place names correspond to stopping points or locations noted in the documentation. Route lines and locations are approximations. Cartography by Sarah Mattics.

The sickness and desertions notwithstanding, the trip was largely uneventful and Deas's journal consists largely of a tally of the towns and geographic features the party passed by. From Gunter's Landing, the boats passed Elk River Shoals and Lamb's Ferry on 21 May and Florence, the Tuscumbia landing, and Waterloo on 22 and 23 May. The pace quickened after the Creeks were transferred to the *Black Hawk* at Waterloo, and accelerated even more when Deas scuttled one of the flatboats at Savannah, Tennessee, on 24 May. The following day, the steamer reached Paducah, Kentucky, and the Creeks encamped in the state of Illinois near the mouth of the Ohio River. On 26 May the party passed New Madrid and the following day arrived in Memphis. The boats did not stop in Memphis because of fears that some refugees would attempt an escape into the Chickasaw country. With the steamboat continuing to travel at night, the *Black Hawk* reached Helena on 27 May and Montgomery's Point on 28 May before passing through the mouth of the White River and the cutoff to the Arkansas River. With the speed of the *Black Hawk* cut in half by the current of the Arkansas, the party passed Pine Bluff on 30 May and reached Little Rock the following day.[23]

By the end of the second week of their journey, the Creeks had grown anxious to reach their destination. When they landed at Little Rock, Deas recorded that "a very few of the people went on shore" and most appeared ready to proceed westward. The party subsequently traveled throughout the night on the last five nights of their journey. They arrived at Fort Gibson on 4 June after passing Fort Smith and Fort Coffee and the mouths of the Canadian and Grand Rivers. The Creeks asked to be landed on the west bank of the Verdigris River near the Creek Agency, and Deas obliged. Immediately after landing onshore, "a large number of them dispersed through the Country" before they could be "re-mustered." The disbursing agent at Fort Gibson, Captain James R. Stephenson, believed that this was the result of the Creeks' "anxiety to visit their friends." Of the 543 Creeks who left Gunter's Landing on 16 May, only 463 arrived on 4 June. Subtracting the 71 escapees, 9 Creeks perished during the journey.[24]

Once again, Deas traveled eastward to locate and enroll the estimated three to four hundred Creek refugees still "lurking in the mountains." Most of these Creeks were living on the edge of survival. One agent discovered a Creek camp with "about 60 destitute of clothing and without any thing to eat." These Creeks gave themselves up, but they escaped back into the woods during the course of the night. The agent tracked some down and found nine Creeks, "5 of them had some little clothing, the other 4, a woman and 3 children, were so nearly in a state of nudity, that I had to send blankets out, for them to cover their Nakedness, before they would come in and without a shoe to their feet." A woman and her children were found in camp wearing only "part of an old blanket, not a yard square." Moreover, the agent observed that "blood was running out of her and her children's legs; they had parched them so by the fire, to keep warm, that where the twigs, touched them, as they came in the blood ran freely." After receiving food and clothing, the woman fled with her children before they could be taken west.[25]

Despite their condition, whenever agents approached, the Creeks hid, fled, or "refused to speak upon the subject of Emigration." Agents appealed to the Cherokees in council for assistance in extracting the Creeks from their territory and were confident that they had secured the cooperation of the council as well as Cherokee headman John Ross. Nevertheless, the Creeks who lived in the Cherokee Nation sent an impassioned letter to the Cherokee chief. Written from Red Clay, the refugees pleaded with Ross and his people to allow them to remain. They appealed to them as brothers, noted that there was no objection raised by their northern neighbors when they first arrived, and reaffirmed that blood or marriage connected most of them to the Cherokee people. After some delay, the Cherokees responded to the agent's request to give up the Creeks. The Cherokee council noted that although they had no power to protect the Creeks and would recommend the Creeks comply with the government's wishes, they would do little to aid the government in rounding up the fugitives. Moreover, the council expressed its confidence that force would not be used to extract the Creeks from their borders. In other words, the Creeks could stay. The council also reaffirmed that "the Creeks and Cherokees had always been friends that the country of each had been a refuge to the other in misfortune." After being allowed to remain, the Creeks formally rejected the agent's request to enroll for removal. Many Creeks had married into Cherokee families and "appear to consider themselves the same people." Although American troops continued apprehending Creeks who had no familial relationship with the Cherokee people, those who had blood or marriage connections were "permitted to share the fate of the Cherokees, to stay as long as they stay and to go when they go."[26]

Back on the Gulf, more than three thousand Creeks remained at Mobile Point waiting for the warriors to be discharged from service in Florida. They had been transferred to the coast in order to avoid the terrorizing whites in central Alabama, but Mobile Point was no place of refuge. The party was "exceedingly unhealthy" and their camp served as a breeding ground for illnesses, including diarrhea, dysentery, and intermittent fever. At their Mobile Point encampment, the Creeks obtained their drinking water by digging holes of up to two feet deep in the sand that were filled by an underground spring. Agents blamed this stagnant water for the Creeks' diarrhea, and the increasing number of deaths on the application of the "severest Indian treatment," an unspecified remedy administered by Creek doctors. The intermittent fever likely was a seasonal disease, however, common along the Gulf Coast during the summer. In fact, New Orleans suffered from a yellow fever outbreak during this time. The first Creek death occurred on 20 March and ninety-three Creeks, many of them children, had died by mid-July. Obsessively concerned with cleanliness and purity, the refugees became "discontented" with their camp's location. Many of the sick were placed inside Fort Morgan and raised off the ground on beds made of planks, which was deemed "necessary for their comfort" and health. The board belonged to the garrison, however, and the soldiers subsequently expropriated the planks, forcing the sick Creeks "to lie on the hard bricks exposed to the dampness of the earth." Some Creeks required extreme treatment. For instance, one Creek Indian required an arm amputation and was transferred to a hospital in Mobile.[27]

The health of the party was also compromised by the inability of the Alabama Emigrating Company to adequately provide full rations. The unexpected removal of the Creeks to the coast stretched the capabilities of the contractors and they were left scrambling to find fresh meat at

FIG. 27. Edward Woolf watercolor "An Indian of the Creek Nation Sketched from Nature at Mobile Alabama," ca. 1837. W. S. Hoole Special Collections Library, University of Alabama, Tuscaloosa AL.

local farms. In the meantime, many Creeks took matters into their own hands. In parties of between five and twenty individuals, they wandered from their encampment in order to hunt white settlers' livestock. Baldwin County residents in south Alabama complained that Creek hunters had killed stock between Mobile Bay and the Perdido River. Oystermen at Bon Secour, Alabama, sold the Creeks ammunition and whiskey, and many residents feared that in addition to the loss of their livestock, the Creeks would join the Seminoles in their war against the United States.[28]

The party was plagued by more bad news in June 1837. First, on 12 June, Brevet Major General Jesup notified the contractors from Tampa Bay that the services of the Creek volunteers would be needed until 10 September. The relocation was therefore suspended for three more months. Worse, the sickness in the Creeks' encampment had not abated and was getting worse. With the promise of an imminent removal over, agents had no choice but to move the Creeks to a healthier location on the Gulf. Captain John Page, and newly promoted Captain Mark W. Bateman, who had returned from accompanying Opothle Yoholo's party to Fort Gibson, subsequently reconnoitered on Dauphin Island in search of healthier ground. On 23 June Lieutenant John G. Reynolds, the assistant surgeon, and thirty-eight Creek headmen traveled on the steamboat *Farmer* to the islands between Mobile Point and Bay St. Louis, Mississippi—including Horn Island, Ship Island, and Cat Island—to look for healthier land. Horn and Ship Islands were rejected by the Creeks "in consequence of the barrenness of the soil, the abundance of musquetoes and the low situation of the ground," while the proprietor of Cat Island, described as an obstinate "old Spaniard," refused to let the Creeks camp at that location. The party reconnoitered as far westward as Lake Borgne in Louisiana before selecting Pass Christian, Mississippi. That site's "high, dry, and airy," environment consisting of "three or four Springs of excellent water and beautifully shaded with large oaks, hickory and other flourishing trees" was a popular place of refuge for residents of New Orleans during the sickly summer season.[29]

In early July the agents and contractors moved the Creeks to the wharf at Mobile Point in preparation for their journey to Pass Christian. What should have been a relatively simple relocation turned into an ordeal that lasted for days, making the refugees' situation even more deplorable. Captain John Page, overseeing the encampment, reported that they had "great difficulty getting [the Creeks] on board the Boat there were a great number sick many of them died on the warf before they could get on board and some died immediately after they embarked and we had to bury them, this detained the Boats some time." On the evening of 7 July 1837 the first party left Mobile Point and arrived at Pass Christian on the afternoon of the following day. Their new camp was established a half mile from the landing. As the boats returned to pick up another party, they ran headlong into a storm that prevented them from docking for nearly two days, which "rendered the situation of the Indians very unpleasant." Despite the storm and the driving rain, the Creeks chose to remain on the wharf because they were unwilling to "spoil their Physic" by returning to their previous, disease-ridden encampment. The last of the parties arrived at Pass Christian on 18 July. Despite the death and disease, there were at least twenty-three births at Mobile Point, according to one muster roll.[30]

Although Pass Christian was a much healthier location, many Creeks who had become ill at Mobile Point died. In fact, within days of arriving at their new encampment, twenty-five Creeks passed away during a two-day period, and by the last day of July, eighty-four Creeks had perished. Most of these were infants or the elderly, and carpenters were hired to build coffins and dig graves for the deceased. Witnesses observed that "these Indians were lying on the wharf, several of them sick and enfeebled under the rays of a meridian sun, without covering, and apparently half famished, as, they were eagerly devouring some water melons that the liberality of some benevolent persons had enabled them to purchase." By the end of August, however, the number of new cases of sickness had decreased sharply. Although sixteen more Creeks died during the last week of August, agents noted that, in general, "the sick are convalescing very rapidly." Agents purchased cloth and made tents for the party and the contractors furnished fresh beef, bacon, corn, and beans, "so the Indians have their choice of Rations." Carpenters were hired to make pine board flooring for the camps, as well as to dig and curb wells in order to access fresh water. The Creek encampment consisted of a series of smaller camps that stretched the entire length of the pass (about three miles) and was located in the woods adjoining a hotel. Each smaller camp belonged to one family or clan. Newspapers describing the composition of the camps noted that "Their tents are rude and slight, though some of them betray a neatness almost amounting to elegance; for even with these children of nature there are evidently classes or grades. There is too, an aristocratic or 'West End' of the encampment, where the squaws are better dressed—where the papoose swings in a neater cradle—and where the lodges are furnished with cleaner beds and culinary utensils than in any other quarter." The Creeks did their best to maintain some semblance of normalcy. They held a ball game while at Pass Christian that was won by Jim Boy and his people. Afterward, the victorious participants danced in celebration. The Creeks, with the agents' permission, left camp for short periods to hunt, fish, and engage in "other necessary amusements." The refugees were granted a five-mile radius from which they could venture; however, a number of Creeks traveled as far as forty miles without the authorization of the agents. And, as was the case at Mobile Point, local residents complained of small bands of four to six Indians "hovering about" and that "signs of killing stock, had in many instances been seen."[31]

The Creeks were also victimized by local whites on the Gulf. Alcohol traders infested the camps and agents were assigned to stand guard near a boat landing and in a small village one mile from the camp to suppress the sale of spirits. When the traders refused to desist from selling alcohol to the Creeks, Lieutenants Reynolds and Sloan confiscated and destroyed the barrels of whiskey. Local authorities at Pass Christian later arrested the two agents and they were arraigned in Bay St. Louis for assault, battery, and inciting a "riot." Both walked away with one hundred dollar fines. The Creeks also obtained alcohol in Biloxi, about sixteen miles from their camp. It was here, far from the protection of federal agents, that the Creeks often fell prey to unscrupulous tradesmen. On one excursion to purchase alcohol in the city, a group of intoxicated Creeks "lost their pocket books or wallets containing considerable amount of money." At a merchant's store in Biloxi, Chisse Harjo tried to exchange fifty dollars for the same amount in silver. The store owner took the Creek man's money but closed the shop before the silver was provided. And despite pleas from the agents for the Creeks to save their money, many did purchase merchandise from local white traders. In fact, by October 1837 the Alabama Emigrating Company estimated that the Creeks had accumulated 199,300 pounds of extra baggage.[32]

The number of Creeks on the Gulf swelled as the volunteers from Florida arrived at various times. Some were discharged from service, while others were given a thirty-day leave of absence to visit their families. On 13 June 171 volunteers from eleven different Creek companies arrived from Fort Brooke on the steamboat *Merchant*. On 19 August 208 Creek volunteers returned from Florida, 157 of whom were from Opothle Yoholo's detachment. On 13 September sixty Creeks, including the Tallassee headman Echo Harjo, returned from Florida on the steamboat *Tomochichi*. Two days later 78 more of Opothle Yoholo's volunteers reached Mississippi, and on 16 September 163 Creek volunteers arrived. Reconnaissance teams also continued apprehending Creeks who had escaped the relocation camps at Mobile Point and Pass Christian or who had never been captured and were participants in the ongoing Second Creek War (which by 1838 had merged with the Second Seminole War). Some Creeks continued hiding in the Florida Territory and in south Alabama and never left.[33]

With the arrival of most of the Florida volunteers, federal officials finally ordered the relocation of the party to Fort Gibson in late 1837. The company and agents finalized the logistics of the journey and procured transportation accordingly. Steamboats were chartered to transport the Creeks to New Orleans. A contractor was sent to Rock Roe to procure wagon teams, some from as far away as Missouri. Still, the company had a number of setbacks that delayed the commencement of the movement. On 31 July Bateman, who likely would have helped conduct the detachment west, died unexpectedly at the Mount Vernon arsenal in Alabama. He had been sick for some time and was suffering from the lingering effects of a horse fall the previous winter. Then, on 22 August, John Page left the party and traveled west after receiving orders to pay out the balance of the Watson contract money to the Creeks in the Indian

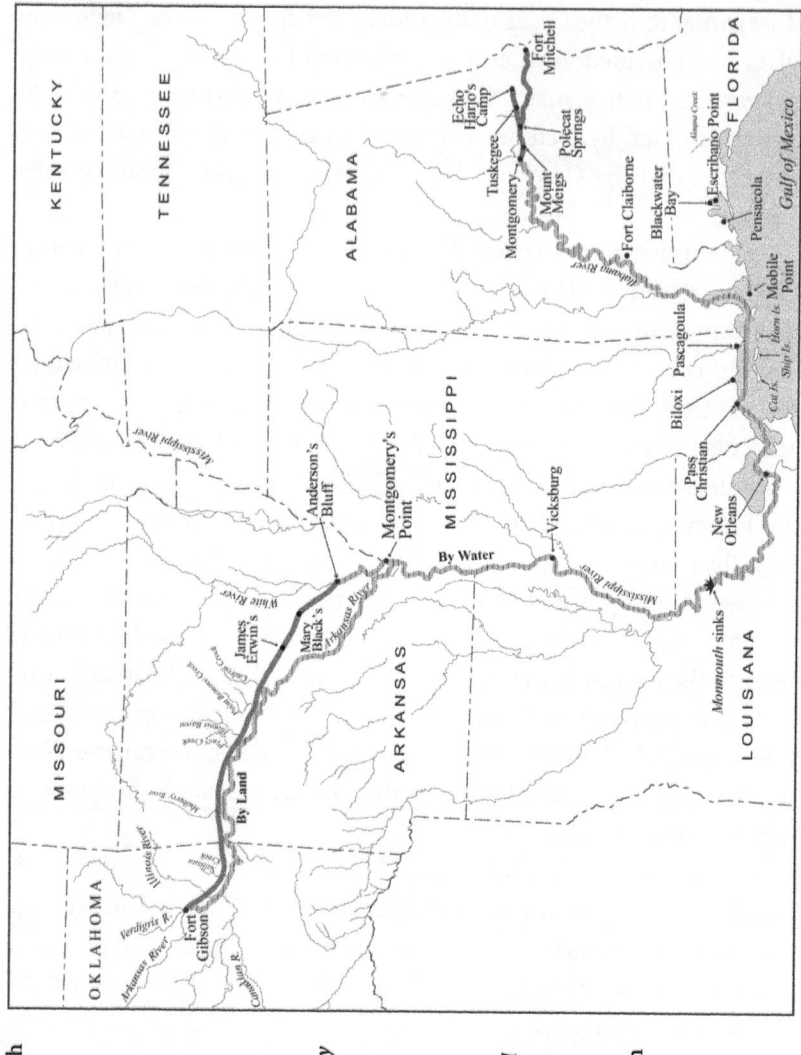

FIG. 28. Route of detachment six, March 1837–December 1837 or January 1838. Place names correspond to stopping points or locations noted in the documentation. Route lines and locations are approximations. Route through the Mississippi Sound to Pass Christian may have required brief passage into the Gulf around Dauphin Island due to shallow water; see Lynn M. Alperin, *History of the Gulf Intracoastal Waterway* (Washington DC: U.S. Army Engineer Water Resources Support Center, 1983), 7–9. The location of Anderson's Bluff (approximately fifty miles south of the mouth of Cache) is from Frank M. Cayton, *Landings on All the Western and Southern Rivers and Bayous, Showing Location, Post-Offices, Distances, &c., Also, Tariff of Premiums on Insurance to All Points* (St. Louis: Woodward, Tiernan and Hale, 1881) and A. E. Sholes, *Directory of the Taxing District of Memphis, Shelby County, Tennessee*, vol. 10 (Memphis: Rogers & Co., 1883), 28. Cartography by Sarah Mattics.

territory. On his way, Page sent back a report on the condition of the western rivers. The news was sobering. The agent warned the contractors that "if you leave the Pass before the first of October you will suffer for water dreadfully—you cannot get further than the mouth of White River by water, and the roads are so bad you cannot get here by land with waggons." Noting that the Arkansas was only two feet deep and too shallow even for keels, Page wishfully declared that "October will do something for us if not God Knows what we are to do." In response to Page's warning and because of the "Epidemic So dreadfully prevailing in" New Orleans (yellow fever), Marine Lieutenant John G. Reynolds, who succeeded Page's command of the party, ordered detachment six's relocation to commence between 5 and 10 October.[34]

The contractors also increasingly came into conflict with federal officials over the rising cost of the operation and the demands placed on the company by government agents. The unexpected relocation of the Creeks to Mobile Point left the company scrambling for boats when the original contract stipulated that the Creeks would travel by land from east-central Alabama. There was also the uncertainty over how long the party would remain on the Gulf, and the company was forced to incur demurrage fees for the *Farmer*, *John Nelson*, and *Navarino* before officials suspended the relocation indefinitely on 12 June. Moreover, before he left for the Indian territory in August, John Page ordered the company to procure a barge for each steamboat to tow in order to provide additional "convenience and safety." The company calculated that each steamboat (registered between 150 and 280 tons), each towing a 60-ton barge, could transport 800 to 1,000 Creeks. When Reynolds assumed command of the party he declined the use of the lighters and instead ordered the company to procure additional steamboats. Reynolds feared that the cramped condition of the barges would foster the spread of disease and that steamboats were a healthier mode of transportation during the Gulf's sickly season. Moreover, federal officials demanded that each steamboat carry no more than five hundred Creeks, which forced the company to procure even more boats than they had initially anticipated. The contractors protested but local steamboat owners and captains upheld the government's estimates and noted that a 150-ton steamer could carry 375 people safely, while a 250-ton boat could hold 500. If the contractors wanted to transport 875 Creeks, the pilots argued, the company would need a 500-ton boat. Moreover, because of the high numbers of convalescent sick, Jesup and Reynolds ordered "double land transportation"—double the number of wagons required by the contract—to carry those who were "too weak to travel on foot." On 23 September contractors wrote Reynolds on behalf of the Alabama Emigrating Company declaring that they were unwilling to comply with the government's request for extra transportation. The following day Reynolds suspended the relocation and sought guidance from Washington.[35]

While Creeks suffered through yet another delay, Reynolds waited for instructions from the commissioner of Indian affairs. Unwilling to allow the Creek warriors from Opothle Yoholo's party (whose family members had moved to Indian territory a year earlier) to wait any longer, Reynolds made preparations to send upwards of three hundred volunteers westward. Meanwhile, the contractors and military agents dickered over the extra transportation as well as compensation for transporting the nearly one hundred tons of extra baggage collected by the Creeks on the Gulf and the approximately forty-three tons of extra baggage left behind by Opothle Yoholo's party a year earlier. The baggage issue was complicated by the Creeks' demands not to be separated from their property during the journey out of fear that their possessions would be misplaced (as had happened to the five detachments of Creeks) or damaged away from their oversight. Yhargee, the son of Big Warrior who led a company of Creek volunteers in Florida from detachment one, for example, complained that his clothing, which was stored at Wetumpka and then Mobile Point, had been ruined by moths and his rifles, plows, and other utensils were all damaged by corrosion.[36]

Once the standoff was resolved, the Alabama Emigrating Company recommenced the business of moving Creeks westward. On 16 October 1837 a small party of Creek volunteers and their headmen, including Jim Boy, arrived in New Orleans on the steamboat *Mazeppa*, with the balance arriving several days later. By the end of October over three thousand Creeks were ascending the Mississippi River in the steamboats *Farmer*, *John Nelson*, *Navarino*, *Monmouth*, *Far West*, *Black Hawk*, and *Cavalier*.

When the *Navarino* hit a snag forty miles above New Orleans and was scuttled, the Creeks were transferred to the steamer *Yazoo*. The party passed Baton Rouge and then Prophet Island to its north without incident. As the *Monmouth*, reportedly laden with 611 Creeks, attempted the same on 31 October, it entered the narrow channel reserved for boats descending the river, leaving it vulnerable to collision from boats traveling south. The darkness of the night and drizzling rain made visibility poor and the pilot of *Monmouth* was unable to see the steamer *Warren* with the *Trenton* in tow until it was too late. The vessels then collided. In an interview, one of the owners of the *Monmouth*, who was also witness to the accident, noted that

> on her passage up the Mississippi, when near the head of Prophet's Island, Mr [Eastman] was standing on the larboard [wheelhouse] of the boat, and hearing the pilot of the Monmouth ring the bell, he immediately went forward and asked why the bell was rung? The pilot had scarcely replied, 'don't you see,' when at that moment the steamer came in contact with a ship with such violence, as to break in the bows of the Monmouth and causing her immediately to be filled with water. As soon as the ship passed by, the steamer was run ashore, and with such lines as could be procured, made fast.
>
> Scarcely had she however reached the shore, when the hull sunk and the cabin floated down stream in two parts, on one of which was Mr E with several of the officers of the boat and probably two hundred Indians. The steamboat Warren which was towing the ship immediately on the happening of the accident, rounded to and made for the portion of the wreck of which we have just spoken, and rendered every possible assistance in saving the lives and property of the Indians.

But many lives were not saved. Newspapers reported that 311 Creeks died in the accident; however, John Page later claimed the number was 288. Some families were left unscathed while others suffered unimaginable losses. Seven of the ten members of Tustunnuggee Emathla's party died in the accident, while Chocoliulishenehaw and his entire family were killed. Four of the victims were Jim Boy's children. Only two whites perished in the disaster—a bartender and a fireman.[37] The *New Orleans True American* opined on the tragedy that the fearful responsibility for this vast sacrifice of human life, rests on the contractors for emigrating the Creek Indians. The avaricious disposition to increase the profits on the speculation, first induced the chartering of rotten, old, and unseaworthy boats because they were of a class to be procured cheaply; and then to make those increased profits still larger, the Indians were packed upon these crazy vessels in such crowds, that not the slightest regard seems to have been paid to their safety, comfort, or even decency. The crammed condition of the decks and cabins, was offensive to every sense and feeling, and kept the poor creatures in a state unfit for human beings.[38]

Accounts of the tragedy that have been passed down through Creek oral tradition described relatives of those who perished on the *Monmouth* walking along the edge of the Mississippi River to identify the bodies of those who had washed up onshore the following day.[39]

Back in Mississippi, agents reconnoitered in the Chickasaw country looking for more Creek refugees. A number of these Creeks had absconded from the 1834–35 voluntary emigrating party as well as from the large forced detachments that passed through Memphis in the fall of 1836. It was estimated that approximately five hundred Creeks lived among the Chickasaws in 1837. Reuben E. Clements, a Lafayette, Tennessee, native and former surveyor in the Creek Nation, was assigned to enroll and remove these Creeks to the Indian territory. Government agents combed Pontotoc, Itawamba, and DeSoto counties looking for fugitives. Creek settlements were found thirty miles east of Pontotoc in Itawamba County, thirty miles south of Memphis, including approximately one hundred living on Horn Lake and on Coldwater River in DeSoto County. In September 1837 Clements established removal camps near those settlements—twenty miles east of Pontotoc, and a second thirty miles from Memphis. Clements met with the Creeks in council in an attempt to entice them into camp. Finding these Creeks, however, proved extremely difficult because they were scattered around a large area and living in a "dispersed situation," and enrolling them was even harder because these refugees simply did not want to move west. Clements considered these Creeks to be "outlaws" because they had "fled from [their] own tribe for murders and crimes they have committed" against their people. Most were afraid of facing punishment in the West. Violence continued, which was fueled by alcohol abuse and a sense of despair, as Clements tried to enroll them for removal. One Creek man attacked another for killing his brother several years earlier and "cut his scull in several places and opened his lungs and would have finished him had he not been prevented by some friends of his victim." Another Creek man was stabbed to death, and threats of death were reported in another case. Clements believed these Creeks to be "the most hostile and savage Indians I have ever Known," and had "great difficulty to get along with them." Moreover, these Creeks were "in a very low state of health and being almost destitute of warm clothing."[40]

Just as difficult as enrolling the Creeks was getting them to commence the journey westward. Clements, who had collected only 297 refugees, placed the primary rendezvous one mile away from a camp of removing Chickasaws. When the agent gave orders for the Creeks to begin their march to Memphis, the refugees "bid defiance and said they would not start untill the Chickasaw started." In fact, one Creek Indian named Billy (or perhaps one of the five family members traveling with him) absconded from the detachment and "run away to the Chickasaw Party." As the detachment began moving from the vicinity of Pontotoc on the last days of October, the agent wrote to his superiors in Washington that he was "just in the rear" of "about one thousand Chickasaws." The Creeks crossed Coldwater River at Cartwright's Ferry (while provision returns suggest that the party may have passed through Mount Pleasant, Mississippi, and Germantown, Tennessee) to Nonconnah Bridge via the Memphis road.[41]

Because of their deteriorated condition and their proclivity to resist orders and escape, federal officials ordered the Creeks to embark on the steamboat *Itasca* at Memphis, despite the fact that it was far cheaper to travel by land. Several hundred Chickasaws accompanied the Creeks on board. The steamer towed a large keelboat containing comfortable berths and places for cooking for the refugees. The water party passed through Little Rock on 24 November and arrived at its destination on 30 November 1837. The land party, consisting of thirty

Creeks and seventy ponies, left Memphis on the same day as the *Itasca* (20 November), and reached the St. Francis River on 25 November and the White River around 1 December. Receipts suggest that the party hit the Arkansas opposite the city of Little Rock and crossed Cadron Creek in a boat before ferrying Point Remove and Palarm Creeks. Sometime around 18 December the Creeks reached Clarksville, Arkansas, before arriving at Fort Gibson on 27 December 1837. Federal officials calculated that the better part of the party was removed to Fort Gibson for $16 per head.[42]

As the Mississippi refugees were moving toward Fort Gibson, the Creeks at Prophet Island were coming to grips with the enormity of the *Monmouth* disaster. On receiving news of the wreck, the steamboats ahead of the *Monmouth* were ordered to stop their progress at the mouth of the White River. Lieutenant Sloan, who was at Vicksburg on the *Black Hawk* when he received the news, returned downriver to investigate the accident and aid the other agents and Creeks who had survived the collision. The steamboat *Yazoo*, traveling behind the *Monmouth*, also came to help. The pilots and hands on board the *Yazoo* discharged the boat's load along the shore and spent three days "coasting below the wreck," aiding in the recovery efforts. Dr. McElvey, who was summoned from St. Francisville, Arkansas, to attend to the wounded Creeks, described his services as "very considerable and disagreeable."[43]

Once the survivors were on board, the *Yazoo* and *John Nelson* continued north to the mouth of the White River where they met the other vessels. The boats ascended the White River with the intention of reaching Rock Roe but could only get as far as Anderson's Bluff, some distance below the mouth of Cache, where low water forced the party to land. The contractors scrambled to bring the wagons down from Rock Roe to meet the party. Due to the infirmity of a headman, an agent agreed to try to ascend the Arkansas River in the *John Nelson*. Approximately 450 of his friends, relatives, and townspeople backtracked down the White River, passed through the cutoff to the Arkansas River, and, despite some close calls, reached Fort Gibson by boat in early December 1837. The balance of the party departed Anderson's Bluff by land and passed Mary Black's and James Erwin's settlements before crossing Piney Creek and

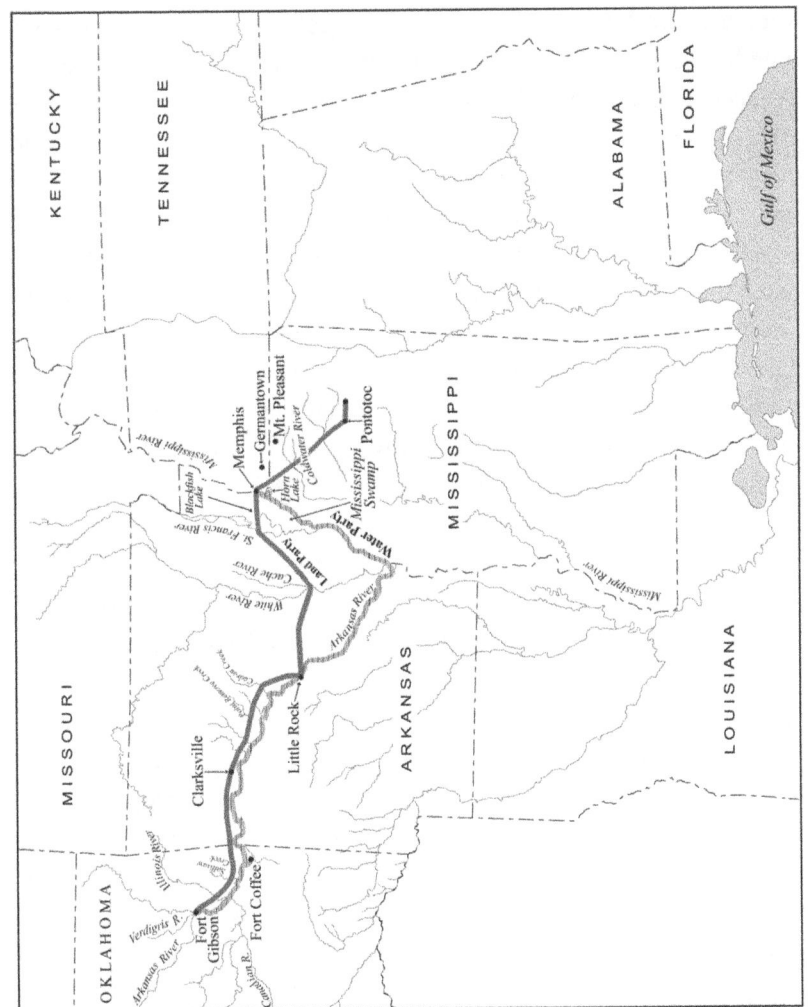

FIG. 29. Route of Creek refugees in Chickasaw country, October–December 1837. Place names correspond to stopping points or locations noted in the documentation. Route lines and locations are approximations. Cartography by Sarah Mattics.

Mulberry Creek farther west. One muster roll notes that approximately nine hundred members of detachment six arrived at Fort Gibson on 28 December 1837. The Alabama Emigrating Company tallied up the arrivals, the deaths, and the prorated cost of transporting Creeks who died along the way. They reported to the government that the company transported 3,471 people from east-central Alabama to Mobile Point and Pass Christian, and 3,352 from Pass Christian to Fort Gibson. They also noted that 296 Creeks died "after leaving Pass Christian," most of whom perished on the *Monmouth*. Among the notables of detachment six who died on the journey west was John Oponee, who was once in line to be a mile chief. The broken headman, who had served in Florida, passed away at the mouth of the Arkansas River. Nearby, Alabama Emigrating Company contractor William J. Beattie died of fever at Montgomery's Point on the last day of November 1837.[44]

Despite the coerced relocations of 1836 and 1837, hundreds of Creeks remained east of the Mississippi River and small parties continued to trickle into the Creek Nation over the next decade. In June 1838 dozens of Creeks were receiving rations at Camp Clanewaugh near Ross's Landing in Tennessee, and in November of that year thirty-seven Creeks were conducted westward by federal agents from the Cherokee country. That same month, thirty-three Creeks were moved within a larger party of 239 Apalachicolas from Blount's town in Florida.[45] Some Creeks continued to remain in Alabama. Clara von Gerstner, who traveled from Austria with her engineer husband, Franz, observed post-removal Alabama on a visit in 1839:

> In the past year the last Indians left Alabama, bringing to 20,000 the number removed from the state during the past three years. The *Federal Government* pays them for land and other real estate, and has them transported across the Arkansas River, where they are settled on new lands. The love the Indians have for their ancestral ground is indescribable; they leave it only with the greatest sorrow. With this final removal the greater part of Alabama's Indians were made to suffer the greed and cruelty of the people who removed them. Although these

people contracted to provide good care as well as transportation, they colluded with officials and gave the Indians not only the worst food but also packed them by hundreds into small boats. Many sickened and died en route; and others, fortunate enough to reach their new home, did not live much longer because the water poisoned them.

Von Gerstner discovered Creeks still hiding in Alabama when she encountered an old Creek man living "in a miserable hut, deep in the woods. Asked why he was hiding here, he answered in an outburst of the deepest unhappiness that the bones of his ancestors rested in this land; and he wanted to die here, too. He begged not to be driven away, because his final hour would come soon, as it already had for two of his comrades, who had stayed here with him and recently died." Some Creeks continued to hide in the swamps of Alabama and were only noticed when they were caught "intruding" on settlers' property. Other Creeks, predominately those of mixed parentage, were able to elude detection by passing themselves off as white Alabamians.[46]

Others avoided traveling in the large detachments of 1836 and 1837 for various reasons, but still chose to move and rejoin family members in the West. Sampson Grayson, the Hillabee man who returned to Alabama and accused John Page of enslaving Creeks on plantations in Mississippi during the 1834 voluntary emigration, self-emigrated with his family in the spring of 1837. James Island, who emigrated with detachment five, returned to Alabama and self-emigrated with a band of Creeks in 1839. Seventeen Creeks and one slave self-emigrated in 1841 under the charge of John Brodnax, who operated as a private emigrating contractor. Some wealthy Creeks remained behind into the 1840s because they were unable to hastily dispose of their property. Paddy Carr, the Cusseta land speculator, returned to Russell County, Alabama, in November 1837 after serving his tour of duty in Florida. Discovering "no indians Left in The old Creek Nation," Carr vowed to stay in Alabama no "longer than I Can Settle up mi Bizzanness." In February 1847 Carr self-emigrated with eleven Creeks and eight slaves. Months later, William Walker, son-in-law of the late Big Warrior, emigrated with his wife to the Indian territory.[47]

There were also dozens of Creeks who were tied to a piece of land in some manner. Their status is unclear, but many may have been day laborers, sharecroppers, or even slaves on a white man's plot of land. Some may have held a life estate that guaranteed the Creek reservee rights to his or her allotment under the 1832 Treaty of Washington until death. Many probably were tricked into working for whites, as Luther Blake reported that a number of Alabamians and Georgians "told them such tales—as would but induce them to remain" through promise of pay only to find themselves living among the whites' black slaves without money. Just how many Creeks were living in this manner was a matter of conjecture, but it was estimated that there were approximately 160 still in Alabama. Luther Blake, who helped conduct the 1829 voluntary emigrating party, reported that there were 51 men, 54 women, and 54 children. Of this total, 44 were slaves. Blake took an interest in these Creeks, hoping to conduct them west for $100 per person, although the government felt the cost too extravagant. Many of the Creeks were anxious to rejoin their townspeople in the West while others pilfered local farms without much apparent desire to leave.[48]

In 1845, Moses K. Wheat, a resident of the Alabama town of Cusseta in Chambers County, secured the contract at $47.25 per person. On 10 January 1846 over sixty Creeks and thirty-nine of their slaves rendezvoused at Montgomery and waited for boats to take them westward. The wait was a bit longer than expected as the party's commencement was delayed by the low stages of the Alabama River. Wheat also had difficulty collecting and even keeping the Creeks in camp because local whites tried to persuade the emigrants to come back to work for them as laborers. Moreover, a "considerable number" of Creeks, primarily women, were being held against their will, allegedly as slaves, in Barbour, Henry, Dale, Covington, and Pike counties. At one point Wheat collected fifty-seven Creeks in Coosa and Talladega counties and directed them to drive a wagon into camp. Before reaching the encampment, whites convinced the Creeks to flee by falsely claiming that the emigrants would be placed in chains and sold as slaves in the Indian territory. While Wheat remained behind collecting more emigrants, the party left under the charge of Arnold Seale, a notorious land speculator in Creek reserves in the mid-1830s, and Leroy Driver.[49]

The Creeks left Montgomery by steamboat and traveled to Mobile and New Orleans. One infant was born on the vessel while crossing Lake Pontchartrain seven miles from New Orleans. The Creeks proceeded up the Mississippi River and overtook a self-emigrating Creek Indian at the mouth of the White River, who then joined the group. The party continued by water and arrived at the Creek Agency on 15 February 1846. On 1 March, two weeks after the party arrived in the West, the adult male who had joined the party at the White River died of exposure. More Creeks remained behind in Alabama for myriad reasons, however. A number of Creeks, reportedly anxious to emigrate, simply stayed behind because they wanted to move solely by land and objected to the contractor's use of steamboat travel. Some, like the approximately twenty members of the Carr family, needed more time to dispose of their property while others had been "deceived and carried off" from the emigration camp by "designing men."[50]

In the spring of 1848, Ward Cochamy (Coachman), who went on to become the principal chief of the Muscogee (Creek) Nation in 1876, traveled back to Alabama from the Indian territory to emigrate a number of his family who still resided on the Coosa River. Cochamy, who was born in Wetumpka in 1823 and then orphaned, had resided with his uncle in Macon County, Alabama, through the relocation of his people. In 1845 he moved to Indian territory. Throughout April and May 1848 Cochamy collected a number of emigrants, including forty in Autauga, Bibb, Coosa, and Talladega counties. These Creeks were sent to Wetumpka, while more than twenty members of Cochamy's family rendezvoused at Montgomery. On 30 May the party of sixty-five Creeks, traveling by boat, left for the Indian territory and reached New Orleans by the first week of June and Fort Smith, Arkansas, on 24 June before taking wagons due to the low stage of the Arkansas River. Echo Fixico's passing at Lewisburg was the only reported death, and for purposes of this book, the last recorded casualty of the Creek removal era.[51]

William Durant, a relative of Cochamy who emigrated with his party, returned to the East in early 1849 to conclude some unsettled business. Arriving in Alabama, Durant was approached by a number of Creeks who were anxious to emigrate to the Indian territory. Some may have been among the hundred or so Creeks that Cochamy claimed still remained as slaves in Alabama and were living "in a deplorable condition." Durant petitioned the federal government for permission and funding to move these Creeks westward. In early May 1849 Durant had collected twenty-eight "Indians and half breeds" at Wetumpka and thirty-six more near Fort Claiborne. Newspapers reported the arrival of a small detachment of Creeks, perhaps from this very party, reaching Fort Gibson in June 1849.[52]

Although Creeks continued emigrating to Indian territory for decades, the major operations of Creek removal and relocation ended in late 1837 or early 1838 when the last of the Creeks from Pass Christian arrived at Fort Gibson. Their arrival coincided with the ten-year anniversary of the departure of the first McIntosh party. Within that decade, approximately twenty-three thousand people were transferred across the Mississippi River. Their land, now the state of Alabama, was almost exclusively occupied by whites and their black slaves. Large-scale cotton agriculture replaced Creek crops. Railroads dissected Creek hunting grounds. American towns, many taking the names of the Creek *talwas* they had displaced, were platted and built. Not all of the Creeks moved west, however. People like Powis Harjo and Neharlocco Harjo, both from Pucantallahassee, had sold their eastern reserves but continued living on the land into the 1840s, apparently with the permission of the white owners. A small number of Creeks went through the tedious legal process of obtaining clear title to their land. Hundreds of Creeks remained undetected and continued living in Alabama. In 1837 a number of Creeks of African descent in Macon County, Alabama, along with a number of Indian countrymen, all of whom were enrolled on the 1832 census as heads of families, requested patents for their land in the former Creek Nation. Other Creeks sought patents for land they claimed from the first article of the 1814 Treaty of Fort Jackson. Under this provision, Creek allies of the United States during the first Creek War could receive a full section of land. In the twentieth century, the descendants of these Creeks organized a council and filed a number of petitions with the U.S. government. In 1984, the Poarch Band of Creek Indians received federal recognition and remain in Alabama to this day.[53]

10 Perseverance

1837–82

Adjusting to life in the Indian territory was extremely difficult for those who relocated to the West in 1836 and 1837. Forced to find new land, construct new homes, and plant new fields, these Creeks struggled to maintain their traditional ways of life in their new country. In the meantime, the new immigrants lived in temporary camps clustered around their headmen, townspeople, and relatives. Some, like those who served in Florida as well as the sick and infirm, lived for an extended period after their arrival in "rotting," government-issue tents. Used on the march westward, the tents were considered "totally wourn out" and unfit for human habitation, although agents observed that "it would be cruel and inhuman to take them from the Indians and Deprive them of the little comfort they derive from being in them." Disease was a problem for the new arrivals and thirty-five hundred people "at the lowest calculation" died of bilious fevers and smallpox within the first months of resettlement. Some estimated that perhaps up to five or six thousand Creeks perished. As was the case during the voluntary emigration period, mortality during the first years of resettlement greatly surpassed the number of deaths en route. Some Creeks were unwilling to start over and, within months of arriving, small parties returned to the East. Opothle Yoholo also was not happy with life in the Indian territory and continued to advocate for a move to Texas. Many Creeks, in fact, held out hope that they would be able to move beyond the jurisdiction of the United States. Some Creeks did go to Texas, including Benjamin Hawkins who fled there after "some misunderstanding with the chiefs" of the McIntosh-led government. Hawkins died (some say he was murdered by the order of his former business partner Sam Houston) a refugee from the Creek Nation prior to 1838. Others did not even have a chance to restart their lives in the West. Neah Micco, a principal headman of Cusseta and one of the leaders of the Second Creek War, perhaps too aged and too tired to start over in a strange new land, died near Fort Gibson in late December 1836, only four months after arriving in the West.[1]

The first order of business for the new Creek settlers was simply to survive the first months of resettlement. The land was not as healthy as federal officials had repeatedly promised. Indeed, some of the earliest instructions sent to David Brearley advised the agent to point out "the better prospects that await them at the west, in soil, in climate and in game." But the Creeks arrived at Fort Gibson in the dead of winter without suitable clothing and shelter. Smallpox then appeared in 1837, reportedly brought west by a steamboat ascending the Missouri River. After killing approximately fifteen thousand people and destroying "nearly all" of the Indian people in the "upper country," the disease spread to the Creek Nation. The Creeks and Seminoles were among the hardest hit. Creek agent James Logan reported that "the mortality was such as you can hardly conceive they were found dead over the whole Country and floating down the water courses." As the deaths mounted, many of the victims' bodies were deposited in hollow or fallen trees and their openings closed with "billets of wood." As described in Isaac McCoy's 1838 *Annual Register*, "a hollow standing tree frequently has an opening near the root; through this opening the corpse was inserted, and extended up the hollow of the trunk of the tree, so that it was left standing on the feet." Many Creeks were not buried during this time, however. Creek custom held that only relatives were allowed to touch and bury bodies, but when whole families died, the corpses often remained where they fell. Major Ethan Allen Hitchcock, who investigated alleged frauds in the supply of provisions to the Indians, noted in 1842 that "when sickness prevailed to a great extent and great numbers died in 1837 and 1838, there were many that died and were not buried, but their bones yet whiten upon the surface of the ground in various parts of the nation." Indeed, in 1839 Agent Logan addressed the Creeks in council and noted that "almost every hollow tree had become a grave for some of them, and that their path was now become white with the bleached bones of the Muscogees."[2]

The Creek prisoners who were forced west the previous July and August 1836 also suffered significantly. In November 1836, before the first large detachments had arrived, a person tending to the Creek prisoners at Fort Gibson lamented that they had all their property taken from them and were "chained and driven like cattle to this sickly climate—where they are now dying like [rotten] sheep not only from the effects of the climate but for the want of blankets &c., which our government justly owe them & ought to ready for them when [they arrive] here." Federal bureaucracy was also partly to blame for the rapid spread of smallpox in 1837–38 because the federal vaccination program was considered by some to be "worse than useless." Moreover, the blankets that were so desperately needed by the indigent Creeks, after their winter clothing was misplaced on a steamboat, finally arrived in March 1837, just as spring was arriving and the worst of winter had passed.[3]

In the face of unimaginable suffering, the Creeks had little choice but to persevere. As they slowly moved away from their temporary encampments, the new residents began the process of rebuilding their lives. They did this despite their deep-seated belief that the Indian territory was unhealthy, and witnesses reported that "a good deal of dissatisfaction exists among them in relation to their location." Soon after the Cowetas and Cussetas of detachment five were enrolled in the Creek Nation in December 1836, they were accompanied by Lieutenant John T. Sprague thirty-five miles beyond Fort Gibson. There, the agent noted that "I encamped them upon a prarie and they soon after scattered in every direction, seeking a desirable location for their new homes." Creeks who had moved west during the voluntary emigrations and had clustered into compact settlements near Fort Gibson also began dispersing after 1836. The thickly settled region near the confluence of the Arkansas and Verdigris rivers—once compared to parts of New England in its composition—was abandoned by the 1850s and its inhabitants "scattered about over their wide territory" on the Verdigris, Arkansas, along the branches of the Canadian, and "some far out on the western borders, where the buffaloes still range." Indeed, missionary Augustus Ward Loomis noted that "scarce a cabin remains" of the Creeks' community near Fort Gibson and the site "bears the name of Tallahassee, or old fields."[4]

Sticking to what they knew, Creek resettlement patterns in Indian territory mirrored those of Alabama and Georgia. In the east, the Creeks had established their fields on the river floodplains of cleared forestland and this method continued, as best as their environment would allow, west of the Mississippi River. In observing Creek farm site selections, Loomis noted that the Creeks assumed "that the best land is likely to be where the timber grew." This, along with a persistent fear of the prairie meant that a vast majority of residents placed their homesteads within the clearings of the woodlands, or failing that, partly in the prairies and partly within these timbered lands. Indeed, travelers to the region often passed over twenty or thirty miles of Creek Nation prairie land without seeing another soul. One missionary did not encounter any Creek houses during a twenty-five-mile stretch of grassland before noting in his journal that the land was prairie, where "the Indians seldom live." Similarly, on his ride to the *talwa* of Oswitchee, Loomis observed a "space for thousands of farms, and pasture" for stock but did not encounter "a habitation in sight; not a person do we meet, nor have we any trail, not even a cattle path." An unintended benefit of living in the timbered lands, however, was that by leaving portions of area uncleared, it created a natural barrier that protected their property from the harsh winter's winds. Still, settling in the limited amount of woodland had long-term consequences for the Creeks. McCoy anticipated back in 1829 that immigrant Indians from "timbered countries" would make their fields in the woodlands and warned that this would eventually create a scarcity of firewood, which indeed was the case by the time Loomis visited in the early 1850s.[5]

Houses were often dismantled and moved to another clearing once the soil or timber became exhausted or simply to be closer to more fertile grazing land, which also depleted timber reserves. In many cases the Creeks simply abandoned their houses, which created, as one witness observed, a line of "dilapidated huts with trifling improvements" because "the owners for some fancy they may have taken to some other location at a distance, better adapted, as they think, to the promotion of their comfort." In many cases, however, these dilapidated houses were grave sites. Visitors to the West noticed that many of the older generation of Creeks continued the practice of burying their dead under the floors of their homes. The survivors would then construct a new domicile, leaving the old house abandoned and falling into "decay, the weeds and bushes covering and almost concealing them." In other instances, family members would bury the body and then erect a small "miniature cabin" over the top of the grave.[6]

Like many others before him, Josiah Gregg, a merchant and explorer who visited the area in 1839, considered the living conditions of most of the Creeks and other frontier Indians to be "undistinguishable" from those of the poorer white settlers in the area. The most common type of Creek homestead generally consisted of a small, square, one-room log house adjacent to a small field, and perhaps a cow pen, and thatch-roofed stable. George Washington Grayson remembered residing as a child in an "exceedingly primitive little log cabin home, with the spaces between the logs composing the house chinked and daubed with red clay," and he noted that all other houses in the region were similarly built. Some houses were not chinked but covered almost completely in earth. Due to the soil composition, the homes of this construction near the Canadian River were bright red, "which gives a quite gay appearance to the house as seen through the woods a little distance off." Loomis visited one Creek homestead, which he called "nothing different from a great many others in the country," and described its construction as a log house,

> covered with long narrow pieces of oak split thin for shingles, and these not nailed, but held to their place by heavy poles laid along the roof. There is not a sawed board about the premises. The floor is of what are called puncheons—thick plank split and hewed tolerably smooth on one side; seats are made of the same material. The table was made with the hatchet, of such boards as cover the roof, and they are

fastened together with small wooden pegs. The doors have wooden hinges and a wooden latch. At the side of the room are holes bored into the logs, and wooden pins driven into the holes—on some of the pins are placed split boards.

Along the inside walls, Loomis observed that the wooden pins held a few articles of dress, wooden hooks could hold a rifle, and plank shelving provided storage for a small number of dishes.[7]

Those considered "well-to-do" were Creeks like Grayson's neighbor, Thlathlo Harjo. The Eufaula man owned several log cabins, "the more pretentious of which were built of split and hewed logs, two being joined together under one roof with a gallery or corridor between, in which the family made their home." Even once-modest homesteads often grew larger as the owners added buildings to the lot commensurate with their rising fortunes. Grayson, for example, noted that their "exceedingly primitive" homestead was later enlarged by adding another log house on the north end of their yard. Similarly, Loomis encountered one of the miccos of Coweta whom he noted lived in a "tolerably comfortable log house" but still felt the need to build an additional structure nearby. Beyond these buildings were "well fenced and well tended fields, good horses, large herds of fine cattle, and many hogs."[8]

The very poorest struggled with food insecurity. Loomis believed that "a majority" of the Creeks were not well off because they had "sickly" corn and few stock animals. The missionary blamed Creek laziness for this, but most of the immigrants arrived in the West with little or nothing and it was costly and laborious to establish new farmsteads. In 1838 agents compiled a list of approximately twenty-three hundred Upper and fifteen hundred Lower indigent Creek Indians, some of whom were listed as blind or "crippled." Moreover, clearing timberland for a field was difficult as the Creeks not only had to fell trees but also clear away thickets and vines that grew to almost six inches in diameter. Even Loomis noted that clearing a field in the timberlands of the richer north side of the Arkansas River "must have been a formidable undertaking." The very poorest Creeks did not own even a small cabin, according to the missionary, and instead "have only camping grounds." As the timberland near the rivers and streams became scarcer due to the settlement of so many people, however, many Creeks were probably forced onto portions of the prairie. Prairie land was inhabitable but difficult to break without large teams, which most Creeks did not have due to the exigencies of relocation. Moreover, the climate continued to be a hindrance to prosperity. Communal farming reemerged in Indian territory among some portions of the population for the first time, perhaps, since the 1832 Treaty of Washington broke the Creek Nation into individual allotments. Gregg reported that the Creeks had "large fields, which are cultivated in common, and the produce proportionally distributed." Loomis saw the common fields of Tallassee, which were dotted with each clan's corn crib. But sickness rendered many of the Creeks bedridden and killed others, which decreased clan productivity. Moreover, Loomis noted that the town and its field were situated on bottomland that was "subject to overflow," which destroyed crops during flooding. In 1856 the Creek Nation was plagued by grasshoppers that destroyed entire fields. And, just as had been the case in the East, alcohol supplied by white traders decreased the impulse to clear, plant, or weed.[9]

Many of the Creeks of modest means organized their homesteads spatially in diffused town sites reminiscent of those in Alabama and Georgia in the late eighteenth and early nineteenth centuries. Moreover, these *talwas* emerged only after the arrival of the main body of Creeks from the six detachments. Indeed, Baptist minister Isaac McCoy noted that no Creek town sites existed in the West by May 1837—the by-product of voluntary immigrants largely huddling near Fort Gibson—but it is noted in his 1838 *Annual Register* that "two or three places begin to assume the appearance of hamlets." According to Gregg, most of the Creeks who lived in these reconstituted *talwas* were among the "lower classes," which, only two years after relocation, probably included a majority of the population. Gregg was even hesitant to call these communities "towns," arguing instead that they were "rather settlements than villages, being but sparse clusters of huts without any regularity." Indeed, when Samuel Washington Woodhouse, a surgeon and naturalist imbedded with a topographical engineering team surveying the Creek Nation boundary

FIG. 30. Selected Creek towns in Indian territory according to Frank G. Speck, ca. 1905. Found in Frank G. Speck, *The Creek Indians of Taskigi Town* (New York: Kraus Reprint, 1964). Cartography by Sarrah Mattics.

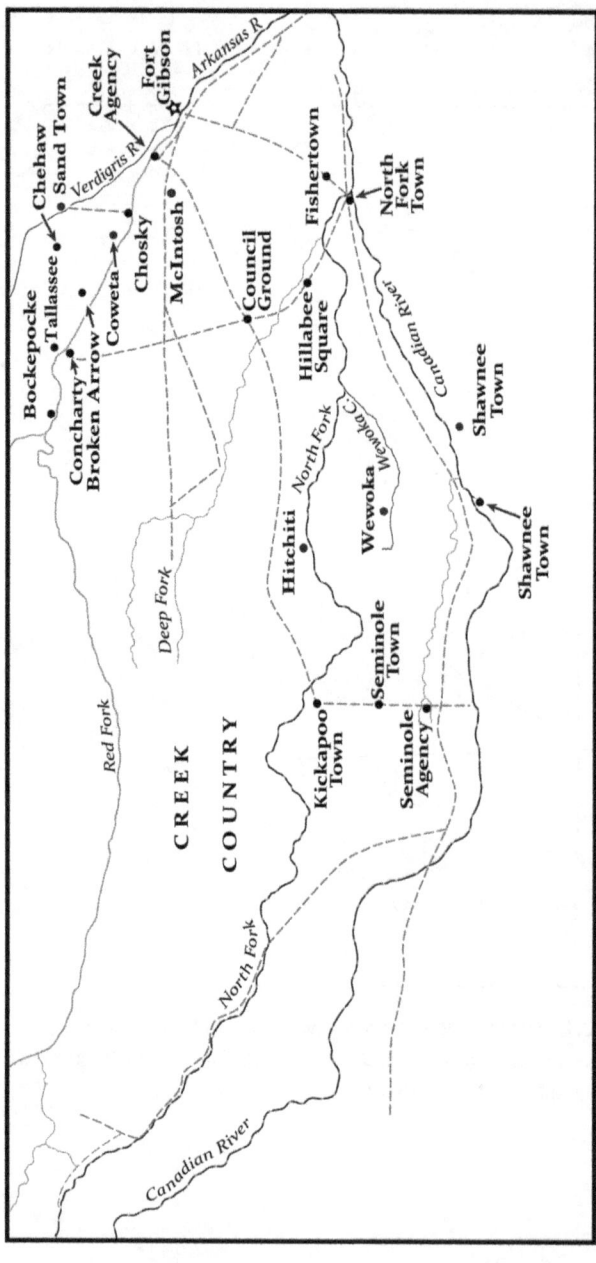

FIG. 31. Indian territory, ca. 1850–59. Drawn from Map 493, Record Group 75, Entry 163, Central Map Files, NARA II, College Park MD; Indian territory, 35th Cong., 1st sess., 1851, H. Exec. Doc. 104, serial no. 958; Boundaries of the Creeks and Seminoles, Map 22, RG 75, Entry 163, Central Map Files, NARA II, College Park MD. Additional town placements from John S. Tomer and Michael J. Brodhead, *A Naturalist in Indian Territory: The Journals of S. W. Woodhouse, 1849–1850* (Norman: University of Oklahoma Press, 1992), 98. Cartography by Sarah Mattics.

line, visited Chehaw in August 1849, he found a "large town extending many miles their houses are at some distance apart," situated along a ridge in the northern part of the territory. Despite calling Chehaw large, towns were much smaller in the West than they had historically been in the East, likely a by-product of the limited amount of timberland available for settlement. Presbyterian ministers, for example, noted that Concharty consisted of approximately two hundred people and was "as large as Indian towns generally are in this country."[10]

As they had done throughout their history in the East, the Creeks incorporated other Indian groups into their nation "as a measure of policy to increase their own strength." This no doubt took on special urgency considering the large number of immigrants who died during the first year of settlement and the continued threat of attack by western Indians. Numbers of relocated Cherokees, Shawnees, Delawares, and Kickapoos were allowed to establish settlements within and around the Creek Nation, while up to six hundred Piankashaws were "domesticated among the Creeks" and "are regarded as a part of the Creek Nation." The Piankashaws were given a small part of the Creek annuity and their headmen were allowed seats on National Councils. Most of these resident Indians lived on the Canadian or Little Rivers. Fifteen hundred Kickapoos, according to Hitchcock, lived fifteen miles up the Canadian from the mouth of Little River, with Shawnee settlements scattered "above and below them." The Piankashaws lived fifteen miles from the Little River's mouth, while seven hundred Delawares lived sixty miles to the west.[11]

The Little River area was also home to a town comprised almost solely of former black slaves. Many of these residents were once Seminole slaves who claimed to have been freed by Thomas S. Jesup during the Second Seminole War. Other residents were free blacks who had been evicted from other Indian nations, while a few were runaways from white owners in the United States. All found refuge among the growing population. Creek headmen tried to close down this settlement, claiming that the runaways had a "very pernicious influence" on not only the Creeks' slaves but also among the "lower class of our people." The complaint was made during a time when Creek leaders were moving toward creating a racial hierarchy and, as Claudio Saunt has argued, "elevate Indians to masters and reduce blacks to slaves." The Creek government passed a series of slave codes and banished abolitionist preachers who ministered to their slaves. In 1842 approximately two hundred slaves escaped from their Creek and Cherokee masters. John D. Lang and Samuel Taylor Jr., who were visiting the Creek Nation, observed that "this caused much excitement, and a posse was sent after them from both nations. Both Church and State seemed aroused on account of these desertions, and ready to make every possible effort to recover them at all hazards, and in future to enact more rigid laws for the government of their slaves, and for binding their chains more strongly upon them."[12]

The wealthiest Creeks operated southern-style plantations, often far away from their *talwas*. Opothle Yoholo, for example, had a net worth of about $80,000 by 1854, and owned a plantation run entirely by black slaves. Noted painter George Catlin visited the western Creek country in the mid-1830s and observed that "it is no uncommon thing to see a Creek with twenty or thirty slaves at work on his plantation." Indeed, Pinkney Hawkins, who voluntarily emigrated with his uncle Benjamin in 1830 and later moved to Texas, established a large plantation run by twenty slaves. Josiah Gregg estimated that the very wealthiest owned more than fifty. Benjamin Marshall reportedly had one hundred. Rich Creeks, some with a large number of slaves to do their bidding, grew myriad crops that they sold on the market. Different types of fruits and vegetables as well as cotton was grown and sold to other Indians and to whites near and far. Wealthy Creeks even sold thousands of bushels of surplus corn to Ireland in the midst of their potato famine in the 1840s. Corn, potatoes, and rice were grown and sold at market in Van Buren, Arkansas, and other nearby cities. Rice was particularly profitable for the Creeks, and many local whites preferred it to the variety brought up the rivers from New Orleans.[13]

For those who lived far away from their towns, which included Creeks who owned more modest farmsteads, *talwas* served two purposes. First, *talwas* served as places of refuge for planters and farmers who lived on the unprotected edges of the Creek Nation. Whenever threatened, these Creeks could seek protection in the "thick settlements" around

Little River and some distance up the Arkansas. Second, *talwas* served as traditional ceremonial centers. As was the case in the East, Creeks who had moved far from the geographic location of their towns returned for the annual Busk and other religious and civic ceremonies. Tuckabatchee was perhaps the most important ceremonial site for Creeks living in the Canadian district, as the town was the only one, according to Hitchcock, to have rebuilt their rotunda by 1842. Hitchcock visited the structure and noted that the Tuckabatchee hothouse was erected with "considerable ingenuity." John Mix Stanley, an artist, portraitist, and explorer, also toured the site and estimated that the conical roof reached a height of thirty feet and was of "singular and peculiar" construction. Mile chief Tuckabatchee Micco, "the great Medicine or Mystery Man of the Creeks," designed the building over a six-day period in which he increased his focus through fasting. The building was built by members of the town who were given miniature sticks resembling the logs they needed to cut. When all the materials came together, Stanley reported that the pieces fit perfectly without any necessary redesign. Beams were lashed with leather and the roof made of shingles. Near the hothouse was a small, enclosed shed that housed the sacred brass and copper plates the Creeks brought from Alabama.[14]

Incredibly resilient, most towns reconstructed their ceremonial sites to some extent upon first arriving in Indian territory. The Chehaws reestablished their council ground on Adams Creek, near the Cherokee line. A map of the Indian territory locates the Hillabee complex just south of the Deep Fork, about ten miles from its junction with the North Fork. The scarcity of timber and the harsh environment meant that some of these public buildings were crudely constructed and difficult to maintain. The Oswitchee "Busk house," according to Presbyterian missionary Augustus Ward Loomis, was located in a "desolate country" some distance from a branch of the Verdigris and was established in the midst of several family settlements. According to Loomis the structure itself was "a rude affair" and consisted of "merely crotches set in the ground, and covered with poles and bushes." At the Tallassee ceremonial grounds Loomis discovered that the structure "was going to ruins; the dancing ground was grown over with weeds," and the chunkey yard pole (used for a Creek ball game played between men and women) "that stood in the centre was fallen down." At the "Kowetah Busk House," located near the Coweta Mission, the sacred conch shells, brought from the East and used for consuming black drink, were stored.[15]

The Creeks took great pains to maintain their traditional spiritual and ceremonial lives during the first years of resettlement. David B. Rollin, an ordained minister, attended a Busk in August 1836, around the time the Creek prisoners were arriving at Fort Gibson. John Mix Stanley attended an 1843 Busk and painted Tomathla Micco, a mile chief of Tuckabatchee, with a Red Stick—in homage to the Creeks' military past—which he carried to the annual ceremony. Loomis, who attended a Green Corn Ceremony in the early 1850s, observed the Creeks doing most of the same preparations they would have done in the East—fasting, cleaning, and repairing their square grounds, and consuming and regurgitating black drink. The Creeks probably brought the yaupon holly plant (*Ilex vomitoria*) with them on their march, although the tree was native to the Texas coast and parts of southern Oklahoma and was probably easily accessible. Cabeza de Vaca, during his time in Texas (ca. 1528–34), observed Indians drink and vomit black drink. In one ceremony during an 1850s Busk, the Creeks danced around the conch shells, carried solemnly from the old Creek Nation, which it was noted were "considered sacred, and may not be touched by any but the appointed officers." And the Tuckabatchees' sacred copper plates continued to feature prominently in their Green Corn Ceremonies, so much so that by the 1870s the plates were noticeably thinner due to their repeated polishing. In fact one Creek woman, who had last seen them around 1876, noted that the original figures and inscriptions engraved on their face had been "scoured out."[16]

The ability of the Creeks to rebuild, however, was often hampered by the geography of Indian territory, the inefficiency of the federal bureaucracy, and the broken promises of federal officials. In 1841 the steamboat *Trident*, laden with annuity goods and rifles, was delayed for months on the river until the water rose sufficiently to ensure its passage. The headmen also repeatedly complained that the government often paid out their annuity in the middle of winter, when traveling was more difficult. This also denied the Creeks adequate time to purchase winter clothes. Declaring that they "suffer a great deal for want of clothing" during the cold months, the headmen demanded that they receive their annuity by September at the latest. Meanwhile, the Creeks often received goods that they had never asked for and subsequently did not want. The 1838 Treaty of Fort Gibson, which compensated Creeks for abandoned and lost property in Alabama and on the march west, guaranteed, among other things, to pay the nation 5 percent annual interest from a $350,000 fund. While interest was paid solely in money the first year, in each subsequent payment, the Creeks were compensated "in money, stock animals, blankets, domestics or such articles of a similar nature as the President of the United States may direct." But according to Opothle Yoholo and other headmen, "such articles" included "fish hooks, and little white pipes, and hobbles for horses and a great many other little things that they did not want." Instead, the Creeks requested money so they could purchase the items themselves. Officials in Washington were not the only ones to blame for bureaucratic inefficiency. When James Logan of Arkansas was appointed agent to the Creeks in 1838, he combed through what few records had been left by previous agents and concluded that "the business of the nation has been conducted very loosely."[17]

All Creeks, regardless of wealth or political affiliation, suffered from federal inattentiveness and bureaucratic red tape. Many of the richest McIntosh party members still had not been compensated for livestock left in the old Creek Nation almost fifteen years after they first emigrated to the West. Despite the signatures of Roly and Chilly McIntosh on the 1838 Treaty of Fort Gibson, the McIntosh party was largely ignored when the payouts were first issued. In a terse 1842 letter to Washington, Roly McIntosh complained that "I was among the first who came to this country. As we gave no trouble to the government, the people have thought it very hard that those who gave the trouble should have their claims obtained and paid while ours have been neglected. It has occasioned a good deal of hard feeling." The Creeks who participated in the Second Creek War were not specifically provided for in the treaty, although due to their "extreme poverty" and the fear that they would "commit depredations on their neighbours," they were allocated ten thousand dollars' worth of stock animals for a year.[18]

Indeed, most of those forced west quickly discovered that the promise of a better life in Indian territory was little more than federal officials' lies, and the Creeks continued to face many of the same problems that had plagued them in the East. Andrew Jackson told the Creeks that emigration would allow them to live unmolested by whites, but encroachment continued to be a point of frustration in the West. Opothle Yoholo, for example, complained that there were "bad white men" living illegally in the Creek Nation, including two who had beaten a woman over the head and "crossed the line," clearly a reference to rape. Moreover, white missionaries and schoolteachers were more prevalent in the West than they had been in the old Creek Nation, in part because the McIntosh-led government had become more receptive to the idea by the 1840s. Many, however, wanted nothing to do with whites. In 1846 a group of Creek headmen addressed their Seminole counterparts and recommended that they "oppose all the ways of the whiteman, such as schools, preaching, fiddle dancing, card playing and the like." Indeed, Loomis discovered firsthand the hostility shown by some toward any white person in the Creek country. As he attempted to engage a town micco in a discussion on religion, the Creek man stopped what he was doing and angrily declared:

> While we were yet in Georgia, and the government agents were trying to get us away, they told us that if we remained there, the whites would settle all around us, and would crowd in amongst us, and by little and little they would teach our people their customs and their laws, and ours would gradually go from us. But, go west, said they—far away beyond the settlements, and you may be by yourselves always, without any fear of intrusion: and we believed their talk, and came west, even away here west of Arkansaw, and now you are on after us again.

The headman's son-in-law, whom Loomis encountered later that day, felt similarly; when approached he hurried away and "with somewhat of bitterness" declared that "when we left the old country it was with the assurance that if we would come to the new reservation, we should never be interfered with in any way."[19]

Many of the early interlopers were speculators from Alabama and Georgia who traveled west in the hopes of acquiring the Creeks' remaining unsold eastern reserves. With disputes over landownership in Alabama unresolved into the late 1830s, the land frauds that had plagued the Creeks in the East continued almost unabated in Indian territory. Whites sought powers of attorney or agreements to purchase Creek land and some Creeks did sell, although headmen complained that the purchasers often did not pay out any actual money. Other speculators, whose claims were rejected because of suspicion of fraud, traveled westward in an attempt to bribe the Creeks into writing false memorials claiming that they had been paid the full amount for their Alabama land. But eastern speculators, fearful that all the remaining land would soon be bought up, created fictitious claims for many of the half-sections in order to thwart the purchases. Some speculators ransomed confiscated property for a profit. Caesar, a black interpreter for Brevet Major General Jesup during the Seminole campaign, entrusted his family and four hundred dollars (with which he intended to use to help purchase his wife's freedom) to a confidante at Tuskegee while he served with the Creeks in Florida. When the custodian died, the money and Caesar's family were turned over to "Ned Hendrick" (probably Montgomery-based land speculator and James C. Watson Company member Edward C. Hanrick), who stole the four hundred dollars and demanded a $3,500 ransom for Caesar's family.[20]

The Creeks were also cheated by white merchants and traders. Some had contracted with the federal government to provide provisions during the march west and during the first year of resettlement. A number of Creeks complained that they did not receive food along the route west, a claim backed up by Lieutenant Edward Deas, who had criticized the lack of provision depots through the Mississippi swamp. Once in Indian territory, many Creeks were given only a small amount of rations to feed large families. Still others were forced to buy their provisions when the contractors ran out of supplies. Major Ethan Allen Hitchcock, hired by the government to investigate the provision frauds, recorded a litany of complaints from people forced west after 1836. Samuel Smith, an Indian of mixed ancestry, objected to the fact that the contractors issued beef overestimated in weight and provided "cows, so poor they could hardly stand." Without provisions, many of those starving were forced to "gather wild salad and boil it and eat it, when they had nothing else to live upon" while others went into the prairie to dig for wild potato. Some of the relocated Creeks were even forced to kill the stock of the old settlers from the voluntary emigrations in order to survive. Hitchcock's diary offers a litany of other grievances the Creeks had with the provision contractors as well as the employees of the Alabama Emigrating Company: "baggage thrown out of the wagons and lost—The Florida warriors, few got rations, got a little money; of the main band, rations issued irregularly; when due, not delivered; and when delivered but half issued." Davy Grayson complained that he never received any provisions and had not received a dollar of the annuity, nor was he paid for driving a wagon from the old Creek Nation to Indian territory. Even Caesar, who in 1842 was still trying to reunite with his wife and three children, was victimized by the provision contractors in Indian territory, who gave him very little beef and "no corn at all, not a grain." Traders, especially those engaged in the sale of spirits, also contributed to the poverty found in the Indian territory as the grog merchants took not only the Creeks' money but also "whatever article of value he would part with." Merchants also preyed on the native inhabitants whenever federal monies were distributed. Benjamin Marshall, for example, argued against paying out any orphan fund money under the 1832 Treaty of Washington because he feared that whites would "commence buying up the claim for [little] or nothing."[21]

Alcohol, brought to the border of Indian territory in large quantities by whites, continued to be a problem in the West. Most of the "ardent spirits" arrived by steamboat to Van Buren or Fort Smith from as far away as Cincinnati. If the water was too low beyond that point, canoes carried the forty-gallon barrels up the Arkansas River. If the water was too low even for canoes, the alcohol was placed on wagons and taken up the "Whiskey Road," a small trail that branched off the military road some six miles from Fort Smith and ran to the mouth of the Illinois

River. The alcohol was then distributed to the Creeks and Cherokees in smaller quantities on the Canadian River. Benjamin Hawkins, for example, was caught smuggling sixty barrels of whiskey into the Indian territory in 1832. Alcohol was a contributing factor to the high mortality rate found in the western Creek Nation. Creeks died from falling off their horses while intoxicated, while one man drowned attempting to cross the Arkansas River. Creek headmen believed that federal officials either did little to stop the problem or, in the case with Brearley, actually contributed to the crisis. Temperance societies were established and by the 1840s the Creeks had passed strict laws against importing alcohol for resale, including execution for a third offense.[22]

Attempts to halt the sale of alcohol in the Creek Nation also highlight the extent to which the Creeks were still subject to American laws in the West, despite assurances that they would be allowed to govern themselves. Because alcohol abuse was such a problem, both Creek and federal law prohibited its sale in Indian territory. In the spring of 1853, when a number of Indians were arrested for trafficking spirits, a U.S. deputy marshal entered the Creek country and apprehended the suspects, only to see a mob of natives impede the arrest and set the men free. This had occurred in an unnamed town where the inhabitants had been brought to Indian territory "in Irons"—meaning they were prisoners who were forced west as coconspirators in the Second Creek War. Although writs for the Creeks' re-arrest were subsequently issued, some military personnel believed that if the suspects were taken into custody, other Indians in nearby settlements who had also come west in chains, along with bands of removed Cherokees, Choctaws, and Chickasaws with "nothing to lose," would join the Creeks in a war against the United States. The Creeks had already placed warriors between their towns and Fort Gibson and sent their women and children away in preparation for battle. With the bitterness of forced removal serving as a backdrop, the mob was protesting the right of Americans to enter their settlements without warning or explanation and "seize and carry off, some of their people." Because the Creeks had their own punishments for lawbreakers, Thomas S. Drew, who served as the head of the Southern Superintendency of Indian Affairs, conceded that "in most cases," jurisdictional confusion would "lead to punnishment of the offender *twice* for the *same offence.*"²³

Most disappointing for the Creeks, the move to the Indian territory did not stop the continued expropriation of Creek land. Andrew Jackson, speaking through Secretary of War John H. Eaton in 1830, told the Creeks in no uncertain terms that "the soil will be yours and the property of your children forever." Nevertheless, the Creeks repeatedly lost territory because of inexperienced surveyors, faulty equipment, bureaucratic oversight, negligence, and outright deceit. This was not just a Creek problem; many eastern Indian nations were led to believe that they would hold their western lands in perpetuity only to be compelled to cede portions of their domain in later years. As Arthur H. DeRosier Jr. has argued, the federal government allotted the Choctaws millions of acres of land in the West, fully aware that they would not retain all of this territory in the future. Similarly, the more than two million acres that was "conveyed and forever secured by the United States, to the said Delaware Nation, as their permanent residence," in present-day Kansas in 1829 was gone by 1866. Moreover, in a number of cases, federal officials consolidated displaced Indian nations onto the same tract of land for logistical expediency. The Chickasaws were initially assigned to the Choctaw reserve and the Creeks and Seminoles were placed together within the Creek Nation. After losing their land in Kansas, many Delawares, because of the dearth of quality unoccupied land, chose to move to the Cherokee country and become members of the Cherokee Nation.²⁴

Although a dispute between the western Creeks and western Cherokees over a tract of the Creek country ceded to the Cherokees in 1828 appeared to be settled in 1833, the Creeks were unhappy with the precise location of the redrawn boundary and complained that they had "lost much country and suffer great wrong" at the hands of the surveyors. Headmen, led by Roly McIntosh, complained that "the Cherokees have the Arkansas as high up as it is navigable; the whole of Grand river and the best part of Verdigris," while the Creeks, according to McIntosh, had only one steamboat landing and no water power for their mills. At the same time, the controversy over whether the Seminoles would live within the Creek Nation under Creek law or as a separate nation altogether remained unresolved through the 1830s. Many Seminoles had refused to live in the Creek Nation because they did not want to relinquish their sovereignty and property, and instead settled in the territories of other Indian peoples. Subsequent complaints by neighboring Indian nations of "numerous and extensive depredations" committed by the Seminoles on their property spurred the federal government to action. In 1845 Creek and Seminole delegates signed a treaty at the Creek Agency that allowed the Seminoles to "make their own town regulations, subject, however, to the general control of the Creek council, in which they shall be represented." The Creeks were financially compensated for incorporating the Seminoles—who because of the Second Seminole War were deemed by Creek leaders to be potentially violent and "troublesome neighbors"—into their national domain (the additional money was also used to assuage the dissatisfaction the Creeks had over the Creek-Cherokee boundary line marked under the 1833 Treaty of Fort Gibson). Because the treaty did not fully separate the two nations, however, the 1845 Treaty of the Creek Agency did little to resolve the Seminole issue. In August 1856 the Creeks finally relented to a cession of their land.[25]

The Creeks also lost a massive amount of territory as punishment for those who joined the Confederacy during the American Civil War. As they had done through much of their history, federal officials used the actions of a faction as an excuse to punish the entire Creek population. In a treaty that normalized relations between the Creek Nation and the American government in 1866, the Creeks were forced to cede "the west half of their entire domain" to the United States. Despite the fact that many Creeks did not join the Confederacy, the federal government determined that the entire nation was "liable to forfeit" their land, annuities, immunities, and protections guaranteed to them in past treaties. The cession was soon inhabited by Potawatomis, Seminoles, Sac and Foxes, Arapahos, and Cheyennes. Of the 3.2 million acres retained by the Creeks, one-third was considered "barren."[26]

Because of their abrupt removal and relocation to the West in 1836 and 1837, the Creeks still had unfinished business in Alabama and Georgia. The Creek orphan fund (from the sale of the twenty sections of land guaranteed them in the 1832 Treaty of Washington) was just one of many loose ends that remained untied decades after the Creeks' resettlement in Indian territory. The twenty reserves were divided into quarter sections and sold at public auction on 25 and 26 April 1836 in Mardisville, Alabama. The unsold quarter sections, along with the reserves that were purchased although the sale was not finalized (due to failure to pay, for instance), were auctioned off in Tuskegee, Alabama, on 8 February 1837. In 1840 federal agents constructed a list of approximately thirteen hundred orphans "who are at this time so destitute as to call for the application of the interest" from their 1836 and 1837 land sales. The proceeds from the sales—$108,713.82—were invested in the stocks of different states, including Tennessee and Virginia (which comprised, among other things, railroad and canal companies). These investments were illegal because the law required the proceeds to be invested in U.S. stocks at an interest rate of not less than 5 percent. Moreover, many of these state stocks had depreciated significantly over time. In addition, federal officials misappropriated approximately $176,000 of the orphan's money that was redirected for "general purposes of the Creek Nation" and to aid loyal Creek refugees who were displaced during the American Civil War. Including the illegal stocks, the orphan fund had lost almost a quarter million dollars. Records show that, interest notwithstanding, money was paid out of the fund only twice—in August 1868 and July 1870—for the benefit of the orphans. In 1879 the Creeks hired William Orrie Tuggle, a Georgia lawyer, to represent them in their orphan fund claims against the federal government. Tuggle ran into a number of roadblocks, as Congress stalled on money bills in the early 1880s in the interest of appearing "economical" to their constituents. Although the United States claimed that, with regard to the interest, "the loss has been made good," the Creek orphans, all of whom had grown into old age and some of whom had already died, still had not received all the compensation from the fund prior to 1882.[27]

In fact, many of the Creeks' outstanding Alabama land claims remained unresolved well after they had moved west, which deprived those forced west of lifesaving monies. The Creeks had complained for years prior to relocation that there were no provisions in the 1832 Treaty of Washington that dealt with cases in which Creek heads of families died before selling their half-section. Administrators, appointed by the orphan courts, often kept the proceeds of the land sale rather than seek out the heirs in Indian territory. Speculators who wanted clear title to this land also complained and LaFayette, Alabama, attorney George D. Hooper, the older brother of Johnson Jones Hooper, represented a number of whites who had purchased these so-called "dead locations." Despite the fraud and the repeated complaints by the Creeks, Jackson refused to attend to the matter and referred it to Congress. The day before Jackson left office, Congress finally passed a sweeping bill that, among other things, authorized the president to sell the Creeks' unsold land in Alabama and confirm the sales made by widows, widows and children, children, or those transferred by "lawful administrators" for reservees who died prior to 4 April 1837 (five years to the day the treaty was ratified).[28]

Despite the passage of the act of 3 March 1837, the Creeks were skeptical that the federal government would conclude their Alabama affairs hastily and pay out any outstanding monies. On 7 October 1837 Creek headmen led by Opothle Yoholo entered into an agreement with a Columbus, Georgia–based land company headed by Charles J. McDonald. Under the terms of the indenture, McDonald and his partners promised to purchase all unsold reserves in Alabama, the half-sections that remained uncertified, land of Creeks who died before selling, and land sold without the approval of the president for $66,500. Although the headmen were no doubt aware of Congress's 3 March act when they agreed to terms with McDonald, they had lost faith in the U.S. government to protect them from future frauds. In pushing for Washington to approve the deal, Opothle Yoholo rhetorically asked, "Does our Father believe if the law of Congress stands and our Lands are sold under it that we or our people will get a twentyeth part of the value of our Lands [?]." Moreover, the headmen had been led to believe that by removing to the West, they would once again operate under their own laws and their own power to negotiate contracts. And with most of those who arrived in 1836 and 1837 destitute and suffering from disease and a shortage of provisions, the Creeks needed money urgently. Although McDonald's offer was low, the headmen believed less money immediately was better than the promise of more money in some distant future and told federal officials as much when they argued that "one dollar to them now will do them more good than five some years hence."[29]

The federal government ultimately rejected the McDonald contract because it ran contrary to the act of 3 March 1837. In 1838 an agent was appointed to sell the lands at public auction, as directed in the first section of the law. Public notice was given and advertisements placed in various newspapers in Alabama and Georgia. Before the auction took place, however, several purchasers came forward with valid claims to a number of reserves and the auction was subsequently postponed. In March 1839 Opothle Yoholo and a number of Creek headmen again wrote Washington complaining that the Creeks still had not received money for their unsold lands and urged federal officials to ratify the McDonald contract. Noting that most of the Creeks "were poor and very much in need of clothes in this cold country," the headmen admonished federal officials and stated that "if you had agreed to the contract we made they could have had their money long ago."[30]

In fact, a number of sections and half-sections allotted under the 1832 Treaty of Washington remained unsold in Alabama decades after the Creeks were relocated to Indian territory. In 1838 the titles to approximately 3,500 reserves transferred by the Creeks were still under federal "examination" while 228 remained unsold. In 1843 a total of 296 cases were still unsettled out of the original 6,696 reserves. Many allotments remained unoccupied while some were improved by white squatters with no title to the soil. By 1848 there were only 66 unsold half-sections, one unsold full section (of deceased Kialigee mile chief Quassad Harjo), and 118 reserves that had been sold but whose sales had not been acted upon by the War Department. Dozens more of the reserves were auctioned off in December 1855 and May 1856. Still, a handful of reserves were not bid on (or were forfeited for nonpayment) and remained unsold almost two decades after the first Creeks were forced from Alabama. In the Creeks' 1856 treaty with the Seminoles, the headmen agreed to quitclaim their rights to all their land east of the Mississippi River with certain exceptions.[31]

Another unresolved controversy was how to compensate Creeks who were accidentally left off the 1832 census and never received a reserve.

When John Page was ordered to leave detachment six at Pass Christian in August 1837 and travel west in order to pay out the remainder of the Watson contract money, he was also directed to make a list of Creeks in the Indian territory who never received land in the old Creek Nation. At a council held on 7 October 1837, Page tallied 212 people left off the 1832 roll. This list was not exhaustive, however, and other Creeks came forward after that date claiming land. Jim Boy, who accompanied a spring 1838 delegation to Washington to petition for ratification of the McDonald contract, used his time in the capital city to urge federal officials to reimburse the eleven Creeks of Thlobthlocco and affiliated towns who were left off the census. No action was taken, however, until 1846, when councils were called to once more ascertain who was eligible for land. At councils held on 22 September and 23 November at the Deep Fork in the Indian territory, government officials revised the census and added 234 names to the roll. In 1852 the number was again revised to 217, with 21 names set aside pending an investigation. In lieu of land, officials compensated the Creeks $1.25 an acre, as guaranteed in the act of March 3, 1837, for the reserves they never received.[32]

The unfulfilled promises and the outright lies of the federal government created an understandable bitterness among the Creek people. In 1842 Ethan Allen Hitchcock observed that many of the Upper Creeks were still "so hostile to the whites and so much exasperated by cheats put upon them in Georgia and Alabama." But the resentment over their relocation also affected Creeks too young to actually remember it. In 1846 two Creeks killed a teamster on the Illinois River near Fort Gibson. One of the suspects escaped while the other, a Yuchi described as "a mere boy," was apprehended by the Creek authorities and soon confessed. The interrogators noted that the child "admits the act, glories in it, even, and speaks of the desire he had to *Kill a white man*."[33]

Most Creeks, however, spent their remaining years rebuilding their lives while wistfully reminiscing about the past. Loomis reported of his visit to Indian territory in the 1850s that the Creeks "were very reluctant to remove; sorry to leave their old fields and orchards, their homes and hunting grounds, their council houses, and the graves of their kinsmen and their braves. To this day, they talk much of the happy country from which they were *driven*, as they express it: they discourse about its springs, and brooks, and rivers; its rich soil, and abundant timber; its hills and valleys, and genial climate." "Nothing," Loomis recorded, "is equal to what they had in Georgia; the summers here are hotter, the winters are colder, the rain is wetter, the crops lighter, the game scarcer, and their people are dying off faster than ever was known in the 'old nation.'" Almost twenty-five years later, in 1879, Tuggle observed a black man sing "a bad song about what a good time he used to have in Ga when he had two wives and was a young man."[34]

For those few Creeks who remained in Alabama after 1837, the pain of relocation was just as sharp, but for a different reason. Although still surrounded by the forests and streams they so cherished, absent were the friends and townspeople who gave that landscape meaning. No one felt the sting of loneliness more than Coffee, a Creek Indian and brother of the famous Chinnabee (an ally of the United States during the first Creek War). While listening to a particularly moving song at a Christian revival in Alabama in the years after the Creeks left Alabama, Coffee abruptly fell "prostrate on his knees in the altar, with an altar full of penitents." The Reverend Joseph Camp, a preacher who later wrote about the incident, observed him weep "as though his heart would break and smiting his breast saying, 'Enokequa sulga'—my heart is sick." Even though they could not speak to each other—Coffee did not understand English— Camp knew exactly why the Creek man was crying. "To think that his people were all in the West," Camp declared, "and he with his wife and few others left behind, cut off from his associates, and he weeping so bitterly." Perhaps overcome a bit himself, Camp sadly noted that he "never had such sympathy for any one in life."[35]

And so, the story ends where it began—with the voluntary emigration of small parties of Creek Indians. Throughout the 1840s and 1850s, dozens and dozens of Creeks in small family-sized detachments self-emigrated to Indian territory. Some may have been prevented from leaving due to outstanding debt owed to white traders. Others probably had been forced to work the fields of Alabama settlers. Most were people who somehow escaped the large relocations only to decide to rejoin their people sometime later. A few were young children who might have been left in the care of a custodian until they were old enough, and healthy enough, to endure the arduous journey west. Safohekee, for example, was an orphan boy who remained in Alabama until leaving to rejoin his people in Indian territory in 1841. John Shepherd of Hitchiti "was left a small boy in Alabama, and came west and found his own mother by whom he was identified" in 1853. Regardless of their circumstances, these Creeks likely had one thing in common; the pull of family and friends was simply too strong to remain where they were. Their Alabama homeland no longer felt like home. Unlike the voluntary parties of the 1820s and early 1830s, which cleaved the Creek Nation in half, these reunification emigrations were attempts to make it somewhat whole. Indeed, when Cosista Harjo and his family left Alabama, they first moved to Texas, but after being "sent for by their people," rejoined their clan in the Creek Nation, Indian territory.[36]

Conclusion
Persistence, 2014

In 1839 British traveler James Silk Buckingham stopped for the night at a local Columbus, Georgia, hotel. Unable to avoid missing the massive portrait of a Creek Indian headman in the lobby, Buckingham marveled at the irony. "Though the people of America seem anxious to get rid of the actual presence of the Indian people, and have them transported to the westward of the Mississippi," Buckingham declared, "they have great admiration for their principal warriors, as if their names and exploits formed part of the national history of their country." Two decades later William Atson marveled at much the same thing. When Atson arrived in Columbus in 1856 on board the Chattahoochee steamer *Cusseta*, he noted that Muskogean place names "are almost the only memorials to remind us, not only of the Indian past, but of our country's past." In that brief, serendipitous collision between the past and the present, Buckingham and Atson believed they had exposed one of the great paradoxes of the removal story: that whites were eager to move the Creeks west while at the same time clinging to their memory. But Buckingham failed to fully grasp why the portrait of that headman was hanging in a Columbus, Georgia, hotel in 1839. As a visitor, he probably did not know exactly how important that Creek Indian was to white Georgia history. But the locals knew; he made the town of Columbus possible. The portrait was of William McIntosh.[1]

Soon after his presidency ended in 1837, Andrew Jackson returned to the Hermitage in Tennessee to live out his final days. So inextricably linked to a place—like Washington's Mount Vernon or Jefferson's

Monticello—Jackson was intimately familiar with the concept of the nurturing home. As he fended off political enemies real or imagined in Washington, Jackson's thoughts often turned to his estate and its tranquility. It was a refuge, he once confided to John Coffee, from the "'corruption and treachery of this wicked world.'" Jackson's wife Rachel was buried there, and he noted on at least one occasion that his "'only ambition is to get to the Hermitage so soon as the interest of my country and the will of the people will permit me, and there to set my house in order and go to sleep along side of my dear departed wife.'" When Jackson died in 1845, he got to sleep next to her once again; they were buried side by side.[2]

At about the same time that Jackson was making his triumphant return to his beloved home, thousands of Creek Indians were dying of smallpox on a cold and unfamiliar ground. Throughout his presidency, Jackson extolled the virtues of the "healthy" Indian territory, a place where native peoples would prosper and be happy. The Creeks, however, repeatedly warned Jackson that the West was "a graveyard." Unmoved, the administration charged ahead with relocating Indians across the Mississippi River. There is little doubt that what occurred in Alabama and Georgia between 1825 and 1837 was ethnic cleansing. It was not, as Jackson asserted, about protecting Indians or preserving their way of life. If the president was interested in the welfare of the native inhabitants he would have reconsidered the emigration program in 1833, when it was reported that 18 percent of the western Creek population died of disease within a three-year period. If he really had the Indians' interests at heart, he surely would not have let three of every four children who were born in the West die. But when the Second Creek War broke out in 1836, Jackson was more than eager to push all Creeks—even those who aided the United States—west. And, that's when the real decimation began. According to a census taken in 1836 and again in 1838, thirty-five hundred people—at minimum—from "the Emigration of 1836" passed away within the first twelve months. The census taker, a man named Alexander (probably James L. Alexander, an Indian countryman coerced west with Opothle Yoholo's detachment in 1836), appears to refer only to those who traveled in the five detachments while seemingly excluding the Creek prisoners, and almost certainly omitting the Florida warriors or their families. If indeed this is the case, then of the 12,648 people from the five detachments that arrived at Fort Gibson (as claimed by the Alabama Emigrating Company), at least 27.6 percent were dead within a year. Even if Alexander included those who participated in the Second Creek War, the number would still be a very high 23 percent. Moreover, Alexander estimated that there were about sixteen thousand Creeks living in 1842, while Claudio Saunt writes that the population stood at about fourteen thousand by 1859. In other words, far from a healthy country, the Creek population steadily declined for at least two decades.[3]

And the Creeks were not the only ones. Isaac McCoy's 1838 *Annual Register* reported that "nearly one half" of the four hundred Seminoles who arrived in the spring of 1836 were dead by the fall of 1837. A number of scholars estimate that four thousand Cherokees died as a direct result of removal out of the sixteen thousand forced west. Russell Thornton argues, however, that taking into account natural population increases had the Cherokees stayed, that "10,138 more Cherokees would have been alive in 1840" if removal had never occurred. Donna L. Akers reports that during the terrible flooding and disease that struck the Indian territory in 1833, mortality among the Choctaws "'since the beginning of fall as far as ascertained, amounts to one-fifth of the whole number.'"[4]

While it is clear that the larger demographic disaster was found in the Indian territory, nothing can downplay the trauma of the actual journey west. Table 1 shows that approximately seven hundred or more Creeks (from the removals and coerced relocations) died before reaching Fort Gibson. Their bodies were hastily buried or left along the side of the road. Like Echo Fixico, they were people without a home. When calculating the mortality rate for the six detachments of relocated Creeks, I have used what is, for lack of a better term, an invoice provided by the Alabama Emigrating Company. Since the Creeks were considered commodities by the contractors, an accurate calculation of the number of people the company successfully transported to the West, as well as those who perished along the way, was required for compensation. Since dead Creeks, even if conducted only a few miles, were worth money to the company, the employees morbidly averaged the distance of all those who died, then sought a prorated sum from the federal government. For example, the

Table 1. Number of Deaths on the Journey West, 1836–37

PARTY	NUMBER IN PARTY	DEATHS
First detachment, Creek prisoners, 1836	2,300	81
Second detachment, Creek prisoners, 1836	193	19
Detachment one, 1836	2,396	78
Detachment two, 1836	3,132	37
Detachment three, 1836–37	2,830	12
Detachment four, 1836	2,366	36
Detachment five, 1836	2,112	25
Detachment six, 1837	3,471+	415+
Refugee (Cherokee Nation), 1837	543	9
Refugee (Chickasaw Nation), 1837	297	N/A
Approximated total	19,600+	700+

company reported that thirty-seven people died from detachment two at an average distance of four hundred miles (about halfway to Fort Gibson). The contractors subsequently claimed half of the $28.50 per capita as stipulated in the contract, and therefore monetized the value of one human life to a mere $14.00.[5]

Legend has it that as the Creeks marched toward Indian territory in 1836 and 1837, they sang songs of encouragement. Passed down through the generations, the modern incarnations of the hymns *Yvmv Estemerketv, Tehoyvnvyof* (When I pass this suffering) and *Ekvnv Pomellvten* (We have an appointed land) are decidedly Christian in nature, but their verses have the unmistakable elements of a long and traumatic journey. Many Oklahoma Creeks claim that their ancestors sang early versions of these songs along the route, and perhaps they did. It would not be surprising after all if, upon reaching Memphis and standing on the edge of that symbolic line demarcating East and West, their old land and their new, if one or more of the Creeks did not sing some variation of *Elkv hvtcen tehoyvnvyof, Tehoyvnvyof, tehoyvnvyof* (When I pass the river of death, When I pass, when I pass). Although they could not at the time foresee the hazards that awaited them in the Indian territory, the Creeks took comfort in the fact that they would survive as a people and rebuild.

FIG. 32. Members of the Muscogee (Creek) Nation at Horseshoe Bend National Military Park, Alabama, 27 March 2014. Photo courtesy of the author.

Although the physical and emotional horrors of Creek Indian removal and relocation are largely indescribable, the larger narrative is not one of death, but of life.[6]

On a warm day in March 2014, approximately three hundred people from the Muscogee (Creek) Nation in Oklahoma gathered on the lawn and under tents to listen to speakers, including Principal Chief George Tiger, commemorate the two hundredth anniversary of the Battle of Horseshoe Bend. The delegates had arrived earlier by a well-traveled route—Interstate

40 through Arkansas to Memphis, U.S. Route 78 (Interstate 22) through Mississippi and Alabama, then U.S. Route 280 to the Horseshoe Bend National Military Park. In doing so, they closely retraced—in the opposite direction—the very route that some of their ancestors had followed on foot approximately 180 years earlier. After the ceremony the Muscogee people walked the grounds. Then, in the afternoon, a few dozen yards away from the running waters of the Tallapoosa, they danced.[7]

ABBREVIATIONS

ABC	Papers of the American Board of Commissioners for Foreign Missions
ADAH	Alabama Department of Archives and History
AF-AG-Clay	Alabama, Governor (1835–37: C. C. Clay), Administrative files, Reels 6–10, ADAH
AG-Jesup	RG 94, Entry 159, Records of the Adjutant General, Thomas S. Jesup Papers
ASP-MA	*American State Papers*, Military Affairs
CGS-IRW	Files of the Office of the Commissary General of Subsistence, Indian Removal to the West, 1832–40, University Publications of America, Bethesda MD
CRR-Misc.	Miscellaneous Creek Removal Records, ca. 1827–59, RG 75, Entry 300, NARA
GA	Georgia Archives
HED 104	House Executive Document 104
HR 25	House Report 25
HR 87	House Report 87
HR 98	House Report 98
HR 826	House Report 826
HRFG	Headquarters Records of Fort Gibson, Indian Territory, 1830–1857, NARA
IPHC	Indian Pioneer History Collection, Works Progress Administration Project S-149, Oklahoma Historical Society

303

IU	Indiana History Mss., Lilly Library, Indiana University
JWA	John William Augustine Sanford Papers, ADAH
LC	Library of Congress
LR-CA	Letters Received by the Office of Indian Affairs, Creek Agency
LR-CAE	Letters Received by the Office of Indian Affairs, Creek Agency Emigration
LR-CAR	Letters Received by the Office of Indian Affairs, Creek Agency Reserves
LR-CAW	Letters Received by the Office of Indian Affairs, Creek Agency West
LR-FS	Letters Received by the Office of Indian Affairs, Florida Superintendency
LR-SAE	Letters Received by the Office of Indian Affairs, Seminole Agency Emigration
LS	Records of the Office of Indian Affairs, Letters Sent
NARA	National Archives and Records Administration
NASP	*The New American State Papers*
NYPL	New York Public Library
OIA	Office of Indian Affairs
PHS-AIC	Presbyterian Historical Society, Philadelphia— American Indian Correspondence
Reynolds-PU	Reynolds journal of a party of Creek Indians, about to Emegrate to the west of the Mississippi, commencing 19th February and Ending 19th October 1837, Box 1, Folder 3, Manuscripts Division, Department of Rare Books and Special Collections, Princeton University Library, Princeton, NJ
RG	Record Group
SD	Senate Document
SFOIA	Special Files of the Office of Indian Affairs
SIAC	Settled Indian Accounts and Claims
VHS	Vermont Historical Society

NOTES

INTRODUCTION

1. Cochamy to Medill, 7 April 1848, LR-CAE, Roll 240, 446-48; Cochamy to Medill, 16 July 1848, LR-CAE, Roll 240, 450-51; Dickson to Medill, 6 June 1848, LR-CAR, Roll 240, 454.
2. Andrew Bell-Fialkoff, "A Brief History of Ethnic Cleansing," *Foreign Affairs* 72, no. 3 (Summer 1993): 110–21; Bell-Fialkoff, *Ethnic Cleansing* (New York: St. Martin's Griffin, 1996); Drazen Petrovic, "Ethnic Cleansing—An Attempt at Methodology," *European Journal of International Law* 5, no. 1 (1994): 1–19; Michael Mann, "The Dark Side of Democracy: The Modern Tradition of Ethnic and Political Cleansing," *New Left Review* 235 (1999): 18–45; Mann, *The Dark Side of Democracy: Explaining Ethnic Cleansing* (Cambridge: Cambridge University Press, 2005); Norman M. Naimark, *Fires of Hatred: Ethnic Cleansing in Twentieth-Century Europe* (Cambridge MA: Harvard University Press, 2001). See also Robert M. Hayden, "Imagined Communities and Real Victims: Self-Determination and Ethnic Cleansing in Yugoslavia," *American Ethnologist* 23, no. 4 (November 1996): 783–801; Jennifer Jackson Preece, "Ethnic Cleansing as an Instrument of Nation-State Creation: Changing State Practices and Evolving Legal Norms," *Human Rights Quarterly* 20, no. 4 (November 1998): 817–42; Rony Blum, Gregory H. Stanton, Shira Sagi, and Elihu D. Richter, "'Ethnic Cleansing' Bleaches the Atrocities of Genocide," *European Journal of Public Health* 18, no. 2 (2008): 204–9. For a comparison of the colonial expansion policies of Nazi Germany and the United States see Carroll P. Kakel, III, *The American West and the Nazi East: A Comparative and Interpretive Perspective* (Houndmills UK: Palgrave Macmillan, 2011). Twenty-three thousand based on number moved west, 1827–49.
3. For varying views on Jackson's Indian policy see Francis Paul Prucha, *American Indian Policy in the Formative Years: The Indian Trade and Intercourse Acts, 1790–1834* (Cambridge MA: Harvard University Press, 1962); Prucha, "Andrew Jackson's Indian Policy: A Reassessment," *Journal of American History* 56, no. 3 (December 1969): 527–39; Ronald N. Satz, *American Indian Policy in the Jacksonian*

Era (Lincoln: University of Nebraska Press, 1975); Michael Paul Rogin, *Fathers and Children: Andrew Jackson and the Subjugation of the American Indian* (New York: Knopf, 1975); Prucha, *Indian Policy in the United States: Historical Essays* (Lincoln: University of Nebraska Press, 1981); Brian W. Dippie, *The Vanishing American: White Attitudes and U.S. Indian Policy* (Middletown CT: Wesleyan University Press, 1982), 56–71; Prucha, *The Great Father: The United States Government and the American Indians*, vol. 1 (Lincoln: University of Nebraska Press, 1984); Robert V. Remini, *The Legacy of Andrew Jackson: Essays on Democracy, Indian Removal, and Slavery* (Baton Rouge: Louisiana State University Press, 1988), 45–82; Satz, "Rhetoric versus Reality: The Indian Policy of Andrew Jackson," in *Cherokee Removal: Before and After*, ed. William L. Anderson (Athens: University of Georgia Press, 1991), 29–54; Remini, *Andrew Jackson and His Indian Wars* (New York: Viking, 2001). See also John Spencer Bassett, *The Life of Andrew Jackson*, vol. 1 (Garden City NY: Doubleday, Page, 1911); Frederic Austin Ogg, *The Reign of Andrew Jackson: A Chronicle of the Frontier in Politics* (New Haven CT: Yale University Press, 1919), 201–16; Marquis James, *The Life of Andrew Jackson* (Indianapolis: Bobbs-Merrill, 1938); John William Ward, *Andrew Jackson: Symbol for an Age* (New York: Oxford University Press, 1955), 13–41; Glyndon G. Van Deusen, *The Jacksonian Era, 1828–1848* (1959; reprint, New York: Harper and Row, 1966), 48–50; Van Deusen, *The Rise and Decline of Jacksonian Democracy* (New York: Van Nostrand Reinhold, 1970), 44–45; James C. Curtis, *Andrew Jackson and the Search for Vindication* (New York: HarperCollins, 1976), 22–23, 105–10; Remini, *The Revolutionary Age of Andrew Jackson* (New York: Harper and Row, 1976), 105–20; Richard B. Latner, *The Presidency of Andrew Jackson: White House Politics 1829–1837* (Athens: University of Georgia Press, 1979), 86–98; Remini, *Andrew Jackson and the Course of American Freedom, 1822–1832*, vol. 2 (New York: Harper and Row, 1981), 201, 220–21; Remini, *Andrew Jackson and the Course of American Democracy, 1833–1845*, vol. 3 (New York: Harper and Row, 1984), 293–314; Thomas R. Hietala, *Manifest Design: Anxious Aggrandizement in Late Jacksonian America* (Ithaca NY: Cornell University Press, 1985), 132–52; Remini, *The Life of Andrew Jackson* (New York: Penguin, 1990), 114–15; Remini, *The Jacksonian Era* (Arlington Heights IL: Harlan Davidson, 1989), 40–52; Harry L. Watson, *Liberty and Power: The Politics of Jacksonian America* (New York: Hill and Wang, 1990), 104–13; Donald B. Cole, *The Presidency of Andrew Jackson* (Lawrence: University Press of Kansas, 1993), 67–74, 109–19; Daniel Feller, *The Jacksonian Promise: America, 1815–1840* (Baltimore: Johns Hopkins University Press, 1995), 179–83; Andrew Burstein, *The Passions of Andrew Jackson* (New York: Knopf, 2003), 182–88; H. W. Brands, *Andrew Jackson: His Life and Times* (New York: Doubleday, 2005), 489–93; Sean Wilentz, *Andrew Jackson* (New York: Times Books, 2005), 66–70; Jon Meacham, *American Lion: Andrew Jackson in the White House* (New York: Random House, 2008), 91–97; William Nester,

The Age of Jackson and the Art of American Power, 1815–1848 (Washington DC: Potomac Books, 2013), 147–57.

4. Scholars of American Indian history have also started using the term: see James Taylor Carson, "'The Obituary of Nations': Ethnic Cleansing, Memory, and the Origins of the Old South," *Southern Cultures* 14, no. 4 (Winter 2008): 6–31; Gary Clayton Anderson, *Ethnic Cleansing and the Indian: The Crime That Should Haunt America* (Norman: University of Oklahoma Press, 2014).

5. See Bernard W. Sheehan, *Seeds of Extinction: Jeffersonian Philanthropy and the American Indian* (Chapel Hill: University of North Carolina Press, 1973), 244; Reginald Horsman, "The Indian Policy of an 'Empire for Liberty,'" in *Native Americans and the Early Republic*, ed. Frederick E. Hoxie, Ronald Hoffman, and Peter J. Albert (Charlottesville: University Press of Virginia, 1999), 37–61; Anthony F. C. Wallace, *Jefferson and the Indians: The Tragic Fate of the First Americans* (Cambridge MA: Harvard University Press, 1999); Christian B. Keller, "Philanthropy Betrayed: Thomas Jefferson, the Louisiana Purchase, and the Origins of Federal Indian Removal Policy," *Proceedings of the American Philosophical Society* 144, no. 1 (March 2000): 39–66; S. Charles Bolton, "Jeffersonian Indian Removal and the Emergence of Arkansas Territory," *Arkansas Historical Quarterly* 62, no. 3 (Autumn 2003): 253–71; Tim Alan Garrison, *The Legal Ideology of Removal: The Southern Judiciary and the Sovereignty of Native American Nations* (Athens: University of Georgia Press, 2002). See also James Monroe, "To Congress—Removal of Indians, 30 March 1824," in *The Writings of James Monroe, Including a Collection of His Public and Private Papers and Correspondence Now for the First Time Printed*, vol. 7: *1824–1831*, ed. Stanislaus Murray Hamilton (1903; reprint, New York: AMS Press, 1969), 14–17.

6. For settler colonialism studies see Patrick Wolfe, "Settler Colonialism and the Elimination of the Native," *Journal of Genocide Research* 8, no. 4 (December 2006): 387–409; Lorenzo Veracini, *Settler Colonialism: A Theoretical Overview* (Houndmills UK: Palgrave Macmillan, 2010); Walter L. Hixson, *American Settler Colonialism: A History* (Houndmills UK: Palgrave Macmillan, 2013). See also Lisa Ford, *Settler Sovereignty: Jurisdiction and Indigenous People in America and Australia, 1788-1836* (Cambridge MA: Harvard University Press, 2011).

7. A nonexhaustive list of works on Indian removal includes Grant Foreman, *Indian Removal: The Emigration of the Five Civilized Tribes of Indians* (1932; reprint, Norman: University of Oklahoma Press, 1972); Dwight L. Smith, ed., "A Continuation of the Journal of an Emigrating Party of Potawatomi Indians, 1838, and Ten William Polke Manuscripts," *Indiana Magazine of History* 44, no. 4 (December 1948): 393–408; Smith, ed., "The Attempted Potawatomi Emigration of 1839," *Indiana Magazine of History* 45, no. 1 (March 1949): 51–80; Smith, ed., "Jacob Hull's Detachment of the Potawatomi Emigration of 1838," *Indiana Magazine of History* 45, no. 3 (September 1949): 285–88; Carl G. Klopfenstein,

"The Removal of the Wyandots from Ohio," *Ohio Historical Quarterly* 66, no. 2 (April 1957): 119–36; Arthur H. DeRosier Jr., *The Removal of the Choctaw Indians* (Knoxville: University of Tennessee Press, 1970); R. David Edmunds, "The Prairie Potawatomi Removal of 1833," *Indiana Magazine of History* 68, no. 3 (September 1972): 240–53; DeRosier, "Myths and Realities in Indian Westward Removal: The Choctaw Example," in *Four Centuries of Southern Indians*, ed. Charles M. Hudson (Athens: University of Georgia Press, 1975), 83–100; Gloria Jahoda, *The Trail of Tears* (New York: Holt, Rinehart and Winston, 1975); Robert A. Trennert, "The Business of Indian Removal: Deporting the Potawatomi from Wisconsin, 1851," *Wisconsin Magazine of History* 63, no. 1 (Autumn 1979): 36–50; James M. McClurken, "Ottawa Adaptive Strategies to Indian Removal," *Michigan Historical Review* 12, no. 1 (Spring 1986): 29–55; Anthony F. C. Wallace, *The Long, Bitter Trail: Andrew Jackson and the Indians* (New York: Hill and Wang, 1993); James Taylor Carson, "State Rights and Indian Removal in Mississippi, 1817–1835," *Journal of Mississippi History* 57, no. 1 (February 1995): 25–42; Donna L. Akers, "Removing the Heart of the Choctaw People: Indian Removal from a Native Perspective," *American Indian Culture and Research Journal* 23, no. 3 (1999): 63–76; Kate A. Berry and Melissa A. Rinehart, "A Legacy of Forced Migration: The Removal of the Miami Tribe in 1846," *International Journal of Population Geography* 9, no. 2 (March/April 2003): 93–112; Donna L. Akers, *Living in the Land of Death: The Choctaw Nation, 1830–1860* (East Lansing: Michigan State University Press, 2004); W. Ben Secunda, "To Cede or Seed? Risk and Identity among the Woodland Potawatomi During the Removal Period," *Midcontinental Journal of Archaeology* 31, no. 1 (Spring 2006): 57–88; Elizabeth Bollwerk, "Controlling Acculturation: A Potawatomi Strategy for Avoiding Removal," *Midcontinental Journal of Archaeology* 31, no. 1 (Spring 2006): 117–41; Claudia B. Haake, *The State, Removal and Indigenous Peoples in the United States and Mexico, 1620–2000* (New York: Routledge, 2007); Amanda L. Paige, Fuller L. Bumpers, and Daniel F. Littlefield Jr., *Chickasaw Removal* (Ada OK: Chickasaw Press, 2010). See also Haake, "Breaking the Bonds of People and Land," in *Removing Peoples: Forced Removal in the Modern World*, ed. Richard Bessel and Claudia B. Haake (Oxford: Oxford University Press, 2009), 79–106.
8. Journal (Bateman), SIAC, Agent (Reynolds), Account (1687), Year (1838), NARA.
9. Interview with Second Chief Alfred Berryhill, Okmulgee, Oklahoma, 23 September 2008.

1. TREASON

1. Michael D. Green, *The Politics of Indian Removal: Creek Government and Society in Crisis* (Lincoln: University of Nebraska Press, 1982), 88–89, 95; Triplett's Testimony, 20 July 1825, HR 98, 388–93; Charles J. Kappler, ed., *Indian Affairs: Laws and Treaties*, vol. 2: *Treaties* (Washington DC: Government Printing Office, 1904), 214–17.

2. Green, *Politics of Indian Removal*, 96–99; Creeks to Gaines, 18 June 1825, HR 98, 596–98; *Cherokee Phoenix*, 28 February 1828; Albert J. Pickett, "The Death of McIntosh, 1825," *Arrow Points* 10, no. 2 (February 1925): 31–32; Peggy and Susannah McIntosh to Campbell and Meriwether, 3 May 1825, LR-CA, Roll 219, 636–38; Hawkins to Campbell and Meriwether, 3 May 1825, LR-CA, Roll 219, 639–41; Letter from Creeks, 14 May 1825, LR-CA, Roll 219, 1595–97; Statement of Creek Chiefs, n.d., SFOIA, SF 136, Roll 27, 969–73; James C. Bonner, "Tustunugee Hutkee and Creek Factionalism on the Georgia-Alabama Frontier," *Alabama Review* 10 (April 1957): 115; Letter on suffering Creeks, 2 February 1825; Benjamin Franklin Cooling, ed., *The New American State Papers, Military Affairs*, vol. 17: *National Development and the Military* (Wilmington DE: Scholarly Resources, 1979), 119–20. For Adams's changing views on Indians, see Lynn Hudson Parsons, "'A Perpetual Harrow upon My Feelings': John Quincy Adams and the American Indian," *New England Quarterly* 46, no. 3 (September 1973): 339–79.

3. Enclosure nos. 1–4, HR 98, 565–67; Hostile Creek Indians Robbed of Samuel Hawkins, LR-CA, Roll 220, 752–54; A list of property taken, LR-CA, Roll 220, 765–66; Spoliation Claims (Hawkins), SFOIA, SF 136, Roll 27, 986–88.

4. Alan Gallay, *The Indian Slave Trade: The Rise of the English Empire in the American South, 1670–1717* (New Haven CT: Yale University Press, 2002); Christina Snyder, "Conquered Enemies, Adopted Kin, and Owned People: The Creek Indians and Their Captives," *Journal of Southern History* 73, no. 2 (May 2007): 255–88; Snyder, *Slavery in Indian Country: The Changing Face of Captivity in Early America* (Cambridge MA: Harvard University Press, 2010); Kathryn E. Holland Braund, "The Creek Indians, Blacks, and Slavery," *Journal of Southern History* 57, no. 4 (November 1991): 601–36; Daniel F. Littlefield Jr., *Africans and Creeks: From the Colonial Period to the Civil War* (Westport CT: Greenwood, 1979), 100–102; List of the Negroes Taken, LR-CA, Roll 220, 751; Hostile Creek Indians Robbed of Samuel Hawkins, LR-CA, Roll 220, 752–54; Creeks to Gaines, 18 June 1825, HR 98, 596–98.

5. Creeks to McIntosh, 5 June 1825, LR-CA, Roll 219, 276–77; Deposition of Marshall, 23 September 1826, SFOIA, SF 136, Roll 27, 1106–7; Wagnon's Certificate, 23 September 1825, SFOIA, SF 136, Roll 27, 857–58.

6. Andrew K. Frank, *Creeks and Southerners: Biculturalism on the Early American Frontier* (Lincoln: University of Nebraska Press, 2004), 96–113; Frank, "The Rise and Fall of William McIntosh: Authority and Identity on the Early American Frontier," *Georgia Historical Quarterly* 86, no. 1 (Spring 2002): 18–48; Green, *Politics of Indian Removal*, 57–62, 69–76, 91; Steven C. Hahn, "The Cussita Migration Legend: History, Ideology, and the Politics of Mythmaking," in *Light on the Path: The Anthropology and History of the Southeastern Indians*, ed. Thomas J. Pluckhahn and Robbie Ethridge (Tuscaloosa: University of Alabama Press, 2006), 57–93; Campbell to Calhoun, 8 January 1825, HR 98, 86–91.

7. Deposition of Ware, 1 September 1826, SFOIA, SF 136, Roll 27, 892–93; Kappler, *Indian Affairs*, 2:214–17; Green, *Politics of Indian Removal*, 82, 91.
8. Adam Hodgson, *Letters from North America, Written During a Tour in the United States and Canada*, vol. 1 (London: Hurst, Robinson, 1824), 127–31; Frank, *Creeks and Southerners*, 43; Robert P. Collins, "A Swiss Traveler in the Creek Nation: The Diary of Lukas Vischer, March 1824," *Alabama Review* 59, no. 4 (October 2006): 269.
9. Kappler, *Indian Affairs*, 2:135–37, 140–44, 170–71, 174–77, 191–95; Arthur H. DeRosier Jr., *The Removal of the Choctaw Indians* (Knoxville: University of Tennessee Press, 1970), 53–69; Bert Anson, *The Miami Indians* (Norman: University of Oklahoma Press, 1970), 177–212; Arrell M. Gibson, *The Chickasaws* (Norman: University of Oklahoma Press, 1971), 80–157; Stephen Warren, *The Shawnees and Their Neighbors, 1795–1870* (Urbana: University of Illinois Press, 2005), 43–68; *Niles' Weekly Register*, 25 July 1829. For more on Lewis Cass, see W. L. G. Smith, *Fifty Years of Public Life: The Life and Times of Lewis Cass* (New York: Derby and Jackson, 1856), 243–48; Andrew C. McLaughlin, *Lewis Cass* (Boston: Houghton, Mifflin, 1891), 155–60; Benjamin F. Comfort, *Lewis Cass and the Indian Treaties: A Monograph on the Indian Relations of the Northwest Territory from 1813 to 1831* (Detroit: Charles F. May, 1923); Frank B. Woodford, *Lewis Cass: The Last Jeffersonian* (New Brunswick NJ: Rutgers University Press, 1950), 122–47, 180–83; Francis Paul Prucha, *Lewis Cass and American Indian Policy* (Detroit: Wayne State University Press, 1967); Francis Paul Prucha and Donald F. Carmony, eds., "A Memorandum of Lewis Cass: Concerning a System for the Regulation of Indian Affairs," *Wisconsin Magazine of History* 52 (Autumn 1968): 35–50; Willis Frederick Dunbar, *Lewis Cass* (Grand Rapids MI: William B Eerdmans, 1970), 41–45, 88–89. Willard Carl Klunder, *Lewis Cass and the Politics of Moderation* (Kent OH: Kent State University Press, 1996), 70–76, writes that Cass's Indian policy was racist.
10. DeRosier, *Removal of the Choctaw Indians*, 53–69; Butler to Lewis, 11 July 1825, Butler Family Papers, MSS 102, Folder 239, The Historic New Orleans Collection, New Orleans LA; Thomas L. McKenney and James Hall, *History of the Indian Tribes of North America, With Biographical Sketches and Anecdotes of the Principal Chiefs. Embellished with One Hundred and Twenty Portraits, From the Indian Gallery in the Department of War, at Washington*, vol. 1 (Philadelphia: Daniel Rice and James G. Clark, 1842), 129–33; Campbell to Calhoun, 8 January 1825, HR 98, 86–91; Testimony of Harris, 12 June 1825, LR-CA, Roll 219, 944–45.
11. Hodgson, *Letters from North America*, 129–31; Auguste Levasseur, *Lafayette in America in 1824 and 1825; or, Journal of a Voyage to the United States*, vol. 2 (1829; reprint, New York: Research Reprints, 1970), 76; Claudio Saunt, *A New Order of Things: Property, Power, and the Transformation of the Creek Indians, 1733–1816* (Cambridge: Cambridge University Press, 1999), 216–17.

12. Bonner, "Tustunugee Hutkee," 118; *Georgia Patriot*, 24 May 1825; Deposition of Lott, 28 August 1826, SFOIA, SF 136, Roll 27, 997; Muster Roll (2nd McIntosh party), SIAC, Agent (Brearley), Account (14,487), Year (1830), NARA; Testimony of Moore, SFOIA, SF 136, Roll 27, 1033; Deposition of Mitchell, 22 September 1826, SFOIA, SF 136, Roll 27, 788–97; Creeks to Gaines, 18 June 1825, HR 98, 596–98; Creeks to Gaines, 9 July 1825, HR 98, 274–75; *Georgia Journal*, 14 June 1825.

13. Peggy and Susannah McIntosh to Campbell and Meriwether, 3 May 1825, LR-CA, Roll 219, 636–38; Hawkins to Campbell and Meriwether, 3 May 1825, LR-CA, Roll 219, 639–41; John Bartlett Meserve, "The MacIntoshes," *Chronicles of Oklahoma* 10, no. 3 (September 1932): 310–25; Kappler, *Indian Affairs*, 2:214–17; Green, *Politics of Indian Removal*, 93–94, 98–100, 211n63; Answers of Francis Flournoy, 9 June 1825, HR 98, 200–201.

14. Green, *Politics of Indian Removal*, 98–117; Gaines to Troup, 10 July 1825, HR 98, 628–30; Andrews to Barbour, 12 June 1825, LR-CA, Roll 219, 268–74; Creek census, HR 98, 257–58. See also Allan Nevins, ed., *The Diary of John Quincy Adams 1794–1845: American Political, Social and Intellectual Life from Washington to Polk* (New York: Longmans, Green, 1928), 346; James W. Silver, *Edmund Pendleton Gaines: Frontier General* (Baton Rouge: Louisiana State University Press, 1949).

15. Butler to Lewis, 1 July 1825, Butler Family Papers, MSS 102, Folder 235, The Historic New Orleans Collection, New Orleans LA; Resolution of the Creek National Council, 29 June 1825, LR-CA, Roll 220, 691–93; Kappler, *Indian Affairs*, 2:1034–35; List of Signers, HR 98, 254–56; *Southern Recorder*, 31 May 1825; Enclosure no. 1, HR 98, 565.

16. Richard J. Hryniewicki, "The Creek Treaty of Washington, 1826," *Georgia Historical Quarterly* 48, no. 4 (Winter 1964): 425–41; Green, *Politics of Indian Removal*, 98–125; John Bartlett Meserve, "Chief Opothleyahola," *Chronicles of Oklahoma* 9, no. 4 (December 1931): 439–53; J. Orin Oliphant, ed., *Through the South and the West with Jeremiah Evarts in 1826* (Lewisburg PA: Bucknell University Press, 1956), 100; John A. Andrew III, *From Revivals to Removal: Jeremiah Evarts, the Cherokee Nation, and the Search for the Soul of America* (Athens: University of Georgia Press, 1992); Creeks to the Secretary of War, 10 December 1825, HR 98, 723–24; *Georgia Messenger*, 15 February 1826.

17. Kappler, *Indian Affairs*, 2:264–68; Green, *Politics of Indian Removal*, 119–25; Creeks to Ridge, 16 December 1826, LR-CA, Roll 220, 480–83; Crowell to Franks, SIAC, Agent (Crowell), Account (15,814), Year (1831), NARA; Crowell to Eaton, 25 May 1829, LR-CA, Roll 222, 77–79; Abstract of Claims, LR-CA, Roll 222, 81–83; Brearley to Barbour, 8 November 1827, LR-CAE, Roll 237, 67–68; Campbell to Calhoun, 8 January 1825, HR 98, 86–91. For more on Fort Mitchell see David W. Chase, "Fort Mitchell: An Archaeological Exploration in Russell County, Alabama," *Alabama Archaeological Society* no. 1 (February 1974): 1–66.

18. Green, *Politics of Indian Removal*, 123; Creeks to Ridge, 16 December 1826, LR-CA, Roll 220, 480–83; Claims for Improvements, SFOIA, SF 207, Roll 61, 37–66; Receipts, LR-CA, Roll 221, 627–28; Angela Pulley Hudson, *Creek Paths and Federal Roads: Indians, Settlers, and Slaves and the Making of the American South* (Chapel Hill: University of North Carolina Press, 2010), 163.

19. Green, *Politics of Indian Removal*, 146; *Acts Passed at the Tenth Annual Session of the General Assembly of the State of Alabama: Begun And Held In The Town of Tuscaloosa, On The Third Monday In November, One Thousand Eight Hundred and Twenty-Eight* (Tuscaloosa AL: M'Guire, Henry and M'Guire, 1829), 65–66; Acts of the General Assembly, LR-CA, Roll 221, 191–93; Tim Alan Garrison, "Beyond *Worcester*: The Alabama Supreme Court and the Sovereignty of the Creek Nation," *Journal of the Early Republic* 19 (Fall 1999): 423–50; Garrison, *The Legal Ideology of Removal:* The Southern Judiciary and the Sovereignty of Native American Nations (Athens: University of Georgia Press, 2002), 155–67.

20. Anthony Finley, "1823 Map of Georgia," in *The New General Atlas* (Philadelphia: A. Finley, 1824); Hudson, *Creek Paths and Federal Roads*, 126. For more on the importance the Creeks placed on boundaries, see Kathryn E. Holland Braund, "'Like a Stone Wall Never to Be Broke': The British-Indian Boundary Line with the Creek Indians, 1763–1773," in *Britain and the American South: From Colonialism to Rock and Roll*, ed. Joseph P. Ward (Jackson: University Press of Mississippi, 2003), 53–79.

21. Woolfolk to Forsyth, 8 February 1828, *Creek Indian Letters, Talks, and Treaties, 1705–1839*, Part 3, 1137, GA; Kathryn E. Holland Braund, *Deerskins and Duffels: The Creek Indian Trade with Anglo-America, 1685–1815* (Lincoln: University of Nebraska Press, 1993), 149; Saunt, *New Order of Things*, 177; Rutherford's journal extract, HR 25, 8–10; Spoliation Claims, CRR-Misc., RG 75, Entry 300, Box 8, NARA.

22. Claim No. 2, 8 July 1828, HR 25, 19; Claim No. 5, 12 July 1828, HR 25, 21; Claim No. 7, 25 July 1828, HR 25, 21–22; Claim No. 30, 12 August 1828, HR 25, 35–36; Claim No. 2, 18 August 1828, HR 25, 68; Claim No. 3, 5 July 1828, HR 25, 69–70; Testimony of Tarver, 9 November 1828, HR 25, 94; Citizens of Lee County to Forsyth, 18 December 1827, *Creek Indian Letters, Talks, and Treaties, 1705–1839*, Part 3, 1129, GA; Watson to Forsyth, 27 November 1827, *Creek Indian Letters, Talks, and Treaties, 1705–1839*, Part 3, 1127, GA; *Tuscumbia Telegraph*, 2 January 1828; Porter to Forsyth, 19 June 1828, *Creek Indian Letters, Talks, and Treaties, 1705–1839*, Part 3, 1141–42, GA; Copy of a Letter from Lee County to the Governor of Georgia, 22 April 1828, HR 25, 6–7; Forsyth to Barbour, 29 November 1827, LR-CA, Roll 221, 323; Crowell to Forsyth, 27 November 1827, LR-CA, Roll 221, 328. See also Larry C. Skogen, *Indian Depredation Claims, 1796–1920* (Norman: University of Oklahoma Press, 1996).

23. G. W. Featherstonhaugh, *Excursion Through the Slave States, from Washington on the Potomac to the Frontier of Mexico; with Sketches of Popular Manners and Geological Notices* (New York: Harper and Brothers, 1844), 144–45, 153; Daniel S. Gray, ed., *Autauga County: The First Hundred Years, 1818–1918* (Prattville AL: Autauga County Prattville Public Library, 1972), 26; John H. Martin, ed., *Columbus, Geo., From Its Selection as a "Trading Town" in 1827, to Its Partial Destruction by Wilson's Raid, in 1865. History—Incident—Personality, Part 1—1827 to 1846* (1874; reprint, Easley SC: Georgia Genealogical Reprints, 1972), 10; Harriet Martineau, *Society in America*, vol. 1 (New York: Saunders and Otley, 1837), 212–13; Hogan to Clay, 30 January 1836, ASP-MA, 6:749; Sol Smith, *Theatrical Management in the West and South for Thirty Years. Interspersed With Anecdotal Sketches* (New York: Harper and Brothers, 1868), 77–79; Anne Royall, *Mrs. Royall's Southern Tour, or Second Series of the Black Book*, vol. 2 (Washington DC, 1831), 142. See also Jeffrey C. Benton, ed., *The Very Worst Road: Travelers' Accounts of Crossing Alabama's Old Creek Indian Territory, 1820–1847* (Eufaula AL: Historic Chattahoochee Commission, 1998). See also Edmund Berkeley and Dorothy Smith Berkeley, *George William Featherstonhaugh: The First U.S. Government Geologist* (Tuscaloosa: University of Alabama Press, 1988), 146–47.

24. Carl David Arfwedson, *The United States and Canada, in 1832, 1833, and 1834*, vol. 2 (1834; reprint, New York: Johnson Reprint, 1969), 26; Royall, *Mrs. Royall's Southern Tour*, 147.

25. Brearley to Barbour, 4 October 1826, LR-CAW, Roll 236, 5–8; Mims to Barbour, 21 July 1826, LR-CA, Roll 220, 425–26; Green, *Politics of Indian Removal*, 128; Ware to Troup, 5 August 1826, *Creek Indian Letters, Talks, and Treaties, 1705–1839*, Part 3, 1097, GA; Letter to Berrien et al., n.d., LR-CAR, Roll 221, 632–38; Tuckabatchee Harjo and Ochteachee Emathla to Eaton, 1 February 1831, SD 512, 2:405–7; Betton to Barbour, 27 June 1827, LR-CA, Roll 221, 60–65; Betton to Barbour, 17 October 1827, LR-CA, Roll 221, 80–84; Betton to Barbour, 4 December 1827, LR-CA, Roll 221, 148–51; Extract of Letter, 23 May 1826, SIAC, Agent (Betton & Mims), Account (10,548), Year (1827), NARA; Letter from Crowell, 17 August 1827, LR-CA, Roll 221, 243–46.

26. Abert to Cass, 11 November 1833, LR-CAR, Roll 241, 144–48; Karl Bernhard, Duke of Saxe-Weimar Eisenach, *Travels Through North America, During the Years 1825 and 1826*, vol. 2 (Philadelphia: Carey, Lea and Carey, 1828), 29; Basil Hall, *Travels in North America, In the Years 1827 and 1828*, vol. 3 (Edinburgh: Cadell and Company, 1829), 288–89; Margaret Hall, *The Aristocratic Journey: Being the Outspoken Letters of Mrs. Basil Hall Written during a Fourteen Months' Sojourn in America, 1827–1828* (New York: G. P. Putnam's Sons, 1931), 237–44; Rutherford's journal extract, HR 25, 8–10.

27. Gregory A. Waselkov, "Changing Strategies of Indian Field Location in the Early Historic Southeast," in *People, Plants, and Landscapes: Studies in Paleoethnobotany*,

ed. Kristen J. Gremillion (Tuscaloosa: University of Alabama Press, 1997), 185–93; Betton to Barbour, 27 June 1827, LR-CA, Roll 221, 60–65; Robbie Ethridge, *Creek Country: The Creek Indians and Their World* (Chapel Hill: University of North Carolina Press, 2003), 169–74; John Worth, "The Lower Creeks: Origins and Early History," in *Indians of the Greater Southeast: Historical Archaeology and Ethnohistory*, ed. Bonnie G. McEwan (Gainesville: University Press of Florida, 2000), 265–98; Scott to Crowell, 17 May 1827, LR-CAR, Roll 241, 518–19; Scott to Barbour, 15 May 1827, LR-CA, Roll 221, 502–4; Abert to Cass, 11 November 1833, LR-CA, Roll 241, 144–48.

28. Letter to Berrien et al., n.d., LR-CAR, Roll 221, 632–38; Scott to Barbour, 15 May 1827, LR-CA, Roll 221, 502–4. See also Betton to Barbour, 27 June 1827, LR-CA, Roll 221, 60–65.

29. Creek census, HR 98, 257–58; H. Thomas Foster II, ed., *The Collected Works of Benjamin Hawkins, 1796–1810* (Tuscaloosa: University of Alabama Press, 2003), 57s–65s; Collins, "A Swiss Traveler in the Creek Nation," 257–58, 258n; Hodgson, *Letters from North America*, 121–22; Map of Chambers County (Map 243); Russell County (Map 238), RG 75, Entry 163, Central Map Files, NARA II, College Park MD; Certificate of Croft, 24 August 1832, LR-CA, Roll 223, 372–73; 1832 Census of Creek Indians Taken by Parsons and Abbott, RG 75, Microcopy 275, Roll 1, NARA; "Names of the Creek Chiefs of the Creek Nation and also the Township and Range in Which Each Town Is Located," LR-CA, Roll 241, 45–59; "Rolls of the Creek Locations of the Creek Lands Made Under the Treaty of March 24, 1832," RG 75, Entry 287, vol. 3, NARA; Memorial of chiefs, 10 November 1833, CRR-Misc., RG 75, Entry 300, Box 1, NARA; United States to Wharton, LR-CA, Roll 222, 537–38. See also H. Thomas Foster II, with contributions by Mary Theresa Bonhage-Freund and Lisa O'Steen, *Archaeology of the Lower Muskogee Creek Indians, 1715–1836* (Tuscaloosa: University of Alabama Press, 2007), 55–59. For descriptions of Upper Creek town life see Joshua Piker, *Okfuskee: A Creek Indian Town in Colonial America* (Cambridge MA: Harvard University Press, 2004), 112–34.

30. Creek census, HR 98, 257–58; Receipts of Okteyoconnee Creeks, SFOIA, SF 207, Roll 61, 831–49; 1832 Creek census, Microcopy 275, Roll 1; Claim No. 1, HR 25, 18; Western Creek Census, 30 September 1833, SD 512, 4:722.

31. Moore to Cass, 29 March 1833, LR-CA, Roll 241, 291–93; Letter, 7 March 1833, LR-CA, Roll 241, 384; Letter from McIntosh, 18 January 1827, LR-CA, Roll 221, 380–82; Gadsden to Jackson, 14 November 1829, LR-SAE, Roll 806.

32. Claim No. 5, HR 25, 71–72.

33. Thomas Hamilton, *Men and Manners in America*, vol. 2 (Philadelphia: Carey, Lea and Blanchard, 1833), 341–42: Charles M. Hudson, ed., *The Southeastern Indians* (Knoxville: University of Tennessee Press, 1976), 408–11; Interrogation of Spencer, HR 98, 206. The ball play was near Drury Spain's, a white man who

ran an inn twenty-eight miles west of the Flint River in Georgia; Hodgson, *Letters from North America*, 1:117.

34. Green, *Politics of Indian Removal*, 130–31; Little Prince to Crowell, 3 June 1827, LR-CA, Roll 221, 221–22; Creeks to Surveyors, 12 January 1827, LR-CA, Roll 221, 527–28; Copy of a letter from James A. Rogers, 23 January 1827, LR-CA, Roll 221, 531–32.

35. Green, *Politics of Indian Removal*, 130–39; Richard J. Hryniewicki, "The Creek Treaty of November 15, 1827," *Georgia Historical Quarterly* 52, no. 1 (March 1968): 1–15.

36. *Southern Advocate*, 8 June 1827; Thomas L. McKenney, *Memoirs, Official and Personal; with Sketches of Travels Among the Northern and Southern Indians; Embracing A War Excursion, and Descriptions of Scenes Along the Western Borders*, vol. 1 (New York: Paine and Burgess, 1846), 187.

2. FISSION

1. Brad Agnew, *Fort Gibson: Terminal on the Trail of Tears* (Norman: University of Oklahoma Press, 1980), 29–31, 206, 218–219n.
2. Provision List, LR-CA, Roll 220, 697–708.
3. Provision List, LR-CA, Roll 220, 697–708; Receipt, SIAC, Agent (Hawkins), Account (13,229), Year (1829), NARA; Gaines to Lewis, 28 August 1829, SIAC, Agent (Marshall), Account (13,231), Year (1829), NARA.
4. Grant Foreman, *Pioneer Days in the Early Southwest* (1926; reprint, Lincoln: University of Nebraska Press, 1994), 69; Brearley to Eaton, 16 April 1829, LR-CAE, Roll 237, 225–26; Brearley to McKenney, 16 May 1826, LR-CAW, Roll 236, 3; Brearley to Barbour, 4 October 1826, LR-CAW, Roll 236, 5–8; Report of A. Balch, Commissioner on the Causes of the Creek Hostilities, 14 January 1837; NASP, 497–507; Barbour to Crowell, 6 October 1826, LS, Roll 3, 179; *Alabama Journal*, 17 November 1826; Barbour to Crowell, 6 October 1826, *Creek Indian Letters, Talks, and Treaties*, Part 3, 1101, GA; Brearley to Barbour, 15 November 1826, LR-CAE, Roll 237, 4–6.
5. Brearley to Barbour, 15 November 1826, LR-CAE, Roll 237, 4–6; Gaines to Barbour, 26 September 1825, HR 98, 560–61; Letter extract, 1 May 1825, HR 98, 328; Randolph to Barbour, 15 May 1827, LR-CA, Roll 221, 444–48.
6. Brearley to Barbour, 15 November 1826, LR-CAE, Roll 237, 4–6; Ware to Troup, 5 March 1826, LR-CA, Roll 220, 565; McIntoshes to Brearley, 28 October 1826, LR-CAW, Roll 236, 13–14.
7. Christopher D. Haveman, "With Great Difficulty and Labour: The Emigration of the McIntosh Party of Creek Indians, 1827–1828," *Chronicles of Oklahoma* 85, no. 4 (Winter 2007–2008): 468–90; Brearley to Barbour, 20 July 1827, LR-CAE, Roll 237, 33–35; Receipt of Brearley, 19 April 1827, SIAC, Agent (Brearley), Account (14,487), Year (1830), NARA; *Alabama Journal*, 23 March 1827; Affidavit

of Nichols, HR 98, 426; Brearley to Barbour, 2 December 1826, LR-CAE, Roll 237, 12–14.

8. Abstract of Disbursements (Exploratory Party), SIAC, Agent (Brearley), Account (14,487), Year (1830), NARA; Brearley to Barbour, 20 July 1827, LR-CAE, Roll 237, 33–35; Baylor to Campbell, 29 October 1831, SD 512, 2:633; Receipts, 19 April and 26 June 1827, SIAC, Agent (Brearley), Account (14,487), Year (1830), NARA; Creeks to Jackson, 25 October 1831, SD 512, 2:633–35; Creeks to Jackson, 22 June 1829, LR-CAW, Roll 236, 85–94. For the steamboats see Bert Neville, *Directory of River Packets in the Mobile-Alabama-Warrior-Tombigbee Trades, 1818–1932* (Selma AL: Selma Printing, 1967), 15, 18; Harry P. Owens, *Steamboats and the Cotton Economy: River Trade in the Yazoo-Mississippi Delta* (Jackson: University Press of Mississippi, 1990), 4, 25.

9. *Macon Telegraph*, 14 August 1827; *Arkansas Gazette*, 25 September 1827; Michael D. Green, *The Politics of Indian Removal:* Creek Government and Society in Crisis (Lincoln: University of Nebraska Press, 1982), 177.

10. *Arkansas Gazette*, 25 September 1827; *Macon Telegraph*, 14 August 1827.

11. Disbursements of Grace, 8 November 1827, SIAC, Agent (Brearley), Account (14,487), Year (1830), NARA; Stambaugh to Cass, 28 February 1834, SFOIA, SF 207, Roll 61, 662–65; Abstract of Disbursements, SIAC, Agent (Brearley), Account (14,487), Year (1830), NARA; Thomas S. Woodward, *Woodward's Reminiscences of the Creek, or Muscogee Indians, Contained in Letters to Friends in Georgia and Alabama* (Montgomery AL: Barrett and Wimbish, 1859), 104; United States to McIntosh (Receipt 23), CRR-Misc., Entry 300, Box 5, NARA.

12. Brearley to Barbour, 5 September 1827, LR-CAE, Roll 237, 58–59; Testimony of Brearley, SFOIA, SF 207, Roll 61, 660; Muster Roll (1st McIntosh party), SIAC, Agent (Brearley), Account (14,487), Year (1830), NARA; Creeks to Jackson, 7 March 1829, LR-CAW, Roll 236, 72–74; SIAC, Agent (Page), Account (17,581), Year (1833), NARA; McKenney to Barbour, 17 January 1828, 20th Cong., 1st sess., 1829, H.R. Doc. 74, serial no. 171, 3–4.

13. Claim of Triplett, SIAC, Agent (Triplett), Account (2743), Year (1839), NARA.

14. Muster Roll (1st McIntosh party), SIAC, Agent (Brearley), Account (14,487), Year (1830), NARA; HR 98, 327, 573; Peggy and Susannah McIntosh to Campbell and Meriwether, 3 May 1825, LR-CA, Roll 219, 636–38; Affidavit of Hambly, 4 July 1825, HR 98, 393–99. See also John Bartlett Meserve, "The Perrymans," *Chronicles of Oklahoma* 15, no. 2 (June 1937): 166–84. For John McIntosh see Journal kept by Richard Blount while serving on the Georgia-Alabama Boundary Survey Commission, 26 June to 6 July 1826, ADAH. For more on the families see Woodward, *Woodward's Reminiscences*, 115.

15. Woodward, *Woodward's Reminiscences*, 104; *Niles' Weekly Register*, 29 December 1827.

16. Brearley to Walker, 8 November 1827, LR-CAE, Roll 237, 71.

17. Muster Roll (1st McIntosh party), SIAC, Agent (Brearley), Account (14,487), Year (1830), NARA; *Niles' Weekly Register*, 29 December 1827.
18. Receipt of Oakchonawa Yoholo and Abstract of Disbursements, SIAC, Agent (Brearley), Account (14,487), Year (1830), NARA; McKenney to Lewis, 6 March 1830, LS, Roll 6, 313; *Arkansas Gazette*, 20 November 1827.
19. Brearley to Barbour, 1 December 1827, LR-CAE, Roll 237, 73; Abstract of Disbursements, Agent (Brearley), Account (14,487), Year (1830), NARA; Disbursements of Grace, 8 November 1827, SIAC, Agent (Brearley), Account (14,487), Year (1830), NARA; Memorial of Expenditures, SIAC, Agent (Brearley), Account (14,487), Year (1830), NARA; *Niles' Weekly Register*, 29 December 1827; *Arkansas Gazette*, 15 January 1828.
20. Brearley to Barbour, 3 August 1827, LR-CAE, Roll 237, 50–51; "Road—Memphis to Tuscumbia," 20th Cong., 1st Sess., H.R. Rep. No. 256, serial no. 179; Brearley to Barbour, 1 December 1827, LR-CAE, Roll 237, 73; Receipts of Thomas Anthony, 11 December 1827, SIAC, Agent (Brearley), Account (14,487), Year (1830), NARA; *Arkansas Gazette*, 15 January 1828; Receipts of Simpson and Livingston, SIAC, Agent (Brearley), Account (14,487), Year (1830), NARA.
21. Abstract of Disbursements, Agent (Brearley), Account (14,487), Year (1830), NARA; Brearley to Barbour, 1 December 1827, LR-CAE, Roll 237, 73. See also Leland D. Baldwin, *The Keelboat Age on Western Waters* (Pittsburgh: University of Pittsburgh Press, 1941), 44–45.
22. Journal (Deas), SIAC, Agent (Reynolds), Account (1687), Year (1838), NARA; Abstract of Disbursements and Receipts, SIAC, Agent (Brearley), Account (14,487), Year (1830), NARA; Brearley to Barbour, 26 January 1828, SIAC, Agent (Brearley), Account (14,487), Year (1830), NARA; *Arkansas Gazette*, 15 January 1828; Brearley to Montgomery and Miller, 17 March 1828, SIAC, Agent (Brearley), Account (14,487), Year (1830), NARA.
23. Brearley to Barbour, 26 January 1828, SIAC, Agent (Brearley), Account (14,487), Year (1830), NARA; *Arkansas Gazette*, 8 and 30 January 1828; United States to McIntosh (Claimant No. 22), CRR-Misc., Entry 300, Box 5, NARA. See also Julie Ward Longnecker, "A Road Divided: From Memphis to Little Rock through the Great Mississippi Swamp," *Arkansas Historical Quarterly* 44, no. 3 (Autumn 1985): 203–19.
24. Brearley to Barbour, 26 January 1828; SIAC, Agent (Brearley), Account (14,487), Year (1830), NARA; *Arkansas Gazette*, 30 January 1828; Abstract of Disbursements, SIAC, Agent (Brearley), Account (14,487), Year (1830), NARA.
25. Abstract of Disbursements, SIAC, Agent (Brearley), Account (14,487), Year (1830), NARA; Creeks to Jackson, 7 March 1829, LR-CAW, Roll 236, 72–75; Carl A. Brasseaux and Keith P. Fontenot, *Steamboats on Louisiana's Bayous: A History and Directory* (Baton Rouge: Louisiana State University Press, 2004), 185.

26. *Arkansas Gazette*, 13 February 1828; Brearley to Barbour, 16 February 1828, LR-CAE, Roll 237, 105–7.
27. *Arkansas Gazette*, 13 February 1828; C. A. Weslager, *The Delaware Indians: A History* (New Brunswick NJ: Rutgers University Press, 1972), 364–66; C. A. Weslager, *The Delaware Indian Westward Migration, with the Texts of Two Manuscripts (1821–22) Responding to General Lewis Cass's Inquiries about Lenape Culture and Language* (Wallingford PA: Middle Atlantic, 1978), 209–50; Willard H. Rollings, *The Osage: An Ethnohistorical Study of Hegemony on the Prairie-Plains* (Columbia: University of Missouri Press, 1992), 254–67; Brearley to Barbour, 16 February 1828, LR-CAE, Roll 237, 105–7; Grant Foreman, *Advancing the Frontier, 1830–1860* (1933; reprint, Norman: University of Oklahoma Press, 1968), 118; Agnew, *Fort Gibson*, 55–57.
28. Van Horne to Gibson, 2 April 1835, CGS-IRW, Roll 5, 772–74; Abstract of Disbursements, SIAC, Agent (Brearley), Account (14,487), Year (1830), NARA; Receipt, February 1828, SIAC, Agent (Brearley), Account (14,487), Year (1830), NARA; *Arkansas Gazette*, 3 January 1826 and 13 February 1828; *Alabama Journal*, 17 October 1828.
29. Brearley to Barbour, 16 February 1828, LR-CAE, Roll 237, 105–7; Abstract of Disbursements, SIAC, Agent (Brearley), Account (14,487), Year (1830), NARA; Rogers to Secretary of War, 27 February 1829, SIAC, Agent (John Rogers), Account (14,999), Year (1831), NARA.
30. Receipt of Thomas Anthony, 23 February 1829, SIAC, Agent (Brearley), Account (14,487), Year (1830), NARA; Receipts, SIAC, Agent (Brearley), Account (14,487), Year (1830), NARA; Claims of Susannah McIntosh and Jane Hawkins, 12 September 1833, LR-CAR, Roll 241, 651; *Cherokee Phoenix*, 14 May 1828; *Arkansas Gazette*, 20 August 1828; Hawkins to Brearley, 1 June 1828, LR-CAE, Roll 237, 162–63.

3. FRENZY

1. McCoy to Porter, 29 January 1829, HR 87, 6–24; Creeks to Adams, 22 January 1829, HR 87, 5; *Alabama Journal*, 30 January 1829. See also Lela Barnes, ed., "Journal of Isaac McCoy for the Exploring Expedition of 1828," *Kansas Historical Quarterly* 5, no. 3 (August 1936): 227–77.
2. Compere to McKenney, 20 May 1828, LR-CA, Roll 221, 704–7; Compere to Bolles, 19 May 1828, American Baptist Board of International Missions Collections, Foreign Mission Correspondence, Box 55, Folder 33, Microfilm No. FM-98, American Baptist Historical Society, Atlanta GA; Memorial of the Rev. W. Capers, containing charges against the Creek Agent Colonel Crowell, HR 98, 24–46; Claudio Saunt, *Black, White, and Indian: Race and the Unmaking of an American Family* (Oxford: Oxford University Press, 2005), 35–36. See also Gary Zellar, *African

Creeks: Estelvste and the Creek Nation (Norman: University of Oklahoma Press, 2007).

3. Compere to McKenney, 10 December 1827, LR-CAE, Roll 237, 78–82; Compere to McKenney, 4 February 1828, LR-CAE, Roll 237, 146–52; McKenney to Crowell, 30 August 1828, LS, Roll 5, 109–10; William G. McLoughlin, "Red, White, and Black in the Antebellum South," *Baptist History and Heritage* 7, no. 2 (April 1972): 69–75; Andrew K. Frank, *Creeks and Southerners: Biculturalism on the Early American Frontier* (Lincoln: University of Nebraska Press, 2005), 91–92. See also Walter Brownlow Posey, *Frontier Mission: A History of Religion West of the Southern Appalachians to 1861* (Lexington: University of Kentucky Press, 1966), 171–74; James Constantine Pilling, ed., *Bibliography of the Muskhogean Languages* (Washington DC: Government Printing Office, 1889), 28.

4. *Macon Telegraph*, 16 June 1828; Testimony of Hudson, 8 March 1828, LR-CA, Roll 221, 877–80; Walker to McKenney, 8 October 1829, LR-CAE, Roll 237, 292–95; Charles M. Hudson, *The Southeastern Indians* (Knoxville: University of Tennessee Press, 1976), 223–24.

5. Brearley to Barbour, 2 December 1826, LR-CAE, Roll 237, 12–14; Deposition of Moore, 24 August 1826, SFOIA, SF 136, Roll 27, 802; Deposition of Moore, 22 August 1826, SFOIA, SF 136, Roll 27, 804; Muster Roll (2nd McIntosh party), SIAC, Agent (Brearley), Account (14,487), Year (1830), NARA; Letter to Crawford, 1 June 1842, LR-CA, Roll 226, 652–54; Walker to Brearley, 8 September 1828, LR-CAW, Roll 236, 33–35; Testimony of Hudson, 8 March 1828, LR-CA, Roll 221, 877–80.

6. Hogan to Gibson, 8 April 1835, ASP-MA, 6:723–24; Hogan to Cass, 8 March 1836, ASP-MA, 6:751–53; *Arkansas Gazette*, 30 December 1834; United States to Dubois, SIAC, Agent (Crowell), Account (15,814), Year (1831), NARA; Frank, *Creeks and Southerners*, 124.

7. Compere to McKenney, 10 December 1827, LR-CAE, Roll 237, 78–82; *Macon Telegraph*, 16 June 1828; Creeks to Brearley, 3 June 1828, LR-CAE, Roll 237, 154–56; Creeks to Gaines, 18 June 1825, HR 98, 596–98; Walker to McKenney, 3 March 1828, LR-CAE, Roll 237, 181–84.

8. *Macon Telegraph*, 16 June 1828; *Alabama Journal*, 17 November 1826; *Cherokee Phoenix*, 8 October 1828; *Tuscumbia Telegraph*, 28 November 1827; *Arkansas Gazette*, 18 November 1828; Walker to McKenney, 3 March 1828, LR-CAE, Roll 237, 181–84; Walker to McKenney, 8 October 1829, LR-CAE, Roll 237, 292–95; Walker to Brearley, 8 September 1828, LR-CAW, Roll 236, 33–35; Creeks to Brearley, 3 June 1828, LR-CAE, Roll 237, 154–56; Certificate of Berryhill, 1 May 1828, LR-CA, Roll 221, 752; Certificate of Reed, 1 May 1828, LR-CA, Roll 221, 750; McKenney to Crowell, 5 January 1828, LS, Roll 4, 233; *Selma Courier*, 2 October 1828; Walker to McKenney, 18 June 1828, LR-CA, Roll 221, 892–94.

9. Creeks to McKenney, 18 July 1828, LR-CAE, Roll 237, 158–59; Walker to McKenney, 8 March 1828, LR-CAE, Roll 237, 174–75; Testimony of Austin, 8 March 1828, LR-CA, Roll 221, 881–83; Testimony of Hudson, 8 March 1828, LR-CA, Roll 221, 877–80; *Alabama Journal*, 11 April 1828; Letter from Creeks, 11 May 1828, LR-CA, Roll 221, 746–48; Walker to McKenney, 18 June 1828, LR-CA, Roll 221, 892–94.

10. *Cherokee Phoenix*, 5 November 1828; Muster Roll (2nd McIntosh party), SIAC, Agent (Brearley), Account (14,487), Year (1830), NARA. Scholars debate the affect wealthy Creeks with white ancestry had on the Creek Nation. See also Claudio Saunt, *A New Order of Things: Property, Power, and the Transformation of the Creek Indians, 1733–1816* (Cambridge: Cambridge University Press, 1999); Theda Perdue, *"Mixed Blood" Indians: Racial Construction in the Early South* (Athens: University of Georgia Press, 2003); Frank, *Creeks and Southerners*.

11. Muster Roll (2nd McIntosh party), SIAC, Agent (Brearley), Account (14,487), Year (1830), NARA; Receipt of Brearley, 19 April 1827, SIAC, Agent (Brearley), Account (14,487), Year (1830), NARA; Thomas S. Woodward, *Woodward's Reminiscences of the Creek, or Muscogee Indians, Contained in Letters to Friends in Georgia and Alabama* (Montgomery AL: Barrett and Wimbish, 1859), 79, 99–100; Frank, *Creeks and Southerners*, 43; "Abstract of Licenses Granted," LR-CA, Roll 219, 92.

12. Muster Roll (2nd McIntosh party, duplicate), SIAC, Agent (Brearley), Account (14,487), Year (1830), NARA; Woodward, *Woodward's Reminiscences*, 46; The United States to Tom Pidgeon, 13 April 1837, SIAC, Agent (Page), Account (1701), Year (1838), NARA. See also Saunt, *Black, White, and Indian*, 10–26.

13. *Alabama Journal*, 31 October 1828; Receipts (Berryhill, Posey, Austin, Hopwood), SIAC, Agent (Brearley), Account (14,487), Year (1830), NARA; *Tuscumbia Telegraph*, 19 July 1828; Survey of Muscle Shoals, 20th Cong., 1st sess., 1828, H.R. Doc. 284, serial no. 175, 5–20; *Arkansas Gazette*, 11 and 18 November 1828; Grant Foreman, *Indians and Pioneers: The Story of the American Southwest before 1830* (1930; reprint, Norman: University of Oklahoma Press, 1967), 258. See also Donald Davidson, *The Tennessee: The Old River; Frontier to Secession*, vol. 1 (New York: Rinehart, 1946), 12–13.

14. *Alabama Journal*, 31 October 1828; Brearley to Porter, 12 December 1828, LR-CAE, Roll 237, 136; *Arkansas Gazette*, 3 January 1826; Abstract of Disbursements, SIAC, Agent (Brearley), Account (14,487), Year (1830), NARA; Receipts, 9 October, 20 November, and 24 November 1828, SIAC, Agent (Brearley), Account (14,487), Year (1830), NARA; Muster Roll (2nd McIntosh party), SIAC, Agent (Brearley), Account (14,487), Year (1830), NARA.

15. *Arkansas Gazette*, 23 December 1828; Brearley to Porter, 12 December 1828, LR-CAE, Roll 237, 136; Brearley to Wheat, 23 January 1829, SIAC, Agent (Brearley), Account (14,487), Year (1830), NARA; Brearley to Stuart, 22 September

1833, SIAC, Agent (Brearley), Account (20,381), Year (1836), NARA; Abstract of Disbursements, SIAC, Agent (Brearley), Account (14,487), Year (1830), Receipt (174), NARA.

16. Anthony to Eaton, 24 June 1829, LR-CAE, Roll 237, 188–93.
17. Brearley to Eaton, 16 April 1829, LR-CAE, Roll 237, 225–26; *Alabama Journal*, 20 March 1829; *Arkansas Gazette*, 8 April and 20 May 1829; Chouteau to Eaton, 18 April 1829, LR-CAE, Roll 237, 227–28. William E. Foley and C. David Rice, *The First Chouteaus: River Barons of Early St. Louis* (Urbana: University of Illinois Press, 1983); Stan Hoig, *The Chouteaus: First Family of the Fur Trade* (Albuquerque: University of New Mexico Press, 2008).
18. McKenney to Crowell, 10 June 1829, LS, Roll 6, 4–5; Brearley to Eaton, 15 June 1829, LR-CAE, Roll 237, 220–22; Blake's Testimony, 21 July 1848, HR 826, 25–26; Michael D. Green, *The Politics of Indian Removal: Creek Government and Society in Crisis* (Lincoln: University of Nebraska Press, 1982), 131; Crowell to Cass, 22 December 1831, LR-CA, Roll 222, 553–54; Marquis James, *The Raven: A Biography of Sam Houston* (New York: Blue Ribbon Books, 1929), 111–12; Creeks to Jackson, 7 March 1829, LR-CAW, Roll 236, 72–75; Anthony to Eaton, 24 June 1829, LR-CAE, Roll 237, 188–93; Anthony to Brearley, 23 March 1829, LR-CAE, Roll 237, 303–4.
19. Robert V. Remini, *The Legacy of Andrew Jackson: Essays on Democracy, Indian Removal, and Slavery* (Baton Rouge: Louisiana State University Press, 1988), 45–82; Letter from Hitchcock, 3 February 1842, LR-CA, Roll 226, 491–505; Austill to Cass, 26 October 1833, LR-CA, Roll 223, 534–36; Allston to Crowell, 28 June 1829, LR-CA, Roll 222, 112–15; List of white intruders living in Creek Nation, LR-CA, Roll 222, 548–51; Letter from Creeks, 27 October 1830, LR-CA, Roll 222, 381–82; Eaton to Newcomb, 10 November 1830, LR-CA, Roll 222, 384. See also Henry DeLeon Southerland Jr. and Jerry Elijah Brown, *The Federal Road through Georgia, the Creek Nation, and Alabama, 1806–1836* (Tuscaloosa: University of Alabama Press, 1989).
20. Allston to Crowell, 28 June 1829, LR-CA, Roll 222, 112–15; Crowell to Eaton, 30 June 1829, LR-CA, Roll 222, 109–10; List of white intruders living in Creek Nation, LR-CA, Roll 222, 548–51; Tuskenehaw to Jackson, 21 May 1831, LR-CA, Roll 222, 441–43.
21. Tuskenehaw to Jackson, 21 May 1831, LR-CA, Roll 222, 441–43; Affidavit of Beck et al., 17 August 1829, LR-CA, Roll 222, 3–5; Citizens to Forsyth, 24 March 1829, LR-CA, Roll 222, 245–47.
22. McKenney to Baldwin, 8 October 1829, LS, Roll 6, 105–7; Crowell to McKenney, 4 February 1830, LR-CA, Roll 222, 303–6; Tuskenehaw to Jackson, 21 May 1831, LR-CA, Roll 222, 441–43; Carl David Arfwedson, *The United States and Canada in 1832, 1833, and 1834* (1834; reprint, New York: Johnson Reprint, 1969), 1:431–33; 2:10–11; Austill to Cass, 5 August 1833, LR-CA, Roll 223, 519–21.

23. Tim Alan Garrison, *The Legal Ideology of Removal: The Southern Judiciary and the Sovereignty of Native American Nations* (Athens: University of Georgia Press, 2002), 104; An Act, LR-CA, Roll 222, 157–58; Tuskenehaw to Jackson, 21 May 1831, LR-CA, Roll 222, 441–43.
24. Blake's Testimony, 21 July 1848, HR 826, 25–26; Crowell to McKenney, 1 August 1829, LR-CA, Roll 222, 118–20; McIntosh to Hitchcock, 28 January 1842, LR-CAE, Roll 240, 255–56; John Bartlett Meserve, "Chief Samuel Checote, with Sketches of Chiefs Locher Harjo and Ward Coachman," *Chronicles of Oklahoma* 16, no. 4 (December 1938): 401–9; United States to Perryman, SFOIA, SF 207, 768; F. M. Moore, *A Brief History of the Missionary Work In the Indian Territory of the Indian Mission Conference, Methodist Episcopal Church South, And an Appendix Containing Personal Sketches of Many of the Early Workers in This Field* (Muskogee: I.T., Phoenix Printing Co., 1899), 199–202; Stidham's testimony, HR 826, 26; United States to Bruner, SFOIA, SF 207, Roll 61, 683; United States to Reed, SFOIA, SF 207, Roll 61, 698; Abstract of Disbursements, SIAC, Agent (Crowell), Account (15,814), Year (1831), NARA; Receipts, SFOIA, SF 207, Roll 61, 45, 785, 817, 819, 827, 839, 849, 860; Creeks to Eaton, 12 April 1829, LR-CAE, Roll 237, 263–64; Creeks to Jackson, 14 August 1829, LR-CAE, Roll 237, 267–68.
25. Creeks to Jackson, 20 November 1829, LR-CA, Roll 222, 37–40; Creeks to Eaton, 12 April 1829, LR-CAE, Roll 237, 263–64; Walker to McKenney, 8 October 1829, LR-CAE, Roll 237, 292–95.
26. Testimony of Hotulke Mahthla, 8 October 1886, SFOIA, SF 285, Roll 77, 114–15; John T. Ellisor, *The Second Creek War: Interethnic Conflict and Collusion on a Collapsing Frontier* (Lincoln: University of Nebraska Press, 2010), 116.
27. Crowell to Eaton, 18 April 1829, LR-CA, Roll 222, 55–57; Stidham's testimony, 21 July 1848, HR 826, 26; Crowell to Eaton, 14 May 1829, LR-CA, Roll 222, 74–75; Blake's testimony, 21 July 1848, HR 826, 25–26.
28. *Arkansas Gazette*, 1, 15, and 22 July 1829; United States to Beshears, 30 June 1829, SIAC, Agent (Crowell), Account (15,814), Year (1831), NARA; United States to Todd, 20 July 1829, SIAC, Agent (Crowell), Account (15,814), Year (1831), NARA; United States to Vann, SFOIA, SF 207, Roll 61, 700; United States to Blake, SIAC, Agent (Crowell), Account (15,814), Year (1831), NARA; Receipts of disbursements, SIAC, Agent (Crowell), Account (15,814), Year (1831), NARA. A receipt shows that William Walker used the steamer *Salina* to overtake the emigrants and perhaps transport the party from Paducah, Kentucky, to Memphis.
29. United States to Fuller, 16 July 1829, SIAC, Agent (Crowell), Account (15,814), Year (1831), NARA; *Arkansas Gazette*, 22 July 1829; Creeks to Jackson, 14 August 1829, LR-CAE, Roll 237, 267–68; United States to Jacobsr, SIAC, Agent (Crowell), Account (15,814), Year (1831), NARA; Receipts of disbursements, SIAC, Agent (Crowell), Account (15,814), Year (1831), NARA.

30. *Arkansas Gazette*, 5, 12, and 19 August 1829; United States to Tarlton, SIAC, Agent (Crowell), Account (15,814), Year (1831), NARA; United States to Bruner, SFOIA, SF 207, Roll 61, 685; United States to Reed, SFOIA, SF 207, Roll 61, 698; United States to Tee-hel-attee, SFOIA, SF 207, Roll 61, 883.
31. *Arkansas Gazette*, 15 July and 12 August 1829; Creeks to Jackson, 14 August 1829, LR-CAE, Roll 237, 267–68; United States to Jacobs, SIAC, Agent (Crowell), Account (15,814), Year (1831), NARA; United States to Gentry, SIAC, Agent (Crowell), Account (15,814), Year (1831), NARA; United States to Turley, SIAC, Agent (Crowell), Account (15,814), Year (1831), NARA.
32. *Arkansas Gazette*, 19 August 1829; Receipts of disbursments, SIAC, Agent (Crowell), Account (15,814), Year (1831), NARA; Blake to Crowell, 4 March 1830, LR-CAW, Roll 236, 161–62; Foreman, *Indians and Pioneers*, 259–60.
33. Houston quote in Foreman, *Indians and Pioneers*, 260; Blake to Crowell, 4 March 1830, LR-CAW, Roll 236, 161–62.
34. McCalla to Atchison, 29 July 1848, HR 826, 25; Herring to Cass, 4 March 1834, LS, Roll 12, 161–62.
35. Hamilton to Campbell, 18 November 1830, SD 512, 2:43–44; Sheffield to Duval, 23 February 1833, LR-FS, Roll 288; Charles J. Kappler, ed., *Indian Affairs: Laws and Treaties, vol. 2: Treaties* (Washington DC: Government Printing Office, 1904), 352; James W. Covington, *The Seminoles of Florida* (Gainesville: University Press of Florida, 1993), 68; Gadsden to Jackson, 12 February 1833, LR-FS, Roll 288; Duval to Herring, 3 March 1833, LR-FS, Roll 288; Census of Seminole towns in Florida, 1833 LR-FS, Roll 288. For more on the Seminoles, see Covington, *Seminoles of Florida*; Brent Richards Weisman, *Unconquered People: Florida's Seminole and Miccosukee Indians* (Gainesville: University Press of Florida, 1999); Edwin C. McReynolds, *The Seminoles* (Norman: University of Oklahoma Press, 1957). James W. Covington, "Federal Relations with the Apalachicola Indians: 1823–1838," *Florida Historical Quarterly* 42, no. 2 (October 1963): 125–41.

4. FRAUD

1. Coffee to Eaton, 16 November 1829, LR-CAE, Roll 237, 248–50; *Macon Telegraph*, 7 January 1828.
2. Crowell to Eaton, 8 August 1830, LR-CA, Roll 222, 319–24; Crowell to Eaton, 30 June 1830, LR-CA, Roll 222, 315–16; Crowell to Eaton, 18 September 1829, LR-CA, Roll 222, 122–24.
3. Creeks to Jackson, 20 March 1829, LR-CA, Roll 222, 14–18; Crowell to Eaton, 8 August 1830, LR-CA, Roll 222, 319–24. For more on the Indian Removal Act and Jackson's use of presidential power, see Gerard N. Magliocca, *Andrew Jackson and the Constitution: The Rise and Fall of Generational Regimes* (Lawrence: University Press of Kansas, 2007), 21–29, 34–47, 69–70; Alfred A. Cave, "Abuse

of Power: Andrew Jackson and the Indian Removal Act of 1830," *Historian* 65, no. 6 (Winter 2000): 1330–53. See also Marilyn J. Anderson, "The Image of the Indian in American Drama during the Jacksonian Era, 1829–1845," *Journal of American Culture* 1, no. 4 (Winter 1978): 800–810; B. Donald Grose, "Edwin Forrest, *Metamora*, and the Indian Removal Act of 1830," *Theatre Journal* 37, no. 2 (May 1985): 181–91; Jill Lepore, *The Name of War: King Philip's War and the Origins of American Identity* (New York: Knopf, 1998; reprint, New York: Vintage, 1999), 192–93, 204–17, 224.

4. Michael D. Green, *The Politics of Indian Removal: Creek Government and Society in Crisis* (Lincoln: University of Nebraska Press, 1982), 155–56; Abert to Cass, 9 November 1833, LR-CAR, Roll 241, 131–142; Jackson to Creeks, 23 March 1829, LS, Roll 5, 373–75; Jackson to Haley, 15 October 1829, Andrew Jackson Papers, 1775–1874, Series 1, Reel 37, 17 April 1829–16 March 1830, No. 14,151–52, Library of Congress, Washington DC; *Acts Passed At The Thirteenth Annual Session of the General Assembly of the State of Alabama, Begun and Held in the Town of Tuscaloosa, on the Third Monday in November, One Thousand Eight Hundred and Thirty-One* (Tuscaloosa AL: Wiley, M'Guire and Henry, 1832), 7–8; Hogan to Cass, 8 March 1835, ASP-MA, 6:751–53; John Yoo, "Andrew Jackson and Presidential Power," *Charleston Law Review* 2 (2007): 521–83.

5. Creeks to Crowell, 13 December 1831, LR-CA, Roll 222, 546–47; Crawford to Robb, 15 September 1832, LR-CA, Roll 223, 54–58; Austill to Cass, 5 August 1833, LR-CA, Roll 223, 519–21.

6. Tuckabatchee Harjo and Octruchee Emathla to Eaton, 1 February 1831, SD 512, 2:405–7; Tuckabatchee Harjo and Octruchee Emathla to Jackson, 18 February 1831, LR-CA, Roll 222, 429–30; Creeks to Crowell, 13 December 1831, LR-CA, Roll 222, 546–47; Crowell to Cass, 15 December 1831, LR-CA, Roll 222, 545; Tuskenehaw to Jackson, 21 May 1831, LR-CA, Roll 222, 441–43; Crowell to Cass, 15 October 1832, LR-CA, Roll 223, 167.

7. Recommendation, LR-CA, Roll 222, 10; Crowell to Eaton, 8 August 1830, LR-CA, Roll 222, 319–24; Porter to Brearley, 30 July 1828, SIAC, Agent (Brearley), Account (20,381), Year (1836), NARA; *Niles' Weekly Register*, 2 October 1830. For more on McKenney and his views on removal, see Herman J. Viola, *Thomas L. McKenney: Architect of America's Early Indian Policy, 1816–1830* (Chicago: Sage Books, 1974).

8. Mitchell to Jackson, 30 December 1829, LR-CA, Roll 222, 240–41; Coffee to Eaton, 24 December 1829, LR-CAE, Roll 237, 252–55; Eaton to Thompson, 15 May 1830, LR-CAE, Roll 237, 334–35; Eaton to Creeks, 20 March 1830, LR-CA, Roll 226, 291–96; Crowell to Eaton, 30 June 1830, LR-CA, Roll 222, 315–16.

9. Creek self-emigration claims, SFOIA, SF 285, Roll 77, 6–7, 27, 30–31, 100–101, 103, 109–10; Thomas S. Woodward, *Woodward's Reminiscences of the Creek, or Muscogee Indians, Contained in Letters to Friends in Georgia and Alabama*

(Montgomery AL: Barrett and Wimbish, 1859), 91; Muster Roll (2nd McIntosh party), SIAC, Agent (Brearley), Account (14,487), Year (1830), NARA; The United States to Theophilus Perryman, SFOIA, SF 207, Roll 61, 673.

10. Eaton to Crowell, 4 June 1830, LS, Roll 6, 449–51; Tuckabatchee Harjo and Octruchee Emathla to Eaton, 1 February 1831, SD 512, 2:405–7; Jackson to Lewis, 25 August 1830, in *Correspondence of Andrew Jackson*, vol. 4: *1829–1832*, ed. John Spencer Bassett (Washington DC: Carnegie Institution, 1929), 176–78.

11. *Macon Telegraph*, 11 September 1830; *Niles' Weekly Register*, 13 November 1830; Creeks to Jackson, 25 April 1830, LR-CA, Roll 222, 298–301; Crowell to Eaton, 8 August 1830, LR-CA, Roll 222, 319–24; Crowell to Randolph, 7 July 1831, LR-CA, Roll 222, 520–22; Muster Roll (2nd McIntosh party), SIAC, Agent (Brearley), Account (14,487), Year (1830), NARA; Copy of the List & Certificate filed by David Conner, Enrolling Agent, SIAC, Agent (Abert), Account (17,572), Year (1833), NARA. See also Claudio Saunt, *Black, White, and Indian: Race and the Unmaking of an American Family* (New York: Oxford University Press, 2005), 30–43.

12. Crowell to Eaton, 30 June 1830, LR-CA, Roll 222, 315–16; Crowell to Eaton, 8 August 1830, LR-CA, Roll 222, 319–24.

13. Crowell to Randolph, 7 July 1831, LR-CA, Roll 222, 520–22; Abert to Cass, 2 June 1833, LR-CA, Roll 223, 399–405; Boykin and Thomas to Gilmer, 1 June 1831, Governor's Subject Files, Gov. George Rockingham Gilmer, RG 1-1-5, Box 13, Georgians to Jackson, 31 May 1831, LR-CA, Roll 222, 564–67; Eaton to Gilmer, 17 June 1831, LS, Roll 7, 279–81; Hamilton to Crowell, 25 July 1831, LS, Roll 7, 306; Parsons to Cass, 10 February 1833, SD 512, 4:74–75.

14. Crowell to Jones, 28 July 1831, LR-CA, Roll 222, 524–25; Crowell to Eaton, 2 July 1831, LR-CA, Roll 222, 518; United States to Wharton, LR-CA, Roll 222, 537–38; Herring to Crowell, 12 January 1832, LS, Roll 8, 137–39; Wharton to Herring, 4 February 1832, LR-CA, Roll 223, 344–46; Crowell to Gilmer, 26 July 1831, Governor's Subject Files, Gov. George Rockingham Gilmer, RG 1-1-5, Box 13, GA.

15. Creeks to Tuckabatchee Harjo and Octruchee Emathla, 7 January 1831, LR-CA, Roll 222, 425–26; Tuckabatchee Harjo and Octruchee Emathla to Eaton, 1 February 1831, LR-CA, Roll 222, 417; Letter from Tuckabatchee Harjo and Octruchee Emathla, 18 February 1831, LR-CA, Roll 222, 428–29; Jackson to Lewis, 25 August 1830, in Bassett *Correspondence of Andrew Jackson*, 4:177; Creeks to Hamilton, 18 February 1831, LR-CA, Roll 222, 427.

16. Creeks to the Secretary of War, 8 April 1831, SD 512, 2:424–25; Letter from Hitchcock, 3 February 1842, LR-CA, Roll 226, 491–505; Crowell to Eaton, 13 January 1831, LR-CA, Roll 222, 464–65; Declaration of Creeks, 15 December 1831, LR-CA, Roll 222, 452–53; Crowell to Cass, 29 February 1832, LR-CA, Roll 223, 117; Crowell to Cass, 25 January 1832, LR-CA, Roll 223, 113; Green, *Politics of Indian Removal*, 159–73; Clara Sue Kidwell, "The Choctaw Struggle for Land and Identity in

Mississippi, 1830–1918," in *After Removal: The Choctaw in Mississippi*, ed. Samuel J. Wells and Roseanna Tubby (Jackson: University Press of Mississippi, 1986), 64–93.

17. Letter from Creeks, 1 March 1832, LR-CA, Roll 223, 86; Brodnax to Cass, 12 March 1832, LR-CA, Roll 223, 28–31; Creeks to Cass, 19 March 1832, LR-CA, Roll 223, 88–93; Green, *Politics of Indian Removal*, 170; Arthur H. DeRosier Jr., "Andrew Jackson and Negotiations for the Removal of the Choctaw Indians," *Historian* 29, no. 3 (May 1967): 343–62.

18. Crowell to Cass, 20 March 1832, LR-CA, Roll 223, 119–20; Enclosure No. 1, HR 98, 565; Creeks to Cass, 5 May 1833, LR-CA, Roll 223, 642–44; Abbott to Cass, May 1833, LR-CAR, Roll 241, 494–500; Ellisor, *Second Creek War*, 72; Green, *Politics of Indian Removal*, 87; Charles J. Kappler, ed., *Indian Affairs: Laws and Treaties*, vol. 2: *Treaties* (Washington DC: Government Printing Office, 1904), 341–43; Miscellaneous Records Concerning Contracts, ca. 1833–1857, RG 75, Entry 298, Box 1, NARA. In lieu of land, Grayson was compensated $1.25 an acre; see Christopher D. Haveman, "'Last Evening I Saw the Sun Set for the Last Time': The 1832 Treaty of Washington and the Transfer of the Creeks' Alabama Land to White Ownership," *Native South* 5 (2012): 83. See also J. Anthony Paredes and Kenneth J. Plante, "A Reëxamination of Creek Indian Population Trends: 1738–1832," *American Indian Culture and Research Journal* 6, no. 4 (1983): 3–28. Jim Boy is more often associated with the town of Thlobthlocco, although he is listed on the 1832 census under the town of Clewalla.

19. Kappler, *Indian Affairs*, 2:341–43; Cass to Abert, 2 May 1833, CRR-Misc., RG 75, Entry 300, Box 1, NARA; Parsons to Cass, 2 May 1833, LR-CA, Roll 223, 1009–11.

20. Kappler, *Indian Affairs*, 2:341–43; Land transfer, 24 January 1833, LR-CA, Roll 241, 638–39; Memorandum, 14 April 1838, LR-CAR, Roll 244, 49; Graham to Balch and Crawford, 24 January 1837, LR-CAR, Roll 244, 176–83. For Napoleon Moore, see Special order of the chiefs, 12 January 1833, CRR-Misc., RG 75, Entry 300, Box 1, NARA; Moore to Crowell, 29 May 1834, CRR-Misc., RG 75, Entry 300, Box 1, NARA; John D. Benedict, *Muskogee and Northeastern Oklahoma, Including the Counties of Muskogee, McIntosh, Wagoner, Cherokee, Sequoyah, Adair, Delaware, Mayes, Rogers, Washington, Nowata, Craig and Ottawa*, vol. 2 (Chicago: S. J. Clarke, 1922), 5–10; List of Claims, LR-CA, Roll 223, 961.

21. Abert to Cass, 5 November 1833, LR-CAR, Roll 241, 110–17; Abert to Cass, 15 October 1834, LR-CAR, Roll 241, 465–76; Tarrant to Herring, 15 August 1833, LR-CAR, Roll 241, 355–56; Crawford to Poinsett, 9 January 1839, LR-CAR, Roll 246, 1052–54; Brodnax to Cass, 28 May 1833, LR-CAR, Roll 241, 210–11.

22. Abert to Cass, 15 October 1834, LR-CAR, Roll 241, 465–76; Copy of Instructions, LR-CAR, Roll 241, 477–80; Ward to Jackson, n.d., LR-CAR, Roll 241, 755–58.

23. Crowell to Cass, 25 January 1832, LR-CA, Roll 223, 113; Gayle to Cass, 2 October 1833, LR-CAR, Roll 241, 230–51; Sanford to Gibson, 14 May 1836, ASP-MA, 6:763.

24. Kappler, *Indian Affairs*, 2:341–43; Act of March 3, 1807, in *The Public Statutes at Large of the United States of America*, ed. Richard Peters (Boston: Charles C. Little and James Brown, 1845), 2:445–46; Austill to Cass, 12 July 1833, LR-CA, Roll 223, 504–6; Austill to Cass, 26 July 1833, LR-CA, Roll 223, 508–13; Notes and accompanying extracts, Lewis Cass Papers, 1774–1924, Manuscript Writings Series, William L. Clements Library, University of Michigan, Ann Arbor MI; Green, *Politics of Indian Removal*, 174–80; Mary Elizabeth Young, "Indian Removal and Land Allotment: The Civilized Tribes and Jacksonian Justice," *American Historical Review* 64, no. 1 (October 1958): 31–45; Young, *Redskins, Ruffleshirts, and Rednecks: Indian Allotments in Alabama and Mississippi* (Norman: University of Oklahoma Press, 1961), 76–81; Note, November [ca. 1832], Bassett, *Correspondence of Andrew Jackson*, 4:493; Gayle to Cass, 20 August 1833, LR-CA, Roll 223, 688–90; Ellisor, *Second Creek War*, 84–85; Frank L. Owsley Jr., "Francis Scott Key's Mission to Alabama in 1833," *Alabama Review* 23, no. 3 (July 1970): 181–92. For more on Jackson's Indian policy and the nullification movement, see William W. Freehling, *Prelude to Civil War: The Nullification Controversy in South Carolina, 1816–1836* (New York: Harper and Row, 1965), 232–34; Richard E. Ellis, *The Union at Risk: Jacksonian Democracy, States' Rights, and the Nullification Crisis* (New York: Oxford University Press, 1987), 25–32; Donald J. Ratcliffe, "The Nullification Crisis, Southern Discontents, and the American Political Process," *American Nineteenth Century History* 1, no. 2 (Summer 2000): 1–30. See also Daniel Feller, *The Public Lands in Jacksonian Politics* (Madison: University of Wisconsin Press, 1984).
25. Cass to Abert and Parsons, 2 May 1833, LR-CA, Roll 223, 432–37.
26. Abert to Cass, 11 November 1833, Roll 241, 144–48; Young, *Redskins, Ruffleshirts, and Rednecks*, 74; Statement of Thomason, 17 March 1835, LR-CAR, Roll 242, 156; Hall to Cass, 21 March 1835, LR-CAR, Roll 242, 154–55; Tyrone Power, *Impressions of America, During the Years 1833, 1834, and 1835*, vol. 2 (London: Richard Bentley, 1836), 134.
27. Report of A. Balch, 14 January 1837, NASP, 9:497–507.
28. Abert to Cass, 14 October 1833, LR-CAR, Roll 241, 103–4; Meigs to Cass, 26 September 1834, LR-CAR, Roll 241, 446–50; Letter from Collins, 26 June 1834, CRR-Misc., RG 75, Entry 300, Box 1, NARA; Creeks to Jackson, 13 June 1835, LR-CA, Roll 224, 273–81; A description and valuation of sections, CRR-Misc., Entry 300, Box 16, NARA.
29. Kappler, *Indian Affairs*, 2:341–43; Tarrant to Herring, 15 May 1833, LR-CAR, Roll 241, 344–47; Abert to Cass, 15 October 1834, LR-CAR, Roll 241, 465–76; Copy of Instructions, LR-CAR, Roll 241, 477–80.
30. Eaton to Creeks, 20 March 1830, LR-CA, Roll 226, 291–96; Letter from Creeks, 7 November 1832, LR-CA, Roll 223, 174–76; Meigs to Cass, 2 August 1834, Native American Manuscripts—Grayson Family, Flap Folder 3, Folder 1, Western History

Collection, University of Oklahoma, Norman OK; Hogan to Cass, 8 March 1836, ASP-MA, 6:751–53.

31. Cass to Abert, 30 September 1833, CRR-Misc., RG 75, Entry 300, Box 1, NARA; Green, *Politics of Indian Removal*, 170–73.

32. Letter from Featherston, 14 December 1833, CRR-Misc., Box 1, NARA; Dudley Randall, 2 September 1834, LR-CAR, 241, 882; Haveman, "Last Evening I Saw the Sun Set for the Last Time," 65–66, 73; Meigs to Cass, 3 September 1834, LR-CAR, Roll 241, 866–69.

33. Young, *Redskins, Ruffleshirts, and Rednecks*, 73–113; Young, "The Creek Frauds: A Study in Conscience and Corruption," *Mississippi Valley Historical Review* 42, no. 3 (December 1955): 411–37; Report of T. Hartley Crawford, 11 May 1838, 25th Cong., 1st sess., 1838, H.R. Doc. No. 452, serial no. 331, 11; Brodnax to Cass, 23 July 1832, LR-CA, Roll 223, 33–39; Kloslitco Investigation, Report Concerning Creek Contracts, 1836, RG 75, Entry 290, NARA; Meigs to Cass, 26 September 1834, LR-CAR, Roll 241, 446–50.

34. Haveman, "Last Evening I Saw the Sun Set for the Last Time," 66–68; Young, *Redskins, Ruffleshirts, and Rednecks*, 73–113; Hogan to Gibson, 3 April 1835, CGS-IRW, Reel 5, 525–28; Testimony of Brinson, 30 October 1835, LR-CAR, Roll 243, 621–24.

35. Thompson to Cass, 11 July 1834, LR-CA, Roll 224, 143.

36. Johnson Jones Hooper, *Some Adventures of Captain Simon Suggs, Late of the Tallapoosa Volunteers; Together with "Taking the Census," and Other Alabama Sketches. By a Country Editor with a Portrait from Life, and Other Illustrations, by Darley* (Philadelphia: Carey and Hart, 1845), 69–81, 142; Haveman, "Last Evening I Saw the Sun Set for the Last Time," 69; Assignment by chiefs of the 29 sections, 4 October 1835, LR-CAR, Roll 242, 692–95; Sanford & Co. to Gibson, 29 October 1835, ASP-MA, 6:755–56; Bright to Herring, 13 May 1834, LR-CAR, Roll 241, 546–47; Tarrant to Cass, 12 October 1835, LR-CAR, Roll 242, 686; Opothle Yoholo to Tarrant, 24 September 1835, LR-CAR, Roll 242, 691; Memorandum, LR-CAR, Roll 246, 314–16; 1832 Census of Creek Indians Taken by Parsons and Abbott, RG 75, Microcopy 275, Roll 1, 106, NARA; Testimony of Marshall, CRR-Misc., RG 75, Entry 300, Box 2, NARA; Woodward, *Woodward's Reminiscences*, 117; Howard Winston Smith, "An Annotated Edition of Hooper's *Some Adventures of Captain Simon Suggs*" (PhD diss., Vanderbilt University, 1965). Most Suggs scholars ignore some of the historical connections in Hooper's work; see W. Stanley Hoole, *Alias Simon Suggs: The Life and Times of Johnson Jones Hooper* (Tuscaloosa: University of Alabama Press, 1952); Robert Hopkins, "Simon Suggs: A Burlesque Campaign Biography," *American Quarterly* 15, no. 3 (Autumn 1963): 459–63; Johnson Jones Hooper, *Adventures of Captain Simon Suggs, Late of the Tallapoosa Volunteers*, intro. Manly Wade Wellman (Chapel Hill: University of North Carolina Press, 1969), ix–xxiv; Howard Winston Smith, "Simon Suggs and the Satiric Tradition,"

in "Essays in Honor of Richebourg Gaillard McWilliams," ed. Howard Creed, *Birmingham-Southern College Bulletin* 63, no. 2 (May 1970): 49–56; Paul Somers Jr., *Johnson J. Hooper* (Boston: Twayne, 1984); Joseph H. Harkey, "Some Adventures of Captain Simon Suggs: The Legacy of Johnson Jones Hooper," in *No Fairer Land: Studies in Southern Literature before 1900*, ed. J. Lasley Dameron and James W. Mathews (Troy NY: Whitston, 1986), 200–210; Johanna Nicol Shields, "A Sadder Simon Suggs: Freedom and Slavery in the Humor of Johnson Hooper," *Journal of Southern History* 56, no. 4 (November 1990): 641–64; Johnson Jones Hooper, *Adventures of Captain Simon Suggs, Late of the Tallapoosa Volunteers; together with "Taking the Census" and Other Alabama Sketches*, intro. Johanna Nicol Shields (Tuscaloosa: University of Alabama Press, 1993), vi–lxix; Shelia Ruzycki O'Brien, "Writing with a Forked Pen: Racial Dynamics and Johnson Jones Hooper's Twin Tale of Swindling Indians," *American Studies* 35, no. 2 (Fall 1994): 95–113; Johanna Nicol Shields, "Writers in the Old Southwest and the Commercialization of American Letters," *Journal of the Early Republic* 27, no. 3 (Fall 2007): 471–505; D. Berton Emerson, "'It's Good to Be Shifty': The Local Democracies of Old Southwestern Humor," *American Literature* 85, no. 2 (June 2013): 273–301; Testimony of Harrison Young, 28 December 1836, SIAC, Agent (Page), Account (1490), Year (1838), NARA; Land Location Registers, ca. 1834–86, "Creek Land Location Register, Treaty of March 24, 1832," Col. James Bright, Vol. I, RG 75, Entry 287, NARA, 54; Woodward, *Reminiscences*, 123–25; Bryan, Lawson, McLemore, & Dudley vs. Menawa, CRR-Misc., Box 15, NARA.
37. Abert to Cass, 3 July 1833, LR-CA, Roll 223, 418–26.
38. Creeks to Cass, 27 September 1832, LR-CA, Roll 223, 95–97; Abert to Cass, 2 June 1833, LR-CA, Roll 223, 399–405.
39. Parsons to Jackson, 12 October 1832, LR-CA, Roll 223, 295–97; Bright to Cass, 8 December 1833, LR-CA, Roll 241, 206–8.
40. Letter from Dougherty, 5 December 1833, LR-CAR, Roll 241, 222–23; Map of Chambers County (Map 243); Russell County (Map 238), RG 75, Entry 163, Central Map Files, NARA II, College Park MD; 1832 Census of Creek Indians Taken by Parsons and Abbott, RG 75, Microcopy 275, Roll 1, NARA, 184; Gregory A. Waselkov, "Changing Strategies of Indian Field Location in the Early Historic Southeast," in *People, Plants, and Landscapes: Studies in Paleoethnobotony*, ed. Kristen J. Gremillion (Tuscaloosa: University of Alabama Press, 1997), 185–93; Efar Tustennugga to Jackson, 25 February 1834, LR-CAR, Roll 241, 618–20; Chiefs' Explanation of Act of Council of 19 July 1834, LR-CAR, Roll 241, 874–79.
41. Hogan to Gibson, 9 May 1835, ASP-ma, 6:724–25; Steven C. Hahn, *The Invention of the Creek Nation, 1670–1763* (Lincoln: University of Nebraska Press, 2004), 119, 189, 259–70. See also Verner Crane, *The Southern Frontier 1670–1732* (Durham NC: Duke University Press, 1928); David H. Corkran, *The Creek Frontier, 1540–1783* (Norman: University of Oklahoma Press, 1967).

42. Robb to Tarrant, 22 November 1832, LS, Roll 9, 382; Cass to Creeks, 21 December 1832, LS, Roll 9, 434–44; Tarrant to Herring, 5 August 1835, LR-CA, Roll 224, 287–88; Tarrant to Herring, 17 October 1835, LR-CA, Roll 224, 302; Tarrrant to Herring, 18 December 1835, LR-CA, Roll 224, 308.

5. ECLIPSE

1. McIntosh to Cass, 28 January 1833, LR-CAE, Roll 237, 390–91; Muster Roll (2nd McIntosh party), SIAC, Agent (Brearley), Account (14,487), Year (1830), NARA; Milton to Cass, 18 June 1833, LR-CAE, Roll 237, 397–99; Herring to Cass, 11 January 1833, LS, Roll 9, 477–78; Herring to McIntosh, 11 February 1833, SD 512, 3:593; Abert to Cass, 18 May 1833, LR-CAE, Roll 237, 372–78.
2. Herring to McIntosh, 4 May 1833, LR-CAE, Roll 237, 393; Abert to Cass, 18 May 1833, LR-CAE, Roll 237, 372–78; Cass to Abert, 25 May 1833, SD 512, 3:703–5.
3. Cass to Abert, 25 May 1833, SD 512, 3:703–5; Compere to McKenney, 15 August 1828, LR-CA, Roll 221, 709–11; Compere to McKenney, 4 February 1828, LR-CAE, Roll 237, 146–52.
4. Abert to Cass, 9–12 June 1833, LR-CAR, Roll 241, 70–89; Crowell to Eaton, 8 August 1830, LR-CA, Roll 222, 319–24; Page to Jesup, 14 November 1831, SD 512, 1:784–85.
5. Milton to Cass, 18 June 1833, LR-CAE, Roll 237, 397–99; Shorter to the Secretary of War, 20 April 1833, SD 512, 4:187–88; Abert to Cass, 9–12 June 1833, LR-CAR, Roll 241, 70–89.
6. Parsons to Herring, 7 June 1833, LR-CA, Roll 223, 1025–27; Gaines to Barbour, 18 July 1825, HR 98, 277–79.
7. Milton to Cass, 18 June 1833, LR-CAE, Roll 237, 397–99; Brown to Gibson, 3 January 1834, CGS-IRW, Roll 5, 40; Van Horne to Gibson, 7 May 1834, CGS-IRW, Roll 5, 186–87; Van Horne to Brown, 25 December 1833, CGS-IRW, Roll 4, 931; Campbell to Herring, 4 September 1833, LR-CAE, Roll 237, 382–83; Campbell to Herring, 18 December 1833, LR-CAE, Roll 237, 385; Muster Roll (McIntosh) LR-CAE, Roll 237, 422–23; Muster Roll (McIntosh), CGS-IRW, Roll 4, 934; Van Horne to Gibson, 21 April 1834, CGS-IRW, Roll 5, 188–91.
8. Van Horne to Gibson, 21 April 1834, CGS-IRW, Roll 5, 188–91; Van Horne to Brown, 18 December 1833, CGS-IRW, Roll 4, 921.
9. Brown to Gibson, 11 October 1834, CGS-IRW, Roll 10, 669–73; Brown to Gibson, 16 October 1834, CGS-IRW, Roll 10, 675–76; Brown to Gibson, 26 October 1834, CGS-IRW, Roll 10, 677–80; Arbuckle to Gibson, 8 April 1834, CGS-IRW, Roll 10, 715; Articles of Agreement (1–9), Records of the Quartermaster Division, Record Group 217, Entry 227, Indian contracts, 1820–1894, Box 1, NARA.
10. Page to Gibson, 15 September 1834, CGS-IRW, Roll 5, 109–12; Hill to Gibson, 18 October 1834, CGS-IRW, Roll 5, 163–64.

11. Cass to Hill, 11 July 1834, CGS-IRW, Roll 5, 159; Page to Gibson, 6 January 1835, CGS-IRW, Roll 5, 134–37; Page to Gibson, 15 September 1834, CGS-IRW, Roll 5, 109–12; Page to Lewis, 24 November 1836, SIAC, Agent (Page), Account (1490), Year (1838), NARA; Page to Gibson, 7 November 1834, CGS-IRW, Roll 5, 114–16.
12. Page to Gibson, 1 May 1835, CGS-IRW, Roll 5, 147–50; Page to Gibson, 3 December 1834, CGS-IRW, Roll 5, 118–19; Page to Gibson, 5 December 1834, CGS-IRW, Roll 5, 124–25; Page to Gibson, 7 November 1834, CGS-IRW, Roll 5, 114–16; Page to Gibson, 4 December 1834, CGS-IRW, Roll 5, 121–22; Page to Gibson, 6 January 1836, CGS-IRW, Roll 5, 134–37; Page to Gibson, 25 April 1835, CGS-IRW, Roll 5, 140–46.
13. Muster Roll (Page), RG 75, Entry 299, Box 2, Vol. 8, NARA; Charles J. Kappler, ed., *Indian Affairs: Laws and Treaties*, vol. 2: *Treaties* (Washington DC: Government Printing Office, 1904), 264–68; Receipt, SIAC, Agent (Crowell), Account (15,814), Year (1831), NARA; Michael D. Green, *The Politics of Indian Removal: Creek Government and Society in Crisis* (Lincoln: University of Nebraska Press, 1982), 87; John T. Ellisor, *The Second Creek War: Interethnic Conflict and Collusion on a Collapsing Frontier* (Lincoln: University of Nebraska Press, 2010), 72.
14. Page to Gibson, 6 January 1835, CGS-IRW, Roll 5, 134–37; Abstract of Disbursements, SIAC, Agent (Page), Account (20,726), Year (1836), NARA; Muster Roll, RG 75, Entry 299, Box 2, Vol. 8, NARA; Sarah Woolfolk Wiggins and Ruth Smith Truss, eds., *The Journal of Sarah Haynsworth Gayle, 1827–1835: A Substitute for Social Intercourse* (Tuscaloosa: University of Alabama Press, 2013), 303; *Niles' Weekly Register*, 24 January 1835.
15. Page to Gibson, 6 January 1835, CGS-IRW, Roll 5, 134–37; Abstract of Disbursements, SIAC, Agent (Page), Account (20,726), Year (1836), NARA.
16. Page to Gibson, 27 April 1835, CGS-IRW, Roll 5, 151–54; Creek petition, LR-CAE, Roll 237, 411–13; Muster Roll (Page), RG 75, Entry 299, Box 2, Vol. 8, NARA.
17. Page to Gibson, 6 January 1835, CGS-IRW, Roll 5, 134–37; Page to Gibson, 25 April 1835, CGS-IRW, Roll 5, 140–46; Letter to Beattie, 2 July 1834, MS 158, Folder 4, VHS; *Arkansas Advocate*, 28 November 1834; Abstract of disbursements, SIAC, Agent (Page), Account (20,726), Year (1836), NARA; Friedrich Gerstäcker, *Wild Sports in the Far West: The narrative of a German Wanderer beyond the Mississippi, 1837–1843*, ed. Edna L Steeves and Harrison R. Steeves (1854; reprint, Durham NC: Duke University Press, 1968), 130; *Arkansas Gazette*, 24 February 1835; SFOIA, SF 62, Roll 7, 356–405; George A. McCall, *Letters From the Frontiers* (1868; reprint, Gainesville: University Press of Florida, 1974), 280–81.
18. Page to Gibson, 25 April 1835, CGS-IRW, Roll 5, 140–46; Brown to Gibson, 1 March 1835, CGS-IRW, Roll 5, 249–50; *Arkansas Gazette*, 24 February 1835.
19. Harris to Gibson, 9 May 1834, CGS-IRW, Roll 1, 462–67; Journal (Harris), CGS-IRW, Roll 1, 327–68; Harris to Gibson, 5 June 1834, CGS-IRW, Roll 1, 470–75; Page to Gibson, 25 April 1835, CGS-IRW, Roll 5, 140–46; Page to Gibson, 1 May 1835,

CGS-IRW, Roll 5, 147–50; Muster Roll (Page), RG 75, Entry 299, Box 2, Vol. 8, NARA.

20. Van Horne to Gibson, 2 April 1835, CGS-IRW, Roll 5, 772–74; Muster Roll (Page), RG 75, Entry 299, Box 2, Vol. 8, NARA; Page to Gibson, 25 April 1835, CGS-IRW, Roll 5, 140–46; Grant Foreman, *Indian Removal: The Emigration of the Five Civilized Tribes of Indians* (1932, reprint; Norman: University of Oklahoma Press, 1974), 128.

21. Page to Gibson, 1 May 1835, CGS-IRW, Roll 5, 147–50; Page to Gibson, 7 November 1834, CGS-IRW, Roll 5, 114–16; Page to Gibson, 25 April 1835, CGS-IRW, Roll 5, 140–46.

22. Estell to Hogan, 3 July 1835, ASP-MA, 6:734; Conner to Hogan, n.d., ASP-ma, 6:734.

23. Circular to Creek Superintendent, 20 March 1835, LR-CAR, Roll 248, 318–24; Hogan to Marcy, 7 April 1845, LR-CAR, Roll 248, 622–27; Hill to Gibson, 12 September 1834, CGS-IRW, Roll 5, 166–68.

24. Hogan to Gibson, 14 May 1835, ASP-ma, 6:725–26; Hogan to Gibson, 9 May 1835, ASP-ma, 6:724–25; Christopher D. Haveman, "'Last Evening I Saw the Sun Set for the Last Time': The 1832 Treaty of Washington and the Transfer of the Creeks' Alabama Land to White Ownership," *Native South* 5 (2012): 87–88n10; List of Land Companies, CRR-Misc., Box 11, NARA; Statement of Billingslea, SIAC, Agent (Townsend), Account (1497), Year (1838), NARA.

25. Hogan to Gibson, 9 May 1835, ASP-MA, 6:724–25; Hogan to Gibson, 8 April 1835, ASP-MA, 6:723–24; Hunter to Hogan, 13 July 1835, ASP-MA, 6:736; Creeks to Jackson, 13 June 1835, LR-CA, Roll 224, 273–81; To The Chiefs & head Men of the different Towns of the Creek & Seminola Nation, February 1833, MS 158, Folder 5, VHS; Creeks to Cass, 17 April 1833, MS 158, Folder 5, VHS; Unsigned letter, 27 March 1834, CRR-Misc., RG 75, Entry 300, Box 1, NARA; Ellisor, *Second Creek War*, 102–3, 115; Jonathan B. Hook, *The Alabama-Coushatta Indians* (College Station: Texas A&M University Press, 1997); Sheri Marie Shuck-Hall, *Journey to the West: The Alabama and Coushatta Indians* (Norman: University of Oklahoma Press, 2008). See also William Bollaert, "Observations on the Indian Tribes in Texas," *Journal of the Ethnological Society of London* 2 (1850): 262–83; Kenneth Wiggins Porter, "The Hawkins' Negroes Go to Mexico: A Footnote from Tradition," *Chronicles of Oklahoma* 24, no. 1 (1946): 55–58; Jean Louis Berlandier, *The Indians of Texas in 1830* (Washington DC: Smithsonian Institution Press, 1969), 104, 124.

26. Hogan to Gibson, 9 May 1835, ASP-MA, 6:724–25; Green, *Politics of Indian Removal*, 96; Ellisor, *Second Creek War*, 115; Jack Gregory and Rennard Strickland, *Sam Houston with the Cherokees, 1829–1833* (Austin: University of Texas Press, 1967), 149–50.

27. Haveman, "Last Evening I Saw the Sun Set for the Last Time," 87–88n10; Letter extract, Hogan to Gibson, 3 June 1835, *ASP-MA*, 6:726; Blue to Hogan, 4 August 1835, *ASP-MA*, 6:740; Hogan to Cass, 8 March 1836, *ASP-MA*, 6:751–53.
28. Page to Herring, 28 June 1835, LR-CA, Roll 224, 231–32; Ellisor, *Second Creek War*, 177. See also Washington Irving, "The Conspiracy of Neamathla: An Authentic Sketch," in *Reviews and Miscellanies, Knickerbocker Edition* (New York: G. P. Putnam's Sons, 1897), 329–40.
29. Parsons to Jackson, 12 October 1832, LR-CA, Roll 223, 295–97; Abert to Cass, 2 June 1833, LR-CA, Roll 223, 399–405; Creeks to Jackson, 13 June 1835, LR-CA, Roll 224, 273–81.
30. Vandeburgh to Hogan, 11 July 1835, *ASP-MA*, 6:736; Estill to Hogan, 4 July 1835, Copy of Estill's report, CGS-IRW, Roll 5, 562; Hargrove to Schley, 6 March 1836, Creek Indian Letters, Talks, and Treaties, 1705–1839, Part 4, 1267, GA; Diary entry, April 1836, Moravian Mission Diaries, Murray County, GA, Vol. 2, GA.
31. Report of A. Balch, 14 January 1837, *NASP*, 9:497–507; Creeks to Jackson, 13 June 1835, LR-CA, Roll 224, 273–81.
32. Louis P. Masur, *1831: Year of Eclipse* (New York: Hill and Wang, 2001), 1–8; Meigs journal, LR-CAR, Roll 241, 845–46. See also Gregory Evans Dowd, "Thinking Outside the Circle: Tecumseh's 1811 Mission," in *Tohopeka: Rethinking the Creek War and the War of 1812*, ed. Kathryn E. Holland Braund (Tuscaloosa: University of Alabama Press, 2012), 30–52; Joel W. Martin, *Sacred Revolt: The Muskogees' Struggle for a New World* (Boston: Beacon Press, 1991), 114–16. For a modern Muscogee take on eclipses, see Jean Chaudhuri and Joyotpaul Chaudhuri, *A Sacred Path: The Way of the Muscogee Creeks* (Los Angeles: UCLA American Indian Studies Center, 2001), 10–12.
33. Hogan to Gibson, 9 May 1835, *ASP-ma*, 6:724–25; Hogan to Gibson, 14 May 1835, *ASP-MA*, 6:725–26; Ward to Lumpkin, 14 March 1835, Creek Indian Letters, Talks, and Treaties, 1705–1839, Part 4, 1191–95, GA; *Niles' Weekly Register*, 21 February 1835; *North Alabamian*, 18 February 1835; Wilson Lumpkin, *The Removal of the Cherokee Indians from Georgia. Including His Speeches in the United States Congress on the Indian Question, as Representative and Senator of Georgia; His Official Correspondence on the Removal of the Cherokees during his two terms as Governor of Georgia, and later as United States Commissioner to the Cherokees, 1827–1841, Together with a Sketch of His Life and Conduct while holding many Public Offices under the Government of Georgia and the United States, prior to 1827, and after 1841*, vol. 1 (Wormsloe GA: Priv. print.; reprint, New York: Dodd, Mead, 1907), 288–89.
34. Connor to Hogan, 6 August 1835, *ASP-MA*, 6:741; Blue to Hogan, 4 August 1835, *ASP-MA*, 6:740; Hogan to Cass, 8 March 1836, *ASP-MA*, 6:751–53; Creeks to Secretary of War, 4 September 1835, LR-CAR, Roll 242, 92–98; Hunter to Gibson, 3

September 1835, CGS-IRW, Roll 5, 580–82; John Howard Payne, "The Green-Corn Dance," *Continental Monthly* 1 (January 1862): 17–29.

35. A Brief of the Transactions Connected with the Formation of the Contract with the Alabama Emigrating Company, SIAC, Agent (Reynolds), Account (1687), Year (1838), NARA; Letter to Hogan, 21 September 1835, ASP-ma, 6:777–78; Iverson to Forsyth, 7 November 1834, LR-CAE, Roll 237, 430–34; Alvin Laroy Duckett, *John Forsyth: Political Tactician* (Athens: University of Georgia Press, 1962), 6. Private contractors were hired for other Indian relocations. See Robert A. Trennert, "The Business of Indian Removal: Deporting the Potawatomi from Wisconsin, 1851," *Wisconsin Magazine of History* 63, no. 1 (Autumn 1979): 36–50. Mary Elizabeth Young, *Redskins, Ruffleshirts, and Rednecks: Indian Allotments in Alabama and Mississippi, 1830–1860* (Norman: University of Oklahoma Press, 1961), 88, states that Alfred Iverson was John Forsyth's nephew.

36. Hogan to Gibson, 24 August 1835, ASP-ma, 6:738; Gibson to Deas, 21 September 1835, ASP-MA, 6:778–79; Creeks to Jackson, 14 January 1836, LR-CA, Roll 225, 38–41; List of Land Companies, CRR-Misc., Box 11, NARA; Young, *Redskins, Ruffleshirts, and Rednecks*, 105–6; United States to Benton, SIAC, Agent (Crowell), Account (15,814), Year (1831), NARA; Daniel Feller, Laura-Eve Moss, Thomas Coens, and Erik B. Alexander, eds., *The Papers of Andrew Jackson*, vol. 9: *1831* (Knoxville: University of Tennessee Press, 2013), 145–47; Iverson to Forsyth, 7 November 1834, LR-CAE, Roll 237, 430–34; Sanford to Abert, 11 November 1834, CRR-Misc., Box 1, NARA; Contract, 17 September 1835, ASP-MA, 6:782–83; Blue to Hogan, 13 July 1835, CGS-IRW, Roll 5, 562–63; Hunter to Hogan, 12 August 1835, ASP-MA, 6:739–40.

37. Cass to Creeks, 27 January 1836, CRR-Misc., Box 2, NARA; Contract, 17 September 1835, ASP-ma, 6:782–83.

38. Contract, 17 September 1835, ASP-MA, 6:782–83.

39. Hogan to Gibson, 5 October 1835, ASP-MA, 6:741; Sanford & Co. to Gibson, 30 September 1835, ASP-MA, 6:753–54; Hogan to Gibson, 6 November 1835, ASP-MA, 6:746; Hogan to Gibson, 12 October 1835, ASP-ma, 6:741–42.

40. Blue to Gibson, 1 December 1835, CGS-IRW, Roll 5, 239; Blue to Gibson, 6 December 1835, CGS-IRW, Roll 5, 236–37; Deas to Gibson, 6 December 1835, CGS-IRW, Roll 5, 318–20; Muster Roll (Deas), LR-CAE, Roll 237, 655–57; Muster Roll (Deas), SIAC, Agent (Page), Account (220), Year (1837), NARA; Memorandum of Expenses (Randall), SIAC, Agent (Page), Account (220), Year (1837), NARA; Hogan to Gibson, 4 November 1835, ASP-MA, 6:744–45. See also Muster Roll (Deas), LR-CAE, Roll 237, 655–57.

41. Deas to Gibson, 21 December 1835, ASP-MA, 6:772–73; Journal (Deas), CGS-IRW, Roll 6, 33–55; John H. Jones, "The Autobiography of John H. Jones, 1814–1882," IU; Gaston Litton, ed., "The Journal of a Party of Emigrating Creek Indians, 1835–1836," *Journal of Southern History* 7, no. 2 (May 1941): 225–42.

42. Journal (Deas), CGS-IRW, Roll 6, 33–55; Deas to Gibson, 28 December 1835, ASP-MA, 6:773.
43. Journal (Deas), CGS-IRW, Roll 6, 33–55; Jones, "Autobiography," IU; R. E. Banta, *The Ohio* (New York: Rinehart, 1949), 294–95; Ingersoll to Howell, 22 December 1835, ASP-MA, 6:758.
44. Journal (Deas), CGS-IRW, Roll 6, 33–55; Jones, "Autobiography."
45. Journal (Deas), CGS-IRW, Roll 6, 33–55; Deas to Gibson, 9 January 1835, ASP-MA, 6:773–74; Jones, "Autobiography."
46. Ingersoll to Howell, 22 December 1835, ASP-MA, 6:758; Journal (Deas), CGS-IRW, Roll 6, 33–55; Jones, "Autobiography."
47. Jones, "Autobiography." *Sofkee*, a corn gruel left to age until it thickens and sours, was not only a favorite dish among the Creeks but also a food with cultural importance. As Amelia Rector Bell has noted, making *sofkee* reasserted a woman's femininity and authority within her family structure. Even among contemporary Creeks in Oklahoma, *sofkee* preparation (by the women) and consumption (by the men) was the symbolic vehicle for signaling a willingness to wed, while the end of *sofkee* production in a household portended the termination of matrimony. Amelia Rector Bell, "Separate People: Speaking of Creek Men and Women," *American Anthropologist* 92, no. 2 (June 1990): 335.
48. Jones, "Autobiography."
49. Jones, "Autobiography"; Journal (Deas), CGS-IRW, Roll 6, 33–55; *Arkansas State Gazette*, 11 April 1837.
50. Journal (Deas), CGS-IRW, Roll 6, 33–55; Litton, "The Journal of a Party of Emigrating Creek Indians," 238; Deas to Gibson, 28 January 1836, ASP-MA, 6:774; Deas to Gibson, 5 February 1836, ASP-MA, 6:774; Muster Roll (Deas), SIAC, Agent (Page), Account (220), Year (1837), NARA.
51. SFOIA, SF 285, Roll 77, 33, 38–45, 48; Tarrant to Herring, 5 August 1835, LR-CA, Roll 224, 287–88; Page to Harris, 20 February 1837, LR-CAE, Roll 238, 544–45.

6. SAND

1. Brad Agnew, *Fort Gibson: Terminal on the Trail of Tears* (Norman: University of Oklahoma Press, 1980), 29–31, 206, 218–219n3; Notes of Hood and Bell, HR 87, 41; Henry Leavitt Ellsworth, *Washington Irving on the Prairie, or, A Narrative of a Tour of the Southwest in the Year 1832*, ed. Stanley T. Williams and Barbara D. Simison (New York: American Book, 1937), 2–4; Benjamin Homans, ed., "Letter from Fort Gibson," *The Military and Naval Magazine of the United States* 3, no. 5 (July 1834).
2. Ellsworth, *Washington Irving on the Prairie*, 6; Gaines to the Secretary of War, 24 July 1825, HR 98, 299–301; Woodruff to Abert, 1 September 1851, HED 104, 20, 32; Logan to Lewis, 18 November 1844, SIAC, Agent (Dawson), Account (1587), Year (1844), NARA; Augustus Ward Loomis, *Scenes in the Indian Country*

(Philadelphia: Presbyterian Board of Publication, 1859), 225–26; Report of Hood and Bell, HR 87, 26. See also Carl Coke Rister and Bryan W. Lovelace, "A Diary Account of a Creek Boundary Survey, 1850," *Chronicles of Oklahoma* 27, no. 3 (Autumn 1949): 268–302.

3. McCoy to Porter, 29 January 1829, HR 87, 15–16.

4. McCoy to Porter, 29 January 1829, HR 87, 21; Woodhouse to Sitgreaves, 20 February 1850, HED 104, 6; Woodhouse to Woodruff, 6 January 1851, HED 104, 25–26; Irving to Paris, 9 October 1832, in Pierre M. Irving, *The Life and Letters of Washington Irving*, vol. 2 (Philadelphia: Lippincott, 1870), 267–68; Grove B. Jones et al., *Soil Survey of Muskogee County, Oklahoma* (Washington DC: Government Printing Office, 1915). See also W. David Baird and Danney Goble, *Oklahoma: A History* (Norman: University of Oklahoma Press, 2008), 3–12.

5. Loomis, *Scenes in the Indian Country*, 8; Creeks to Jackson, 21 October 1831 LR-CAE, Roll 237, 348–54; McCoy to Porter, 29 January 1829, HR 87, 21; Logan to Lewis, 18 November 1844, SIAC, Agent (Dawson), Account (1587), Year (1844), NARA.

6. McCoy to Cass, 6 March 1832, SD 512, 3:230–41; Notes of Hood and Bell, HR 87, 43; Woodhouse to Woodruff, 6 January 1851, HED 104, 26–27; Woodhouse to Sitgreaves, 20 February 1850, HED 104, 6.

7. Notes of Hood and Bell, HR 87, 41; McCoy to Porter, 29 January 1829, HR 87, 14; Eugene Current-Garcia and Dorothy B. Hatfield, eds., *Shem, Ham, & Japheth: The Papers of W. O. Tuggle, Comprising His Indian Diary, Sketches & Observations, Myths & Washington Journal in the Territory & at the Capital, 1879–1882* (Athens: University of Georgia Press, 1973), 101; Woodruff to Abert, 1 September 1851, HED 104, 20–21; McCoy to Cass, 6 March 1832, SD 512, 3:230–41; W. Stanley Hoole, ed., "Echoes from the 'Trail of Tears,' 1837," part 2, *Alabama Review* 6, no. 3 (July 1953): 222–32.

8. McCoy to Porter, 29 January 1829, HR 87, 14; Woodhouse to Sitgreaves, 20 February 1850, HED 104, 5; Hoole, "Echoes from the 'Trail of Tears,' 1837," part 2; Notes of Hood and Bell, HR 87, 41; Loughridge to Lowrie, 25 May 1843, Box 9, Reel 1, Letter 8, PHS-AIC; Map of Indian Territory (1866), Map 492, Record Group 75, Entry 163, Central Map Files, NARA II, College Park MD.

9. Loomis, *Scenes in the Indian Country*, 37; Journal (Sprague), SIAC, Agent (Reynolds), Account (1687), Year (1838), NARA; Notes of Hood and Bell, HR 87, 43; McCoy to Porter, 29 January 1829, HR 87, 14; George F. Spaulding, ed., *On the Western Tour with Washington Irving: The Journal and Letters of Count de Pourtalès* (Norman: University of Oklahoma Press, 1968), 58.

10. William P. Trent and George S. Hellman, eds., *The Journals of Washington Irving (Hitherto Unpublished)*, vol. 3 (New York: Haskell House, 1970), 134; Cochamy to Medill, 16 July 1848, LR-CAE, Roll 240, 450–51; Page to Reynolds, 1 September

1837, SIAC, Agent (Reynolds), Account (1687), Year (1838), NARA; Map of Indian Territory (1866), Map 492, Record Group 75, Entry 163, Central Map Files, NARA II, College Park MD; Thomas Nuttall, *A Journal of Travels into the Arkansa Territory, During the Year 1819. With Occasional Observations on the Manners of the Aborigines* (Philadelphia: Thomas H. Palmer, 1821), 168; Gen. Thomas James, *Three Years among the Indians and Mexicans*, ed. Milo Milton Quaife (New York: Citadel, 1966), 116; McCoy to Cass, 6 March 1832, SD 512, 3:230–41; Woodruff to Abert, 1 September 1851, HED 104, 19, 21; Woodhouse to Sitgreaves, 20 February 1850, HED 104, 5–6.

11. McCoy to Cass, 6 March 1832, SD 512, 3:230–41; Woodruff to Abert, 1 September 1851, HED 104, 19–21; McCoy to Porter, 29 January 1829, HR 87, 14; Van Horne to Gibson, 7 October 1834, CGS-IRW, Roll 5, 211–18. See also James H. Irwin, "Water Resources," in *Geography of Oklahoma*, ed. John W. Morris (Oklahoma City: Oklahoma Historical Society, 1977), 25–38.

12. Campbell to Herring, 18 June 1833, LR-CAW, Roll 236, 356–57; Campbell to Herring, 15 July 1833, LR-CAW, Roll 236, 359–60; Notes of Hood and Bell, HR 87, 41; Van Horne to Gibson, 7 October 1834, CGS-IRW, Roll 5, 211–18.

13. Brearley to Barbour, 20 July 1827, LR-CAE, Roll 237, 33–35; McCoy to Cass, 6 March 1832, SD 512, 3:230–41; Woodruff to Abert, 1 September 1851, HED 104, 19, 21; Logan to Crawford, 7 June 1840, LR-CA, Roll 226, 197–98.

14. Grant Foreman, *The Five Civilized Tribes* (Norman: University of Oklahoma Press, 1934), 148; Richard A. Sattler, "Cowboys and Indians: Creek and Seminole Stock Raising, 1700–1900," *American Indian Culture and Research Journal* 22, no. 3 (1998): 79–99; Woodruff to Abert, 1 September 1851, HED 104, 19, 21; Notes of Hood and Bell, HR 87, 41; Van Horne to Gibson, 7 October 1834, CGS-IRW, Roll 5, 211–18; Ellsworth, *Washington Irving on the Prairie*, 11; Abert to Brown, 26 April 1850, LR-CA, Roll 228, 365–67; Woodhouse to Woodruff, 6 January 1851, HED 104, 25; Loomis, *Scenes in the Indian Country*, 12.

15. Woodhouse to Sitgreaves, 20 February 1850, HED 104, 5–8, 14–15; journal extract, PHS-AIC, Box 9, Roll 1, Letter 62; Foreman, *Five Civilized Tribes*, 148; George Catlin, *Letters and Notes on the Manners, Customs, and Condition of the North American Indians. Written During Eight Years' Travel Amongst the Wildest Tribes of Indians in North America, In 1832, 33, 34, 35, 36, 37, 38, and 39*, vol. 2 (1841; reprint, Minneapolis: Ross and Haines, 1965), 46; Woodhouse to Woodruff, 6 January 1851, HED 104, 25–26; John Uri Lloyd, "Citrullus Colocynthis," *The Western Druggist* (June 1898): 3–11. See also James H. Gardner, "One Hundred Years Ago in the Region of Tulsa," *Chronicles of Oklahoma* 11, no. 2 (June 1933): 765–85.

16. Testimony of Harris, 12 June 1825, LR-CA, Roll 219, 944–45; Foreman, *Five Civilized Tribes*, 148; Woodruff to Abert, 1 September 1851, HED 104, 21; *Alabama Journal*,

22 August 1828; Jack D. Tyler and Wendy J. Anderson, "Historical Accounts of Several Large Mammals in Oklahoma," *Proceedings of the Oklahoma Academy of Science* 70 (1990): 51–55; Rister and Lovelace, "A Diary Account of a Creek Boundary Survey, 1850," 268–302; Woodhouse to Woodruff, 6 January 1851, HED 104, 25; Woodhouse to Sitgreaves, 20 February 1850, HED 104, 8.

17. Journal extract, PHS-AIC, Box 9, Roll 1, Letter 62; Charles M. Hudson, ed., *The Southeastern Indians* (Knoxville: University of Tennessee Press, 1976), 284.

18. McCoy to Porter, 29 January 1829, HR 87, 17; *Niles' Weekly Register*, 25 July 1829; Sarah Fountain, ed., *Authentic Voices: Arkansas Culture, 1541–1860* (Conway: University of Central Arkansas Press, 1986), 120–21; Campbell to Calhoun, 8 January 1825, HR 98, 86–91; Hopkins to Clark, 12 August 1831, Vol. 6, Reel 95, MS 95, 273–76, Kansas State Historical Society, Topeka; James Stuart, *Three Years in North America*, vol. 2 (Edinburgh: Robert Cadell, 1833), 159. For descriptions of Choctaw land, see Emmanuel-Henri-Dieudonné Domenech, *Seven Years' Residence in the Great Deserts of North America*, vol. 1 (London: Longman, Green, Longman, and Roberts, 1860), 152–59.

19. Ellsworth to Cass, 14 December 1832, SD 512, 3:557–58; Herring to Ellsworth and Schermerhorn, 1 June 1833, SD 512, 3:706–07; Herring to Ellsworth and Schermerhorn, 30 November 1833, SD 512, 3:835; Joseph T. Manzo, "Emigrant Indian Objections to Kansas Residence," *Kansas History* 4 (1981): 247–54; McCabe to Armstrong, 5 April 1835, LR-CAW, Roll 236, 598–99. See also David La Vere, *Contrary Neighbors: Southern Plains and Removed Indians in Indian Territory* (Norman: University of Oklahoma Press, 2000).

20. Gaines to the Secretary of War, 24 July 1825, HR 98, 299–301; Blake to Lewis, 13 March 1832, SIAC, Agent (Crowell), Account (16,806), Year (1833), NARA; Creeks to Jackson, 29 October 1831, in *The Papers of Andrew Jackson: A Microfilm Supplement*, ed. Harold D. Moser [et al.] (Wilmington DE: Scholarly Resources, 1986), Roll 18, 1145–52; *New York Observer*, 18 October 1834.

21. Garrick Alan Bailey, *Changes in Osage Social Organization, 1673–1906* (Eugene: University of Oregon, 1973), 58; Willard H. Rollings, *The Osage: An Ethnohistorical Study of Hegemony on the Prairie-Plains* (Columbia: University of Missouri Press, 1992); Louis F. Burns, *A History of the Osage People* (Tuscaloosa: University of Alabama Press, 2004); John Joseph Mathews, *The Osages: Children of the Middle Waters* (Norman: University of Oklahoma Press, 1961); A. M. Gibson, *The Kickapoos: Lords of the Middle Border* (Norman: University of Oklahoma Press, 1963), 100–101; Sitgreaves to Abert, 14 February 1850, HED 104, 4; McCoy to Cass, 6 March 1832, SD 512, 3:230–41; Chouteau to Clark, 28 June 1831, SD 512, 2:498–500; Treaty, 10 May 1831, SD 512, 2:504–6; Treaty, 18 May 1831, SD 512, 2:500–503; Herring to Cass, 19 November 1831, LS, Roll 7, 475–83; Arbuckle to Eaton, 21 May 1831, LR-CAW, Roll 236, 206–8; McCabe to Armstrong, 5 April 1835, LR-CAW, Roll 236, 598–99.

22. John P. Bowes, *Exiles and Pioneers: Eastern Indians in the Trans-Mississippi West* (Cambridge: Cambridge University Press, 2007), 122–23. Gibson, *Kickapoos*, 176–78.
23. Foreman, *Five Civilized Tribes*, 151; Western Creek census, 30 September 1833, SD 512, 4:722; Van Horne to Gibson, 7 October 1834, CGS-IRW, Roll 5, 211–18; Vaill to Green, 10 January 1831, ABC, Roll 779, 330–33; Fleming to Green, 29 October 1833, ABC, Roll 779, 209–11; Fleming to Green, 4 June 1834, ABC, Roll 779, 223–29; *Arkansas Gazette*, 19 March 1828 and 2 March 1835; Solomon Peck, "History of the Missions of the Baptist General Convention," in *History of American Missions to the Heathen, From their Commencement to the Present Time* (1840; reprint, New York: Johnson Reprint, 1970), 547; Valuation of Improvements, SFOIA, SF 207, Roll 61, 570–83; Spaulding, *On the Western Tour*, 42; Dawson to Macomb, 2 November 1831, Letters Received by the Topographical Bureau of the War Department, 1824–1865, Microcopy 506, Roll 18, 1–10; McCoy to Cass, 6 March 1832, SD 512, 3:230–41.
24. Foreman, *Five Civilized Tribes*, 149–51; *Niles' Weekly Register*, 25 July 1829; Valuation of Improvements, SFOIA, SF 207, Roll 61, 570–83; Provision Return, SIAC, Agent (Brearley), Account (14,487), Year (1830), NARA; Herring to Crowell, 7 February 1832, LS, Roll 8, 81; McKenney to Crowell, 22 March 1830, LS, Roll 6, 348; Gibson to Van Horne, 19 May 1835, CGS-IRW, Roll 7, 742–44; Van Horne to Gibson, 7 October 1834, CGS-IRW, Roll 5, 211–18; Brown to Gibson, 4 February 1835, CGS-IRW, Roll 10, 796.
25. Cass to Jackson, 16 February 1832, LS, Roll 8, 275; Valuation of Improvements, SFOIA, SF 207, Roll 61, 570–83; Claims for Lost Property, SIAC, Agent (Jacob Brown), Account (20,258), Year (1836), NARA; Bert Hodges, "Notes on the History of the Creek Nation and Some of Its Leaders," *Chronicles of Oklahoma* 43, no. 1 (Spring 1965): 9–18; Washington Irving, *A Tour on the Prairies*, ed. John Francis McDermott (1859; reprint, Norman: University of Oklahoma Press, 1956), 211.
26. Valuation of Improvements, SFOIA, SF 207, Roll 61, 570–83; Foreman, *Five Civilized Tribes*, 149.
27. *Alabama Journal*, 22 August 1828 and 17 October 1828; Campbell to Eaton, 12 April 1830, LR-CAW, Roll 236, 141–42; Grant Foreman, *Advancing the Frontier, 1830–1860* (1933; reprint, Norman: University of Oklahoma Press, 1968), 16; Foreman, *Five Civilized Tribes*, 149; Van Horne to Gibson, 7 October 1834, CGS-IRW, Roll 5, 211–18; Pekka Hämäläinen, *The Comanche Empire* (New Haven CT: Yale University Press, 2008), 153–54.
28. Irving, *A Tour on the Prairies*, 20, 22, 213; Trent and Hellman, *Journals of Washington Irving*, 134–36; *Christian Mirror and N. H. Observer*, 22 July 1830; Catlin, *Letters and Notes*, 2:122.
29. List of signers to the treaty at Indian Springs, HR 98, 254; Josiah C. Nott, *The Physical History of the Jewish Race* (Charleston SC: Steam-Power Press of Walker

and James, 1850), 27; John Bartlett Meserve, "Chief Samuel Checote, With Sketches of Chiefs Locher Harjo and Ward Coachman," *Chronicles of Oklahoma* 16, no. 4 (December 1938): 401–9; Isaac McCoy, *The Annual Register of Indian Affairs, in the Western (or Indian) Territory, 1835–1838* (Springfield MO: Particular Baptist Press, 2000), 20–21, 70; Armstrong to Medill, 27 November 1846, LR-CA, Roll 227, 549–50; Declaration of western Creeks, SIAC, Agent (Kendall Lewis), Account (18,271), Year (1834), NARA.

30. Campbell to Herring, 15 July 1833, LR-CAW, Roll 236, 359–60; Margaret Smith Ross, ed., "Three Letters of Cephas Washburn," *Arkansas Historical Quarterly* 16, no. 2 (Summer 1957): 174–91; Campbell to Herring, 4 September 1833, LR-CAE, Roll 237, 382–83; Campbell to Herring, 20 November 1833, LR-CAW, Roll 236, 370; Western Creek census, 30 September 1833, SD 512, 4:722; Irving, *A Tour on the Prairies*, 27–28; Weed to Greene, 24 May 1833, ABC, Roll 779, 186–87; Weed to Greene, 18 October 1832, ABC, Roll 779, 182–85; Loomis, *Scenes in the Indian Country*, 194, 234–35, 243. See also David Lewis Jr. and Ann T. Jordan, eds., *Creek Indian Medicine Ways: The Enduring Power of Mvskoke Religion* (Albuquerque: University of New Mexico Press, 2002).

31. Logan to Crawford, 3 March 1845, LR-CA, Roll 227, 447–49.

32. Baylor to Porter, 20 January 1829, LR-CAW, Roll 236, 96; McIntosh Voucher, 6 January 1829, LR-CAW, Roll 236, 97; Creeks to the Secretary of War, 8 April 1831, SD 512, 2:424–25; Braden to Eaton, 19 June 1830, LR-CAE, Roll 237, 298–300.

33. Charles Joseph Latrobe, *The Rambler in North America MDCCCXXXII–MDCCCXXXIII*, vol. 1 (New York: Harper and Brothers, 1835), 134; Hoole, "Echoes from the 'Trail of Tears,' 1837" part 2; Creeks to Jackson, 7 March 1829, LR-CAW, Roll 236, 72–75; Logan to Armstrong, January 1845, LR-CA, Roll 227, 351–57; Joel D. Boyd, "Creek Indian Agents, 1834–1874," *Chronicles of Oklahoma* 51, no. 1 (1973): 37–58; Armstrong to Herring, 3 April 1837, LR-CA, Roll 225, 233–34; Creeks to Jackson, 12 June 1830, in *Papers of Andrew Jackson: A Microfilm Supplement*, ed. Harold D. Moser [et al.] (Wilmington DE: Scholarly Resources, 1986), Roll 15, 1348–56; Christopher D. Haveman, "'Last Evening I Saw the Sun Set for the Last Time': The 1832 Treaty of Washington and the Transfer of the Creeks' Alabama Land to White Ownership," *Native South* 5 (2012): 65; *Arkansas State Gazette*, 4 May 1842, 8 June 1842, 17 July 1844, and 30 October 1844. See also C. Edwards Lester, *The Life of Sam Houston (The only Authentic Memoir of him ever published)* (New York: J. C. Derby, 1855), 54–57.

34. Charles J. Kappler, ed., *Indian Affairs: Laws and Treaties*, vol. 2: Treaties (Washington DC: Government Printing Office, 1904), 288–92, 385–91; McCoy to Porter, 29 January 1829, HR 87, 20; Creeks to Jackson, 21 October 1831, LR-CAE, Roll 237, 348–54; Valuation of Improvements, Western Creeks, SFOIA, SF 207, Roll 61, 570–83; Improvements, SIAC, Agent (Jacob Brown), Account (20,258), Year (1836), NARA.

35. Kappler, *Indian Affairs*, 2:344–45, 388–91, 756–63; John K. Mahon, "Two Seminole Treaties: Payne's Landing, 1832, and Ft. Gibson, 1833," *Florida Historical Quarterly* 41, no. 1 (July 1962): 1–21; Herring to Thompson, 7 July 1834, LS, Roll 13, 126–27; Armstrong to Crawford, 27 February 1841, LR-CA, Roll 226, 233–34; Muster Roll of Upper Towns, RG 75, Entry 299, Box 1, NARA; Kevin Mulroy, *Freedom on the Border: The Seminole Maroons in Florida, the Indian Territory, Coahuila, and Texas* (Lubbock: Texas Tech University Press, 1993), 35–36; Mulroy, *The Seminole Freedmen: A History* (Norman: University of Oklahoma Press, 2007), 53–58; Jane F. Lancaster, *Removal Aftershock: The Seminoles' Struggles to Survive in the West, 1836–1866* (Knoxville: University of Tennessee Press, 1994), 13–15, 24–62, 115; Stambaugh to Crawford, 30 March 1842, LR-CA, Roll 226, 597–603. For slavery among the Seminoles, see Christina Snyder, *Slavery in Indian Country: The Changing Face of Captivity in Early America* (Cambridge MA: Harvard University Press, 2010), 213–43.
36. Blake's testimony, 21 July 1848, HR 826, 25–26; Stidham's testimony, 21 July 1848, HR 826, 26; *Alabama Journal*, 22 August 1828; Thomas S. Woodward, *Woodward's Reminiscences of the Creek, or Muscogee Indians, Contained in Letters to Friends in Georgia and Alabama* (Montgomery AL: Barrett and Wimbish, 1859), 22.

7. CHAINS

1. Gibson to Page, 16 April 1836, CGS-IRW, Reel 7, 846; Sanford & Company to Gibson, 28 March 1836 and 12 April 1836, ASP-MA, 6:762; Hogan to Gibson, 7 January 1836, ASP-MA, 6:747.
2. Hogan to Gibson, 30 January 1836, ASP-MA, 6:748–49; Hogan to Clay, 30 January 1836, ASP-MA, 6:749; Letter Extract, Hogan to Gibson, 23 January 1836, ASP-MA, 6:748; Hogan to Cass, 5 February 1836, ASP-MA, 6:750–51; Hogan to Cass, 8 March 1836, ASP-MA, 6:751–53.
3. Hogan to Cass, 8 March 1836, ASP-MA, 6:751–53.
4. Page to Cass, 8 May 1836, LR-CAR, Roll 243, 1327–32; Muster Roll of Emigrant Creek Indians, LR-CAE, Roll 238, 735; Muster Roll (Opothle Yoholo's slaves), SIAC, Agent (Opothle Yoholo), Account (1618), Year (1838), NARA.
5. Page to Cass, 8 May 1836, LR-CAR, Roll 243, 1327–32; Graham to Polk, 1 March 1836, in *Correspondence of James K. Polk*, vol. 3: *1835–1836*, ed. Herbert Weaver and Kermit L. Hall (Nashville: Vanderbilt University Press, 1975), 519–23.
6. Hogan to Cass, 8 March 1836, ASP-MA, 6:751–53; Sanford & Company to Gibson, 30 March 1836, ASP-MA, 6:761; Hogan to Jackson, 22 April 1836, LR-CAR, Roll 243, 892–99; Sanford & Company to Cass, 1 March 1836, ASP-MA, 6: 759–60; Hogan's examination in Sanford's District, LR-CAR, Roll 243, 937–65; Copy of a Correspondence between Capt. W. Walker & Col. Hogan, 14 April 1836, LR-CAR, Roll 243, 900–905.

7. Hogan to Cass, 8 March 1836, ASP-ma, 6:751–53; Sanford & Company to Gibson, 30 March 1836, ASP-MA, 6:761; Thomas L. McKenney and James Hall, *History of the Indian Tribes of North America, with Biographical Sketches and Anecdotes of the Principal Chiefs. Embellished with One Hundred and Twenty Portraits, from the Indian Gallery in the Department of War, at Washington*, vol. 2 (Philadelphia: Daniel Rice and James G. Clark, 1842), 23–24; List of Land Companies, CRR-Misc., Box 11, NARA.

8. Mitchell to Howard, 7 May 1836, ASP-MA, 6:576; Charles M. Hudson, ed., *The Southeastern Indians* (Knoxville: University of Tennessee Press, 1976), 411.

9. Creeks to Eaton, 8 April 1831, SD 512, 2:424–25.

10. Creeks to Jackson, 6 February 1836, LR-CA, Roll 225, 43–44.

11. Hogan to Cass, 8 March 1836, ASP-MA, 6:751–53; Page to Gibson, 9 April 1836, ASP-MA, 6:767–68; Page to Gibson, 11 April 1836, ASP-MA, 6:768.

12. John T. Ellisor, *The Second Creek War*: Interethnic Conflict and Collusion on a Collapsing Frontier (Lincoln: University of Nebraska Press, 2010), 185–86; Kenneth L. Valliere, "The Creek War of 1836: A Military History," *Chronicles of Oklahoma* 57, no. 4 (1979–80): 463–85; Report of A. Balch, 14 January 1837, NASP, 9:497–507.

13. Ellisor, *Second Creek War*, 157, 160, 305; Hogan to Cass, 5 February 1836, ASP-MA, 6:750–51; Page to Gibson, 8 May 1836, ASP-MA, 6:768–69; Page to Gibson, 27 March 1836, ASP-MA, 6:766–67; Lieutenant Joseph Harris' Florida Removal, Estimate of Funds for the 4th Quarter, 10 September 1836, LR-FS, Roll 288. For the Second Seminole War, see John Bemrose, *Reminiscences of the Second Seminole War*, ed. John K. Mahon (Gainesville: University of Florida Press, 1966); John K. Mahon, *History of the Second Seminole War, 1835–1842* (Gainesville: University of Florida Press, 1967); Frank Laumer, *Massacre!* (Gainesville: University of Florida Press, 1968); Laumer, *Dade's Last Command* (Gainesville: University Press of Florida, 1995); John Missall and Mary Lou Missall, *The Seminole Wars: America's Longest Indian Conflict* (Gainesville: University Press of Florida, 2004).

14. Ellisor, *Second Creek War*, 182–200, 248–49; Page to Gibson, 8 May 1836, ASP-MA, 6:768–69; Page to Gibson, 16 May 1836, ASP-MA, 6:771; Patterson to Clay, 22 June 1836, AF-AG-Clay, Reel 6, ADAH. See also E. G. Richards, "Reminiscenses of the Early Days in Chambers County," *Alabama Historical Quarterly* 4, no. 3 (Fall 1942): 417–45.

15. Ellisor, *Second Creek War*, 223; Clay to Cass, 3 June 1836, AF-AG-Clay, Roll 6, ADAH; Creeks to the Secretary of War, 10 May 1836, LR-CA, Roll 225, 46–48; Page to Gibson, 12 May 1836, ASP-MA, 6:770–71; Salli to Cass, 13 May 1836, LR-CA, Roll 225, 151–52.

16. Memorandum, 19 May 1836, LR-CA, Roll 225, 23–24; Cass to Jesup, 19 May 1836, ASP-MA, 7:312–13; Gibson to Hogan, 20 May 1836, ASP-MA, 6:776; Cass to

Shorter, 21 May 1836, LS, Roll 18, 447–48; Page to Harris, 15 August 1838, SIAC, Agent (Alabama Emigrating Company), Account (2282), Year (1838), NARA.
17. Ellisor, *Second Creek War*, 211–14, 244–48, 256; Creeks to the Secretary of War, 10 May 1836, LR-CA, Roll 225, 46–48; Creeks to Jesup, 26 June 1836, AG-Jesup, Box 15, Folder: "Letters Received During the Creek War, 1836–38, From Camps and Forts," NARA; Lomax to Jesup, 19 June 1836, AG-Jesup, NARA.
18. Shackleford and Pascalis to Clay, 21 May 1836, AF-AG-Clay, Reel 6, ADAH; Shackleford to Clay, 22 May 1836, AF-AG-Clay, Reel 6, ADAH; Goldthwaite to Clay, 4 June 1836, AF-AG-Clay, Reel 6, ADAH; McIntosh to Jesup, 13 August 1836, AG-Jesup, Box 12, Folder: "Letters Received from Officers of the Army, names beginning with 'Me' and 'Mackay,'" NARA; *Independent American*, 2 February 1859; Clay to Patterson, 6 June 1836, AF-AG-Clay, Reel 6, ADAH.
19. Wood to Jesup, 15 August 1836, JWA, Container 1, Folder 3, ADAH.
20. Page to the Commissary General of Subsistence [extract], 2 July 1836, ASPMA, 7:953; Jacob Rhett Motte, *Journey into Wilderness: An Army Surgeon's Account of Life in Camp and Field during the Creek and Seminole Wars 1836–1838*, ed. James F. Sunderman (Gainesville: University of Florida Press, 1953), 20; Barry to Gibson, 12 July 1836, SIAC, Agent (Barry), Account (507), Year (1837), NARA; *Army and Navy Chronicle*, 28 July 1836; *Niles' Weekly Register*, 23 July 1836.
21. Ellisor, *Second Creek War*, 206, 301–5; Eugene Current-Garcia and Dorothy B. Hatfield, eds., *Shem, Ham, & Japheth: The Papers of W. O. Tuggle, Comprising His Indian Diary, Sketches & Observations, Myths & Washington Journal in the Territory & at the Capital, 1879–1882* (Athens: University of Georgia Press, 1973), 46; *Army and Navy Chronicle*, 28 July and 11 August 1836; Robert M. Howard, *Reminiscences* (Columbus GA: Gilbert Printing Co., 1912), 2.
22. Motte, *Journey into Wilderness*, 19–20; Muster Roll (Barry), RG 75, Entry 299, Box 1, NARA; Barry to Gibson, 12 July 1836, SIAC, Agent (Barry), Account (507), Year (1837), NARA; Grant Foreman, *Indian Removal: The Emigration of the Five Civilized Tribes of Indians* (1932; reprint, Norman: University of Oklahoma Press, 1972), 153–54; Tuskenehaw to Jesup, 29 September 1836, AG-Jesup, Box 1a, NARA.
23. Barry to Jesup, 16 July 1836, AG-Jesup, Box 11, Folder: "Letters Received from Officers of the Army, 1836–37, Names beginning with 'B,'" NARA; Page to Iverson, 8 July 1837, SIAC, Agent (Sanford), Account (691), Year (1837), NARA; Hogan to Herring, 20 July 1836, LR-CAR, Roll 243, 935–36; Hogan's examination in Sanford's District, LR-CAR, Roll 243, 942–50; *Army and Navy Chronicle*, 16 November 1837; Milton to Jesup, 18 July 1836, AG-Jesup, Box 12, Folder: "Letters Received from Officers of the Army, 1836–37, Names beginning with 'M.'" For more on Creek-Yuchi relations, see Steven C. Hahn, "'They Look upon the

Yuchis as Their Vassals': An Early History of Yuchi-Creek Political Relations," in *Yuchi Indian Histories before the Removal Era*, ed. Jason Baird Jackson (Lincoln: University of Nebraska Press, 2012), 123–53.

24. Milton to Jesup, 18 July 1836, AG-Jesup, Box 12, Folder: "Letters Received from Officers of the Army, 1836–37, Names beginning with 'M,'" NARA.

25. Barry to Gibson, 16 July 1836, CGS-IRW, Roll 5, 829–30; Foreman, *Indian Removal*, 154; Hogan to Herring, 20 July 1836, LR-CAR, Roll 243, 935–36; Barry to Jesup, 16 July 1836, AG-Jesup, Box 11, Folder: "Letters Received from Officers of the Army, 1836–37, Names beginning with 'B,'" NARA; Barry to Gibson, 19 July 1836, CGS-IRW, Roll 5, 820–21; Auguste Levasseur, *Lafayette in America in 1824 and 1825; or, Journal of a Voyage to the United States*, vol. 2 (1829; reprint, New York: Research Reprints, 1970), 87–88; Abadie to Gibson, 21 July 1836, CGS-IRW, Roll 5, 804–5. The shallow passage between Mobile Bay and Dauphin Island oftentimes forced boats into the Gulf regardless of the weather conditions. Lynn M. Alperin, *History of the Gulf Intracoastal Waterway* (Washington DC: U.S. Army Engineer Water Resources Support Center, 1983), 7–9.

26. Barry to Gibson, 19 July 1836, CGS-IRW, Roll 5, 820–21; *Army and Navy Chronicle*, 11 August 1836; Abadie to Gibson, 21 July 1836, CGS-IRW, Roll 5, 804–5; *Arkansas Gazette*, 2 August 1836; *Niles' Weekly Register*, 6 August 1836; *New-Orleans Bee*, 22 July 1836. See also Franz Anton Ritter von Gerstner, *Early American Railroads: Franz Anton Ritter von Gerstner's Die innern Communicationen (1842–1843)*, ed. Frederick C. Gamst, trans. David J. Diephouse and John C. Decker (Stanford CA: Stanford University Press, 1997), 745–54. The account of Neah Emathla refusing a blanket is reported in W. H. Sparks, *The Memories of Fifty Years: Containing Brief Biographical Notices of Distinguished Americans, and Anecdotes of Remarkable Men; Interspersed with Scenes and Incidents Occurring During a Long Life of Observation Chiefly Spent in the Southwest* (Philadelphia: Claxton, Remsen and Haffelfinger, 1872), 476, who incorrectly states that the event happened in winter.

27. Barry to Gibson, 20 July 1836, CGS-IRW, Roll 5, 834; Barry to Gibson, 23 July 1836, CGS-IRW, Roll 5, 836–37; Abadie to Gibson, 21 July 1836, CGS-IRW, Roll 5, 804–5; Foreman, *Indian Removal*, 155–57; *New-Orleans Bee*, 22 July 1836. Abadie writes that the keelboat deck collapsed off Columbia, Mississippi, a town on the Pearl River, but he probably meant Columbia, Arkansas, in Chicot County; Abadie to Gibson, 20 October 1836, CGS-IRW, Roll 5, 800–802; G. W. Featherstonhaugh, *Excursion Through the Slave States, from Washington on the Potomac, to the Frontier of Mexico; with Sketches of Popular Manners and Geological Notices* (New York: Harper and Brothers, 1844), 137.

28. Barry to Gibson, 10 August 1836, CGS-IRW, Roll 5, 823–24; Abadie to Gibson, 14 August 1836, CGS-IRW, Roll 5, 807–8.

29. Barry to Gibson, 10 August 1836, CGS-IRW, Roll 5, 823–24; Barry to Gibson, 14 August 1836, CGS-IRW, Roll 5, 816–17.
30. Barry to Gibson, 14 August 1836, CGS-IRW, Roll 5, 816–17; Abadie to Gibson, 21 July 1836, CGS-IRW, Roll 5, 804–5; Abadie to Gibson, 14 August 1836, CGS-IRW, Roll 5, 807–8; Barry to Gibson, 10 August 1836, CGS-IRW, Roll 5, 823–24.
31. Abadie to Gibson, 20 October 1836, CGS-IRW, Reel 5, 800–802; Abadie to Gibson, 21 July 1836, CGS-IRW, Roll 5, 804–5; Abadie to Gibson, 14 August 1836, CGS-IRW, Roll 5, 807–8; Muster Roll (Barry), SIAC, Agent (Sanford), Account (691), Year (1837); Foreman, *Indian Removal*, 156–57. For more on Blind King, see Ellisor, *Second Creek War*, 32, 254–55; Samuel G. Drake, *Biography and History of the Indians of North America. From Its First Discovery To The Present Time; Comprising Details In The Lives Of All The Most Distinguished Chiefs And Counsellors, Exploits Of Warriors, And The Celebrated Speeches Of Their Orators; Also, A History Of Their Wars, Massacres And Depredations, As Well As The Wrongs And Sufferings Which The Europeans And Their Descendants Have Done Them; With An Account Of Their Antiquities, Manners And Customs, Religion And Laws; Likewise Exhibiting An Analysis Of The Most Distinguished, As Well As Absurd Authors, Who Have Written Upon The Great Question Of The First Peopling Of America*, Book 4 (Boston: Antiquarian Institute, 1837), 96.
32. Harris to Butler, 1 December 1836, LS, Roll 20, 190–247; *Army and Navy Chronicle*, 29 September 1836; Solomon Peck, "History of the Missions of the Baptist General Convention," in *History of American Missions to the Heathen, from Their Commencement to the Present Time*, ed. Joseph J. Kwiat (1840; reprint, New York: Johnson Reprint, 1970), 549.
33. Journal (Belton), LR-CAE, Roll 237, 520–26; Muster Roll (Belton), Entry 299, Box 1, NARA; Foreman, *Indian Removal*, 158; J. F. Belton, Biography of F. S. Belton, Belton-Kirby-Dawson-Todd Families Papers, Manuscripts and Archives Division, NYPL; Belton to his wife, 26 July 1836, NYPL; Belton to Gibson, August 1836, CGS-IRW, Roll 5, 870–71; For more on the Pontchartrain Railroad, see von Gerstner, *Early American Railroads*, 747–50.
34. Journal (Belton), LR-CAE, Roll 237, 520–26; Belton to his wife and son, 20 August 1836, NYPL; Contract with Mahon, 22 August 1836, SIAC, Agent (Belton), Account (2195), Year (1838), NARA; Contract with Jones, 10 August 1836, SIAC, Agent (Belton), Account (528), Year (1837), NARA.
35. Journal (Belton), LR-CAE, Roll 237, 520–26; Receipts, SIAC, Agent (Belton), Account (528), Year (1837), NARA; Belton to his wife, 10 September 1836, NYPL.
36. Harris to Brown, 28 November 1836, LS, Roll 20, 181–83; Harris to Boyd, 28 November 1836, SIAC, Agent (Boyd), Account (505), Year (1837), NARA; Watson to Harris, 14 January 1837, LR-CAE, Roll 238, 893–97.
37. Cass to Jesup, 19 May 1836, ASP-MA, 7:312–13; Page to Gibson, 20 July 1836, SIAC, Agent (Sanford), Account (66), Year (1837), NARA.

8. COERCION

1. Jesup to Bateman, 3 October 1836, SIAC, Agent (Reynolds), Account (1687), Year (1838), NARA; Campbell to Poinsett, 22 May 1838, SIAC, Agent (Reynolds), Account (1687), Year (1838); Cass to Jesup, 19 May 1836, ASP-MA, 7:312–13; Letter, Jesup, 31 August 1839, SIAC, Agent (Bateman), Account (3797), Year (1839), NARA; Theda Perdue and Michael D. Green, *The Cherokee Nation and the Trail of Tears* (New York: Viking, 2007), 123–28.

2. Cass to Shorter, 21 May 1836, LS, Roll 18, 447–48; "A List of the Friendly Indians Enrolled & now being furnished with provisions," AG-Jesup, Box 15, Folder: "Letters Received During the Creek War, 1836–38, from Camps and Forts," NARA; Page to Gibson, 20 July 1836, SIAC, Agent (Sanford), Account (66), Year (1837), NARA; Sprague to Harris, 1 April 1837, LR-CAE, Roll 238, 739–56.

3. Order No. 63, 17 August 1836, AG-Jesup, Box 25, Folder: "Orders and Letters Sent by Gen. Jesup, Aug., 1836 (1 of 4)"; The U.S. in account current with the Alabama Emigrating Company, SIAC, Agent (Reynolds), Account (1687), Year (1838), NARA; The United States to Noah Felton, SIAC, Agent (Bateman), Account (3797), Year (1839), NARA; Journal (Screven), SIAC, Agent (Reynolds), Account (1687), Year (1838), NARA.

4. Order No. 67, 22 August 1836, SIAC, Agent (Reynolds), Account (1687), Year (1838), NARA; Journal (Deas, Sprague), SIAC, Agent (Reynolds), Account (1687), Year (1838), NARA; Deas to Gibson, 27 September 1836, CGS-IRW, Roll 6, 121–25; Sprague to Harris, 1 April 1837, LR-CAE, Roll 238, 739–56; Sprague to Jesup, 4 September 1836, AG-Jesup, Box 19, Folder: "Letters Received from Various USMC Officers, 1836–1838"; Page to Iverson, 8 July 1837, SIAC, Agent (Reynolds), Account (1687), Year (1838), NARA; Sprague to Ervin, 5 September 1836, SIAC, Agent (Sprague), Account (547), Year (1837), NARA; Muster Roll (Marshall), SIAC, Agent (Reynolds), Account (1687), Year (1838), NARA.

5. Opothle Yoholo to Jesup, 26 August 1836, LR-CAR, Roll 243, 1067–71; Creeks to the Secretary of War, 4 September 1835, LR-CAR, Roll 242, 92–98; Report of A. Balch, 14 January 1837, NASP, 9:497–507; Grant Foreman, ed., *A Traveler in Indian Territory: The Journal of Ethan Allen Hitchcock, Late Major-General in the United States Army* (1930; reprint, Norman: University of Oklahoma Press, 1996), 128; Albert James Pickett, *History of Alabama and Incidentally of Georgia and Mississippi, From the Earliest Period* (1851; reprint, Birmingham AL: Birmingham Book and Magazine, 1962), 83. For more on the plates see James Adair, *The History of the American Indians*, ed. Kathryn E. Holland Braund (Tuscaloosa: University of Alabama Press, 2005), 208–9.

6. Mose Wiley interview, 22 November 1937, IPHC, Roll 16, Vol. 49, 380–81; Simon Johnson interview, 22 September 1937, IPHC, Vol. 31, Roll 11, 299–302.

7. Comments upon the statement of "facts & principals," SIAC, Agent (Reynolds), Account (1687), Year (1838), NARA; United States to the Alabama Emigrating

Company, 1836, SIAC, Agent (Reynolds), Account (1687), Year (1838), NARA; Testimony of Gandy, 24 March 1838, SIAC, Agent (Reynolds), Account (1687), Year (1838), NARA; John T. Ellisor, "'Like So Many Wolves': Creek Removal in the Cherokee Country, 1835–1838," *Journal of East Tennessee History* no. 71 (1999): 10; Mary Grayson interview, 5 August 1937, IPHC, Vol. 105, Roll 35, 474–77; Sprague to Harris, 1 April 1837, LR-CAE, Roll 238, 739–56; Report of A. Balch, 14 January 1837, NASP, 9:497–507; Angela Pulley Hudson, *Creek Paths and Federal Roads: Indians, Settlers, and Slaves and the Making of the American South* (Chapel Hill: University of North Carolina Press, 2010), 163; Land Location Registers, ca. 1834–66, "Creek Land Location Register, Treaty of March 24, 1832," RG 75, Entry 287, Col. James Bright, Vol. 1, NARA; Christopher D. Haveman, "'Last Evening I Saw the Sun Set for the Last Time': The 1832 Treaty of Washington and the Transfer of the Creeks' Alabama Land to White Ownership." *Native South* 5 (2012): 77–78; Abstracts of Approved Contracts for Sales of Reservations, 1839–42, RG 75, Entry 295, Box 1, NARA.

8. Jesup to Bateman, 3 October 1836, SIAC, Agent (Reynolds), Account (1687), Year (1838), NARA; Creeks to Conway, 7 November 1836, AG-Jesup, Box 1a; Opothle Yoholo to Arbuckle, 14 November 1836, SIAC, Agent (Reynolds), Account (1687), Year (1838), NARA.

9. Page to Gibson, 9 November 1836, SIAC, Agent (Barry), Account (507), Year (1837), NARA; Order No. 63, 17 August 1836, AG-Jesup, Box 25, Folder: "Orders and Letters Sent by Gen. Jesup, Aug., 1836 (1 of 4)"; Journal (Bateman, Deas, Screven, Sprague), SIAC, Agent (Reynolds), Account (1687), Year (1838), NARA; Bateman to Jesup, 12 September 1836, AG-Jesup, Box 11, Folder: "Letters Received from Officers of the Army, 1836–37, letters beginning with 'B'"; Sprague to Harris, 1 April 1837, LR-CAE, Roll 238, 739–56; Deas to Jesup, 30 August 1836, AG-Jesup, Box 15, Folder: "Letters Received During the Creek War, 1836–38, From Camps and Forts"; Deas to Gibson, 27 September 1836, CGS-IRW, Roll 6, 121–25; Letter (Sommerville), 24 March 1838, SIAC, Agent (Reynolds), Account (1687), Year (1838), NARA; Notes relative to the claim of the Alabama Emigrating Company, SIAC, Agent (Reynolds), Account (1687), Year (1838), NARA.

10. Campbell to Crawford and Balch, 22 October 1836, LR-CAR, Roll 243, 433–39; Jesup to Cass, 30 August 1836, LR-CA, Roll 225, 75–80; Haveman, "Last Evening I Saw the Sun Set for the Last Time," 75; Journal, 1836–1838, RG 75, Entry 291, NARA; Screven to Page, 31 August 1836, Ethan Allen Hitchcock Collection on Indian Removal, Box 5, Folder 25, Beinecke Rare Book & Manuscript Library, Yale University, New Haven CT; Page to Gibson, 9 November 1836, SIAC, Agent (Barry), Account (507), Year (1837), NARA; Robert Saunders Jr., *John Archibald Campbell, Southern Moderate, 1811–1889* (Tuscaloosa: University of Alabama Press, 1997), 20–30, 104, 152; Henry G. Connor, *John Archibald Campbell: Associate Justice of the United States Supreme Court, 1853–1861* (Boston: Houghton Mifflin, 1920).

11. Haveman, "Last Evening I Saw the Sun Set for the Last Time," 75–77; Screven to Page, 31 August 1836, Box 5, Folder 25, Beinecke Rare Book & Manuscript Library, Yale University, New Haven CT. Tuscoona Harjo's name appears on other copies of the contract, Assent of John Ward, CRR-Misc., RG 75, Entry 300, Box 13, NARA.

12. Haveman, "Last Evening I Saw the Sun Set for the Last Time," 75–77; Letter from Hitchcock, 3 February 1842, LR-CA, Roll 226, 491–505; Campbell to Crawford and Balch, 22 October 1836, LR-CAR, Roll 243, 433–39; The Watson Company included William Walker, Peter C. Harris, Edward Hanrick, and John Peabody; see Harris to Butler, 17 February 1837, LR-CA, Roll 225, 412–23.

13. Pickett, *History of Alabama*, 83; *Arkansas State Gazette*, 25 April 1837; Statement of Dubois, 12 April 1838, SIAC, Agent (Reynolds), Account (1687), Year (1838), NARA; United States to the Alabama Emigrating Company, SIAC, Agent (Reynolds), Account (1687), Year (1837), NARA; Sprague to Harris, 1 April 1837, LR-CAE, Roll 238, 739–56; Comments upon the statement of "facts & principals," SIAC, Agent (Reynolds), Account (1687), Year (1838), NARA; Journal (Bateman, Deas, Screven, Sprague), SIAC, Agent (Reynolds), Account (1687), Year (1838), NARA; Sprague to Gibson, 16 October 1836, LR-AE, Roll 237, 640–42; Testimony of Whalock, March 1838, SIAC, Agent (Reynolds), Account (1687), Year (1838), NARA; Deas to Gibson, 27 September 1836, CGS-IRW, Roll 6, 121–25.

14. Thomas L. McKenney and James Hall, *History of the Indian Tribes of North America, with Biographical Sketches and Anecdotes of the Principal Chiefs. Embellished with One Hundred and Twenty Portraits, from the Indian Gallery in the Department of War, at Washington*, vol. 2 (Philadelphia: Daniel Rice and James G. Clark, 1842), 104–5; Haveman, "Last Evening I Saw the Sun Set for the Last Time," 77.

15. Deas to Jesup, 30 August 1836, AG-Jesup, Box 15, Folder: "Letters Received During the Creek War, 1836–38, From Camps and Forts"; Sprague to Harris, 1 April 1837, LR-CAE, Roll 238, 739–56; Tuskenehaw to Jesup, 29 September 1836, AG-Jesup, Box 1a, NARA; Journal (Bateman, Screven), SIAC, Agent (Reynolds), Account (1687), Year (1838), NARA.

16. Sprague to Harris, 1 April 1837, LR-CAE, Roll 238, 739–56.

17. Deas to Gibson, 27 September 1836, CGS-IRW, Roll 6, 121–25; The U.S. in account current with the Alabama Emigrating Company, SIAC, Agent (Reynolds), Account (1687), Year (1838), NARA; Sprague to Harris, 1 April 1837, LR-CAE, Roll 238, 739–56; Sprague to Jesup, 4 September 1836, AG-Jesup, Box 19, Folder: "Letters Received from Various USMC Officers, 1836–1838"; Certificate of Indians who joined the Party No. 5, SIAC, Agent (Reynolds), Account (1687), Year (1838), NARA; Muster Roll (Marshall), SIAC, Agent (Reynolds), Account (1687), Year (1838), NARA; Page to Iverson, 8 July 1837, SIAC, Agent (Reynolds), Account

(1687), Year (1838), NARA; Sprague to Gibson, 16 October 1836, LR-CAE, Roll 237, 640–42; Iverson to Harris, 18 July 1837, SIAC, Agent (Reynolds), Account (1687), Year (1838), NARA; Creek self-emigration claims, SFOIA, SF 285, Roll 77, 156.

18. Journal (Deas), SIAC, Agent (Reynolds), Account (1687), Year (1838), NARA; Deas to Lewis, 13 February 1838, SIAC, Agent (Deas), Account (3594), Year (1839), NARA; *National Intelligencer*, 10 October 1836.
19. Journal (Bateman, Screven), SIAC, Agent (Reynolds), Account (1687), Year (1838), NARA; Bateman to Jesup, 12 September 1836, AG-Jesup, Box 11, Folder: "Letters Received from Officers of the Army, 1836–37, letters beginning with 'B'"; Notes relative to the claim of the Alabama Emigrating Company, SIAC, Agent (Reynolds), Account (1687), Year (1838), NARA; Letter (Sommerville), 24 March 1838, SIAC, Agent (Reynolds), Account (1687), Year (1838), NARA.
20. Journal (Sprague), SIAC, Agent (Reynolds), Account (1687), Year (1838), NARA.
21. Sprague to Abercrombie and Gibson, 24 September 1836, SIAC, Agent (Reynolds), Account (1687), Year (1838), NARA; Journal (Bateman, Deas, Sprague), SIAC, Agent (Reynolds), Account (1687), Year (1838), NARA; Bateman to Commissary General of Subsistence, 12 September 1836, CGS-IRW, Roll 5, 859; Matthew William Clinton, *Tuscaloosa, Alabama: Its Early Days, 1816–1865* (Tuscaloosa AL: Zonta Club, 1958), 66.
22. Journal (Bateman, Deas, Screven), SIAC, Agent (Reynolds), Account (1687), Year (1838), NARA; Deas to Gibson, 27 September 1836, CGS-IRW, Roll 6, 121–25; Sprague to Harris, 1 April 1837, LR-CAE, Roll 238, 739–56.
23. Journal (Sprague), SIAC, Agent (Reynolds), Account (1687), Year (1838), NARA; Sprague to Harris, 1 April 1837, LR-CAE, Roll 238, 739–56.
24. Journal (Bateman, Deas, Sprague), SIAC, Agent (Reynolds), Account (1687), Year (1838), NARA; Creeks to President of the United States, 25 December 1836, Box 3, Folder 13, Beinecke Rare Book & Manuscript Library, Yale University, New Haven CT.
25. Journal (Bateman), SIAC, Agent (Reynolds), Account (1687), Year (1838), NARA; Creeks to Jesup, 9 October 1836, AG-Jesup, Box 24, Folder: "Letters Received Regarding Creek/Seminole Affairs, Sept–Dec 1836"; United States to James Alexander, 13 December 1836, SIAC, Agent (Bateman), Account (3797), Year (1839), NARA; Sprague to Spickernagle, 19 October 1836, SIAC, Agent (Sprague), Account (547), Year (1837), NARA; John H. Love, 21 March 1838, SIAC, Agent (Reynolds), Account (1687), Year (1838), NARA.
26. Journal (Sprague, Screven), SIAC, Agent (Reynolds), Account (1687), Year (1838), NARA.
27. Journal (Bateman, Deas, Sprague, and Screven), SIAC, Agent (Reynolds), Account (1687), Year (1838), NARA; Fergusson to Fergusson, 14 October 1836, Fergusson Family Papers, 1784–1927, Box 12, Folder 4, Tennessee State Library and Archives.

28. Creeks to Jesup, 9 October 1836, AG-Jesup, Box 24, Folder: "Letters Received Regarding Creek/Seminole Affairs, Sept–Dec 1836"; Haveman, "Last Evening I Saw the Sun Set for the Last Time," 77–78.
29. Journal (Bateman, Deas, Sprague, and Screven), SIAC, Agent (Reynolds), Account (1687), Year (1838), NARA; Sprague to Harris, 1 April 1837, LR-CAE, Roll 238, 739–56.
30. Journal (Deas, Sprague), SIAC, Agent (Reynolds), Account (1687), Year (1838), NARA; Robert Gudmestad, *Steamboats and the Rise of the Cotton Kingdom* (Baton Rouge: Louisiana State University Press, 2011), 78–96.
31. *Arkansas State Gazette*, 15 November 1836; Journal (Sprague, Deas), SIAC, Agent (Reynolds), Account (1687), Year (1838), NARA; Testimony of Gandy, 24 March 1838, SIAC, Agent (Reynolds), Account (1687), Year (1838), NARA.
32. Journal (Deas, Sprague), SIAC, Agent (Reynolds), Account (1687), Year (1838), NARA; Deas to Gibson, 22 November 1836, LR-CAE, Roll 237, 553–56.
33. Journal (Sprague), SIAC, Agent (Reynolds), Account (1687), Year (1838), NARA; Deas to Gibson, 22 November 1836, LR-CAE, Roll 237, 553–56; Sprague to Harris, 1 April 1837, LR-CAE, Roll 238, 739–56; Ted R. Worley, "Arkansas and the 'Hostile' Indians, 1835–1838," *Arkansas Historical Quarterly* 6, no. 2 (Summer 1947): 155–64.
34. Journal (Bateman, Deas, Screven), SIAC, Agent (Reynolds), Account (1687), Year (1838), NARA.
35. Journal (Bateman, Sprague), SIAC, Agent (Reynolds), Account (1687), Year (1838), NARA; Sprague to Harris, 1 April 1837, LR-CAE, Roll 238, 739–56; *Arkansas State Gazette*, 20 December 1836 and 17 January 1837. In another letter Sprague reports that the *John Nelson* arrived with the 395 Creeks at Fort Gibson on 22 November. Tuckabatchee Harjo may have refused to move because of sickness; see *Arkansas State Gazette*, 24 January 1837.
36. Journal (Deas), SIAC, Agent (Reynolds), Account (1687), Year (1838), NARA.
37. Journal (Bateman), SIAC, Agent (Reynolds), Account (1687), Year (1838), NARA; Bateman to Harris, 20 December 1836, LR-CAE, Roll 237, 532; Stuart to Jones, 15 January 1837, LR-CAE, Roll 238, 19–22; Arbuckle to Harris, 18 December 1836, LR-CAE, Roll 238, 9–10; Harris to Page, 6 February 1837, SIAC, Agent (Reynolds), Account (1687), Year (1838), NARA; Page to Harris, 20 February 1837, SIAC, Agent (Reynolds), Account (1687), Year (1838), NARA; Notes relative to the claim of the Alabama Emigrating Company, SIAC, Agent (Reynolds), Account (1687), Year (1838), NARA, 41–44.
38. Sprague to Harris, 1 April 1837, LR-CAE, Roll 238, 739–56; Journal (Deas, Sprague), SIAC, Agent (Reynolds), Account (1687), Year (1838), NARA; J. W. Stephens interview, 22 March 1938, IPHC, Roll 23, Vol. 68, 109–24; William Benson interview, 22 September 1937, IPHC, Roll 5, Vol. 14, 410–15; Stuart to Jones,

15 January 1837, LR-CAE, Roll 238, 19–22; *Arkansas State Gazette*, 3 January 1837; Charles M. Hudson, ed., *The Southeastern Indians* (Knoxville: University of Tennessee Press, 1976), 327–28.

39. Sprague to Harris, 1 April 1837, LR-CAE, Roll 238, 739–56; Journal (Bateman, Deas, Screven, Sprague), SIAC, Agent (Reynolds), Account (1687), Year (1838), NARA; The U.S. in account current with the Alabama Emigrating Company, SIAC, Agent (Reynolds), Account (1687), Year (1838), NARA.
40. Friedrich Gerstäcker, *Wild Sports in the Far West: The narrative of a German Wanderer beyond the Mississippi, 1837–1843*, ed. Edna L. Steeves and Harrison R. Steeves (1854; reprint, Durham nc: Duke University Press, 1968), 277.
41. Conway to Opothle Yoholo, 10 November 1836, SIAC, Agent (Reynolds), Account (1687), Year (1838), NARA; Opothle Yoholo to Arbuckle, 14 November 1836, SIAC, Agent (Reynolds), Account (1687), Year (1838), NARA; *Niles' Weekly Register*, 12 November 1836; Van Horne to Gibson, 23 August 1836, CGS-IRW, Roll 10, 270–72; Bateman to Harris, 8 January 1837, LR-CAE, Roll 238, 47–48; *Arkansas State Gazette*, 10 January 1837; Armstrong to Harris, 24 December 1836, LR-CAE, Roll 238, 6–7.
42. McKenney and Hall, *History of the Indian Tribes*, 103–5; John T. Ellisor, *The Second Creek War: Interethnic Conflict and Collusion on a Collapsing Frontier* (Lincoln: University of Nebraska Press, 2010), 330–31.

9. DEFIANCE

1. Churchill to Jesup, 29 September 1836, AG-Jesup, Box 15, Folder: "Letters Received During the Creek War 1836, Headquarters Fort Mitchell," NARA; Sprague to Jesup, 7 September 1836, AG-Jesup, Box 19, Folder: "Letters Received from Various USMC Officers, 1836–1838," NARA; John T. Ellisor, *The Second Creek War: Interethnic Conflict and Collusion on a Collapsing Frontier* (Lincoln: University of Nebraska Press, 2010), 335–70.
2. Journal (Bateman), SIAC, Agent (Reynolds), Account (1687), Year (1838), NARA; Sprague to Jesup, 4 September 1836, AG-Jesup, Box 19, Folder: "Letters Received from Various USMC Officers, 1836–1838," NARA; Jesup to Chambers, 28 August 1836, LR-CAE, Roll 237, 592–93; List of Creek volunteers, AG-Jesup, Box 1a, NARA; John T. Sprague, *The Origin, Progress, and Conclusion of the Florida War* (1848; reprint, Gainesville: University of Florida Press, 1964), 162; Ellisor, *Second Creek War*, 339; Screven's Muster Roll shows that ten Creeks from detachment two volunteered to fight the Seminoles; Muster Roll (Screven), RG 75, Entry 299, vol. 2, NARA.
3. Jesup to Chambers, 28 August 1836, LR-CAE, Roll 237, 592–93; Page to Harris, 9 February 1837, LR-CAE, Roll 238, 508–10; Christina Snyder, *Slavery in Indian Country: The Changing Face of Captivity in Early America* (Cambridge

MA: Harvard University Press, 2010), 219–20; Opothle Yoholo to Arbuckle, 14 November 1836, SIAC, Agent (Reynolds), Account (1687), Year (1838), NARA; Crawford and Balch to Butler, 13 December 1836, 24th Cong. 2nd sess., 1837, S. Doc. No. 180, serial no. 298, 6–7. For a list of additional promises made to the Creek headmen and complaints that these promises were not kept see Hitchcock to Spencer, 28 May 1842, AG-Jesup, Box 37, Folder "General Scott's Operation in Florida and Creek Country, 2 of 3," NARA.

4. Jesup to Freeman, 9 September 1837, SIAC, Agent (Reynolds), Account (1687), Year (1838), NARA; Jesup to Butler, 7 March 1837, LR-CAE, Roll 238, 395–96.

5. Ellisor, *Second Creek War*, 264–96, 335–415; Tate to Lewis, 8 January 1837, LR-CAE, Roll 238, 441–43.

6. Page to Harris, 9 February 1837, LR-CAE, Roll 238, 508–10; Letter from Sloan, 31 March 1837, LR-CAE, Roll 238, 403–6.

7. Ellisor, *Second Creek War*, 344–52; Page to Harris, 3 February 1837, LR-CAE, Roll 238, 504–6; Letter from Sloan, 31 March 1837, LR-CAE, Roll 238, 403–6; Sloan to Page, 7 February 1837, LR-CAE, Roll 238, 514–18.

8. Ellisor, *Second Creek War*, 358–59; Reynolds to Wilson, 31 March 1837, John G. Reynolds Journal, Reynolds-PU; Grant Foreman, *Indian Removal: The Emigration of the Five Civilized Tribes of Indians* (1932; reprint, Norman: University of Oklahoma Press, 1972), 182.

9. Howard Corning, ed., *Letters of John James Audubon, 1826–1840*, vol. 2 (Boston: Club of Odd Volumes, 1930), 145–46; Richard Rhodes, *John James Audubon: The Making of an American* (New York: Knopf, 2004), 397–98; Phineas Taylor Barnum, *The Life of P. T. Barnum* (New York: Redfield, 1855), 193–96; Page to Harris, 9 February 1837, LR-CAE, Roll 238, 508–10.

10. The U.S. in account current with the Alabama Emigrating Company, SIAC, Agent (Reynolds), Account (1687), Year (1838), NARA; Scott to Harris, 14 April 1837, LR-CA, Roll 225, 352–53; Ellisor, *Second Creek War*, 178–79; *Montgomery Advertiser*, 8 March 1837.

11. Ellisor, *Second Creek War*, 358–59; Timeline, John G. Reynolds Journal, Reynolds-PU; *National Intelligencer*, 3 April 1837; United States to the Alabama Emigrating Company, SIAC, Agent (Reynolds), Account (1687), Year (1838), NARA; Polk to Lewis, n.d., SIAC, Agent (Alabama Emigrating Company), Account (2282), Year (1838), NARA; Extract of letters from Gen[era]l Jesup, LR-CAE, Roll 238, 587; Wilson to Jesup, 20 May 1837, AG-Jesup, Box 1B, Folder XYZ, NARA.

12. Jesup to Harris, 18 July 1837, LR-CAE, Roll 238, 424–26; Jesup to Poinsett, 11 April 1837, AG-Jesup, Box 27, Folder: "Letters Sent, April 1837," NARA; Returns of Troops in Florida, AG-Jesup, Box 32, Folder: "Returns of Troops, June 1837, 2 of 2," NARA.

13. *Alabama Journal*, 4 September 1829; Timeline, John G. Reynolds Journal, Reynolds-PU; United States to William Turner, SIAC, Agent (Page), Account

(1701), Year (1838), NARA; United States to Zachariah McGirth, SIAC, Agent (Page), Account (1701), Year (1838), NARA.

14. Reynolds to Wilson, 4 June 1837, Reynolds-PU; Wilson to Harris, 4 September 1837, LR-CAE, Roll 238, 931–33; Ellisor, *Second Creek War*, 384–87; Brian R. Rucker, "West Florida's Creek Indian Crisis of 1837," *Florida Historical Quarterly* 69, no. 3 (January 1991): 315–34.
15. Deas to Harris, 30 March 1837, LR-CAE, Roll 238, 199–202; Deas to Moore, 16 May 1837, LR-CAE, Roll 238, 237–38; The U. States to James Childress, SIAC, Agent (Deas), Account (1180), Year (1837), NARA; Wool to Poinsett, 31 March 1837, 25th Cong., 1st sess., 1837, H.R. Doc. No. 46, serial no. 311, 68–70; The U. States to Tarkey, SIAC, Agent (Deas), Account (1180), Year (1837), NARA; The U. States to Fors-hach-fixico, SIAC, Agent (Deas), Account (1180), Year (1837), NARA; Muster Roll (Deas), SIAC, Agent (Reynolds), Account (1687), Year (1838), NARA.
16. Journal (Deas), LR-CAE, Roll 238, 251–81; Hembree to Tedder, 26 April 1837, Tedder Papers, Correspondence, III-G-1, Folder 14, Tennessee State Library and Archives; Creeks to Ross, 14 August 1837, LR-CAE, Roll 238, 456–57.
17. Muster Roll (Deas), SIAC, Agent (Reynolds), Account (1687), Year (1838), NARA; Journal (Deas), LR-CAE, Roll 238, 251–81; Deas to Harris, 10 May 1837, LR-CAE, Roll 238, 214–17; Stephenson to Harris, 13 June 1837, LR-CAE, Roll 238, 815.
18. Journal (Deas), LR-CAE, Roll 238, 251–81.
19. Journal (Deas), LR-CAE, Roll 238, 251–81; Muster Roll (Deas), SIAC, Agent (Reynolds), Account (1687), Year (1838), NARA; Theda Perdue, *Cherokee Women: Gender and Culture Change, 1700–1835* (Lincoln: University of Nebraska Press, 1998), 33; Charles M. Hudson, ed., *The Southeastern Indians* (Knoxville: University of Tennessee Press, 1976), 324; Grant Foreman, ed., *A Traveler in Indian Territory: The Journal of Ethan Allen Hitchcock, late Major-General in the United States Army* (1930; reprint, Norman: University of Oklahoma Press, 1996), 130. See also Bernard Romans, *A Concise Natural History of East and West Florida*, ed. Kathryn E. Holland Braund (Tuscaloosa: University of Alabama Press, 1999), 148.
20. Journal (Deas), LR-CAE, Roll 238, 251–81.
21. Journal (Deas), LR-CAE, Roll 238, 251–81.
22. Muster Roll (Deas), SIAC, Agent (Reynolds), Account (1687), Year (1838), NARA; Journal (Deas), LR-CAE, Roll 238, 251–81; Deas to Harris, 10 May 1837, LR-CAE, Roll 238, 214–17.
23. Journal (Deas), LR-CAE, Roll 238, 251–81.
24. Journal (Deas), LR-CAE, Roll 238, 251–81; Stephenson to Harris, 13 June 1837, LR-CAE, Roll 238, 815; Stephenson to Harris, 18 June 1837, LR-CAE, Roll 238, 824; Muster Roll (Deas), SIAC, Agent (Reynolds), Account (1687), Year (1838), NARA.

25. Smith to Harris, 29 May 1837, LR-CAE, Roll 238, 792–94.
26. Deas to Harris, 2 August 1837, LR-CAE, Roll 238, 302–4; Creeks to Ross, 14 August 1837, LR-CAE, Roll 238, 456–57; Lindsay to Poinsett, 21 September 1837, LR-CAE, Roll 238, 454–55; Deas to Harris, 9 September 1837, LR-CAE, Roll 238, 321–23; Ellisor, *Second Creek War*, 336–39; Ellisor, "Like So Many Wolves: Creek Removal in the Cherokee Country, 1835–1838," *Journal of East Tennessee History* no. 71 (1999): 1–24.
27. Woodfin to Reynolds, 13 June 1837, Reynolds-PU; Nott to Reynolds, 31 July 1837, Reynolds-PU; Reynolds to Page, 31 July 1837, Reynolds-PU; Bateman to Harris, 18 June 1837, LR-CAE, Roll 238, 106–7; Reynolds to Belton, 12 June 1837, Reynolds-PU; Reynolds to Belton, 10 June 1837, Reynolds-PU; Woodfin to Reynolds, 10 June 1837, Reynolds-PU; Timeline, 23 May 1837, Reynolds-PU.
28. Wilson to Harris, 11 May 1837, LR-CAE, Roll 238, 915; Citizens to Poinsett, 17 June 1837, LR-CAE, Roll 238, 377–79.
29. Jesup to Beattie, 12 June 1837, SIAC, Agent (Alabama Emigrating Company), Account (2282), Year (1838), NARA; Bateman to Harris, 18 June 1837, LR-CAE, Roll 238, 106–7; United States to W. J. Beattie, SIAC, Agent (Page), Account (1701), Year (1838), NARA; Reynolds to Page, 27 June 1837, Reynolds-PU; Woodfin to Reynolds, 27 June 1837, Reynolds-PU.
30. Page to Jesup, 27 July 1837, AG-Jesup, Box 16, Folder: "Misc. Letters Received, 5 of 6," NARA; Timeline, 7 July 1837, Reynolds-PU; United States to Hien, 26 August 1837, SIAC, Agent (Reynolds), Account (4083), Year (1840), NARA; Muster Roll (Reynolds), SIAC, Agent (Reynolds), Account (1687), Year (1838), NARA.
31. Reynolds to Page, 31 July 1837, Reynolds-PU; Woodfin to Reynolds, 26 August 1837, Reynolds-PU; *New-Orleans Bee*, 10 and 15 August 1837; Reynolds to Harris, 27 August 1837, Reynolds-PU; Page to Jesup, 27 July 1837, AG-Jesup, Box 16, Folder: "Misc. Letters Received, 5 of 6"; Wiedeman to Reynolds, 2 September 1837, Reynolds-PU; Reynolds to Harris, 2 September 1837, LR-CAE, Roll 238, 655–57; Page to Harris, 15 August 1837, LR-CAE, Roll 238, 607; Foreman, *Indian Removal*, 186; *Arkansas State Gazette*, 29 August 1837; Circular, 2 September 1837, Reynolds-PU; Reynolds to Harris, 9 September 1837, Reynolds-PU; Receipts, SIAC, Agent (Reynolds), Account (4083), Year (1840), NARA.
32. Page to Harris, 4 August 1837, LR-CAE, Roll 238, 599; Reynolds to Harris, 2 September 1837, LR-CAE, Roll 238, 655–57; Ogden to Harris, 4 September 1837, LR-CAE, Roll 238, 484; Reynolds to Wooldridge, 30 September 1837, SIAC, Agent (Page), Account (1701), Year (1838), NARA; Sloan to Wooldridge, 3 October 1837, SIAC, Agent (Page), Account (1701), Year (1838), NARA; Jesup to Freeman, 9 September 1837, SIAC, Agent (Reynolds), Account (1687), Year (1838), NARA; Polk to Lewis, 5 February 1839, SIAC, Agent (Alabama Emigrating Company), Account (2755), Year (1839), NARA.

33. Reynolds to Harris, 13 September 1837, Reynolds-PU; Timeline, 19 August 1837, 15 and 16 September 1837, Reynolds-PU; Ellisor, *Second Creek War*, 396–415; Jesup to Freeman, 9 September 1837, SIAC, Agent (Reynolds), Account (1687), Year (1838), NARA; List of Creek volunteers, AG-Jesup, Box 1a, NARA; Wilson to Harris, 4 September 1837, LR-CAE, Roll 238, 931–33.
34. Page to Reynolds, 1 September 1837, SIAC, Agent (Reynolds), Account (1687), Year (1838), NARA; Blake to Harris, 31 July 1837, LR-CAE, Roll 238, 118–19; Page to Harris, 7 March 1837, LR-CAE, Roll 238, 561; Campbell to Poinsett, 22 May 1838, SIAC, Agent (Reynolds), Account (1687), Year (1838), NARA; Testimony of Gandy, 2 March 1838, SIAC, Agent (N/A), Account (4785), Year (1840), NARA; Page to Harris, 10 November 1837, LR-CAR, Roll 245, 259–60; Sloan to Campbell, 13 April 1838, SIAC, Agent (N/A), Account (4785), Year (1840), NARA; Reynolds to Mayor of New Orleans, 14 September 1837, Reynolds-PU; Woodfin to Reynolds, 15 September 1837, Reynolds-PU.
35. Reynolds to Wiedeman, 19 September 1837, Reynolds-PU; Campbell to Reynolds, 15 September 1837, Reynolds-PU; Reynolds to Campbell and Beattie, 18 September 1837, Reynolds-PU; Maynard et al. to Woodfin, 21 September 1837, Reynolds-PU; Page to Campbell, 12 May 1838, SIAC, Agent (Reynolds), Account (1687), Year (1838), NARA; Page to Harris, 15 August 1838, SIAC, Agent (Alabama Emigrating Company), Account (2282), Year (1838), NARA; Beattie and Campbell to Reynolds, 23 September 1837, Reynolds-PU; Reynolds to Harris, 25 September 1837, Reynolds-PU; Reynolds to Campbell and Beattie, 24 September 1837, Reynolds-PU.
36. Beattie to Reynolds, 6 October 1837, Reynolds-PU; Reynolds to Beattie, 7 October 1837, Reynolds-PU; Reynolds to Harris, 8 October 1837, Reynolds-PU; Reynolds to Harris, 5 September 1837, Reynolds-PU.
37. Foreman, *Indian Removal*, 186–88; Sloan to Harris, 3 November 1837, LR-CAE, Roll 238, 863–64; United States to the Alabama Emigrating Company, SIAC, Agent (Reynolds), Account (1687), Year (1838), NARA; Testimony of Latham, 19 March 1839, SIAC, Agent (N/A), Account (4785), Year (1840), NARA; Iverson to Lewis, 16 November 1838, SIAC, Agent (N/A), Account (4785), Year (1840), NARA; Sloan to Campbell, 13 April 1838, SIAC, Agent (N/A), Account (4785), Year (1840), NARA; *New-Orleans Bee*, 31 October 1837; *New Orleans True American*, 7 November 1837; Abstract of Disbursements and receipts, SIAC, Agent (Boyd), Account (3041), Year (1839), NARA; Muster Roll (Felton), SIAC, Agent (Reynolds), Account (1687), Year (1838), NARA; *New-Orleans Bee*, 25 and 30 October 1837; Polk to Lewis, 5 February 1839, SIAC, Agent (Alabama Emigrating Company), Account (2755), Year (1839), NARA; *Army and Navy Chronicle*, 16 November 1837; Thomas L. McKenney and James Hall, *History of the Indian Tribes of North America, with Biographical Sketches and Anecdotes of the Principal Chiefs. Embellished with*

One Hundred and Twenty Portraits, from the Indian Gallery in the Department of War, at Washington, vol. 2 (Philadelphia: Daniel Rice and James G. Clark, 1842), 95–96; *Macon Telegraph*, 13 November 1837; Robert Gudmestad, *Steamboats and the Rise of the Cotton Kingdom* (Baton Rouge: Louisiana State University Press, 2011), 78; *Army and Navy Chronicle*, 16 November 1837.

38. *Arkansas State Gazette*, 28 November 1837.
39. *Arkansas State Gazette*, 28 November 1837; Foreman, *Indian Removal*, 187–88; Bert Neville, *Directory of River Packets in the Mobile-Alabama-Warrior-Tombigbee Trades 1818–1932* (Selma AL: Selma Printing Service, 1967), 23. Thomas Barnett interview, 24 June 1937, IPHC, Roll 5, Vol. 13, 453–58.
40. Clements to Harris, 25 September 1837, LR-CAE, Roll 238, 161; Patterson's receipt, 10 October 1837, SIAC, Agent (Morris), Account (1837), Year (1838), NARA; Upshaw to Harris, 13 September 1837, LR-CAE, Roll 238, 885; Clements to Harris, 20 September 1837, LR-CAE, Roll 238, 163–64; Upshaw to Harris, 21 July 1837, LR-CAE, Roll 238, 883; Clements to Harris, 11 October 1837, LR-CAE, Roll 238, 174; Clements to Harris, 18 November 1837, LR-CAE, Roll 238, 179–81; Clements to Harris, 1 November 1837, LR-CAE, Roll 238, 176–77; Morris's report, 9 April 1838, LR-CAE, Roll 239, 19–29.
41. Muster Roll (Clements), RG 75, Entry 299, Vol. 7, Box 2, NARA; Clements to Harris, 1 November 1837, LR-CAE, Roll 238, 176–77; Receipts, SIAC, Agent (Morris), Account (1837), Year (1838), NARA; *Memphis Enquirer*, 18 November 1837.
42. Morris's report, 9 April 1838, LR-CAE, Roll 239, 19–29; Brown to Morris, 6 April 1838, LR-CAE, Roll 239, 30–34; *Arkansas State Gazette*, 28 November 1837; Amanda L. Paige, Fuller L. Bumpers, and Daniel F. Littlefield Jr., *Chickasaw Removal* (Ada OK: Chickasaw, 2010), 121.
43. Sloan to Collins, 4 November 1837, SIAC, Agent (N/A), Account (4785), Year (1840), NARA; Officers of the steamboat *Yazoo*, 16 November 1837, SIAC, Agent (Reynolds), Account (1687), Year (1838), NARA; Chinn to Crawford, 11 April 1840, LR-CAE, Roll 240, 22–23.
44. United States to the Alabama Emigrating Company, SIAC, Agent (Reynolds), Account (1687), Year (1838), NARA; The U.S. in account current with the Alabama Emigrating Company, SIAC, Agent (Reynolds), Account (1687), Year (1838), NARA; Testimony of Cravens, 2 August 1838, SIAC, Agent (Alabama Emigrating Company), Account (2755), Year (1839), NARA; Campbell to Poinsett, 22 May 1838, SIAC, Agent (Reynolds), Account (1687), Year (1838), NARA; Muster Roll (Sloan), SIAC, Agent (Reynolds), Account (1687), Year (1838), NARA; Arbuckle to Jones, 16 December 1842, LR-CA, Roll 226, 386–87; Iverson to Lewis, 24 June 1839, SIAC, Agent (N/A), Account (4785), Year (1840), NARA; Nowland to Beattie, 29 March 1838, MS 158, Folder 6, VHS. For the location of Anderson's Bluff see Frank M. Cayton, *Landings on All the Western and Southern Rivers and*

Bayous, Showing Location, Post-Offices, Distances, &c., Also, Tariff of Premiums on Insurance to All Points (St. Louis: Woodward, Tiernan and Hale, 1881), and A. E. Sholes, *Directory of the Taxing District of Memphis, Shelby County, Tennessee*, vol. 10 (Memphis: Rogers & Co., 1883), 28.

45. *Arkansas State Gazette*, 21 November 1837; Muster Roll (Boyd), RG 75, Entry 299, Box 3, NARA; James L. Douthat, ed., *Creek Ration Book: Records Taken in June 1838 at Camp Clanewaugh near Ross' Landing in Tennessee* (Signal Mountain TN: Mountain Press, 1999).

46. Frederic Trautmann, "Alabama through a German's Eyes: The Travels of Clara von Gerstner, 1839," *Alabama Review* 36, no. 2 (April 1983): 129–42; Lewis to Lewis, 12 December 1843, LR-CAE, Roll 240, 308.

47. Creek Self-Emigration Claims, 1886–1904, SFOIA, SF 285, Roll 77, 35, 96, 112, 119, 162; Muster Roll (Brodnax), LR-CAE, Roll 240, 522; Muster Roll (Carr), LR-CAE, Roll 240, 428; Wheat to Medill, 13 July 1846, LR-CAE, Roll 240, 418–19; Lovett and Carr to Lewis, 15 December 1846, LR-CAE, Roll 240, 424; Logan to Medill, 9 November 1847, LR-CAE, Roll 240, 430; Carr to Seminoles, 16 November 1837, AG-Jesup, Box 4, Folder: "Col. A. G. W. Fanner, 2 of 2," NARA; Articles of Agreement, CRR-Misc., RG 75, Entry 300, Box 11, NARA.

48. Blake to Abert, 8 May 1841, LR-CAE, Roll 240, 129; Blake to Crawford, 8 June 1844, LR-CAE, Roll 240, 298; Blake to Crawford, 25 June 1841, LR-CAE, Roll 240, 142–43; War Dept. to Blake, 7 July 1841, LR-CAE, Roll 240, 150; Blake to Crawford, 21 August 1841, LR-CAE, Roll 240, 145; Crawford to Porter, 17 November 1843, LR-CAE, Roll 240, 284–87; Lewis to Lewis, 12 December 1843, LR-CAR, Roll 240, 308.

49. Cherry to Crawford, 28 August 1845, LR-CAE, Roll 240, 344–47; Muster Roll (Wheat), LR-CAE, Roll 240, 393; Cherry to Crawford, 3 October 1845, LR-CAE, Roll 240, 356–57; Wheat to Commissioner of Indian Affairs, 20 January 1846, LR-CAE, Roll 240, 412–13.

50. Logan to Medill, 29 July 1846, LR-CAE, Roll 240, 405; Logan to Medill, 5 March 1846, LR-CAE, Roll 240, 387–88; Muster Roll (Wheat), LR-CAE, Roll 240, 393; Abstract of Provisions, LR-CAE, Roll 240, 389; Wheat to Medill, 8 May 1846, LR-CAE, Roll 240, 415–16; Wheat to Medill, 13 July 1846, LR-CAE, Roll 240, 418–19.

51. Cochamy to Medill, 7 April 1848, LR-CAE, Roll 240, 446–48; John Bartlett Meserve, "Chief Samuel Checote, with Sketches of Chiefs Locher Harjo and Ward Coachman," *Chronicles of Oklahoma* 16, no. 4 (December 1938): 401–9; Dickson to Medill, 6 June 1848, LR-CAR, Roll 240, 454; Cochamy to Medill, 16 July 1848, LR-CAE, Roll 240, 450–51.

52. Durant to Medill, 7 March 1849, LR-CAE, Roll 240, 500–501; Cochamy to Medill, 16 July 1848, LR-CAE, Roll 240, 450–51; Durant to Medill, 2 May 1849, LR-CAE, Roll 240, 503; H. F. O'Beirne and E. S. O'Beirne, *The Indian Territory: Its Chiefs,*

Legislators and Leading Men (St. Louis: C. B. Woodward, 1892), 341–43; *Fort Smith Herald*, 6 June 1849.

53. Shortridge to Crawford, 10 December 1840, LR-CAR, Roll 247, 384–85; Abbott to Harris, 30 April 1837, LR-CAR, Roll 244, 6–8; J. Anthony Paredes, "Back from Disappearance: The Alabama Creek Indian Community," in *Southeastern Indians since the Removal Era*, ed. Walter L. Williams (Athens: University of Georgia Press, 1979), 123–41; George Roth, "Federal Tribal Recognition in the South," in *Anthropologists and Indians in the New South*, ed. Rachel A. Bonney and J. Anthony Paredes (Tuscaloosa: University of Alabama Press, 2001), 49–70. See also Lucius F. Ellsworth and Jane E. Dysart, "West Florida's Forgotten People: The Creek Indians from 1830 until 1970," *Florida Historical Quarterly* 59, no. 4 (April 1981): 422–39; Dysart, "Another Road to Disappearance: Assimilation of Creek Indians in Pensacola, Florida, during the Nineteenth Century," *Florida Historical Quarterly* 61, no. 1 (July 1982): 37–48; Marie West Cromer, *Modern Indians of Alabama: Remnants of the Removal* (Birmingham AL: Southern University Press, 1984), 83–95; Gregory A. Waselkov, "Formation of the Tensaw Community," in *Red Eagle's Children: Weatherford vs. Weatherford et al.*, ed. J. Anthony Paredes and Judith Knight (Tuscaloosa: University of Alabama Press, 2012), 36–45.

10. PERSEVERANCE

1. Sloan, Sommerville, and Felton to Page, n.d., SIAC, Agent (Page), Account (1701), Year (1838), NARA; Grant Foreman, ed., *A Traveler in Indian Territory: The Journal of Ethan Allen Hitchcock, Late Major-General in the United States Army* (1930; reprint, Norman: University of Oklahoma Press, 1996), 119–20; Ethan Allen Hitchcock Notebooks, Creeks, 31 January 1842, Box 4, Folder 17, Beinecke Rare Book & Manuscript Library, Yale University, New Haven CT; Isaac McCoy, *The Annual Register of Indian Affairs, In the Western (or Indian) Territory 1835–1838* (Springfield MO: Particular Baptist Press, 2000), 276; J. Leitch Wright Jr., *Creeks and Seminoles: The Destruction and Regeneration of the Muscogulge People* (Lincoln: University of Nebraska Press, 1986), 312–13; Armstrong to Harris, 10 May 1837, LR-CA, Roll 225, 240–41; Stambaugh to Leavenworth, 26 May 1834, LR, HRFG, Roll 2, 92–94; H. F. O'Beirne and E. S. O'Beirne, *The Indian Territory: Its Chiefs, Legislators, and Leading Men* (St. Louis: C. B. Woodward, 1892), 171; *Arkansas State Gazette*, 10 January 1837.

2. Porter to Brearley, 30 July 1828, SIAC, Agent (Brearley), Account (20,381), Year (1836), NARA: McCoy, *Annual Register*, 248–49, 278; Letter from Logan, 3 June 1844, SIAC, Agent (Logan), Account (892), Year (1844), NARA; G. Foreman, *Traveler in Indian Territory*, 139; *Arkansas State Gazette*, 27 March 1839; Edward R. Roustio, ed., *Early Indian Missions: As Reflected in the Unpublished Manuscripts of Isaac McCoy* (Springfield MO: Particular Baptist Press, 2000), 184–85.

3. Dodge to Greene, 3 November 1836, ABC, Roll 779, 288–93; Armstrong to Harris, 15 March 1837, LR-CA, Roll 225, 230–31; McCoy, *Annual Register*, 249.
4. McCoy, *Annual Register*, 276; Sprague to Harris, 1 April 1837, LR-CAE, Roll 238, 739–56; Augustus Ward Loomis, *Scenes in the Indian Country* (Philadelphia: Presbyterian Board of Publication, 1859), 9–10. See also Douglas A. Hurt, "Defining American Homelands: A Creek Nation Example, 1828–1907," *Journal of Cultural Geography* 21, no. 1 (Fall/Winter 2003): 19–43.
5. Robbie Ethridge, *Creek Country: The Creek Indians and Their World* (Chapel Hill: University of North Carolina Press, 2003), 55–60, 144–46; Loomis, *Scenes in the Indian Country*, 10–11, 136; Journal extract, PHS-AIC, Box 9, Roll 1, Letter 62; McCoy to Porter, 29 January 1829, HR 87, 21.
6. Josiah Gregg, *Commerce of the Prairies*, vol. 2 (1844; reprint; Philadelphia: J. B. Lippincott, 1962), 317; Loomis, *Scenes in the Indian Country*, 10–11, 137, 195–96.
7. Gregg, *Commerce of the Prairies*, 2:317–18; Loomis, *Scenes in the Indian Country*, 124–25; G. W. Grayson, *A Creek Warrior for the Confederacy: The Autobiography of Chief G. W. Grayson*, ed. W. David Baird (Norman: University of Oklahoma Press, 1988), 33; G. Foreman, *Traveler in Indian Territory*, 116.
8. Grayson, *Creek Warrior for the Confederacy*, 33–34, 39; Loomis, *Scenes in the Indian Country*, 11, 167–68.
9. Loomis, *Scenes in the Indian Country*, 12, 147, 163, 198; Muster Roll of Upper Towns, RG 75, Entry 299, Box 1, NARA; Muster Roll of the Lower Towns, RG 75, Entry 299, Box 1, NARA; McCoy to Porter, 29 January 1829, HR 87, 21; Gregg, *Commerce of the Prairies*, 2:317; G. Foreman, *Traveler in Indian Territory*, 127–28; Claudio Saunt, *Black, White, and Indian: Race and the Unmaking of an American Family* (New York: Oxford University Press, 2005), 66.
10. McCoy, *Annual Register*, 20, 69, 162, 254, 276; Gregg, *Commerce of the Prairies*, 2:317; John S. Tomer and Michael J. Brodhead, *A Naturalist in Indian Territory: The Journals of S. W. Woodhouse 1849–1850* (Norman: University of Oklahoma Press, 1992), 134; Ramsay to Lowrie, 1 February 1850, PHS-AIC, Box 12, Roll 2, Letter 4. For the locations of western Creek towns see Muster Roll of Upper Towns, RG 75, Entry 299, Box 1, NARA; Muster Roll of Lower Towns, RG 75, Entry 299, Box 1, NARA; Map of Indian Territory, Map 492, RG 75, Entry 163, Central Map Files, NARA II, College Park MD; Map of the Boundary of the Creek Country, HED 104; Tomer and Brodhead, *Naturalist in Indian Territory*, 98, 134, 149–50, 201; Angie Debo, *Tulsa: From Creek Town to Oil Capital* (Norman: University of Oklahoma Press, 1943), 14; Loughridge to Lowrie, 24 April 1849, PHS-AIC, Box 9, Roll 1, Letter 144; Ramsay to Wilson, 29 September 1859, PHS-AIC, Box 6, Roll 1, Letter 229; Boundaries of the Creeks and Seminoles, 1871, RG 75, Entry 163, Central Map Files, NARA II, College Park MD; Map of Boundary of the Creek Country, HED 104; Carolyn Thomas Foreman, "North

Fork Town," *Chronicles of Oklahoma* 29, no. 1 (Spring 1951): 79–111; Albert S. Gatschet, *A Migration Legend of the Creek Indians: Texts and Glossaries in Creek and Hitchiti, with a Linguistic, Historic, and Ethnographic Introduction and Commentary*, vol. 2 (1888; reprint, New York: Kraus Reprint, 1969), 184–89; Frank G. Speck, *The Creek Indians of Taskigi Town* (Millwood NY: Kraus Reprint, 1974).

11. G. Foreman, *Traveler in Indian Territory*, 257; Map of Indian Territory, Map 492, RG 75, Entry 163, Central Map Files, NARA II; Arrell M. Gibson, *The Kickapoos: Lords of the Middle Border* (Norman: University of Oklahoma Press, 1963), 142, 163, 168, 176. See also Grant Foreman, *The Last Trek of the Indians* (Chicago: University of Chicago Press, 1946), 162–63.

12. Logan to Medill, 12 January 1847, LR-CA, Roll 227, 579–80; Creeks to Commissioner of Indian Affairs, 29 March 1848, LR-CA, Roll 228, 64–66; Saunt, *Black, White, and Indian*, 72–75; John D. Lang and Samuel Taylor Jr., *Report of a Visit to Some of the Tribes of Indians, Located West of the Mississippi River* (New York: M. Day, 1843), 30.

13. Virginia Clay-Clopton, *A Belle of the Fifties: Memoirs of Mrs. Clay, of Alabama, covering Social and Political Life in Washington and the South, 1853–66, Gathered and Edited by Ada Sterling* (New York: Doubleday, Page, 1904), 107–9; George Catlin, *Letters and Notes on the Manners, Customs, and Condition of the North American Indians, Written during Eight Years' Travel amongst the Wildest Tribes of Indians in North America, in 1832, 33, 34, 35, 36, 37, 38, and 39*, vol. 2: 1841 (Minneapolis: Ross and Haines, 1965), 122; O'Beirne and O'Beirne, *Indian Territory*, 171–72; Gregg, *Commerce of the Prairies*, 2:317; Angie Debo, *The Road to Disappearance* (Norman: University of Oklahoma Press, 1941), 110; John T. Ellisor, *The Second Creek War: Interethnic Conflict and Collusion on a Collapsing Frontier* (Lincoln: University of Nebraska Press, 2010), 421; *Fort Smith Herald*, 22 November 1850; *Arkansas State Gazette*, 14 September 1842. See also David A. Chang, *The Color of the Land: Race, Nation, and the Politics of Landownership in Oklahoma, 1832–1929* (Chapel Hill: University of North Carolina Press, 2010).

14. McIntosh to Mason, 5 March 1845, LR, HRFG, Roll 3, 791–92. Logan to Crawford, 6 March 1845, LR-CA, Roll 227, 443–45; G. Foreman, *Traveler in Indian Territory*, 113–15; John Mix Stanley, *Portraits of North American Indians, with Sketches of Scenery, Etc.* (Washington DC: Smithsonian Institution, 1852), 12–13.

15. Tomer and Brodhead, *Naturalist in Indian Territory*, 134–35n8; Map of Indian Territory, Map 492, RG 75, Entry 163, Central Map Files, NARA II, College Park MD; Loomis, *Scenes in the Indian Country*, 136–37, 162–67, 247; *Arkansas State Gazette*, 14 September 1842; O'Beirne and O'Beirne, *Indian Territory*, 194–96. Loomis blamed the decaying Tallassee ceremonial complex on the lack of interest among the younger generation of Creeks, but it may have also been due to the diffusion of the population away from the junction of the Arkansas and Verdigris Rivers where the site was located.

16. Loomis, *Scenes in the Indian Country*, 241–48; Stanley, *Portraits of North American Indians*, 10, 12. See also, Kathryn E. Holland Braund, "Red Sticks," in *Tohopeka: Rethinking the Creek War and the War of 1812* (Tuscaloosa: University of Alabama Press, 2012), 98–99; William L. Merrill, "The Beloved Tree: *Ilex vomitoria* among the Indians of the Southeast and Adjacent Regions," in *Black Drink: A Native American Tea*, ed. Charles M. Hudson (Athens: University of Georgia Press, 1979), 40–82; Solomon Peck, "History of the Missions of the Baptist General Convention," in *History of American Missions to the Heathen, from their Commencement to the Present Time*, ed. Joseph J. Kwiat (1840; reprint, New York: Johnson Reprint, 1970), 548–49. See also Carmine Stahl and Ria McElvaney, *Trees of Texas: An Easy Guide to Leaf Identification* (College Station: Texas A&M University Press, 2003), 82; Eugene Current-Garcia and Dorothy B. Hatfield, eds., *Shem, Ham, & Japheth: The Papers of W. O. Tuggle, Comprising His Indian Diary, Sketches & Observations, Myths & Washington Journal in the Territory & at the Capital, 1879–1882* (Athens: University of Georgia Press, 1973), 42. For modern ceremonies see Frank G. Speck, *Ethnology of the Yuchi Indians* (1909; reprint, Lincoln: University of Nebraska Press, 2004); W. L. Ballard, *The Yuchi Green Corn Ceremonial: Form and Meaning* (Los Angeles: University of California–Los Angeles, American Indian Studies Center, 1978); Jason Baird Jackson, *Yuchi Ceremonial Life: Performance, Meaning, and Tradition in a Contemporary American Indian Community* (Lincoln: University of Nebraska Press, 2003).
17. Armstrong to Crawford, 25 November 1841, LR-CA, Roll 226, 258; Hitchcock to Spencer, 30 April 1842, LR-CA, Roll 226, 478–79; Charles J. Kappler, ed., *Indian Affairs: Laws and Treaties*, vol. 2: *Treaties* (Washington DC: Government Printing Office, 1904), 524–25; Hitchcock to Spencer, 2 May 1842, LR-CA, Roll 226, 484–85; Logan to Harris, 14 May 1838, LR-CA, Roll 225, 651–52.
18. Memoranda, from Gen. McIntosh, 28 January 1842, LR-CA, Roll 226, 472–74; Kappler, *Indian Affairs*, 2:524–25.
19. Opothle Yoholo's remarks, 3 February 1842, LR-CA, Roll 226, 491–505; Journal extract, PHS-AIC, Box 9, Roll 1, Letter 62; Loomis, *Scenes in the Indian Country*, 167–79.
20. Christopher D. Haveman, "'Last Evening I Saw the Sun Set for the Last Time': The 1832 Treaty of Washington and the Transfer of the Creeks' Alabama Land to White Ownership," *Native South* 5 (2012): 79, 83; G. Foreman, *Traveler in Indian Territory*, 149–50; Mary E. Young, *Redskins, Ruffleshirts, and Rednecks: Indian Allotments in Alabama and Mississippi, 1830–1860* (Norman: University of Oklahoma Press, 1961), 90, 102–3, 106.
21. Synopsis of documents and statements accompanying the preceding report, no. 68, *NASP*, 10:461-76; Statement of George Shirley, no. 72, 30 January 1842, *NASP*, 10:529–30; Statement of Little Sims, no. 65, 25 January 1842, *NASP*, 10:524–25; Statement of Benjamin Marshall, no. 64, 25 January 1842, *NASP*, 10:522–24;

G. Foreman, *Traveler in Indian Territory*, 143, 149–52; Loomis, *Scenes in the Indian Country*, 209–13; Marshall to Armstrong, 25 November 1846, LR-CA, Roll 227, 551–52.

22. Journal extract, PHS-AIC, Box 9, Roll 1, Letter 62; Eaton to Jackson, 23 September 1829, in *The Papers of Andrew Jackson: A Microfilm Supplement*, ed. Harold D. Moser [et al.] (Wilmington DE: Scholarly Resources, 1986), Roll 13, 1406–9; Robb to Campbell, 16 August 1832, LS, Roll 9, 168–70; Herring to Vashon, 10 January 1834, LS, Roll 12, 21–22; Dawson to Davenport, 10 July 1843, LR, HRFG, Roll 3, 173–74; *Choctaw Telegraph*, 23 August 1849; Armstrong to Crawford, 22 April 1843, LR-CA, Roll 227, 23; Dodge to Greene, 23 April 1835, ABC, Roll 779, 282–83; Dodge to Greene, 20 January 1835, ABC, Roll 779, 285–86; *Christian Mirror and N. H. Observer*, 22 July 1830; *Arkansas State Gazette*, 29 June 1842; Jack Gregory and Rennard Strickland, *Sam Houston with the Cherokees* (Austin: University of Texas Press, 1967), 78; Campbell to Cass, 17 October 1832, LR-CAW, Roll 236, 283–84; Stambaugh to Leavenworth, 26 May 1834, LR, HRFG, Roll 2, 92–94.

23. Little to Cooper, 14 September 1853, LR, HRFG, Roll 1, 236–37.

24. Eaton to Creeks, 20 March 1830, LR-CA, Roll 226, 291–96; Arthur H. DeRosier Jr., "Myths and Realities in Indian Westward Removal: The Choctaw Example," in *Four Centuries of Southern Indians*, ed. Charles M. Hudson (Athens: University of Georgia Press, 1975), 83–100; Kappler, *Indian Affairs*, 2:304–5; C. A. Weslager, *The Delaware Indians: A History* (New Brunswick NJ: Rutgers University Press, 1972), 359–464; Wendy St. Jean, *Remaining Chickasaw in Indian Territory, 1830s–1907* (Tuscaloosa: University of Alabama Press, 2011), 8–26; Muriel H. Wright and Peter J. Hudson, "Brief Outline of the Choctaw and the Chickasaw Nations in the Indian Territory 1820 to 1860," *Chronicles of Oklahoma* 7, no. 4 (December 1929): 388–418; Gaston L. Litton, "The Negotiations Leading to the Chickasaw-Choctaw Agreement, January 17, 1837," *Chronicles of Oklahoma* 17, no. 4 (December 1939): 417–27. See also Angie Debo, *And Still the Waters Run: The Betrayal of the Five Civilized Tribes* (Princeton, NJ: Princeton University Press, 1940); Donald L. Fixico, *The Invasion of Indian Country in the Twentieth Century: American Capitalism and Tribal Natural Resources* (Niwot: University Press of Colorado, 1998).

25. Creeks to Secretary of War, 15 January 1842, LR-CA, Roll 226, 604–8; Hitchcock to Spencer, 9 April 1842, LR-CA, Roll 226, 464–65; Kappler, *Indian Affairs*, 2:388–91, 550–52, 756–63. For a more detailed account of the problems between the Creeks and Seminoles in Indian territory see Jane F. Lancaster, *Removal Aftershock: The Seminoles' Struggles to Survive in the West, 1836–1866* (Knoxville: University of Tennessee Press, 1994), 13–15, 24–62, 115.

26. Kappler, *Indian Affairs*, 2:931–37; Map of Indian Territory, Map 490, Record Group 75, Entry 163, Central Map Files, NARA II; Map of Indian Territory, Map

493, Record Group 75, Entry 163, Central Map Files, NARA II; J. H. Beadle, *The Undeveloped West; or, Five Years in the Territories: Being a Complete History of that Vast Region Between the Mississippi and the Pacific, Its Resources, Climate, Inhabitants, Natural Curiosities, Etc., Etc. Life and Adventure on Prairies, Mountains, and the Pacific Coast. With Two Hundred and Forty Illustrations, From Original Sketches and Photographic Views of the Scenery, Cities, Lands, Mines, People, and Curiosities of the Great West* (Philadelphia: National, 1873), 386; 47th Cong., 1st sess., 1882, H.R. Rep. No. 310, serial no. 2065. See also Christine Schultz White and Benton R. White, *Now the Wolf Has Come: The Creek Nation in the Civil War* (College Station: Texas A&M University Press, 1996); Lela J. McBride, *Opothleyaholo and the Loyal Muskogee: Their Flight to Kansas in the Civil War* (Jefferson NC: McFarland, 2000).

27. A Schedule of Creek Orphan Children, LR-CAR, Roll 247, 70–89; Docket Books, 1836–1838, Record Group 75, Entry 292, Docket A, Box 1, NARA; 47th Cong., 1st sess., 1882, H.R. Rep. No. 310, serial no. 2065; "The United States in Account Current," SIAC, Agent (Secretary of War) Account (7261), Year (1842), NARA; List of Orphans Receiving Payment, SIAC, Agent (Logan), Account (6538), Year (1848), NARA; Current-Garcia and Hatfield, *Shem, Ham & Japheth*, 3, 90, 203.

28. Armstrong to Harris, 10 May 1837, LR-CA, Roll 225, 240–41; Act of March 3, 1837, in *The Public Statutes at Large of the United States of America*, vol. 5, ed. Richard Peters (Boston: Little, Brown, 1856), 186.

29. Haveman, "Last Evening I Saw the Sun Set for the Last Time," 81–82.

30. War Department, Office of Indian Affairs to S. Cooper, 15 May 1838, LR-CAR, Roll 245, 705–6; Creeks to Poinsett, 5 May 1838, LR-CAR, Roll 245, 166–68; War Department, Office of Indian Affairs to Iverson, 12 June 1838, LR-CAR, Roll 245, 409; Creeks to Poinsett, 28 March 1839, LR-CAR, Roll 246, 933–35.

31. OIA to Poinsett, 26 October 1838, LR-CAR, 245, 66–67; Crawford to Poinsett, 24 December 1840, LR-CAR, 247, 375–77; War Department to Hunter, 24 December 1840, LR-CAR, 247, 379–380; "List of Tracts of Land . . . ," LR-CAR, 248, 868–89; WDOIA to Fitzpatrick, 21 August 1843, LR-CAR, 248, 404–5; A Joint Resolution of the State of Alabama, 30 December 1842, LR-CAR, 248, 402; *Letter from the Acting Secretary of War, Transmitting, In pursuance of a resolution of the House of Representatives of the 13th of March last, a report from the Commissioner of Indian Affairs, relative to the Creek Indian reservations under the treaty of 1832*, 30th Cong., 1st sess., 1848, House Executive Document 66, serial no. 521, 1–15; "List of Creek Indian Lands in Alabama sold under the act of Congress of the 3d of March, 1837," Miscellaneous Records Concerning Contracts, ca. 1833–1857, RG 75, Entry 298, Box 2, NARA; "List of Creek Indian lands in Alabama which do not appear to have been disposed of . . . ," Miscellaneous Records Concerning Contracts, ca. 1833–1857, RG 75, Entry 298, Box 2, NARA; *Fort Smith Herald*, 23 August 1856; Kappler, *Indian Affairs*, 2:756–63.

32. Page's list of Creeks entitled to land, LR-CAR, Roll 245, 425–33; Haveman, "Last Evening I Saw the Sun Set for the Last Time," 80, 82–83; Jim Boy to Harris, 16 April 1838, LR-CAR, Roll 245, 272–77; Logan to Medill, 24 November 1846, LR-CAR, Roll 248, 691–92; Roll of Creek Indians entitled to land, LR-CAR, Roll 248, 693–705; OIA to Stuart, May 1852, LR-CAR, Roll 248, 739–45.

33. G. Foreman, *Traveler in Indian Territory*, 112; Creeks to Manypenny, 19 July 1856, LR-CA, Roll 229, 605–12; Cady to Prentiss, 22 March 1846, LR, HRFG, Roll 1, 165–66. For reports of dissatisfaction of Indians in the West see *Letter from the Secretary of War, Upon the Subject of a Hostile disposition upon the part of the Indians on the Western Frontier*, H.R. Doc no. 434, 1838, 25th Cong., 2nd Sess., Serial Set 331, 1–10. Mexican agents, sensing that embittered Indians may join in an alliance, sent emissaries to Indian territory in the 1840s. Roly McIntosh rejected the overtures. Dawson to Crawford, 25 May 1843, LR-CA, Roll 227, 80; Logan to Spencer, 2 May 1842, LR-CA, Roll 226, 561–63; Amelia W. Williams and Eugene C. Barker, eds., *The Writings of Sam Houston, 1813–1863*, vol. 2 (Austin: University of Texas Press, 1939), 50–51; Joseph Milton Nance, *Attack and Counterattack: The Texas-Mexican Frontier, 1842* (Austin: University of Texas Press, 1964), 140–41; Gary Clayton Anderson, *The Conquest of Texas: Ethnic Cleansing in the Promised Land, 1820–1875* (Norman: University of Oklahoma Press, 2005), 134; Brian DeLay, *War of a Thousand Deserts: Indian Raids and the U.S.-Mexican War* (New Haven CT: Yale University Press, 2008), 4, 64; Dawson to Crawford, 5 June 1843, LR-CA, Roll 227, 82–83. See also Stephen L. Moore, *Savage Frontier*, vol. 2: *1838–1839: Rangers, Riflemen, and Indian Wars in Texas* (Denton: University of North Texas Press, 2006), 147; Morfit to Forsyth, 27 August 1836, RG 59, General Records of the Department of State, 1763–2002, Microcopy T-728, Despatches from United States Ministers to Texas, 1836–45, Roll 1, 26–32, NARA. Senator John C. Calhoun once argued that southeastern Indians who were friendly to the United States might serve as an effective protective barrier between white frontiersmen and the western Indians. Remarks, 16 February 1837; Clyde N. Wilson, ed., *The Papers of John C. Calhoun*, vol. 13: *1835–1837* (Columbia: University of South Carolina Press, 1980), 436.

34. Loomis, *Scenes in the Indian Country*, 7–8; Current-Garcia and Hatfield, *Shem, Ham, & Japheth*, 84.

35. Reverend Joseph Camp, *An Insight into an Insane Asylum* (Published for the Author, 1882), 122–26. Camp (or his father, who was also named Joseph) was a land speculator who had Kloslitco arrested and bound because of a debt (see chapter 4). Kloslitco investigation, RG 75, Entry 290, Report Concerning Creek Contracts, 1836, NARA.

36. Self-emigration Claims, SFOIA, SF 285, Roll 77, 6, 119, 122, 139, 164. John Dannely, threatened by Menawa at an 1829 ball game for his advocacy of voluntary emigration, self-emigrated with his family in 1836.

CONCLUSION

1. William Atson, *Heart Whispers; or, A Peep Behind the Family Curtain, Interspersed with Sketches of a Tour Through Nine Southern States. Contained in a Series of Letters to His Wife* (Philadelphia: H. Cowperthwait, 1859), 167–68; J. S. Buckingham, *The Slave States of America*, vol. 1 (London: Fisher, Son, 1842), 247.
2. Jon Meacham, *American Lion: Andrew Jackson in the White House* (New York: Random House, 2008), 189; Andrew Burstein, *The Passions of Andrew Jackson* (New York: Knopf, 2003), 207.
3. Alexander counted "a few over 11,000" at Fort Gibson in December 1836, before detachment three arrived at the garrison. Alexander reported that the population did begin to rebound in the late 1830s and early 1840s. Western Creek Census, 30 September 1833, SD 512, 4:722; Ethan Allen Hitchcock Notebooks, Creeks, 31 January 1842, Box 4, Folder 17, Beinecke Rare Book & Manuscript Library, Yale University, New Haven CT; The U.S. in Account Current with the Alabama Emigrating Company, SIAC, Agent (Reynolds), Account (1687), Year (1838), NARA; Alexander to Hitchcock, 31 January 1842, *NASP*, 10:530–33; Claudio Saunt, *Black, White, and Indian: Race and the Unmaking of an American Family* (New York: Oxford University Press, 2005), 66.
4. Isaac McCoy, *The Annual Register of Indian Affairs, In the Western (or Indian) Territory 1835–1838* (Springfield MO: Particular Baptist Press, 2000), 278; Michael F. Doran, "Population Statistics of Nineteenth Century Indian Territory," *Chronicles of Oklahoma* 53, no. 4 (Winter 1975–1976): 492–515; Russell Thornton, *The Cherokees: A Population History* (Lincoln: University of Nebraska Press, 1990), 71–77; Thornton, "The Demography of the Trail of Tears Period: A New Estimate of Cherokee Population Losses," in *Cherokee Removal: Before and After*, ed. William L. Anderson (Athens: University of Georgia Press, 1991), 75–95; Thornton, "Cherokee Population Losses during the Trail of Tears: A New Perspective and a New Estimate," *Ethnohistory* 31, no. 4 (Autumn 1984): 289–300; Donna L. Akers, "Removing the Heart of the Choctaw People: Indian Removal from a Native Perspective," *American Indian Culture and Research Journal* 23, no. 3 (1999): 63–76; Akers, *Living in the Land of Death: The Choctaw Nation, 1830–1860* (East Lansing: Michigan State University Press, 2004), 112–13. See also Benjamin Madley, "Reexamining the American Genocide Debate: Meaning, Historiography, and New Methods," *American Historical Review* 120, no. 1 (February 2015): 98–139.
5. It is unclear if the numbers for detachment six include those who fought the Seminoles in Florida. Journal (Belton), LR-CAE, Roll 237, 520–26; Abadie to Gibson, 20 October 1836, CGS-IRW, Roll 5, 800–802; The U.S. in account current with the Alabama Emigrating Company, SIAC, Agent (Reynolds), Account (1687), Year (1838), NARA.

6. George Tiger speech, 27 March 2014, courtesy of Mvskoke Media, Okmulgee, Oklahoma; David Farthing, ed., *Creek Hymnal* (Coweta, OK: George Doyle, 1996); *Nakcokv Esyvhiketv: Muskogee Hymns* (Westminister Press, n.d.).

7. Kathryn E. Holland Braund, "'Resolved Not to Yield': Tohopeka Two Hundred Years On," *Alabama Review* 67, no. 3 (July 2014): 211–18. George Tiger speech, 27 March 2014.

BIBLIOGRAPHY

ARCHIVAL SOURCES

Alabama Department of Archives and History, Montgomery AL
    Administrative Files, Alabama Governor—C. C. Clay
    John William Augustine Sanford Papers, 1754–1917
    Richard A. Blount Papers
    U.S. Land Office, Tallapoosa Land District, Plat Books

American Baptist Historical Society, Atlanta GA
    American Baptist Board of International Missions Collections, Foreign Mission Correspondence

Beinecke Rare Book & Manuscript Library, Yale University, New Haven CT
    Diary of Thomas Sidney Jesup, 1836
    Ethan Allen Hitchcock Collection on Indian Removal

Birmingham Public Library, Birmingham AL
    Cartography Collection

Columbus State University, Columbus GA
    Henry Benning–Seaborn Jones Collection (MC 6)

Georgia Archives, Morrow GA
    Creek Indian Letters, Talks, and Treaties, 1705–1839, Parts 2–4
    Governor's Papers
    Indian Letters, 1782–1839
    Moravian Mission Diaries, Murray County GA

Harvard University, Cambridge MA
    Papers of the American Board of Commissioners for Foreign Missions
        ABC 18: Missions on the American Continents and to the Islands of the Pacific, 1811–1919, Chicasaw Mission (ABC 18.4.4), Volume 1: Chicasaws, Creeks, Osages; Letters (ABC 18–19), 1830–1837, Reel 779, Woodbridge CT: Research Publications, 1985

Historic New Orleans Collection, New Orleans LA
    Butler Family Papers, MSS 102

Kansas State Historical Society, Topeka KS
    William Clark Papers, 1807–55, Volume 6, Reel MS 95
Library of Congress, Washington DC
    Presidential Papers Microfilm
        Andrew Jackson Papers, 1775–1874, Series 1, Reel 37
Lilly Library, Indiana University, Bloomington IN
    Indiana History Manuscripts
        Autobiography of John H. Jones, 1814–82
National Archives and Records Administration, Washington DC
    Record Group 59, General Records of the Department of State, 1763–2002
        Despatches from Diplomatic Officers, 1789–1906, Microfilm
            Microcopy T-728—Despatches from United States Ministers to Texas, 1836–45, Roll 1
    Record Group 75, Records of the Bureau of Indian Affairs, 1793–1989, Documents
        Records Relating to Indian Removal, 1817–86
            Entry 287—Land Location Registers, ca. 1834–66
            Entry 290—Report Concerning Creek Contracts, 1836
            Entry 291—Journal, 1836–38
            Entry 292—Docket Books, 1836–38
            Entry 295—Abstracts of Approved Contracts for Sales of Reservations, 1839–42
            Entry 298—Miscellaneous Records Concerning Contracts, ca. 1833–57
            Entry 299—Emigration Lists, 1836–38.
            Entry 300—Miscellaneous Creek Removal Records, ca. 1827–59
    Record Group 75, Records of the Bureau of Indian Affairs, 1793–1989, Microfilm
        Microcopy 21—Records of the Office of Indian Affairs, Letters Sent, Rolls 4–9, 12–13, 18, 20
        Microcopy 234—Letters Received by the Office of Indian Affairs, 1824–81
            Creek Agency, 1824–76, Rolls 219–27
            Creek Agency Emigration, 1826–49, Rolls 237–40
            Creek Agency Reserves, 1832–50, Rolls 241-48
            Creek Agency West, 1826–36, Roll 236
            Florida Superintendency, 1824–53, Roll 288
            Seminole Agency Emigration, 1824–76, Roll 806
        Microcopy 275—1832 Census of Creek Indians Taken by Parsons and Abbott, Roll 1
        Microcopy 574—Special Files of the Office of Indian Affairs, 1807–1904.
            Special File 62, Roll 7—James Erwin and Erwin & Greathouse, claims for losses under contracts made in 1834–35 for transporting and providing subsistence for Creek and Seminole Indians, 1847–55

Special File 136, Roll 27—McIntosh party, claims for property destroyed by hostile Creek Indians in 1825, 1825–26
Special File 207, Roll 61—Creek claims for property left in the East and lost during removal, 1838
Special File 285, Roll 77—Creek self-emigration claims, 1886–1904
Microcopy 1466—Headquarters Records of Fort Gibson, Indian Territory, 1830–57, Rolls 1–5
Record Group 77—Records of the Office of the Chief of Engineers, 1789–1996
Letters Received by the Topographical Bureau of the War Department, 1824–65, Microcopy 506, Roll 18
Record Group 94—Records of the Adjutant General's Office, 1780s–1917
Entry 159, Records of Thomas S. Jesup
Record Group 217—Records of the Accounting Officers of the Department of the Treasury
Entry 227, Indian Contracts, 1820–94
Entry 525, Settled Indian Accounts and Claims, 1794–1894
National Archives and Records Administration II, College Park MD
Record Group 75
Entry 163, Central Map Files
New York Public Library, New York NY
Belton-Kirby-Dawson-Todd families papers, ca. 1763–1892, Manuscripts and Archives Division; Astor, Lenox, and Tilden Foundations
Oklahoma Historical Society, Oklahoma City OK
Indian Pioneer History Collection, Works Progress Administration Project S-149
Presbyterian Historical Society, Philadelphia PA
American Indian Correspondence, Collection of Missionaries' Letters, 1833–93, Box 6, Reel 1, Westport CT: Greenwood, 1978
Princeton University, Department of Rare Books and Special Collections, Princeton NJ
John G. Reynolds Journal
Tennessee State Library and Archives, Nashville TN
Fergusson Family Papers, 1784–1927
Tedder Papers, Correspondence
University of Alabama, Libraries Division of Special Collections, Tuscaloosa AL
Edward Woolf watercolor
University of Oklahoma, Western History Collection, Norman OK
Native American Manuscripts—Grayson Family
University of Tennessee, Knoxville TN
The Papers of Andrew Jackson: A Microfilm Supplement, Rolls 13, 15, 18, Wilmington DE: Scholarly Resources, 1986
University Publications of America, Bethesda MD

Files of the Office of the Commissary General of Subsistence, Rolls 1, 4–6, 7, 10
Indian Removal to the West, 1832–40
Vermont Historical Society, Barre VT
Beattie Family Papers
William L. Clements Library, University of Michigan, Ann Arbor MI
Lewis Cass Papers, 1774–1924

PUBLISHED SOURCES

Acts Passed at the Tenth Annual Session of the General Assembly of the State of Alabama: Begun And Held In The Town of Tuscaloosa, On The Third Monday In November, One Thousand Eight Hundred and Twenty-Eight. Tuscaloosa AL: M'Guire, Henry and M'Guire, 1829.

Acts Passed at the Thirteenth Annual Session of the General Assembly of the State of Alabama, Begun and Held In The Town of Tuscaloosa, On The Third Monday In November, One Thousand Eight Hundred and Thirty-one. Tuscaloosa AL: Wiley, M'Guire and Henry, 1832.

Adair, James. *The History of the American Indians*. Edited by Kathryn E. Holland Braund. Tuscaloosa: University of Alabama Press, 2005.

Agnew, Brad. *Fort Gibson: Terminal on the Trail of Tears*. Norman: University of Oklahoma Press, 1980.

Akers, Donna L. *Living in the Land of Death: The Choctaw Nation, 1830–1860*. East Lansing: Michigan State University Press, 2004.

———. "Removing the Heart of the Choctaw People: Indian Removal from a Native Perspective." *American Indian Culture and Research Journal* 23, no. 3 (1999): 63–76.

Alperin, Lynn M. *History of the Gulf Intracoastal Waterway*. Washington DC: U.S. Army Engineer Water Resources Support Center, 1983.

Alvarez, Alex. *Native America and the Question of Genocide*. Lanham MD: Rowman & Littlefield, 2014.

The American Almanac and Repository of Useful Knowledge, For the Year 1831. Boston: Gray and Bowen, 1831.

American State Papers: Documents, Legislative and Executive of the Congress of the United States. Vols. 6–7, *Military Affairs*. Washington DC: Gales and Seaton, 1861.

Anderson, Gary Clayton. *The Conquest of Texas: Ethnic Cleansing in the Promised Land, 1820–1875*. Norman: University of Oklahoma Press, 2005.

———. *Ethnic Cleansing and the Indian: The Crime That Should Haunt America*. Norman: University of Oklahoma Press, 2014.

Anderson, Marilyn J. "The Image of the Indian in American Drama during the Jacksonian Era, 1829–1845." *Journal of American Culture* 1, no. 4 (Winter 1978): 800–810.

Andrew, John A., III. *From Revivals to Removal: Jeremiah Evarts, the Cherokee Nation, and the Search for the Soul of America*. Athens: University of Georgia Press, 1992.

Anson, Bert. *The Miami Indians.* Norman: University of Oklahoma Press, 1970.
Arfwedson, Carl David. *The United States and Canada in 1832, 1833, and 1834.* Vols. 1–2. 1834; reprint, New York: Johnson Reprint, 1969.
Atkinson, James R. *Splendid Land, Splendid People: The Chickasaw Indians to Removal.* Tuscaloosa: University of Alabama Press, 2004.
Atson, William. *Heart Whispers; or, A Peep Behind the Family Curtain, Interspersed with Sketches of a Tour Through Nine Southern States. Contained in a Series of Letters to His Wife.* Philadelphia: H. Cowperthwait, 1859.
Audubon, John James. *Letters of John James Audubon, 1826–1840.* Vol. 2. Edited by Howard Corning. Boston: Club of Odd Volumes, 1930.
Bailey, Garrick Alan. *Changes in Osage Social Organization, 1673–1906.* Eugene: University of Oregon, 1973.
Baird, W. David, and Danney Goble. *Oklahoma: A History.* Norman: University of Oklahoma Press, 2008.
———. *The Quapaw Indians: A History of the Downstream People.* Norman: University of Oklahoma Press, 1980.
Baldwin, Leland D. *The Keelboat Age on Western Waters.* Pittsburgh: University of Pittsburgh Press, 1941.
Ballard, W. L. *The Yuchi Green Corn Ceremonial: Form and Meaning.* Los Angeles: University of California, American Indian Studies Center, 1978.
Banner, Stuart. *How the Indians Lost Their Land: Law and Power on the Frontier.* Cambridge MA: Harvard University Press, 2005.
Banta, R. E. *The Ohio.* New York: Rinehart, 1949.
Barnes, Lela., ed. "Journal of Isaac McCoy for the Exploring Expedition of 1828." *Kansas Historical Quarterly* 5, no. 3 (August 1936): 227–77.
Barnum, Phineas Taylor. *The Life of P. T. Barnum.* New York: Redfield, 1855.
Bassett, John Spencer, ed. *Correspondence of Andrew Jackson.* Vol. 4. Washington DC: Carnegie Institution, 1929.
———. *The Life of Andrew Jackson.* Vol. 1. Garden City NY: Doubleday, Page, 1911.
Beadle, J. H. *The Undeveloped West; or, Five Years in the Territories: Being a Complete History of that Vast Region Between the Mississippi and the Pacific, Its Resources, Climate, Inhabitants, Natural Curiosities, Etc., Etc. Life and Adventure on Prairies, Mountains, and the Pacific Coast. With Two Hundred and Forty Illustrations, From Original Sketches and Photographic Views of the Scenery, Cities, Lands, Mines, People, and Curiosities of the Great West.* Philadelphia: National Publication Company, 1873.
Bell, Amelia Rector. "Separate People: Speaking of Creek Men and Women." *American Anthropologist* 92, no. 2 (June 1990): 332–45.
Bell-Fialkoff, Andrew. "A Brief History of Ethnic Cleansing." *Foreign Affairs* 72, no. 3 (Summer 1993): 110–21.
———. *Ethnic Cleansing.* New York: St. Martin's Griffin, 1996.

Bemrose, John. *Reminiscences of the Second Seminole War*. Edited by John K. Mahon. Gainesville: University of Florida Press, 1966.

Benedict, John D. *Muskogee and Northeastern Oklahoma: Including the Counties of Muskogee, McIntosh, Wagoner, Cherokee, Sequoyah, Adair, Delaware, Mayes, Rogers, Washington, Nowata, Craig and Ottawa*. Vols. 1–2. Chicago: S. J. Clarke, 1922.

Benton, Jeffrey C., ed. *The Very Worst Road: Travellers' Accounts of Crossing Alabama's Old Creek Indian Territory, 1820–1847*. Eufaula AL: Historic Chattahoochee Commission, 1998.

Berkeley, Edmund, and Dorothy Smith Berkeley. *George William Featherstonhaugh: The First U.S. Government Geologist*. Tuscaloosa: University of Alabama Press, 1988.

Berlandier, Jean Louis. *The Indians of Texas in 1830*. Washington DC: Smithsonian Institution, 1969.

Bernhard, Karl, Duke of Saxe-Weimar Eisenach. *Travels Through North America, During the Years 1825 and 1826*. Vol. 2. Philadelphia: Carey, Lea and Carey, 1828.

Berry, Kate A., and Melissa A. Rinehart. "A Legacy of Forced Migration: The Removal of the Miami Tribe in 1846." *International Journal of Population Geography* 9, no. 2 (March/April 2003): 93–112.

Blum, Rony, Gregory H. Stanton, Shira Sagi, and Elihu D. Richter. "'Ethnic Cleansing' Bleaches the Atrocities of Genocide." *European Journal of Public Health* 18, no. 2 (2008): 204–9.

Bollaert, William. "Observations on the Indian Tribes in Texas." *Journal of the Ethnological Society of London* 2 (1850): 262–83.

Bollwerk, Elizabeth. "Controlling Acculturation: A Potawatomi Strategy for Avoiding Removal." *Midcontinental Journal of Archaeology* 31, no. 1 (Spring 2006): 117–41.

Bolton, S. Charles. *Arkansas 1800–1860: Remote and Restless*. Fayetteville: University of Arkansas Press, 1998.

———. "Jeffersonian Indian Removal and the Emergence of Arkansas Territory." *Arkansas Historical Quarterly* 62, no. 3 (Autumn 2003): 253–71.

Bonner, James C. "Journal of a Mission to Georgia in 1827." *Georgia Historical Quarterly* 44, no. 1 (March 1960): 74–97.

———. "Tustunugee Hutkee and Creek Factionalism on the Georgia-Alabama Frontier." *Alabama Review* 10 (April 1957): 111–25.

Bowes, John P. *Exiles and Pioneers: Eastern Indians in the Trans-Mississippi West*. Cambridge: Cambridge University Press, 2007.

Boyd, Joel D. "Creek Indian Agents, 1834–1874." *Chronicles of Oklahoma* 51, no. 1 (1973): 37–58.

Brands, H. W. *Andrew Jackson: His Life and Times*. New York: Doubleday, 2005.

Brasseaux, Carl A., and Keith P. Fontenot. *Steamboats on Louisiana's Bayous: A History and Directory*. Baton Rouge: Louisiana State University Press, 2004.

Braund, Kathryn E. Holland. "The Creek Indians, Blacks, and Slavery." *Journal of Southern History* 5, no. 4 (November 1991): 601–36.

———. *Deerskins & Duffels: Creek Indian Trade with Anglo-America, 1685–1815*. Lincoln: University of Nebraska Press, 1993.

———. "'Like a Stone Wall Never to Be Broke': The British-Indian Boundary Line with the Creek Indians, 1763–1773." In *Britain and the American South: From Colonialism to Rock and Roll*, edited by Joseph P. Ward, 53–79. Jackson: University Press of Mississippi, 2003.

———. "'Resolved Not to Yield': Tohopeka Two Hundred Years On." *Alabama Review* 67, no. 3 (July 2014): 211–18.

Buckingham, J. S. *The Slave States of America*. Vol. 1. London: Fisher, Son, 1842.

Burns, Louis F. *A History of the Osage People*. Tuscaloosa: University of Alabama Press, 2004.

Burstein, Andrew. *The Passions of Andrew Jackson*. New York: Knopf, 2003.

Camp, Joseph. *An Insight into an Insane Asylum*. Published for the Author, 1882.

Carson, James Taylor. "'The Obituary of Nations': Ethnic Cleansing, Memory, and the Origins of the Old South." *Southern Cultures* 14, no. 4 (Winter 2008): 6–31.

———. "State Rights and Indian Removal in Mississippi, 1817–1835." *Journal of Mississippi History* 57, no. 1 (February 1995): 25–42.

Carter, Clarence Edwin, ed. *The Territorial Papers of the United States*. Vol. 21: *The Territory of Arkansas, 1829–1836*. Washington DC: Government Printing Office, 1954.

Catlin, George. *Letters and Notes on the Manners, Customs, and Condition of the North American Indians. Written During Eight Years' Travel amongst the Wildest Tribes of Indians in North America, in 1832, 33, 34, 35, 36, 37, 38, and 39*. Vol. 2. 1841; reprint, Minneapolis: Ross and Haines, 1965.

Cave, Alfred A. "Abuse of Power: Andrew Jackson and the Indian Removal Act of 1830." *Historian* 65, no. 6 (Winter 2000): 1330–53.

Cayton, Frank M. *Landings on All the Western and Southern Rivers and Bayous, Showing Location, Post-Offices, Distances, &c., Also, Tariff of Premiums on Insurance to All Points*. St. Louis: Woodward, Tiernan and Hale, 1881.

Champagne, Duane. *Social Order and Political Change: Constitutional Governments among the Cherokee, the Choctaw, the Chickasaw, and the Creek*. Stanford CA: Stanford University Press, 1992.

Chang, David A. *The Color of the Land: Race, Nation, and the Politics of Landownership in Oklahoma, 1832–1929*. Chapel Hill: University of North Carolina Press, 2010.

Chase, David W. "Fort Mitchell: An Archaeological Exploration in Russell County, Alabama." *Alabama Archaeological Society* no. 1 (February 1974): 1–66.

Chaudhuri, Jean, and Joyotpaul Chaudhuri. *A Sacred Path: The Way of the Muscogee Creeks*. Los Angeles: UCLA American Indian Studies Center, 2001.

Clay-Clopton, Virginia. *A Belle of the Fifties: Memoirs of Mrs. Clay, of Alabama, covering Social and Political Life in Washington and the South, 1853–66, Gathered and Edited by Ada Sterling.* New York: Doubleday, Page, 1904.

Clifton, James A. *The Prairie People: Continuity and Change in Potawatomi Indian Culture, 1665–1965.* Lawrence: Regents Press of Kansas, 1977.

Clinton, Matthew William. *Tuscaloosa, Alabama: Its Early Days, 1816–1865.* Tuscaloosa AL: Zonta Club, 1958.

Cole, Donald B. *The Presidency of Andrew Jackson.* Lawrence: University Press of Kansas, 1993.

Collins, Robert P. "A Swiss Traveler in the Creek Nation: The Diary of Lukas Vischer, March 1824." *Alabama Review* 59, no. 4 (October 2006): 243–84.

Comfort, Benjamin F. *Lewis Cass and the Indian Treaties: A Monograph on the Indian Relations of the Northwest Territory from 1813 to 1831.* Detroit: Charles F. May, 1923.

Connor, Henry G. *John Archibald Campbell: Associate Justice of the United States Supreme Court, 1853–1861.* Boston: Houghton Mifflin, 1920.

Cooling, Benjamin Franklin, ed. *The New American State Papers, Military Affairs.* Vol. 17: *National Development and the Military.* Wilmington DE: Scholarly Resources, 1979.

Corkran, David H. *The Creek Frontier, 1540–1783.* Norman: University of Oklahoma Press, 1967.

Cotterill, R. S. *The Southern Indians: The Story of the Civilized Tribes before Removal.* Norman: University of Oklahoma Press, 1954.

Covington, James W. "Federal Relations with the Apalachicola Indians: 1823–1838." *Florida Historical Quarterly* 42, no. 2 (October 1963): 125–41.

———. *The Seminoles of Florida.* Gainesville: University Press of Florida, 1993.

Crane, Verner W. *The Southern Frontier, 1670–1732.* Durham NC: Duke University Press, 1928.

Cromer, Marie West. *Modern Indians of Alabama: Remnants of the Removal.* Birmingham AL: Southern University Press, 1984.

Current-Garcia, Eugene, and Dorothy B. Hatfield, eds. *Shem, Ham, & Japheth: The Papers of W. O. Tuggle, Comprising His Indian Diary, Sketches & Observations, Myths & Washington Journal in the Territory & at the Capital, 1879–1882.* Athens: University of Georgia Press, 1973.

Curtis, James C. *Andrew Jackson and the Search for Vindication.* New York: HarperCollins, 1976.

Davidson, Donald. *The Tennessee: The Old River; Frontier to Secession.* Vol. 1. New York: Rinehart, 1946.

Davis, Clyde Brion. *The Arkansas.* New York: Farrar and Rinehart, 1940.

Davis, Ethan. "An Administrative Trail of Tears: Indian Removal." *American Journal of Legal History* 50, no. 1 (January 2008–2010): 49–100.

Debo, Angie. *And Still the Waters Run: The Betrayal of the Five Civilized Tribes*. Princeton NJ: Princeton University Press, 1940.
———. *The Road to Disappearance*. Norman: University of Oklahoma Press, 1941.
———. *Tulsa: From Creek Town to Oil Capital*. Norman: University of Oklahoma Press, 1943.
DeLay, Brian. *War of a Thousand Deserts: Indian Raids and the U.S.-Mexican War*. New Haven CT: Yale University Press, 2008.
DeRosier, Arthur H., Jr. "Andrew Jackson and Negotiations for the Removal of the Choctaw Indians." *Historian* 29, no. 3 (May 1967): 343–62.
———. "Myths and Realities in Indian Westward Removal: The Choctaw Example." In *Four Centuries of Southern Indians*, edited by Charles M. Hudson, 83–100. Athens: University of Georgia Press, 1975.
———. *The Removal of the Choctaw Indians*. Knoxville: University of Tennessee Press, 1970.
De Smet, P. J., SJ. *Western Missions and Missionaries: A Series of Letters*. 1859; reprint, Shannon: Irish University Press, 1972.
Dippie, Brian W. *The Vanishing American: White Attitudes and U. S. Indian Policy*. Middletown CT: Wesleyan University Press, 1982.
Domenech, Emmanuel-Henri-Dieudonné. *Seven Years' Residence in the Great Deserts of North America*. Vol. 1. London: Longman, Green, Longman, and Roberts, 1860.
Doran, Michael F. "Population Statistics of Nineteenth Century Indian Territory." *Chronicles of Oklahoma* 53, no. 4 (Winter 1975–76): 492–515.
Doster, James F. *Creek Indians: The Creek Indians and Their Florida Lands, 1740–1823*. Vol. 2. New York: Garland, 1974.
Douglas, Mary. *Purity and Danger: An Analysis of the Concepts of Pollution and Taboo*. 1966; reprint, New York: Routledge and Kegan Paul, 1978.
Douthat, James L., ed. *Creek Ration Book: Records Taken in June 1838 at Camp Clanewaugh near Ross' Landing in Tennessee*. Signal Mountain TN: Mountain Press, 1999.
Dowd, Gregory Evans. "Thinking Outside the Circle: Tecumseh's 1811 Mission." In *Tohopeka: Rethinking the Creek War and the War of 1812*, edited by Kathryn E. Holland Braund, 30–52. Tuscaloosa: University of Alabama Press, 2012.
Drake, Samuel G. *Biography and History of the Indians of North America. From Its First Discovery To The Present Time; Comprising Details In The Lives Of All The Most Distinguished Chiefs And Counsellors, Exploits Of Warriors, And The Celebrated Speeches Of Their Orators; Also, A History of Their Wars, Massacres And Depredations, As Well As The Wrongs And Sufferings Which The Europeans And Their Descendants Have Done Them; With An Account Of Their Antiquities, Manners And Customs, Religion And Laws; Likewise Exhibiting An Analysis Of The Most Distinguished,*

As Well As Absurd Authors, Who Have Written Upon The Great Question Of The First Peopling Of America. Book 4. Boston: Antiquarian Institute, 1837.

Drinnon, Richard. *Facing West: The Metaphysics of Indian-Hating and Empire Building*. Minneapolis: University of Minnesota Press, 1980.

Duckett, Alvin Laroy. *John Forsyth: Political Tactician*. Athens: University of Georgia Press, 1962.

Dunbar, Willis Frederick. *Lewis Cass*. Grand Rapids MI: William B. Eerdmans, 1970.

Dysart, Jane E. "Another Road to Disappearance: Assimilation of Creek Indians in Pensacola, Florida, during the Nineteenth Century." *Florida Historical Quarterly* 61, no. 1 (July 1982): 37–48.

Edmunds, R. David. *The Potawatomis: Keepers of the Fire*. Norman: University of Oklahoma Press, 1978.

———. "The Prairie Potawatomi Removal of 1833." *Indiana Magazine of History* 68, no. 3 (September 1972): 240–53.

Ellis, Richard E. *The Union at Risk: Jacksonian Democracy, States' Rights, and the Nullification Crisis*. New York: Oxford University Press, 1987.

Ellisor, John T. "Like So Many Wolves: Creek Removal in the Cherokee Country, 1835–1838." *Journal of East Tennessee History*, no. 71 (1999): 1–24.

———. *The Second Creek War: Interethnic Conflict and Collusion on a Collapsing Frontier*. Lincoln: University of Nebraska Press, 2010.

Ellsworth, Henry Leavitt. *Washington Irving on the Prairie; or, A Narrative of a Tour of the Southwest in the Year 1832*. Edited by Stanley T. Williams and Barbara D. Simison. New York: American Book, 1937.

Ellsworth, Lucius F., and Jane E. Dysart. "West Florida's Forgotten People: The Creek Indians from 1830 until 1970." *Florida Historical Quarterly* 59, no. 4 (April 1981): 422–39.

Emerson, D. Berton. "'It's Good to Be Shifty': The Local Democracies of Old Southwestern Humor." *American Literature* 85, no. 2 (June 2013): 273–301.

Ethridge, Robbie. *Creek Country: The Creek Indians and Their World*. Chapel Hill: University of North Carolina Press, 2003.

Farthing, David., ed. *Creek Hymnal*. Coweta OK: George Doyle, 1996.

Featherstonhaugh, George William. *Excursion Through the Slave States, from Washington on the Potomac to the Frontier of Mexico; with Sketches of Popular Manners and Geological Notices*. New York: Harper and Brothers, 1844.

Feller, Daniel. *The Jacksonian Promise: America, 1815–1840*. Baltimore MD: Johns Hopkins University Press, 1995.

———. *The Public Lands in Jacksonian Politics*. Madison: University of Wisconsin Press, 1984.

Feller, Daniel, Laura-Eve Moss, Thomas Coens, and Erik B. Alexander, eds., *The Papers of Andrew Jackson* Vol. 9: *1831*. Knoxville: University of Tennessee Press, 2013.

Finley, Anthony. "1823 Map of Georgia." In *The New General Atlas*. Philadelphia: A. Finley, 1824.

Fixico, Donald L. *The Invasion of Indian Country in the Twentieth Century: American Capitalism and Tribal Natural Resources*. Niwot: University Press of Colorado, 1998.

Foley, William E., and C. David Rice. *The First Chouteaus: River Barons of Early St. Louis*. Urbana: University of Illinois Press, 1983.

Ford, Lisa. *Settler Sovereignty: Jurisdiction and Indigenous People in America and Australia, 1788-1836*. Cambridge MA: Harvard University Press, 2011.

Foreman, Carolyn Thomas. "North Fork Town." *Chronicles of Oklahoma* 29, no. 1 (Spring 1951): 79-111.

Foreman, Grant. *Advancing the Frontier, 1830-1860*. 1933; reprint, Norman: University of Oklahoma Press, 1968.

———. *The Five Civilized Tribes*. 1934; reprint, Norman: University of Oklahoma Press, 1966.

———. *Indian Removal: The Emigration of the Five Civilized Tribes of Indians*. 1932; reprint, Norman: University of Oklahoma Press, 1974.

———. *Indians and Pioneers: The Story of the American Southwest, before 1830*. 1930; reprint, Norman: University of Oklahoma Press, 1967.

———. *The Last Trek of the Indians*. Chicago: University of Chicago Press, 1946.

———. *Lore and Lure of Eastern Oklahoma*. Muskogee Chamber of Commerce, 1947.

———. *Pioneer Days in the Early Southwest*. 1926; reprint, Lincoln: University of Nebraska Press, 1994.

———, ed. *A Traveler in Indian Territory: The Journal of Ethan Allen Hitchcock, Late Major-General in the United States Army*. 1930; reprint, Norman: University of Oklahoma Press, 1996.

Foster, H. Thomas, II. With contributions by Mary Theresa Bonhage-Freund and Lisa O'Steen. *Archaeology of the Lower Muskogee Creek Indians, 1715-1836*. Tuscaloosa: University of Alabama Press, 2007.

———, ed. *The Collected Works of Benjamin Hawkins, 1796-1810*. Tuscaloosa: University of Alabama Press, 2003.

Fountain, Sarah, ed. *Authentic Voices: Arkansas Culture, 1541-1860*. Conway: University of Central Arkansas Press, 1986.

Frank, Andrew K. *Creeks and Southerners: Biculturalism on the Early American Frontier*. Lincoln: University of Nebraska Press, 2005.

———. "The Rise and Fall of William McIntosh: Authority and Identity on the Early American Frontier." *Georgia Historical Quarterly* 86, no. 1 (Spring 2002): 18-48.

Freehling, William W. *Prelude to Civil War: The Nullification Controversy in South Carolina, 1816-1836*. New York: Harper and Row, 1965.

Gallay, Alan. *The Indian Slave Trade: The Rise of the English Empire in the American South, 1670-1717*. New Haven CT: Yale University Press, 2002.

Gardner, James H. "One Hundred Years Ago in the Region of Tulsa." *Chronicles of Oklahoma* 11, no. 2 (June 1933): 765–85.

Garrison, Tim Alan. "Beyond *Worcester*: The Alabama Supreme Court and the Sovereignty of the Creek Nation." *Journal of the Early Republic* 19 (Fall 1999): 423–50.

———. *The Legal Ideology of Removal: The Southern Judiciary and the Sovereignty of Native American Nations*. Athens: University of Georgia Press, 2002.

Gatschet, Albert S. *A Migration Legend of the Creek Indians: Texts and Glossaries in Creek and Hitchiti, with a Linguistic, Historic, and Ethnographic Introduction and Commentary*. Vol. 2: *1888*. New York: Kraus Reprint, 1969.

Gerstäcker, Friedrich. *Wild Sports in the Far West: The narrative of a German Wanderer beyond the Mississippi, 1837–1843*. Edited by Edna L. Steeves and Harrison R. Steeves. 1854; reprint, Durham NC: Duke University Press, 1968.

Gibson, Arrell M. *The Chickasaws*. Norman: University of Oklahoma Press, 1971.

———. *The Kickapoos: Lords of the Middle Border*. Norman: University of Oklahoma Press, 1963.

Gray, Daniel S., ed. *Autauga County: The First Hundred Years, 1818–1918*. Prattville AL: Autauga County Prattville Public Library, 1972.

Grayson, G. W. *A Creek Warrior for the Confederacy: The Autobiography of Chief G. W. Grayson*. Edited by W. David Baird. Norman: University of Oklahoma Press, 1988.

Green, Michael D. *The Politics of Indian Removal: Creek Government and Society in Crisis*. Lincoln: University of Nebraska Press, 1982.

Gregg, Josiah. *Commerce of the Prairies*. Vol. 2. 1844; reprint, Philadelphia: J. B. Lippincott, 1962.

Gregory, Jack, and Rennard Strickland. *Sam Houston with the Cherokees, 1829–1833*. Austin: University of Texas Press, 1967.

Griffith, Benjamin W., Jr. *McIntosh and Weatherford, Creek Indian Leaders*. Tuscaloosa: University of Alabama Press, 1988.

Grose, B. Donald, "Edwin Forrest, *Metamora*, and the Indian Removal Act of 1830." *Theatre Journal* 37, no. 2 (May 1985): 181–91.

Gudmestad, Robert. *Steamboats and the Rise of the Cotton Kingdom*. Baton Rouge: Louisiana State University Press, 2011.

Haake, Claudia B. "Breaking the Bonds of People and Land." In *Removing Peoples: Forced Removal in the Modern World*, edited by Richard Bessel and Claudia B. Haake, 79–106. Oxford: Oxford University Press, 2009.

———. *The State, Removal and Indigenous Peoples in the United States and Mexico, 1620–2000*. New York: Routledge, 2007.

Hahn, Steven C. "The Cussita Migration Legend: History, Ideology, and the Politics of Mythmaking." In *Light on the Path: The Anthropology and History of the Southeastern Indians*, edited by Thomas J. Pluckhahn and Robbie Ethridge, 57–93. Tuscaloosa: University of Alabama Press, 2006.

———. *The Invention of the Creek Nation, 1670–1763*. Lincoln: University of Nebraska Press, 2004.

———. "'They Look upon the Yuchis as Their Vassals': An Early History of Yuchi-Creek Political Relations." In *Yuchi Indian Histories before the Removal Era*, edited by Jason Baird Jackson, 123–53. Lincoln: University of Nebraska Press, 2012.

Hall, Basil. *Travels in North America, in the Years 1827 and 1828*. Vol. 3. Edinburgh: Cadell, 1829.

Hall, Margaret Hunter. *The Aristocratic Journey: Being the Outspoken Letters of Mrs. Basil Hall Written during a Fourteen Months' Sojourn in America, 1827–1828*. New York: G. P. Putnam's Sons, 1931.

Hämäläinen, Pekka. *The Comanche Empire*. New Haven CT: Yale University Press, 2008.

Hamilton, Stanislaus Murray, ed. *The Writings of James Monroe, Including A Collection of His Public and Private Papers and Correspondence Now for the First Time Printed*. Vol. 7: 1824–1831. 1903; reprint, New York: AMS Press, 1969.

Hamilton, Thomas. *Men and Manners in America*. Vol. 2. Philadelphia: Carey, Lea, and Blanchard, 1833.

Harkey, Joseph H. "Some Adventures of Captain Simon Suggs: The Legacy of Johnson Jones Hooper." In *No Fairer Land: Studies in Southern Literature before 1900*, edited by J. Lasley Dameron and James W. Mathews, 200–210. Troy NY: Whitston, 1986.

Haveman, Christopher D. "'Last Evening I Saw the Sun Set for the Last Time': The 1832 Treaty of Washington and the Transfer of the Creeks' Alabama Land to White Ownership." *Native South* 5 (2012): 61–94.

———. "With Great Difficulty and Labour: The Emigration of the McIntosh Party of Creek Indians, 1827–1828." *Chronicles of Oklahoma* 85, no. 4 (Winter 2007–2008): 468–90.

Hayden, Robert M. "Imagined Communities and Real Victims: Self-Determination and Ethnic Cleansing in Yugoslavia." *American Ethnologist* 23, no. 4 (November 1996): 783–801.

Hietala, Thomas R. *Manifest Design: Anxious Aggrandizement in Late Jacksonian America*. Ithaca NY: Cornell University Press, 1985.

Hixson, Walter L. *American Settler Colonialism: A History*. Houndmills UK: Palgrave Macmillan, 2013.

Hodges, Bert. "Notes on the History of the Creek Nation and Some of Its Leaders." *Chronicles of Oklahoma* 43, no. 1 (Spring 1965): 9–18.

Hodgson, Adam. *Letters from North America, Written During a Tour in the United States and Canada*. Vol. 1. London: Hurst, Robinson, 1824.

Hoig, Stan. *Beyond the Frontier: Exploring the Indian Country*. Norman: University of Oklahoma Press, 1998.

———. *The Chouteaus: First Family of the Fur Trade.* Albuquerque: University of New Mexico Press, 2008.

———. *Tribal Wars of the Southern Plains.* Norman: University of Oklahoma Press, 1993.

Homans, Benjamin, ed. "Letter from Fort Gibson." In *The Military and Naval Magazine of the United States.* Vol. 3. Washington DC: Wm. Moore, 1834, 383–85.

Hook, Jonathan B. *The Alabama-Coushatta Indians.* College Station: Texas A&M University Press, 1997.

Hoole, W. Stanley. *Alias Simon Suggs: The Life and Times of Johnson Jones Hooper.* Tuscaloosa: University of Alabama Press, 1952.

———, ed. "Echoes From the 'Trail of Tears.'" 1837. *Alabama Review* 6, no. 2 (April 1953): 135–52.

———, ed. "Echoes From the 'Trail of Tears.'" 1837. Part 2. *Alabama Review* 6, no. 3 (July 1953): 222–32.

Hooper, Johnson Jones. *Adventures of Captain Simon Suggs, Late of the Tallapoosa Volunteers.* Introduction by Manly Wade Wellman, ix–xxiv. Chapel Hill: University of North Carolina Press, 1969.

———. *Adventures of Captain Simon Suggs, Late of the Tallapoosa Volunteers; Together with "Taking the Census" and Other Alabama Sketches.* Introduction by Johanna Nicol Shields, vii–lxix. Tuscaloosa: University of Alabama Press, 1993.

———. *Some Adventures of Captain Simon Suggs, Late of the Tallapoosa Volunteers; Together with "Taking the Census," and Other Alabama Sketches. By a Country Editor. With a Portrait from Life, and Other Illustrations, by Darley.* Philadelphia: Carey and Hart, 1845.

Hopkins, Robert. "Simon Suggs: A Burlesque Campaign Biography." *American Quarterly* 15, no. 3 (Autumn 1963): 459–63.

Horsman, Reginald. "The Indian Policy of an 'Empire for Liberty.'" In *Native Americans and the Early Republic,* edited by Frederick E. Hoxie, Ronald Hoffman, and Peter J. Albert, 37–61. Charlottesville: University Press of Virginia, 1999.

———. *Josiah Nott of Mobile: Southerner, Physician, and Racial Theorist.* Baton Rouge: Louisiana State University Press, 1987.

———. *The Origins of Indian Removal, 1815-1824.* East Lansing: Michigan State University Press, 1970.

Howard, Robert M. *Reminiscences.* Columbus GA: Gilbert, 1912.

Hryniewicki, Richard J. "The Creek Treaty of November 15, 1827." *Georgia Historical Quarterly* 52, no. 1 (March 1968): 1–15.

———. "The Creek Treaty of Washington, 1826." *Georgia Historical Quarterly* 48, no.4 (December 1964): 425–41.

Hudson, Angela Pulley. *Creek Paths and Federal Roads: Indians, Settlers, and Slaves and the Making of the American South.* Chapel Hill: University of North Carolina Press, 2010.

Hudson, Charles M. *The Southeastern Indians*. Knoxville: University of Tennessee Press, 1976.

Hurt, Douglas A. "Defining American Homelands: A Creek Nation Example, 1828–1907." *Journal of Cultural Geography* 21, no. 1 (Fall/Winter 2003): 19–43.

Hurt, R. Douglas. *The Indian Frontier, 1763–1846*. Albuquerque: University of New Mexico Press, 2002.

Hyde, George E. *The Pawnee Indians*. Norman: University of Oklahoma Press, 1974.

Irving, Pierre M. *The Life and Letters of Washington Irving*. Vol. 2. Philadelphia: Lippincott, 1870.

Irving, Washington. "The Conspiracy of Neamathla: An Authentic Sketch." In *Reviews and Miscellanies*. Knickerbocker Edition. New York: G. P. Putnam's Sons, 1897.

———. *The Journals of Washington Irving (Hitherto Unpublished)*. Vol. 3. Edited by William P. Trent and George S. Hellman. New York: Haskell House, 1970.

———. *A Tour on the Prairies*. Edited by John Francis McDermott. 1835; reprint, Norman: University of Oklahoma Press, 1956.

Irwin, James H. "Water Resources." In *Geography of Oklahoma*, edited by John W. Morris, 25–38. Oklahoma City: Oklahoma Historical Society, 1977.

Jackson, Jason Baird. *Yuchi Ceremonial Life: Performance, Meaning, and Tradition in a Contemporary American Indian Community*. Lincoln: University of Nebraska Press, 2003.

Jahoda, Gloria. *The Trail of Tears*. New York: Holt, Rinehart and Winston, 1975.

James, Marquis. *The Life of Andrew Jackson*. Indianapolis IN: Bobbs-Merrill, 1938.

———. *The Raven: A Biography of Sam Houston*. New York: Blue Ribbon Books, 1929.

James, Thomas. *Three Years among the Indians and Mexicans*. Edited by Milo Milton Quaife. New York: Citadel, 1966.

Jones, Grove B., Cornelius Van Duyne, Ewing Scott, and H. W. Hawker. *Soil Survey of Muskogee County, Oklahoma*. Washington DC: Government Printing Office, 1915.

Kakel, Carroll P., III. *The American West and the Nazi East: A Comparative and Interpretive Perspective*. Houndmills UK: Palgrave Macmillan, 2011.

Kappler, Charles, J., ed. *Indian Affairs: Laws and Treaties*. Vol. 2: *Treaties*. Washington DC: Government Printing Office, 1904.

Keller, Christian B. "Philanthropy Betrayed: Thomas Jefferson, the Louisiana Purchase, and the Origins of Federal Indian Removal Policy." *Proceedings of the American Philosophical Society* 144, no. 1 (March 2000): 39–66.

Kidwell, Clara Sue. "The Choctaw Struggle for Land and Identity in Mississippi, 1830–1918." In *After Removal: The Choctaw in Mississippi*, edited by Samuel J. Wells and Roseanna Tubby, 64–93. Jackson: University Press of Mississippi, 1986.

Klopfenstein, Carl G. "The Removal of the Wyandots from Ohio." *Ohio Historical Quarterly* 66, no. 2 (April 1957): 119–36.

Klunder, Willard Carl. *Lewis Cass and the Politics of Moderation*. Kent OH: Kent State University Press, 1996.

Lancaster, Jane F. *Removal Aftershock: The Seminoles' Struggles to Survive in the West, 1836–1866.* Knoxville: University of Tennessee Press, 1994.

Lang, John D., and Samuel Taylor. *Report of a Visit to Some of the Tribes of Indians, Located West of the Mississippi River.* New York: M. Day, 1843.

Latner, Richard B. *The Presidency of Andrew Jackson: White House Politics 1829–1837.* Athens: University of Georgia Press, 1979.

Latrobe, Charles Joseph. *The Rambler in North America, MDCCCXXXII–MDCCCXXXIII.* Vol. 1. New York: Harper and Brothers, 1835.

Laumer, Frank. *Dade's Last Command.* Gainesville: University Press of Florida, 1995.

———. *Massacre!* Gainesville: University of Florida Press, 1968.

La Vere, David. *Contrary Neighbors: Southern Plains and Removed Indians in Indian Territory.* Norman: University of Oklahoma Press, 2000.

Lepore, Jill. *The Name of War: King Philip's War and the Origins of American Identity.* New York: Knopf, 1998; reprint, New York: Vintage, 1999.

Lester, C. Edwards. *The Life of Sam Houston (The only Authentic Memoir of him ever published).* New York: J. C. Derby, 1855.

Levasseur, Auguste. *Lafayette in America in 1824 and 1825; or, Journal of a Voyage to the United States*, Vol. 2. Philadelphia: Carey and Lea, 1829; reprint, New York: Research Reprints, 1970.

Lewis, David, Jr., and Ann T. Jordan, eds., *Creek Indian Medicine Ways: The Enduring Power of Mvskoke Religion.* Albuquerque: University of New Mexico Press, 2002.

Littlefield, Daniel F., Jr. *Africans and Creeks: From the Colonial Period to the Civil War.* Westport CT: Greenwood, 1979.

Litton, Gaston L. "The Journal of a Party of Emigrating Creek Indians, 1835–1836." *Journal of Southern History* 7, no. 2 (May 1941): 225–42.

———. "The Negotiations Leading to the Chickasaw-Choctaw Agreement, January 17, 1837." *Chronicles of Oklahoma* 17, no. 4 (December 1939): 417–27.

Lloyd, John Uri. "Citrullus Colocynthis." *Western Druggist* (June 1898): 3–11.

Longnecker, Julie Ward. "A Road Divided: From Memphis to Little Rock through the Great Mississippi Swamp." *Arkansas Historical Quarterly* 44 (Autumn 1985): 203–19.

Loomis, Augustus Ward. *Scenes in the Indian Country.* Philadelphia: Presbyterian Board of Publication, 1859.

Lumpkin, Wilson. *The Removal of the Cherokee Indians from Georgia. Including His Speeches in the United States Congress on the Indian Question, as Representative and Senator of Georgia; His Official Correspondence on the Removal of the Cherokees during his two terms as Governor of Georgia, and later as United States Commissioner to the Cherokees, 1827–1841, Together with a Sketch of His Life and Conduct while holding many Public Offices under the Government of Georgia and the United States, prior to 1827, and after 1841.* Vol. 1. Wormsloe GA: Priv. print.; reprint, New York: Dodd, Mead, 1907.

Maddox, Lucy. *Removals: Nineteenth-Century American Literature and the Politics of Indian Affairs*. New York: Oxford University Press, 1991.
Madley, Benjamin, "Reexamining the American Genocide Debate: Meaning, Historiography, and New Methods." *American Historical Review* 120, no. 1 (February 2015): 98–139.
Magliocca, Gerard N. *Andrew Jackson and the Constitution: The Rise and Fall of Generational Regimes*. Lawrence: University Press of Kansas, 2007.
Mahon, John K. *History of the Second Seminole War, 1835–1842*. Gainesville: University of Florida Press, 1967.
———. "Two Seminole Treaties: Payne's Landing, 1832, and Ft. Gibson, 1833." *Florida Historical Quarterly* 41, no. 1 (July 1962): 1–21.
———. *The War of 1812*. Gainesville: University of Florida Press, 1972.
Mann, Michael. *The Dark Side of Democracy: Explaining Ethnic Cleansing*. Cambridge: Cambridge University Press, 2005.
———. "The Dark Side of Democracy: The Modern Tradition of Ethnic and Political Cleansing." *New Left Review* 235 (1999): 18–45.
Manzo, Joseph T., "Emigrant Indian Objections to Kansas Residence." *Kansas History* 4, no. 4 (Winter 1981): 246–54.
Martin, Joel W. *Sacred Revolt: The Muskogee's Struggle for a New World*. Boston: Beacon, 1991.
Martin, John H., ed. *Columbus, Geo., From Its Selection as a "Trading Town" in 1827, to Its Partial Destruction by Wilson's Raid, in 1865. History—Incident—Personality. Part 1—1827 to 1846*. 1874; reprint, Easley SC: Georgia Genealogical Reprints, 1972.
Martineau, Harriet, *Society in America*. Vol. 1. New York: Saunders and Otley, 1837.
Masur, Louis P. *1831: Year of Eclipse*. New York: Hill and Wang, 2001.
Mathews, John Joseph. *The Osages: Children of the Middle Waters*. Norman: University of Oklahoma Press, 1961.
McBride, Lela J. *Opothleyaholo and the Loyal Muskogee: Their Flight to Kansas in the Civil War*. Jefferson NC: McFarland, 2000.
McCall, George A. *Letters From the Frontiers*. 1868; reprint, Gainesville: University Presses of Florida Press, 1974.
McClurken, James M. "Ottawa Adaptive Strategies to Indian Removal." *Michigan Historical Review* 12, no. 1 (Spring 1986): 29–55.
McCoy, Isaac. *The Annual Register of Indian Affairs, in the Western (or Indian) Territory 1835–1838*. Springfield MO: Particular Baptist Press, 2000.
———. *History of Baptist Indian Missions: Embracing Remarks on the Former and Present Condition of the Aboriginal Tribes; Their Settlement Within the Indian Territory, and Their Future Prospects*. Washington DC: William M. Morrison, 1840.
———. *Remarks on the Practicability of Indian Reform, Embracing their Colonization*. New York: Gray and Bunce, 1829.

McKenney, Thomas L. *Memoirs, Official and Personal; with Sketches of Travels Among the Northern and Southern Indians; Embracing A War Excursion, and Descriptions of Scenes Along the Western Borders.* Vol. 1. New York: Paine and Burgess, 1846.

McKenney, Thomas L., and James Hall. *History of the Indian Tribes of North America, With Biographical Sketches and Anecdotes of the Principal Chiefs. Embellished with One Hundred and Twenty Portraits, From the Indian Gallery in the Department of War, at Washington.* Vols. 1–2. Philadelphia: Daniel Rice and James G. Clark, 1842.

McLaughlin, Andrew C. *Lewis Cass.* Boston: Houghton, Mifflin, 1891.

McLoughlin, William G. "Red, White, and Black in the Antebellum South." *Baptist History and Heritage* 7, no. 2 (April 1972): 69–75.

McReynolds, Edwin C. *The Seminoles.* Norman: University of Oklahoma Press, 1957.

Meacham, Jon. *American Lion: Andrew Jackson in the White House.* New York: Random House, 2008.

Merrill, William L. "The Beloved Tree: *Ilex vomitoria* among the Indians of the Southeast and Adjacent Regions." In *Black Drink: A Native American Tea,* edited by Charles M. Hudson, 40–82. Athens: University of Georgia Press, 1979.

Meserve, John Bartlett. "Chief Opothleyahola." *Chronicles of Oklahoma* 9, no. 4 (December 1931): 439–53.

———. "Chief Samuel Checote, with Sketches of Chiefs Locher Harjo and Ward Coachman." *Chronicles of Oklahoma* 16, no. 4 (December 1938): 401–9.

———. "The MacIntoshes." *Chronicles of Oklahoma* 10, no. 3 (September 1932): 166–84.

———. "The Perrymans." *Chronicles of Oklahoma* 15, no. 2 (June 1937): 310–25.

Missall, John, and Mary Lou Missall. *The Seminole Wars: America's Longest Indian Conflict.* Gainesville: University Press of Florida, 2004.

Monroe, James. "To Congress—Removal of Indians, 30 March 1824." In *The Writings of James Monroe, Including A Collection of His Public and Private Papers and Correspondence Now for the First Time Printed.* Vol. 7: 1824–1831, edited by Stanislaus Murray Hamilton, 14–17. 1903; reprint, New York: AMS Press, 1969.

Moore, F. M. *A Brief History of the Missionary Work In the Indian Territory of the Indian Mission Conference, Methodist Episcopal Church South, And an Appendix Containing Personal Sketches of Many of the Early Workers in This Field.* Muskogee: I.T., Phoenix Printing Co., 1899.

Moore, Stephen L. *Savage Frontier.* Vol. 2: 1838–1839: *Rangers, Riflemen, and Indian Wars in Texas.* Denton: University of North Texas Press, 2006.

Motte, Jacob Rhett. *Journey into Wilderness: An Army Surgeon's Account of Life in Camp and Field during the Creek and Seminole Wars, 1836–1838.* Edited by James F. Sunderman. Gainesville: University of Florida Press, 1953.

Mulroy, Kevin. *Freedom on the Border: The Seminole Maroons in Florida, the Indian Territory, Coahuila, and Texas*. Lubbock: Texas Tech University Press, 1993.

———. *The Seminole Freedmen: A History*. Norman: University of Oklahoma Press, 2007.

Naimark, Norman M. *Fires of Hatred: Ethnic Cleansing in Twentieth-Century Europe*. Cambridge MA: Harvard University Press, 2001.

Nakcokv Esyvhiketv: Muskogee Hymns. Westminister Press, n.d.

Nance, Joseph Milton. *Attack and Counterattack: The Texas-Mexican Frontier, 1842*. Austin: University of Texas Press, 1964.

Nester, William. *The Age of Jackson and the Art of American Power, 1815–1848*. Washington DC: Potomac Books, 2013.

Neville, Bert. *Directory of River Packets in the Mobile-Alabama-Warrior-Tombigbee-Trades 1818–1932*. Selma al: Selma Printing, 1967.

———. *Directory of Tennessee River Steamboats (1821–1928)*. Selma al: Coffee Printing, 1963.

Nevins, Allan, ed. *The Diary of John Quincy Adams 1794–1845: American Political, Social and Intellectual Life from Washington to Polk*. New York: Longmans, Green, 1928.

Nott, Josiah C. *The Physical History of the Jewish Race*. Charleston SC: Steam-Power Press of Walker and James, 1850.

Nuermberger, Ruth Ketring. *The Clays of Alabama: A Planter-Lawyer-Politician Family*. Lexington: University of Kentucky Press, 1958.

Nuttall, Thomas. *A Journal of Travels into the Arkansa Territory, During the Year 1819. With Occasional Observations on the Manners of the Aborigines*. Philadelphia: T. H. Palmer, 1821.

O'Beirne, H. F., and E. S. O'Beirne. *The Indian Territory: Its Chiefs, Legislators and Leading Men*. St. Louis: C. B. Woodward, 1892.

O'Brien, Shelia Ruzycki. "Writing with a Forked Pen: Racial Dynamics and Johnson Jones Hooper's Twin Tale of Swindling Indians." *American Studies* 35, no. 2 (Fall 1994): 95–113.

Ogg, Frederic Austin. *The Reign of Andrew Jackson: A Chronicle of the Frontier in Politics*. New Haven CT: Yale University Press, 1919.

Oliphant, J. Orin, ed. *Through the South and the West with Jeremiah Evarts in 1826*. Lewisburg PA: Bucknell University Press, 1956.

Opler, Morris Edward. "The Creek 'Town' and the Problem of Creek Indian Political Reorganization." In *Human Problems in Technological Change: A Casebook*, edited by Edward H. Spicer, 165–80. New York: Russell Sage, 1952.

Owens, Harry P. *Steamboats and the Cotton Economy: River Trade in the Yazoo-Mississippi Delta*. Jackson: University Press of Mississippi, 1990.

Owsley, Frank L., Jr. "Francis Scott Key's Mission to Alabama in 1833." *Alabama Review* 23, no. 3 (July 1970): 181–92.

Paige, Amanda L., Fuller L. Bumpers, and Daniel F. Littlefield Jr. *Chickasaw Removal.* Ada OK: Chickasaw, 2010.

Paredes, J. Anthony. "Back from Disappearance: The Alabama Creek Indian Community." In *Southeastern Indians since the Removal Era*, edited by Walter L. Williams, 123–41. Athens: University of Georgia Press, 1979.

Paredes, J. Anthony, and Kenneth J. Plante. "A Reëxamination of Creek Indian Population Trends: 1738–1832." *American Indian Culture and Research Journal* 6, no. 4 (1983): 3–28.

Parsons, Lynn Hudson. "'A Perpetual Harrow upon My Feelings': John Quincy Adams and the American Indian." *New England Quarterly* 46, no. 3 (September 1973): 339–79.

Pate, James P., ed. *The Reminiscences of George Strother Gaines: Pioneer and Statesman of Early Alabama and Mississippi, 1805–1843.* Tuscaloosa: University of Alabama Press, 1998.

Payne, John Howard. "The Green-Corn Dance." *Continental Monthly* (January 1862): 17–29.

Pearce, Roy Harvey. *The Savages of America: A Study of the Indian and the Idea of Civilization.* Baltimore: Johns Hopkins University Press, 1953.

Peck, Solomon, "History of the Missions of the Baptist General Convention." In *History of American Missions to the Heathen, From Their Commencement to the Present Time*, edited by Joseph J. Kwiat. 1840; reprint, New York: Johnson Reprint, 1970.

Perdue, Theda. *Cherokee Women: Gender and Culture Change, 1700–1835.* Lincoln: University of Nebraska Press, 1998.

———. *"Mixed Blood" Indians: Racial Construction in the Early South.* Athens: University of Georgia Press, 2003.

Perdue, Theda, and Michael D. Green. *The Cherokee Nation and the Trail of Tears.* New York: Viking, 2007.

Peters, Richard, ed. *The Public Statutes at Large of the United States of America.* Vol. 2. Boston: Charles C. Little and James Brown, 1845.

———. *The Public Statutes at Large of the United States of America.* Vol. 5. Boston: Little, Brown, 1856.

Petrovic, Drazen. "Ethnic Cleansing—An Attempt at Methodology." *European Journal of International Law* 5, no. 1 (1994): 1–19.

Pickett, Albert James. "The Death of McIntosh, 1825." *Arrow Points* 10, no. 2 (February 1925): 31–32.

———. *History of Alabama and Incidentally of Georgia and Mississippi, From the Earliest Period.* 1851; reprint, Birmingham AL: Birmingham Book and Magazine, 1962.

Piker, Joshua. *Okfuskee: A Creek Indian Town in Colonial America.* Cambridge MA: Harvard University Press, 2004.

Pilling, James Constantine, ed. *Bibliography of the Muskhogean Languages.* Washington DC: Government Printing Office, 1889.

Porter, Kenneth Wiggins. "The Hawkins' Negroes Go to Mexico: A Footnote from Tradition." *Chronicles of Oklahoma* 24, no. 1 (1946): 55–59.
Posey, Walter Brownlow. *Frontier Mission: A History of Religion West of the Southern Appalachians to 1861*. Lexington: University of Kentucky Press, 1966.
Power, Tyrone. *Impressions of America During the Years 1833, 1834, and 1835*. Vol. 2. London: Richard Bentley, 1836.
Preece, Jennifer Jackson. "Ethnic Cleansing as an Instrument of Nation-State Creation: Changing State Practices and Evolving Legal Norms." *Human Rights Quarterly* 20, no. 4 (November 1998): 817–42.
Prucha, Francis Paul. *American Indian Policy in the Formative Years: The Indian Trade and Intercourse Acts, 1790–1834*. Cambridge MA: Harvard University Press, 1962.
———. "Andrew Jackson's Indian Policy: A Reassessment," *Journal of American History* 56, no. 3 (December 1969): 527–39.
———. *The Great Father: The United States Government and the American Indians*. Vol. 1. Lincoln: University of Nebraska Press, 1984.
———. *Indian Policy in the United States: Historical Essays*. Lincoln: University of Nebraska Press, 1981.
———. *Lewis Cass and American Indian Policy*. Detroit: Wayne State University Press, 1967.
Prucha, Francis Paul, and Donald F. Carmony, eds. "A Memorandum of Lewis Cass: Concerning a System for the Regulation of Indian Affairs." *Wisconsin Magazine of History* 52, no. 1 (Autumn 1968): 35–50.
Ratcliffe, Donald J. "The Nullification Crisis, Southern Discontents, and the American Political Process." *American Nineteenth Century History* 1, no. 2 (Summer 2000): 1–30.
Read, William A. *Indian Place Names in Alabama*. 1937; reprint, Tuscaloosa: University of Alabama Press, 1984.
Reid, John, and John Henry Eaton. *The Life of Andrew Jackson*. Philadelphia, 1817; reprint, Tuscaloosa: University of Alabama Press, 1974.
Remini, Robert V. *The Age of Jackson*. Columbia: University of South Carolina Press, 1972.
———. *Andrew Jackson*. 1966; reprint, New York: Harper and Row, 1969.
———. *Andrew Jackson and His Indian Wars*. New York: Viking, 2001.
———. *Andrew Jackson and the Course of American Democracy, 1833–1845*. Vol. 3. New York: Harper and Row, 1984.
———. *Andrew Jackson and the Course of American Freedom, 1822–1832*. Vol. 2. New York: Harper and Row, 1981.
———. *The Election of Andrew Jackson*. Philadelphia: J. B. Lippincott, 1963.
———. *The Jacksonian Era*. Arlington Heights IL: Harlan Davidson, 1989.
———. *The Legacy of Andrew Jackson: Essays on Democracy, Indian Removal, and Slavery*. Baton Rouge: Louisiana State University Press, 1988.

———. *The Life of Andrew Jackson*. New York: Penguin, 1990.

———. *The Revolutionary Age of Andrew Jackson*. New York: Harper and Row, 1976, 105–20.

Rhodes, Richard. *John James Audubon: The Making of an American*. New York: Knopf, 2004.

Richards, E. G. "Reminiscenses of the Early Days in Chambers County." *Alabama Historical Quarterly* 4, no. 3 (Fall 1942): 417–45.

Rister, Carl Coke, and Bryan W. Lovelace. "A Diary Account of a Creek Boundary Survey, 1850." *Chronicles of Oklahoma* 27, no. 3 (Autumn 1949): 268–302.

Rogin, Michael Paul. *Fathers and Children: Andrew Jackson and the Subjugation of the American Indian*. New York: Knopf, 1975.

Rollings, Willard H. *The Osage: An Ethnohistorical Study of Hegemony on the Prairie-Plains*. Columbia: University of Missouri Press, 1992.

Romans, Bernard. *A Concise Natural History of East and West Florida*. Edited by Kathryn E. Holland Braund. Tuscaloosa: University of Alabama Press, 1999.

Ronda, James P. "'We Have A Country': Race, Geography, and the Invention of Indian Territory." *Journal of the Early Republic*, 19 (Winter 1999): 739–55.

Ross, Margaret Smith, ed. "Three Letters of Cephas Washburn." *Arkansas Historical Quarterly* 16, no. 2 (Summer 1957): 174–91.

Roth, George. "Federal Tribal Recognition in the South." In *Anthropologists and Indians in the New South*, edited by Rachel A. Bonney and J. Anthony Paredes, 49–70. Tuscaloosa: University of Alabama Press, 2001.

Roustio, Edward R., ed. *Early Indian Missions: As Reflected in the Unpublished Manuscripts of Isaac McCoy*. Springfield MO: Particular Baptist Press, 2000.

Royall, Anne. *Mrs. Royall's Southern Tour; or, Second Series of the Black Book*. Vol. 2. Washington DC, 1830.

Rucker, Brian R. "West Florida's Creek Indian Crisis of 1837." *Florida Historical Quarterly* 69, no. 3 (January 1991): 315–34.

Sattler, Richard A. "Cowboys and Indians: Creek and Seminole Stock Raising, 1700–1900." *American Indian Culture and Research Journal* 22, no. 3 (1998): 79–99.

Satz, Ronald N. *American Indian Policy in the Jacksonian Era*. Lincoln: University of Nebraska Press, 1975.

———. "Rhetoric Versus Reality: The Indian Policy of Andrew Jackson." In *Cherokee Removal: Before and After*, edited by William L. Anderson, 29–54. Athens: University of Georgia Press, 1991.

Saunders, Robert, Jr. *John Archibald Campbell, Southern Moderate, 1811–1889*. Tuscaloosa: University of Alabama Press, 1997.

Saunt, Claudio. *Black, White, and Indian: Race and the Unmaking of an American Family*. New York: Oxford University Press, 2005.

———. *A New Order of Things: Property, Power, and the Transformation of the Creek Indians, 1733–1816*. Cambridge: Cambridge University Press, 1999.

Schultz White, Christine, and Benton R. White. *Now the Wolf Has Come: The Creek Nation in the Civil War.* College Station: Texas A&M University Press, 1996.

Secunda, W. Ben. "To Cede or Seed? Risk and Identity among the Woodland Potawatomi during the Removal Period." *Midcontinental Journal of Archaeology* 31, no. 1 (Spring 2006): 57–88.

Sheehan, Bernard W. *Seeds of Extinction: Jeffersonian Philanthropy and the American Indian.* Chapel Hill: University of North Carolina Press, 1973.

Shields, Johanna Nicol. "A Sadder Simon Suggs: Freedom and Slavery in the Humor of Johnson Hooper." *Journal of Southern History* 56, no. 4 (November 1990): 641–64.

———. "Writers in the Old Southwest and the Commercialization of American Letters." *Journal of the Early Republic* 27, no. 3 (Fall 2007): 471–505.

Sholes, A. E. *Directory of the Taxing District of Memphis, Shelby County, Tennessee.* Vol. 10. Memphis: Rogers & Co., 1883.

Shuck-Hall, Sheri Marie. *Journey to the West: The Alabama and Coushatta Indians.* Norman: University of Oklahoma Press, 2008.

Silver, James W. *Edmund Pendleton Gaines: Frontier General.* Baton Rouge: Louisiana State University Press, 1949.

Skogen, Larry C. *Indian Depredation Claims, 1790–1920.* Norman: University of Oklahoma Press, 1996.

Smith, Dwight L., ed. "The Attempted Potawatomi Emigration of 1839." *Indiana Magazine of History* 45, no. 1 (March 1949): 51–80.

———, ed. "A Continuation of the Journal of an Emigrating Party of Potawatomi Indians, 1838, and Ten William Polke Manuscripts." *Indiana Magazine of History* 44, no. 4 (December 1948): 393–408.

———, ed. "Jacob Hull's Detachment of the Potawatomi Emigration of 1838." *Indiana Magazine of History* 45, no. 3 (September 1949): 285–88.

Smith, Howard Winston. "An Annotated Edition of Hooper's *Some Adventures of Captain Simon Suggs.*" PhD dissertation, Vanderbilt University, 1965.

———. "*Simon Suggs* and the Satiric Tradition." In "Essays in Honor of Richebourg Gaillard McWilliams," ed. Howard Creed. *Birmingham-Southern College Bulletin* 63, no. 2 (May 1970): 49–56.

Smith, Sol. *Theatrical Management in the West and South for Thirty Years. Interspersed With Anecdotal Sketches.* New York: Harper and Brothers, 1868.

Smith, W. L. G. *Fifty Years of Public Life: The Life and Times of Lewis Cass.* New York: Derby and Jackson, 1856.

Snyder, Christina. "Conquered Enemies, Adopted Kin, and Owned People: The Creek Indians and Their Captives." *Journal of Southern History* 73, no. 2 (May 2007): 255–88.

———. *Slavery in Indian Country: The Changing Face of Captivity in Early America.* Cambridge MA: Harvard University Press, 2010.

Somers, Paul, Jr. *Johnson J. Hooper.* Boston: Twayne, 1984.

Southerland, Henry DeLeon Jr., and Jerry Elijah Brown. *The Federal Road through Georgia, the Creek Nation, and Alabama, 1806–1836.* Tuscaloosa: University of Alabama Press, 1989.

Sparks, W. H. *The Memories of Fifty Years: Containing Brief Biographical Notices of Distinguished Americans, and Anecdotes of Remarkable Men; Interspersed with Scenes and Incidents Occurring During a Long Life of Observation Chiefly Spent in the Southwest.* Philadelphia: Claxton, Remsen and Haffelfinger, 1872.

Spaulding, George F., ed. *On the Western Tour with Washington Irving: The Journal and Letters of Count de Pourtalès.* Norman: University of Oklahoma Press, 1968.

Speck, Frank G. *The Creek Indians of Taskigi Town.* New York: Kraus Reprint, 1964.

——. *Ethnology of the Yuchi Indians.* 1909; reprint, Lincoln; University of Nebraska Press, 2004.

Sprague, John T. *The Origin, Progress, and Conclusion of the Florida War.* 1848; reprint, Gainesville: University of Florida Press, 1964.

Stahl, Carmine, and Ria McElvaney. *Trees of Texas: An Easy Guide to Leaf Identification.* College Station: Texas A&M University Press, 2003.

Stanley, John Mix. *Portraits of North American Indians, With Sketches of Scenery, Etc.* Washington DC: Smithsonian Institution, 1852.

St. Jean, Wendy. *Remaining Chickasaw in Indian Territory, 1830s–1907.* Tuscaloosa: University of Alabama Press, 2011.

Stuart, John. *Three Years in North America.* Vol. 2. Edinburgh: Robert Cadell, 1833.

Swanton, John. *Creek Religion and Medicine.* Lincoln: University of Nebraska Press, 2000.

——. *Early History of the Creek Indians and Their Neighbors.* Washington DC: Government Printing Office, 1922.

——. "Religious Beliefs and Medicinal Practices of the Creek Indians." In *Forty-Second Annual Report of the Bureau of American Ethnology.* Washington DC: Government Printing Office, 1928.

Takaki, Ronald T. *Iron Cages: Race and Culture in Nineteenth-Century America.* New York: Knopf, 1979.

Thornton, Russell. *American Indian Holocaust and Survival: A Population History since 1492.* Norman: University of Oklahoma Press, 1987.

——. "Cherokee Population Losses during the Trail of Tears: A New Perspective and a New Estimate." *Ethnohistory* 31, no. 4 (Autumn 1984): 289–300.

——. *The Cherokees: A Population History.* Lincoln: University of Nebraska Press, 1990.

——. "The Demography of the Trail of Tears Period: A New Estimate of Cherokee Population Losses." In *Cherokee Removal: Before and After*, edited by William L. Anderson, 75–95. Athens: University of Georgia Press, 1991.

Tiro, Karim M. *The People of the Standing Stone: The Oneida Nation from the Revolution through the Era of Removal.* Amherst: University of Massachusetts Press, 2011.

Tomer, John S., and Michael J. Brodhead. *A Naturalist in Indian Territory: The Journals of S. W. Woodhouse, 1849–1850*. Norman: University of Oklahoma Press, 1992.

Trautmann, Frederic. "Alabama through a German's Eyes: The Travels of Clara von Gerstner, 1839." *Alabama Review* 36, no. 2 (April 1983): 129–42.

Trennert, Robert A. "The Business of Indian Removal: Deporting the Potawatomi from Wisconsin, 1851." *Wisconsin Magazine of History* 63, no. 1 (Autumn 1979): 36–50.

Tyler, Jack D., and Wendy J. Anderson. "Historical Accounts of Several Large Mammals in Oklahoma." *Proceedings of the Oklahoma Academy of Science* 70 (1990): 51–55.

Unrau, William E. *The Rise and Fall of Indian Country, 1825–1855*. Lawrence: University Press of Kansas, 2007.

U.S. Congress. House Document 25. *Letter from the Secretary of War, Transmitting The Correspondence between that Department and the Executive of Georgia, relative to depredations committed by the Creek Indians on the frontier inhabitants of that State*. 21st Congress, 1st Session, 1830, Serial Set 196.

———. House Document 46. *Message from the President of the United States, Transmitting The Proceedings of the Court of Inquiry in the case of Brevet Brigadier General Wool*. 25th Congress, 1st Session, 1837, Serial Set 311.

———. House Document 74. *Letter from the Secretary of War, Transmitting the Information required by a resolution of the House of Representatives, of the 15th inst. In Relation to the Number of Creek Indians Which Have Removed West of the Mississippi, And the expense attending the same*. 20th Congress, 1st Session, 1828, Serial Set 171.

———. House Document 284. *Letter from the Secretary of War, Transmitting The information required by a resolution of the House of Representatives of the 16th January last, In Relation to an Examination of the Muscle Shoals in Tennessee River, with a View to Removing the Obstructions to the Navigation thereof, and the Construction of a Canal Around the Same*. 20th Congress, 1st Session, 1828, Serial Set 175.

———. House Document 434. *Letter from the Secretary of War, Upon the Subject of a Hostile disposition upon the part of the Indians on the Western Frontier*. 25th Congress, 2nd Session, 1838, Serial Set 331.

———. House Document 452. *Message from the President of the United States, Transmitting Information in relation to Alleged Frauds on the Creek Indians in the Sale of their Reservations*. 25th Congress, 2nd session, 1838, Serial Set 331.

———. House Executive Document 66. *Letter from the Acting Secretary of War, Transmitting, In pursuance of a resolution of the House of Representatives of the 13th of March last, a report from the Commissioner of Indian Affairs, relative to the Creek Indian reservations under the treaty of 1832*. 30th Congress, 1st session, 1848, Serial Set 521.

———. House Executive Document 104. *Letter from the Secretary of War, Transmitting Reports of Captains Sitgreaves and Woodruff of the survey of the Creek Indian boundary line.* 35th Congress, 1st Session, 1858, Serial Set 958.

———. House Report 87. *Remove Indians Westward.* 20th Congress, 2nd Session, 1829, Serial Set 190.

———. House Report 98. *Report of the Select Committee of the House of Representatives, To Which Were Referred The Messages of the President U.S. Of the 5th and 8th February, and 2d March, 1827, With Accompanying Documents and A Report and Resolutions of the Legislature of Georgia.* 19th Congress, 2nd Session, 1827, Serial Set 161.

———. House Report 256. *Road—Memphis to Tuscumbia.* 20th Congress, 1st Session, 1828, Serial Set 179.

———. House Report 310. *The Creek Orphan Fund.* 47th Congress, 1st Session, 1882, Serial Set 2065.

———. House Report 826. *Creek Nation of Indians.* 30th Congress, 1st Session, 1848, Serial Set 526.

———. Senate Document 180. *Documents Relating To the Sale of Creek Reservations, under the Treaty of March 24, 1832.* 24th Congress, 2nd Session, 1837, Serial Set 298.

———. Senate Document 379. *Letter from the Secretary of War, in reply to the resolution of the House of Representatives of the 24th ultimo, relative to the plan proposed for the defense of the western frontier; also, what tribes of Indians inhabit the country immediately west of Arkansas and Missouri,* 13 April 1840. 26th Congress, 1st Session, Serial Set 359.

———. Senate Document 512. *Correspondence on the Subject of the Emigration of Indians, Between the 30th November, 1831, and 27th December, 1833, With Abstracts of Expenditures By Disbursing Agents, in the Removal and Subsistence of Indians, &c. &c.* 23rd Congress, 2nd Session, 1834–35, Vols. 1–5, Serial Sets 244–48.

Valliere, Kenneth L. "The Creek War of 1836: A Military History." *Chronicles of Oklahoma* 57, no. 4 (1979–80): 463–85.

Van Deusen, Glyndon G. *The Jacksonian Era, 1828–1848.* 1959; reprint, New York: Harper and Row, 1966.

———. *The Rise and Decline of Jacksonian Democracy.* New York: Van Nostrand Reinhold, 1970.

VanDevelder, Paul. *Savages and Scoundrels: The Untold Story of America's Road to Empire through Indian Territory.* New Haven CT: Yale University Press, 2009.

Veracini, Lorenzo. *Settler Colonialism: A Theoretical Overview.* Houndmills UK: Palgrave Macmillan, 2010.

Viola, Herman J. *Thomas L. McKenney: Architect of America's Early Indian Policy, 1816–1830.* Chicago: Sage Books, 1974.

von Gerstner, Franz Anton Ritter. *Early American Railroads: Franz Anton Ritter von Gerstner's Die innern Communicationen (1842–1843).* Edited by Frederick C.

Gamst, translated by David J. Diephouse and John C. Decker. Stanford CA: Stanford University Press, 1997.
Wallace, Anthony F. C. *Jefferson and the Indians: The Tragic Fate of the First Americans.* Cambridge MA: Harvard University Press, 1999.
———. *The Long, Bitter Trail: Andrew Jackson and the Indians.* New York: Hill and Wang, 1993.
Ward, John William. *Andrew Jackson: Symbol for an Age.* New York: Oxford University Press, 1955.
Warren, Stephen. *The Shawnees and Their Neighbors, 1795–1870.* Urbana: University of Illinois Press, 2005.
Waselkov, Gregory A. "Changing Strategies of Indian Field Location in the Early Historic Southeast." In *People, Plants, and Landscapes: Studies in Paleoethnobotony,* edited by Kristen J. Gremillion, 179–94. Tuscaloosa: University of Alabama Press, 1997.
———. *A Conquering Spirit: Fort Mims and the Redstick War of 1813–1814.* Tuscaloosa: University of Alabama Press, 2006.
———. "Formation of the Tensaw Community." In *Red Eagle's Children: Weatherford vs. Weatherford et al.,* edited by J. Anthony Paredes and Judith Knight, 36–45. Tuscaloosa: University of Alabama Press, 2012.
Waselkov, Gregory A., and Kathryn E. Holland Braund, eds. *William Bartram on the Southeastern Indians.* Lincoln: University of Nebraska Press, 1995.
Watson, Harry L. *Liberty and Power: The Politics of Jacksonian America.* New York: Noonday, 1990.
Weaver, Herbert, and Kermit L. Hall. *Correspondence of James K. Polk, 1835–1836.* Vol. 3. Nashville TN: Vanderbilt University Press, 1975.
Weisman, Brent Richards. *Unconquered People: Florida's Seminole and Miccosukee Indians.* Gainesville: University Press of Florida, 1999.
Weslager, C. A. *The Delaware Indian Westward Migration, with the Texts of Two Manuscripts (1821–22) Responding to General Lewis Cass's Inquiries about Lenape Culture and Language.* Wallingford PA: Middle Atlantic, 1978.
———. *The Delaware Indians: A History.* New Brunswick nj: Rutgers University Press, 1972.
Whalen, Brett E. "A Vermonter on the Trail of Tears, 1830–1837." *Vermont History* 66, no. 1 (1998): 31–38.
Wiggins, Sarah Woolfolk, and Ruth Smith Truss, eds., *The Journal of Sarah Haynsworth Gayle, 1827–1835: A Substitute for Social Intercourse.* Tuscaloosa: University of Alabama Press, 2013.
Wilentz, Sean. *Andrew Jackson.* New York: Times Books, 2005.
Williams, Amelia W., and Eugene C. Barker, eds. *The Writings of Sam Houston, 1813–1863.* Vol. 2. Austin: University of Texas Press, 1939.

Wilson, Clyde N., ed. *The Papers of John C. Calhoun*. Vol. 13: *1835–1837*. Columbia: University of South Carolina Press, 1980.

Wilson, Samuel, Jr. *Southern Travels: Journal of John H. B. Latrobe, 1834*. New Orleans: Historic New Orleans Collection, 1986.

Wolfe, Patrick. "Settler Colonialism and the Elimination of the Native." *Journal of Genocide Research* 8, no. 4 (December 2006): 387–409.

Woodford, Frank B. *Lewis Cass: The Last Jeffersonian*. New Brunswick NJ: Rutgers University Press, 1950.

Woodward, Thomas S. *Woodward's Reminiscences of the Creek, or Muscogee Indians, Contained in Letters to Friends in Georgia and Alabama*. Montgomery AL: Barrett and Wimbish, 1859.

Worley, Ted R. "Arkansas and the 'Hostile' Indians, 1835–1838." *Arkansas Historical Quarterly* 6, no. 2 (Summer 1947): 155–64.

Worth, John E, "The Lower Creeks: Origins and Early History." In *Indians of the Greater Southeast: Historical Archaeology and Ethnohistory*, edited by Bonnie G. McEwan, 265–98. Gainesville: University Press of Florida, 2000.

Wright, Amos J., Jr. *Historic Indian Towns in Alabama, 1540–1838*. Tuscaloosa: University of Alabama Press, 2003.

Wright, J. Leitch, Jr. *Creeks and Seminoles: The Destruction and Regeneration of the Muscogulge People*. Lincoln: University of Nebraska Press, 1986.

Wright, Muriel H., and Peter J. Hudson. "Brief Outline of the Choctaw and the Chickasaw Nations in the Indian Territory, 1820 to 1860." *Chronicles of Oklahoma* 7, no. 4 (December 1929): 388–418.

Yoo, John. "Andrew Jackson and Presidential Power." *Charleston Law Review* 2 (2007): 521–83.

Young, Mary E. "The Creek Frauds: A Study in Conscience and Corruption." *Mississippi Valley Historical Review* 42, no. 3 (December 1955): 411–37.

———. "Indian Removal and Land Allotment: The Civilized Tribes and Jacksonian Justice." *American Historical Review* 64, no. 1 (October 1958): 31–45.

———. *Redskins, Ruffleshirts, and Rednecks: Indian Allotments in Alabama and Mississippi, 1830–1860*. Norman: University of Oklahoma Press, 1961.

Zellar, Gary. *African Creeks: Estelvste and the Creek Nation*. Norman: University of Oklahoma Press, 2007.

INDEX

Abadie, Eugene, 189, 191, 193
Abbott, Thomas, 183
Abercrombie, Charles, 215, 217
Abert, John James, 29, 30, 91, 95, 103–4, 109; emigration strategy of, 84–85, 116; as locating agent, 103–4
Adams, John Quincy, 6, 12, 20
agents: dishonesty of, 70, 171–72; inefficiency of, 120; instructed to promote emigration, 128–29. *See also* Barry, John Waller; Bateman, Mark W; Belton, Francis Smith; Brearley, David; Clements, Reuben E.; Crowell, John; Deas, Edward; Hill, Alexander; Hogan, John B.; Logan, James; Page, John; Reynolds, John G.; Screven, R. B.; Sloan, Thomas; Sprague, John T.
Ahalocco Yoholo, 112
Akers, Donna L., 298
Alabama: asserts legal jurisdiction over Creek lands in, 3, 24, 85, 100, 183; Creek land in under Treaty of Washington, 22; Creeks remaining in, 234, 264–65, 266, 268–69, 294; Creeks resettle in, 31–38 (*see also* Poarch Band of Creek Indians; refugees, Creek); discriminatory laws against Creeks in, 3, 24; land quality in, 29

Alabama Artillery Number One, 187–88
Alabama Emigrating Company, 200, 207, 210, 214, 221, 244, 255, 258; calculation of deaths by, 231, 264, 298–99; complaints against, 286; conflicts of with Sprague, 215, 217; and detachment six, 258; negligence of, 215, 225, 226, 250. *See also* contractors
Alabamas and Coushattas, 130
alcohol, 5, 18, 70, 180, 233; contributes to starvation, 91, 276; at councils, 132; in enrollment camps, 140; in Indian territory, 276, 286–87; and land fraud, 107; laws against, 287; on route west, 51, 117, 140, 144, 146, 196, 209, 254, 261
alcohol abuse, 25, 73, 82, 91
Alexander, James L., 297–98
allotments. *See* reserves, individual
Alpha (steamboat), 142–47
Anderson's Bluff, Arkansas, 256, 262
Andrews, Timothy P., 20
Angelico Island, Arkansas, 196
annuity, 28, 73, 120, 132, 148, 205, 206, 236, 279, 282–83, 289
Anthony, Thomas, 52
Arbeka Tustunnuggee, 45, 47, 49

395

Arbuckle, Matthew, 55, 150, 232
Arfwedson, Carl David, 27, 73
Arkansans, 193
Arkansas, 204–5
Arkansas Post, 53, *78*, *197*, 229
Arkansas River, 146–47, 155, 156, 246; color of, 155; flooding of, 157; ice, 157; low stages of, 156; sandbars on, 125, 146, 147, 246; snags, 146–47, 246
Asseemee, 45, 49
Atson, William, 296
Audrain, Francis, 172
Audubon, John James, 239
Austin, Pleasant, 68

Balch, Alfred, 102, 133, 180
Balize, Louisiana, 189
ball game, 7–8, 38–39, 83, 135, 179; on journey west, 190, 254
Barclay, H. G., 244
Barnett, Holo, 89
Barnum, P. T., 239, 240
Barry, John Waller, 187, 189, 190, 191, 193
Bateman, Mark W., 9, 201, 204, 209, 214, 220; on alcohol, 214; choice of routes by, 213; death of, 255; describes conditions on journey west, 217, 218, 225–26, 228; with detachment six, 252
Baylor, John W., 170
Beattie, William J., 123, 140, 187, 188, 264
Belton, Francis Smith, 195, 196
Benton, Samuel C., 138
Berryhill (family), 170
Berryhill, Alfred, 9
Berryhill, John, 64, 71
Berryhill, Pleasant, 66
Berryhill, Samuel, 70
Berryhill, Togo Micco, 9, 156

Betton, Solomon, 29
Big Warrior, 12, 16, 21; father-in-law of Barent Dubois, 62; father-in-law of Kendall Lewis, 16, 65; father-in-law of William Walker, 50, 61, 62; father of Tuskenehaw, 64; opposes preaching, 59–60
Billingslea, Clement, 129
Biloxi, Mississippi, 254–55, 256
Black, Mary, 119, 123, *124*, 196, *197*, 256, 262
black drink, 137, 282
Black Hawk (steamboat), 244–48, 258, 262
blacks: Creek attack on, 59, 60–61; in Indian territory, 279–80. *See also* slaves, black
Blake, Luther, 76, 77, 79, 266; and land speculation, 171, 178; as Sanford & Company member, 138, 178, 180; as western Creek subagent, 171–72
Blind King, 194
Blount, John, 80–81
blown water ceremony, 170
Bolivar, Tennessee, 215, *219*, 220, 224, 229
Bonnets O Blue (steamboat), 240
Brearley, Charles, 52
Brearley, David, 50, 127; accusations against, 70, 171; commissioned to conduct McIntosh party, 43–44; on Indian territory, 157; instructed to promote Indian territory, 271; and journey west, 51, 52, 54, 55; promotion of emigration by, 63; relieved of duties, 70; use of Indian countrymen to promote emigration, 45–46, 61
Brodnax, John H., 92, 93, 265
Brown, Jacob, 119
Brown's Ferry, *247*; Creeks escape near, 245–46

Bruner, Thomas, 74
Bryan, Joseph, 108
Bryan, Theophilus, 38
Buckingham, James Silk, 296
buffer, erosion of, 25–28
burial, 271, 274; Creek's fear of improper burial along route, 223, 231; desecration of Creek burial sites, 176; during journey west, 54, 79, 218, 246, 253
Busk, 7–8, 31–32, 135, 137, 185; implements used in, 203, 282; in Indian territory, 170, 281, 282; on the route, 190–91
Butler, Edward G. W., 17

Caesar, 285, 286
California, McIntosh Creeks travel to, 174
Camp, Joseph, 294
Campbell, Duncan Greene, 17, 19, 22
Campbell, John, 157, 206, 207, 236
camps, detachment six: establishment of, 236; at Pass Christian, 252–55; relocation of to Fort Gibson, 262–63; relocation of to Mobile Point, 240–41; unhealthiness of, 250, 252; whites' attacks on, 237–39
camps, emigration: attacks on, 57, 63, 72, 74, 75; camp life en route, 145; Creeks harassed by whites at Harpersville, 48; establishment of, 48; rendezvous at Autauga County, 140; rendezvous at Centreville, 121; rendezvous at Fort Strother, 63, 64, 65; rendezvous at Sylacauga, 76
camps, relocation: camp life on route, 211; cleansing rituals in, 214; conditions in, 206, 220–21, 225–26; Creeks ordered into, 201; days of rest along route, 214; establishment of, 201–2; leave-taking rituals in, 202–3
camps, removal: alcohol procured at, 196; in New Orleans, 189–90; at Old Ursuline Convent, 195; possible Busk at, 190–91
Canadian River, 155, 156; Creeks settle on, 119, 165, 166–67, 233, 274; description of, 46, 155; environment surrounding, 153, 157; fishing on, 161; water quality of, 155
Cantonment Gibson, 46, 149–50. See also Fort Gibson
Capers, William, 59, 60
Carr, Paddy, 182, 235; as land speculator, 178; self-emigrates west, 265
Cass, Lewis, 8, 16, 198; on use of contractors, 139; goals of for Treaty of Washington, 95, 105; and land cessions, 16; and McIntosh's emigration operations, 115–16; plans of for ethnic cleansing, 201; response of to Second Creek War, 183–84
Catawba (steamboat), 46
Cat Island, Mississippi, 189, 252, 256
Catlin, George, 160, 168, 280
Cavalier (steamboat), 258
census (1832), 94–95, 108, 292–93
census, western Creek Nation (1833), 164–65
Centreville, Alabama, 121, 124, 216
ceremonial lives: closure of in Alabama, 202–3; effects of Treaty of Washington on, 110–12; maintenance of, 7–8, 31–32, 135, 137, 185; reestablishment of in Indian territory, 281–82
Champion (steamboat), 242
Checote, Samuel, 74

Chehaw, 180; Creeks from, hunt in Georgia, 26; in Indian territory, 279, 281; and Second Creek War, 175, 181
Cherokee Agency, Treaty of, 16
Cherokees: affected by Treaty of Washington, 22; as counselors to Creek headmen, 40; Creek refugees among, 38, 133, 234, 242–44, 249–50; mortality rate of, 126, 298; and Trail of Tears, 200; and Treaty of Cherokee Agency, 16; western Creek land ceded to, 172–73, 288; in western Creek Nation, 279
Chickasaws, 16; Creek refugees among, 122–23, 133, 234, 242, 260–62; dissatisfaction of with Indian territory, 151; exploration of Indian territory by, 58–59; in Indian territory, 288; placed within Choctaw reserve, 162; removal of, 261
Chippewa (steamboat), 27, 240
Choctaws: anticipated emigration of, 118; Creek asylum among, 133; and Dancing Rabbit Creek agreement, 93, 94; dissatisfaction of with Indian territory, 151; exploration of Indian territory by, 58–59; loss of land in Indian territory by, 288; mortality rate of, 298; reserve of, other Indians moved to, 162; and Treaty of Doak's Stand, 16, 17
cholera, 80, 126, 169–71, 193, 226
Chouteau (family), 55, 69–70, 157, 158, 160, 167
Christianity, 59–60. *See also* missionaries
Cimarron River, 155, 156; description of, 155; environment surrounding, 153–54, 158; low stages of, 156; water quality of, 155, 156

Clarksville, Arkansas, 163, 262
Clay, Clement Comer, 100, 240
cleanliness, Creeks' concern with, 144, 245, 250
Clements, Reuben E., 260–62
Clermont, 56, 164
climate, of Indian territory, 150–51, 153
Coachman, Ward. *See* Cochamy, Ward
Cochamy, Ward, 1, 267
Coffee, 294
Colonel Blue, 11
Columbia (steamboat), 46
Columbia, Arkansas, 192; Creek child killed near, 190
Columbia River, McIntosh Creeks travel to, 174
Columbus, Georgia, 73, 96, 181, 182, 233, 296; home to speculators and alcohol traders, 5, 25, 73, 106, 117, 138, 291; residents of, 91, 176, 178; as source of income for Creeks, 27, 186
Columbus, Mississippi, 122, 123, 124
compensation: for Creeks left off census, 293; for lost property, 283; for removal, 15–16, 24, 28–29, 83, 174
Compere, Lee, 59, 62–63; supports emigration, 60–61, 116
Concharty, 279
conch shells, 203, 282
consolidation strategy, 131–32
Constellation (frigate), 241
contractors, for emigration/removal/relocation, 137–39, 148, 214; conflict of with federal officials, 257–58; Creeks suspicious of, 138; and fifth voluntary party, 141–48; lack of influence of, 213; loss of emigrants' property by, 230; negligence of, 144, 215, 225, 227; and relocation of detachment six, 258; transport of prisoners by, 187–93; treatment

of emigrants by, 215, 217; trouble recruiting emigrants, 140. *See also* Alabama Emigrating Company; Sanford & Company

cooking, 145

Coosada, 48, 53, 65, 76; in west, 165

Cotton Gin Port, Mississippi, 122, *124*, 205, *212*, 213

council grounds, 47, 110–12, 135; in west, 281–82

councils, 132

Courtland, Alabama, 51, *53*, 67, 141, *143*, 206, *219*, 229

Coweta: Coweta Resolution, 112; mile chiefs of, 95, 121, 132; and relocation, 202, 203, 204, 209, 222; and Treaty of Indian Springs, 15, 20; in West, 165, 233, 272, 275, 282.

Coweta Tustunnuggee, 11

Cowles, Thomas M., 129

Cowockcochee Emarthla, 169

Cowyka: and forced removal, 187; in Indian territory, 165; land of, stolen, 187

credit, and land fraud, 106–7

Creek Agency, closure of, 89, 113

Creek Agency, Treaty of, 40, 289

Creek Agency, western, 156–57, 170

Creek country, western: encroachment on by other Indians, 162; land in, 151–53; loss of territory in, 288–89; map of, *159*; Seminoles in, 173–74. *See also* Creek Nation, western; Indian territory; resettlement

Creek Nation: conditions in, 71–73, 74, 82, 90–92, 177; corrupting influences of whites on, 17–18; decline of, 1; and defense of territory, 112; despair in, 179; destruction of in East, 112; divisions in, 70–71, 94–95, 132; governance of, 39–40, 61, 112 (*see also* headmen); removal of (*see* emigration; removal). *See also* Creeks

Creek Nation, western, 14–15; considered illegitimate, 112; founding of, 42; government of, 57, 168–69, 194 (*see also* McIntosh, Chilly; McIntosh, Roly); incorporation of other Indian groups into, 279; population of, 165, 169–70; relation of with headmen in east, 88; as subject to American laws, 287–88. *See also* Creek country, western; Indian territory; resettlement

Creek National Council: and defense of territory, 112; and disputed land in Georgia, 39–40

Creeks: attacks on, 176; change in demeanor of, 114, 133–35; desperation of, 133–35; land-use traditions of, 102–5; remaining in Alabama, 234, 264–65, 266, 268–69, 294 (*see also* refugees, Creek); remaining in South, 234–35; settlement patterns, 102; as slaves, 266, 268; trusting nature of, 109. *See also* Creek Nation

Creeks, Lower: division of 29 sections, 96; reaction of to relocation of Florida volunteers' families, 241; in Second Creek War, 182; selection of mile chiefs, 94–95

Creeks, Upper: division of 29 sections, 96; in Second Creek War, 184; selection of mile chiefs, 94–95

crops, Indians' failure to plant, 28, 72, 90–91, 120, 177, 182

Crowell, John, 14, 22, 27, 83, 84, 92, 103, 178; on Creeks' starvation, 26, 73; dismissal of, 113; and dispute

Crowell, John (*continued*)
with Troup, 20; emigration strategy of, 116; on headmen's campaign against emigration, 83, 84; on Indian countrymen, 88; and merging of eastern and western agencies, 70, 171; opposition of to preaching, 59–60; oversees emigration, 70, 71, 76; plan of to introduce more whites into Creek Nation, 86; presses Creeks to cede Georgia strip, 39–40, 47; proposes Creeks take land in allotments, 93–94, 97; provides rations to hungry Creeks, 29; on retribution against emigrants, 91; in Second Creek War, 182; on stopping of government-funded emigration, 90–91, 116–17; on treatment of Creeks by settlers, 86

Crowell, Thomas, 60, 76, 77

Cumberland (barque), 190

Cusseta, 65, 110, 140; Creeks from, hunt in Georgia, 26; description of prior to 1826, 31; and Second Creek War, 175, 181; near West Point or Tuskenehaw Chooley's Town, 34–35; and relocation, 202, 204, 208, 209, 213, 222; and removal, 187, 190; removal from Georgia, 7; and resettlement in Indian territory, 272; Secharlitcha, 31, 34–37, 94; Tolarnulkarhatchee, 36–37, 178

Dancing Rabbit Creek, Treaty of, 93, 94

Danely, Jim, 83

Danely, John, 83

Dardanelle, Arkansas, 46, 53, 56, 67, 78, 118, 227, 229; as crossing point over Arkansas River, 56, 68, 119

Davis, John, 4, 60

Dawson, James L., 172

Deas, Edward, 141, 142, 144, 209, 214, 215, 217, 223, 225, 230, 244, 245–46, 248; accompanies detachment three, 202; appointed to remove Creeks in Cherokee Nation, 242–43; complains of lack of provisions on route, 226, 285; describes camp life, 211; frustrations with Menawa and Tuscoona Harjo, 227–28; reports on sinking of keelboat, 147

deaths: after resettlement, 169–71, 270, 271, 287, 297–98, 365n3; claimed by Alabama Emigrating Company, 298–99; Echo Fixico's, 1, 3, 267; during emigration, 68, 79, 80, 118, 298; during McIntosh's emigration operations, 118; in *Monmouth* disaster, 259–60, 264; of prisoners, 190, 193–94, 195, 196, 198; of refugees, 246; during relocation, 214, 218, 231, 232, 253, 264, 298–99, 299; in Sanford & Company's contract, 139

debt, 25, 106–7, 131, 140, 180, 206, 209

Decatur, Alabama, 51, 53, 76, 78, 205, 219, 245, 247

Delawares, 55–56, 162, 279, 288

Deposit Landing (ferry), 205, 224

Derasaw (family), 12, 49, 140

Derasaw, Jacob, 169

DeRosier, Arthur H., Jr., 288

desertion, 9; of black slaves, 187; during Chilly McIntosh's 1833 party, 118; of Creek prisoners, 186; of Creek refugees, 245–46; during fourth voluntary party, 120, 122–23, 127; during relocation, 235; during second McIntosh party, 63, 66

DeSoto County, Mississippi, 260

disease: cholera, 80, 126, 169–71, 193, 226; dysentery, 126, 169, 193, 244,

246, 250; in Indian territory, 151, 169–71, 270, 298; influenza, 126; measles, 126; of refugees, 244; smallpox, 80, 82, 92, 271, 272, 297; tuberculosis, 246; yellow fever, 250, 257. *See also* deaths
Ditto's Landing, 245, *247*
Doak's Stand, Treaty of, 16, 17
Drew, Thomas S., 287
Dubois, Barent, 62, 129, 201
Dudley, Peter, 108
Durant, William, 268
Dwight Mission, *219*
dysentery, 126, 169, 193, 244, 246, 250

Eaton, John H., 71, 88, 288
Echo Harjo, 202, 235; relocation camp of, 236, 238
eclipse, 134, *136*
Efar Emathla, 103, 178
Ellisor, John T., 181
Ellsworth, Henry Leavitt, 150, 158
Elyton, Alabama, 76, 141, *143*, 205, 206, 213, *216*, 229
emigration, voluntary: collected by Wheat (1845), 266–67; conducted by Cochamy (1848), 267; conducted by Durant (1849), 268; conducted by McIntosh (1833), 114–16, 117–18; cost of, 80, 127, 138, 266; decision to stop government funding of, 116; emigrants' return to Alabama, 171; end of, 183; fifth voluntary party, 141–48, *143*; first McIntosh party, 49–57, *53*; fourth voluntary party, 83, 118–27, *125*; headmen's opposition to, 44, 47, 49, 57, 61, 63–64, 83–84, 119 (*see also* resistance); motivations for, 74–75, 149; promotion of, 45; routes of parties, 2, *53*, 67, *78*, 124, *143*; second McIntosh party, 65–69, 67; self-emigration, 88–89, 148, 265, 294–95; third voluntary party, 76–80, *78*, 83
emigrations, reunification, 295
employment, of Creeks, 27
encampments, Jones on, 145–46
encroachment: by Indians in the west, 162, 164; by whites in Alabama, 25, 57, 71–72, 74, 81, 82, 84–86, 93, 97, 100, 115, 132, 134, 148, 175–76; by whites in the west, 284
enrollment, of emigrants, 40–41, 74; McIntosh's attempts at, 115; by Sanford & Company, 140, 175. *See also* camps, emigration
Erwin, James, *192*, 193, 196, *197*, 256, 262
ethnic cleansing: forms of, 3; goal of in Treaty of Washington, 95; justification of by Second Creek War, 185, 198; plans for, 201; removal as, 4, 297; systematic process of, 4; treaties designed for, 22
etničko čišćenje (ethnic cleansing), 3
Etommee Tustunnuggee, 11, 12
Eufaula, 5, 85, *87*; Creeks from, hunt in Georgia, 26; in Indian territory, 165, 275; in Second Creek War, 181
Eufaula Harjo, 122, 123
Evarts, Jeremiah, 21
extension laws, 85, 100, 183

Facility (steamboat), 55, 56, 68
families: and clan justice, 75; effects of emigration on, 66; reunification of, 295
Farmer (steamboat), 220, 221, 240, 252, 257, 258
farming: decline of, 101–2; in Indian territory, 167, 276. *See also* crops
Far West (steamboat), 258
Featherstonhaugh, George William, 27

fields, clearing, 275
fires, town, 203
firewood, 153, 273
fish, in Indian territory, 161
Fixico, Echo, 1, 3, 267
flooding, 156–57, 298
Florence, Alabama, 66, *67*, 78, 142, *247*, 248
Florida volunteers, Creek, 235–39, 252, 255
food insecurity, 275. *See also* starvation
food shortages, 91, 133. *See also* starvation
Forshatch Fixico, 235
Fort Adams (steamboat), 45
Fort Bainbridge, 16, *67*, 74, 76, *78*; emigrants threatened and attacked at, 63, 64, 75
Fort Claiborne, 242, *256*, 268
Fort Coffee, *247*, 248, 263
Fort Gaines, 48, *53*
Fort Gibson, Indian territory, 150, 158. *See also* Cantonment Gibson
Fort Gibson, Treaty of, 173, 283, 289
Fort Hull, 120, 124, 131
Fort Jackson, Treaty of, 16, 268–69
Fort Mitchell, Alabama, 22, 23, 28, 60, *124*, *192*
Fort Morgan, Alabama, 250
Fort Smith, Arkansas, 2, *53*, 55, 56, *67*, 68, 69, *78*, *143*, 147, 150, 166, 229, *247*, 248, 267, 286
Fort Strother, 65–66, *67*, 68; emigrants driven from, 63–64
funding, for emigration, 76, 80, 89
Fushatchee Micco, 169

Gaines, Edmund P., 20, 43, 44, 117, 150, 151
gamblers, 132
game, in Indian territory, 160–61

Gayle, John, 100
Gayle, Sarah Haynsworth, 121–22
Georgia: Creeks forced out of, 23–24; Creeks' loss of land in, 22, 40, 45; Creeks prohibited from entering, 73–74; Creeks' refusal to leave, 26–27; disputed land in, 39–40, 47, 60; effects of settlement of, 180–81; reminiscences of, 293–94; white immigrants in, 40
Georgian (steamboat), 182
Gerstäcker, Friedrich, 232
Gibson, Felix G., 215, 217
Gibson, George, 127
Goodwin, John, 108
Goodwin, Thomas, 108
government, federal: attempts of to entice Creeks to emigrate, 148; bitterness towards, 293; Creek Nation's appeals to, 86, 92–93, 179; funding for emigration by, 76, 80, 89; neglect of Indian territory by, 171–74; and plans for 1835 emigration party, 128–29; refusal of to fund small parties, 120; refusal of to help Indians, 91–93. *See also* Cass, Lewis; funding, for emigration; Jackson, Andrew
Grand River, 46, 148, 149, 153, 163, 248, 288
graves, desecration of, 176–77
Grayson (family), 90
Grayson, Davy, 286
Grayson, George, 95
Grayson, George Washington, 274
Grayson, Sampson, 130, 265; accuses Page of neglect on route, 127–28
Grayson, Thomas, 65, 90
Grayson, Walter, 66, 90
Grayson, William, 65, 90
Greathouse, Daniel, *78*, 196, *197*

Green, Michael D., 40
Green Corn Ceremony. *See* Busk
Gregg, Josiah, 274, 276, 280
Gunter's Landing, Alabama, 66, 67, 68, 76, 78, 205, 219, 224, 244, 247, 248; refugee Creeks encamped at, 210, 244, 246

Hahn, Steven C. 112
Hall, Basil, 29, 72
Hanrick, Edward C., 285
Hardage, Siah, 169
Harpersville, Alabama, 48, 50, 53
Harris, Carey A., 194
Harris, Peter C., 131
Harry Hill (steamboat), 123, 125
Hatcheechubba: and forced removal, 187; in Indian territory, 165, land of, stolen, 187
Hawkins (family), 13, 15–16, 18–19
Hawkins, Benjamin (agent), 3, 31
Hawkins, Benjamin (of Hillabee), 43, 118; attempted execution of, 12; attempts to promote emigration, 44, 88; in Cherokee country, 173; death of, 270–71; as emigrating agent, 118; emigration of, 49, 57; exploration of Indian territory by, 45; property of in Indian territory, 167; smuggling of whiskey by, 287; and Texas, 130–31
Hawkins, Eliza, 49
Hawkins, Jane, 19; emigration of, 57
Hawkins, Pinkney, 280
Hawkins, Samuel, 12, 13
Hawkins, Stephen, 18
headmen: accused of being controlled by land speculators, 129–32, 138, 178; attempts to use diplomacy, 86, 179; mile chiefs, 94–95; opposition of to emigration, 44, 47, 49, 57, 61, 63–64, 80, 83–84, 119; relations with western Creek Nation, 88; relations with whites in Creek Nation, 62; resistance of during relocation, 211–13, 226–28; in Second Creek War, 181, 182, 184; suppression of information about Treaty of Washington by, 110; of western Creek Nation, 168–69
health. *See* disease
Helena, Arkansas, 229, 247, 248
Henry, Jim, 186
Herring, Elbert, 115
Hill, Alexander, 120, 121, 123, 127, 128, 138
Hill, Seaborn, 172
Hitchcock, Ethan Allen, 271, 281, 285–86, 293
Hitchiti, 26; and emigration, 65, 74; in West, 165; and resettlement within Alabama, 32, 36–37; and Second Creek War, 175, 180, 181
Hodgson, Adam, 16, 17, 31
Hogan, John B., 62, 128, 137, 180, 181, 187, 233; appointment of, 128; difficulties of in recruiting emigrants, 129, 131, 139; dismissal of, 183; feud of with Sanford & Company, 177–78; investigates land frauds, 177–78, 206; opposes use of contractors, 138, 188; warns of impending war, 176
homesteads, 275
Hooper, George D., 291
Hooper, Johnson Jones, 107–9
Hopwood, Samuel, 68
Horn Island, Mississippi, 189, 256; environment of, 252
Horn Lake, 260, 263
horses, during emigration, 144, 225
Horseshoe Bend, 300–301
houses, in Indian territory, 273–75

Houston, Sam, 79–80, 271
Howell, John D., 138, 187, 188
hunger, 72. See also starvation
hunting, 102, 163
Huntsville, Alabama, 205, 224; description of camp life at, 211
Hyperion (steamboat), 182

illegals, white, 6, 25, 71–72, 82, 85, 148
illness. See disease
impersonation, 107. See also land fraud
indebtedness, 25, 106–7, 131, 140, 180, 206, 209
Indian Bay, Arkansas, 219, 226
Indian countrymen, 16; arrest/expulsion of, 86, 88; emigration of, 5; promotion of emigration by, 50, 61, 62; threats against, 61–62; used to promote emigration, 45–46
"An Indian of the Creek Nation Sketched from Nature at Mobile Alabama" (Woolf), 251
Indian relocation. See emigration; ethnic cleansing; removal
Indian Removal Act, 84
Indians, western: conflicts of with Creek immigrants, 162–64. See also Osages
Indian Springs, Treaty of, 6; abrogation of, 6, 21–22; effects of, 5, 12, 24–29, 58; as emigration document, 40; and guarantee of McIntosh party's protection, 19, 20; illegality of, 11, 20; motivations of signers of, 14–18; negotiations for, 17, 162; opposition to, 12; as removal document, 11, 19–20; retribution for signing of, 12–14, 19–20; role of federal officials in signing of, 16–17; signing of, 11
Indian territory: climate of, 150–51, 153; conflicts between Indians in, 162–64; difficulties faced in, 149, 270–71; disease in, 151, 169–71, 298; dissatisfaction with, 161–62, 165, 272; evaluation of, 47; exploration of, 45–46, 58–59; farming in, 167; fish in, 161; flooding in, 156–57; game in, 160–61; government neglect of, 171–74; hunting in, 163; Indians' loss of land in, 172–73, 288–89; land in, 151–53; map of, 159, 278; plant species in, 160; power of McIntosh party in, 174; reactions of voluntary emigrants to, 152; resettlement in (see resettlement); soil quality in, 157; timber in, 152–53, 157, 162; unhealthiness of, 129, 130, 150, 271; water in, 153–57; whites' view of, 158, 160. See also Creek country, western; Creek Nation, western
Ingersoll, Stephen Miles, 138, 140
Irving, Washington, 166, 168, 170
Irwinton, Alabama, 85, 87
Island, James, 184, 202, 203, 210, 265
Itasca (steamboat), 261–62
Itawamba County, Mississippi, 260

Jackson, Andrew, 3, 7, 75, 79, 80, 86, 103, 114, 123, 200, 240, 291, 296–97; administration's policies, 104, 105, 113, 116, 120; approves Watson's contract, 207–8; Creeks' appeal to, 72, 81, 84, 134, 152, 171; disregard of for concerns of Creeks, 138; election of, 82, 84; justifies moving Creeks west, 4, 5, 71, 148, 198, 200, 201, 284, 288; merges eastern and western agencies, 70; and nullification, 129; pressures headmen to emigrate, 89–90; refusal of to help Indians, 71, 81, 84, 91–92, 179; removal of legal protections for Creek Nation

by, 89–90; responsibility of for atrocities against Indians, 5–6; role of in land cession treaties, 16, 17, 27; stops government-sponsored emigration, 89–90; supports Alabama's extension laws, 85; whites appeal to, 91–92
Jefferson, Thomas, 6
Jesup, Thomas S., 8, 184, 236, 241, 279; concessions to Creeks, 206; extension of Creeks' service, 236–37; recruitment of Florida volunteers, 206; and relocation of Creeks, 201–2; and removal of prisoners, 195, 200
Jim Boy, 95, 130, 202, 254, 258, 293; family of in *Monmouth* disaster, 259; and Second Creek War, 182, 184; serves in Florida, 202, 235; signs Watson contract, 207; threatens emigrants, 64
John Nelson (steamboat), 220, 222, 225–27, 230–31, 240, 257, 258, 262, 350n35; runs aground, 229
Johnson, Dick, 75
Jones, James, 195, 196
Jones, John Hewitt, 142, 145, 147
justice, clan, 75

keelboat, sinking of, 146–47
Kennard, Daniel, 45
Kialigee, 102; and relocation, 221
Kickapoos, 162, 163, 164, 279
Kotchar Tustunnuggee, 174
Kymulga, 48, 49–50, 53

Lady Byron (steamboat), 220, 222–23, 226
LaFayette, Alabama, 182, 202, 229, 291
La Grange, Tennessee, 212, 216, 220
Lake Borgne, 189, 195, 197
Lake Pontchartrain, 189, 197, 267

Lamplighter (steamboat), 190
land: Creeks' loss of in Georgia, 22, 40, 45; Creeks' use of, 102–5; disputed, in Georgia, 39–40, 47, 60; Indians' loss of in Indian territory, 172–73, 288–89; in Indian territory, 151–53; in Treaty of Fort Jackson, 268–69. *See also* reserves, individual
land, western. *See* Indian territory
land claims, 120, 132, 206, 236, 290–92
land fraud, 106–9, *108*, 113, 133, 137, 138, 148, 178, 180, 291
land fraud investigations, 177–78, 181, 183
land ownership, 104–5, 113, 131
land reserves, individual. *See* reserves, individual
land speculators, 175, 176, 207, 285; competition among, 178; control of headmen, 129–32, 138, 178; murder of, 179–80; partnerships of with contractors, 138; support of for removal, 132–33
Lang, John D., 280
Lashley, Alexander, 49, 57
Latrobe, Charles Joseph, 171
Lawson, Irvin, 108
Leighton, Alabama, 51, 53
Levasseur, Auguste, 18
Lewis, Kendall, 16, 17, 65, 166, 169, 173
Lewisburg, Arkansas, 1, 2, *143*, 146, 267
Lewis Cass (steamboat), 187, 194–95
Little Doctor, 204, 207
Little Prince, 14, 39, 40, 44, 47
livestock: and diffusion of Creek towns, 110; hunting of, 25–26, 252; suitability of Indian territory for, 157–58; and water scarcity, 156
Logan, James, 170, 172, 271, 272, 283
loneliness, of Creeks remaining in Alabama, 294

Loomis, Augustus Ward, 170, 273, 274–75, 276, 281, 282, 284, 293–94
Lott, Benjamin, 65
Lott, William, 18, 19, 70
Loughridge, Robert McGill, 158, 161

Mad Blue, 204, 207
Mad Tiger, 47
Majestic (steamboat), 190
Maplesville, Alabama, 212
Marshall, Benjamin, 43, 93, 103, 144, 202, 210, 280, 286; in government of western Creek Nation, 169; individual reserve of, 96, 98, 99; joins Sanford & Company, 140; member of McIntosh party, 21; in Second Creek War, 184; signs Treaty of Indian Springs, 14
Marshall, Joseph, 14
Mazeppa (steamboat), 195, 258
McCann, Joseph D., 202
McCoy, Isaac, 151, 152–53, 154, 155, 156, 161, 163, 165, 169, 172, 273, 276, 298
McDonald, Charles J., 291–92
McDonald contract, 291–92, 293
McDougald, Daniel, 176, 178
McIntosh, Chilly, 14, 50, 59, 161, 283; character of, 117–18; decision of to emigrate, 18; as emigrating agent, 115–16, 117, 118; in exile, 13; in first McIntosh party, 48, 49–50, 51, 54; in government of western Creek Nation, 169; return of to Alabama, 114–15; signing of Treaty of Indian Springs, 11
McIntosh, David, 65
McIntosh, Hagy, 12, 49
McIntosh, John, 49
McIntosh, Peggy, 19; emigration of, 57
McIntosh, Roly, 14, 49, 74, 162, 164, 283; complaints against agents, 70; elected leader of McIntosh party, 18, 21; in exile, 13; fears power struggle, 174, 194; in government of western Creek Nation, 57, 168–69; insistence of on reconnaissance of Indian territory, 45; knowledge of Indian territory, 17, 47; meets with Opothle Yoholo, 232–33; protests loss of land in Indian territory, 152, 172–73, 288; returns to Alabama, 88; sends slaves west, 65; signing of Treaty of Indian Springs by, 11
McIntosh, Susannah, 18, 19; emigration of, 57; in Indian territory, 173
McIntosh, William: charisma, 19; execution of, 12; losses to estate of, 13; motivations of, 14–18; negotiation of Treaty of Indian Springs by, 162; portrait of, 296; power of, 14–15; signing of Treaty of Indian Springs by, 6, 11
McIntosh party: exile of, 19; exploration of Indian territory by, 45–46; first emigration party of, 49–57; in government of western Creek Nation, 168–69; lack of compensation for, 283; in negotiations for Treaty of Washington, 21; number of, 44–45; protection guaranteed to, 19, 20; provisions provided by, 167; relation of with headmen in east, 88; return of to homes, 20–21; second emigration party of, 65–69; violence against for signing of treaty, 12–14
McKenney, Thomas L., 17, 40, 70, 86
McLemore, Charles, 109
medicine, Creek, 170, 250
Meigs, Return J., 104, 134
Memphis, Tennessee, 52

Menawa, 184, 202, 208–9, 223, 227, 228, 233
Merchant (steamboat), 255
Meridian (steamboat), 187–88
Meriwether, James, 17, 19
Mexico, 130–31. *See also* Texas
Micco Foseke, 95
mile chiefs, 94–95, 174
Miller, Charles, 49
Miller, Samuel, 49
Miller, William, 12, 49
Milton, John, 188
Mims, Linah, 28
missionaries, 59–61, 62–63, 116, 158, 194. *See also* Loomis, Augustus Ward
Mississippi Swamp, 52, 53, 67, 77, 78, 124, 143, 216, 220, 221, 224, 225, 229, 263, 285; descriptions of, 54, 144, 223; during winter, 123
Missouri, Creeks in, 162
Mitchell, David B., 19
Mobile Point, 240–41, 250, 252, 256
Moniac, Alexander, 64
Monmouth (steamboat), 258, 259–60, 262, 264
Monroe, James, 6
Montevallo, Alabama, 141, 143, 205, 216
Montgomery's Point, 53, 67, 192, 195, 197, 247, 248, 256, 264
Moore, James, 18, 61–62
Moore, John P., 154, 171–72
Moscow, Tennessee, 212, 218
Motte, Jacob Rhett, 187
Moulton, Alabama, 141, 143, 213
Mount Meigs, Alabama, 76, 256; Barnum sees Creeks at, 240; families of Florida volunteers moved to, 239
Mt. Pleasant, Mississippi, 261, 263
Muscogee (Creek) Nation, 9, 203, 267, 300

narratives, 203, 230
Narticker Tustunnuggee, 225
Natchez, Mississippi, 190, *192*
National Council: relocation of to Indian territory, 174; usurpation of power of, 183; at Wetumpka, 46–47
Navarino (steamboat), 240, 257, 258–59
Neah Emathla, 75, 132, 181, 188, 189, 190, 194
Neah Micco: arrival of in western Creek Nation, 194; complaints of to Crowell, 86; death of, 271; during emigration, 190, 191; land speculators' influence on, 138, 178; and Second Creek War, 181, 184; slaves' desertion of, 187; and violent resistance, 132; warned not to interfere with emigration, 119
New Madrid, 248; Creeks settle at, 162
New Orleans, Creek prisoners in, 189–90
Nichols, Lemuel B., 45, 49
North Fork River, 154, 155, 156
nullification, 100, 129, 240

Oakchonawa Yoholo, 50
Octruchee Emathla, 92, 93, 181–82
Okfuskee Yoholo, 184
Okteyoconnee, 32–33
Old Dwight Mission, *197*, 219, 229
Old Ursuline Convent, 195
Oponee, John, 121; death of, 264; denied full reserve, 95
Opothle Yoholo, 59–60, 69, 75, 88, 103, 168, 204–5, 206, 283, 284; and 1826 Treaty of Washington, 21; and 1832 Treaty of Washington, 93, 94, 110; accused of being controlled by land speculators, 129; advocates move to Texas, 129–31, 132, 270; arrives in Indian territory, 231; assigned to

Opothle Yoholo (*continued*)
  detachment one, 201; ceremonial life of, 137; debt of, 100, 131, 140; and McDonald contract, 291–92; meets with McIntosh party, 232–33; as mile chief, 95; opposes use of contractors, 138; opposes voluntary emigration, 61–62; opposition of to Treaty of Creek Agency, 40; opposition of to Treaty of Indian Springs, 11; orders detachment two to follow in his path, 211–12; plantation of in Indian territory, 280; predicts end of world, 134–35; prepares for relocation, 8, 202–3; refusal of to board boats, 223; relationship with Dubois, 62; and relocation, 208, 209, 214, 218, 228; resigned to emigrate, 137, 177; and sale of reserves, 207; and Second Creek War, 182–83, 184, 198; sends slaves west, 177; service of his people in Second Seminole War, 235, 236, 241, 255, 258; and Watson contract, 207
orphan fund, 96, 286, 289–90
Osages, 47, 55–56, 69–70, 163–64
Oswitchee, 26, 131–32; emigration of, 65; in Indian territory, 273, 281; and Second Creek War, 181
Otellewhoyanunau, 32, 36–37
Ottawas, 58–59
Owens, Hardiman, 101
ownership, land, 104–5, 113, 131

Pacific Ocean, McIntosh Creeks travel to, 174
Paducah, Kentucky, 142, *143*, 245, 248
Page, John, 119, 120, 132, 155, 177, 181, 183, 199, 201, 252, 257, 259; accused of neglect, 127–28, 165; conducts 1834 party, 121–27; as disbursing agent, 128, 180, 184; oversees detachment six, 238, 240, 252, 253; pays out Watson money, 255; takes census in Indian territory, 293
Parsons, Enoch, 110
Pass Christian, Mississippi, 252–55, 256
Payne, John Howard, 137
Payne's Landing, Treaty of, 173–74
Perry & Company, 178
Perryman, Benjamin, 74, 168, 169, 173
Perryman, Daniel, 49
Perryman, Samuel, 168
Perryman, Theophilus, 89
personation (impersonation), 107
Petit Jean Mountain, 3
Piankashaws, in Creek country, 279
Pickett, Albert James, 208
Pidgeon, David, 66
Pidgeon, Joseph, 66
Pidgeon, Thomas, 66
Pine Bluff, Arkansas, 77, *247*, 248
plantations, in Indian territory, 280
plant species, in Indian territory, 160
plates, sacred, 203, 208, 282
Poarch Band of Creek Indians, 7, 269
Pocahontas (steamboat), 76
Poinsett, Joel, 240
Polecat Springs, 236, 238, 256; Creek prisoners escape at, 186
Pontotoc, Mississippi, 205, 210, 260, 261, 263
Pontotoc County, Mississippi, 260
Posey, Thomas, 66
Porter, Peter B., 88
Potawatomis, 58–59
poverty: after resettlement, 165–66, 286; of emigrants, 120, 126, 209–10
Power, Tyrone, 101–2
prairie, 152, 273, 276
preaching, banning of, 59
primacy, in creation stories, 14–15

prisoners, Creek: escape attempts by, 186–87, 188; execution of, 186; marched to Montgomery, 185–86; negotiations of with relocated headmen, 204–5; removal of, 187–93, 194–98; suicides by, 186
propaganda: anti-emigration, 63; pro-emigration, 62–63
property, emigrants': compensation for losses of, 283; contractors' mistreatment of, 144; damage to, 258; delayed arrival of, 272; destruction of, 64, 91; Indian territory as refuge for, 177; limits on, 139, 204; loss of, 77, 215, 230; stolen by whites, 209
Purdy, Tennessee, 214, *219*, 220, 221, *224*, *229*
purity, Creeks' concern with, 154, 185, 245, 250

Quapaws, 162
Quassad Harjo, 292

Rabbit Town, 221
Raleigh, Tennessee, 220–21, *229*
Red Clay, 243, *247*; home to Creek refugees, 243, 244, 249
Reed, John, 64
Reed, Vicey, 74, 77
refugees, Creek, 235; among Cherokees, 38, 133, 234, 242–44, 249–50; among Chickasaws, 122–23, 133, 234, 242, 260–62; among Seminoles, 234; condition of, 244, 249, 260–61; deaths of, 243, 245, 246, 248, 299; desertion on route, 245–46; desert relocation camps, 235; enrollment of in Mississippi, 260–61; escape to Cherokee country, 38, 133; escape to Chickasaw country, 122–23, 133; escape to Florida, 38, 133, 181; resistance to removal, 243, 245–46, 261; route of, *247*, *263*; search for in Cherokee country, 242–44, 248–50; search for in Chickasaw country, 260–61; search for in Florida, 241–44; transport of to Indian territory, 244–48; violence against, 242, 243–44
relocation, coerced: Alabama camps, 202, 235, 237–39; arrival of Creeks at Fort Gibson, 231; camp life on route, 211; cost of, 200, 206, 299; deaths during, 231, 253, 259, 299; definition of, 200; departure days, 208; fatigue during, 217–20, 226, 228–30; lack of legal right to move, 200; leave-taking rituals in camps, 202–3; *Monmouth* disaster, 259–60, 262; problem with contractors, 215–17, 257; relocation to Mobile Point, 240; relocation to Pass Christian, 252–53; resistance during, 211–13, 226–28; routes of, *212*, *215*, *219*, *224*, *229*, *256*; sickness of detachment six, 250, 253; steamboat travel during, 222–23; through Mississippi Swamp, 223–25; transportation of conch shells, 203; transportation of copper plates, 208; transportation of town fire, 203. *See also* ethnic cleansing
removal, forced, 185; deaths during, 186–87, 189, 190, 193–94, 198, 299; definition of, 200; departure of detachment one, 187; departure of detachment two, 194; possible Busk during, 190–91; prisoners marched to Montgomery, 185–86; resistance during, 186–87, 188, 191; routes of, *192*, *197*. *See also* ethnic cleansing

reserves, individual, 81, 82, *98*, *99*, 117; assignment of, 96; and Creeks left off census, 292–93; lack of resolution regarding, 290–92; location of, Lower Creek, *34–38*; and McDonald contract, 291–92, 293; proposal of, 93–94; quality of land in, 101–3; sale of, 105–6, 204, 206–8, 209, 221; and Watson contract, 207–8. *See also* land claims; land fraud; Washington, Treaty of (1832)

resettlement: and ceremonial lives, 281–82; deaths after, 169–71, 270, 271, 287, 297–98; difficulties in, 270–71; and farming, 275, 276; and food insecurity, 275; and government inefficiency, 282; houses built after, 273–75; incorporation of other Indian groups into Creek Nation, 279; lack of provisions after, 285–86; patterns of, 272–73; plantations built after, 280; and starvation, 286; towns built after, 276, *277*, 279, 280–81

resistance, 6–9; during relocation, 211–13, 226–28; during removal, 186–87, 188, 191, 243, 245–46, 261. *See also* refugees, Creek; Second Creek War; violence

reunification emigrations, 295

Revenue (steamboat), 190, 191

Reynolds, John G., 238, 239, 252, 257, 258

Ridge, John, 40

rivers, in Indian territory, 153–57

rivers of sand, 9

robbery, 135

Rock Roe, *67*, 68, 119, 123, *124*, 190, 191, *192*, 212, *216*, 219, 220, 221–22, 224, 225–26, 229, 255, 262

Ross, John, 249

Ross Landing, 244, *247*

routes: of captured refugees, *247*, *263*; of detachment five during relocation, *229*; of detachment four during relocation, *224*; of detachment six during relocation, *256*; of detachment three during relocation, *219*; of detachment two during relocation, *216*; of Echo Fixico's party, *2*; of fifth voluntary party, *143*; of first detachment of prisoners, *192*; of first McIntosh party, *53*; of fourth voluntary party, *125*; proposed by Brown, 119; during relocation, 205, 220; of second detachment of prisoners, 194–98, *197*; of second McIntosh party, *67*; of third voluntary party, *78*

Royall, Anne, 27, 28

Russellville, Alabama, 213, *216*, 218

Salina (steamboat), 322n28

Salli, George F., 183

Salt Lake, McIntosh Creeks travel to, 174

Sanford & Company, 138–39, 148, 198; competition of with other land speculators, 178; and fifth voluntary party, 141–48; Hogan on, 188; Hogan's feud with, 177–78; plans of for enrollment, 175; transport of prisoners by, 187–93. *See also* Alabama Emigrating Company; contractors

Saunt, Claudio, 60, 279, 298

Savannah, Tennessee, 205, *224*, *247*; Creek girl dies near, 246; flatboat scuttled at, 248

Sawokli, 95; and emigration, 121; and forced removal, 187; in Indian territory, 165; land of, stolen, 187; in Second Creek War, 181

Scott, Gustavus H., 30
Screven, R. B., 202, 209, 211, 214
Second Creek War, 3, 113, 237, 297; arrest of leaders of, 184–85; causes of, 133, 180–81, 183; as excuse for ethnic cleansing, 185, 198; as excuse for forced removal, 5–6, 185; outbreak of, 181–82; repercussions of, 198
Second Seminole War, 181, 241, 289
self-emigration, 88–89, 148, 265, 294–95
Sells, Sam, 88–89
Seminoles: anticipated emigration of, 118; in Cherokee country, 174; Creek refugees among, 133, 234; in Indian territory, 288; mortality rate of, 298; Second Seminole War, 181, 241, 289 (*see also* Florida volunteers, Creek); and smallpox, 271; and Treaty of Payne's Landing, 173–74; within western Creek Nation, 173–74, 288–89
Senecas, 162
settlements, Creek. *See* towns, Creek
settlers. *See* illegals, white; whites
Shawnees, in Creek country, 279
Shelly, Jacob D., 202
Ship Island, Mississippi, 189, 256; environment of, 252
sickness. *See* disease
slaves, black, 13–14, 27–28, 187, 279–80
slaves, Creeks as, 266, 268
Sloan, Thomas, 238, 262
smallpox, 82, 92, 271, 272, 297
soil quality, in Indian territory, 157
soldiers, Creek, 235–39, 252, 255
Some Adventures of Captain Simon Suggs (Hooper), 107–9
Somerville, Alabama, 51, 53, 67, 68, 76, 78, 205, 215, 219

Somerville, Tennessee, 219, 220, 224, 229
songs, sung on journey west, 145–46, 299
South Florence, Alabama, 52, 53
spiritual lives, 7–8, 31–32, 135, 137, 185, 190–91, 203, 282
Sprague, John T., 202, 209, 210, 213, 215, 217, 226, 230
square grounds, 110–12, 203
squatters, 6, 25, 71–72, 82, 85, 148
Stanley, John Mix, 281, 282
starvation, 26, 40, 82, 91–92, 177, 183; caused by treaties, 28–29; in Indian territory, 286; and Second Creek War, 180
stealing, punishment for, 191
steamboats: *Alpha*, 142–47; *Black Hawk*, 244–48, 258, 262; *Bonnets O Blue*, 240; *Catawba*, 46; *Cavalier*, 258; *Champion*, 242; *Chippewa*, 27, 240; *Columbia*, 46; conditions on, 222–23; for detachment six, 257–58; *Farmer*, 220, 221, 240, 252, 257, 258; *Far West*, 258; *Fort Adams*, 45; *Georgian*, 182; *Harry Hill*, 123, 125; *Hyperion*, 182; *Itasca*, 261–62; *John Nelson*, 220, 222, 225–27, 229, 230–31, 240, 257, 258, 262, 350n35; *Lady Byron*, 220, 222–23, 226; *Lamplighter*, 190; *Lewis Cass*, 187, 194–95; *Majestic*, 190; *Mazeppa*, 195, 258; *Merchant*, 255; *Meridian*, 187–88; *Monmouth*, 258, 259–60, 262, 264; *Navarino*, 240, 257, 258–59; objections to, 267; *Pocahontas*, 76; *Revenue*, 190, 191; *Salina*, 322n28; *Thomas Yeatman*, 126; *Tomochichi*, 255; travel by, 123, 125, 142, 144–47; *Virginia*, 77; *Watchman*, 241; *Wheeling*, 142; *Yazoo*, 259, 262

Stidham, George W., 74
Stidham, John, 95
Stiggins, George, 93, 94
Stuart, James, 162
Stuart, John, 231
Suddi Micco, 108
suicides, 133, 186, 241
Sylacauga, 64, 76, *78*

Talladega, Alabama, 202, 205, 208, 209, 210, *219*, 224
Talladega County, Alabama, 105, 202, 266, 267
Talladega Creeks, 56–57, 202, 243; in Indian territory, 165; and relocation, 221
Tallahassee, Treaty of, 80
Tallassee, 184, 185, 201, 215; and council ground of, 111–12, 207; and emigration, 65; in Indian territory, 276, 281–82, 360n15; and relocation, 202, 209
Tallasseehatchee: and emigration, 65; and reserves of, 101; and relocation, 221
Tallassee Fixico, 184
talwas. See towns, Creek
Tawarsa council house, 110
Taylor, Samuel, Jr., 280
Ten Islands emigration camp, 64, *67*
Texas, 129–31, 270–71
Thlakatchka: council at, 20; Creeks from, hunt in Georgia, 26; and emigration, 65, 66; in Indian territory, 165
Thlathlo Harjo, 275
Thomas Yeatman (steamboat), 126
Thornton, Russell, 298
Tiger, Robert, 114
timber, in Indian territory, 152–53, 157, 162, 273

Toma Micco, 95
Tomathla Micco, 112, 282
Toma Yoca, 165
Tomochichi, 255
Tomoc Micco, 20
towns, Creek: attempts to rebuild, 31; council grounds in, 110–12, 135; dispersal of, 30–31, 110; Eufaula, 5, 85, *87*; in Indian territory, 276, 277, 279, 280–81; maps of, *33–38*; relocation of, 203
traders, in Indian territory, 286
Trail of Tears (Cherokee), 200
transience, 8, 38, 40, 114, 175, 177
treaties: designed to disrupt Creek life, 22; effects of, 16–17; Osages cajoled into, 55; Treaty of Cherokee Agency, 16; Treaty of Creek Agency, 40, 289; Treaty of Dancing Rabbit Creek, 93, 94; Treaty of Doak's Stand, 16, 17; Treaty of Fort Gibson, 173, 283, 289; Treaty of Fort Jackson, 16, 268–69; Treaty of Payne's Landing, 173–74; Treaty of Tallahassee, 80. See also Indian Springs, Treaty of; Washington, Treaty of (1826); Washington, Treaty of (1832)
trees, in Indian territory, 152–53. See also timber
Trident (steamboat), 282
Troup, George M., 13, 19, 20, 21
tuberculosis, 246
Tuckabatchee, in Alabama, 63, 94, 95, 110, 134: Busk at, 137; and plates of, 202–03, 208, 282; and relocation, 201–02, 221.
Tuckabatchee, in Indian territory, 281
Tuckabatchee Harjo, 92, 93, 119, 184, 201, 202, 213, 226–27
Tuckabatchee Micco, 93, 204, 207, 281
Tuggle, William Orrie, 290, 294

Tuscaloosa, Alabama, 24, 121–22, *124*, 205, 211, *216*; Creeks camped in, 121–22, 214; Eufaula Harjo's speech given in, 122
Tuscoona Harjo, 202, 223, 227, 228
Tuscumbia, Alabama, 51, *53*, 67, *78*, *143*, *216*, *219*, 229, 247
Tuskenehaw, 59, 64, 66, 131–32, 178, 181
Tuskenehaw of Cusseta, 72, 74
Tustunnuggee Chopco, 184, 207

Upatoi, 24; Creeks from, hunt in Georgia, 26

vaccination program, 272
Van Buren, Arkansas, *143*, 147, *219*, 229, 280, 286
Van Buren, Martin, 3, 6
vandalism, 135
Van Horne, Jefferson, 158
Vann, David, 40
Verdigris River, 154, 156
Vicksburg, Mississippi, *256*, 262
violence: committed by Creeks, 237, 238; contact and, 179; Creeks' turn to, 135; Hogan's warnings about, 176; intensification of, 175. *See also* Second Creek War
Virginia (steamboat), 77
Vischer, Lukas, 31
von Gerstner, Clara, 264–65

Walker, William, 50, 61, 64, 76, 79, 131, 175, 265
Ward, John, 97
Ware, Robert J., 129
Washington, Treaty of (1826), 6–7; Creeks resettle within Alabama, 31–38; effects of, 5, 24–29, 40, 58; as emigration document, 40; lack of enforcement of, 83; negotiations for, 21–22; as removal document, 11; resistance to, 25–26; terms of, 22–24
Washington, Treaty of (1832), 117, 183, 276, 286, 292; design of, 82; effects of, 81, 82, 100, 101–2, 109–12; goal of ethnic cleansing in, 95; headmen's motivations in adopting, 113; incompatibility of with Creek culture, 101–5; lack of provision for transfer of land to heirs in, 106; and legalization of encroachment by whites, 100–101; negotiations for, 94; and orphan fund, 96, 286, 289–90; and quality of land in reserves, 101–3; stipulations of, 94–97; ulterior motives in, 105. *See also* land claims; land fraud; reserves, individual
Watchman (steamboat), 241
water: in Indian territory, 153–57; scarcity of during coerced relocation, 218; scarcity of in Indian territory, 153, 154; whites' view of, 154
Waterloo, Alabama, 76, *78*, 142, *143*, 244, *247*, 248
Watson, James C., 207
Watson contract, 255, 293
Weogufka, and emigration, 65
West (region). *See* Indian territory
West Point, Georgia, 25, 30–31, 71, 117, 182, 208, *229*; James Island's encampment near, 202. *See also* Cusseta, near West Point
Wetumpka (*talwa*), 8, 32–33, 185, 267
Wetumpka, Alabama, 2, 27, 140, *143*, 182, 202, 205, 208, 209, 211, *216*, 230, 235, 258, 267, 268
Wetumpka Council House, 46, 47, 110, *111*
Wharton, William, 92
Wheat, Moses K., 266

Wheeling (steamboat), 142
whites: attacks on relocation camps by, 237–39; attempts to thwart emigration, 132; corrupting influences of, 17–18; encroachment by, 25, 71–72, 82, 85, 148, 284; and erosion of buffer with Creeks, 25–28; in Georgia, 40; Indians' bitterness towards, 293; Indians' desire to avoid, 233, 284, 285; in Indian territory, 284, 285–86; legalization of encroachment by, 100–101; married to Creek women (*see* Indian countrymen); proximity to, 25–28; and Second Creek War, 180; threats of to prosecute Creeks, 100; treatment of Creek prisoners by, 195; treatment of Creeks on Gulf by, 254–55; treatment of emigration parties by, 50, 209; view of water, 154; violence against Indians by, 242, 243–44
Wills, William J., 64, 66
winter, 122–26, 127, 128
Wirt, William, 92
Woodhouse, Samuel Washington, 158, 160, 276
Woodward, Thomas, 49, 131, 175
Woolf, Edward, 251
Works Progress Administration, 203
Wynn, John, 49, 70

Yazoo (steamboat), 259, 262
Yelko Harjo, 202
yellow fever, 250, 257
Yoholo Micco, 60, 122
Young, Bird H., 108
Young, Harrison, 109
Young's Ferry, 140
Yuchis, 38, 179–80; Creeks from, hunt in Georgia, 72; driven from enrollment camps, 63–64, 65; emigration of, 74; forced removal of, 187; and Second Creek War, 181; and starvation of, 29; resistance of, during removal, 191

IN THE INDIANS OF THE SOUTHEAST SERIES
The Payne-Butrick Papers, Volumes 1, 2, 3
The Payne-Butrick Papers, Volumes 4, 5, 6
Edited and annotated by William L. Anderson, Jane L. Brown, and Anne F. Rogers

Deerskins and Duffels: The Creek Indian Trade with Anglo-America, 1685–1815
By Kathryn E. Holland Braund

Searching for the Bright Path: The Mississippi Choctaws from Prehistory to Removal
By James Taylor Carson

Demanding the Cherokee Nation: Indian Autonomy and American Culture, 1830–1900
By Andrew Denson

The Second Creek War: Interethnic Conflict and Collusion on a Collapsing Frontier
By John T. Ellisor

Cherokee Americans: The Eastern Band of Cherokees in the Twentieth Century
By John R. Finger

Creeks and Southerners: Biculturalism on the Early American Frontier
By Andrew K. Frank

Choctaw Genesis, 1500–1700
By Patricia Galloway

The Southeastern Ceremonial Complex: Artifacts and Analysis
The Cottonlandia Conference
Edited by Patricia Galloway
Exhibition Catalog by David H. Dye and Camille Wharey

The Invention of the Creek Nation, 1670–1763
By Steven C. Hahn

Rivers of Sand: Creek Indian Emigration, Relocation, and Ethnic Cleansing in the American South
By Christopher D. Haveman

Bad Fruits of the Civilized Tree: Alcohol and the Sovereignty of the Cherokee Nation
By Izumi Ishii

Epidemics and Enslavement: Biological Catastrophe in the Native Southeast, 1492–1715
By Paul Kelton

An Assumption of Sovereignty: Social and Political Transformation among the Florida Seminoles, 1953–1979
By Harry A. Kersey Jr.

Up from These Hills: Memories of a Cherokee Boyhood
By Leonard Carson Lambert Jr.
As told to Michael Lambert

The Caddo Chiefdoms: Caddo Economics and Politics, 700–1835
By David La Vere

The Moravian Springplace Mission to the Cherokees, Volume 1: 1805–1813
The Moravian Springplace Mission to the Cherokees, Volume 2: 1814–1821
Edited and introduced by Rowena McClinton

The Moravian Springplace Mission to the Cherokees, Abridged Edition
Edited and with an introduction by Rowena McClinton

Keeping the Circle: American Indian Identity in Eastern North Carolina, 1885–2004
By Christopher Arris Oakley

Choctaws in a Revolutionary Age, 1750–1830
By Greg O'Brien

Choctaw Resurgence in Mississippi: Race, Class, and Nation Building in the Jim Crow South, 1830–1977
By Katherine M. B. Osburn

Cherokee Women: Gender and Culture Change, 1700–1835
By Theda Perdue

The Brainerd Journal: A Mission to the Cherokees, 1817–1823
Edited and introduced by Joyce B. Phillips and Paul Gary Phillips

Seminole Voices: Reflections on Their Changing Society, 1970–2000
By Julian M. Pleasants and Harry A. Kersey Jr.

The Yamasee War: A Study of Culture, Economy, and Conflict in the Colonial South
By William L. Ramsey

The Cherokees: A Population History
By Russell Thornton

Buffalo Tiger: A Life in the Everglades
By Buffalo Tiger and Harry A. Kersey Jr.

American Indians in the Lower Mississippi Valley: Social and Economic Histories
By Daniel H. Usner Jr.

William Bartram on the Southeastern Indians
Edited and annotated by Gregory A. Waselkov and Kathryn E. Holland Braund

Powhatan's Mantle: Indians in the Colonial Southeast
Edited by Peter H. Wood, Gregory A. Waselkov, and M. Thomas Hatley

Creeks and Seminoles: The Destruction and Regeneration of the Muscogulge People
By J. Leitch Wright Jr.

To order or obtain more information on these or other University of Nebraska Press titles, visit nebraskapress.unl.edu.

www.ingramcontent.com/pod-product-compliance
Lightning Source LLC
LaVergne TN
LVHW041207250326
834689LV00016BA/154/J